INTERNATIONAL LAW AND DISPUTE SETTLEMENT

International dispute settlement plays a fundamental role in maintaining the fabric of the international legal order, reflecting the desire of States, and increasingly non-State actors, to resolve their differences through international dispute procedures and other legal mechanisms. This edited collection focuses upon the growth and complexity of such legal methods, which includes judicial settlement (courts and tribunals), arbitration and other legal (or what might be termed 'extra-legal') means (international organisations, committees, inspection panels, and ombudsmen).

In this important collection, such mechanisms are compared and evaluated side-by-side to provide, in one volume, a detailed and analytical account of the current framework. Ranging from key conceptual issues of proliferation of legal mechanisms and the associated risks of fragmentation through to innovations in dispute settlement mechanisms in many topical areas of international law, including international trade law, collective security law and regional law, this collection, written by leading international lawyers, provides a major study in the ongoing trends and emerging problems in this crucial area of international law.

This edited collection is published to mark the retirement of Professor John Merrills, Emeritus Professor of International Law, University of Sheffield, who has written widely on international law and human rights law, but is probably best known for his work on the settlement of international disputes, evidenced by the enduring appeal of his leading text *International Dispute Settlement*, now in its fourth edition.

Volume 28 in the series Studies in International Law

Studies in International Law

Volume 1: Between Light and Shadow: The World Bank, the International Monetary Fund and International Human Rights Law
Mac Darrow

Volume 2: Toxics and Transnational Law: International and European Regulation of Toxic Substances as Legal Symbolism
Marc Pallemaerts

Volume 3: The Chapter VII Powers of the United Nations Security Council
Erika de Wet

Volume 4: Enforcing International Law Norms Against Terrorism
Edited by Andrea Bianchi

Volume 5: The Permanent International Criminal Court
Edited by Dominic McGoldrick, Peter Rowe and Eric Donnelly

Volume 6: Regional Organisations and the Development of Collective Security
Ademola Abass

Volume 7: Islamic State Practices, International Law and the Threat from Terrorism: A Critique of the 'Clash of Civilizations' in the New World Order
Javaid Rehman

Volume 8: Predictability and Flexibility in the Law of Maritime Delimitation
Yoshifumi Tanaka

Volume 9: Biotechnology and International Law
Edited by Francesco Francioni and Tullio Scovazzi

Volume 10: The Development of Human Rights Law by the Judges of the International Court of Justice
Shiv Bedi

Volume 11: The Environmental Accountability of the World Bank to Third Party Non-State Actors
Alix Gowlland-Gualtieri

Volume 12: Transnational Corporations and Human Rights
Edited by Olivier De Schutter

Volume 13: Biotechnologies and International Human Rights
Edited by Francesco Francioni

Volume 14: Human Security and International Law: Prospects and Problems
Barbara Von Tigerstrom

Volume 15: The Arms Trade and International Law
Zeray Yihdego

Volume 16: Africa: Mapping New Boundaries in International Law
Edited by Jeremy Levitt

Volume 17: Forced Migration, Human Rights and Security
Edited by Jane McAdam

Volume 18: The Use of Nuclear Weapons and the Protection of the Environment during International Armed Conflict
Erik Koppe

Volume 19: The Shifting Allocation of Authority in International Law: Considering Sovereignty, Supremacy and Subsidiarity
Edited by Tomer Broude and Yuval Shany

Volume 20: Counterterrorism: Democracy's Challenge
Edited by Andrea Bianchi and Alexis Keller

Volume 21: Amnesty, Human Rights and Political Transitions
Louise Mallinder

Volume 22: Property Rights and Natural Resources
Richard Barnes

Volume 23: Human Dignity and the Foundations of International Law
Patrick Capps

Volume 24: Sovereignty and the Stateless Nation: Gibraltar in the Modern Legal Context
Keith Azopardi

Volume 25: The International Court of Justice and Self-Defence in International Law
James A Green

Volume 26: State Liability in Investment Treaty Arbitration: Global Constitutional and Administrative Law in the BIT Generation
Santiago Montt

Volume 27: Reappraising the Resort to Force: International Law, Jus ad Bellum and the War on Terror
Lindsay Moir

Volume 28: International Law and Dispute Settlement: New Problems and Techniques
Edited by Duncan French, Matthew Saul and Nigel D White

International Law and Dispute Settlement

New Problems and Techniques

Edited by
Duncan French
Matthew Saul
and
Nigel D White

•HART•
PUBLISHING
OXFORD AND PORTLAND, OREGON
2010

Published in the United Kingdom by Hart Publishing Ltd
16C Worcester Place, Oxford, OX1 2JW
Telephone: +44 (0)1865 517530
Fax: +44 (0)1865 510710
E-mail: mail@hartpub.co.uk
Website: http://www.hartpub.co.uk

Published in North America (US and Canada) by
Hart Publishing
c/o International Specialized Book Services
920 NE 58th Avenue, Suite 300
Portland, OR 97213-3786
USA
Tel: +1 503 287 3093 or toll-free: (1) 800 944 6190
Fax: +1 503 280 8832
E-mail: orders@isbs.com
Website: http://www.isbs.com

British Library Cataloguing in Publication Data
Data Available

ISBN: 978-1-84113-912-8

Typeset by Compuscript Ltd, Shannon
Printed and bound in Great Britain by
TJ International Ltd, Padstow, Cornwall

Foreword

Settling disputes lies at the heart of the legal enterprise. Law seeks to structure, order and facilitate the interactions between those subject to its reach. Providing means and mechanisms for resolving the inevitable conflicts and difficulties which such regulation generates is an essential attribute of an effective legal system. Yet all too often the question of what comprises an effective system of dispute resolution in the international arena becomes focussed on the presence—or on the absence—of courts; on the scope—or on the restrictions on the scope—of their jurisdiction; and on the capacity to enforce—or, more usually, the lack of capacity to enforce—their decisions or judgments. All of the above, and more besides, are of course vitally important questions which contribute to a critique of international dispute settlement. However, there is very much more to be considered and the work of Professor Merrills has played a seminal role in broadening our understanding of the processes of dispute settlement. These Essays honour that work by further illustration and illumination of the complexities involved.

At one level, that complexity is reflected in the forms of dispute settlement available—the political, the non-judicial, the quasi-judicial and the judicial itself. In this the international legal system follows domestic systems, all of which have variants of such approaches nuanced to reflect the nature of the disputes in question and the subjects which they serve. However, the consensual and dispersed nature of the sources of international legal obligation pose an additional challenge which is not faced in so stark a fashion by municipal systems. States have proven adept at constructing bespoke systems of dispute resolution concerning particular forms of subject matter or which are operable within particular treaty regimes, or within particular regional contexts or within international organisations. Overlaying all of this are the more general principles of State responsibility and means of accountability, both through international claims and, ultimately, the threat or use of a coercive or forceable response.

Those unfamiliar with international law sometimes point to the dearth of judicial fora having a general and compulsory jurisdictional reach as evidence of its poverty as a system of legal control. An alternative view is that the nature of the international legal enterprise is such that issues of 'dispute resolution' pervade all of its aspects and are already embedded in its systems of norm generation, of patterns of obligation and responsibility, of its interface with domestic legal systems, both public and private, and of course with political agencies, national and international.

A further complexity arises from a changing understanding of what might be called the purpose of international law. From being generally understood as a fairly static system which primarily spoke to the interactions between States and operated to fill what would otherwise be the vacuums between, it has become a venue for the generation of forms of international public policy which reach back into the States themselves. Just as the public policy of States exists to inform the regulation of the private, so does international law increasingly concern itself with matters previously thought well beyond its practical reach. As international legal discourse increasingly becomes a venue for policy debate and social control, the need becomes all the greater for appropriately nuanced and suitably affective means of addressing the disputes which are the product of the constraints which are generated.

Settling disputes is not just about 'settling disputes'. It is also about how issues are addressed, regulated and engaged with. It is about *how* law is generated, about *what* law is generated and about the manner in which it is engaged with and responded to. It is also about the means and mechanisms for solving problems and adjudicating outcomes, of securing remedies and securing the interests of those who it is there to serve. All of these themes, and more besides, permeate the work of Professor Merrills and are properly and appropriately reflected in the contributions to this collection in his honour, which it is an honour to introduce.

Malcolm D Evans
Professor of Public International Law
at the University of Bristol
July 2009

Preface

Professor John Merrills has a worldwide reputation as a scholar of international law. His impressive writing and work in international law is itemised towards the end of this book. His reputation was built from Sheffield University, where he started as an Assistant Lecturer in 1964, becoming Professor of Public International Law in 1985 until his retirement in 2007. John Merrills remains active within the Law School as an Emeritus Professor. It is fitting that a collection of essays in his honour should combine contributions from international lawyers both from Sheffield and elsewhere. Sheffield's reputation as a centre for international legal research owes a great deal to John Merrills.

Professor John Merrills has written widely on International Law and Human Rights Law, but is probably best known for his work on the settlement of international disputes, evidenced by the enduring appeal of his leading text *International Dispute Settlement* published by Cambridge University Press and now in its fourth edition. In this book Professor Merrills divided dispute settlement up into diplomatic and non-judicial methods (negotiation, mediation, inquiry, conciliation), and legal or judicial methods such as (arbitration and international tribunals). Later chapters examined the delicate relationship between legal and diplomatic methods in the law of the sea and in international trade. The book finishes with a review of political institutions (the UN and regional organisations) and their roles in dispute settlement.

The idea behind this collection of essays is not to reproduce Professor Merrills' seminal text on dispute settlement—that would not be possible—but in a way to try to complement it by further exploring by means of a number of different perspectives the area of legal and judicial means and methods of settling disputes, specifically new problems and new techniques in these areas. It re-considers the role of international courts and tribunals, but also looks at other quasi-judicial methods (trade disputes under the WTO, the human rights committees, even the Security Council) as well as alternative processes of dispute resolution involving third parties such as ombudsmen and inspection panels. In so doing it inevitably raises wider issues of responsibility, accountability and access to justice, all themes that Professor Merrills has contributed significantly to during his academic career.

Thanks go to Ali Bohm who acted as editorial assistant on this book and to the School of Law, University of Sheffield, for its financial help in this regard.

Duncan French, Matthew Saul and Nigel D White
School of Law, University of Sheffield
June 2009

Contents

List of Contributors

Tawhida Ahmed
Lecturer in Law, University of Sheffield

Kisch Beevers
Honorary Senior Lecturer in Law, University of Sheffield

Paul James Cardwell
Lecturer in Law, University of Sheffield

Robin Churchill
Professor of International Law, University of Dundee

James Crawford
Whewell Professor of International Law; Director, Lauterpacht Centre for International Law, University of Cambridge

Malgosia Fitzmaurice
Professor of Public International Law, Queen Mary, University of London

Duncan French
Professor of International Law, University of Sheffield

Sandy Ghandhi
Professor, School of Law, University of Reading

Richard Kirkham
Lecturer in Law, University of Sheffield

Vaughan Lowe
QC, Chichele Professor of Public International Law and Fellow of All Souls College, Oxford University

Sorcha MacLeod
Lecturer in Law, University of Sheffield

Gino J Naldi
Senior Lecturer, Norwich Law School, University of East Anglia

Matthew Saul
Lecturer in Law, Durham University, formerly PhD student at the University of Sheffield

Karen N Scott
Senior Lecturer, School of Law, University of Canterbury, New Zealand

Surya P Subedi
OBE, Barrister (Middle Temple), Professor of International Law, University of Leeds

Nigel D White
Professor of Public International Law, University of Nottingham, formerly Professor of International Law at the University of Sheffield

List of Abbreviations

AAT	Australian Antarctic Territory
ADR	Alternative dispute resolution
ATA	Antarctic Treaty Area
ATCM	Antarctic Treaty Consultative Meetings
ATS	Antarctic Treaty System
AU	African Union
BERR	Department for Business, Enterprise and Regulatory Reform (UK Government)
BIT	Bilateral investment treaty
CAT	Committee Against Torture
CCAMLR	Convention on the Conservation of Antarctic Marine Living Resources
CEDAW	Committee on Elimination of Discrimination Against Women
CERD	Committee on the Elimination of Racial Discrimination
CFI	Court of First Instance (of the ECJ)
CFSP	Common Foreign and Security Policy
CITES	Convention on International Trade in Endangered Species
CoE	Council of Europe
COP	Communications on Progress
CORE	Corporate Responsibility Coalition
CRAMRA	Convention on the Regulation of Antarctic Mineral Resource Activities (Wellington Convention)
CSR	Corporate social responsibility
CSW	Commission on the Status of Women
DAW	Division for the Advancement of Women
DPRK	North Korea (Democratic People's Republic of Korea)
DSM	Dispute Settlement Mechanism
DSU	Dispute Settlement Understanding
EC	European Community
ECHR	European Convention on Human Rights
ECJ	European Court of Justice
ECOSOC	Economic and Social Council of the UN
ECOWAS	Economic Community of West African States
ECtHR	European Court of Human Rights
EEZ	Exclusive Economic Zone
ENMOD	Convention on the Prohibition of Military or Any Other Hostile Use of Environmental Modification Techniques

EU	European Union
EUFOR	EU Force
FAO	Food and Agriculture Organization (of the UN)
GA	General Assembly
GAOR	General Assembly Ordinary Resolution
GATT	General Agreement on Tariffs and Trade
GC	Global Compact
GEF	Global Environment Facility
HRC	Human Rights Commission
IAATO	International Association of Antarctic Tour Operators
IAEA	International Atomic Energy Agency
ICC	International Criminal Court
ICCAT	International Commission for the Conservation of Atlantic Tunas
ICCPR	International Covenant on Civil and Political Rights
ICESCR	International Covenant on Economic, Social and Cultural Rights
ICJ	International Court of Justice
ICPDR	International Commission for the Protection of the Danube River
ICRW	International Convention for the Regulation of Whaling
ICTR	International Criminal Tribunal for Rwanda
ICTY	International Criminal Tribunal for the former Yugoslavia
IFOR	Implementation Force
IGO	Inter-governmental organisation
IGY	International Geophysical Year
ILC	International Law Commission
IMO	International Maritime Organization
INGO	International non-governmental organisation
ITLOS	International Tribunal for the Law of the Sea
IUU	Illegal, unreported and unregulated
IWC	International Whaling Commission
KFOR	Kosovo Force
LRTAP	Convention on Long-range Transboundary Air Pollution
MARPOL	International Convention for the Prevention of Pollution from Ships
MTBE	Methyl tertiary-butyl ether
NAFTA	North American Free Trade Agreement
NATO	North Atlantic Treaty Organization
NCP	National Contact Points (ch 4); Non-compliance procedure (ch 9)
NGO	Non-governmental organisation
OAU	Organization of African Unity

OECD	Organisation for Economic Co-operation and Development
OHCHR	Office of the High Commissioner for Human Rights
OP	Optional Protocol
OSPAR	Convention for the Protection of the Marine Environment of the North-East Atlantic
PDVSA	Petróleos de Venezuela SA
PJC	Police and Judicial Cooperation
RAID	Rights and Accountability in Development
RFMO	Regional Fisheries Management Organisation
SADC	Southern African Development Community
SC	Security Council
SFOR	Stabilisation Force
SME	Small and medium enterprises
STL	Special Tribunal for Lebanon
TEU	Treaty on European Union
TNC	Trans-national corporation
TUC	Trades Union Congress
UDHR	Universal Declaration of Human Rights
UNCITRAL	UN Commission on International Trade Law
UNCLOS	United Nations Convention on the Law of the Sea
UNCTC	UN Commission on Transnational Corporations
UNEP	United Nations Environment Programme
UNIFIL	United Nations Interim Force in Lebanon
UNMIK	United Nations Mission in Kosovo
UNSC	UN Security Council
UNTS	UN Treaty Series
WHO	World Health Organization
WTO	World Trade Organization

Introduction

DUNCAN FRENCH, MATTHEW SAUL
AND NIGEL D WHITE

DISPUTE RESOLUTION IS a crucial aspect of any legal system or legal order, and in the international legal order there are numerous different means and methods, including a growing number of judicial mechanisms (courts, tribunals, arbitral panels) and more widely what can be labelled other quasi-judicial, legal or extra-legal means (committees, inspection panels, ombudsmen, etc). The growth and complexity of judicial and legal methods of dispute settlement reflects the evolution of the international legal order, arguably towards further entrenchment of the rule of law, though the centrality of courts and other legal mechanisms in the international legal order continues to be the focus of detailed consideration. This entails not only looking at quite specific issues of legal dispute settlement in particular areas of international law—more specifically in environmental law, human rights law, trade law, law of the sea, and collective security—it also requires a consideration of a number of more far-reaching conceptual issues.

The book includes analyses of aspects of the work of the leading tribunals, but the wider purpose is to consider the trends and developments in the area of dispute settlement. To provide focus the book does not have specific chapters on political, non-legal means, such as diplomacy and negotiation, though these form the backdrop of all the contributions. The very presence of legal means of dispute settlement may well encourage parties to the dispute to settle by means of negotiation.

The aim of the book is to explore developments and trends in judicial, legal and what may be called extra-legal means and methods of international dispute settlement. By focusing on legal means, the book comes squarely into wider debates about the direction and development of international law. The contribution of both courts and alternative legal methods to the development of international law and to methods of dispute settlement, in areas such as responsibility and accountability, are considered throughout the book, but are raised in particular in Part 1. Part 2 focuses on dispute settlement in substantive areas of international law, including private international law, while Part 3 contains discussion of judicial methods in the regional domain.

I. THE CHANGING FACE OF INTERNATIONAL ADJUDICATION

In chapter 1 Vaughan Lowe sets the scene by examining the choices of dispute settlement made by governments, particularly in bilateral investment treaties, whereby governments bind their freedoms by giving rights in private law—if not in international law—to foreign individuals and companies investing in their countries, and by providing for dispute settlement, ultimately by arbitral tribunal. This is a development that reflects the *de facto* power of private corporations on the international stage. Orthodoxy speaks about international law made by States *for* States, but the reality is very different. The chapter considers the issue of whether the arbitral hearings arising from bilateral investment disputes should be held in private, allowing of no public interest representations, in effect reflecting the private legal nature of the dispute. However, given that these disputes can, and often do, involve environmental and human rights issues, the chapter critically evaluates the trend towards allowing *amicus* briefs, by inter alia non-governmental organisations. This also calls into question the limited use of *amicus* briefs in the WTO settlement system. In raising the issues of 'public participation in private dispute settlement' (more widely 'whether private justice could adequately secure public interests'), concepts that can be applied to more traditional cases between States before inter alia the International Court of Justice, the chapter provides a suitably thought-provoking entry into the book. Later chapters therefore consider the contribution of such bodies as the International Court, the Dispute Settlement Body of the WTO and the dispute settlement mechanisms under the Law of the Sea Convention, as well as noting the role of an increasingly diverse array of litigants in utilising (and by utilising, thus defining the relevance of) international adjudication. Vaughan Lowe's chapter causes us to think about the nature of the international legal order and whether it is suited to secure public interests through legal dispute settlement.

In chapter 2, by Malgosia Fitzmaurice, the work of the International Court of Justice is appraised with reference to a particular area of international law, namely the protection of the environment. Does the ICJ help to shape a legal framework to protect the environment in cases that are essentially settling disputes between States? Malgosia Fitzmaurice discusses this from the perspective of the infringement of rights in multilateral treaties within the context of the 'inherent bilateralism of relations between States'. Does bilateralism constitute a 'stumbling block in cases in which the vindication of wider community values is at stake'? Or to re-phrase this, have dispute settlement techniques been adapted to take full account of community values? The chapter considers these issues in the light of the doctrines of obligations *erga omnes* and *erga omnes partes*, and the question of third-party intervention in International Court cases through the 1974 and 1995 *Nuclear Test* cases. The author concludes that 'the limited scope of the right of intervention ... makes it a rather ineffective tool for the redress of community concerns regarding environmental issues before the ICJ'. Having said that, the author then reviews the Court's contribution to the development of general principles of environmental law such as sustainable development, the precautionary principle, environmental impact assessment and intergenerational equity, in looking at contentious cases and advisory opinions in nuclear law, water law, transboundary air pollution and damage to land. The chapter contains a wealth of discussion of cases, which show the Court applying and developing principles of environmental law, including the yet to be decided *Aerial Herbicide Spraying* case arising out of the use of toxic herbicides on illicit coca and poppy plantations by Columbia on its frontier with Ecuador, a case that promises to further develop the seminal arbitral judgment in the *Trail Smelter* case. The chapter finishes with an analysis of the best judicial forum for the settlement of environmental disputes—the ICJ or a specialised international tribunal? The lengthy process of adjudication by the ICJ and the problem it has in fairly addressing shared and community interests, have to be balanced against the fragmentary problems that creating alternative fora will cause.

The limitations on the International Court, and to a lesser extent other State-based methods of dispute settlement, are reflected in Duncan French and Richard Kirkham's account, in chapter 3, of complaint and grievance mechanisms. These accountability techniques, such as the ombudsman and inspection panels, represent a 'transformation from a model premised upon a narrow conception of inter-governmentalism and formal legalism to one that is increasingly receptive to broader constitutional notions, including ideals such as enhancing legitimacy and promoting good governance'. By seeking to 'engage a range of communities beyond the intergovernmental level' such techniques, emerging primarily though not exclusively in the World Bank and other international financial institutions, have rebalanced to some extent the hitherto domination of dispute settlement by governments. The authors point out that such techniques not only provide means of securing redress for individuals but also serve the wider more constitutional purpose of holding organisations to account and thereby helping to develop better governance within those bodies. Though the 'grievance' (perhaps more technically accurate than 'dispute') is normally bilateral, between the individual or group and the organisation, the public interest can be served by these techniques in a way that traditional techniques of dispute settlement may not. The argument for creating an institution-wide UN ombudsman, with a wide-reaching remit, though undoubtedly radical and with many obstacles towards its implementation, is strong.

Sorcha MacLeod takes forward an examination of accountability techniques for transnational corporations in chapter 4. The concept of corporate social responsibility, signifying that 'businesses have obligations beyond the financial and commercial and which includes social obligations, particularly in the sphere of human rights and the environment', has 'developed steadily but the model adopted has not been that of … a traditional adjudicatory framework—ie courts, tribunals or arbitration'. The move has not simply been away from traditional dispute settlement but towards 'alternative dispute prevention and settlement strategies with an emphasis on involving *all* of the relevant actors including States, business and civil society'. Corporate social responsibility approaches at the UN (principally the Global Compact) and the OECD (through the National Contact Points) have become more central in the international legal order. Despite this 'the provision of effective remedies for human rights violations by business is the area in most need of serious attention'. Though such developments are to be welcomed there is still a long way to go to ensure that they protect both the interests of the individual as well as the interests of the community.

II. PROBLEMS AND TECHNIQUES IN SUBSTANTIVE AREAS OF INTERNATIONAL LAW

Part 2 of the book contains evaluations of means of dispute settlement within key areas of public and private international law, developing the initial discussions of human rights law, environmental law, etc, found in Part 1. In chapter 5, Sandy Ghandhi, considers the practice and procedure of dispute settlement in individual communication cases within the Human Rights Committee and the Committee on the Elimination of Discrimination against Women. In it he considers whether the overlapping dispute settlement work of these quasi-judicial bodies is coherent, or whether it is an example of an issue of increasing concern to international lawyers, namely fragmentation. Contrary to some evaluations, and many expectations, the conclusion is that 'CEDAW is intent on developing a jurisprudence that is both congruent and consistent with that of the other UN treaty-monitoring bodies, especially the HRC'. Sandy Ghandhi does, however, contrast this congruence with divergence elsewhere in the human rights system, leading to calls for a unified standing treaty body. Giving remedies to individuals within the international legal order is crucial, but the enduring legitimacy of this development will only be ensured if there is consistency. On CEDAW itself, given the relative newness of its Optional Protocol, only 'time will tell whether CEDAW can vindicate the rights of women in the individual communication procedure as successfully as the HRC'. Again this chapter provides another view on non-traditional methods that provide avenues for individuals seeking redress, in this case for human rights violations. In light of the limitations on this and the other non-traditional forms of dispute settlement considered in the course of this book, and in particular the *ex ante* requirement of State consent to many of these processes, this is a clear indication that such processes are grafted onto the existing system of international law, rather than being based on alternative precepts.

Once a State has signed up to an individual complaints procedure under a human rights treaty regime, then it has no choice but to answer the complaints brought against it. Though based on original consent, the element of compulsion is present thereafter, although as Ghandhi notes some governments have attempted to limit the competence of the relevant Committee through reservations to individual complaints procedures. Though the optional clause is present within the Statute of the International Court of Justice, its effects have been severely curtailed by States signing up to it, limiting the development of this type of quasi-compulsory competence within the leading international tribunal. In chapter 6, Robin Churchill shows how compulsory means of dispute settlement have developed and increased within an area in which the International Court of Justice has traditionally been concerned—the Law of the Sea. The methods of dispute settlement in this classic area of international law are predictably traditional in their form—judicial and quasi-judicial—but the move towards compulsion presses against the consensual nature of international law. The myriad of alternative choices within the Convention, including the International Tribunal for the Law of the Sea, and the International Court of Justice, does not detract from the fact that parties cannot escape appearing before a tribunal of some sort, given the fallback provided of an Annex VII arbitral tribunal. Despite this machinery, only just over a handful of cases have been subject to compulsory judicial settlement, which, given that there are over 200 unresolved maritime boundaries, seems to be a less than satisfactory record. Robin Churchill addresses this claim and also considers disputes which are more than bilateral and essentially private between States, namely those relating to mining in the International Seabed Area. Whether these methods are robust enough to cope with the wider community interests underlying these disputes remains to be seen, as the first contracts for the exploration of the Area were not signed until 2001. In considering dispute settlement mechanisms outside the Law of the Sea Convention, under fisheries and marine pollution treaties, the chapter shows the progress being made in dispute settlement, but also that the underuse of these mechanisms maybe due to a 'reluctance to use judicial means to settle disputes that have strong policy (rather than legal) content', as well as problems of *locus standi*, which does not seem to bode well in tackling the problems of over-exploitation of maritime resources, and increasing pollution of the seas.

However, although 'much of this diverse dispute settlement machinery is unused', a 'good deal of it is of very recent origin' and may well play a significant role, at least in resolving bilateral issues, in the future.

In contrast to the judicial means found in the Law of the Sea, in chapter 7, Surya Subedi considers the WTO dispute settlement mechanism to be 'neither fully judicial nor completely a non-judicial mechanism', more specifically describing this as a new technique for settling disputes in international law being a 'blend of diplomacy, negotiation, mediation, arbitration and adjudication'. It shares with the Law of the Sea mechanisms the element of compulsory jurisdiction, but in contrast to those methods outlined in the Law of the Sea, the popularity of the WTO dispute settlement machinery cannot be doubted with nearly 380 cases being referred to it. However, the weaknesses of the system must not be forgotten, especially 'when it come to enforcing the rulings of the [Dispute Settlement Body] against major powers', and further the contention that it 'does not provide an effective remedy for those non-State business actors which suffer from injustices and distortions in international trade'. Here we are reminded that business actors may well also be victims of violations of international law and should have access to justice in such disputes. The chapter also reminds us of the public interest issues that often arise in trade disputes in discussing the role of *amicus curiae.* Though restricted 'it should be noted … that the issue relating to what kind of access the public might have to panel proceedings or their input into the procedure by means of *amicus curiae* briefs is one of the subjects being discussed within the DSB under the Doha mandate'. Nevertheless, the author concludes that while the DSB has performed well as a quasi-judicial mechanism for settling trade disputes it is debatable whether it can 'deliver justice in the broader sense of the term'.

A different blend of non-judicial features of dispute settlement can be found in the most ambiguous and powerful of all international bodies, the UN Security Council. In chapter 8, Nigel White and Matthew Saul consider what they broadly label as the quasi-judicial powers of the Security Council, within the context of its traditional dispute settlement techniques (contained in Chapter VI of the Charter) as well as its exceptional coercive powers (under Chapter VII). In considering the Security Council as an 'integral part of the post-1945 international legal order', and its powers to seize itself of disputes, of investigation, judgment, and implementation, the authors argue that 'in trying to achieve order in international relations, the Security Council must also strive to achieve justice, and it is this constant balancing which permeates all decisions on matters of collective security—where the security imperative meets the rights of States or individuals'. Given that the Security Council has the power to bind Member States and furthermore such binding decisions can, subject to limitations identified by the authors, override inconsistent treaty obligations and can be enforced by the Security Council using Chapter VII, the potential of the Security Council as a 'settler' of disputes is huge, but it is a power that is accompanied by responsibility to act consistently, fairly (for instance by conforming with basic principles of natural justice when imposing measures upon States or individuals) and with respect to general axioms of international law.

One might wonder whether an all-powerful executive might have success in other areas such as international environmental law, which has been built on a multilateral treaty approach. By way of counter-argument to this in chapter 9, Karen Scott considers non-compliance procedures (NCPs) and dispute resolution mechanisms under multilateral international environmental agreements. Relatively unknown until recently, 'today there are over 20 non-compliance procedures that actively seek to support and facilitate compliance with international obligations in areas such as air pollution, climate change, marine environmental protection, biodiversity conservation, environmental impact assessment, fisheries management, freshwater resources and transboundary movement of chemicals, pesticides and waste'. One of the earliest developed under the 1979 Bern Convention on the Conservation of European Wildlife and Habitats 'remains innovative almost 30 years on owing to its status as one of the few NCPs to permit non-governmental organisations … and individuals to indirectly initiate action against a [State] party in alleged non-compliance with their obligations under the Convention'. NCPs seem to be a combination of prevention of disputes by providing assistance to enable States to comply with their environmental treaty obligations, and the adoption of coercive measures if the facilitative approach fails—what Karen Scott labels the 'good-cop-bad-cop approach'. This is normally overseen by a compliance committee or similar, often consisting of representatives drawn from a small number of State parties. The remit of these committees can go beyond the individual cases to consider the implementation of treaty obligations more generally, raising the prospect of that body being able to consider the wider public interest. This prospect is enhanced given that 'many (but by no means all) non-compliance procedures permit some form of public participation within the procedure'. 'Non-compliance procedures have been developed in order to respond to the very specific challenges faced by traditional dispute resolution mechanisms within environmental regimes, which generally create *erga omnes*—as opposed to strictly reciprocal—obligations', thus contrasting NCPs and their accompanying compliance committees with the approach of the International Court of Justice considered by Malgosia Fitzmaurice in chapter 2.

In an intriguing contribution in chapter 10 on the Antarctic treaty after 50 years, James Crawford looks at a treaty regime that seems to work in effect by suspending disputes, with little by way of formal dispute resolution or any form of powerful executive. As the author states, the 'Antarctic Treaty is the reduction to writing of a disagreement about status; a truce called on claims'. In answer to the question of how the treaty works—how it is implemented—James Crawford identifies it as a 'system of self-policing in which under Article VII the parties could designate observers to carry out inspections'. While showing that a quite limited, in some ways traditional, treaty regime can work, the author is realistic about over-claiming on the value of the legal structures—'if the Treaty remains a success after 50 years, one major reason for its stability is the continued relative isolation of Antarctica and the relative absence of economically exploitable resources'. Should extraction of those resources become economically viable then the dormant claims to areas of Antarctic territory and underlying disputes will become live and another dispute settlement mechanism might have to be considered. This would encounter the range of legal issues that the present approach has left unresolved, such as whether the claimant States can legitimately be seen as 'coastal' States for the purposes of the Law of the Sea Convention, and, most fundamentally, whether Antarctica 'has the same characteristics as other terrestrial territories, including the character as a space capable of being subject to sovereignty'. Overall, the author concludes that 'legal difficulties have not stood in the way of the continuing political success of the Antarctic Treaty and its system'. Disputes have been avoided because the 'parties have managed to incorporate aspirants and even opponents into the system without—apparently—diluting it too much'. A combination of the economic realities of trying to extract the resources of the region and an unwillingness of the key actors to try and enforce their claims 'at the expense of the system as a whole' have meant that thus far formal disputes have been avoided and the treaty regime continues to successfully govern the Antarctic.

In chapter 11 the book takes what seems like a detour into the world of private international law, moreover into what we would label a non-legal means of dispute settlement—mediation. In her essay on cross-border family mediation, Kisch Beevers demonstrates that lessons for public international law can be learned from private international law (and vice versa), and also that the line between legal and non-legal means is far from clear. For instance, to claim that the non-compliance mechanisms in environmental protection are 'legal' is going too far, for as Karen Scott states in chapter 9, while they have become increasingly 'legalised' they are still political in origin. Furthermore, the chapter by Kisch Beevers gives further insights into the benefits of non-judicial methods of settlement, with mediation producing 'the facilitation of better communication and understanding between the parties in a safe environment and improvement in their ongoing relationship through the development of constructive workable solutions to their dispute'. Furthermore, the 'avoidance of litigation brings more than [these] practical benefits, for it reduces the conflict often attached to the adversarial process', which may further undermine the wider policies being sought to be protected, whether it be the best interests of the child or, by analogy, the protection of the environment. 'Moreover, if mediation achieves an agreed settlement, then this settlement is perceived to have been achieved through a self-determinative process: a process that the parties entered into voluntarily, participated in and ultimately resolved without that resolution being imposed by the courts'. Such an approach is important when the disputes involve individuals from different countries, given that 'cross-border mediation will often mean cross-cultural mediation where differing underlying traditions, presumptions, beliefs and expectations need to be dealt with sympathetically', elements that a court is not best suited for.

III. THE REGIONAL DIMENSION

Part 3 contains three chapters which consider trends and techniques within regional processes of dispute settlement, specifically looking at judicial means. In chapter 12 Gino Naldi considers the African Court of Justice and Human Rights. An African Court was agreed in principle as part of the OAU's successor the AU, which came into being in 2002, and which marked a departure from the original African Organization's 'hesitation to put in place a judicial body' for the resolution of inter-African disputes. A Protocol of 2003 which would have created a court with similar competence to the International Court of Justice in relation to inter-State disputes was 'stillborn, as the AU decided that the Court of Justice should be merged with the African Court on Human and Peoples' Rights into one single judicial body'—the African Court of Justice and Human Rights. The merger provides an interesting case study on whether such a court, dealing with inter-State disputes on the one hand, and cases brought by individuals and NGOs on the basis of alleged human rights violations by a State on the other, can work. Arguably though, the amalgamation gives the African Court a greater chance to play a constitutional role than does the International Court of Justice, a perception that is strengthened by the fact that the African Court is expressly given powers to review all acts, decisions, regulations and directives of the AU organs. Its model may thus be seen as the European Court of Justice rather than the International Court of Justice. As the Statute of the Court is not yet in force, the workability and effectiveness of such a court outside the European region however remains to be seen.

In the final two chapters the issue of judicial competence over human rights within the EU and Council of Europe, and the European Court of Justice's competence as a constitutional court, are considered. In chapter 13, Tawhida Ahmed looks at the EU, the ECHR and the effective protection of human rights for individuals. The issue is one of consistency, for as the author notes 'the direction and development of international dispute settlement is certainly being challenged, as well as enhanced, by the multiplicity of international courts and tribunals'. In general the chapter considers the impact of judgments by the courts of one regional system concerning the protection of human rights in the other system, more specifically it centres on the European Court of Human Rights' rather tentative approach in this regard in its decision in the *Bosphorus* case. In the case the Court adopted an approach that presumes that the 'EU provides a level of protection "equivalent" ("comparable", not identical) to those found in the ECHR system in both substance and procedure and therefore closer scrutiny of whether the EU law in question specifically guarantees the right in the case before it is unnecessary'. This approach, while preserving 'harmonious relations both between the EU and the ECHR and between the ECJ and the ECtHR', seems to undermine the 'very essence of the protection promised by the ECHR: the guarantee of Convention rights *to individuals,* which are *enforceable by those individuals*'. The chapter serves admirably as a 'general account of the current stage of the law in relation to the interactions (conflicting or otherwise) in human rights dispute settlement between the two European courts in focus'.

In chapter 14, Paul James Cardwell examines the European Court of Justice as a constitutional court and considers the implications for the EU and international legal orders. It focuses on the developing relationship between the European Court of Justice and other regional and international courts, but also more profoundly between the Community/Union legal order and public international law. The chapter considers two related points: 'the increasingly blurred nature of international dispute resolution between States who are also members of the European Union, and the complexity of recognising how the EU's distinct legal order fits within the international legal system, within the context of the growth of new dimensions in the European integration process'. The chapter then concentrates on three major judgments of the ECJ since 2005, which range across the three pillar structure of the EU—*Pupino, Kadi,* and *Mox Plant*—drawing out what they tell us about the 'present state of the constitutional order of the EU and dispute resolution'.

By focusing on recent trends in international and regional judicial means of dispute settlement and alternative quasi-judicial, legal and what may be called extra-legal methods of dispute settlement, it is hoped that this book will make a significant contribution to the literature in the area and to a wider understanding of the value and importance of dispute settlement in international relations. In this way it should provide a fitting tribute to the contribution of Professor John Merrills to international law and dispute settlement.

Part 1

The Changing Face of International Adjudication

1

Private Disputes and the Public Interest in International Law

VAUGHAN LOWE

THIS SHORT PAPER is offered as a token of friendship and esteem to John Merrills, who, for four decades, has been a pillar of international law scholarship in the United Kingdom. His scholarship combines breadth and knowledge with a remarkable sense of balance and practicality which draws upon his grasp of history. While his contributions to international law have touched upon many aspects of the subject, this paper sprang from my admiration for his classic study of International Dispute Settlement, now in its fourth edition. My paper addresses, within the context of international law, some aspects of the question of whether private justice can secure the fulfilment of public values.

The question is a general one, and it underlies many of the choices which the governments of States make about the structure of the public order within the State. For example, in England, incitements to racial hatred are matters which engage the criminal law.[1] The police and other public bodies may become involved in the enforcement of that law, and perpetrators of that crime may be punished in the name of the State by the imposition of a fine or a term of imprisonment. Persons convicted of the offence acquire a criminal record, which (within certain limits) they may be obliged to disclose to potential employers and others.[2] Straightforward verbal abuse, on the other hand, is not prohibited, at least if it does not rise to the level of a breach of the peace. It is repressed by informal social sanctions—remonstrations by the target or by bystanders, and so on—if it is repressed at all.

Contracts, above all things, are regarded as personal matters, in relation to which third parties may not consider that it is appropriate for them to

[1] Public Order Act 1986 Pt III.
[2] Police Act 1997 Pt V.

intervene even with simple social sanctions.[3] If one party fails to fulfil its obligations under the contract, it is up to the other party to take action to secure its enforcement. That other party may choose not to do anything, but rather to tolerate the breach of contract; or not to go beyond informal requests and social pressures in attempts to bring the other party back into compliance with its obligations. Or the party may decide to seek enforcement through the courts, in public proceedings within the State's legal system. But, while public interest in the integrity of the legal process is engaged if the matter does go to court, the decisions on what is done in respect of the breach of contract, and on whether to have recourse to that legal process in the first place, are entirely a matter for the parties themselves. The obligations which are in question are also created and defined by the parties themselves.

False allegations of dishonest or disgraceful behaviour are dealt with in yet another way: by permitting the victim to sue the alleged wrongdoer for libel—for breach of norms created and defined not by the parties but by the legal system, in a private suit which is controlled by the parties and which the parties may settle on such terms as they see fit. All three categories of behaviour may violate the standards and norms of a society; but the violations may be handled in very different ways.

Sometimes the approaches overlap. The US antitrust laws, which play an immensely important role in the structuring of economic activity in (and, indeed, beyond) the USA, may be enforced by private actions. Companies injured by the activities of unlawful cartels may sue in treble damage actions for three times the loss that they have suffered. Antitrust laws may also be enforced by criminal actions or by civil proceedings instituted by the Department of Justice, acting in the broader public interest.

There is, it will be noted, a public interest even in the enforcement of private obligations. There may be no *public* interest in ensuring that the plumber that I hire does the work that he has contracted to do properly, or that I pay him as I have agreed to do. But if one of us believes that the other has failed to fulfil the contract, and goes to court to seek its enforcement, there *is* a public interest in ensuring that private contractual rights are upheld in fair, transparent and just proceedings in the court. The public interest here does not concern our *substantive* rights and duties, which are a matter between the plumber and me, but rather the integrity of the procedure by which our private rights are enforced.

[3] Programmes on radio and television highlighting the sufferings of consumers at the hands of suppliers, and consumer columns in newspapers, are interesting exceptions. They sometimes lead to the enactment of consumer protection legislation criminalising certain commercial practices, and so completing the translation of the contractual relations from the private to the public sphere.

The focus upon the integrity of the procedure, rather than upon the substantive rights, is reflected in the fact that the plumber and I may choose not to refer any dispute arising from the contract to the courts but rather to arbitration—to settlement by a tribunal chosen by us, sitting and deciding the case in private, so that the public need never know that we have had recourse to arbitration, or what we said to the tribunal, or what the tribunal decided. But again, if one of us fails to comply with the award of the arbitral tribunal, the other may go to the public courts to obtain an order from the courts to enforce the award. If necessary, the successful party may invoke the assistance of the law enforcement agencies of the State in the coercive enforcement of the court order. Here, again, the public interest is engaged once the matter comes within the court system.[4]

These observations are directed at the position in municipal law; but the essential distinction between public and private interest is one that has great importance in international law, too.

There is, in the eyes of many international lawyers, a serious issue arising from the convergence of two developments in international behaviour, both of them obvious and well-known. The first is the growth in the scale and the pervasiveness of the power of private corporations, and of the dependence of individuals and societies upon them. The impact upon my daily life of decisions taken by News International or Microsoft or the various companies that purport to operate travel services in this country is enormous, and certainly on a scale comparable with the influence of government decisions on my daily life. If corporate action threatens to isolate my rights or to disrupt the social order, public regulatory authorities, operating under national law, may step in.[5] The Competition Commission may intervene to prevent the abuse of a dominant position on the market; regulators may intervene in the pricing of services on which I am dependent. But here the second development comes in.

States around the world have, over the past 30 or 40 years, and particularly in the past 20 years, entered into large numbers of legally binding agreements which regulate the treatment of foreign investors. Some are regional: the detailed provisions of the North American Free Trade Agreement (NAFTA), protecting Canadian, Mexican and US investors in each other's States, for example. Many are bilateral. There are around 2,500 bilateral investment treaties under which States bind themselves to observe certain standards in the treatment of investors who are nationals

[4] The courts will also exercise a supervisory jurisdiction over the arbitral process, in order to offer a guarantee that it meets minimum standards of procedural fairness and efficiency. See Arbitration Act 1996.

[5] This was written before the spectacular banking failures of October 2008, which may have prompted a more cautious view of the ability of regulatory bodies to protect the public interest.

of the other State party. Typically, these are obligations not to expropriate their property except under certain conditions and with proper compensation, to treat the investment fairly and equitably, to give full protection and security to the investment, and not to discriminate against investors. In these ways, public authorities bind their freedom of action by giving private rights to foreign investors. Moreover, though I speak of 'States' doing this, it is of course governments who do this, usually acting under their power, within the national constitutional order, to make treaties.

This last point is significant. If the governments were establishing these rights for investors by legislation, or by the decision of Executive officials, there would be an opportunity for scrutiny and debate in Parliament, and for challenges to Government decisions in the courts. But by establishing private rights in international treaties, both possibilities may in practice be excluded in many States whose constitutional provisions give the Executive a more or less free hand in the areas of treaty-making and the conduct of foreign affairs.

The rights of investors under bilateral investment treaties are extensive. I have already mentioned the substantive right of investors, notably the right to 'fair and equitable' treatment and to 'full protection and security' for their investments—both terms of art employed in investment treaties. If these terms sound vague, that is a reflection of their remarkable breadth. An investor may be treated in a manner that is in complete accordance with national law (the enactment, amendment and repeal of which is, of course, likely to be within the control of the Government); but the treatment may nonetheless be unfair and inequitable. To put the point another way, there may be no legal right of the investor under the law of the host State that has been infringed; but the investor may nevertheless be entitled to a legal remedy under the bilateral investment treaty if its investment has been treated by the State in a manner that is judged to be unfair or unreasonable,[6] or if its investment is harmed by any third party and it is judged that the State should have protected it from that harm.[7] Under the treaty, the investor would in principle be entitled to recover from the State the full extent of the loss that it has suffered.

The bilateral investment treaties typically give investors—private corporations and individuals—the right to invoke arbitration in the event of a dispute. The investor and the respondent State each appoint one arbitrator, and they agree upon a third, presiding, arbitrator, failing which some designated impartial authority, such as the President of the International Court of Justice, will make the appointment. The system

[6] See, eg *Metalclad Corp v Mexico* ICSID Case No ARB(AF)/97/1.

[7] *CME Czech Republic BV v The Czech Republic (Partial Award)* (2002) 14:3 *World Trade and Arbitration Materials* 109.

is tight and effective: the investor can insist upon the constitution of an arbitral tribunal to rule upon its claim; and even if the State refuses to participate the tribunal will nonetheless proceed to hear and decide upon the claim.

One of the characteristics of arbitration is the principle of confidentiality that attaches to it,[8] to which I have already referred. Another aspect of the essentially private nature of arbitration is the principle that no third party is entitled to intervene in the proceedings of the arbitral tribunal without the consent of the parties, which may be given either specifically or by the inclusion of some provision for intervention in the rules that the parties have chosen to govern the arbitration.[9] In the municipal courts, in contrast, there are procedural devices such as the right of the court to appoint an *amicus curiae* to represent the public interest or the interest of a non-party, and the right of the court to permit or compel a third person to be joined as a party to the proceedings.[10]

Let me give two examples to illustrate the point. First, the *Tecmed* case: there the Mexican government's environmental agency decided not to renew a Spanish investor's permit to operate a landfill site. The decision was justified by Mexico on environmental grounds and also on the basis of local opposition to the operation of the landfill site. The investor argued that the non-renewal amounted to an expropriation of its property, in violation of its rights under the bilateral investment treaty between Spain and Mexico. The arbitral tribunal agreed, and awarded $5.5m damages to the investor (a relatively modest sum: the Czech Republic was ordered to pay over $350m to Ronald Lauder for breaches of duties which the Republic owed under bilateral investment tribunals to a television company that he had set up jointly with local Czech partners). The Government decision in *Tecmed* was lawful and effective in Mexican law, and the investor would have had no remedy and no right to reverse the decision in the Mexican courts. The decision was, moreover, defended by Mexico by reference to the responsibility of the Mexican government for safeguarding the environment, and its responsibility to listen to and take account of the views of the citizens from whom it derives its powers and to whom its laws and decisions are primarily applied.

The *Tecmed* tribunal, sitting in Washington DC, could hear witnesses put forward by the two parties, Tecmed and the Mexican Government; but it did not have other witnesses representing the interests of the local

[8] See, eg C Knahr, 'Transparency, Third Party Participation and Access to Documents in International Investment Arbitration' (2007) 23 *Arbitration International* 327–35.

[9] JDM Lew, LA Mistelis and S Kröll, *Comparative International Commercial Arbitration* (The Hague, Kluwer, 2003) 389–92; C Chinkin, *Third Parties in International Law* (Oxford, Oxford University Press, 1993) 281–82.

[10] Civil Procedure Act 1997 s 1; CPR 19.

community and what might be said to be the impersonal 'interests' of the environment.[11] The proceedings were not opened to the public; and while the award was in fact published with the agreement of the parties, they were not obliged to give that agreement.

As a second example, let me take the *Methanex* case. *Methanex,* like *Tecmed,* arose under the NAFTA. But it is typical of the cases that are arising in considerable numbers under bilateral investment treaties.

The *Methanex* case arose from a dispute over the production and sale of methyl tertiary-butyl ether (MTBE), an additive for petrol which replaced the use of lead. The State Government of California had allocated $500,000 from public funds to the University of California to investigate and report on 'the human health and environmental risks and benefits, if any' associated with the use of MTBE. In addition, the Governor of California, then Mr Gray Davis, issued an Executive Order recording that there was a significant risk to the environment arising from the use of MTBE. The Order was issued in March 1999 and required the California Energy Commission to develop by July 1999 a timetable for the removal of MTBE from gasoline by the end of 2002.

Methanex, a Canadian corporation, based in Vancouver, was the world's largest producer of methanol, and a leading producer of MTBE. It complained that the Californian measures (which, under well-established principles of international law, were attributed to the United States[12]) were a disguised restriction on trade and investment intended to protect the US ethanol industry, which produced products that competed directly with MTBE. Methanex argued that MTBE was safe, and approved for use by the *federal* authorities in the USA, and in Europe. It said that ethanol, in contrast, is harmful to human health. Nonetheless, ethanol production was heavily subsidised by tax breaks in the USA, where ethanol was produced from corn.

Plainly, the case raised important questions of public policy, and the proceedings were a matter of considerable public interest.

The tribunal eventually held that Methanex had not proved its allegations, noting that California, far from encouraging the use of ethanol, was moving towards a phasing-out of all such additives, and that almost half of US methanol came from domestic producers in the USA who were

[11] Plainly, 'the environment' does not have 'interests' of its own. There are groups who argue for particular causes of action and do so by reference to objectives which are defined or described in terms of effects upon 'the environment' (itself a term that could usefully be subjected to further analysis). This raises the question of the basis upon which one might properly identify those who are interested in any particular matter. See further 'Part II: Contemporary Environmental Ethics' in D Jamieson (ed), *A Companion to Environmental Philosophy* (Oxford, Blackwell, 2001).

[12] See International Law Commission's Articles on the Responsibility of States for Internationally Wrongful Acts Art 4 UN Doc A/56/10 (2001).

affected by the Californian measures in the same way as Methanex. But the question here is, how should we accommodate the public interest in such cases? It would be unthinkable for the government of the UK or the European Community to be able to adopt measures such as those in question in *Methanex*, and for a legal challenge to them to be heard and decided *in camera*, and for the decision to remain 'confidential'. Should the position be any different where such measures are the focus of an investment dispute heard by an international arbitration tribunal?

To break the question down, what kinds of public interest are appropriate to be put before international tribunals, and who should decide that question? Who should be permitted to make representations in the public interest? Elected local councils? State agencies, such as environmental agencies established by the government of a State? International scientific bodies? Organisations with an explicit political agenda, such as Greenpeace or Amnesty International? You? Me? The Church of Scientology? And again, who decides?

And how should the public interest be presented and represented in the proceedings? By the submission of written briefs? By the making of oral presentations? And should the parties be allowed, or required, to respond to arguments and analyses introduced by intervenors—and if the parties do respond, should the intervenor have any right of reply? And what should the tribunal then do with the arguments and facts concerning the public interest which are put before it? Could they prevail over the rights of the parties?

Bilateral Investment Treaties gave no guidance on these questions. There are no provisions explaining how environmental, health, or political interests are to be reconciled with the explicit rights of investors in a State. There are no provisions directing a tribunal hearing a dispute on how it should deal with requests to intervene and put arguments and facts relating to the public interest.

One reason for choosing the *Methanex* case as an example is that the tribunal there faced exactly these questions. The claim was filed by Methanex in December 1999; and in August 2000 the International Institute for Sustainable Development, an NGO based in Canada, requested permission to intervene. The request was followed shortly afterwards by two similar requests, from Communities for a Better Environment, and the Earth Island Institute, two California-based NGOs. NAFTA was silent on the admissibility of *amicus* briefs, as were the UNCITRAL arbitration rules under which the tribunal was operating. The only relevant rules were those empowering the tribunal to 'conduct the arbitration in such manner as it considers appropriate' and stipulating that the oral 'hearings shall be held *in camera* unless the parties agree otherwise.'

The *Methanex* tribunal concluded that it had the power to accept written *amicus curiae* briefs, and that it would do so, although it would not give the intervenors access to the papers submitted by the parties in the arbitration. The decision was based explicitly on considerations of the public interest in the arbitration and on the desirability of transparency in the NAFTA arbitration process. The tribunal recognised, however, that the intervenors were likely to adopt a pro-environment stance and to tend towards supporting the Respondent (the United States) rather than the applicant Methanex, and that the Applicant might therefore need some procedural protection—such as additional time to respond to interventions—in order to safeguard its position.

The approach of the *Methanex* decision to the admission of *amicus* briefs is mirrored in decisions in other investment arbitrations, and was in effect brought in as part of the institutional structure of such arbitrations by the inclusion of similar provisions in the 2006 amendments of the rules of the International Centre for the Settlement of Investment Disputes, in what is now Rule 37(2) of the Arbitration Rules.[13]

Similar developments have been taking place elsewhere. In 2004 the United States published a new Model Bilateral Investment Treaty (BIT)[14]—a template for the treaties which it negotiates with other countries. The 2004 Model Treaty, perhaps surprisingly, displays considerable enthusiasm on the part of the United States Government for *amicus* interventions in investment cases. It expressly states, in Article 28(3), that a tribunal hearing on investment dispute 'shall have the authority to accept and consider *amicus curiae* submissions from a person or entity that is not a disputing party.' But it goes further than that, and also requires the Respondent State to transmit to the intervening *amicus* copies of the pleadings and papers submitted to the tribunal, and to make those documents available to the public.

In this respect the 2004 US Model BIT marks a decisive break with the past tradition of confidential arbitrations—though it must be said that in the field of investment arbitrations, while the proceedings and award are in principle private, it has become common during the past decade for parties to choose to release the relevant documentation, at least after the close of the proceedings. The 2004 Model BIT provisions clearly recognise the public interest in what the law has traditionally regarded as private proceedings.

This recognition is, however, not universal. The World Trade Organization has a sophisticated and very active system of dispute settlement, operating through impartial quasi-judicial Panels and equipped with its own appeal procedure. The dispute settlement provisions empower

[13] ICSID, Rules of Procedure for Arbitration Proceedings, http://icsid.worldbank.org/ICSID/ICSID/RulesMain.jsp.

[14] See www.ustr.gov/assets/Trade_Sectors/Investment/Model_BIT/asset_upload_file847_6897.pdf.

Panels to 'seek information and technical advice from any individual or body which it deems appropriate'. When the Panel hearing the *Shrimp-Turtle* dispute,[15] which concerned restrictions imposed by the USA on imports of shrimps caught by methods said to kill significant numbers of endangered species of turtle, was offered *amicus* briefs by interested NGOs, it refused to accept them. The WTO Appellate Body,[16] however, ruled in 1998 that Panels had the right (though not the duty) to accept unsolicited *amicus* briefs, as well as the undoubted right to ask NGOs and others to make representations to the Panel. A little later, in the *Asbestos* dispute,[17] it was confirmed that WTO Panels, and the Appellate Body itself, could receive *amicus* briefs; but the position remains controversial.

In 2000 Egypt requested a special meeting of the WTO General Council to consider the question;[18] and most States, other than the USA, were critical of the position taken by the Appellate Body. While the Appellate Body has not withdrawn from its position on the admissibility of *amicus* briefs, it has in fact accepted relatively few and refused to accept many of those offered to it.[19]

These developments in investment tribunals, in the NAFTA and investment treaties, and in the WTO, are part of a clear trend towards increasing what might, somewhat tendentiously, be called 'public participation' in private dispute settlement.[20] The trend is by no means universal. The International Court of Justice, for example, does not accept *amicus* submissions into the record of proceedings before it—although its librarian is, I believe, willing to accept them into the Court's library, where the judges are free to read them, or not, as they wish. But the trend is clear, and is clearly borne out of a concern to promote the transparency and what is termed the legitimacy (which seems often to mean little more than the ability to fend off authoritative or organised criticism) of decisions taken by tribunals adjudicating upon disputes which implicate questions of serious public concern.

[15] *United States—Import Prohibition of Certain Shrimp and Shrimp Products*, Report of the Panel (15 May 1998) WT/DS58/R [7.7]–[7.8].

[16] *United States—Import Prohibition of Certain Shrimp and Shrimp Products*, Report of the Appellate Body (12 October 1998) WT/DS58/AB/R [79]–[91].

[17] *EC—Measures Affecting Asbestos and Products Containing Asbestos*, Report of the Appellate Body (12 March 2001) WT/DS135/AB/R [50]–[57].

[18] WTO General Council, Minutes of Meeting Held on 22 November 2000 (23 January 2001) WT/GC/M/60.

[19] B Paterson, '*Trasformismo* at the World Trade Organization', ch 4 in M McNally and J Schwarzmantel (eds) *Gramsci and Global Politics: Hegemony and Resistance*. (New York: Routledge, 2009). [ISBN: 9780415474696]

[20] See, eg: O Nisja, 'Confidentiality and Public Access in Arbitration—The Norwegian Approach' [2008] *International Arbitration Law Review* 187–92; C Knahr and A Reinisch, 'Transparency versus Confidentiality in International Investment Arbitration' (2007) 6 *Law & Practice of International Courts and Tribunals* 97–118; A Mourre, 'Are *Amici Curiae* the Proper Response to the Public's Concerns on Transparency in Investment Arbitration?' (2006) 5 *Law & Practice of International Courts and Tribunals* 257–71.

The trend, and the principles to which it relates, has a wider significance. Public participation is regarded as a free-standing goal, worthy of protection and advancement in international agreements. The 1998 Åarhus Convention on Access to Information, Public Participation in Decision-Making and Access to Justice in Environmental Matters[21] does what its name suggests. The 41 States parties, from Ireland and the UK in the west to Tajikistan and Turkmenistan in the east, have bound themselves to guarantee prescribed minimum rights of access to information and to public participation in environmental decision-making. Perhaps the idea will one day catch on in other areas of public life.

One might push the point further, and say that public participation is simply one aspect of the broader role which it is now recognised non-State entities can and should play in the international legal system.[22] While human rights instruments have long given individuals, and corporations, a place on the international juridical stage, the instrument that epitomises this broader principle is the UN Global Compact,[23] launched (these days legal instruments which have a high inspirational content are not 'adopted' but 'launched', like the *Titanic*) in 2000. The Compact is described by its secretariat as 'a framework for businesses that are committed to aligning their operations and strategies with ten universally accepted principles in the areas of human rights, labour, the environment, and anti-corruption'. While the Principles may be thought to lack something in specificity—Principle 1 reads 'Businesses should support and respect the protection of internationally proclaimed human rights'—it is the conception of the instrument that is significant. It recognises that States have no monopoly when it comes to the development of effective international principles and standards, and that it is necessary to involve non-State actors in the processes of law-making and implementation. The Global Compact claims to have over 3,000 participating companies world-wide, and a key element of its programme is the encouragement that it gives to companies to 'engage in dialogue with the company's stakeholders'—that is, to bring the whole of civil society within the great enterprise.

That observation brings me full circle. I began by considering some of the questions to which the settlement of disputes between States—governments—and private corporate investors give rise, and asked whether private justice could adequately secure public interests. I have moved to the question of the involvement of civil society as a whole in

[21] UN Doc ECE/CEP/43, opened for signature 25 June 1998, entered into force 30 October 2001.

[22] For a recent survey, see S Ripinsky and P Van den Bossche, *NGO Involvement in International Organizations* (London, BIICL, 2007).

[23] www.unglobalcompact.org.

the development and implementation of principles and rules of international law. But I need now to return to the fundamental question, this time posed at a higher level of abstraction.

In municipal legal systems, we think of laws as being made by the legislature,[24] which is generally appointed so as to be representative in some way of the community for which the laws are made. We regard laws as having greater importance in the public arena than contracts, which are essentially private arrangements. Indeed, the essence of a contract is that it is an exercise of individual autonomy, creating rights and obligations within the limits set by legislation. In international law, the picture is very different. There are very, very few mandatory rules of international law which impose limitations upon the freedom of States to enter into binding obligations of their own choosing. A handful of peremptory norms—rules of *jus cogens*—prohibit, for example, the making of agreements to engage in genocide or aggressive war or slavery; and any such agreement would be null and void. But that leaves immense scope for States to reach agreements setting out the rules of conduct that will bind them. In this sense, international law is overwhelmingly consensual, contractual, in nature.

But how can the public interest be secured in this context? What are we to make of a position where, for example, States which are bound by a duty to conserve and manage the living resources of the seas reach an agreement setting unsustainable quotas on fish catches; or when States whose nationals are subjected to detention and interrogation in circumstances that would amount to a violation of international law, choose not to complain about that treatment but to waive the right to object and to defend their nationals? What do we say if—as the World Trade Organization's General Agreement on Tariffs and Trade (GATT) specifically permits[25]—a State complaining that another State is acting inconsistently with its GATT obligations reaches a 'satisfactory adjustment': in other words, if they strike a side deal?

The significance of such side deals must not be underestimated. Sometimes they have a relatively minor impact on the more generally observed rules—or serve even to strengthen those rules. For example, the 1982 Law of the Sea Convention leaves unsettled important questions as to the content of the right of innocent passage through a State's territorial sea, but a side deal between the USA and the then USSR defining that content as between the two of them effectively set the standard for all other States.[26] Sometimes side deals are more disruptive: the UK opt-outs

[24] These observations apply equally to judge-made common law.

[25] Art XXIII.

[26] Uniform Interpretation of Norms of International Law Governing Innocent Passage (USA–USSR) (23 September 1989) in (1989) 14 United Nations, Law of the Sea Bulletin 12–13.

in EU law[27] might be thought to be examples of side deals which do little to strengthen the legal regime to which they are attached, even though they may enhance (at least in some quarters) the political acceptability of that regime. But some, such as the restraints on international trade in textiles set out in the Multi-Fibre Arrangement,[28] which effectively re-wrote the basic trade rules in the GATT, do not simply modify the norm, they *become* the norm for most practical purposes. Looking only at the 'basic' legal rules would give a misleading view of the position: one must look also at the ways in which States have tweaked their own specific obligations under those rules, in order to understand properly the normative framework in international matters.

These are examples of agreed modifications to the legal obligations of States under international law, entered into as a result of negotiations conducted by governments—by the Executive—often without the need for any legislative approval or judicial scrutiny in their own States. And functionally they are similar, within the international legal system, to the private settlement of disputes. So let me put the initial question again, but in a slightly different way. Given the nature of international law, is it possible for the international legal system adequately to protect the public interest? Or does its predominantly consensual, contractual nature impede, or even preclude, the achievement of that goal?

The answer to the question is of fundamental importance. It is—or at least should be—the key factor delimiting our expectations of international law and our ambitions for it. To take two extreme positions on the question, we might say that we should look to international law to constrain the actions of irresponsible and wicked governments, and that when municipal legal remedies prove incapable of preventing, punishing or remedying violations of, say, human rights or environmental rules, international law should step in.

On the other hand, we might say that the nature of international law is such that it can never effectively fulfil that role, and that we—and I mean

[27] See the Protocol on Certain Provisions relating to the United Kingdom of Great Britain and Northern Ireland attached to the Treaty on European Union [1992] OJ C191 (opt-out from the Economic and Monetary Union); and the Protocol on the application of certain aspects of Article 7a of the Treaty establishing the European Community to the United Kingdom and to Ireland, attached to the Treaty of Amsterdam [1997] OJ C340 (opt-out from the Schengen acquis). Further opt-outs have been negotiated by the UK with respect to the Treaty of Lisbon: see, eg Protocol on the application of the Charter of Fundamental Rights of the European Union to Poland and to the United Kingdom [2007] OJ C306.

[28] The *Arrangement regarding International Trade in Textiles* (adopted 20 December 1973, entered into force 2 January 1974 (provisionally), 17 January 1974 (definitively)) 930 UNTS 166, was originally intended to apply for four years; however it remained in force until 1994 (through consecutive renewals).

here not simply readers of papers on international law, but humankind as a whole—must seek our remedies on the municipal level.

There has for centuries been a tendency to respond to this and similar questions by focusing upon the lack of sanctions in international law. I think that is both an incorrect appraisal of the situation and a misdirected focus of attention. Incorrect, because while international law lacks the uniformed police who do such a fine job of maintaining law and order on the streets of London, Harare, Mogadishu and elsewhere, it has a wide range of mechanisms for attaching unpleasant and costly consequences to violations of legal rules, and therefore unattractive. For example, in its dispute with Venezuela over the alleged mistreatment of its investments in that country by the Venezuelan Government, in breach of Venezuela's obligations under international law, Exxon obtained within a matter of weeks an order from a US court freezing around $300m of the assets of Petróleos de Venezuela SA (PDVSA), the Venezuelan State-owned oil company, and orders from courts in the UK and the Netherlands freezing a further $12 billion of PDVSA assets.[29]

The focus on the question of the sanctions available to international law is, furthermore, misdirected, in my opinion; and for two reasons. First, compliance with *any* system of law is motivated primarily by factors other than sanctions. It is not fear of incurring penalties under the Road Traffic Act that leads me to drive on the left-hand side of the road in England; nor fear of prosecution that leads me to refrain from murder, rape and burglary.

Second—and this is the most important point—focus on sanctions under international law directs attention away from the fact that the rules of international law, whether complied with or violated, can be modified by States, because international law is a predominantly consensual system. If the rules are unattractive or inconvenient, States can almost always decide not to sign up to them (as with the USA on the Kyoto Protocol), to strike a side deal (as in the Multi-Fibre Agreement), or to exercise whatever right there may be to withdraw from them (as Venezuela is threatening to do in respect of the Convention on the Settlement of Investment Disputes).[30] Again, it should be emphasised that decisions on these matters are decisions for the Government, for the Executive; and in

[29] S Bodzin and M Walter, 'Venezuela to Fight Exxon's $12 Billion Asset Freeze' *Bloomberg.com* (8 February 2008), www.bloomberg.com/apps/news?pid=20601087&sid=aMaMx3TW91KQ&refer=home. The freezing order was subsequently set aside by the High Court: *Mobil Cerro Negro Ltd v Petróleos de Venezuela SA* [2008] EWHC 532 (Comm).

[30] F Cabrera Diaz, 'South American Alternative to ICSID in the Works as Governments Create an Energy Treaty' *Investment Treaty News* (6 August 2008) www.investmenttreatynews.org/. In fact Bolivia was the first state to withdraw from the ICSID Convention: 'Bolivia Submits a Notice under Article 71 of the ICSID Convention' *ICSID News Release* (16 May 2007), http://icsid.worldbank.org.

many States these decisions fall within a barely-constrained prerogative power (whether the Royal Prerogative of the British Constitution[31] or the marginally more rational foreign affairs prerogative that exists in many other States).

If one wishes to hold a State to its international legal obligations, one must make sure that it remains bound by those obligations before one seeks to enforce them. It is, I think, at the very least arguable that the fight to keep a State bound by specific rules of international law is a fight that must in the nature of things be fought primarily at the local level—by political and legal pressure on the governments of States, brought to bear primarily through domestic channels and institutions. That is a consequence of the fact that the political duties and responsibilities of governments are owed to their internal electorates, and not to some hypothesised 'international community'.

So, can international law adequately protect public interests? Not entirely, in my view. International law is a flexible, valuable, indispensable tool. But, like the Swiss Army knife and the iPhone, not even international law can do everything. Some battles must be fought at home, on the domestic stage.

[31] *R (Bancoult) v Secretary of State for Foreign and Commonwealth Affairs* [2008] UKHL 61, [2007] EWCA Civ 498, [2006] EWHC 1038 (Admin).

2

The International Court of Justice and Environmental Disputes

MALGOSIA FITZMAURICE

I. INTRODUCTION

THE SUBJECT OF the role of the International Court of Justice (ICJ) in relation to environmental issues and disputes has attracted considerable interest among both theorists and practitioners in recent years; and there are a number of cases currently pending before the Court which hold out the promise of further development and crystallisation of the norms of international environmental law. Overall, the number of cases having an environmental element has grown significantly since the first essays on this subject were published.[1]

The present chapter will cover not only particular cases before the Court which have an environmental aspect, but also a number of general doctrinal issues which underlie the adjudication of cases which have an impact on the development of international environmental law and which have been the subject of consideration in the jurisprudence of the Court, although not necessarily in those particular cases which have directly involved environmental issues. Analysis of these, which will be presented in the first Part of the chapter, will involve some consideration of the work of other law-developing forums besides the Court itself, in particular the International Law Commission (ILC). The second part of the chapter will cover the cases of the Court having a direct environmental element (both those already decided and those currently pending). Finally, in the third part of the chapter, there will be a brief discussion of the subject of the possible establishment of an environmental court, and of the actual establishment of the ICJ's Chamber for Environmental Matters.

[1] See, eg: PN Okowa, 'Environmental Dispute Settlement: Some Reflections on Recent Developments' in M Evans (ed), *Remedies in International Law* (Oxford, Hart Publishing, 1998); M Fitzmaurice, 'Environmental Protection and the International Court of Justice', in V Lowe and M Fitzmaurice (eds), *Fifty Years of the International Court of Justice. Essays in Honour of Sir Robert Jennings* (Cambridge, Cambridge University Press, 1996).

II. PART ONE: SOME GENERAL ISSUES CONSIDERED BY THE ICJ WHICH ARE RELEVANT TO ENVIRONMENTAL DISPUTES

In this part, we will consider aspects of the nature of international environmental norms and related issues concerning bilateralism and multilateralism in relation to treaties and to the law of State responsibility, the starting point of which is the work of the ILC on the subject of State responsibility (Section A). This subject involves, of course, the issue—and it is one to which the realm of environmental protection is particularly relevant—of the concept of *erga omnes*, including that of obligations *erga omnes partes* within multilateral treaty regimes. These issues lead on naturally to the question of the concept of an injured State, and thence to the issue of countermeasures, the right to invoke State responsibility and *locus standi* before the ICJ (Section B). The third section (Section C) in this part considers the issues of the community interest and the obligation *erga omnes* and that of third party intervention, with particular reference to the treatment of these issues by the ICJ in the *Nuclear Tests* Cases of 1974 and 1995 (more specifically environmental issues arising in these cases is considered in Part III of the chapter).

A. The Legal Nature of Environmental Norms

i. Nature of International Environmental Norms and Relevance of Bilateralism and Multilateralism

The special character of norms of international environmental law was recognised by the ILC during its codification of the law concerning State responsibility, in relation to types of, and legal consequences arising from, multilateral obligations.[2] In particular, it was recognised that, despite superficial similarities, the legal characters of human rights obligations and environmental obligations are distinct. According to the Special Rapporteur, James Crawford, 'human rights obligations are specifically formulated in terms of the rights of individuals, whereas for example international environmental instruments speak of the obligations of States'.[3] The Special Rapporteur presented a comprehensive analysis of the legal nature and effects of bilateralism and multilateralism in international relations. It is quite notable that classical international law is predicated upon bilateralism. This was evidenced by comments of certain members of the

[2] J Crawford, ILC, 'Third Report on State Responsibility', Fifty-second session, Geneva, 1 May–9 June; 10 July; 18 August 2000, A/CN.4/507, paras 82–119. See also 2001 Draft Articles on State Responsibility, in particular, Arts 42 and 48, http://untreaty.un.org/ilc/texts/instruments/english/draft%20articles/9_6_2001.pdf.

[3] Crawford, ibid, para 89.

ILC and of States on the occasion of the adoption in 1985 of Draft Article 40 of the Draft Articles on State Responsibility, dealing with the notion of an injured State.[4] One of the main difficulties concerning this Article was reconciling the concept of 'standing' in cases concerning infringements of rights arising from multilateral treaties with the inherent bilateralism of relations between States, in particular the very specific notions of an 'injured State' and 'legal interest' which in traditional international law are very precisely defined and constitute a stumbling block in cases in which the vindication of wider community values is at stake.

There are various classifications of multilateral obligations, the most fundamental of which was submitted by Sir Gerald Fitzmaurice as a Rapporteur of the ILC during its work on the codification of the law of treaties.[5] Analysis of the full theory of Fitzmaurice exceeds the framework of this study; suffice it to note that in his basic classification, he drew a distinction between reciprocal (concessionary) and multilateral obligations, which in turn were divided into absolute and integral or interdependent obligations. This last type of obligation presupposes the interest of all States in their observance, although in fact their legal nature may vary widely. Absolute obligations are predicated on the premise that the performance of such obligations is not dependent upon the behaviour of other States in respect of such obligations, and that there are no benefits linked to compliance with them. It is suggested that this type of obligation may be extended to the environmental field in treaties which express their standard-setting nature by referring to the object of protection as a 'common heritage of mankind' or 'good of mankind' or by emphasising the 'intrinsic' value of nature.[6] In contrast to absolute obligations, in the case of interdependent obligations, all States have an interest in the performance of the obligations of all other States, as the non-performance by one State imperils the whole purpose of undertaking such an obligation by every State. According to Fitzmaurice, an example of such interdependent obligations is provided by obligations in the field of disarmament.

Environmental law obligations may be given as a modern example of such obligations, where, in the case of global Multilateral Environmental Agreements (MEAs), non-performance by one party defeats the whole purpose of the treaty (eg, the protection of the ozone layer, or the prevention or control of climate change). It may be noted that that from a doctrinal point of view the differentiation between the legal character of

[4] *Yearbook of the ILC* (1985) vol II (pt 2) 25–27.

[5] G Fitzmaurice, *Second Report*, Draft Art 19(1)(iv), *Yearbook of the ILC* (1957), vol II 31; ibid Draft Art18(3)(e), *Yearbook of the ILC* (1959), vol II, 46.

[6] CH Tams, *Enforcing Obligations Erga Omnes in International Law* (Cambridge, Cambridge University Press, 2005) 57.

these types of multilateral obligations is very challenging, owing to their very nuanced differences.[7]

The classification of Fitzmaurice gave rise to the distinction drawn by Crawford between types of multilateral obligations referred to in Draft Article 40. The first type included obligations towards the international community as a whole (*erga omnes*). The second type—obligations *erga omnes partes*—are particularly important regarding the field of environmental protection. According to the Special Rapporteur, this latter type of obligation is based on the premise that there is a common legal interest of all State parties in the maintenance and implementation of the international regime. Examples of such obligations may be found in the field of the environment, such as in relation to biodiversity or global warming. The relevant feature of such obligations is that, although it is conceivable that one of a few States may be especially affected by the breach, such an event is unlikely and is in any event 'without prejudice to the general interest in the subject matter which is shared by all States parties collectively.'[8] Finally, mention must be made of obligations to which some or many States are parties but in respect of which a particular State or group of States is recognised as legally interested, that is, in cases of multilateral obligations (including obligations *erga omnes*) they have a specific interest in compliance with these obligations. It must be observed that these categories are not mutually exclusive.

The following States are entitled to invoke responsibility in respect to multilateral obligations: obligations *erga omnes*—all States; obligations *erga omnes partes*—all States parties (as in case of the integral obligation); multilateral obligations generally—unless otherwise provided, any State 'specially affected by the breach or regarded as having a special interest'.[9] It is worth noting that the category of obligations *erga omnes partes* is not without controversy. It has been suggested that there is no need to distinguish such a category of obligations at all, for several reasons, the most important being that the legal regime governing obligations *erga omnes partes* first and foremost depends on the express or implied terms of the treaty of which they form part. As a consequence, the rules governing the various obligations *erga omnes partes*:

> are considerably more diverse than those governing obligations *erga omnes* … whereas obligations *erga omnes* and *erga omnes partes* are similar in that all States bound by the obligation have a legal interest in seeing it performed, the applicable rules may be very different. Since treaties often expressly regulate under which circumstances all States have a legal interest on seeing the treaty

[7] Ibid 57.
[8] Crawford above n 2, para 106(b).
[9] Ibid para 107.

> observed, and how the legal interest can be vindicated, the regime governing obligations *erga omnes partes* is considerably more flexible.[10]

Owing to these considerations, the same author expresses doubts whether 'anything approaching a coherent legal regime of obligations *erga omnes partes* has yet emerged'.[11]

ii. The Relevance of the Injured State

The thorny issue of the invocation of State responsibility by an injured State was covered by two of the Draft Articles, Articles 42 (previously 43) and 48 (previously 49). The legal issues concerning the invocation of State responsibility by a State, the standing of a State in case of countermeasures, and the standing of a State to bring a claim before the ICJ are inexorably linked together.

Within the realm of the law of treaties Article 60 of the 1969 Vienna Convention on the Law of Treaties gives a State the possibility of redress for material breach of a treaty. This Article is constructed in a way that combines the traditional bilateralism in relationships between States with the possibility of multilateral action under certain strictly regulated conditions in the event of material breach.[12] The structure of Article 60 followed Fitzmaurice's classification of obligations. However, as Tams observes, 'decentralised responses to breaches are only permitted where there is an exchange of benefits between States', as consequence of which 'in the absence of individually sustained injury, decentralised reactions are only permitted in response to breaches of interdependent obligations'.[13] Tams continues:

> In contrast, outside that narrowly defined category, the general interest of each and every State in the observance of reciprocal or absolute obligations is not sufficient to trigger an individual right of response.[14]

B. Countermeasures, Right to Invoke State Responsibility and Standing before the ICJ

The issues covered under this heading are among the most challenging in international law and this section will give an outline of these problems

[10] Tams, above n 6, 125, 127–28.

[11] Ibid 128.

[12] The detailed analysis of Art 60 exceeds the framework of this chapter. See on this subject M Fitzmaurice and O Elias, *Contemporary Issues in the Law of Treaties* (Utrecht, Eleven International Publishing, 2005).

[13] Tams, above n 6 at 63.

[14] Ibid.

as a general background to the issues arising in environmental claims before the ICJ.

Countermeasures are an institution of customary international law. Article 49 of the Articles on State Responsibility defines their object in the following manner:

> 1. An injured State may only take countermeasures against a State which is responsible for an internationally wrongful act in order to induce that State to comply with its obligations.

There is direct link between the permissibility of the recourse to countermeasures by a State and the dispute pending before an international judicial body which has authority to take a binding decision on the issue between the parties. In such an event, countermeasures are not permissible, owing to Article 52(3)(a).[15] This means that when a dispute is before the ICJ, countermeasures cannot be taken or, if already started, must be suspended without undue delay. Notwithstanding differences between countermeasures and judicial proceedings before the ICJ, their purpose is to put 'pressure on a State that has violated international law.'[16] Recourse to both procedures is subject to many conditions and limitations. The main question which still remains a challenge is the legal possibility of the adoption of countermeasures by States which are not directly and individually injured in relation to breaches of the obligations *erga omnes*. There has been a very heated debate concerning this issue. One view expressed by many scholars is that there is insufficient practice (and also a lack of *opinio juris*) to support the existence in customary international law of such a right to take countermeasures; however, a contrary proposition also has support and is based on the premise that contemporary international law recognises the right of all States to adopt countermeasures in response to large-scale or systematic breaches of obligations *erga omnes*.[17]

Articles 42 and 48 are predicated upon the distinction between the narrow definition of an injured State (Article 42) and a broader definition (Article 48) of States which may invoke State responsibility. In relation to what Crawford has referred to as 'victimless' breaches of community obligations—that is, those without a specific, identifiable victims, for example in the event of certain obligations *erga omnes* in the environmental field, such as involving an injury to global commons—if restitution is materially impossible, then other States may be limited to seeking cessation, satisfaction and assurances against repetition. As the Special Rapporteur stressed,

[15] See also Air Services Case, France v United States (1978), 18 RIAA 416.
[16] Tams, above n 6 at 25.
[17] Ibid 250.

> [a]gain, however, these are significant in themselves, and any State party to the relevant collective obligation should be entitled to invoke responsibility in these respects.[18]

The standing of parties in the pursuit of redress of violations of various types of obligation, both bilateral and multilateral (including obligations *erga omnes* and *erga omnes partes*), depends on particular rules of standing before the ICJ within the realm of invocation of State responsibility (countermeasures). Tams suggests that in the *Barcelona Traction* case, the Court appeared 'to accept that standing to institute proceedings would follow the general rules of responsibility'.[19] He continued: 'Hence damage suffered by shareholders in *Barcelona Traction* did not justify a "diplomatic claim" nor involved "responsibility"'.[20] The same author argues that the final rejection of the Applicant's judicial claim by the ICJ was in fact implying that they had no right to invoke the Defendant's responsibility. Likewise, he further says, certain decisions of the ICJ relating to standing to institute proceedings have been acknowledged as having defined the general rules of standing to invoke State responsibility.[21] These issues are closely linked, but not coterminous. However, their legal proximity may lead to the conclusion that in cases where 'a State can establish a general right to invoke another State's responsibility, it may be presumed to have standing' before the ICJ.[22]

C. Community Concerns before the ICJ in Environmental Matters

i. Obligations Erga Omnes *Before the Court and the 1974 Nuclear Tests Cases*[23]

Both Applicants in this case—ie, Australia and New Zealand—relied on obligations *erga omnes* in their pleadings, citing the *Barcelona Traction* case for the purpose of establishing their standing before the Court.[24] Australia asserted that the prohibition of nuclear testing and the duty of observance of this prohibition existed in international customary law and

18 Above n 2, para 379.

19 Tams, above n 6 at 39.

20 Ibid, quoting from Barcelona Traction, Light and Power Co Ltd (Belgium v Spain) [1970] ICJ Rep 36, para 46.

21 Tams, n 6 above, 39–40.

22 Ibid 40.

23 Nuclear Tests (Australia v France) Judgment [1974] ICJ Rep 253; Nuclear Tests Cases (New Zealand v France) Judgment [1974] ICJ Rep 457 (Nuclear Tests Cases I).

24 Australian Memorial, *ICJ Pleadings*, vol I, 331 and 334, paras 431 and 448; New Zealand Memorial, vol II, 204, para 191.

that these involved the same kind of legal obligations as exist in relation to the law concerning the basic rights of the human person as mentioned in paragraph 34 of the Judgment in the *Barcelona Traction* case—ie, obligations *erga omnes*. The Applicant further argued that in consequence the right of States in relation to observance of the prohibition of nuclear testing corresponds with the duty of each State not to breach the prohibition. This duty is owed by each State to each and every other State. New Zealand pleaded, on the other hand, that it follows from the character of obligations *erga omnes* that its claim against France relates to a right of all States—of the whole of the international community—and that such a right is not owed to each member of that community on a bilateral basis.[25]

The individual opinion of judges in this case differed considerably in relation to the *locus standi* before the Court in redress of obligations *erga omnes*. Judge de Castro in his Dissenting Opinion referred expressly to the *Barcelona Traction* case. He commented first of all upon the question of standing in cases where an issue of general interest arose, such as in general humanitarian cases, in which an Applicant State did not suffer damage to its tangible interests. Judge de Castro, having analysed the Opinion of Judge Jessup in the *Barcelona Traction* case, interpreted standing in such cases restrictively, as limited to States which can assert a legal interest based on a treaty. It would appear that these obligations are what State responsibility terms obligations *erga omnes partes*.

Judge de Castro's approach generally to obligations *erga omnes* had been sceptical and he referred to the *obiter* in the *Barcelona Traction* case regarding these obligations as needing to be taken '*cum grano salis*'.[26] He wrote, in relation to the *Barcelona Traction* case, as follows:

> [i]t seems to me that the *obiter* reasoning expressed therein should not be regarded as amounting to recognition of the *actio popularis* in international law; it should be interpreted more in conformity with the general practice accepted as law. I am unable to believe that by virtue of this dictum, the Court would regard as admissible, for example, a claim by State A against State B that State B was not applying 'principles and rules concerning the basic rights of the human person' (*I.C.J. Reports* 1970, p. 32, para. 34) with regard to the subjects of State B or even C. Perhaps in drafting the paragraph in question the Court was thinking of the case where State B injured subjects of State A by violating the fundamental rights of the human person. It should also be borne in mind that the Court appears to restrict its dictum on the same lines Judges Jessup and Tanaka

[25] New Zealand Memorial, para 207.

[26] Judge de Castro Dissenting Opinion, *Australia v France Nuclear Tests Case* [1974] ICJ Rep 253, 387.

> when referring to 'international instruments of a universal or quasi-universal character' (*I.C.J. Reports* 1970, p. 32, para. 34).[27]

Absolutely opposite views were expressed by the *ad hoc* Judge Sir Garfield Barwick. Judge Barwick agreed with the view of the Applicant that the prohibition of the nuclear testing and the corresponding duty of observance of this prohibition to each and every State constitute an obligation *erga omnes*. He stated as follows:

> if this submission were accepted, the Applicant would, in my opinion, have the requisite legal interest, the *locus standi* to maintain this basis of its claim. The right it claims in its dispute with France would be *its* right: the obligation it claims France to be under, namely an obligation to refrain from the atmospheric testing of nuclear weapons, would be an obligation owed to Australia. The parties would be in dispute as to their respective rights.[28]

In the view of the present author this is a very interesting statement: on one hand Judge Barwick agrees with the view of the Applicant (Australia) that the prohibition of nuclear weapons testing is an obligation *erga omnes*; on the other hand, however, the *locus standi* of Australia against France is of a bilateral nature. France is 'under an obligation owed to Australia' and 'the parties would be in dispute as to their respective rights'. Therefore, the procedural side of the obligations *erga omnes*—ie, the question of standing—involves a return to classical bilateral international law. This clearly was a way, according to Judge Barwick, in which the notoriously complicated and contentious issue of standing in respect of obligations *erga omnes* would be resolved.

Judges Onyeama, Dillard, Jiménez de Aréchaga and Sir Humphrey Waldock in their Joint Dissenting Opinion presented yet a different view on the issues of *locus standi* and legal interest in these cases. They approached the question of Australia's legal interest firstly from the point of view of classical international law—ie, the legal interest in the defence of the inherent right to the Applicant's territorial sovereignty, which by its very nature is uncontested. However, the Dissenting Judges were much more cautious regarding legal interest and standing regarding atmospheric nuclear testing. Interestingly, they suggested that the question of legal interest should be part of the general legal merits of the case—ie, the alleged existence of a general rule of international law prohibiting atmospheric nuclear testing. If the alleged rule exists, the Court would have to determine what is the precise character and content of such a rule and in particular whether it confers on every State individually standing to prosecute a claim to enforce it. Thus the question

[27] Ibid.

[28] Judge Barwick's Dissenting Opinion, *Australia v France Nuclear Tests Case* [1974] ICJ Rep 253, 437.

of legal interest is part and parcel of the substantive legal issue of the existence and the scope of the alleged rule of customary international law prohibiting nuclear atmospheric testing. Finally, in this connection, they stated that:

> [a]lthough we recognize that the existence of so-called *actio popularis* in international law is a matter of controversy, the observations of this Court in the *Barcelona Traction, Light and Power Company, Limited* case suffice to show that the question is one that may be considered as capable of rational legal argument and a proper subject of litigation before the Court.[29]

Thus, the Dissenting Judges appear to be very measured in the support of obligations *erga omnes*, and unlike Judge de Castro, allow the possibility of standing for other States in order to enforce such an obligation, providing the existence of a substantive rule of international customary law has been sufficiently evidenced.

Judge Pétren, in his Separate Opinion, made some general observations on the development of the obligations *erga omnes*. He stated:

> [i]t is only an evolution subsequent to the Second World War which has made the duty of States to respect the human rights of all, including their own nationals, an obligation under international law towards all States members of international community. The Court alluded to this in its Judgment in the case concerning the *Barcelona Traction, Light and Power Company, Limited*.[30]

The same judge argued that a similar evolution was taking place in an 'allied field, that of the protection of the environment'.[31] Judge Pétren, however, regretted that this universal recognition of human rights was not accompanied by a corresponding development in the jurisdiction of international judicial organs. He argued, however, that the rule prohibiting nuclear atmospheric weapons testing had not emerged by the time of the filing of the application. Therefore the dispute was inadmissible in the absence of the existence of such a rule in general international law.

In conclusion, the 1974 *Nuclear Tests* Cases show the diverse views of judges as to the existence of obligations *erga omnes*. It may be stated, however, that the majority of judges gave them limited recognition, at the same time being mindful of the difficulties concerning the issue of standing to redress violations of these obligations in international judicial proceedings.

[29] Judges Onyeama, Dillard, Jiménez de Aréchaga and Sir Humphrey Waldock, Joint Dissenting Opinion, *Australia/France Nuclear Tests Case* [1974] ICJ Rep 253, 369–70, para 117. See also ibid 370, para 118.

[30] Judge Pétren Separate Opinion, *Australia v France Nuclear Tests Case* [1974] ICJ Rep 253, 305.

[31] Ibid.

ii. The 1974 and 1995 Nuclear Tests[32] *Cases and the Question of Intervention*

The above-mentioned cases were also important from the point of view of another aspect of the 'multi-faceted'[33] character of environmental disputes which is challenged by the essentially bilateral nature of judicial proceedings before the ICJ, namely, the question of third party intervention.[34] In general the interventions in both *Nuclear Tests Cases* were based on Article 62 of the ICJ Statute (in case of *Nuclear Tests Case II* also Article 63 of the ICJ Statute). Article 62 of the Statute of the Court reads as follows:

> 1. Should a State consider that it has an interest of a legal nature which may be affected by the decision in the case, it may submit a request to the Court to be permitted to intervene.
> 2. It shall be for the Court to decide upon this request.

Article 81 of the 1978 Rules of Procedure of the Court contains precise requirements for the submission of an application to intervene.

> 1. An application for permission to intervene under the terms of Article 62 of the Statute, signed in the manner provided for in Article 38, paragraph 3, of these Rules, shall be filed as soon as possible, and not later than the closure of the written proceedings. In exceptional circumstances, an application submitted at a later stage may however be admitted.
> 2. The application shall state the name of an agent. It shall specify the case to which it relates, and shall set out:
>   (a) the interest of a legal nature which the State applying to intervene considers may be affected by the decision in that case;
>   (b) the precise object of the intervention;
>   (c) any basis of jurisdiction which is claimed to exist as between the State applying to intervene and the parties to the case.

The legal aspects of intervention have been the subject of many cases before the Court and of many academic publications, full consideration of which is outside the realm of this chapter. Suffice it to say that some of the general aspects of the institution of intervention based on Article 62, such as the jurisdictional link, were the subject of discussion by judges in the *Nuclear Tests I* case.[35] However, for the purpose of the enforcement of community concerns in environmental cases, the institution of intervention

[32] Request for Examination of the Situation in Accordance with Paragraph 63 of the Court's Judgment of 20 December 1974 in the *Nuclear Tests (New Zealand v France) Case* [1995] ICJ Rep 288 (*Nuclear Tests Case II*).

[33] Okowa, above n 1 at 164.

[34] There are several publications on general aspects of third-party intervention; see, eg S Rosenne, *Intervention in the International Court of Justice* (Dordrecht, Martinus Njihoff, 1993) and C Chinkin, *Third Parties in International Law* (Oxford, Clarendon Press, 1993) 148.

[35] On the detailed analysis of relevant cases see Rosenne, above n 34 at 126, 160.

appears to have a limited impact. As Okowa correctly observes, the Court in the *Gulf of Fonseca* case[36] explained that intervention has a restricted purpose and scope. The Court stated that the intervening State cannot be considered to be a party to the dispute. The rights of such a State are limited to the protection of its interests; and for that reason it is not bound by the Judgment of the Court. Therefore one has to agree with Okowa that '[i]ntervention cannot therefore be regarded as an appropriate mechanism for protecting community values'.[37] However, in the same case the Chamber of the Court decided that in order to be granted permission to intervene no jurisdictional link is necessary.[38]

In the *Nuclear Tests I* case, Fiji sought to intervene on the basis of Article 62 of the Stature of the International Court of Justice, claiming that its own legal interests were affected by the nuclear tests of France.[39] In its Application the Government of Fiji argued:

> as a consequence of the French programme of atmospheric nuclear weapon testing radioactive fallout has been deposited on Fiji territory including its waters, giving rise to measurable concentration of radionuclides in foodstuffs and in man and has therefore resulted in additional radiation doses to persons living in Fiji.[40]

No objection was filed either by the Government of Australia or of New Zealand to Fiji's request to intervene (France ignored the request in line with its general attitude towards this case). The Court did not make any pronouncements on the substantive issues concerning the intervention request by Fiji, as it terminated the case in 1974, and consequently found that Fiji's Application for permission to intervene lost its purpose and that no further action on the part of the Court was called for.[41] However, several judges expressed views disagreeing with the reasoning of the Court's Order.[42] Judge Onyeama argued that at the time material to the proceedings before the Court there was no jurisdictional link between Fiji and France and consequently the Court should reject the Application on the basis of Article 62.[43] Similar views were expressed by Judges Dillard and Sir Humphrey Waldock in their Joint Declaration. They disagreed with

[36] Land, Island and Maritime Frontier Dispute (EL Salvador/Honduras: Nicaragua Intervening) [1992] ICJ Rep 350.
[37] Okowa, above n 1 at 165.
[38] Above n 36 at 422, para 100.
[39] Application for Permission to Intervene Submitted by the Government of Fiji, www.icj-cij.org/docket/files/58/9441.pdf.
[40] Ibid 149.
[41] *Nuclear Tests Case,* (*Australia v France*) Application to Intervene, Order of 20 December 1974 [1974] ICJ Rep 530.
[42] See on this aspect Sir E Lauterpacht, *Aspects of the administration of International Justice* (Cambridge, Cambridge University Press, 1993) 27.
[43] Declaration of Judge Onyeama, 531, www.icj-cij.org/docket/files/58/6085.pdf.

the Order of the Court on the ground that the jurisdictional link between France and Fiji should have been examined by the Court 'in order to determine whether or not there existed a sufficient jurisdictional link between Fiji and France to justify the former's intervention under Article 62 of the Court's Statute'. They continued by saying: '[f]urthermore, in our view an opportunity should have been given to Fiji to be heard on the issue before the determination was made'.[44]

Judge de Arechaga presented the following argument. First, he was of the view the dismissal of the Fiji's Application should have been on the basis of the lack of jurisdictional title in relation to France (Fiji was neither a party to the 1928 General Act nor to the optional clause system). De Arechaga argued that:

> in order to be entitled to intervene under Article 62 of the Statute for the purpose of asserting a right as against the respondent a State must be in a position in which it could itself bring the respondent before the Court.[45]

He relied on the history of the drafting of Article 62 of the Statue of the Permanent Court of International Justice (PCIJ) which was predicated on the assumption that the intervening State would have its own title of jurisdiction relating to the respondent, due to the fact that the draft Statute then provided for general compulsory jurisdiction. When this system was replaced by the optional clause, Article 62 remained unchanged, 'but it must be interpreted and applied as still subject to this condition'.[46] Any other interpretation would result in unreasonable consequences, conflicting with basic principles such as those of equality of parties before the ICJ and strict reciprocity of States accepting the Court's jurisdiction regarding their rights and obligations. De Arechaga explained that a State which cannot be brought before the Court as a respondent by another State is unable to become an applicant regarding this State or an intervener against the same State, entitled to make submissions arguing its own interest. De Arechaga said that in his view that the provision in Article 62, paragraph 2 of the 1972 Rules of the Court requiring a statement of law and of fact justifying intervention must be in the circumstances of the *Nuclear Tests I* case 'be interpreted as including the requirement of establishing an independent jurisdictional link between intervener and respondent'.[47]

In the 1995 *Nuclear Tests II* case, five States (Australia, Solomon Islands, Micronesia, Marshall Islands and Samoa) sought to intervene, arguing in their applications for an intervention that their own legal interests were affected by French nuclear tests. Australia argued that its legal interest in

[44] Ibid 532.
[45] Ibid 533.
[46] Ibid.
[47] Ibid.

its Application for permission to intervene on the basis of Article 62 of the Statute is closely linked to the character of the obligations *erga omnes*, as pleaded by New Zealand in the *Nuclear Tests Case I*.[48] Australia in its Application made an attempt to overcome the inherent bilateralism of the settlement of disputes between States and the multilateralism of obligations *erga omnes*, arguing as follows:

> this is not to suggest that New Zealand in bringing the claim is purporting to represent and speak on behalf of the international community as a whole. The *dispute* which forms the basis of the proceedings, and which New Zealand asks to the Court to determine, is a bilateral dispute between New Zealand and France. Other States may or may not agree with New Zealand that the proposed conduct of France would violate an *erga omnes* obligation under international law. Furthermore, by virtue of Article 59 of the Statute, it is only the parties to the case, and not the international community as a whole, which would be bound by the judgment of the Court. However, while the *dispute* between New Zealand and France is bilateral, it remains the case that in determining the merits of the New Zealand claim, the Court would necessarily be required to pronounce on the rights of all States. The legal interests of every member of the international community, even those States not bound by the judgment are thus 'affected' or '*en cause*' within the meaning of Article 62 of the Statute.[49]

Australia further pleaded that the community concerns in this case made it different from the other cases of applications for leave to intervene based on Article 62 in which the Court refused the right of intervention. In situations where the *erga omnes* obligations (or interests of the community of States) are at stake, legal interests of the claimant State are identical with those of the Applicant State (ie, in this particular case the interests of New Zealand and Australia).[50] It may observed that Australia was not the only State which relied on the obligations *erga omnes* to substantiate its intervention request. This was also present (to a more limited extent) in other Applications, for example, in the Application of Solomon Islands.[51]

Apart from general grounds—ie, community concerns—for the right to intervene, all States relied on ecological arguments, relating to the harmful influence of such tests on the environment, in particular the marine environment. All States asking for the permission to intervene, with the

[48] Application for the Permission to Intervene Under the Terms of Article 62 of the Statute submitted by the Government of Australia, 9–10, www.icj-cij.org/docket/files/97/13317.pdf.

[49] Ibid para 20.

[50] Ibid para 21.

[51] Application for Permission to Intervene Under Article 62 and Declaration of Intervention under Article 63, Submitted by Solomon Islands, 5, para 25(a), www.icj-cij.org/docket/files/97/7189.pdf.

exception of Australia, based their claim as well on Article 63 of the ICJ Statute:

1. Whenever the construction of a convention to which States other than those concerned in the case are parties is in question, the Registrar shall notify all such States forthwith.
2. Every State so notified has the right to intervene in the proceedings; but if it uses this right, the construction given by the judgment will be equally binding upon it.

and on Article 82 of the Rules of Procedure of the Court, which specifies the following requirements:

1. A State which desires to avail itself of the right of intervention conferred upon it by Article 63 of the Statute shall file a declaration to that effect, signed in the manner provided for in Article 38, paragraph 3, of these Rules. Such a declaration shall be filed as soon as possible, and not later than the date fixed for the opening of the oral proceedings. In exceptional circumstances a declaration submitted at a later stage may however be admitted.
2. The declaration shall state the name of an agent. It shall specify the case and the convention to which it relates and shall contain:
   (a) particulars of the basis on which the declarant State considers itself a party to the convention;
   (b) identification of the particular provisions of the convention the construction of which it considers to be in question;
   (c) a statement of the construction of those provisions for which it contends;
   (d) a list of the documents in support, which documents shall be attached.

All the States concerned relied on the construction of the 1986 Noumea Convention to file their declaration for intervention. However, the Court never considered either the applications for the permission to intervene or the declarations in accordance with Article 82 of the Rules, as by the Order of September 1995 it decided that the case 'does not fall within the provisions of the said paragraph 63 and must consequently be dismissed'.[52] Consequently, the applications for permission to intervene as well as declarations to intervene were dismissed.

In conclusion it may be said that, as was observed above, the limited scope of the right of intervention, only infrequently allowed by the Court, makes it a rather ineffective tool for the redress of community concerns regarding environmental issues before the ICJ. In general, the strict rules relating to the standing of parties before the Court are not very well suited to the pursuit of claims with multiple parties and harmful effects affecting

[52] Order of 22 September 1995 Request for an Examination of the Situation in Accordance with Paragraph 63 of the Court's Judgment of 20 December 1974 in the *Nuclear Tests (New Zealand v France) Case* [1995] ICJ Rep 288.

more than one State. The lack of acknowledgement of an *actio popularis* in international law also exacerbates the situations in which

> large areas of State activity or those under State control that cause harm to the global environment will be immune from censure, for the reason that they affect collective interests, and under the circumstances where no State could claim that its proprietary or specific legal interests have been infringed.[53]

III. PART TWO—SUBSTANTIVE ISSUES OF INTERNATIONAL ENVIRONMENTAL LAW BEFORE THE ICJ

In this part, substantive issues of international environmental law will be discussed. The following fields of international environmental law have been the subject of cases before the Court: nuclear law (nuclear tests and nuclear weapons); water law; transboundary air pollution; and damage to land. In deciding of some of these cases, the Court, as well as individual judges, also made pronouncements regarding certain general principles of international environmental law, such as sustainable development, the precautionary principle, environmental impact assessment and intergenerational equity; and these general principles will also be discussed.

A. Nuclear Law and the Environment

This section will focus on the aspects of nuclear law as considered by the ICJ. It will concern nuclear testing (*Nuclear Tests I and II* cases, see above) as well as the legality of nuclear weapons (1996 *Advisory Opinion on the Threat or Use of Nuclear Weapons*).[54]

i. Nuclear Tests I and II *Cases*

The *Nuclear Tests I and II* cases may be said to constitute an example illustrating the principle elaborated by the Court in the *Corfu Channel* case, in which the famous statement was made by the Court that 'every State's obligation not to allow knowingly its territory to be used for acts contrary to the rights of other States'.[55] However, the manner and extent of the application of this principle in environmental law is somewhat unclear;

[53] Okowa, above n 1 at 166. See generally: T Stephens, *International Courts and Environmental Protection* (Cambridge, Cambridge University Press, 2009).

[54] Legality of the Threat or Use of Nuclear Weapons, Advisory Opinion [1996] ICJ Rep 226.

[55] Corfu Channel Case (United Kingdom v Albania) Judgment [1949] ICJ Rep 1. 22.

and the Court itself in this case did not specify the exact content of the rights concerned.[56] The Court has not subsequently been called upon to elaborate or clarify this principle in any case.

As is widely acknowledged, this principle had enormous influence, not least in constituting one of foundations of the 1972 Stockholm and 1992 Rio Declarations and of the work of the ILC in its several drafts concerning prevention of transboundary harm from hazardous activities and liability arising out of acts not prohibited by international law. This concept also lies behind the conclusion of a number of multilateral environmental agreements. The *Nuclear Tests* cases might have presented the Court with an opportunity to further develop the principle laid down in the *Corfu Channel* case. However, in both of these the Court chose not decide on their substantive issues—ie, broadly, issues relating to legal responsibility for the transboundary effects of nuclear testing. The legal aspects of nuclear testing, both atmospheric and underground, were extensively discussed by both Australia and New Zealand in the 1974 cases and by New Zealand in the 1995 case, as well as by the intervening States.

In the 1974 cases, Australia and New Zealand claimed that French nuclear testing in the Pacific caused nuclear fallout infringing their sovereignty in a manner contrary to international law and resulting in environmental damage. The pleadings in this case relied very strongly on the damage done to the environment by nuclear testing. In the submission of Australia, it was expressly stated that nuclear tests not only adversely affect human beings and animals, but also contaminate the environment. It was alleged by the Australian Government that the main radioactive contamination of the environment by a nuclear explosion is caused by radioactive fall-out deposited on the surface of the earth, including direct contamination of soil, of the water of oceans, lakes, rivers and reservoirs and of vegetation. It was claimed that nuclear fall-out also affects the atmosphere, contributing to changes in meteorological conditions. The French nuclear explosions resulted in tropospheric fall-out on States and territories in the Southern hemisphere and on the oceans of that hemisphere. Australia submitted that the radioactive 'cloud' of debris in the troposhere might make several transits around the globe before being depleted by radioactive decay and deposit.[57] The application of New Zealand was very similar in stressing the dangers of radiation to people and animals, such as by causing malignant disease.

[56] P Birnie, A Boyle and C Redgwell, *International Law and the Environment*, 3rd edn (Cambridge, Cambridge University Press, 2009) 143–45.

[57] Above n 23, *ICJ Pleadings, Oral Arguments*, Documents Application, vol I, 9–10.

In legal terms, the main argument put forward by Australia was based on the assumption that the deposit of radioactive fall-out on the territory of Australia and its dispersion in Australia's airspace, without Australian consent, constituted a violation of Australian sovereignty over its territory, impaired Australia's independent right to determine what acts would take place within its territory and exposed people to radiation from artificial sources. Australia also observed that the interference with ships and aircraft on the high seas and the superjacent airspace, and the pollution of the high seas by radioactive fall-out, constituted infringements of the freedom of high seas.[58] Thus the main argument presented by Australia was based on alleged infringement of sovereignty rather than on environmental damage. However, the environmental effects of nuclear testing were also brought into consideration. In this respect, Australia argued that the 'effects of the French nuclear tests upon the resources of the sea or the conditions of the environment can never be undone and would be irremediable by any payment of damages.'[59]

Issues relating to the environmental effects of nuclear testing were also put forward in Australia's oral pleadings. Mr Ellicott, counsel for Australia, stressed these issues quite forcefully. He relied on Principle 21 of the 1972 Stockholm Declaration, arguing that the obligation contained in this Principle is absolute and without any qualification. He remarked on the emerging rule of international customary law that prohibits States from engaging in conduct 'tending towards pollution and the creation of hazards to human health and the environment and in particular a rule prohibiting the conduct of atmospheric nuclear tests'.[60] Interestingly, he pointed out that the Stockholm Declaration reflects the changing standards of environmental protection adopted by the international community.[61] It may be noted that New Zealand also relied on the 1972 Conference on Human Environment and the principles enshrined in the Stockholm Declaration.[62]

While the judgment of the Court in the *Nuclear Tests I* Case did not itself refer to these substantive issues, some elucidation of the individual judges' approaches to environmental matters in general, and to the effects of nuclear testing in particular, can be found in their opinions. Judge Petrén, in his Separate Opinion, posed the question whether there existed a norm of customary international law whereby States are prohibited from causing the deposit of radioactive fall-out on the territory of other States, through carrying out atmospheric tests.[63] Having analysed the

[58] Ibid 103.
[59] Ibid 104.
[60] Ibid 104.
[61] Mr Ellicott, *ICJ Pleadings*, n 23 above, vol II, 56–57.
[62] Submission of Mr Finlay, ibid 100.
[63] Judge Petrén Separate Opinion, above n 30 at 304.

existing practice of States, he came to the conclusion that such a rule did not exist.[64] Judge Petrén saw the attempt at prohibition of atmospheric nuclear tests as a political rather than a legal act, outside the confines of international law, as it existed in 1974. Judge de Castro in his Dissenting Opinion submitted a different view. He invoked as a basic principle of international environmental law: the principle *sic utero tuo ut alineum non laedes*. He also referred to the above-mentioned *Corfu Channel* case and the award in the *Trail Smelter* arbitration. Judge de Castro thus indirectly admitted the possibility of the existence of a rule of international customary law that would prohibit the emissions of noxious fumes from neighbouring properties, thus implying that deposit of radioactive fall-out on the territory of another State is by analogy illegal.[65]

The *Nuclear Tests II* case had a dramatically different character from the environmental point of view than the earlier case. Although environmental issues were not fully reflected in the Court's Order terminating the case, New Zealand's Request for an Examination of the Situation[66] and the pleadings in this case (written and oral), were all centered on environmental questions. The Request was filed by New Zealand on the basis of paragraph 63 of the 1974 Judgment. These cases are an excellent illustration exemplifying the growing concern for environmental issues. The Request analysed the alleged environmental impact, in particular on the marine environment, of underground nuclear tests conducted by France on the Polynesian atolls of Mururoa and Fangataufa. New Zealand contested the legality of France's nuclear testing in the South Pacific as being unacceptable in international law and in contravention of developments in environmental matters. New Zealand also relied on general principles of international environmental law, namely, the principle of environmental impact assessment (EIA), a requirement for which was incorporated in the 1986 Convention for the Protection of the Natural Resources and Environment of the South Pacific (the Nuomea Convention), and the precautionary principle.[67] It argued that France should have carried out an EIA, as an obligation under international customary law, before conducting underground nuclear tests.[68] Furthermore, New Zealand was of the view that by virtue of the application of the precautionary principle in international environmental law, the burden of proof fell on

64 He wrote: 'The example given by China when it exploded a very powerful bomb in the atmosphere is sufficient to demolish the contention that there exists at present a rule of customary international law prohibiting atmospheric nuclear tests' ibid 388–89.

65 Judge de Castro Dissenting Opinion, above n 26 at 388.

66 *Nuclear Tests Case* (*New Zealand v France*), Request for an Examination of the Situation, above n 52.

67 Text of the Convention in (1987) ILM 38.

68 See, eg *Request for an Examination of the Situation New Zealand v France* 36, www.icj-cij.org/docket/files/97/7187.pdf; see also *Verbatim Record*, 12 September 1995, CR95/20.

a State proposing to engage in activities with potentially harmful effect on the environment, to demonstrate that these activities would not result in contamination. Sir Kenneth Keith, who pleaded on behalf of New Zealand, put forward the following suggestions in the course of his oral submission:

(i) States must ensure that activities within their jurisdiction or control do not cause damage to the environment of other States or of areas beyond the limits of their jurisdiction;
(ii) Any addition of radioactive material to the environment or exposure of individuals to radiation must be justified. Such addition or exposure must be for good reason;
(iii) Any disposal or introduction of artificially created radioactive material into the marine environment is heavily circumscribed. It is in general forbidden;
(iv) Any introduction of radioactive material into the marine environment as a result of nuclear tests is forbidden. The world community no longer accepts that testing of nuclear weapons can be used to justify marine contamination.[69]

By the Order of 22 September 1995, the Court ruled that the Request of New Zealand for the resumption of the proceedings did not fall within the remit of paragraph 63 of the 1974 Judgment in 1974 *Nuclear Tests I* case (the basis of its 1974 Judgment had not been 'affected', as required by this paragraph) and dismissed the case. The new Application related to underground nuclear testing, while the 1974 case was concerned solely with atmospheric tests, and on that basis the Court declined its jurisdiction. Even so, in paragraph 64 of the Order, the Court, mindful of environmental aspects of the case, made this statement:

> the present Order is without prejudice to the obligations of States to respect and protect the natural environment, obligations to which both New Zealand and France have in the present instance reaffirmed their commitment.

Judges Weeramantry, Koroma and Judge *ad hoc* Sir Geoffrey Palmer appended dissenting opinions, in which in very persuasive terms they expressed their support for environmental protection. Judge Weeramantry discussed several principles of international environmental law as relevant to nuclear testing, such as intergenerational rights (equity), the precautionary principle, the principle of environmental impact assessment (described by him as 'gathering strength and international acceptance').[70] He also emphatically stressed the illegality of introducing nuclear waste into the marine environment.[71] Judge Koroma in his Dissenting Opinion noted the evolution in environmental knowledge and law and argued

[69] CR95/20, 10.
[70] Judge Weeramantry Dissenting Opinion [1995] ICJ Rep 288, 317, 345.
[71] Ibid 345.

that the Court should have taken into consideration all these new developments and allowed New Zealand's Request.[72] A similar stand was adopted by Sir Geoffrey Palmer, who noted the great development of international environmental law and its principles as enshrined in both the Stockholm and the Rio Declarations, therefore according merit to the Request of New Zealand. He was, furthermore, of the view that the principle of environmental impact assessment and the precautionary principle had already entered the body of international customary law.[73]

Analysis of the two *Nuclear Tests* cases clearly indicates the extent to which, in intervening years between them, environmental issues had become an important aspect of the Court's judicial process. States appearing before the Court, and judges, took seriously the ecological and legal issues relating to nuclear testing and embraced the emerging principles of international environmental law. The decision of the Court in the *Nuclear Tests II* case is perhaps disappointing from the point of view of the attention accorded by the Court to environmental matters; but opinions of several of the judges and pleadings of New Zealand clearly show the changing approaches to environmental matters and the acceptance of principles enshrined in both Stockholm and Rio Declarations, such as the fundamental Principle 21 of the Stockholm Declaration.

ii. Requests for Advisory Opinion Regarding the Threat or Use of Nuclear Weapons

A further question concerning nuclear activities, this time relating to the threat or use of nuclear weapons by States, appeared before the Court in connection with two Requests for Advisory Opinions: one submitted by the World Health Organisation (WHO) on 14 May 1993 and the second one by the United Nations General Assembly on 15 December 1994. The Court was asked by the WHO whether:

> [i]n view of the health and environmental effects ... would use of nuclear weapons by a State in war or other armed conflicts be a breach of its obligation under international law including the WHO Constitution.[74]

The second Request (by the UN General Assembly) was phrased as follows: '[i]s the threat or use of nuclear weapons in any circumstances permitted under international law?'.[75]

[72] Judge Koroma Dissenting Opinion [1995] ICJ Rep 288, 363.
[73] Judge *ad hoc* Sir Geoffrey Palmer [1995] ICJ Rep 288, 381.
[74] Legality of the Use by a State of Nuclear Weapons in Armed Conflict, Advisory Opinion [1996] ICJ Rep 66, 73.
[75] Legality of the Threat or use of Nuclear Weapons, Advisory Opinion [1996] ICJ Rep 226.

The first of these requests (by the WHO) was declined by the Court on the grounds that issues of the legality or illegality of nuclear weapons did not fall within the WHO's sphere of functions as required by Article 92(2) of the UN Charter. However, dissenting judges in the two Applications had no doubt that environmental obligations had an effect on the methods and means of warfare.[76] Judge Weeramantry, in his Dissenting Opinion in relation to the WHO request, emphasised environmental obligations of States, which have evolved dramatically, and opined that there is a close link between health and the impact of nuclear weapons on the environment. Therefore, in his view, the request submitted by the WHO fell within its Constitution.[77] Similar comments were made by Judge Koroma, who stressed the importance of environmental obligations of States in relation to nuclear weapons, especially that they are enshrined in international customary law and the Geneva Conventions.[78]

During written and oral statements in relation to both requests, many States argued the illegality of the use of nuclear weapons by reference to existing norms relating the protection of the environment. States relied on the provisions of the Additional 1977 Protocol I to the 1949 Geneva Conventions, that is, Article 35(3) and the 1977 Convention on the Prohibition of Military or Any other Hostile Use of Environmental Modification Techniques (Article 18, ENMOD Convention). States also referred to general environmental law, such as, respectively, Principles 21 and 2 of the Stockholm and Rio Declarations. Certain States argued that these instruments and other provisions relating to the safeguarding and protecting of the environment were to apply at all times, in war as well as in peace. It was stated that they would be violated by the use of nuclear weapons the consequences of which would be widespread and would have transboundary effects. However, these views were challenged by other States, which questioned the binding nature of fundamental norms of environmental law, denied the applicability of the ENMOD Convention to the use of nuclear weapons in hostilities, and, in relation to the Additional Protocol I, argued that they were not generally bound by its terms or relied on their reservations in respect of Article 35(3). Some States took the view that the principal purpose of environmental

[76] On jurisdictional issues relating to the WHO request for an Advisory Opinion, see in particular E Lauterpacht, 'Judicial Review of the Acts of International Organisations', in L Boisson de Chazournes and P Sands (eds), *International Law, The International Court of Justice and Nuclear Weapons* (Cambridge, Cambridge University Press, 1996), 92–102.

[77] Judge Weermanatry Dissenting Opinion [1996] ICJ Rep 66, 101. For further development of Judge Weeramantry's views on the substantive issues relating to nuclear weapons and the environment, see his Dissenting Opinion in the UN General Assembly Request [1996] ICJ Rep 429.

[78] Judge Koroma Dissenting Opinion [1996] ICJ Rep 66, 101, 172.

treaties and norms was to protect the environment in time of peace. It was observed that these treaties made no mention of nuclear weapons, that warfare in general, and nuclear warfare in particular, were not mentioned in their texts, and that it would have a destabilising effect on the rule of law and confidence in international negotiations if those treaties were now interpreted in such a manner as to prohibit the use of nuclear weapons.

In the second Advisory Opinion, the Court recognised that the environment is under daily threat and that the use of nuclear weapons could constitute 'a catastrophe for the environment'. The Court also stated that:

> the environment is not an abstraction but represents a living space, the quality of life and the very health of human beings, including generations unborn. The existence of the general obligation of States to ensure that activities within their jurisdiction and control respect the environment of other States or areas beyond their national control is now part of the corpus of international law relating to the environment.[79]

The Court's focus in its analysis of treaties including norms on environmental protection was, however, not 'whether the treaties in question are or are not applicable during an armed conflict, but rather whether the obligations stemming from these treaties were intended to be obligations of total restraint during military conflict'. The Court concluded that these treaties were not intended 'to deprive a State of the exercise of its right of self-defence under international law[80] because of its obligations to protect the environment'.[81] The Court found that States must take the environment into consideration 'when assessing what is necessary and proportionate in the pursuit of legitimate military objectives.'[82] The Court was of the view that respect for the environment is one of the elements to be taken into account while assessing whether military action conforms to the principles of necessity and proportionality, which is supported by Principle 24 of the Stockholm Declaration.

The Court also mentioned Articles 35(3) and 55 of Additional Protocol I, which, taken together, provide additional protection for the environment—ie, grant a general obligation to protect the natural environment against widespread, long-term and severe environmental damage. The Court stated that all the obligations which States must follow regarding the protection of the environment during warfare are powerful

[79] Above n 75 at para 29.
[80] Ibid para 30.
[81] Ibid.
[82] Ibid.

constraints for all States having subscribed to these provisions.[83] The ICJ also relied on the 1992 UN General Assembly 47/37 Resolution on the Protection of the Environment in Times of Armed Conflict.[84]

In conclusion, the Court found that while existing international law relating to the protection and safeguarding of the environment does not specifically prohibit the use of nuclear weapons, it noted important environmental factors that have to be properly considered in the context of the implementation of the principles and rules of law applicable in armed conflict.[85]

The effects of nuclear weapons on the environment were also discussed by Judge Weeramantry, who, in his Dissenting Opinion, noted that nuclear weapons have the potential to destroy the entire ecosystem of the planet. He also commented on the disastrous effects of ionising radiation in coniferous forests, crops, the food chain, livestock and marine ecosystems; and he raised the question of the long-lasting and not fully known effects of nuclear weapons on future generations within the concept of intergenerational equity. He was of the view that this latter concept, together with the one of common heritage of mankind, are both well-established in international law; and that the legality of the use of nuclear weapons should be analysed within their framework.[86]

During oral presentations, issues of intergenerational equity within the context of the use of nuclear weapons were mentioned as well.[87] In this respect, however, Brown-Weiss observed that the mention of future generations by the Court did not fully reflect the principle of intergenerational equity to a similar extent as did Judge Weeramantry.[88]

In relation to this Advisory Opinion, the view has been expressed that the existing rules of environmental law and humanitarian law, if applied jointly, could grant sufficient protection to the environment during armed conflict.[89] However, some critical comments have also been expressed regarding the Court's approach to environmental protection during armed conflict. First of all, it was noted that the Court did not make reference to environmental considerations in its decision and that such a

[83] Ibid.
[84] Ibid para 32.
[85] Ibid para 33.
[86] Judge Weeramantry Dissenting Opinion, above n 77, [1996] ICJ Rep, 226, ,454.
[87] Eg by the representatives of New Zealand and the Philippines, CR 95/25 and CR/95/27. See also E Brown-Weiss, 'Opening the Door to the Environment and Future Generations' above n 76 at 349–53.
[88] Ibid 349–50.
[89] Momtaz wrote, 'Ces principes tirés du droit international de l'environment et du droit international humanitaire, s'ils étaient appliqéues conjointement et de bonne foi, purraient ofrir une protection suffisante a l'enviornment': D Momtaz, 'Le Recours A L'Arme Nucleaire et La Protection de L'Environment: L'Apport de la Court Internationale de Justice', above n 76 at 374.

'cautious' attitude appeared to be 'unwarranted'. The Court, by including a reference to the environment, would further have developed the integration of environmental considerations in implementing international law related to armed conflict.[90]

Since the *Nuclear Tests* Cases, the Court had developed its approach to matters of ecology, as evidenced, for instance, by placing it beyond doubt that the obligation enshrined in Principles 21 and 2 of the Stockholm and Rio Declarations had acquired the legal status of binding norms of international customary law; by giving serious consideration to the necessity of the protection of the environment for future generations; and through analysing the relevant legal instruments relating to environmental protection during the use of nuclear weapons both within the realm of international humanitarian law and international environmental law.

B. Water Law and the Environment

i. Gabčikovo-Nagymaros Project

The main case thus far in which the Court has made some pronouncements on international water law and the protection of the environment was the *Gabčikovo-Nagymaros Project* case,[91] concerning which there are numerous existing publications.[92] In this case environmental considerations played a pivotal role, as they constituted the main theme of pleadings submitted by Hungary.[93] However, it would be an over-simplification to claim that the main theme of this case was exclusively environmental law. It presented a complicated problem which consisted of general issues of international

[90] E Brown-Weiss, above n 87 at 348.

[91] Case Concerning the Gabčikovo-Nagymaros Project (Hungary/Slovakia) [1997] ICJ Rep 7.

[92] J Lammers, 'The *Gabčikovo-Naygmaros Case* Seen in Particular from the Perspective of the Law of International Watercourses and the Protection of the Environment' (1998) 11 *Leiden Journal of International Law* 287–320; S Schwebel, 'The Judgment of the International Court of Justice in the *Case* Concerning *the Gabčikovo-Nagymaros Project* (*Hungary/Slovakia*) (2002) *Resolution of International Water Disputes*, Permanent Court of Arbitration, Peace Palace Papers, PCA, International Law Seminar, 8 November 2002 (The Hague, Kluwer, 2003) 247–59; B Fuyane and F Madai, 'The Hungary-Slovakia Danube River Dispute: Implications for Sustainable Development and Equitable Utilization of Natural Resources in International Law' (1997) 1 *International Journal of Global Environmental Issues* 329–44; S Stec and G E Eckstein 'Of Solemn Oaths and Obligations: The Environmental Impact of the ICJ's Decision in the *Case Concerning the Gabčikovo-Nagymaros Project*' (1997) 8 *Yearbook of International Environmental Law* 41–50; J Sohnle '*Irruption du Droit del'Environment dans la Jurisprudence de la C.I.J.: L'Affaire Gačikovo-Nagymaros*' (1998) 102 *Revue Général de Droit International Public* 86.

[93] Memorial of the Republic of Hungary, vol 1, 2 May 1992 (vol I: www.icj-cij.org/docket/files/92/10921.pdf; vol II: www.icj-cij.org/docket/files/92/10929.pdf).

law, such as the law of treaties,[94] the law of State responsibility[95] and the law of State succession.[96]

Briefly, the subject-matter of the dispute was the construction and operation of the Gabčikovo-Nagymaros barrage system on the River Danube on the basis of the 1977 Treaty together with two subsequent Protocols, signed by Hungary and Czechoslovakia. Owing to far-reaching political and social changes in Eastern and Central Europe, Hungary decided first to suspend and later to terminate the project. The Czechoslovak Government, and subsequently the Slovak Government (since 1993), decided to continue the project and initiated the so-called 'Variant C', which was a unilateral diversion of the Danube on the territory of the Slovak Republic. The main argument of Hungary for abandoning the Treaty was the alleged existence of 'a state of ecological necessity'.[97]

Hungary provided several ecological reasons to substantiate its claim, such as a dramatic deterioration in water quality and threat to habitat. The Court, inter alia, analysed the concept of a state of necessity in general and had to determine to what extent transboundary detrimental interference with the environment or the utilisation of natural resources may give rise to a state of necessity and to what extent the invocation of state of necessity could exonerate Hungary from otherwise unlawful suspension and termination of the 1997 Treaty.[98] The Court acknowledged that the concerns expressed by Hungary for its natural environment related to an 'essential interest' of Hungary within the meaning of this concept in the realm of State responsibility.[99] However, the Court expressed some doubts as to whether in 1989 Hungary's essential interests could have been threatened by a 'grave and imminent peril' and whether the steps adopted by Hungary to suspend and abandon work could be regarded as the only available means to safeguard its essential interests against grave and imminent peril.[100] The Court noted that Hungary frequently referred only to 'uncertainties' in 1989 as to the possible impact on the environment of the erection of a barrage system. Having examined the definition

[94] M Fitzmaurice, 'The *Gabčikovo-Nagymaros* case and the Law of Treaties' (1998) 11 *Leiden Journal of International Law* 321–44.

[95] R Lefeber, 'Case Analysis: The *Gabčikovo-Nagymaros Project* and the Law of State Responsibility' (1998) 11 *Leiden Journal of International Law* 609–32.

[96] J Klabbers, 'Cat on a Hot Tin Roof: The World Court, State Succession and the *Gabčikovo-Nagymaros* Case' (1998) 11 *Leiden Journal of International Law* 345–55.

[97] Above n 91 at paras 50–52.

[98] Lammers, above n 92 at 298–99.

[99] The Court relied on its statement regarding the importance of environmental protection made in the 1996 Advisory Opinion regarding the Threat or Use of Nuclear Weapons (see above).

[100] Above n 91 at para 54; Lammers, above n 89 at 301.

and conditions of the existence of 'peril' in State responsibility, the Court concluded that 'possible' peril was not sufficient according to the rules of State responsibility and that peril when established must be of a 'grave' and 'imminent' character. It further concluded that the situation which would have existed upon the erection of the barrage system would not have constituted a grave and imminent peril at the time when Hungary suspended the Treaty.

The argument put forward by Slovakia that the operation of Variant C was a countermeasure for the breach of treaty obligations by Hungary was not accepted by the Court on the grounds that it was not proportionate as it did not conform to the principle of equitable and reasonable share of natural resources of the Danube. The Court relied on the principle of equitable and reasonable utilisation of international watercourses as a principle of general international law, which is derived from the principle of equality of all riparian States in relation to navigational uses.[101] This principle underlies the 1997 United Nations Convention on Non-Navigational Uses of International Watercourses.

As regards general international environmental law, Hungary argued that it was justified in terminating the 1977 Treaty owing to the emergence of new standards (requirements) of international environmental law, even though it did not argue that any of these norms was of a *jus cogens* character.[102] However the Court observed that the 1977 Treaty granted the possibility of incorporating new norms as Articles 15, 19 and 20 contained general, evolving and continuing obligation requiring the Parties, while implementing the Treaty, to take into consideration the quality of water in the Danube River, the protection of nature and new environmental norms. This was a joint responsibility, implementation of which should have been effected through a process of consultation and negotiation, aimed at translating these general obligations into specific ones.[103]

The Court emphasised, in other parts of the judgment, the necessity and fundamental importance of observation of the obligations prescribed by Articles 15, 19 and 20 arising from the special nature of environmental protection in which 'vigilance and prevention are required on account of the often irreversible character of damage to the environment and the limitations inherent in the very mechanism of reparation in relation to this type of damage.'[104] However, these obligations do not appear to have been a point of disagreement between the Parties, which, as the Court

[101] Territorial Jurisdiction of the International Commission of the River Oder [1929] PCIJRep Series A, No 23.
[102] Above n 91 at para 112.
[103] Ibid para 112.
[104] Ibid para 140.

observed, took environmental concerns seriously and agreed on precautionary measures, even though:

> [t]hey fundamentally disagree[d] on the consequences this has for the joint Project. In such a case, third-party involvement may be helpful and instrumental in finding a solution, provided each of the Parties is flexible in its position.[105]

Further, regarding general issues of international environmental law, the Court also mentioned the concept of sustainable development:

> Such new norms have to be taken into consideration, and such new standards given proper weight, not only when States contemplate new activities but also when continuing with activities begun in the past. This need to reconcile economic development with protection of the environment is aptly expressed in the concept of sustainable development.[106]

In the view of the present author the rather cursory mention of the concept of sustainable development is regrettable. At the time of the passing of the judgment in this case, this concept was already quite well analysed, despite the fact that its legal status still was unclear. A more profound statement from the Court regarding this concept would have been of assistance in clarification of its legal nature and content.[107]

It must be observed that from the point of view of clarification of rules of international environmental law, it was Vice-President Judge Weeramantry who, in his Separate Opinion, discussed the principle of sustainable development in a more detailed a manner. This was perceived by him as an established principle of contemporary international law. Judge Weeramantry acknowledged that the right to development and the right to environmental protection are part and parcel of international law and may conflict with each other; and that the role of the principle of sustainable development is to reconcile these two rights. This principle, according to Judge Weeramantry, was not new as it was present in many religions and cultures. It is derived from similar principles of trusteeship of natural resources and the protection of fauna and flora, intergenerational equity and respect of land. The principle of sustainable development is closely related to that of environmental impact assessment, which has to be conducted in a continuous manner, as long as the project is in operation.[108] Judge Weeramantry also raised the question of human rights

[105] Ibid para 113.

[106] Ibid para 140. See similarly Lammers, above n 92 at 318.

[107] There are numerous publications on this subject. See, eg: D French, *International Law and Policy of Sustainable Development* (Manchester, Manchester University Press; New York, Juris Publishing, Melland Schill Studies in International Law, 2005); P Brandon and P Lombardi, *Evaluating Sustainable Development* (Oxford, Blackwell, 2005); T Strange and A Bayley, *Sustainable Development. Linking Economy, Society and Environment* (Paris, OECD, 2008).

[108] Vice-President Weeramantry, Separate Opinion 88–119.

and environmental rights, where he said that environmental rights are human rights and that the Court cannot endorse action violating human rights under a treaty which was drafted at a time when such an action was not a violation of human rights.[109]

ii. Kasikili/Sedudu *Case*[110]

Mention must be made of the *Kasikili/Sedudu* case. This case also illustrates how general international law and international environmental law issues (water law) cannot be separated in a dispute. This case related to, inter alia, flow of water in the river—but one of the main general law issues was the interpretation of the 1890 Treaty between Great Britain and Germany. In this case Judge Weeramantry emphasised the importance of environmental considerations in boundary delimitation, which he noted should take into account the interests of ecosystems. He also endorsed taking into account equitable principles of riparian law, which play a significant role in determining riparian boundaries, where there is room for a difference of opinion.[111] The principle of equitable and reasonable utilisation of international watercourses was acknowledged by Judge Kooijmans in his Separate Opinion as widely accepted for both navigational and non-navigational utilisation of international watercourses. He mentioned as an example of the uses of this principle the 1997 Convention on Non-Navigational Uses of International Watercourses.[112]

iii. Pulp Mills on the River Uruguay *Case*

A case currently pending before the ICJ also relates to the problems concerning international water law and international environmental law, namely, *Pulp Mills on the River Uruguay* (*Argentina v Uruguay*). On 4 May 2006, Argentina instituted proceedings against Uruguay on the basis of Article 60 of the 1975 Statute of the River Uruguay, concluded between Argentina and Uruguay (entered into force in 1976), and asked the Court for indication of provisional measures.[113] Argentina alleged breach by

[109] 'Environmental rights are human rights. Treaties that affect human rights cannot be applied in such a manner as to constitute a denial of human rights as understood at the time of their application. A Court cannot endorse actions which are a violation of human rights by the standards of their time merely because they are taken under a treaty which dates back to a period when such action was not a violation of human rights.' Ibid 114.

[110] Kasikili/Sedudu Island (Botswana/Namibia) Judgment [1999] ICJ Rep 1045.

[111] Judge Weeramantry, Dissenting Opinion [1999] ICJ Rep 1045, 1184, 1177, paras 91–92, 77.

[112] Judge Kooijmans, Separate Opinion, [1999]ICJ Rep 1045,1151, paras 36–37.

[113] Order of 13 July 2006 for the Indication of Provisional Measures, *Case Concerning Pulp Mills On The River Uruguay* (*Argentina v Uruguay*) 13 July 2006 General List No 135; M Fitzmaurice, 'Pulp Mills on the River Uruguay (or not, as the case may be)' *The Hague Justice Portal*, www.haguejusticeportal.net/eCache/DEF/5/048.html.

Uruguay of its obligations under this Statute. In its Application Argentina alleged that the breach arose from 'the authorization, construction and future commissioning of two pulp mills on the River Uruguay', with reference in particular 'to the effects of such activities on the quality of the waters of the River Uruguay and on the areas affected by the river'. Argentina submitted that a joint régime was established for the use of the river. According to Argentina, the purpose of the 1975 Statute was to establish the joint machinery necessary for the optimum and rational utilisation of that part of the River Uruguay which is shared by the two States and which constitutes their common boundary. The Statute regulates activities such as conservation, utilisation and development of other natural resources; imposes obligations on the Parties regarding the prevention of pollution and the liability resulting from damage inflicted as a result of pollution and sets up an 'Administrative Commission of the River Uruguay' (CARU), whose functions include regulation and coordination.

Argentina submitted, in particular, that Articles 7–13 of the Statute provided for an obligatory procedure for prior notification and consultation through CARU for any party planning to carry out works liable to affect navigation, the regime of the river, or the quality of its waters. Argentina alleged that the Government of Uruguay, in October 2003, unilaterally authorised the Spanish company ENCE to construct a pulp mill nearby, and argued that this was done in breach of the notification and consultation procedure. Further, Argentina claimed that Uruguay had aggravated the dispute by authorising the Finnish company Oy Metsä-Botnia AB in 2005 to construct a second pulp mill without following the procedures included in the 1975 Statute. The hearings took place on 8 and 9 June 2006. Argentina relied on its previous arguments and pleaded that Uruguay breached its obligation not to cause environmental pollution or consequential economic losses, for example, to tourism, and authorised works against which Argentina had lodged objections. It also asserted that such a project would represent 'real and present damage' and would cause 'a serious risk of irreparable prejudice to the rights in issue'.

Uruguay stated that it did not dispute that Article 60 of the 1975 Statute constituted a prima facie basis for the jurisdiction of the Court, but only as far as it related to the indication of provisional measures in relation to Argentina's claims concerning the 1975 Statute. Uruguay argued that disputes such as those concerning tourism, urban and rural property values, etc, and those regarding other aspects of environmental protection in transboundary relations between the two States, fell outside the Court's jurisdiction. It submitted that it had complied fully with the obligation of informing Argentina of the existence of the pulp mill projects and that it was the first time in 31 years that Argentina had claimed a procedural right under the Statute and decided to block Uruguay from initiating projects during the procedural stages.

Uruguay also asserted that the dispute between Uruguay and Argentina over the pulp mills had in fact been settled by an agreement concluded in 2004, which stipulated that the CMB mill could be built according to the Uruguayan plan. According to that Agreement, Uruguay would provide Argentina with information regarding its specifications and operation and CARU would monitor the quality of the river water once the mill became operational in order to ensure compliance with the Statute. Moreover, according to Uruguay there was no current or imminent threat to any right of Argentina. Uruguay also assured the Court of its ongoing commitment to respect the provisions of the 1975 Statue.

The Court observed that, in dealing with a request for provisional measures, it was not necessary to satisfy itself that it has jurisdiction on the merits of the case. However, it would not indicate such measures unless the provisions invoked by the Applicant appeared, prima facie, to constitute a basis on which the jurisdiction of the Court might be based. The Court observed that environmental concerns are taken by the Court very seriously as evidenced in its Advisory Opinion *on the Legality of the Threat or Use of Nuclear Weapons* and in its judgment in the *Case Concerning the Gabčikovo-Nagymaros Project*. Argentina, however, had not persuaded the Court that the construction of the mills presented a risk of irreparable damage to the environment, nor had it sufficiently demonstrated that the construction of the mills currently constituted a threat of irreparable economic and social damage, or provided evidence suggesting that any pollution resulting from the commissioning of the mills would be of a nature to cause irreparable damage to the River Uruguay. The Court found, in view of the above, and the ongoing commitment of Uruguay to comply with the 1975 Statute, that the circumstances of the case were not such as to require the indication of a provisional measure ordering the suspension by Uruguay of the authorisation to construct the pulp mills or the suspension of the actual construction works. In paragraph 80 of the Order, the Court noted that:

> the present case highlights the importance of the need to ensure environmental protection of shared natural resources while allowing for sustainable economic development, whereas it is in particular necessary to bear in mind the reliance of the Parties on the quality of the water of the River Uruguay for their livelihood and economic development; whereas from this point of view, account must be taken of the need to safeguard the continued conservation of the river environment and of the rights of economic development of the riparian States.[114]

The Court stated that Argentina has the right to submit a new request for the indication of provisional measures, based on new facts.[115]

[114] Order for Provisional Measures, above n 113 at para 80.
[115] Ibid para 86.

This case is also a very good example of the potential practical application of the global 1997 United Nations Convention on the Non-Navigational Uses of International Watercourses. This Convention contains both substantive rights (as to the equitable utilisation of international watercourses) and procedural rights (such as a right to be notified of planned measures) of States in relation to the utilisation of a common watercourse. The Convention also has provisions on the protection of the riparian environment, a major issue in this case. In the 1957 *Lake Lanoux Arbitration* (*Spain v France*), similar substantive and procedural rights of States were discussed, as well as the extent of a State's unilateralism in adopting decisions which may affect the other State.

On 29 November 2006, Uruguay submitted in turn to the Court a request for the indication of provisional measures.[116] Uruguay claimed that organised groups of Argentine citizens had blockaded a vital international bridge over the Uruguay River, shutting off commercial and tourist travel from Argentina to Uruguay which would result in the loss of hundreds of millions of dollars in lost trade and tourism and that the blockade would extend beyond the bridges to the river itself to prevent river traffic with supplies for Botnia. The Court declined to indicate provisional measures and reiterated the statement from its previous Order that both States should implement in good faith the consultation and cooperation procedures provided for by the 1975 Statute, with the CARU constituting the envisaged forum in this regard; and that the Parties should, in the meantime, refrain from any actions which might render more difficult the resolution of the dispute.

French has noted that requests for provisional measures in general have become a significant factor in international environmental litigation in different international fora, with, however, 'subtly different approaches to such matters', which, as this author observes, may affect the choice of forum.[117]

There is no doubt that when this case has been decided on the merits it will enrich the growing body of international water law. But numerous other interesting questions are raised here (some of them are also discussed in the *Gabčikovo-Nagymaros Project*), such as issues regarding the joint management of the river, which, according to the Court, is the optimal manner in which riparian States should administer a shared waterway. The case will also contribute to the development of general international law, as it also involves consideration of the state

[116] Order of 21 January 2007 Request For the Indication of Provisional Measures *Case Concerning Pulp Mills On the River Uruguay)* (*Argentina v Uruguay*) 23 January 2007, General List No 135.

[117] D French, 'Environmental Dispute Settlement: The First (Hesitant) Signs of Spring?' (2006) 14 *The Hague Yearbook of International Law* 14.

of the law relating to shared natural resources and of the law of State responsibility.

C. Transboundary Air Pollution and the Environment—The *Aerial Herbicide Spraying* Case

In 2008 a case was filed by Ecuador against Columbia concerning aerial herbicide spraying.[118] Ecuador alleged that Colombia engaged in aerial spraying of toxic herbicides at locations near, at and across its border with Ecuador. The targets of this spraying have been illicit coca and poppy plantations in the frontier area. Ecuador claims that the spraying has already caused serious damage to people, crops, animals and the natural environment on the Ecuadorian side of the frontier, and poses a grave risk of further damage over time. Ecuador requested the Court to order Colombia to:

(a) respect the sovereignty and territorial integrity of Ecuador;
(b) take all steps necessary to prevent the use of any toxic herbicides in such a way that they could be deposited onto the territory of Ecuador;
(c) prohibit the use, by means of aerial dispersion, of such herbicides on or near any part of its border with Ecuador; and
(d) indemnify Ecuador for any loss or damage caused by its internationally unlawful acts.

Ecuador alleged that the impact of Colombia's spraying had not been confined to its side of the border and had had significant effects, such as impairment to health and farming, in Ecuador. Bilateral negotiations have proved unsuccessful.

This case, which is only in its early stages, will without doubt further develop findings made in the famous and often misunderstood *Trail Smelter Case*.[119] In that case, the Arbitral Tribunal said as follows:

> Under the principles of international law, as well as the law of the United States, no State has the right to use or permit to use its territory in such a manner as to cause injury by fumes on or to the territory of another or the properties or

[118] *Aerial Herbicide Spraying* (*Ecuador v Columbia*) Application, www.icj-cij.org/docket/files/138/14474.pdf.

[119] Trail Smelter Case (USA v Canada), Awards of 16 April 1938 and 11 March 1941, Reports of International Arbitral Awards (RIAA), vol III, 1905. See on this subject RM Batspies and, RA Miller (eds), Transboundary Harm in International Law. Lessons from Trail Smelter Arbitration (Cambridge, Cambridge University Press, 2006). See in particular critical analysis of the case J Knox, 'The Flawed Trail Smelter Procedure: The Wrong Tribunal, the Wrong Parties, and the Wrong Law' 66–78.

> persons therein, when the case is of serious consequence and the injury is established by clear and convincing evidence.

This statement led to the formulation of the obligation of States in Principles 21 and 2 respectively of the Stockholm and Rio Declarations. The changes in industrial activities of States, development in science, and in law, rendered many of the findings of the Arbitral Tribunal obsolete. As Okowa observes, the new problem of long-term transboundary pollution that has emerged since the *Trail Smelter* Arbitration is the impossibility of the establishment of a direct causal nexus of the kind that existed in this case (eg, inability to trace sources of pollution, such as nuclear pollution).[120] The same author asserts that the *Trail Smelter* legacy is more suitable to be relied upon in small transboundary claims, in private law actions of a civil law nature.[121] Therefore it is even more interesting whether and to what extent both Ecuador and Columbia are going to rely on this case. There are, however, some of the findings of the Tribunal in the *Trail Smelter Case* which are a lasting contribution to the development of international environmental law, such as the determination of what kind of property-related harm should trigger State responsibility, and the methods of assessing such harm. The Tribunal also provided for a limited regulatory regime, which was an innovation at that time.[122]

D. Land Degradation and Environmental Law—The *Nauru* Case[123]

Land degradation was the subject-matter of the *Nauru* case. Broadly, this case concerned breach of the obligation by, and the responsibility of, Australia as a Trusteeship Authority for land degradation due to unsuitable phosphate mining. Nauru was seeking compensation which also included the costs of rehabilitating the worked-out damaged land. The Pleadings before the Court mainly concerned the legal nature of the Trusteeship Agreement. However, as it was observed:

> It is nevertheless significant that the Court was considered by the applicant as an appropriate forum for the determination of the relevant legal issues, including compensation for harm to the environment.[124]

[120] P Okowa, 'The Legacy of *Trail Smelter* in the Filed of Transboundary Air Pollution' in Bastpies and Miller (eds), above n 119 at 198.

[121] Ibid 204.

[122] Ibid 204–07.

[123] *Certain Phosphates in Nauru* (*Nauru v Australia*) [1990] ICJ Rep, vol I, Pleadings Memorial of Nauru.

[124] Okowa, above n 1 at 162.

This case was never decided on the merits as it was settled outside the Court.

IV. PART THREE—ENVIRONMENTAL FORUMS

A. The Best Judicial Forum for Settlement of Environmental Disputes—The ICJ or a Specialised International Tribunal?

The question of the suitability of the Court to decide environmental disputes was particularly topical at the time of the Court's establishment, in 1993, of the Chamber of the Court for Environmental Matters (see below). The discussion at that time was focused on the question whether the Court was well equipped to deal with such matters or whether there was a need to create a special international forum to deal with environmental disputes.[125]

The majority of problems relating to the ICJ as a forum suitable for the settlement of international environmental disputes derive from the special character of protected interests, such as shared and community interests.[126] The rigidity of the right of standing in cases before the Court and the non-recognition of *actio popularis* are the main issues which might prevent the ICJ from being an entirely suitable court to decide environmental matters. Other obstacles which have been mentioned are the lengthy process of adjudication before the Court, when environmental degradation requires swift action and the allegedly very technical character of environmental law, which requires specialist knowledge. This latter argument, in the view of the present author, is not persuasive as the ICJ can use experts, if necessary.[127]

The lack of standing of non-State actors, in particular NGOs, is also put forward as another argument against the Court as a suitable forum to decide on environmental matters. However, to a limited extent, NGOs can voice their opinions before the Court, at least in Advisory Opinions, on the basis of Article 66(2) of the ICJ Statute. In contentious proceedings, the role of NGOs probably cannot be sustained as Article 34(2)

[125] See, eg Sir R Jennings, 'Need for Environmental Court?' (1992) 20 *Environmental Policy and Law* 313–14; A Postiglione, 'An International Court for the Environment' (1993) 23 *Environmental Policy and Law*, 73; E Valencia Ospina, 'The International Court of Justice and International Environmental Law (1994) 2 *Asian Yearbook of International Law* 1–10; E Hey, *Reflections on an International Environmental Court* (The Hague, Kluwer, 2000); Fitzmaurice, above n 1 at 302–08; L Rajamani, in book review of E Hey (above in this note), (2001) 10 *Review of European Community and International Environmental Law* 350–51.

[126] See eg Valencia-Ospina, n 125 above, 2–3.

[127] Ibid. See also: G White, 'The Use of Experts by International Court' in Lowe and Fitzmaurice, n 1 above, 528–41.

of the ICJ Statute refers to 'public international organizations', a term which the ICJ Rules of Procedure defines as organisations consisting of States.[128] The role of NGOs was very significant (if controversial) during the Court's proceedings regarding the 1996 Advisory Opinion on Nuclear Weapons.[129]

For all these reasons, the view was put forward that establishment of a special international court for environmental matters was necessary. The chief proponent of such a court was Judge Postiglione.[130] His main argument was based on the existence of an individual human right to a clean environment, including in particular the right of access to environmental information, the right to participate in administrative and judicial proceedings and the right of access to courts. However, as subsequent developments indicate, these arguments are not at present easy to sustain. Furthermore, there is already extensive jurisprudence of international courts (in particular the European Court of Human Rights) and quasi-judicial bodies on human rights which deal with environmental issues notwithstanding the absence of a special environmental human right; and within the context of the UN Economic Commission for Europe, there is the 1998 Convention on Access to Information, Public Participation in Decision-making and Access to Justice in Environmental Matters (Aarhus Convention), which grants—to a certain extent—a procedural environmental right.

At the same time, there were numerous arguments submitted against the establishment of an environmental court, which, it was alleged, would give rise to unnecessary multiplication of international courts and tribunals, which might lead to further fragmentation of international law. It was also claimed that what constitutes an international environmental legal dispute is ill-defined, and therefore not suitable to be brought before a special environmental court. It was considered that in many instances, national courts were better suited to adjudicate environmental disputes.[131]

[128] See: D Shelton, '*The Participation of Nongovernmental Organizations in International Judicial Proceedings*' (1994) 88 *AJIL* 619–28.

[129] M Mohr, 'Advisory Opinion of the International Court of Justice on the Legality of the use of Nuclear Weapons under International Law—a Few Thoughts on its Strengths and Success' (1997) 316 *International Review of Red Cross* 92–102; S Charnowitz, 'Non Governmental Organisations and International Law' (2006) 100 AJIL 364. See very critical comments on the involvement of NGOs in the Advisory Opinion of Judges Guillaume and Oda [1996] ICJ Rep 234, para 13 and 388, para 2; and Judge Oda [1996] ICJ Rep 335–36, para 8; and regarding the request by WHO, [1996] ICJ Rep 92–96, paras 15–16.

[130] He is a founder of ICEF (International Court of the Environment Foundation), an NGO registered in 1992 in Rome as a non-profit foundation. See also Stephens above n 53, 56-61, who has provided a valid criticism of the establishing of such a Court.

[131] Hey, above n 125 at 3–4. Hey is of the view that although international organisations should be held accountable before international courts, she discounts the idea of an environmental court as a suitable forum for this purpose, 3–4. See also comments of Rajamani, on the same issue above n 125.

The former President of the ICJ, Judge Jennings, was a great supporter of the ICJ as being the most suitable forum for environmental disputes. He, correctly in the view of this author, argued that notwithstanding the complex and specialist nature of environmental problems, environmental issues remain part and parcel of general international law, such as the law of treaties and the law of State responsibility, a view supported by the close relationship of these general issues with environmental issues in the *Gabčikovo-Nagymaros* case. In fact, Judge Jennings claimed, the authority of the Court to develop and crystallise international law might prove beneficial for the development of international environmental law, and that the presence on the Court of judges from different legal systems and civilisations renders the Court the best forum to deal with environmental disputes. Finally he relied on Article 94 of the UN Charter, as giving additional weight to the Court's decisions.[132]

The discussion concerning a special international environmental court, which was current in the 1990s, was revived in November 2008, when Stephen Hockman QC argued that an international court (based on the ICJ) should be established to enforce international agreements on cutting greenhouse gas emissions; to impose fines on States which fail to protect wildlife (endangered species) and which fail to enforce the right to a healthy environment.[133] However, this proposal was met with a critical response. It was observed that there are very deeply-rooted conflicts in international environmental law and policy between developed and developing countries, which would make it difficult to achieve a consensus to establish such a court. Furthermore, the existence of the right to a healthy environment is debatable and there are as yet no clear standards in international environmental law, such as the level of pollution, which would make it more problematic for such a court to reach decisions.[134] Apart from these issues, it may be added in any event that, were there to be a special environmental court along these lines, it probably should not be based unconditionally on the ICJ, as one of main problems of its suitability to adjudicate environmental claims (as was stated above) is the bilateralism of the Court's jurisdiction and the exclusively State participation in contentious cases.

In general, proposals for the establishment of an international environmental court have been largely abandoned. During the intervening

[132] Jennings above n 125 at 313–14.
[133] L Gray, 'Lawyers call for international court for the environment' *Daily Telegraph* (London 28 November 2008) www.telegraph.co.uk/earth/environment/climatechange/3530607/Lawyers-call-for-international-court-for-the-environment.html.
[134] OW Pedersen, 'An International Environmental Court' *International Law Observer* http://internationallawobserver.eu/2008/11/29/an-international-environmental-law-court/.

years, environmental matters were present before various judicial forums besides the ICJ, such as the International Tribunal for the Law of the Sea (ITLOS); and World Trade Organization (WTO) and various arbitration tribunals. Environmental issues were linked closely with general international law and other specific branches of international law, which brings forward the issue of fragmentation. However, as French argues, a more positive emphasis still needs to be placed on international environmental law by international courts and tribunals as involving 'potential horizontal issues, crossing a range of other sub-disciplines'.[135]

B. The Chamber of the ICJ for Environmental Matters

In 1993, the Court established a Special Chamber for Environmental Matters, on the basis of Article 26(1) of the Court's Statute.[136] However, no case has ever been brought before it and in 2006 the Court took the decision not to reconstitute the Chamber. The apparent lack of success of the Chamber was foreseen by some writers at the time of its establishment. First, it was argued that exactly the same rules of access to the Court were applicable to the Chamber—ie, excluding individuals and non-State actors. It was asserted that there was no evidence that the Chamber would offer any more expedient, cheaper or less formal procedure than the full Court; or that the judges who were appointed the members of this Chamber had a wider knowledge of international environmental law.

Furthermore, at that time, the body of international environmental law was still evolving and no fast rules had been formed. It was thought that it would be more expedient to allow, at least for the time being, the full Court to develop and crystallise the rules of international environmental law to form a coherent body of environmental jurisprudence before the Chamber was established. Most importantly, the argument was put forward that it was uncertain what disputes would be classified as environmental and whether parties would have full freedom to select the

[135] French above n 117 at 31.

[136] The Court made the following statement: 'in the past the Court considered the question of the possible formation of a chamber to deal with environmental matters. On those occasions it took the view that it was not yet necessary to set up a standing special chamber, emphasizing that it was able to respond to rapidly to requests for the constitutions of so-called "ad hoc" Chamber (pursuant to Article 26, paragraph 2 of the Statute) which could deal also with any environmental case. In the view of the developments in the field of environmental law and protection which have taken place in the last few years, and considering that it should be prepared to the fullest possible extent to deal with any environmental case falling within its jurisdiction, the Court has now deemed it appropriate to establish a seven-member Chamber for Environmental Matters': the Court's Communiqué N.93/20 19 July 1993.

Chamber for other than environmental reasons; and whether in such an event the Chamber would have power to refuse to accept the dispute and refer parties to the full Court.[137] In the event, as the practice of the Court has shown, all cases with an environmental element have been adjudicated by the full Court. It was very clear in the *Gabčikovo-Nagymaros Case* that both environmental and general international law issues formed the fabric of the case which could therefore not be characterised as an exclusively environmental dispute. The Slovak Republic rested its defence almost entirely on the law of treaties, so that it may be regarded as doubtful whether it would have consented to the case being brought before the Environmental Chamber.

V. PART IV—CONCLUSION

In the view of this author, the discussion concerning the suitability of the ICJ as a forum for settlement of environmental disputes should not be focused any more on whether it is in principle suitable to decide environmental cases but rather on the extent of its contribution to the development and crystallisation of the body of norms of international environmental law and their integration within the body of general international law. Past case law of the Court indicates that in fact it has already dealt with an extensive number of cases with an environmental component, and the Court's docket for the near future shows that their number is increasing.

Practitioners and scholars are mindful of the structure of the Court; its rigid rules on the right of access to its proceedings that appear not to be the most suitable for the adjudication of environmental disputes, where frequently community concerns are at stake and non-State actors play a fundamental role. Despite these factors, the Court dealt many times with questions of environmental law, including its fundamental principles such as sustainable development. The Court's analysis of certain issues of international environmental law might not have been sufficiently profound; but it must be noted that it has been facing a difficult task as certain norms of international environmental law are still developing and perhaps even lack a definite normative content.

Historically, we can distinguish certain periods in the Court's approach to environmental matters and in its contribution to the development of international environmental law. Viñuales in his insightful essay distinguished three such periods.[138] The first period included the general

[137] Okowa, above n 1 at 168–69.

[138] JE Viñuales, 'The Contribution of the International Court of Justice to the Development of International Environmental Law' (2008) 32 *Fordham International Law Journal* 232–258.

international law cases which had an impact of environmental protection such as the *Corfu Channel Case*, the *Barcelona Traction Case* and the *Nuclear Tests I Case* (which at least in its pleadings contained some environmental elements); the second period, including the *Gabčikovo-Nagymaros Case* and the *Advisory Opinion on Nuclear Weapons*, was characterised by Viñuales as focused on consolidating previous findings of the Court and linked international environmental law with other branches of international law, such as humanitarian law. Finally, the third period—which is contemporary—will be focused on clarification of specific norms of international environmental law.

The same author correctly surmises that the Court's contribution to the development of international environmental law may be assessed by some as quite modest in comparison to the exponential development of multilateral environmental treaties from 1970s. Such an impression, however, would not be entirely justified. As Viñuales observes, we could easily overlook the most important function of the Court, the integration of particular branches of international law into both the fabric of general international law and its various other branches. We must agree with this author that:

> the main role of the ICJ with regard to the development of international law is arguably not that of a ground-breaking body but rather of a stock-taking institution or, to put it in somewhat more colorful terms, that of being the gate-keeper and guardian of general international law.[139]

We should also note that other international courts and tribunals will develop norms of international environmental law, while adjudicating cases which in principle belong to human rights law, humanitarian law or the law of the sea. However, undoubtedly the ICJ will contribute the most to linking international environmental law to general international law.

[139] Ibid, 258.

3

Complaint and Grievance Mechanisms in International Dispute Settlement

DUNCAN FRENCH AND RICHARD KIRKHAM

I. INTRODUCTION

IN THE RULES and principles that guide and regulate international organisations, there has been a gradual, yet noticeable, transformation from a model premised upon a narrow conception of inter-governmentalism and formal legalism to one that is increasingly receptive to broader constitutional notions, including ideals such as enhancing legitimacy and promoting good governance.[1] In this process, concepts such as accountability, transparency, public participation and due administration have become prevalent both in the rhetoric and everyday reality of international organisations. This chapter focuses upon one element of this wider discourse, namely the increased adoption within the international community of complaint and grievance mechanisms that operate outside the traditional legal framework.

Such mechanisms are often administrative in nature, and thus clearly distinguishable from both judicial[2] and quasi-judicial[3] dispute settlement

[1] On the law relating to international organisations, see, eg CF Amerasinghe, *Principles of the Institutional Law of International Organizations*, 2nd edn (Cambridge, Cambridge University Press, 2005). As regards changing perceptions of international organisations see, eg T Franck, *Fairness in International Law and Institutions* (Oxford, Oxford University Press, 1995), J Nye, 'Globalization's Democratic Deficit: How to Make International Institutions More Accountable' *Foreign Affairs* (July/August 2001) and N Woods, 'Good Governance in International Organizations' (1999) 5 *Global Governance* 39–61.

[2] The reference to 'judicial' should be read expansively to include both judicial settlement *per se* (such as the proceedings of the International Court of Justice (ICJ) and the European Convention of Human Rights), binding arbitration (such as that facilitated by the Permanent Court of Arbitration (PCA)) and those systems (such as that within the World Trade Organization (WTO)), which employ a combination of both arbitration and judicial settlement (*viz*, the Appellate Body).

[3] The reference to 'quasi-judicial' refers, in particular, to the jurisdiction of autonomous international human rights bodies (such as the Human Rights Committee and the European Committee of Social Rights) to receive allegations of violations of human rights.

procedures, on the one hand, and more traditional diplomatic processes,[4] on the other. Moreover, though forming only one procedure amongst an array of 'accountability' techniques increasingly employed by international organisations,[5] including *ante hoc* (eg, public document disclosure and consultation procedures), *post hoc* (eg, evaluation and audit) and *ad hoc* (eg, committees of inquiry), the complaint and grievance mechanism stands out as an interesting, innovative and instrumental tool, both for affected stakeholders and for the organisations themselves. What is particularly encouraging is that such mechanisms seek to engage a range of communities beyond the intergovernmental level and incorporate the views and interests of civil society, which had previously been largely marginalised in the operation of such processes.

As this chapter will note, complaint and grievance mechanisms have been established within a wide array of international organisations, including both international financial institutions (eg, the World Bank and regional development banks) and as part of the structure of internationally-administered territorial entities (including the so-called 'Kosovo ombudsperson'). Moreover, as the report from the One World Trust highlights, accountability mechanisms have begun to be established not only within intergovernmental organisations (IGOs), but also within international non-governmental organisations (INGOs) and transnational corporations (TNCs).

Of course, international complaint and grievance mechanisms take many forms and, as the chapter will show, some of these differences necessarily point to significant variations both in theoretical underpinning and operational practice. Moreover, substantial gaps remain; most of the current mechanisms that exist in the UN system, for instance, are exclusively concerned with personnel matters, rather than complaints arising from *outside* the organisation.[6] Nevertheless, the idea of establishing a mechanism to hear public grievances, however putative the notion still is within many organisations, is increasingly emerging as integral to the broader discourse on what is required for good global governance.[7]

[4] As regards the role of methods such as negotiation, mediation, conciliation, and inquiry, see JG Merrills, *International Dispute Settlement*, 4th edn (Cambridge, Cambridge University Press, 2005) chs 1–4.

[5] For instance, the non-governmental organisation, the One World Trust, publishes an annual *Global Accountability Report*, which contains four principal areas of analysis: transparency, participation, evaluation, and complaint and response mechanisms, www.oneworldtrust.org/?display=index_2007_home.

[6] This is not, in any way, to imply that internal complaints mechanisms, including appropriate procedures to handle matters raised by 'whistle-blowing', are not intrinsic to good governance.

[7] M Zwanenburg, *Accountability of Peace Support Operations* (Leiden, Brill, 2005) 300: 'the concept of the ombudsman does exist at the international level. It has developed mainly as

This development is belatedly mirroring the trend towards 'alternative dispute resolution' (ADR) that has occurred over the last 50 years at the national level.[8]

Many of the complaint and grievance mechanisms in existence at the international level are reflective, perhaps even derivative, of processes and functions that already exist in the domestic sphere. The most prominent and wide-ranging form of ADR to have evolved at the national level is the office of the ombudsman, which is enshrined in many national constitutional, administrative and private structures.[9] Given the potential within the ombudsman model, this chapter explores the impact of the idea in public international law. However, in recognising the sheer diversity in the range of national (and regional) ombudsmen, this chapter seeks neither to describe the 'characteristic' ombudsman nor to consider whether it has been adopted at the global level. Rather, the aim of this chapter is more nuanced: to consider to what extent core attributes of national ombudsmen and ombudsmen-like processes can be ascertained in international complaint and grievance mechanisms.

Many of the underlying issues inherent within any ombudsman scheme are particularly relevant when placed in the international context. Questions such as 'who is entitled to complain?', 'what level of operational independence should a complaint and grievance mechanism enjoy?', 'what is the extent of the mechanism's mandate and jurisdiction?', and 'what powers can the mechanism employ to achieve its purpose?' all raise complex institutional issues. A further question, but one that is arguably particularly interesting in this context is 'what are the objectives of a complaint and grievance mechanism?' These objectives could range from reviewing the organisation's compliance with its own procedures, fostering friendly solutions to disputes, investigating maladministration and/or promoting human rights, through to promoting a 'lessons learnt' approach within the wider institution. Of course, all of these questions are inherently generic and applicable to any level of governance, however

a corollary of the demand for accountability of international organizations, and in particular accountability towards individuals'.

[8] It should be noted that the use of methods such as conciliation, fact-finding and mediation at the international level have a much longer history: see generally Merrills, above n 4. As regards the continued use of ADR methods between States, see also suggestions for the establishment of an ombudsman within the WTO as a precursor and supplement to the formal dispute settlement system that operates between member States (see *The Multilateral Trade Regime: Which Way Forward? The report of the first Warwick Commission*, www2.warwick.ac.uk/research/warwickcommission, 33: 'This would offer an initial non-litigious avenue for settlement and would also serve to inform consultations in the next stage of the dispute settlement process should the informal mediation fail to deliver amicable settlement'.

[9] See, eg R Gregory and P Giddings (eds), *Righting Wrongs: The Ombudsman in Six Continents* (Amsterdam, IOS Press, 2000).

they are potentially more interesting, if not also contentious, when placed within the global arena. International organisations, which have so long had to carefully balance sovereign membership with limited institutional independence, are now also having to balance such autonomy with popular concerns of accountability and transparency.

In addressing these issues, the chapter is divided into four parts. Part II reviews the theoretical arguments in favour of complaint and grievance mechanisms outside the traditional legal/judicial model. It also considers some of the lessons that can be derived from the experiences gained at the national level from the use of perhaps the most advanced form of complaint and grievance mechanism outside the courts, the ombudsman. Part III provides a brief overview of the development of complaint and grievance mechanisms within international organisations and analyses the extent to which ombudsman characteristics have been embedded within international models. Part IV then offers some thoughts on the potential for greater use to be made of the ombudsman institution in the United Nations more generally.

The chapter will then contend in Part V that the key attributes of ombudsman-like processes and offices are arguably central to implementing the ubiquitous notions of good governance[10] and due process—thus further supporting the cross-fertilisation of ideas inherent with the discourse on global administrative law. But the international community still has a long way to go before it embraces fully the potential contained within the ombudsman concept, even though concurrently it is also arguable that automatic replication of national ombudsmen should be avoided. Complaint and grievance mechanisms at the international level are innovative both in their contribution to the operation of international organisations and as an alternative model vis-à-vis traditional dispute settlement procedures. Nevertheless, in truth it is the structural limitations of such mechanisms, as much as the opportunities they provide, which reveal a more complete analysis of the recurring tensions within global governance. Yet the inherent weaknesses of non-judicial complaints and grievance mechanisms are also a potential strength. Such 'softer' forms of dispute resolution, which are able to bend more easily to the strictures of a system of law ultimately grounded in the sovereignty of nation-states, rather than break when confronted directly against them, are arguably more amenable to the incorporation of ideals of legitimacy and governance than traditional dispute resolution regimes.

[10] For an overview of good governance and, in particular, its linkages with the development of complaint and grievance mechanisms, both nationally and internationally, see L Reif, *The Ombudsman, Good Governance and the International Human Rights System* (Leiden, Martinus Nijhoff, 2004) ch 3.

II. THE THEORY BEHIND COMPLAINT AND GRIEVANCE MECHANISMS

The existence of complaint and grievance mechanisms at the global level, especially if made available to affected civil society and local communities, could rightly be heralded as a milestone in the organisation of international affairs. This development is a sign of a gradual shift away from a purely intergovernmental approach to one premised upon broader notions of global regulation and administration. As the impact and reach of such organisations increasingly transcend State boundaries and thus have the capacity to affect the lives and livelihoods of individuals, the call for greater accountability of such organisations was perhaps inevitable.[11] The fact that many organisations remain resistant to wholesale change, or hold on to the 'old' premise that they are primarily engaged in technical matters and thus outside popular concern, should not disguise the fact that the discourse on global governance has changed dramatically over recent years.

Such change has been mirrored by a shift in perspective on the role of global organisations within the broader parameter of international relations. As Krisch and Kingsbury note:

> central pillars of the international legal order are seen from a classical perspective as increasingly challenged: the distinction between domestic and international law becomes more precarious, soft forms of rule-making are ever more widespread, the sovereign equality of states is gradually undermined, and the legitimacy of international law is increasingly in doubt.[12]

One response to such challenges has been to import values—traditionally dominant within the domestic and regional sphere—into the global consciousness. For want of a better name, such analysis is often referred to as global administrative law.

> It starts from the observation that much of global governance can be understood as regulation and administration ... the increasing exercise of public power in these structures has given rise to serious concerns about legitimacy and accountability, prompting patterns of responses to those concerns in many areas of global governance.[13]

While recognising the merits of some of the insights of the global administrative law approach, there is an equal recognition that 'classical' international law remains very much the dominant paradigm. There are thus

[11] More generally, see D Bodansky, 'The Legitimacy of International Governance: A Coming Challenge for International Environmental Law' (1999) 93 *American Journal of International Law* (*AJIL*) 610: 'the more international environmental law resembles domestic law, the more it should be subject to the same standards of legitimacy that animate domestic law'.

[12] N Krisch and B Kingsbury, 'Introduction: Global Governance and Global Administrative Law in the International Legal Order' (2006) 17 *European Journal of International Law* 1. On the issue of legitimacy at the international level, more generally, see Franck, above n1, ch 2.

[13] Ibid.

noticeable tensions between demands for greater legitimacy and transparency, on the one hand, and a retrenched belief in the traditional notions of sovereignty and political autonomy, on the other. It is the response of international organisations in reconciling such considerations that is very much the driving force behind recent attempts to establish complaint and grievance mechanisms as a novel means of dispute resolution.

The significance of complaint and grievance mechanisms is that they can contribute to the promotion of a variety of constitutional values. Perhaps of most importance is their capacity to provide a realistic route by which grievances can be effectively pursued by those most immediately affected. Thus, the existence of such mechanisms compensates for the classic critique of the ability of judicial bodies to uphold the rule of law only when it falls within the narrow strictures of a particular factual matrix, as well as reflecting the almost universal truth that formal processes tend to be difficult to take advantage of and are prohibitively expensive and intimidating for the average litigant. With the work of international organisations increasingly impacting directly on the lives of individual citizens, these are important considerations if those same institutions are to obtain legitimacy. Moreover, the lack of a comprehensive judicial framework at the international level, particularly one which does not provide individuals with any meaningful role—other than the existence of a few human rights courts which permit individual claims against States—exacerbates both the general problem and highlights the need for alternative procedures.

But the value of complaint and grievance mechanisms can go further than securing redress. Complaint and grievance mechanisms cannot only call to account the actions of international organisations, but they can provide tangible evidence to the wider community that they are accountable and, at the same time, provide heightened incentives for international organisations to focus on the promotion of internal good governance. Furthermore, if permitted, complaint and grievance mechanisms can also monitor the responses of international organisations to their investigations and even work with them to identify potential areas for institutional improvement.

Operating along these lines there are now a considerable number of complaint and grievance mechanisms at the international level that are worthy of study. Problems exist within many of these mechanisms and the potential gains from this form of dispute resolution have only just begun to be identified. In particular, it is evident that the global community has yet to adopt in full the ombudsman model, which has proved so popular at the national level. This must be considered a possible area for future exploration as it has been amply demonstrated at the nation-state level that the ombudsman can be a particularly useful tool in the resolution of those disputes with a quasi-political dimension. Given this potential, it could be that over the next 20 to 30 years we will see ever more ambitious models of complaint and grievance mechanisms playing an increasingly significant role in the further development of international dispute resolution.

A. The Ombudsman Technique—Lessons From the National Level

The technique of 'ombudsmanry' has been described by one author as 'the jurisprudential development of the 20th century',[14] whilst others have charted the incredible growth in the popularity of the idea in the latter half of the last century.[15] There are now national, local and State ombudsmen in operation in approximately 120 countries[16] and a growing body of academic literature is dedicated to this form of complaint and grievance mechanism.[17] At the national level there have also been significant developments in theoretical and practical thinking as to how best to resolve disputes, which has resulted in at least a partial shift away from dispute resolution led by lawyers and an ever growing emphasis on so-called 'alternative dispute resolution mechanisms', of which the ombudsman is the most important example.

As with complaint and grievance mechanisms at the international level, there is much to differentiate the various models of ombudsmen adopted around the world.[18] With a few notable exceptions,[19] most are relatively

[14] N Lewis, 'World Ombudsman Community: aspects and prospects' (1993) 39 *Indian Journal of Public Administration* 676.

[15] Gregory and Giddings, above n 9.

[16] See the International Ombudsman Institute website for details, www.law.ualberta.ca/centres/ioi/About-the-I.O.I./History-and-Development.php.

[17] While the notion of 'complaint and grievance mechanism' is sufficiently broad to incorporate the office of the ombudsman, at the national level it is generally more appropriate to refer to 'ombudsman' as that is the principal—though not exclusive—mechanism by which grievances are aired outside the formal legal context. However, see Reif, above n 10 at 366, in which she makes a distinction between the office of ombudsman and mechanisms such as the World Bank's inspection panel—'a classical ombudsman is a non-judicial, soft mechanism having only the sanctions of recommendation and public reporting. The inspection panel has even more limited functions and powers'.

[18] Ombudsman institutions are given a range of different titles. As the website for the International Ombudsman Institute, www.law.ualberta.ca/centres/ioi/About-the-I.O.I./History-and-Development.php, explains, 'Defensor del Pueblo is the title of the ombudsman office in a number of Spanish-speaking countries (such as in Spain, Argentina, Peru and Colombia). Parliamentary Commissioner for Administration (Sri Lanka, United Kingdom), Médiateur de la République (such as France, Gabon, Mauritania, Senegal), Public Protector (South Africa), Protecteur du Citoyen (Québec), Volksanwaltschaft (Austria), Public Complaints Commission (Nigeria), Provedor de Justiça (Portugal), Difensore Civico (Italy), Investigator-General (Zambia), Citizen's Aide (Iowa), Wafaqi Mohtasib (Pakistan), and Lok Ayukta (India) are the titles of some other ombudsman offices around the world'.

[19] In particular, the office of the Swedish Ombudsman (*Justitieombudsman*) is 200 years old in 2009.

young institutions. The vast majority of ombudsmen now in operation around the world were established in the last 50 years and, in many cases, the last 20 years. As a consequence, in many countries there is still a lack of full appreciation and knowledge as to how the institution operates and what it is fully capable of. Thus, the concept of ombudsmanry is still in its infancy. Moreover, the development of the practice has been hampered by a number of factors. Commonly, new ombudsman institutions are required to spend a significant amount of institutional energy embedding their place within the constitutional order and gaining the acceptance of both citizens and established public authority, including the courts. Other barriers to successful operation include securing adequate funding, maintaining independence and persuading authorities to implement their recommendations. Such institutional barriers, coupled with the relative newness of this form of dispute resolution mechanism, means that there is still little agreed understanding, and few practical examples, as to the full capacity of the ombudsman institution.[20] These inherent problems put into context the relative underdevelopment of the idea at the international level and, at the same time, highlight a key lesson; that the strength of ombudsman schemes owes much to the background political and institutional support that they receive.

A generic observation that can be made about ombudsmanry at the national level is the lack of uniformity in the model that has been adopted. Although there have been efforts to describe the 'classical ombudsman',[21] in truth the key feature of the ombudsman institution is its flexibility and the ability for the office to be moulded to meet a variety of different needs and situations. A few examples serve to demonstrate the point. In Latin America, where the ombudsman (the *Defensor del Pueblo*) has become an important part of the constitutional scene, the office is normally established along the model developed in Spain and Portugal. This entails that the primary focus of the institution has been to promote and protect human rights and uphold human rights legislation and treaties. A similar development can be seen to have occurred in Eastern Europe and in several countries in Africa. By contrast, in the Nordic countries, where the modern ombudsman began, the onus has been on using the institution as an upholder of the law, with there being an explicit crossover between the work of the courts and the ombudsman. In common law countries, however, much less emphasis is placed on the ombudsman pursuing breaches of the law, with instead ombudsmen empowered to investigate

[20] For a more detailed exposition, see T Buck, R Kirkham and B Thompson, *The Ombudsman Enterprise and Administrative Justice* (Ashgate, 2010, forthcoming).

[21] DG Gottehrer and M Hostina, *Essential Characteristics of a Classical Ombudsman* (1998). Available on the United States Ombudsman Association website, www.usombudsman.org/en/references/more_references/.

alleged breaches of more equitable standards, such as maladministration or denial of fairness.

Thus, the ombudsman model has proved to be an extremely adaptable tool that has contributed to dealing with a variety of jurisprudential problems in a range of different jurisdictions. The concept has also crossed over from the public to the private sector and has been used to tackle issues as diverse as the environment and corruption.[22] Given that the ombudsman has proved to be flexible at the national level, it is hardly surprising that it has been identified as a potentially useful device at the international level, despite the very different issues of governance that arise.

In so far as there is such a thing as a 'classical ombudsman' model, the key is the specific institutional features that the ombudsman ordinarily possesses.[23] Above all, ombudsmen are seen as independently appointed officers of the State or parliament who operate autonomously of the executive and public authority more generally. The most significant evidence of their autonomy are the wide-ranging powers that they possess to summon witnesses and discover documents. However, in stark contrast to their investigatory powers, ombudsmen do not ordinarily possess any powers of legal enforcement. Indeed, such enforcement powers are considered to be contradictory to the overall methodology of the ombudsman. Rather than being an institution of legal authority and force, the key technique of the ombudsman is one of intellectual authority and powers of persuasion, backed up, if necessary, by access to means of political pressure and embarrassment.

There are further flexibilities inherent in the ombudsman technique that are also key to their popularity and potential. Although the primary aim of the institution is to resolve grievances and secure redress, the ombudsman is capable of achieving much more. Owing to its design, the ombudsman has an inherent capacity to promote accountability and institutional learning. Its strong investigatory powers enable it to obtain information that classic techniques of legal dispute resolution can find hard to uncover, while the softer approach necessitated by the lack of powers of enforcement generally facilitates a more positive cooperative relationship with the public authorities investigated.[24] At its best, the nature of this relationship, backed up by the ombudsman's broad inquisitorial powers, enables the ombudsman to uncover information and arrive at an understanding of events that adds significantly to the wider constitutional efforts to secure

[22] Eg in Hungary there is now a Parliamentary Commissioner for the Rights of Future Generations, who is responsible for environmental protection, and in India a lead function of the 'Lok Ayukta' is to investigate allegations of fraud.

[23] Gottehrer and Hostina, above n 21.

[24] M Hertogh, 'Coercion, Cooperation, and Control: Understanding the Policy Impact of Administrative Courts and the Netherlands' (2001) 23 *Law and Policy* 47.

the accountability of public authorities. More than that though, the softer approach of the ombudsman can encourage the public authority involved to take on board the complaints handling process as an opportunity to learn rather than a challenge to resist. While ombudsmen may deliver firm conclusions, which can have a significant long-term impact, in general ombudsmen seek to emphasise potential solutions and ways forward to address the errors made. Again, given the frequently politically sensitive overtone of activities undertaken by international organisations, such a soft law approach to dispute resolution has many attractions.

As argued above, the full potential of the ombudsman institution is only just beginning to be properly explored at the national level. There is, however, an argument to suggest that the ombudsman is a particularly useful institution in those areas where law meets politics and/or where dispute resolution is complicated by the existence of a number of different competing political and social interests. Lon Fuller famously argued that courts were not a good place to resolve what he described as polycentric disputes.[25] In polycentric disputes there are a range of conflicting interests involved, with it being highly probable that not all affected parties are represented in the dispute. In such disputes often there are also moral judgments to be made and difficult issues of resource allocation to face up to. In short, the dispute is politically and morally complex with contentious issues which, taken together, make the balancing exercise that has to be then undertaken by the dispute resolution mechanism beyond the boundaries of traditional legal reasoning. Yet there is still a dispute to be resolved. An argument in favour of the ombudsman technique being used to resolve such complex disputes is that it is not restricted by the arguments presented by the immediate parties and has wide investigatory powers to pursue all the issues involved. Perhaps of even more importance, though, is the idea that because it has no binding powers of enforcement the ombudsman cannot rely upon its legal authority to force a solution. Instead, the ombudsman is driven by necessity to make logically consistent and defensible findings and to use his tools of persuasion, as well as logical reasoning, to arrive at workable solutions:

> It may be stated that this inability to force change represents the central strength of the office and not its weakness. It requires that recommendations must be based on a thorough investigation of all facts, scrupulous consideration of all perspectives and vigorous analysis of all issues. Through this application of reason, the results are infinitely more powerful than through the application of coercion.[26]

[25] L Fuller, 'The Forms and Limits of Adjudication' (1978–79) 92 *Harvard Law Review* 353.

[26] S Owen, 'The Ombudsman: Essential Elements and Common Challenges' in L Reif, M Marshall and C Ferris (eds), *The Ombudsman: Diversity and Development* (Edmonton, International Ombudsman Institute, 1992) 52.

All of the characteristics noted above make the ombudsman institution an extremely interesting jurisprudential device. It is no doubt because of these features that the number of ombudsmen around the world has grown significantly over the last 50 years. At the same time in many countries the limitations of the court mechanism have become steadily more apparent, so further fuelling the search for other solutions. Evidently, there are certain issues that are best resolved in the courts and in general it is understood that questions of legal interpretation should remain the prerogative of the courts. Yet in many other instances the highly procedural, cumbersome and restrictive way in which legal disputes are resolved is inappropriate, excessively expensive and often not particularly relevant to the needs of either side of the dispute. On a wider constitutional level, it is also of concern that while the court process provides a very strong form of accountability, it does not always make a particularly positive long-term contribution towards improved governance within public bodies. In these two senses, the ombudsman's flexibility allows it to provide a much more tailored and positive service.

III. COMPLAINT AND GRIEVANCE MECHANISMS AT THE INTERNATIONAL LEVEL

The aim of this part is to consider how far the underlying values of the ombudsman have been endorsed at the international level through the development of complaint and grievance mechanisms. With the exception of the European Ombudsman, it is difficult to find any examples of fully fledged ombudsman systems along the lines established at the nation-state level. Nevertheless, there does exist a range of complaint and grievance mechanisms that adopt various aspects of the technique and/or pursue similar objectives. In one sense, complaint and grievance mechanisms are reasonably well established in international organisations. Thus, for instance, one area where the introduction of complaint and grievance mechanisms has been profound has been in areas of internal dispute resolution between international organisations and their staff.[27] To name but a few, the United Nations, the World Health Organization, the World Bank Group, the International Monetary Fund and the World Trade Organization all employ some form of workplace ombudsman or mediator to deal with staff grievances. But as Reif notes,

> [t]his type of ombudsman mechanism should not be overly controversial or threatening to either international organization or member state interests. Rather,

[27] For a general overview of such international ombudsmen, see Reif, above n 10 at 336–46.

> the model is designed to settle secretariat employment disputes informally, avoid the more legalistic and expensive formal dispute settlement alternatives and thereby improve both staff morale and organizational efficiency.[28]

This is, of course, an interesting and important development. Not only does it demonstrate a healthy commitment from international organisations towards taking the rights of their employees seriously, but it also provides evidence of awareness of the benefits of alternative dispute resolution mechanisms. However, these internal forms of dispute resolution only touch upon the surface of what such mechanisms can offer.

In this part, some of the more far-reaching forms of complaint and grievance mechanisms are considered. What can be noticed is that though such mechanisms might, at first glance, appear rather distinctive from traditional notions of the ombudsman, there are also key similarities. These include that the aim of such mechanisms is to resolve grievances without recourse to formal judicial proceedings, that they are established to operate independently and autonomously and that the authority of their office derives not from any designated powers of enforcement but purely from the persuasiveness of their arguments. Of course, there are significant divergences in approach—as there are at the national level—but such differences should not mask the very real synergies that nevertheless exist between such mechanisms.

A. World Bank Inspection Panel: A Radical, Yet Conservative, Innovation

One of the earliest, and certainly one of the most discussed, complaint and grievance mechanisms at the international level is the World Bank's[29] Inspection Panel.[30] Established in 1993, its creation was an institutional

[28] Ibid 364–65.

[29] Technically, the 'World Bank' is shorthand for the International Bank for Reconstruction and Development (IBRD) and the International Development Association (IDA). It is these two institutions which jointly established the Inspection Panel, and over whose activities the Panel may receive complaints. As regards other institutional components of the World Bank group, both the International Finance Corporation (IFC) and Multilateral Investment Guarantee Agency (MIGA) have developed an alternative model, the office of the Compliance Advisor Ombudsman (CAO), whose role combines the investigation of complaints, overseeing compliance reviews of IFC/MIGA activities and providing independent advice to IFC/MIGA management on environmental and social aspects of their policies.

[30] See generally, D Clark, *Demanding Accountability: Civil Society Claims and the World Bank Inspection Panel* (New York, Rowman & Littlefield Publishers, 2003), I Shihata, *The World Bank Inspection Panel: In Practice*, 2nd edn (New York, Oxford University Press, 2000), S Schlemmer-Schulte, 'The World Bank's Experience with its Inspection Panel' (1998) 58 *Zeitschrift für ausländisches öffentliches Recht und Völkerrecht* 353–88, and C Chinkin, 'Alternative Dispute Resolution under International Law' in M Evans (ed), *Remedies in International Law: The Institutional Dilemma* (Oxford, Oxford University Press, 1998) 134–37.

response to criticism that the World Bank was failing to follow its own internal policies and procedures, specifically with regard to the negative impact World-Bank sponsored large infrastructural projects were having on local environments and communities.[31] Significantly, such criticism did not just come from civil society, but also included some of the Bank's own members, most noticeably the United States.[32] In the light of such pressure, the World Bank had little choice but to respond. The Inspection Panel was rightly heralded as the first international organisation to seek to address such accountability concerns, though it is perhaps more conservative than radical in its actual operation, certainly as compared to other, more recent, mechanisms.[33]

The function of the Inspection Panel is to consider allegations from persons, and in certain circumstances their representatives, whose:

> rights or interests have been or are likely to be directly affected by an action or omission of the Bank as a result of a failure of the Bank to follow its operational policies and procedures with respect to the design, appraisal and/or implementation of a project financed by the Bank … provided in all cases that such failure has had, or threatens to have, a material adverse effect.[34]

The Inspection Panel—though housed in the World Bank—is independent of the World Bank's management and reports directly to the Board of Executive Directors, individuals who are either appointed or selected by the Bank's member State constituencies. The three members who make up the Inspection Panel are appointed for one five-year term and though as officials of the Bank, are subject to the requirement of exclusive loyalty to the Bank,[35] appointment is based upon, inter alia, 'their ability to deal thoroughly and fairly with the requests brought to them, their integrity and their independence from the Bank's Management'.[36]

The Inspection Panel is neither a binding nor a judicial process; its purpose is to investigate allegations and to report its findings to the Bank's Board of Executive Directors, which will—together with receipt of the

[31] For the range of issues that beset the World Bank in the early 1990s, see K Horta, 'The World Bank and the International Monetary Fund' in J Werksman (ed), *Greening International Institutions* (London, Earthscan, 1996) 132–33.

[32] I Bowles and C Kormos, 'Environmental Reform at the World Bank: The Role of the US Congress' (1995) 35 *Virginia Journal of International Law* 777–839.

[33] For a comprehensive analysis of such mechanisms within multilateral development banks and related institutions, see D Bradlow, 'Private Complainants and International Organizations: A Comparative Study of the Independent Inspection Mechanisms in International Financial Institutions' (2005) 36 *Georgetown Journal of International Law* 403–91.

[34] Resolution No IBRD 93-10/Resolution No IDA 93-6 (22 September 1993) para 12.

[35] Ibid para 4.

[36] Ibid. For a more detailed account of how the Inspection Panel operates, see A Gowlland Gualtieri, 'The Environmental Accountability of the World Bank to Non-State Actors: Insights from the Inspection Panel' (2001) LXXII *British Yearbook of International Law* 213–53.

management's response and, where appropriate, its recommendations for remedial action—'consider' the matter.[37] The Inspection Panel procedure is a two-stage process: first, a determination whether an allegation requires investigation; and second, the investigation itself. Since 1999, as regards the first stage of the process, the Executive Board has automatically authorised an investigation 'without making a judgement on the merits of the claimants' request', so long as certain 'technical eligibility criteria' are met.[38]

As regards investigations, several key points are worth noting. First, the Panel is entitled to access all relevant Bank staff and to all pertinent Bank records in undertaking its investigations. Second, the Panel will, where necessary, consult with other internal Bank accountability and evaluation bodies, including the independent evaluation group[39] and the internal auditor. Third, where inspections are to take place in the territory of the borrower country, they shall not be carried out unless prior consent has been given, though there is equally an explicit assumption that consent will be granted. During such visits, though the Bank recognises that Panel members will wish 'to gather information through consultations with affected people',[40] the rules governing Panel activities do very carefully note that such in-country investigations should 'be kept as low[-profile] as possible in keeping with its role as a fact-finding body on behalf of the Board. The Panel's methods of investigation should not create the impression that it is investigating the borrower's performance'.[41] This language is particularly interesting as it reflects the diverse pressures between improving global governance, on the one hand, and respecting domestic sovereignty, on the other.

The Inspection Panel has now been in existence for over 15 years, and has conducted an increasing number of important investigations. The results of these investigations have prompted the Bank's management to make significant changes to a number of high-profile projects,[42] as well as

[37] Merrills, above n 4 at 62: 'The findings of the Panel are not binding, but based as they are on impartial investigation … carry considerable weight. As evaluation has a quasi-judicial aspect, Panel reports go beyond inquiry in the strict sense, but clearly incorporate a significant fact-finding element'.

[38] See 1999 Clarification of the Board's Second Review of the Inspection Panel, para 9.

[39] As the mandate of the Director-General, World Bank Evaluations states, 'The independent evaluation function is responsible for the assessment of the relevance, efficacy, and efficiency of World Bank Group operational programs and activities, and their contribution to development effectiveness. Evaluation enhances accountability and informs the formulation of new directions, policies and procedures, and country and sector strategies for the Bank's work' (footnote reference omitted), www.worldbank.org/ieg/dge_mandate.html.

[40] 1999 Clarification, above n 38 at para 12.

[41] Ibid.

[42] R Bissell, 'Recent Practice of the Inspection Panel of the World Bank' (1997) 91 AJIL 741–44. See also the annual reports of the Inspection Panel, www.worldbank.org/inspectionpanel.

affecting the operation of its overall project cycle.[43] It can also be claimed that as a result of the Inspection Panel's work there is 'much greater sensitivity in the institutions to their own operational policies and procedures'.[44] As Bissell, a one-time chairman of the panel, has commented, the Inspection Panel is both 'enriching and modifying the Bank's approach to its legal obligations'.[45] Changes are, of course, most likely to occur when the project remains at an early stage of implementation. Those projects reviewed at a later stage of development have, therefore, proved much more difficult to remedy.

A significant weakness identified by a number of commentators is the lack of ongoing supervision.

> The Inspection Panel does not have oversight authority over the implementation of those remedial measures; nor is it able to provide the Board with an assessment of whether Management's proposed remedial measures would satisfy the concerns of the claimants and/or bring the project into compliance with Bank policy.[46]

This is a significant weakness and one that some of the subsequent mechanisms established in the wake of the Inspection Panel have sought to resolve. The Compliance Review Panel of the Asian Development Bank, for instance, monitors implementation of remedial measures and reports to the Board annually on issues of implementation.[47] More recently, there have been examples where the World Bank Board of Executive Directors has itself asked the Inspection Panel to review the Bank Management's progress reports on implementing its action plans.[48] This is a positive step forward, but one which should be codified within the legal framework which established the Panel, particularly as such an innovation would seem, in fact, to be contrary to the stated expectations of how the Panel would operate, as set out in the initial Bank resolutions on the matter.[49]

Moreover, there is also some argument that the very existence of the Inspection Panel (along with the World Bank's safeguard policies which the Panel monitors) has had a potentially detrimental effect on how the Bank operates *in practice*. It has been suggested that such innovations not

43 See Bradlow, above n 33 at 409–10.

44 Ibid.

45 Bissell, above n 42 at 744.

46 D Clark, 'The World Bank and Human Rights: The Need for Greater Accountability' (2002) 15 *Harvard Human Rights Journal* 218.

47 Bradlow, above n 33 at 431.

48 See 2006–07 Inspection Panel's Annual Report, 15: 'During fiscal year 2007, the Panel also reviewed, at the Board's request, Management's Progress report on its Action Plan in response to the Panel's Investigation Report on the Mumbai Urban Transport Project'.

49 1999 Clarifications, above n 38 at para 16: 'The Board should not ask the Panel for its view on other aspects of the action plans nor would it ask the Panel to monitor the implementation of the action plans'.

only encourage Bank staff to focus too specifically on 'panel-proofing' Bank activities, but also they provide a negative incentive within the Bank to water down the policies on which the Panel reports.

> When the Bank first adopted environmental safeguard policies, the policies tended to be comprehensive and demanding. The Bank saw the policies as guiding principles, rather than as binding rules. When civil society began demanding compliance with these policies, the conversion process weakened them in an attempt to make them easier to meet.[50]

Of course, if true, this clearly suggests that—at one level—the Inspection Panel must be operating reasonably successfully, otherwise there would be no need for such a reactive response. Politically, however, civil society and its member States should seek to ensure that positive institutional change, such as the establishment and effective operation of the Inspection Panel, does not prompt retreat in other areas, notably the normative and procedural standards under which the Bank operates.

Overall, the Inspection Panel must be considered an important institutional development both within the World Bank itself and as a precursor to the development of other mechanisms elsewhere, specifically within other international financial organisations. Nevertheless, as Hunter notes, '[t]he Panel is still a work in progress ... the short-term benefits that come from the added attention brought by filing a Panel claim do not necessarily translate into long-term sustainable benefits'.[51] This seems also to be the benchmark that the Panel sets itself: as it noted in its 2006–07 annual report, '[w]e hope that our work will contribute to ensuring sustainable and equitable development, an important goal of the World Bank'.[52] High rhetoric, of course, but also a certain element of truth; as with much of the general movement towards accountability and good governance in the international arena, the changes are not intended to be the end-goal, but will hopefully also improve the *delivery* of the organisation's wider aims and purposes.

B. Mechanisms Within Other International Institutions

The World Bank may have been the first multilateral development bank to adopt such a mechanism for external grievances and complaints, but many other institutions, particularly—though not exclusively—international financial institutions, have also responded to such demands for accountability to create their own procedures and systems.

[50] N Bridgeman, 'World Bank Reform in the "Post-Policy" Era' (2001) 13 *Georgetown International Environmental Law Review* 1024.

[51] D Hunter, 'Using the World Bank Inspection Panel to Defend the Interests of Project-Affected People' (2003) 4 *Chicago Journal of International Law* 210.

[52] 2006–07 Inspection Panel's Annual Report, 16.

Though it is beyond the limits of this chapter to review these mechanisms, there are certain general themes surrounding the development of complaint and grievance mechanisms in international law which can be noted. Bradlow, in his work on complaint mechanisms within international financial organisations, for instance, highlights a number of key issues. First, he argues that the range of functions that such mechanisms undertake vary greatly to include not only compliance-review (as with the World Bank's Inspection Panel) but also, in some instances, problem-solving/mediation and significantly, at the culmination of an investigation, a 'lessons learnt'/dissemination of good practice role. Both of these additional functions are important, if for slightly different reasons. As regards problem-solving/mediation, he argues '[i]n reality, non-state actors are more interested in having the problems caused by the organisation's operations solved than they are in ensuring that the staff and management comply with the applicable operational policies and procedures'.[53]

As regards the inclusion of a 'lessons learnt' function, this can 'demonstrate to the organization's staff and management and to its member states that the purpose of the mechanism is not "finger pointing" but improvement in the operations of the organization'.[54] Civil society will also wish to know that the international organisation has learnt from its mistakes and will—hopefully—not replicate the same errors again. On both issues the World Bank Inspection Panel lags behind some—though not all—of the other institutional mechanisms. On the issue of 'lessons learnt', Bradlow sees this as a particular failing as it means that the World Bank's Executive Board and Management 'are currently being deprived of ... unique knowledge about the impact of their operations on affected communities and about the implementation of their operational policies and procedures'.[55]

Second, he notes a progression—what he refers to as 'generations' of inspection procedures—within such institutions.[56] What he means by this is relatively nuanced but essentially it is the narrative of how complaint and grievance mechanisms have evolved from the model established by the World Bank ('first generation'), to incorporating problem-solving within the compliance function ('second generation'), through to retaining these diverse functions but ensuring they are administered separately ('third generation').[57] This 'generational' account would seem to be a

53 Bradlow, above n 33 at 484–85.
54 Ibid 486.
55 Ibid 462.
56 Ibid 484.
57 *cf* Reif, n 10 above, 365: 'all of the mechanisms are limited to an examination of the organization's policies and procedures and do not have the freedom to look at other legal norms or fairness considerations'.

reasonably accurate description of the development of such mechanisms, though it must also be recognised that there is also room for over-generalisation, especially outside the financial arena. For instance, a small (yet increasing) number of UN institutions[58] which permit consideration of external complaints have not established bespoke mechanisms but have rather 'opened-up' their internal procedures for external complaints.[59] This may be far from ideal, though it does again indicate the inherent flexibility and broad span of approaches currently taken, as well as, perhaps, a disinclination to endorse complex institutional arrangements in all instances.

C. The Kosovo Ombudsperson

One of the most notable examples of a recent complaints mechanism established through the framework of international law—though, in reality, had more of the appearance of a domestic procedure, or at least a hybrid of the two—was the creation of the 'Ombudsperson Institution' by the United Nations Interim Administration Mission in Kosovo (UNMIK). Established in June 2000[60] by the Special Representative of the UN Secretary-General under authority given to him by the UN Security Council to administer the territory, the role of the ombudsperson was to:

> promote and protect the rights and freedoms of individuals and legal entities and ensure that all persons in Kosovo are able to exercise effectively the human rights and fundamental freedoms safeguarded by international human rights standards, in particular the European Convention on Human Rights and its Protocols and the International Covenant on Civil and Political Rights.[61]

Though established by the UN, the ombudsperson institution was, in fact, developed by the Organization for Security and Co-operation in Europe (OSCE) as part of the broader multi-agency approach to tackling the range of complex administrative, institutional, economic, security, and political issues in Kosovo, subsequent to NATO's intervention in 1999.[62] The creation of the ombudsperson was considered particularly necessary as the international community, in establishing UNMIK, had ranged beyond

[58] Such as the UN Development Programme, the UN Environment Programme and the World Food Programme.

[59] See 2007 Global Accountability Report, above n 5 at 53.

[60] UNMIK/REG/2000/38 (30 June 2000).

[61] Ibid s 1.1.

[62] For a succinct history of the establishment of the Kosovo Ombudsperson, see C Waters, 'Human Rights in an International Protectorate: Kosovo's Ombudsman' (2000) 4 *The International Ombudsman Yearbook* 141–52. More generally, on the role of ombudsmen as a feature of post-conflict peace-building, see Reif, above n 10, ch 8.

its normal functional capacities to undertake one of the most ambitious tasks in its history. Along with the UN Transitional Administration in East Timor (UNTAET),[63] the undertaking of 'international territorial administration'[64] in Kosovo raised a variety of institutional and practical questions, as well as generating more fundamental issues around the very 'act' of international organisations administering a territory.[65] In effect, the UN and its institutional partners were not just behaving as—but for a significant period of time were—the governing administration of Kosovo, together with all the incumbent rights and legitimate expectations of how such a government should operate. Thus, by acting in this enlarged role of domestic administration, it is of little surprise that there was a concurrent demand for accountability mechanisms similar to those that exist in many national jurisdictions.

Of course, such accountability is not a legal prerequisite, per se; nothing is formally required beyond the normative force of a UN Security Council resolution.[66] However, it is unimaginable that UNMIK should not also seek domestic support, if not broader legitimacy, for its actions, particularly as such institutional control raises both political and jurisprudential issues about the very special relationship between the UN and those it is seeking to protect. As the Kosovo ombudsperson noted in Special Report No 1 (2001), 'UNMIK acts as a surrogate state'.[67] Of course, the creation of an accountability mechanism is not the only—or, by itself, the exclusive—means to generate such legitimacy; in particular, a traditional ombudsman is rarely considered an adequate replacement—rather than as a corollary and supplement—to the rule of law, as administered by the courts. Nevertheless, ensuring that the local population can 'air' their grievances has increasingly been accepted as having a significant role in the wider machinery of government. It is also important to note that the function of the Kosovo ombudsperson was never just limited to receiving—and

[63] UNTAET was in operation between 1999–2002. See also Reif, above n 10 at 285: 'In the case of East Timor, UN transitional administration lasted less than three years and a UNTAET Ombudsperson operated for about one year before East Timor became an independent state—although it was a welcome development, there was not much time for the office to be formalized or developed'.

[64] On this issue, see R Wilde, Territorial Administration by International Organizations: How Trusteeship and the Civilizing Mission Never Went Away (Oxford, Oxford University Press, 2008).

[65] As regards the very different issues which arose resolving post-conflict tension in Bosnia and Herzegovina and the role of the ombudsman therein, see AL Wetzel, 'Post-Conflict National Human Rights Institutions: Emerging Models from Northern Ireland and Bosnia & Herzegovina' (2007) 13 *Columbia Journal of European Law* 427–70.

[66] In this case, UN Security Council Resolution 1244 (1999) 10 June 1999.

[67] Special Report No 1 on the compatibility with recognised international standards of UNMIK Regulation No 2000/47 on the Status, Privileges and Immunities of KFOR and UNMIK and Their Personnel in Kosovo (18 August 2000) and on the Implementation of the above Regulation (26 April 2001) para 23.

investigating—complaints against the international administration of the territory, but also 'to provide oversight for local self-governing bodies, bodies which have grown in importance as UNMIK's role has shrunk'.[68]

There was, however, a second—and arguably more fundamental—reason which justified the creation of an ombudsman-like process within UNMIK. It was that in administering Kosovo during this period, the United Nations maintained the traditional view that international organisations and their staff possessed legal immunity from local jurisdiction. This clearly separated them from national governments, especially those in liberal democracies, which are subject to judicial review and/or oversight by municipal courts. As the ombudsperson again noted, quite pointedly in the same first special report:

> No democratic state operating under the rule of law accords itself total immunity from any administrative, civil or criminal responsibility. Such blanket lack of accountability paves the way for the impunity of the state … the actions and operations of [the executive and legislative] branches of government must be subject to the oversight of the judiciary, as the arbiter of legality in a democratic society.[69]

The creation of the ombudsperson was, in part, to counter this lack of accountability; indeed, a *total* lack of accountability would undoubtedly be incompatible with recognised standards of human rights. Though the level of control and compulsion exerted by an ombudsman, in contrast to a judicial body, is ultimately based upon persuasiveness rather than legal authority, this is not necessarily an obstacle to effectiveness. Nevertheless, it should be noted that in most national systems, the office of ombudsman co-exists alongside a fully functioning judicial structure. Whether an ombudsman is able to operate as completely and successfully without this supporting pillar of the rule of law is debatable.[70]

Notwithstanding such reservations, the creation of the Kosovo ombudsperson remains an important innovation in this area of international law. Moreover, the role of the ombudsperson (to 'ensure that all persons in Kosovo are able to exercise effectively … [their] human rights and fundamental freedoms') would seem to be encouragingly broad. However, it should be noted that this generously-worded purpose is somewhat narrowed by a noticeably more specific jurisdictional remit. First, though the ombudsperson was to investigate complaints 'concerning human

[68] C Waters, 'Nationalisaing Kosovo's Ombudsperson' (2007) 12 *Journal of Conflict and Security Law* 140.

[69] Special Report No1, above n 67 at paras 23, 24.

[70] P Nikiforos Diamandouros, 'The role of the Ombudsman in strengthening accountability and the rule of law' (Speech by the European Ombudsman, at the Constitution Unit, University College London, London, 29 November 2005) www.ombudsman.europa.eu/speeches/en/2005-11-29.htm.

rights violations and actions constituting an abuse of authority by the interim civil administration or any emerging central or local institution', the ombudsperson was denied jurisdiction over complaints against the 'international security presence'[71] until such time as the commander of KFOR, the international security force, entered into an agreement with the ombudsperson. This, in fact, never occurred, thus placing one of the most significant areas of potential complaints outside the reach of the ombudsperson's jurisdiction. However, while this prevented the ombudsperson from receiving complaints directly concerning the international security presence, this did not prevent the ombudsperson from imaginatively ensuring that more general issues which affected *both* the civil and military aspects of the international framework were effectively scrutinised. In his work on the possible establishment of ombudsmen in peace support operations, Zwanenburg notes that the Kosovo ombudsperson did not shy away from incorporating references to KFOR when required, thus suggesting that the office 'indirectly exercises jurisdiction … in spite of the lack of a formal basis for jurisdiction'.[72] This is perhaps too strong a conclusion, though it does highlight the inherent flexibility which is entrusted to an ombudsman, especially where the competence is of a sufficiently broad character.

It is also worth noting, in this regard, that such flexibility was also used by the ombudsperson to 'stretch' the applicable law to include consideration not just of human rights standards but also, arguably rather tentatively, to include basic tenets of international humanitarian law, where applicable.[73] This again underlines the rather difficult task of accurately demarcating *in practice* the remit of an ombudsman, particularly when the original mandate would appear to conflict with what the ombudsman him-/herself considers to be fair and in accordance with general principles of good governance and the rule of law.

The second limitation on the jurisdiction of the ombudsperson was its focus on human rights violations; though commendable that the function of the ombudsperson was so intrinsically tied to the protection of recognised standards of human rights, there was some regret that there was not a more general role in the investigation of maladministration, as more generally understood.[74] Maladministration is a key aspect of many domestic complaint- and grievance-style mechanisms. In reality, this may not have been a particularly serious issue; as has been commented upon, 'the Ombudsperson seems to interpret the term "abuse of authority"

[71] UNMIK Reg 2000/38, s 3.4.
[72] Zwanenburg, above n 7 at 310.
[73] Ibid 308–10.
[74] Waters, above n 62 at 145.

broadly to include many elements of maladministration as defined by, for example, the European Ombudsman'.[75]

Third, the ombudsperson was precluded from investigating disputes between the international administration and its staff.

Fourth, as the political situation changed in Kosovo, and following the arguably premature nationalisation of the ombudsperson in 2006,[76] oversight of UNMIK became less transparent as accountability was transferred from the ombudsperson to a less independent Human Rights Advisory Panel.[77]

Thus, it is very clear that within the very fabric of the jurisdiction of the ombudsperson institution itself existed some very obvious limitations, reflecting significant political and institutional tensions concerning both its initial set-up and the extent of its mandate. And while it would be wrong to suggest that the work of the ombudsperson was thus hamstrung from the start, it is reasonably clear that despite playing an important, if limited part, in the rebuilding and reconstruction of Kosovo, this was perhaps despite, rather than because of, the political will to support proactively the work of the ombudsperson. As Hoffman and Mégret cautiously observe:

> [d]espite … successes, this image of emerging accountability has been substantially blurred. The ombudsperson is essentially an OSCE institution, tolerated rather than supported by the UN. The UN's cooperation and responsiveness record vis-à-vis the ombudsperson has been dismal.[78]

The same authors conclude that the principal lesson to be learnt from the Kosovan experience is that though 'there seems to be nothing impossible in theory about having ombudspersons exercise vigorous scrutiny over the UN itself', actual practice suggests all is dependent upon political support, especially where 'institutional resistance remains high'.[79]

IV. A UN OMBUDSMAN?

Thus, when compared to the operation of ombudsmen at the national level, even the most advanced of complaint and grievance mechanisms at the international level, whilst innovative, are nevertheless structurally limited. However, achievements can be identified and their institutional

[75] Zwanenburg, above n 7 at 307.

[76] See Waters, above n 68 at 139–48.

[77] Ibid 144–45. See also B Knoll and RJ Uhl, 'Too little, too late: The Human Rights Advisory Panel in Kosovo' (2007) 5 *European Human Rights Law Review* 534–49.

[78] F Hoffmann and F Mégret, 'Fostering Human Rights Accountability: An Ombudsman for the United Nations?' (2005) 11 *Global Governance* 56.

[79] Ibid 57.

designs can be viewed as realistic, given the political context within which they were established. The question becomes how much further can the non-judicial concept of complaint and redress mechanisms go at the international level? Already, the experience of the Kosovo ombudsman has led others to call for more ambitious complaint and grievance mechanisms either in discrete areas previously devoid of such procedures (such as the gradual emergence of accountability mechanisms in peacekeeping, 'peace support' and humanitarian operations) or, more radically, for the UN as a whole. Certainly, some action, if of variable and limited nature, has already taken place, though undoubtedly such processes could be greatly strengthened in both instances.

As regards accountability innovations in discrete areas of UN activity, there have, for instance, been obvious developments in the use of accountability mechanisms during peacekeeping and peace support operations. After several high profile human rights and sexual abuse scandals, involving particularly peacekeepers in various zones of conflict in Africa, which highlighted to many for the first time[80] that the UN—through its staff—was able to commit breaches of, rather than promote, human rights,[81] the UN has recently sought to act proactively in seeking to deal with the problem.[82]

As the UN's Under-Secretary-General for Peacekeeping Operations noted in a letter printed in the British newspaper, *The Independent*, in 2007:

> we have established conduct and discipline teams and independent investigative offices in all of our largest peacekeeping operations and training on prevention of sexual exploitation and abuse is now mandatory for all of our peacekeeping personnel in the field. Missions have established networks of focal points to receive complaints of this nature and premises where prostitution is known or suspected to occur are placed off-limits to our personnel and patrolled. Other measures such as curfews, 'non-fraternization' policies and 'hotlines' for anonymous complaints are also in place in many missions. It may be impossible to completely ensure zero incidents, but we can and do mandate zero tolerance.[83]

This would appear to be an impressive response—at least from a particularly low base—and accountability forms just one part of a much more

[80] *cf* ibid 44: 'Already during the UN operation in the Republic of Congo (1960-1964), for example, concerns were raised about the possibility that troops operating under UN command had violated international humanitarian law'.

[81] See, eg F Hoffmann and F Mégret, 'The United Nations as a Human Rights Violator?' (2003) 25 *Human Rights Quarterly* 314–42.

[82] Secretary-General's Bulletin: Special measures for protection from sexual exploitation and sexual abuse (ST/SGB/2003/13, 9 October 2003).

[83] Jean-Marie Guéhenno, 'USG Guéhenno responds on sexual exploitation and abuse by UN peacekeepers', *Independent* (London 9 January 2007).

complex package of measures that the UN is increasingly attempting to put in place to try to ensure that not only are past wrongs not repeated but that institutional responses are in place if they do reoccur.

However, there remains a residual concern amongst some that senior diplomats in the UN are unconvinced, despite the general acceptance for greater accountability to deal with such shocking acts, of the need for even greater and more radical institutional change. As has been argued, the UN adopts a 'somewhat ambiguous attitude towards its *own* accountability'[84] traversing somewhere between accepting responsibility and seeking to ensure that others, such as the State providing the peacekeepers, take the lead in ensuring the necessary measures are adopted. Though such criticism perhaps underplays the extent to which the UN does accept responsibility both in *law* and in *practice* for actions that are attributable to it,[85] it nevertheless highlights a perennial issue for those individuals who are seeking redress in being able to identify the relevant body responsible. Such a problem is, unsurprisingly, greatly exacerbated at the international level where delimitation of roles and responsibilities, particularly between the plenary jurisdiction of the State and the more limited role of international institutions, is usually less than clearly defined.

More radical still, there have also been suggestions that the UN would benefit from a wide-ranging ombudsman, with a significant overview of much of what the UN does. Of course, all organisations within the UN family do have accountability mechanisms to a certain extent already, ranging from offices of audit and internal oversight[86] to work-place ombudsmen and, in a few cases, external complaint mechanisms. As noted above, the UN General Assembly itself established an office of ombudsman in 2002, though its function is limited to 'address[ing] the employment-related problems of staff members'.[87]

Nevertheless, for those who view accountability as a prerequisite of good governance and, in particular, a means to uphold key norms and values, especially the protection of human rights within international institutions, a more radical answer is required.

[84] Hoffmann and Mégret, above n 78 at 47. Emphasis added.

[85] P Sands and P Klein, *Bowett's Law of International Institutions*, 5th edn (London, Sweet and Maxwell, 2001) 520: 'Breaches of international obligations by members of UN peacekeeping forces have been inevitably attributed to the organisation itself, rather than to the member states providing the contingent to which the peacekeepers concerned were attached'.

[86] UNGA Res 48/218 (12 August 1994): 'The purpose of the Office of Internal Oversight Services is to assist the Secretary-General in fulfilling his internal oversight responsibilities in respect of the resources and staff of the Organization through the exercise of the following functions: (i) Monitoring … (ii) Internal audit … (iii) Inspection and evaluation … (iv) Investigation … [and] (v) Implementation of recommendations and reporting procedures'.

[87] UN Secretary-General's Bulletin: Office of the Ombudsman—appointment and terms of reference of the Ombudsman (ST/SGB/2002/12, 15 October 2002) s 1.

> [I]f the UN wanted to send a strong signal to the world community that it was serious about accountability, the best solution would point in the direction of a new, sui generis organ along the lines of the EU ombudsperson ... Although legitimate concerns about costs are bound to arise, centralizing the tasks of the ombudsperson ... would probably be a much more cost-effective measure than the multiplication of theatre- or agency-specific mechanisms.[88]

How such an ombudsman office would in fact work would, of course, be subject to a plethora of practical and political objections. Key issues that would need to be resolved include the appointment and tenure of such an ombudsman, the extent of its jurisdiction,[89] the scope of its investigatory powers, the range of ADR techniques at its disposal (ie, whether it would be focused on compliance-review or also mediation), and the line of authority (ie, to whom would an ombudsman report?). These are, of course, general matters relating to any ombudsman; but one can also think of some institutional-specific difficulties, including—as merely examples of how difficult it will be to demarcate between the permissible and impermissible—how far would such an ombudsman be able to receive complaints about the work of the UN's political organs including the Security Council, should the ombudsman be able to receive complaints if it also involves activities of States, and how should the work of the ombudsman relate to the role of the International Court of Justice as the principal judicial body within the UN system? Moreover, who would be entitled to make a complaint and how would the UN ensure that those who depend upon the UN the most—those most marginalised in the global South—benefit from simply another administrative innovation far removed from their daily existence. These are all difficult issues, and while similar matters have been raised at the national level and not proved insurmountable to resolve, the scale of the project at the international level is recognised to be of a significantly different magnitude.

Notwithstanding the myriad of practical and political hurdles which would bedevil such a project, the existence of greater accountability mechanisms would arguably not only serve to enhance the reputation of individual UN operations, but would also improve the legitimacy of the organisation of the UN as a whole. However, what becomes quickly apparent is that just as States, which fervently protect their own national interests wherever they are perceived to be at risk, international institutions are equally defensive of their own rights and responsibilities. In this

88 Hoffmann and F Mégret, above n 78 at 60.

89 This includes the very contentious issue of how far the mandate *ratione materiae* of such an ombudsman should range beyond procedural issues to incorporate matters of substance and policy. For instance, should a UN ombudsman be able to receive complaints about the lack of sanitation in a UN-run refugee camp from its inhabitants? (Thanks to a member of the audience at Brunel Law School during a presentation of this chapter for this example).

regard, the 'opening up' of institutions through complaint and grievance mechanisms is often viewed with a certain level of suspicion and mistrust as to how far the process will undermine the traditional approach as to how such organisations (should) function. What is often missing in such deliberations, however, is the realisation that such accountability mechanisms are now viewed as integral to the implementation of good governance, which itself is increasingly essential to ensuring international organisations possess both political credibility and, more fundamentally, normative legitimacy.

V. COMPLAINT MECHANISMS: INCREASING SYNERGIES, AVOIDING UNFAIR COMPARISONS

One of the central rationales of this chapter has been that a well-functioning complaint and grievance mechanism (including the office of the ombudsman) can go a long way towards promoting and achieving accountability within a governance structure and defending the rule of law, whether that be at the national, regional or global level. There is inevitably some debate as to whether such processes can only ever truly work where there is a sufficient link between the institution and the complainant, most clearly shown in the connexion between national and local administrations and the *demos* they serve.[90] But it has been argued in this chapter that such mechanisms are also useful at the international level to ensure improved operational performance and accountability to stakeholders.

This may, at first glance, suggest a relatively restrictive understanding of the place of such mechanisms within international institutions, which focuses upon their utility in increasing the overall effectiveness of such organisations rather than recognising the broader constitutional significance of complaint and grievance mechanisms.[91] However, as has been highlighted above, the establishment of innovative accountability

[90] This is not to suggest that there are not increased links between private individuals and international organisations, but rather that the connexion between them is usually more distant than the connexion between the individual and the administrative apparatus of his/her State. This is, of course, not as true as once it were; as the work of the European Union, United Nations and the World Bank—to a greater or less extent—shows, international organisations are now affecting the lives and behaviours of individuals much more directly, and with less direct State involvement (see also Bodansky, above n 11).

[91] For an alternative understanding on the role and status of complaint and grievance mechanisms at the international level, see the 'concentric circles' approach of Reif, above n 10 at 364–65: the 'inner circle of activity' of the workplace ombudsman, the middle circle 'representing an organization's attempts to improve the relationship among member states' (Reif notes that this 'has not been the site of the development of the ombudsman', but see the Warwick Commission, above n 8) and the outer circle 'provid[ing] an external accountability mechanism for non-state actors affected by its activities'.

mechanisms also plays a significant role in ensuring the development of increased standards of good governance and legitimacy within international institutions. There can be little denying how important the existence of transparent, accessible and administratively-workable accountability mechanisms have become, both within those international organisations that have adopted such procedures and, more generally, within the broader dialogue on the future direction of international institutional governance.

Moreover, it is not just the existence of complaint and grievance mechanisms that is important per se—though undoubtedly they are both novel and innovative in their own right—it is the role of such mechanisms in allowing private individuals and local communities to complain, to a greater or lesser extent, about the policies and procedures of previously hermetically-sealed international institutions that truly underlines their overall importance. As well as reflecting what Zwanenburg previously referred to as 'a corollary of the demand for accountability of international organizations, *and in particular accountability towards individuals*',[92] the 'opening up' of such mechanisms to individuals and local communities is, equally, a substantive contribution to the incorporation of the individual as a participant in international law.[93]

Thus, it must be recognised that the role of individuals in these processes is far from purely instrumental—the individual *qua* catalyst for complaint handling and institutional review—what is actually happening is that individuals are, in fact, seeking to enforce *their* interests. These interests may not necessarily always be legal rights or entitlements in the traditional sense of the term, though, as with the Kosovo Ombudsman, if the complaints are human-rights based, this does suggest a potential amalgam of *private* complaint and *legal* right. Thus, such mechanisms permit, if not also directly encourage, individuals to assert that which they were unable to protect previously at the international level, and in an increasingly expansive number of international organisations. In short, not only is this an important—if still putative—constitutional sea-change in the status of the individual in international law, but it heralds an emerging expectation in how international organisations should operate and treat non-State interests. This may, of course, be overstating the actuality of the current situation and how, in particular, such mechanisms operate in practice, but one cannot deny that a fundamental shift has now taken place.

[92] Above n 7. Emphasis added.

[93] Moreover, without seeking to question the validity of Franck's general work on the legitimacy of international law, in which he propounds four 'indicators': determinacy, symbolic validation, coherence and adherence (above n 1 at 30–46), it might be tentatively suggested that consideration also be given to a fifth, *participation*—both at the stage of formation of the rule/policy and, in this context, at the stage of *post hoc* accountability.

Moreover, as noted above, there is a strong argument that much of what has happened at the global level is reflective of changing patterns in institutional behaviour, which were first introduced at the national and regional level. To this extent, it is unsurprising that many of the same issues arise concerning how such mechanisms operate in practice and the continuing obstacles they face. This linkage between the global and national is not all one-way either. There is also evidence that the international community is aware of the positive benefits that can be gained through the development of these and other methods of ADR. In recent years, many international organisations have promoted the work of such mechanisms at the national level in contributing towards the implementation of standards of good governance and human rights, often as part of a wider development agenda.[94]

However, any attempt to make direct comparisons between the techniques adopted at the global and national levels has to be approached cautiously, especially given the very different approaches to, and attributes of, governance that exist. To that extent, it would be a mistake to argue for a 'one model fits all' approach to the utility of the ombudsman and other complaint and grievance mechanisms. Thus, a preliminary conclusion must inevitably be that automatic replication of such mechanisms should be avoided, and concurrently any such proposal must therefore always take into account the particular institutional framework in which it is to operate.

This is not to say that there are not certain fundamental features which all such mechanisms should demonstrate, but rather that they should be applied flexibly and with due care for the overarching governance structure already in place. Moreover, it should also not be ignored that though such mechanisms are rarely considered a form of 'dispute settlement' in the formal sense of the term—'dispute avoidance' often considered a better description—they share very similar goals. Though complaint and grievance mechanisms do not have the inherent characteristics of either judicial proceedings or arbitration, at a generic level, their purpose in seeking to resolve differences, to ensure accountability and perhaps to provide redress, are ultimately not very far apart.[95] Thus, complaint and grievance mechanisms should be viewed not only as innovative in the way international organisations operate but also as an alternative model

[94] See, for instance, Reif, above n 10 at 70: 'In proposing ideas for strengthening good governance, the [United Nations Development Programme] has suggested the establishment of ombudsman and human rights oversight bodies'.

[95] On a related point, see Merrills, above n 4 at 315–16: 'the role of law and the role of adjudication are two issues, not one … While it is difficult to imagine adjudication without law, law without adjudication is actually the normal situation in international affairs … although international disputes are generally resolved without adjudication, law will frequently play a significant part in defining the points in issue'.

vis-à-vis traditional dispute settlement procedures. Of course, complaint and grievance mechanisms are not an institutional panacea for the perceived failings of international dispute settlement, and the truth is that such mechanisms should at best be considered supplementary procedures, and only then within certain institutional settings.

Nevertheless, what might originally appear to be the weaknesses in such complaint and grievance mechanisms—their limited jurisdiction, their lack of binding authority, their dependence on political goodwill for subsequent implementation—are also potential strengths. It is relatively clear that many of the international organisations, which have incorporated a complaint and grievance mechanism within their governance model, would be wholly unwilling to establish more intrusive procedures—with greater legal enforcement powers—over the same subject-matter. This is not a viable political alternative; it is simply unrealistic to expect the World Bank, for instance, to permit independent judicial supervision of its operating policies and procedures, rather than through the present practice of accountability via the in-house Inspection Panel. Such 'softer' forms of dispute resolution, which are able to respond more flexibly to the competing demands of an international governance system so very obviously predicated on national and institutional interests, reflect more accurately the political contours of the current international system.[96]

In any event, it is not at all clear that 'harder' procedures would be any more effective in incorporating the ideals of legitimacy and governance within international institutions. In this area of international law and policy, the maxim, 'the perfect is the enemy of the good' seems particularly apt; in fact, it is not at all clear that other—binding—processes could achieve as much as complaint and grievance mechanisms have the *potential* to do. The goal of international institutions must now be to refine and build upon the mechanisms that already exist to ensure that such 'good' is realised still further.

[96] Moreover, as is clear from this chapter, it is not yet the situation that all international organisations are prepared to adopt even 'soft' accountability mechanisms. See Shihata, n 30 above, 264: 'Once accountability to the affected public is postulated as an efficient complementary element in the overall accountability system of an international organization, it is difficult to see why such an element should be restricted to … multilateral development institutions. Obviously, this would not be case if the function were to contradict or dilute existing systems of governance and accountability in the organization involved *or otherwise hinder its efficient operation*' (emphasis added).

4

Stuck in the Middle With You?: Alternative Approaches to Realising Accountability for Human Rights Violations by Business

SORCHA MACLEOD*

> It is recognized that global policy responses represent the best solution to issues surrounding the regulation of Multinational Enterprises, with a regional solution, on either a country or product basis, second best, and actions by individual host countries only a third best solution.[1]

I. INTRODUCTION

A CHAPTER ON the responsibility of transnational corporations (TNCs) and business enterprises for human rights violations does not appear to sit naturally in a collection of works on the subject of international dispute settlement, given that no global dispute resolution mechanism exists for addressing such breaches.[2] As Brewer and Young note above, a coherent international reaction would seem to be the only possible logical response to corporate misbehaviour which takes place internationally, but this has not been the case.[3] Since the early 1990s the

* I would like to express my thanks to Nigel White, Duncan French and Amanda Warren Jones for their helpful comments on drafts of this paper. Thanks are also due to Scarlett McArdle for her invaluable research assistance. Flaws, of course, remain my own.

[1] TL Brewer and S Young, *The Multilateral Investment System and Multinational Enterprises* (Oxford, Oxford University Press, 2000) 96.

[2] The term 'transnational corporation' was adopted by the UN in the early 1970s in preference to 'multinational' in order 'to underline the extent of the cross-border activities involved'. See Brewer and Young, ibid 88.

[3] For a comprehensive approach to alleged business human rights violations see the Report of the Special Representative of the Secretary-General on the issue of human rights and transnational corporations and other business enterprises, Addendum 2, *Corporations*

concept of Corporate Social Responsibility (CSR) has developed steadily but the model adopted has not been that of what could be described as a traditional international adjudicatory framework, that is, courts, tribunals or arbitration.

Defining the term CSR remains a difficult task as there is no one favoured definition, with stakeholders adopting positions which are frequently poles apart. At a basic level CSR has become a term of art which symbolises that all businesses have obligations beyond the financial and commercial, and which includes social obligations, particularly in the spheres of human rights and the environment. Historically, there has always been a tension between those advocating a hard law regulatory approach to CSR (usually NGOs and trade unions) in the form of treaties or statutory frameworks and those businesses promoting voluntarism in the form of non-binding external measures or codes of conduct.[4] Traditionally, the majority of States have supported the latter view.[5] Thus this tension has played out in every international organisation in which there has been a debate about CSR. The so-called business case for voluntarism has generally prevailed and as a result no adversarial-style dispute settlement mechanism has developed. Various organisational players have attempted over the last decade or so, however, to construct a variety of alternative mechanisms to implement and adjudicate CSR standards and, as a consequence, the framework for addressing business misbehaviour in relation to human rights has become diverse, disparate and chaotic. There have also been well documented attempts at the national level to impose corporate accountability by invoking existing legal provisions such as the US Alien Tort Claims Act.[6] Such national endeavours have had limited success and in any event are outside the scope of this chapter. At the global level, however, despite two aborted attempts within the UN at creating the framework for a treaty

and human rights: a survey of the scope and patterns of alleged corporate-related human rights abuse, A/HRC/8/5/Add.2, 23 May 2008.

[4] See, eg H Ward, 'Corporate Social Responsibility in law and policy' in N Boeger, R Murray and C Villiers (eds), *Perspectives on Corporate Social Responsibility* (Cheltenham, Edward Elgar, 2008) 8–38.

[5] See, eg State responses to the consultation conducted by the OHCHR on the proposed 'Norms' and which became part of the 'Report of the United Nations High Commissioner on Human Rights on the responsibilities of transnational corporations and related business enterprises with regard to human rights E/CN.4/2005/91,15 February 2005. Excerpts from the submissions to the OHCHR can be viewed here: http://reports-and-materials.org/UN-submissions-excerpts-16-Nov-2004.doc. Although many States objected to the perceived ultra vires activities of the Sub-Committee for the Promotion and Protection of Human Rights, most were concerned about the idea that business enterprises would become objects of international law.

[6] Alien Tort Statute 28 USC 1350; see, eg *Maria Aguinda et al v Texaco Inc* 175 FRD 50 (US District Court, SD New York) (12 August 1997); *John Doe et al v Unocal Corp* 963 F Supp 880.

which would have imposed legally binding norms upon TNCs, all of the currently active mechanisms are non-binding and offer no right of individual complaint as such (although the OECD economic grouping comes close with the Specific Instance procedure) let alone establishing dispute resolution apparatus. There is therefore, no unifying approach to, or mechanism for, ensuring adherence to CSR standards.[7]

This is not to say that such initiatives are inherently inferior. Given the continued debate over the status of business enterprises as subjects of international law, the existing traditional human rights channels available to individuals such as the Human Rights Committee are simply unavailable when the allegations are made against non-State actors.[8] What is being witnessed, therefore, is a shift in focus from conventional international dispute settlement mechanisms to alternative dispute prevention and settlement strategies with an emphasis on involving all of the relevant actors including States, business and civil society—although not necessarily those on the receiving end of corporate misbehaviour. As a consequence, specific CSR projects at the UN, such as the Global Compact, and other international organisations such as the OECD are becoming increasingly concerned with corporate misbehaviour and the implementation of novel strategies for addressing it. So, for example, the National Contact Points for the OECD's Guidelines on Multilateral Enterprises are assuming ever more importance. There is a clear swing away from the adversarial international court- and tribunal-based dispute settlement approach found in other areas of international concern towards more inclusive, multistakeholder preventative techniques and dispute resolution. Such methods can be seen to a certain extent at the global level, via the Global Compact as already mentioned, and to a different extent within economic groupings, for example the OECD. The significance of this shift has not escaped the notice of the UN Special Representative to the Secretary-General for Business and Human Rights, John Ruggie. In his final report under his 2005 Mandate, Ruggie unveiled his benchmark standard of 'Promote, Protect and Remedy', which is significant for acknowledging the 'baseline' responsibility of corporations to respect human rights; but he also points out that:

> The business and human rights debate currently lacks an authoritative focal point. Claims and counter-claims proliferate, initiatives abound, and yet no

[7] For a discussion of the regulatory options see RG Steinhardt, 'Corporate Responsibility and the International Law of Human Rights' in P Alston et al (eds), *Non-State Actors and Human Rights* (Oxford, Oxford University Press, 2005) 180–212.

[8] JG Ruggie, 'Business and Human Rights: The Evolving International Agenda' (2007) 101 AJIL 832. See also ND White and S MacLeod, 'EU Operations and Private Military Contractors: Issues of Corporate and Institutional Responsibility' (2008) 19 *European Journal of International Law* 965–88.

effort reaches significant scale. Amid this confusing mix, laggards—States as well as companies—continue to fly below the radar.[9]

Aiming to rectify this and implement the Protect, Respect and Remedy agenda, the new 2008 mandate granted by the Human Rights Council specifically authorises Ruggie 'to identify, exchange and promote best practices and lessons learned' in the field of CSR and to consult with 'international and regional organizations,' among others, on CSR issues.[10] This is to be done while taking account of the underlying principles of 'Protect, Respect and Remedy', namely the primary duty of the State to protect citizens from human rights abuses, secondly the active obligation incumbent upon business and corporations to respect and protect human rights (essentially to 'do no harm')[11] and finally, the necessity of ensuring access to adequate remedies for those who have suffered human rights violations at the hands of business. The provision of effective remedies for human rights violations by business is the area most in need of serious

[9] Protect, Respect and Remedy: a Framework for Business and Human Rights Report of the Special Representative of the Secretary-General on the issue of human rights and transnational corporations and other business enterprises, John Ruggie A/HRC/8/5, 7 April 2008 ('Protect, Respect and Remedy').

[10] 4(e) and (g) Human Rights Council Resolution 8/7. Mandate of the Special Representative of the Secretary-General on the issue of human rights and transnational corporations and other business enterprises, 18 June 2008. Cooperation between stakeholders and agencies is emphasised throughout the Mandate:

'(a) To provide views and concrete and practical recommendations on ways to strengthen the fulfilment of the duty of the State to protect all human rights from abuses by or involving transnational corporations and other business enterprises, including through international cooperation;
(b) To elaborate further on the scope and content of the corporate responsibility to respect all human rights and to provide concrete guidance to business and other stakeholders;
(c) To explore options and make recommendations, at the national, regional and international level, for enhancing access to effective remedies available to those whose human rights are impacted by corporate activities;
(d) To integrate a gender perspective throughout his work and to give special attention to persons belonging to vulnerable groups, in particular children;
(e) Identify, exchange and promote best practices and lessons learned on the issue of transnational corporations and other business enterprises, in coordination with the efforts of the human rights working group of the Global Compact;
(f) To work in close coordination with United Nations and other relevant international bodies, offices, departments and specialized agencies, and in particular with other special procedures of the Council;
(g) To promote the framework and to continue to consult on the issues covered by the mandate on an ongoing basis with all stakeholders, including States, national human rights institutions, international and regional organizations, transnational corporations and other business enterprises, and civil society, including academics, employers' organizations, workers' organizations, indigenous and other affected communities and non-governmental organizations, including through joint meetings;
(h) To report annually to the Council and the General Assembly'.

[11] Protect, Respect and Remedy, above n 9 at 9 para 24 and 17 paras 54 and 55.

attention and in the opinion of Ruggie is seriously 'underdeveloped' 'patchwork' and 'flawed' and can only be satisfactorily addressed by combining the three principles.[12] In order to address this inchoate state of affairs Ruggie has outlined the minimum elements required for an effective remedy. An effective remedy should be 'legitimate,' 'accessible,' 'predictable,' 'equitable,' 'rights-compatible' and 'transparent', which in essence means that it ought to be independent, non-discriminatory, fair and with clearly defined procedures.[13]

To that end, Ruggie's Preliminary Work Plan outlines the so-called 'operational phase' of the Mandate and represents a response to those critics who were unhappy with what they perceived to be a merely principled approach to the problem, lacking in concrete action.[14] It is evident that a multistakeholder approach is crucial to this phase and he is very keen to see 'what works, what doesn't, and where the gaps are' by drawing upon the experiences of all international institutions involved with business and human rights.[15] This high-profile experiential methodology is to be welcomed, as in recent years there has been reluctance in some quarters, most notably on the part of the European Union, to learn from the practice of others.[16] Ruggie is seeking to amass this shared information to create what is described as 'a backdrop to the mandate's own processes of developing guiding principles.'[17] It is Ruggie's belief that in doing so it will 'strengthen the overall international architecture in the business and human rights domain.'[18] The question is whether existing initiatives have anything positive to contribute to this architecture. In submitting his final report under the original mandate Ruggie recognises throughout that the 'Protect, Respect and Remedy' mantra is simply a framework for action and acknowledges that it is a merely a baseline, or starting point, and clearly indicates the aspiration for practical tactics for moving the process forward. But how is this to be realised?

[12] Ibid 9 para 26 and 22 para 87.

[13] Ibid 22 para 92.

[14] Preliminary Work Plan Mandate of the Special Representative on the Issue of Human Rights and Transnational Corporations and other Business Enterprises 1 September 2008–30 June 2011 (10 October 2008), www.reports-and-materials.org/Ruggie-preliminary-work-plan-2008-2011.pdf ('Ruggie Work Plan'). For criticisms of Ruggie see, eg Earthrights International, 'Ominous Outlook for the Norms,' 22 March 2006, www.earthrights.org/legalfeature/ominous_outlook_for_the_un_norms.html; Á deRegil, 'Business and Human Rights: Upholding the market's social Darwinism', Report by Jus Semper, October 2008, www.jussemper.org/Resources/Corporate%20Activity/Resources/BHRRUpholding_Mkts_Darwinis.pdf.

[15] Ruggie,Work Plan, above n 14 at 3.

[16] See S MacLeod, 'Reconciling Regulatory Approaches to Corporate Social Responsibility: The European Union, OECD and United Nations Compared' (2007) 13 *European Public Law* 671–702; see also ND White and S MacLeod, above n 8.

[17] Ruggie Work Plan, above n 14 at 3.

[18] Ibid 4.

With this in mind, this chapter examines two specific organisational examples of fresh approaches to CSR execution and considers their efficacy: the UN and the OECD, and in particular the UK's Specific Instance procedure. Do such novel tactics represent innovative and realistic methods for ensuring the protection of human rights in the face of corporate misbehaviour, or are they simply a botched compromise in light of intransigence by all parties? What can they contribute to the work of the Special Representative, if anything? Do they offer adequate remedies? The chapter concludes that while there is no doubt that the international community has a long way to go in implementing an effective CSR strategy, both the UN and OECD have much to contribute on a practical level and such strategies should not be immediately dismissed as inferior to traditional dispute settlement mechanisms or indeed a binding, global CSR apparatus. Absent an internationally binding mechanism, while they are not the answer to the problem of 'bad' business practices, with careful development they could be useful tools in ensuring a modicum of adherence to CSR standards at the global level.

II. UNITED NATIONS

For nearly 40 years, the UN has attempted to address the problems posed by errant business enterprises and to that end numerous diverse projects were undertaken with varying success. This section, while touching on the role of the UN Commission on Transnational Corporations (UNCTC) and the Norms on the Responsibility of Transnational Corporations and Other Business Entities with Regards to Human Rights (the Norms[19]), focuses in detail on the effectiveness of the preventative and regulatory techniques utilised by the Global Compact with additional attention paid to the principles and proposals of Special Representative Ruggie.

Starting with the UNCTC's endeavours in the 1970s and continuing into the twenty-first century with the Norms project of the Sub-Commission for the Promotion and Protection of Human Rights, the UN's initial attempts at regulatory capture sought the creation of a treaty-based apparatus for the enforcement of human rights obligations against business enterprises but both resulted in a failure to agree on a unified approach to CSR standards and ultimately the projects collapsed, albeit for different reasons.[20] Initially at least it seems that the UN (and/or its

[19] UN Doc E/CN.4/Sub.2/2003/12/Rev 2 of 26 August 2003.

[20] Commission on Transnational Corporations and the Sub-Committee on the Promotion and Protection of Human Rights Norms on the Responsibility of Transnational Corporations and Other Business Entities with Regards to Human Rights . For an overview of the work of the UNCTC, see P Muchlinski, *Multinational Enterprises*, 2nd edn (Oxford, Oxford University Press, 2007); Brewer and Young, above n 2 at 88 ff. For more on the UNCTC and the Norms, see S MacLeod in Boeger, Villiers and Murray, above n 4 at 64–84.

constituent members) was unable or unwilling to put in place a credible device for the enforcement of human rights obligations against business enterprises. Looking back at the first UN project to address the responsibility of business on the international plane, the UNCTC, it is clear that all of what would be considered modern and familiar CSR issues were considered during the drafting of its putative Code of Conduct for TNCs, that is: voluntarism versus legally binding measures; addressees (should the Code apply to States alone, to TNCs alone or to both?); monitoring and sanctions. Ultimately it was decided in the absence of any kind of agreement, that the Draft Code should be 'an instrument of moral persuasion' rather than a binding document.[21] State involvement with the UNCTC was highly politicised, with regional and economic groupings disagreeing fundamentally. Developing nations in particular objected to TNCs in principle, while seeking to protect their fledgling sovereignty while the developed, industrialised nations perceived the draft Code as a constraint on business activities and therefore resisted its implementation. Writing at the time, Hellman noted that 'the developing countries are not willing at this point to renounce part of their newly gained sovereignty to promote control over multinational corporations.'[22] The overarching general preoccupation with defending State sovereignty meant that there was little objection to the notion of a legally binding international instrument which would apply directly to corporations and bring them to account for their actions. In particular there was no objection to human rights obligations being imposed upon TNCs but in any event the enforcement and reporting mechanisms were weak.[23] Despite the ultimate failure of the UNCTC its efforts live on in the ongoing work of UNCTAD.[24] More modern regulatory attempts came in the controversial guise of the Sub-Committee on the Promotion and Protection

[21] ECOSOC, Report of the Group of Eminent Persons on the Impact of MNC on the Development Process and International Relations (New York, UN, 1974) 55.

[22] R Hellman, Transnational Control of Multinational Corporations (New York, Praeger, 1977).

[23] Proposed Text of the Draft Code of Conduct on Transnational Corporations, 31 May 1990, UN Doc E/1990/94 of 12 June 1990. Paras 14 and 15 addressed human rights and apartheid respectively and lacked detail, so para 14 reads:

> 'Respect for human rights and fundamental freedoms
> 14. Transnational corporations shall respect human rights and fundamental freedoms in the countries in which they operate. In their social and industrial relations, transnational corporations shall not discriminate on the basis of race, colour, sex, religion, language, social, national and ethnic origin or political or other opinion. Transnational corporations shall conform to government policies designed to extend equality of opportunity and treatment.'

[24] Eg the World Investment Reports; UNCTAD also publishes the journal Transnational Corporations.

of Human Rights Norms. The Committee endeavoured to draft a convention template which would impose human rights obligations upon business and included a proposal for the monitoring and enforcement of those obligations. This agenda was driven by particular members of the Committee and was opposed wholesale by the members from the western and industrialised States. Many States viewed the imposition of rights and duties upon business enterprises as a direct challenge to the international legal status quo and as such opposed them vociferously. Accordingly the Norms were met with powerful opposition from many quarters with States such as the USA criticising the imposition of human rights obligations on companies as being contrary to international law.[25] Others such as Norway praised the Committee for its endeavours and in particular commended the attempt to put in place any type of dispute settlement mechanism.[26]

Ultimately the opponents prevailed and the Norms were dropped from the agenda, but not before stimulating a great deal of debate about the merits of adopting a hard law approach to corporate misbehaviour with its attendant dispute settlement mechanism. The Norms project ended in ignominy with the Sub-Committee accused of exceeding its mandate.[27] John Ruggie has gone further and described the Norms as a 'train wreck'.[28]

The Global Compact, conversely, has never tried to realise either a hard law approach or an enforcement mechanism. It demonstrates a more nuanced, alternative approach to corporate accountability and one that Special Representative Ruggie is obliged to engage with under his 2008 Mandate, specifically through the GC's Human Rights Working Group.[29] From its inception, however, it was made clear that the GC was intended to be a voluntary organisation.[30] Business and civil society around the globe were encouraged to become 'participants' in the GC but it was

[25] US submission to the UNHCHR for the Report of the United Nations High Commissioner on Human Rights on the responsibilities of transnational corporations and related business enterprises with regard to human rights, E/CN.4/2005/91, 15 February 2005.

[26] Norway's submission, ibid.

[27] US Submission to the UNHCHR, ibid.

[28] Remarks by John G Ruggie, UN Special Representative for Business and Human Rights, Delivered at a Forum on Corporate Social Responsibility Co-Sponsored by the Fair Labor Association and the German Network of Business Ethics Bamberg, Germany, 14 June, 2006, http://198.170.85.29/Ruggie-remarks-to-Fair-Labor-Association-and-German-Network-of-Business-Ethics-14-June-2006.pdf, at 2. The remarks regarding the Norms were subsequently repeated in 2007.

[29] 4(e). Identify, exchange and promote best practices and lessons learned on the issue of transnational corporations and other business enterprises, in coordination with the efforts of the human rights working group of the Global Compact.

[30] See the Ten Principles at www.unglobalcompact.org/AboutTheGC/TheTenPrinciples/index.html and the Overview of the GC 2000.

always made clear that there would be no binding regulatory structure. Corporate members voluntarily agree to abide by the Compact's Ten Principles on human rights, the environment and corruption and incorporate them into the fabric of the business, as well as adhering to the reporting requirements.[31]

By 2008, however, there had been a subtle but important change of emphasis, with the GC describing the initiative as 'global and local; private and public; *voluntary yet accountable*' (emphasis added).[32] The 'collaborative solutions' to the 'challenges facing business and society' are to be achieved by harnessing the 'moral authority and convening power' of the UN and the diverse problem-solving expertise of the private sector and civil society. In addition to signing the Compact, participants are invited to enrol in one of the eighty Local Networks established under the GC. This 'bottom-up' approach of these Local Networks aims to ensure that 'local priorities and needs' are addressed, but it is impossible to measure the success or otherwise of the networks. The GC itself states that the:

> networks provide opportunities for participants to improve understanding and share experiences on the Ten Principles and partnerships, as well as how to report on progress in these areas. Collective action campaigns and government policy dialogues are also increasingly organised through the Local Networks.[33]

It also points to the fact that the Secretary-General has had meetings with several of the Local Networks and concludes that this is indicative of their growing importance.[34] Likewise numerous examples of meetings, workshops and conferences are held up as examples of the success of the networks. Overall 60 per cent of active participating companies are part of a local network, which is useful in terms of disseminating information to the 'converted', but it seems as if the networks could be doing more in terms of outreach in relation to non-participating companies. Certainly there is nothing to indicate that concrete developments have taken place such as involving new participants in the GC or indeed that corporate misbehaviour has been averted as a result of the efforts of the networks. It would be useful to have this information. Only one example of tangible action on the ground is cited. The Mexican Local Network, along with Mexican businesses, a US NGO and sporting and entertainment celebrities, was involved in the creation

[31] www.unglobalcompact.org/AboutTheGC/TheTenPrinciples/index.html and www.unglobalcompact.org/HowToParticipate/Business_Participation/index.html.

[32] Overview of the GC at http://www.unglobalcompact.org/AboutTheGC/

[33] Annual Review 2008 at 18.

[34] Ibid.

of an emergency hotline for the anonymous reporting of child sexual exploitation.[35] An advertising campaign was also undertaken. While this campaign is admirable, and necessary, particularly in the context of a burgeoning tourist industry, the businesses involved are adopting a more traditional philanthropic role, historically adopted by a variety of industries over the years. There are no illustrations of situations where a Local Network has addressed the specific issue of human rights violations by business itself. The 2008 Annual Review is silent on this point and it appears that the preventative role of the GC is restricted to the promulgation of information.

Notwithstanding its voluntary nature and its current limited modes of activity, as an organisation the GC has introduced some novel approaches to preventing business violations of agreed standards in the areas of human rights, the environment and corruption in addition to seeking a measure of accountability where breaches do occur. The fact that more businesses than ever are actively participating in the GC and are submitting Communications on Progress (COP) is to be applauded and may very well be as a result of the activities of the Local Networks. Without solid details it is impossible to determine this. Furthermore the GC has adopted a truly effective stakeholder approach by involving NGOs, trade unions, academics and other elements of civil society in all aspects of its operations. The Mexican child safety hotline demonstrates this well but it can also be seen in the reports and documents being produced which are clearly harnessing cross-sector expertise.[36] Many of those documents also rely on the work of Special Representative Ruggie and it is significant to note this move towards a more joined up approach by international organisations to the problem of business and human rights. This truly multistakeholder involvement is one of the great strengths of the GC and is why the dissemination programme will be successful in ensuring greater respect for human rights standards, at least where businesses want to be involved.

Despite the progress, the GC, now in its ninth year of operation, continues to face many of the regulatory challenges it encountered at its outset

[35] Annual Review 2008 at 21. For more information about the Mexican Local Network see http://www.unglobalcompact.org/NetworksAroundTheWorld/display.html?id=MX and http://www.unglobalcompact.org/docs/networks_around_world_doc/Annual_Reports_2007/Mexico_Annual_Activity_Report_2007.pdf.

[36] See, eg *Human Rights Translated: A Business Reference Guide 2008*, which has been published by a consortium comprising the Castan Centre for Human Rights Law, Monash University, the Office of the High Commissioner for Human Rights, the International Business Leaders Forum and the Global Compact itself. The publication aims to explain the content of international human rights and to act as 'a tool for companies wanting to engage in activities in support of human rights' (at xiii).

and throughout its existence.[37] In its Annual Report for 2008 the recurring themes around corporate failure to meet the specific communication obligation under the Global Compact loom large.[38] While there has been a 25 per cent increase from 2007 in the number of participants submitting Communications on Progress (COP), at the same time over 400 companies were delisted in 2008 for failing to submit a COP at all.[39] It seems clear, therefore, that there are different categories of business operating. Firstly, there are the businesses which are willing and able to adhere to the GC principles, for example, submitting a COP or belonging to a Local Network. These tend to be the big high-profile, high-street names which respond to reputational carrots.[40] Next, there are those businesses which are willing but unable to adhere to GC commitments such as submitting COPs. The vast majority of delinquent participants fall within the small and medium enterprise sector (SME) and the naming and shaming stick used in previous years to embarrass participants into meeting their obligations is less likely to have a positive effect than previously.[41] SMEs generally have a lower public profile and it must therefore be assumed that they are less susceptible to bad publicity and the consumer campaigns and boycotts which often plague the larger high-profile businesses and act as a lever for better behaviour.[42] Finally, there are businesses which are simply unwilling to become involved with initiatives such as the GC at all. It is this renegade group which presents the greatest challenge for voluntary schemes. If one of the aims of the CSR project is to convince industry that CSR is good for business then ways of reaching those businesses which 'fly under the radar' need to be developed over and above those which reach businesses that are responsive to the threat of losing consumer confidence or their reputation. This is the crux of the matter as the businesses currently engaged in human rights violations will never be persuaded by the reputational carrot held out by voluntary initiatives.[43]

[37] For an overview of the work of the GC see www.unglobalcompact.org/AboutTheGC/.

[38] United Nations Global Compact, 'Annual Review 2008' (New York, UN Global Compact Office, March 2009) www.unglobalcompact.org/docs/news_events/9.1_news_archives/2009_04_08/GC_2008AR_FINAL.pdf.

[39] A total of 404 companies were delisted in 2008, which amounts to over 800 delisted companies in total.

[40] See for example DaimlerChrysler in the earliest days of the GC.

[41] Only 32% of SMEs are active participants in comparison to 67% for other companies which have been participants for more than two years. The overall figure is a much higher 76% when new participants are included: 2008 Annual Review at 53.

[42] See, eg the footwear industry, eg NIKE, Reebok and the changes to operating practices after consumer boycotts.

[43] See 'Human Rights Translated' at vii–viii 'Good human rights practice may bring commercial rewards … Companies implicated in human rights scandals often see their reputations and brand images suffer, resulting in the loss of share value, and face increased

Companies out of the public eye are far less susceptible to the notion of the 'price of getting it wrong' and this is why it is necessary to establish a parallel top-down *international* regulatory architecture which will apply to all business.[44]

In light of these ongoing difficulties, the GC will have to work hard to address the problem of non-communicating participants and inactive/delisted companies. This is being addressed partly through the implementation of a quality reporting programme which is designed to help businesses draft their COPs, encourage 'greater transparency' among existing participants and standardise the COPs.[45] Such a scheme will be of unquestionable value for SMEs, who struggle with the administrative burden of institutional paperwork and red tape at the best of times. Nevertheless, the GC will also have to demonstrate that it is more than a mere talking shop or opportunity for charitable works and move towards material prevention of human rights violations by business. There is no question that the dissemination of information about human rights standards (and the rest) is valuable in terms of ensuring respect for principles but there are ongoing breaches which require urgent attention and the GC remains unable to tackle them. While the GC is an important tool in relation to encouraging adherence to some aspects of CSR, nevertheless, the current institutional arrangements are simply not capable of addressing ongoing violations of human rights and certainly do not fully meet Ruggie's requirements for an 'effective remedy.'[46] The GC was never designed with any sort of enforcement mechanism or punishment in mind for active human rights breaches and while the bottom-up reporting approach and dissemination activities are commendable in terms of preventing business misbehaviour, huge cracks appear in the system when businesses simply refuse to meet their reporting obligations and the system itself cannot remedy ex post facto situations of human rights abuse. Special Representative Ruggie wants to identify examples of existing good practice in relation to business and human rights. There is no doubt that the GC has much to offer in this regard via the COPs and Local Networks in particular. The GC is doing good work in the promotion of human rights standards, and consequently protection, but it is simply not in a position to offer any kind of remedy or redress for human rights violations by business unless its terms of reference change.

security and insurance costs, as well as expensive lawsuits such as those pursued under the Alien Tort Claims Act, and consumer boycotts. The price of getting it wrong cannot be underestimated.'

[44] Ibid.

[45] Practical Guide to the Communication on Progress, 'Human Rights—A Call to Action', September 2008.

[46] Protect, Respect and Remedy, above n 9 at 24 para 92.

III. ORGANISATION FOR ECONOMIC CO-OPERATION AND DEVELOPMENT (OECD)

In some respects the OECD adopts a truly cooperative approach to business and human rights and one which operates at the international and national levels. It harnesses the consensual authority of an international instrument coupled with institutional clout and national mechanisms to bring a degree of accountability to the behaviour of corporate actors. In so doing, it seems to be clearly adhering to Ruggie's (and international law's) concept that States have the primary obligation to protect individuals from human rights abuses, but also recognises that business has obligations too and that human rights can only be protected, respected and remedied by a combined arrangement. In other words the OECD adopts a top-down/bottom-up approach, albeit a flawed one.

Much like the UN the OECD has a lengthy history in relation to CSR. Its 1976 Guidelines on Multinational Enterprises (the Guidelines) created a set of recommendations endorsed by Member States and to be adhered to by corporate actors. The UK Government describes the Guidelines as 'the only comprehensive, multilaterally endorsed code of conduct for multinational enterprises.'[47] Despite the fact that the Guidelines are not legally binding (they emphasise self-regulation and reporting mechanisms[48]) they do specifically address the issue of human rights (as well as the environment and particular labour issues) and there is much to be learned from the OECD experience overall, both positive and negative.[49] This is particularly true in relation to accountability attempts. This makes the OECD's embryonic experiences in attempting to regulate business behaviour different from the GC and demonstrates something which might warrant classification as Ruggie's 'remedy.' Notwithstanding this positive aspect, the OECD system exhibits structural difficulties which have hampered openness, transparency and the involvement of civil society as well as classic problems in relation to enforcement and remedies.

From the beginning, an open, multistakeholder approach was adopted at the highest level of the OECD in relation to business and human rights. As the Guidelines fall within the sphere of responsibility of the Committee on International Investment and Multinational Enterprises (CIME) it is required to coordinate 'exchanges of views' with stakeholders.[50]

[47] Department for Business Enterprise and Regulatory Reform, www.berr.gov.uk/whatwedo/sectors/lowcarbon/cr-sd-wp/nationalcontactpoint/page45873.html. See also eg Statement by the United Kingdom National Contact Point (NCP) for OECD Guidelines for Multinational Enterprises: DAS Air, 17 July 2008, para 2.

[48] OECD Guidelines on Multinational Enterprises 2000, http://www.oecd.org/dataoecd/56/36/1922428.pdf. II(3), (6), (7) III(1), (2), (3) and (4).

[49] Guideline II(2).

[50] Council Decision, June 2000 II(1).

Relevant stakeholders include the Business Industry Advisory Council (BIAC), the Trade Union Advisory Council (TUAC)[51] as well as 'other non-governmental organisations'.[52] However, a clear distinction was drawn, at least initially, between the various stakeholders as regards their involvement. The role of both TUAC and BIAC is specifically formalised in the Guidelines and they are officially regarded as operating on an equal footing, with an emphasis being placed on 'strict parallelism of treatment'.[53] Conversely, although NGOs may be consulted by CIME as relevant stakeholders, in practice they have been formally excluded from the Guidelines' international implementation process and this has resulted in much historical dissatisfaction.[54] More recently, however, NGOs have become actively involved in the 'monitoring and reviewing' efforts of CIME and although their participation has not become formalised it certainly demonstrates a desire on the part of the OECD to increase and augment the involvement of civil society within the overarching framework of the Guidelines.

Notwithstanding this evidently inclusive attitude, there is some support for the assertion that the Guidelines are not being applied effectively and this is largely to do with the structure of the National Contact Points (NCP). In the view of Ruggie in particular, they have 'failed to meet their potential'. To say that they have failed to meet their potential is to suggest that they could have achieved more, but it is not clear how this would be possible given the current systemic limitations imposed by the adherent States themselves. NCPs are only as effective as their structure allows and this is entirely the responsibility of adherent States. Fault lies with the adherent States, not the NCPs. So what mechanisms are in fact in place within the OECD system and how effective are they at holding businesses to account for human rights abuses? After the revision of the Guidelines in 2000, each OECD Member State was required to create an NCP for the purpose of, inter alia, monitoring the implementation of the Guidelines and to contribute to the resolution of complaints. The NCPs take a variety of forms but disappointingly the vast majority do not formally include NGOs, trade unions or even business within their constitution

[51] BIAC is consists of representatives from both industry and employers' associations within OECD member States. Similarly TUAC is composed of national trade union organisations from all OECD members. Both TUAC and BIAC have secretariats are based in Paris and engage in formal and informal contact with the OECD. See OECD document 'Relations with BIAC and TUAC' 7 June 2001.

[52] OECD Council Decision, June 2000, II(1) and (2).

[53] Ibid.

[54] 'NGO Statement on the OECD Guidelines for Multinational Enterprises' in *OECD Guidelines for Multinational Enterprises: Global Instruments for Corporate Responsibility*, Annual Report 2001 (OECD, 2001) at 46 'The unconvincing explanation given is that the NGOs are not organised in a similar fashion as BIAC and TUAC.'

which is a major weakness and some distance from the evolving and arguably enlightened multistakeholder approach of the OECD itself.[55] Encouragingly 11 of the 39 NCPs adopt a tripartite or even a quadripartite structure and work together with business and civil society mostly in the form of trade unions, although the Finnish and Chilean NCPs also embrace NGOs.[56] This is a noteworthy improvement on previous years mostly as 'a result of choices made by new adherents' to the Guidelines.[57] It is worth noting that while many NCPs do not formally engage with trade unions, NGOs or even the business sector, a great many of them 'use advisory committees or permanent consultative bodies whose members include non-government partners' while others meet or consult informally with stakeholders.[58] It would seem that there has been a conscious effort on the part of some but not all States to do this and also to restructure NCPs in order to step away from purely government-based institutions and to make them more transparent.[59] At the G8 Heilegendamm Summit in 2007 States made clear that they are actively seeking 'better governance' via the NCPs, hence this restructuring.[60]

Nevertheless, it is undeniable that there has been a disparate response to the 'better governance' agenda because NCP arrangements are left to the discretion of individual adhering States. Further, it seems to be the case that this lack of a coherent approach stems from the belief of States that 'there is no perfect structure' for NCPs.[61] As a consequence, many adherent States cling to an 'in-house' scheme where the NCP is rooted entirely in government departments and which seems to fly in the face of the multipartite ethos which underpins the Guidelines. The arguments in favour of such a policy are set out in the NCP Review 2008. States point to the fact that it is governments that 'are the primary guarantors of the

[55] Report of the 2007 Annual Meeting of the National Contact Points, 19–20 June 2007, OECD at 4. Of the 39 NCPs 20 are composed of a single government department, seven involve multiple government departments, one is bipartite (government and business), nine are tripartite (government, business and trade unions) and two are quadripartite (government, business, trade unions and NGOs).

[56] Belgium, Denmark, Estonia, France, Latvia, Lithuania, Luxembourg, Norway and Sweden.

[57] Estonia, Latvia, Lithuania and Romania. 'Review of NCP Performance: Key Findings 2008' (background document to the OECD-ILO Conference on Corporate Social Responsibility, 23–24 June 2008, Paris) at 4.

[58] Ruggie, above n 9; OECD, above n 55 at 4.

[59] Review of NCP Performance: Key Findings, Background Paper to the OECD-ILO conference on corporate social responsibility *Employment and Industrial Relations: Promoting Responsible Business Conduct in a Globalising Economy* 23–24 June 2008, OECD Conference Centre, Paris, at 4 ('Review of NCP Performance'). The Netherlands NCP is now made up of independent experts appointed to work with selected government advisors as opposed to its previous inter-departmental incarnation.

[60] G8 Summit Declaration Heiligendamm, 'Growth and Responsibility in the World Economy' Germany 7 June 2007 at para 24.

[61] Review of NCP Performance 2008 at 5.

Guidelines' and they also have the requisite economic expertise to deal with the issues, and thus it makes sense for the NCP to be based solely within government.[62] Quite clearly this does not adequately justify the apparent formal exclusion of civil society from many NCP structures. Furthermore, States point to the difficulties of reaching consensus on contentious issues when civil society is included in the process, but the evidence demonstrates that such snags can be dealt with in a straightforward manner.[63] So, for example, in Sweden the chair of the NCP retains a casting vote. Proclamations by adherent States highlighting the fact that civil society can be involved with the process irrespective of the structure of the NCP betray the inherent overarching multistakeholder architecture of the Guidelines. It is also difficult to see how an entirely government based NCP ensures proper accountability. Certainly proponents of the multipartite approach argue that true 'objectivity, transparency and accountability' can only be realised within an inclusive, multistakeholder NCP structure.[64] A coherent and consistent configuration across adherent States can only add to the esteem of the NCPs, ensuring the proper application and protection of human rights standards.

In addition to the monitoring function, the NCPs play a crucial role in contributing to the 'resolution of issues that arise relating to implementation of the Guidelines in specific instances.'[65] As with the GC, the NCPs are expressly non-judicial in nature, which in and of itself is not problematic; as has already been demonstrated, non-judicial approaches can be a valuable tool for protecting human rights, but it inevitably raises further issues around lack of enforcement and binding redress.[66]

Certainly this is borne out to an extent by the experience of the UK NCP, although it suffered from a variety of additional systemic problems since it was first established. It came under fire as a result of chronic delays, lack of transparency and accountability, and general mismanagement.[67] In response to the criticisms the UK government has restructured its NCP, removing it from the sole domain of the Department for Business, Enterprise and Regulatory Reform (BERR) and formalising the roles of the Foreign and Commonwealth Office and the Department for

62 Ibid 6.

63 Ibid 7–8.

64 Ibid 7.

65 Guidelines, at 47, pt C Implementation in Specific Instances.

66 Guidelines II(3), (6) and (7). Also III(1), (2) and (3).

67 RAID/CORE/TUC, 'Fit for Purpose? A Review of the UK National Contact Point (NCP) for the Organisation for Economic Co-operation and Development (OECD) Guidelines for Multinational Enterprises 2008,' a report by Rights and Accountability in Development (RAID) in association with The Corporate Responsibility (CORE) Coalition and The Trades Union Congress (TUC) November 2008, www.corporatejustice.org/IMG/pdf/NCP_report_2008.pdf ('Fit for Purpose? A Review of the UK National Contact Point').

International Development. Furthermore, it has created a Steering Group and implemented the Specific Instance procedure. Notwithstanding the restructuring, criticisms continue to be expressed by stakeholders. A report published by RAID, CORE and the TUC highlights the limitations of the current structure:

> The NCP is a non-judicial mechanism that provides a degree of accountability for the environmental and human rights impacts of British companies operating abroad. It does not have any powers of enforceability, cannot impose penalties on companies or award compensation to victims. It has some capacity to investigate complaints brought to it by NGOs or unions directly, by seeking information from parties to the dispute, and plays a mediating role in trying to bring them together to facilitate dialogue and a resolution to the case. If there is no resolution, the NCP can review the evidence, consult experts, make a determination and issue a statement on the case.[68]

Irrespective of the recent changes, trade unions and NGOs are firmly of the view that the UK NCP procedure is no substitute for judicial proceedings, particularly in relation to the lack of enforcement measures and penalties. Nonetheless, there is clear evidence of States moving towards a more effective Specific Instance process and many of Ruggie's requirements for an effective remedy are present. For example, the UK and the Netherlands have adopted a policy of naming the parties to initial assessments for Specific Instance proceedings, and some NCPs publicise the acceptance of a Specific Instance on their website.[69] Transparency is therefore achieved on at least one level.[70] On the other hand, where a case is rejected, every NCP, with the exception of The Netherlands, keeps the parties anonymous. It is important to note, however, that an NCP may only mediate a resolution in relation to a complaint and may only make recommendations. Even so, the final statements issued by an NCP at the end of the Specific Instance process are becoming more detailed and are generally always published even if there has been no mediated agreement. The statement of the UK NCP in relation to Afrimex illustrates the strengths and weaknesses of the Specific Instance procedure.[71] It is one of only two condemnatory statements made by the UK NCP.[72]

[68] Ibid ii.

[69] Review of NCP Performance at 11. Specifically UK, Brazil and Japan.

[70] Ibid 14.

[71] Final Statement by the UK National Contact Point for the OECD Guidelines for Multinational Enterprises: Afrimex (UK) Ltd, 28 August 2008, URN 08/1209 (Afrimex Final Statement),www.berr.gov.uk/whatwedo/sectors/lowcarbon/cr-sd-wp/nationalcontactpoint/page45873.html.

[72] The other being Das Air. Final Statement by the UK National Contact Point (NCP) for the OECD Guidelines for Multinational Enterprises: Das Air, 21 July 2008, www.berr.gov.uk/whatwedo/sectors/lowcarbon/cr-sd-wp/nationalcontactpoint/page45873.html.

In February 2007 the NGO Global Witness lodged a complaint against Afrimex (UK) Ltd with the UK NCP on the basis of its investigations into the British-registered company's activities in the Democratic Republic of Congo. Specific allegations were made regarding the use of child labour and forced labour in mines within a conflict zone which supplied minerals to companies linked to Afrimex. Furthermore there were allegations that Afrimex had paid 'taxes' to rebel forces in Congo which contributed to the conflict. The company disputed the allegations on the basis that there was no link between it and the alleged human rights violations because it was removed from the mining process and it had never paid 'taxes' to rebel forces.[73] The existence of a conflict was significant to the outcome of the procedure not least because the UN Security Council's Panel of Experts on the Illegal Exploitation of Natural Resources had stated previously that companies such as Afrimex were the 'engines' of conflict.[74] After an unsuccessful attempt at mediation between the parties, the NCP made a determination. Significantly the determination is rooted in Ruggie's notion of due diligence, that is, the practical implementation of the obligation to protect human rights: 'the steps a company must take to become aware of, prevent and address adverse human rights impacts.'[75] The NCP concluded that Afrimex had failed to exercise due diligence in relation to its supply chain and was in breach of a multitude of provisions of the Guidelines.[76] Specifically the NCP stated that it was 'unacceptable' for Afrimex to fail to impose conditions on its suppliers 'given the context of conflict and human rights abuses taking place.'[77] It went on to declare in no uncertain terms that Afrimex had funded a conflict which 'prevented the economic, social and environmental progress key to achieving sustainable development and contributed to human rights abuses'. The NCP made several recommendations at the centre of which was the practical integration of the contents of a corporate responsibility policy. It proposed that the policy document should make explicit reference to international human rights instruments and sought assurances that the document would change corporate culture and not be a 'worthless piece of paper'.[78] In making its recommendations the NCP again explicitly reverts to Ruggie by advising Afrimex to adopt the due diligence standard and to require that its suppliers 'do no harm.'[79] It also recommends that Afrimex

[73] Afrimex Final Statement at 5.
[74] Afrimex Final Statementat at 3.
[75] Protect, Respect and Remedy, above n 9 at 17, para 56.
[76] Guidelines II(1), II(2), II(10), IV(1)(b), IV(1)(c) and IV(4)(b).
[77] Afrimex Final Statement, at 10–11, para 47.
[78] Ibid para 66.
[79] Ibid paras 64, 65 and 66.

monitor its suppliers to ensure compliance with these standards as well as referring the company to a number of tools to assist with the development and application of its policy.[80] Despite the non-binding nature of the recommendations the NCP's determination has been welcomed. Global Witness stated in a Press Release that it sent the 'right message' to business and that the 'British government's ruling provides positive guidance to help … change … practices.'[81] The message *is* unequivocal: 'The UK government expects British companies to exercise the highest levels of due diligence in situations of widespread violence and systematic human rights abuses.'[82] There is no doubt that this new enhanced procedure offers a measure of accountability, the question is whether it can also offer realistic protection against human rights abuses in the absence of a binding mechanism or an effective remedy. The NGO and trade union community says that it does not and recommends a new body with the power of sanctions and remedies for individuals.[83] Ruggie too emphasises that an effective remedy is one which will 'investigate, punish, and redress abuse' and it is clear that while the Specific Instance procedure involves an investigation of business behaviour, and an outcome which may act as a deterrent, it neither punishes nor provides redress for human rights abuses. Nevertheless, Afrimex is now firmly on the human rights 'radar' and even absent any punishment or redress it is to be hoped that the inevitable monitoring of its future activities will be a sufficient deterrent to breaches of the Guidelines.

IV. CONCLUSION

These examples of regulatory capture are a definitive move away from conventional adjudicatory techniques of international dispute resolution towards a more unconventional approach which eschews courts and tribunals and embraces collaborative stakeholder practices, emphasises the local, and may even act as a deterrent to future human rights abuses. What is also being witnessed is a move away from a traditional top-down application of international legal rules and a treaty-based system towards a structure whereby entirely new or existing international multistakeholder mechanisms are utilised in an attempt to protect human

[80] Eg the OECD Risk Awareness Tool for Multinational Enterprises in Weak Governance Zones; the Sanctions Unit at the Foreign and Commonwealth Office.

[81] Global Witness Press Release, 'UK company Afrimex broke international guidelines, says British government' 28 August 2008.

[82] Afrimex Final Statement at 16, para 75.

[83] Fit for Purpose? A Review of the UK National Contact Point, above n 67 at iv.

rights standards from bad business behaviour. Witness the rise of the GC's Local Networks and the OECD's NCPs. Such initiatives are not comparable to the much criticised voluntary codes of conduct adopted by many businesses and business organisations since the birth of the CSR movement. Furthermore it is axiomatic that they are not comparable to traditional international law as they are not legally binding upon business actors who either choose to adopt certain standards of behaviour—eg all GC participants—or fall within their remit by virtue of their geographical location—eg Afrimex. The Global Compact falls within the former category, being an entirely voluntary enterprise although it does rely upon internationally agreed and binding (at least on States) human rights standards. The OECD goes further by basing its regulatory system upon an existing international agreement and the State structures which emanate from it to hold business to account at the national level. Nevertheless while these mechanisms offer useful alternative approaches to CSR, questions arise as to the efficacy of them when it comes to actually remedying human rights abuses. So within the NCP Specific Instance procedure what happens after a complaint is investigated and upheld? What is the carrot or stick for good behaviour? Why should a business care about a negative determination? As Ruggie states, redress should be effective and 'could include compensation, restitution, guarantees of non-repetition, changes in relevant law and public apologies.' Neither the GC nor NCPs have the capability to provide such redress. Furthermore, there is a clear regulatory gap in relation to those businesses which choose not to engage with the GC or which are not registered within an OECD member State. It is all very well to articulate that one of the aims of the CSR project is to convince industry that CSR is good for business so that it voluntarily engages but there needs to be some sort of stick or leverage over those that choose to ignore the project. The problem is that they 'fly under the radar' because either they have no contact with end-users, for example, natural resource companies, or disengage part-way through the process, for example, SMEs. So while the GC and the OECD can be regarded as successful in protecting human rights to a certain extent, the absence of teeth in the mechanisms means that even those businesses captured by their regulatory structures escape penalties and many more simply continue to fly under the radar whereas those affected by their misconduct continue to be denied adequate redress.

It is for these reasons that, in addition to strengthening and honing the existing alternative mechanisms, an effective overarching international architecture must be developed to work in tandem with enhanced bottom-up initiatives. History teaches us that States are unable and/or unwilling to regulate business enterprises within a multilateral covenant framework so can a workable, meaningful and effective middle ground be achieved? Prevention of human rights abuses is obviously the key and there is no question that the existing dissemination of information to and education of the business community will go a long way towards prevention. Likewise convincing business that adhering to standards is good for the bottom line. If the reputational carrot is insufficient to engage business with human rights standards, then effective sticks need to be explored. A variety of options could be implemented, particularly within a structure such as an NCP. So for example, a business could be fined, training could be required, export credit benefits could be linked with compliance[84] or access to public procurement could be linked with compliance. Such techniques would send out a message to business that human rights abuses are unacceptable. Other stronger and most likely unpopular options such as withdrawing the advantages of corporate status or pursuing company officers could also be utilised. Employing such methods would do much to satisfy the 'punish' and 'redress' elements of Ruggie's 'effective remedy' requirement.'

There is no doubt that the GC, OECD and NCPs have much to contribute to the debate on business and human rights. The lack of an effective redress mechanism, however, coupled with disengaged business means that as it stands they cannot solve the global issue of business abusing human rights. Nevertheless they offer a useful starting point for ensuring a measure of adherence to human rights standards.

[84] The Netherlands has done this in relation to compliance with the OECD Guidelines: OECD, 'Relations with BIAC and TUAC', 7 June 2001 (Paris, OECD).

Part 2

Problems and Techniques in Substantive Areas of International Law

5

Practice and Procedure of Dispute Settlement in Individual Communication Cases within the Human Rights Committee and the Committee on the Elimination of Discrimination against Women: Congruence or Conflict?

SANDY GHANDHI

I. INTRODUCTION

HUMAN RIGHTS HAVE been described as the 'idea of our time'.[1] The Charter of the United Nations, which was signed on 26 June 1945 in San Francisco, at the conclusion of the United Nations Conference on International Organization, and entered into force 24 October 1945, heralded in this new dawn for the international rights of man.[2] The central importance of human rights in the UN Charter is confirmed by the second preambular paragraph which was drafted by Field-Marshal Smuts and hardly altered in its final form, which proclaims that:

> WE THE PEOPLES OF THE UNITED NATIONS DETERMINED
>
> … to reaffirm faith in fundamental human rights, in the dignity and worth of the human person, in the equal rights of men and women and of nations large and small …
>
> HAVE RESOLVED TO COMBINE OUR EFFORTS TO ACCOMPLISH THESE AIMS.[3]

[1] L Henkin, *The Rights of Man Today* (London, Stevens & Sons, 1979) Preface.

[2] See generally: B Simma et al (eds), *The Charter of the United Nations: A Commentary*, 2nd edn (Oxford, Oxford University Press, 2002).

[3] Smuts pressed for the inclusion of human rights clauses in the Charter. At the 6th Plenary Session, 6 May 1945, he suggested that: 'the Charter should contain at its very

The Charter then goes on to contain seven explicit references to human rights on an obligatory basis.[4] These are known collectively as the human rights clauses of the Charter. This elevation of the protection of human rights on to the international arena on a principled and conceptualised basis for the first time resonates fully with the view expressed by Sir Hersch Lauterpacht in a lecture at Chatham House, London on 27 May 1941 when he described '[t]he protection of human personality and of its fundamental human rights' as 'the ultimate purpose of all law, national and international'.[5] In addition, every Article that refers to the Purposes and Principles of the Charter refers by implication also to human rights. The peremptory norm of non-discrimination, which is a fundamental concern of both of the human rights treaty bodies, the Human Rights Committee (HRC) and the Committee on Elimination of Discrimination Against Women (CEDAW) being examined in this paper, plays a central role in the human rights clauses.[6] This is exemplified by the very first reference to it in Article 1(3), which specifies that one of the four main purposes of the UN is 'to achieve international co-operation in … promoting and encouraging respect for human rights and for fundamental freedoms for all without distinction as to race, sex, language, or religion'. Subsequently, the Charter refers to non-discrimination in Articles 13(1)(b), 55(c) and 76(c). Professor John Humphrey has described the human rights clauses as running through

outset and in the preamble, a declaration of human rights and of common faith which has sustained the Allied Peoples in their bitter struggle for the vindication of these rights and that faith. … We have fought for justice and decency and for the fundamental freedom and rights of man, which are basic to all human advancement and progress and peace'.

[4] The obligatory nature of the Charter pronouncements on human rights is discussed fully in: A Petrenko, 'The Human Rights Provisions of the UN Charter' (1978) 9 *Manitoba Law Journal* 141; LB Sohn, 'The Human Rights Clauses of the Charter' (1977) 12 *Texas International Law Journal* 129; FC Newman, 'Interpreting the Human Rights Clauses of the Charter' (1972) 5 *Human Rights Journal* 283; J Robinson, *Human Rights and Fundamental Freedoms in the Charter of the United Nations: A Commentary* (New York, Institute of Jewish Affairs of the American Jewish Congress and World Jewish Congress, 1946); see also the Advisory Opinion of the ICJ on the *Legal Consequences for States of the Continued Presence of South Africa in Namibia (SW Africa) notwithstanding Security Council Resolution 276* (1970) ICJ Reports (1971) 16. There is a huge amount of literature analysing the Court's opinion; see, in particular: E Schwelb, 'The International Court of Justice and the Human Rights Clauses of the Charter' (1972) 66 *American Journal of International Law* (*AJIL*) 337.

[5] International Law: Being the Collected Papers of H Lauterpacht (II) (Cambridge, Cambridge University Press, 1975) 47.

[6] See generally A Orakhelashvili, *Peremptory Norms in International Law* (Oxford, Oxford University Press, 2006).

the Charter 'like a golden thread'.[7] This development was quite 'revolutionary in character'.[8]

Thus, it is clear that non-discrimination on grounds of, for example, race (the concern of the Committee on the Elimination of Racial Discrimination (CERD)) or gender (the concern of CEDAW) is the cornerstone of the human rights clauses of the Charter. The Universal Declaration of Human Rights 1948 (UDHR), adopted on the night of 10 December 1948 by the General Assembly in Paris, develops in greater detail the meaning of the expression 'human rights and fundamental freedoms' in the provisions of the Charter.[9] The whole document is underpinned by the general non-discrimination clause in Article 2, which declares that '[e]veryone is entitled to all the rights and freedoms set forth in this Declaration, without distinction of any kind, such as race, colour, sex, language, religion, political or other opinion, national or social origin, property, birth or other status'. In addition, Article 7 states that '[a]ll are equal before the law and are entitled without any discrimination to equal protection of the law. All are entitled to equal protection against any discrimination in violation of this Declaration and against any incitement to such discrimination'. Furthermore, Article 16 deals with issues particularly relevant to women: the right to marry and found a family; equality of rights between spouses 'as to marriage, during marriage and at its dissolution'; the principle of 'free and full consent' of the

[7] JP Humphrey, 'The International Law of Human Rights in the Middle Twentieth Century' in M Bos (ed), The Present State of International law and Other Essays: Written in Honour of the Centenary Celebration of the International Law Association 1873–1973 (Deventer, Kluwer, 1973).

[8] JP Humphrey, 'The International Protection of Human Rights' (1948) 255 *Annals of the American Academy of Political & Social Sciences* 21.

[9] Res 217A (III) adopted without any dissenting votes (the whole of the Communist bloc—Byelorussia, Czechoslovakia, Poland, Ukraine, Yugoslavia and the USSR—abstained, together with Saudi Arabia and South Africa); see generally: G Alfredsson and A Eide, *The Universal Declaration of Human Rights: A Common Standard of Achievement* (The Hague, Martinus Nijhoff, 1999); see in particular: H Lauterpacht, 'The Universal Declaration of Human Rights' (1948) 25 *British Year Book of International Law* 354; R Cassin, 'Looking Back at the Universal Declaration of 1948' (1968) 15 *Review of Contemporary Law* 13; R Cassin, '*La Déclaration Universelle et la Mise en Oeuvre des Droits de l'Homme*' (1951) 79 *Recueil des Cours* 237; JL Kunz, 'United Nations Declaration of Human Rights' (1949) 43 *AJIL* 316; P Alston, 'The Universal Declaration at 35: Western and Passé or Alive and Universal' (1983) 31 *Review of the International Commission of Jurists* 60; JP Humphrey, 'The Universal Declaration of Human Rights: Its History, Impact and Juridical Character' in BG Ramcharan (ed), *Human Rights: Thirty Years After the Universal Declaration* (The Hague, Martinus Nijhoff, 1979); A Verdoodt, 'The Present Significance of the Universal Declaration of Human Rights' (1965) 7 *World Justice* 158; A Verdoodt, *Naissance et Signification de la Déclaration Universelle des Droits de l'Homme* (Louvain, Nauwelaerts, 1964); N Robinson, *The Universal Declaration of Human Rights: Its Origin, Significance, Application and Interpretation* (New York, Institute of Jewish Affairs, 1958); E Schwelb, *Human Rights and the International Community: The Roots and Growth of the Universal Declaration of Human Rights 1948–1963* (Chicago, Quadrangle Books, 1964).

intending spouses; and finally, the pre-eminence given to the concept of the 'family'.[10] Most of the representatives present at the Paris session of the General Assembly did not believe that they were adopting a Declaration that would be binding in law. In order to clarify the matter and leave no room for argument, some delegations endorsed this interpretation expressly. Of course, it is true that over the passage of time, many of the provisions of the Declaration have become binding as part of customary international law or as general principles of law recognised by civilised nations.[11] As soon as the Declaration had been adopted, the Commission on Human Rights started work on the next stage of the international bill of rights, namely the translation of the rights contained in the Declaration into legally binding form. After much debate, the decision was taken to draft two documents called Covenants (rather than Conventions, to symbolise the concept of a sacred trust), one containing civil and political rights and the other containing economic, social and cultural rights. Both instruments contain general non-discrimination clauses in similar format. Thus, the International Covenant on Civil and Political Rights (ICCPR) states in its Article 2(1) that:

> [e]ach State Party to the present Covenant undertakes to respect and to ensure to all individuals within its territory and subject to its jurisdiction the rights recognized in the present Covenant, without distinction of any kind, such as race, colour, sex, language, religion, political or other opinion, national or social origin, property, birth or other status.[12]

The ICCPR also contains some provisions which are of especial concern for women (Article 23 family law rights, in part rather similar to Article 16 of the UDHR but without the Declaration's immediacy of obligation in respect of the rights of spouses as to marriage, during marriage and

[10] See also Art 25(2) dealing with motherhood, inter alia.

[11] See: PR Ghandhi, 'The Universal Declaration of Human Rights at 50 Years: Its Origins, Significance and Impact' (1998) 41 *German Yearbook of International Law* 206.

[12] 999 United Nations Treaty Series (UNTS) 171. See also Art 26 of the ICCPR, which declares that '[a]ll persons are equal before the law and are entitled without any discrimination to the equal protection of the law. In this respect, the law shall prohibit any discrimination and guarantee to all persons equal and effective protection against discrimination on any ground such as race, colour, sex, language, religion, political or other opinion, national or social origin, property, birth or other status'. Note that Art 26 does not merely duplicate the guarantees of Art 2(1); see the discussion in: PR Ghandhi, *The Human Rights Committee and the Right of Individual Communication: Law and Practice* (Aldershot, Ashgate Publishing Company, 1998) 166–71; see also: G Moon, 'Complying with its International Obligations: The United Kingdom and Article 26 of the International Covenant on Civil and Political Rights' [2003] *European Human Rights Law Review* 283; TA Choudhury, 'The Drafting of Article 26 of the International Covenant on Civil and Political Rights' [2002] *European Human Rights Law* Review 591; TA Choudhury, 'Interpreting the Right to Equality under Article 26 of the International Covenant on Civil and Political Rights' [2003] *European Human Rights Law Review* 24.

at its dissolution;[13] and, Article 24 dealing with the rights of children).[14] Similarly, the International Covenant on Economic, Social and Cultural Rights (ICESCR) states in its Article 2(2) that:

> [t]he States Parties to the present Covenant undertake to guarantee that the rights enunciated in the present Covenant will be exercised without discrimination of any kind as to race, colour, sex, language, religion, political or other opinion, national or social origin, property, birth or other status.[15]

Here too, there are additional provisions targeted at the rights of women (such as Article 10, dealing with aspects of the family, motherhood and protection of children).

Thus, these two Covenants, the central pillars of the international bill of rights, stipulate for a general norm of non-discrimination which also protects persons of all races and whichever gender. Specific norms in relation to gender-based (and race-based) discrimination were adopted only subsequently by the relevant United Nations bodies.

II. THE ORIGINS OF THE GENDER-BASED PRESCRIPTIONS ADOPTED BY THE UNITED NATIONS

The impetus for the development of norms in relation to gender-based discrimination was provided by the Commission on the Status of Women (CSW). Cast originally in 1946 as a sub-commission of the former Commission on Human Rights, the CSW soon acquired the status of a full commission.[16] The brief of the CSW included 'the preparation of recommendations relating to urgent problems requiring the immediate attention in the field of women's rights with the object of implementing the principle that men and women should have equal rights, and the development of proposals to give effect to such recommendations'. In a spate of legislation, the CSW was the catalyst for the adoption of a series of instruments in the field of women's rights, including the Convention on the Political Rights of Women 1952,[17] the Convention on the Nationality of Married Women 1957[18] and the Convention on Consent to Marriage, Minimum Age for

[13] The obligation is only one of progressive achievement, contrary to the general principle of immediacy of obligation in respect of this Covenant.

[14] See generally: PR Ghandhi and E MacNamee, 'The Family in UK Law and the International Covenant on Civil and Political Rights 1966' (1991) 5 *International Journal of Law and the Family* 104.

[15] 993 UNTS 3.

[16] The constitutional basis for the creation of the CSW may be traced to Art 68 of the UN Charter.

[17] 193 UNTS 135.

[18] 309 UNTS 65.

Marriage and Registration of Marriages 1962.[19] Apart from in these specific areas of discrimination experienced by women, women's rights were protected by the provisions of the general human rights treaties (ICCPR and ICESCR) outlined above. Such generic protection supplemented by certain very specific protection was never going to be entirely satisfactory in dealing with the generalised discrimination faced by women globally. Thus the CSW was mandated by the Economic and Social Council (ECOSOC), following a request by the General Assembly,[20] to prepare a draft declaration to deal comprehensively with the entirety of the discrimination faced by women. The CSW began the process of drafting such a declaration in 1965. After a lengthy drafting process, the Declaration on the Elimination of Discrimination against Women was adopted on 7 November 1967.[21] Even this piece of soft law engendered much discord during the drafting process, especially in regard to its Article 6, which deals with the contentious issue of the equality of spouses in various familial contexts. The issue revolved around whether it was possible, even if it was desirable, to abolish discriminatory customary practices within marriage by legislation, rather than by a process of gradual re-education.

In the late 1960s, a greater appreciation of the discrimination faced by women on a generalised basis provoked a number of NGOs working in the field to demand greater protection. In 1972 the CSW began to consider the possibility of the introduction of a legally binding text to translate the soft law of the Declaration into the hard law of internationally binding treaty stipulations. After much preliminary work by its Working Group tasked to reflect on the development of a legally binding framework for the rights of women, in 1974 the CSW decided to press ahead with the preparation of a general treaty, without prejudice to later efforts at eliminating discrimination against women in targeted fields. Extensive drafting work took place in the CSW and the Third Committee of the General Assembly from 1977–79. The Convention on the Elimination of All Forms of Discrimination against Women[22] was adopted finally on 18 December 1979 by the General Assembly by 130 votes to none (10 States abstained).[23] On 3 September 1981, 30 days after its 20th ratification (in accordance with its Article 27(1)), the Convention entered into force.[24] As of 15 December

[19] 521 UNTS 231; see also: Recommendation on Consent to Marriage, Minimum Age for Marriage and Registration of Marriages, UNGA Res 2018(XX) of 1 November 1965.

[20] UNGA Res 1921 (XVIII) of 5 December 1963.

[21] UNGA Res A/RES/2263 (XXII) of 7 November 1967.

[22] 1249 UNTS 13.

[23] UNGA Res 34/180.

[24] See generally: 'Progress achieved in the Implementation of the Convention on the Elimination of All Forms of Discrimination against Women: Report by the Committee on the Elimination of Discrimination against Women' (A/CONF.177/7) from which this description of events is drawn, and which the author duly acknowledges.

2009, there are 186 States parties to the Convention. At the time of entry into force of the Convention, under Article 17 of the Convention, CEDAW began to exercise the functions with which it was entrusted with a complement of 18 independent experts. Today, CEDAW has a membership of 23 experts, including only one man: Mr Cornelis (Cees) Flinterman (Netherlands).[25] As of 1 January 2008, the servicing of CEDAW has been transferred from the Division for the Advancement of Women (DAW) to the Office of the High Commissioner for Human Rights (OHCHR).

One of the key issues which have plagued the implementation of this Convention has been the matter of reservations.[26] Essentially, the text of the Convention permits the deposit of reservations made by States parties at the same time as ratification or accession. However, Article 28(2) states that: '[a] reservation incompatible with the object and purpose of the present Convention shall not be permitted'. Many States parties have entered reservations to particular Articles (especially Article 16, which deals with the elimination of discrimination against women in all matters relating to marriage and family relations) on the grounds that 'national law, tradition, religion or culture' is not compatible with the Convention. Other States parties have entered a reservation to Article 2 (which contains the core undertakings under the Convention to eliminate discrimination against women) on the basis that their own national constitutions specifically exclude all discrimination against women. In short, the Convention is undermined systematically with reservations which, for many States parties, make a mockery out of their fundamental obligations under the

[25] On the UN Human Rights Treaty Body System as a whole see A Bayefsky, *The UN Human Rights Treaty System: Universality at the Crossroads* (Ardsley, Transnational Publishers, 2001); on CEDAW generally see: AH Robertson and JG Merrills, *Human Rights in the World: An Introduction to the Study of the International Protection of Human Rights* Manchester, Manchester University Press, 1996) 101–04; A Byrnes, 'The "Other" Human Rights Treaty Body: The Work of CEDAW' (1991) 14 *Yale Journal of International Law* 1; C Flinterman, 'United Nations Human Rights Reform: Some Reflections of a CEDAW Member' (2003) 21 *Netherlands Quarterly Human Rights* 621; R Jacobson, 'The Committee on Elimination of Discrimination Against Women' in P Alston (ed), *The United Nations and Human Rights: A Critical Appraisal* (Oxford, Clarendon Press, 1992); MR Bustelo, 'The Committee on Elimination of Discrimination Against Women at the Crossroads' in P Alston and J Crawford (eds), *The Future of UN Human Rights Treaty Monitoring* (Cambridge, Cambridge University Press, 2000); H Shin, 'CEDAW and Women's Human Rights: Achievements and Obstacles', Paper presented at the Castan Centre for Human Rights Law's Annual Conference—Human Rights 2004: The Year in Review, 3 December 2004, www.law.monash.edu.au/castancentre/events/2004/heisoo-shin-paper.pdf.

[26] There is a significant amount of literature on the subject of reservations to human rights treaties generally and some studies of the position as regards this Convention. See generally: L Lijnzaad, *Reservations to UN Human Rights Treaties: Ratify and Ruin?* (The Hague, Martinus Nijhoff, 1995); see in particular: B Clarke, 'The Vienna Convention Reservations Regime and the Convention on Discrimination Against Women' (1991) 85 *AJIL* 281; R Cook, 'Reservations to the Convention on the Elimination of All Forms of Discrimination Against Women' (1990) 30 *Virginia Journal of International Law* 643.

Convention.[27] As Article 28(2) permits reservations unless they conflict with the 'object and purpose' of the treaty (or with the provisions of general international law), States have had an almost unlimited license to destroy the heart of their obligations while paying lip service to the general principle of non-discrimination on grounds of gender.

In its 1997 preliminary conclusions on reservations to normative multilateral treaties including human rights treaties, the International Law Commission (ILC) stated that:

> where these treaties are silent on the subject, the monitoring bodies established thereby are competent to comment upon and express recommendations with regard, inter alia, to the admissibility of reservations by States, in order to carry out the functions assigned to them.[28]

Nevertheless, the ILC considered still that it was not appropriate for human rights treaty bodies to decide on the consequences of an invalid reservation and that it was the reserving State party that had the responsibility to take appropriate action. Thus, a State party may: (1) maintain its reservation, after examining its propriety in good faith; (2) withdraw its reservation; (3) replace the impermissible reservation with an amended and permissible one; or (4) denounce the treaty in question. In July 2003, members of the ILC met with members of the HRC to discuss the HRC's General Comment No 24 and the 1997 preliminary conclusions. Since then, it seems that the position of the ILC has changed; the Special Rapporteur of the ILC on Reservations to Treaties, Professor Alain Pellet, has proposed draft guideline 3.2.1, which states that: 'where a treaty establishes a body to monitor application of the treaty, that body shall be competent, for the purpose of discharging the functions entrusted to it, to assess the validity of reservations formulated by a State'.[29] This text has not been adopted yet by the ILC.[30] CEDAW has made two General Recommendations (Numbers 4 and 20)[31] and a Statement[32] on reservations in an attempt to persuade States parties to remove or modify their reservations.[33] In addition, in

[27] See CEDAW/SP/2006/2: 'Declarations, Reservations, Objections and Notifications of Withdrawal of Reservations relating to the Convention on the Elimination of All Forms of Discrimination against Women'; see also HB Schöpp-Schilling, 'Rservations to CEDAW: An Unresolved Issue or (No) New Developments?' in I Ziemele (ed), *Reservations to Human Rights Treaties and the Vienna Convention Regime: Conflict, Harmony or Reconciliation,* (Leiden, Martinus Nijhoff, 2004).

[28] A/52/10, para 157.

[29] A/CN.4/558/Add 2, annex.

[30] See CEDAW/C/2008/II/WP 2, 'Working Paper on Reservations in the Context of Individual Communications', dated 20 May 2008.

[31] There have been 25 General Recommendations altogether.

[32] UN GAOR 53rd Session, Supplement No 38 (A/53/38/Rev 1), Report of the Committee on the Elimination of Discrimination against Women, vol II, ch I A, para 8.

[33] See www.un.org/womenwatch/daw/cedaw/reservations.htm, which provides the basis of the remarks on reservations and which the author duly acknowledges.

its Recommendation Number 21 on Equality in Marriage and Family Relations, CEDAW addressed reservations to Article 16; it noted that a number of States parties had made reservations in whole or in part to Article 16 and required States to progress to the stage where reservations, particularly to Article 16, will be withdrawn. These pleas seem to be bearing fruit as recently a number of States have withdrawn reservations to the Convention or have expressed the intention of doing so. However, withdrawal of reservations to either Article 2 or 16 still needs further impetus.

III. THE OPTIONAL PROTOCOL TO THE CONVENTION ON THE ELIMINATION OF ALL FORMS OF DISCRIMINATION AGAINST WOMEN

The International Convention on the Elimination of All Forms of Racial Discrimination contains within Article 14 an optional right of individual communication. The International Covenant on Civil and Political Rights contains a similar right, but in its attached Protocol (OP).[34] By contrast, the Convention on the Elimination of All Forms of Discrimination against Women contained no such right at the outset, because, although the matter was discussed, one of the reasons for the failure to include it was that some, such as the representative of Hungary in the CSW, considered that gender-based discrimination did not merit such a procedure, as it did not equate to 'serious international crimes' such as apartheid and race discrimination. This was a grave weakness. An individual communication system would have strengthened considerably the implementation of the engagements entered into by the State parties by reaching deep into the heart of a State party's domestic law systems, beyond the reach of the more generalised reporting procedure. The first substantial impetus for the development of such a procedure was provided at the World Conference on Human Rights in Vienna in June 1993. The Vienna Declaration and Programme of Action in its paragraph 40 states that:

> [n]ew procedures should be adopted to strengthen implementation of the commitment to women's equality and the human rights of women. The Commission on the Status of Women and the Committee on the Elimination of Discrimination against Women should quickly examine the possibility of introducing the right of petition through the preparation of an optional protocol to the Convention on the Elimination of Discrimination against Women.[35]

[34] 999 UNTS 171.

[35] UN doc A/CONF 157/24, para 40; PR Ghandhi, *Blackstone's International Human Rights Documents*, 6th edn (Oxford, Oxford University Press, 2008) 464; the desirability of an optional protocol had also been suggested by Theodor Meron: see 'Enhancing the Effectiveness of the Prohibition of Discrimination against Women' (1990) 84 *AJIL* 213.

Between 29 September and 1 October 1994 an Expert Group Meeting on the Adoption of an Optional Protocol to the Convention on the Elimination of All Forms of Discrimination against Women was organised by the Women in the Law Project (International Human Rights Group) and the Maastricht Centre for Human Rights at the University of Limburg, which attracted members of CEDAW, CERD and the HRC and many other experts in the field on international human rights law and the human rights of women. It produced a draft Optional Protocol (OP).

Between January and February 1995, CEDAW adopted Suggestion No 7 outlining possible elements of an optional protocol. In March 1995, at the invitation of the CSW, Governments, IGOs, and NGOs submitted their views via the Secretary-General of the UN. Fresh impetus was provided by the Fourth World Conference on Women at Beijing in September 1995, which requested the support of all member States of the UN in the elaboration of an optional protocol.[36]

In March 1996 CSW formed an open-ended Working Group on the OP and began discussion. The CSW recommended that the Working Group continue its discussions in 1997, but in order to facilitate its task requested the Secretary-General to provide reports on: (1) other international individual procedures; and (2) the views of Governments, IGOs and NGOs.

Serious elaboration of an optional protocol commenced in March 1997, when the open-ended Working Group discussed a draft prepared by the chairperson (Ms Worgetter). A representative of CEDAW (Ms Cartright) was invited to be present as a resource person and various NGOs made statements. Progress was made. A first reading of the full draft was concluded. The text of some of the Articles was agreed and some elaborations and amendments were suggested to the remaining Articles.

The open-ended Working Group continued its elaboration in March 1998. It is interesting to note that at this comparatively early stage, in addition to Ms Cartright (of CEDAW) being present again as a resource person, a member of the HRC was also invited to be present to elaborate on its practice and procedure under the OP, together with a representative of the OHCHR, to provide more generalised information on the operation of other individual communication procedures and a representative from the Secretariat Office of Programme Planning, Budget and Accounts to advise on budgetary matters. Very substantial progress was made, including a complete second reading of the chairperson's draft and an agreement that a short preamble be incorporated to introduce the document. The discussions were informed by a report of the Secretary-General comparing the draft protocol with existing international human rights instruments.

[36] UN doc A/CONF 177/20, Platform for Action, 97, para 230(k).

In March 1999, the Open-ended Working Group continued its elaboration and finally adopted the protocol as did the CSW together with a draft resolution for the Economic and Social Council (ECOSOC) to adopt, which it did.

The General Assembly adopted the OP on 6 October 1999, without reference to a Main Committee.[37] The instrument was opened for signature and ratification on 10 December 1999, and entered into force on 22 December 2000 subsequent to receipt of its tenth instrument of ratification.[38] As of 31 July 2008, there were 90 States parties to the OP, including the UK.

IV. A COMPARATIVE ANALYSIS OF THE OPTIONAL PROTOCOL TO CONVENTION ON ELIMINATION OF ALL FORMS OF DISCRIMINATION AGAINST WOMEN

The OP to the Women's Convention is the sole method of dispute settlement for that instrument.[39] From a detailed textual examination of the OP, it is manifest that the drafters took as their inspiration the terms of the OP to the ICCPR together with the jurisprudence generated thereon by the HRC under the individual communication procedure. Of course, the drafters also had the benefit of being able to review the practice of CERD under the International Convention on the Elimination of All Forms of Racial Discrimination[40] and CAT under the Convention Against Torture and Other Cruel, Inhuman or Degrading Treatment or Punishment (Torture Convention).[41]

[37] A/RES/54/4.

[38] The account of the drafting process is drawn from: www.un.org/womenwatch/daw/cedaw/protocol/history.htm and which the author gratefully acknowledges. See also: A Byrnes, 'Slow and Steady Wins the Race? The Development of an Optional Protocol to the Women's Convention' (1997) 91 *Proceedings of the American Society of International Law* 383; A Byrnes and J Connors, 'Enforcing the Human Rights of Women: A Complaints Procedure for the Women's Convention?' (1996) 21 *Brooklyn Journal of International Law* 682; S Cartright, 'Rights and Remedies: the Drafting of an Optional Protocol to the Convention on the Elimination of All Forms of Discrimination Against Women' (1998) 9 *Otago Law Review* 239; A Worgetter, 'The Draft Optional Protocol to the Law on the Elimination of All Forms of Discrimination Against Women' (1997) 2 *Austrian Review of International and European Law* 261; U O'Hare 'Ending the "Ghettoisation": The Rights of Individual Petition to the Women's Convention' (1997) 5 *Web Journal of Current Legal Issues*; U O'Hare, 'Realizing Human Rights of Women' (1999) 21 *Human Rights Quarterly* 364.

[39] See generally I Boerefijn, 'The Women's Convention'(2005) 1 *International Studies Journal* 1; see especially C Tomuschat, 'Learning from the Committee's Experience: The Optional Protocol to the Convention Banning Discrimination Against Women' in H von Jörn Ipsen and E Schmidt-Jortzig (eds), *Festchrift für Dieter Rausching* (Köln, Carl Heymans Verlag KG, 2001); 'Issues arising under the Optional Protocol to the Convention on the Elimination of All Forms of Discrimination against Women', which the author respectfully acknowledges; see also CEDAW/C/2004/I/WP.2, dated 19 November 2003, prepared by Dr I Boerefijn.

[40] 660 UNTS 195.

[41] 1465 UNTS 85.

Some particular provisions of the dispute settlement provisions of the OP to the Women's Convention will be examined now to determine if a coherent or fragmentary picture emerges in the Human Rights Treaty Body Systems under discussion here. In addition, reference will be made to the jurisprudence of CEDAW where relevant. To date, 18 communications have been registered since the OP to the Women's Convention entered into force. At its 40th session, CEDAW discontinued consideration of one communication which had become moot. Decisions have been reached in 10 decided cases, involving issues as diverse as domestic violence, effects of divorce, social security benefits, enforced sterilisation, succession to titles of nobility, wearing of headscarves, asylum/deportation and transfer of nationality. Significantly, all these cases have concerned European States members of the Council of Europe and (with the exception of Turkey) the European Union.

Article 1 of both the OP to the ICCPR and to the Women's Convention is quite similar. However, Article 1 of the OP to the Women's Convention is short and succinct. It outlines simply the basic competence of CEDAW to receive and consider individual communications. Unlike Article 1 of the OP to the ICCPR ('individuals … who claim to be victims of a violation'), it does not mention the 'victim' requirement at this stage.

However, there is one very important difference between the Article 1 OP texts of both instruments: the OP to the ICCPR specifies that only individuals 'subject to its jurisdiction' may bring admissible communications against a State party; this is a reflection of the requirement in Article 2(1) of the ICCPR itself that State parties have the obligation to respect and to ensure the rights recognised in that instrument to 'all individuals within its territory and subject to its jurisdiction'. It is not surprising that that this conflicting phraseology has caused the Human Rights Committee some considerable difficulty in interpretation and attracted much controversy by its pronouncements that sometimes jurisdiction can be extra-territorial.[42] As there is no such similar clause in the Women's

[42] See PR Ghandhi, *The Human Rights Committee and the Right of Individual Communication: Law and Practice* (Aldershot, Ashgate, 1998) 125–39; in General Comment No 31 [80] at para 10, the HRC has said: 'States parties are required by Article 2, paragraph 1, to respect and to ensure the Covenant rights to all persons who may be within its territory and to all persons subject to their jurisdiction. This means that a State party must respect and ensure the rights laid down in the Covenant to anyone within the power or effective control of that State party, even if not situated within the territory of that State party. … This principle also applies to those within the power or effective control of the forces of a State party acting outside its territory, regardless of the circumstances in which such power or effective control was obtained, such as forces constituting a national contingent of a State party assigned to an international peace-keeping or peace-enforcement operation' (CCPR/C/21/Rev.1/Add.13, 26 May 2004); this formulation was criticised heavily in the UK's 6th Periodic Report at para 59(b) (CCPR/C/GBR/6, 18 May 2007); for a recent attack over the claimed jurisdictional reach of the ICCPR, see 'Comments by the Government of the United States of America on the Concluding Observations of the Human Rights Committee' CCPR/C/USA/CO/3/Rev 1/Add 1, 12 February 2008.

Convention, it was unnecessary obviously to insert an equivalent provision in its OP. However, it should be noticed that Article 2 of the OP to the Women's Convention (discussed below) does use the expression 'under the jurisdiction of a State party'. Nevertheless, it is obvious from the nature of the Women's Convention that in its case, the obligations undertaken by the State party are exclusively territorial: a State party cannot eliminate gender-based discrimination outside its own territory. This is certainly a point of fragmentation between the texts of the two different instruments and the interpretation of them by the treaty bodies concerned. This situation has been fragmented further by the recent Order of the International Court of Justice at The Hague declaring that 'there is no restriction of a general nature in CERD relating to its territorial application' and that '[the] provisions of CERD generally appear to apply … to the actions of a State party when it acts beyond its territory'.[43] This is certainly very controversial. There is nothing in the *travaux préparatoires* to indicate that the drafters had anything in mind other than a strictly territorial jurisdiction. As with the Women's Convention, a State party cannot eliminate race discrimination extra-territorially. It also ignores the circumstances that gave rise to the drafting of Race Discrimination Convention.

Article 2 of the OP to the Women's Convention departs in some significant details from the approach adopted by the OP to the ICCPR. Article 2 of the OP to the ICCPR specifies that only 'individuals' may bring claims for violation of their Covenant rights against a State party. Thus, the OP to the ICCPR adopted a very restrictive terminology, which from its earliest days the Human Rights Committee had to develop constructively in its jurisprudence to meet the demands of proper actionability of appropriate claims. Indeed, the present Rules of Procedure of the HRC state that:

> [n]ormally, the communication should be submitted by the individual personally or by that individual's representative; a communication submitted on behalf of an alleged victim may, however, be accepted when it appears that the individual in question is unable to submit the communication personally.[44]

Naturally, this seemingly straight forward provision has resulted in a detailed case-law development by the HRC. In essence, the HRC has held over a number of decisions that:

(1) if the individual victim can bring a claim, so too can groups of individuals;
(2) legal representatives, counsel and lawyers may necessarily bring claims on behalf of their clients;

[43] Case Concerning the Application of the International Convention on the Elimination of All Forms of Racial Discrimination, Order of the Court, 15 October 2008, www.icj-cij.org/docket/files/140/14801.pdf.
[44] CCPR/C/3/Rev 8, 22 September 2005.

(3) other cases where the author may be accepted as having the necessary authority include:
 (a) those who can show a close family connection; and
 (b) unrelated third parties where they can show some genuine link;

 the author has to show clear evidence of the grounds and circumstances justifying his action on behalf of the alleged victim;

 the onus of proof is on the author to justify his authority;

 in addition to showing the grounds and circumstances justifying his action, the author must give reasons for believing that the alleged victim would approve him acting on his behalf and also why he believes that the alleged victim is unable to act on his own behalf;

 in such cases a power of attorney or some other documented proof that the author is authorised to act on behalf of the alleged victim is required;

(4) an organisation as such cannot submit a valid communication as personal standing is required; and
(5) unincorporated associations and companies cannot sue for lack of *locus standi*.[45]

Lessons have been learned from the experience of the HRC and, in order to create a harmonised system, the text of Article 2 of the OP to the Women's Convention inserts more detail in several respects than the equivalent provision in the OP to the ICCPR. In particular, the text makes clear that communications may be submitted by those other than the actual 'victim' and can be submitted by 'groups of individuals'. It is particularly important to allow 'groups of individuals' and NGOs to petition in the case of a convention dealing with group rights, in this case the group rights of women. Indeed, it was predicted in 1997 that the NGOs would make great use of the OP.[46] Unfortunately, this has not yet happened. To date only three cases have been brought by NGOs; two of these cases were brought by the Vienna Intervention Centre Against Domestic Violence and the Association for Women's Access to Justice;[47] one of these cases was brought by the European Roma Rights Centre and Legal Defence Bureau for National and Ethnic Minorities.[48] In addition, the author has been represented by legal counsel in only one case.[49] One

[45] See PR Ghandhi, above n 42 at 84–90.

[46] See MA Freeman, 'The Human Rights under the CEDAW Convention: Complexities and Opportunities of Compliance' (1997) 91 *Proceedings of the American Society of International Law* 378, 382.

[47] *H Goekce, H Goekce and G Goekce v Austria* (CEDAW/C/39/D/5/2005) and *B Akbak, G Khan and M Özdemir v Austria* (CEDAW/C/39/D/6/2005).

[48] *AS v Hungary* (CEDAW/C/36/D/4/2004).

[49] *Kayhan v Turkey* (CEDAW/C/34/D/8/2005).

can only speculate about the minimal involvement of the NGO sector in individual communications to date. Certainly, NGOs working in the field of Women's Rights are aware of the possibilities. Training sessions have been held by the Law Society's International Human Rights Committee and other members of civil society generally. The most plausible explanation is that at present NGOs prefer to channel communications to the European Court of Human Rights (ECtHR) at Strasbourg or the HRC in Geneva where the facts permit such a submission. CEDAW will need to reflect carefully on this issue. Awareness and training are key factors, but there may be others that need addressing. In particular, the responsibility of the State party in this dimension is a critical feature. CEDAW has made it clear that States parties must take prime responsibility and concrete measures to make the Women's Convention and its OP widely known: this includes public awareness and training programmes initiated by the State party, together with the duty incumbent on it to raise awareness among women of their rights under the Convention and its communication procedures; it includes also the duty to make the jurisprudence of CEDAW an integral part of educational curricula, including for legal education, and the training of judicial officers, judges, lawyers and prosecutors. The UK Government has failed signally to discharge this duty.[50]

Furthermore, it is also stated explicitly in the second sentence of the text of Article 2 of the OP to the Women's Convention that: '[w]here a communication is submitted on behalf of individuals or groups of individuals, this shall be with their consent unless the author can justify acting on their behalf without their consent'. This seems in basic harmony with the jurisprudence of the HRC. However, it is suggested that unintentionally the wording of the OP to the CEDAW provision may actually be more restrictive in as much as under the OP to the ICCPR only unrelated third parties and not close relatives seem to be required to satisfy the additional requirement of showing 'consent'. It may be assumed that CEDAW will follow the jurisprudence of the HRC in determining when an author can justify acting without 'consent' when he or she is not a close relative. Thus, Rule 68(3) of CEDAW's Rules of Procedure specifies that where an author is acting on behalf of an alleged victim without her consent, she/he must provide written reasons justifying such action.[51] Equally, CEDAW will find the jurisprudence of the HRC on the meaning of 'groups of individuals' instructive, particularly when grappling with the difficult issue of when an unrelated third party

[50] See in particular Concluding Observations of CEDAW: UK of Great Britain and Northern Ireland, 5th and 6th Periodic Reports, CEDAW/C/GBR/CO/6, 18 July 2008.

[51] Rules of Procedure of CEDAW, UN GAOR, 56th Session, Supp No 38 (A/56/38), annex 1.

may be permitted to act on behalf of such a group without their consent. It is suggested that, the second sentence of Article 2 of the OP to the Women's Convention is not intended to cover situations where national legislation might infringe women's rights as a whole or generally, but rather where discrimination is visited on a finite group of women. The drafters never envisaged the possibility that CEDAW would entertain allegations of breaches of the Convention *in abstracto* by way of an *actio popularis* in this regard.[52] This is fully consonant with the application of the OP to the ICCPR, and presents a unified picture with that of the UN Human Rights Treaty Monitoring Bodies collectively. Article 2 of the OP to the Women's Convention also endorses the requirement that valid complaints can only be received from those persons claiming to be 'victims of a violation' or by those authorised to act on their behalf. In this connection, it is logical to assume that CEDAW will have appropriate regard to the meaning of the notion of the 'victim' developed by the HRC in its jurisprudence in order to ensure consistency of interpretation and application.[53]

Article 4(1) of the OP to the Women's Convention deals with the requirement to exhaust all available domestic remedies. This applies unless the application of the remedies is unreasonably prolonged. This is a normal requirement in general international law based on the need to ensure that the State party is given the opportunity to deal with any alleged infringement of its international obligations through its own national legal order and administrative systems. This mirrors the provision in Article 5(2)(b) of the OP to the ICCPR. However, the version in the OP to the Women's Convention goes much further and adds that the requirement to exhaust all domestic remedies shall also not apply where it is 'unlikely to bring effective relief'. The addition of this requirement is hardly surprising given that the drafters had in mind the constant jurisprudence of the HRC that only remedies that are effective in principle (the burden of showing that such remedies exist being on the State party) need be exhausted (unless there are special circumstances) in accordance with the generally accepted principles of international law with regard to the exhaustion of domestic remedies as applied in the field of human rights.[54] In accordance with these well established principles, in *Dung Thi Thuy Nguyen v The Netherlands*,[55] CEDAW declared that particular appeal proceedings would be 'unlikely to bring relief' and therefore

[52] See Reports of the UN Secretary-General, UN doc E/CN.6/1996/10, paras 64–74 dated 10 January 1996 and UN doc E/CN.6/1997/5, paras 80–98 dated 18 February 1997.

[53] See PR Ghandhi, above n 42 at 90–117.

[54] See PR Ghandhi, above n 42 at 239–75.

[55] CEDAW/C/36/D/3/2004.

did not have to be exhausted on grounds of futility.[56] Similarly, in *AS v Hungary*,[57] CEDAW held that special or extraordinary remedies do not have to be exhausted in congruence with the jurisprudence of the HRC.[58]

The classic operation of the general principle is illustrated by *B-J v Germany*,[59] in which divorce proceedings initiated by the author's husband in May 1999 became final on 28 July 2000 together with the matter of the equalisation of pensions. CEDAW noted that separate proceedings regarding the equalisation of accrued gains and maintenance after termination of marriage had not been settled finally at the date of CEDAW's decision on 14 July 2004. The author did not deny that this was the case nor had she argued convincingly in the view of the majority of the Committee that the proceedings had been unreasonably prolonged or unlikely to bring effective relief. Accordingly, the claims were inadmissible for failure to exhaust all available domestic remedies. However, two members of CEDAW, Ms Krisztina Morvai and Ms Meriem Belmihoub-Zerdani, dissented on this issue. The dissentients argued that the proceedings for accrued gains and spousal maintenance had been on going for about five years and still no final decision had been reached. In highly emotive language, the dissentients argued that the subject matter of these proceedings concerned 'the determination and granting of the financial/material sources of the survival of the author'. The dissentients considered various factors such as the age of the author (57 years old), the length of the marriage (some 30 years), the devotion of the author's whole married life to unpaid work for the family allowing her husband to advance his career and the fact that at her age she would have very little prospect of securing a job on the open labour market in view of her lack of work experience. The dissentients held that in these circumstances the domestic courts should have determined and granted a decent maintenance for her a long time ago. A legal system that permitted the finalisation of contested divorce proceedings

[56] A similar conclusion was reached in H Goekce, H Goekce and G *Guekce (descendants of the deceased) v Austria* (CEDAW/C/39/D/5/2005); see also the factually almost identical case of *B Akbak, G Khan and M Özdemir (descendants of the deceased) v Austria* (CEDAW/C/39/D/6/2005), where CEDAW confirmed that the moment for deciding whether an applicant has exhausted domestic remedies is the moment of consideration of the communication generally, following the jurisprudence of the HRC in cases such as *Taright, Touadi, Remli and Yousfi v Algeria* (communication no 1085/2002) and *Koi v Portugal* (communication no 925/2000); the influence and jurisprudence of established international human rights instances, especially that of the HRC, is obviously considered by CEDAW to be of great importance in establishing a coherent and congruent jurisprudence across the whole UN Human Rights Treaty Body System.

[57] CEDAW/C/36/D/4/2004.

[58] See PR Ghandhi, above n 42 at 267–68.

[59] CEDAW/C/31/D/1/2003.

in approximately one year (May 1999 to July 2000), should be able to finalise post-divorce maintenance and accrued gains with similar speed and efficiency. This delay amounted to a serious violation of the author's human rights. Thus, in all the circumstances, the application of the remedies was unreasonably prolonged and accordingly the exception to the need to exhaust domestic remedies applied in this case. The plight of the author was certainly a matter of deep concern, but it is doubtful whether the dissentients were right in law, as the author herself had not argued convincingly that the proceedings were unreasonably prolonged or unlikely to bring effective relief.[60]

By contrast, *AT v Hungary*[61] involved a very serious case of regular domestic gender-based violence inflicted on the author by her common law husband (who possessed a firearm) and threats to kill the author and rape the children of the partnership, one of whom was severely brain damaged. The author stated that she had not gone to a shelter for battered wives because there did not exist any shelter in the country that could accommodate a fully disabled child together with his sister and the author. The State party conceded that the currently available remedies in Hungary were incapable of providing immediate protection to the author from the ill-treatment meted out to her by her husband. Thus, CEDAW was not precluded from considering the communication on the ground of non-exhaustion of domestic remedies under Article 4(1) of the OP.

Article 4(2)(a) of the OP to the Women's Convention deals with the issue of exhaustion of other international remedies as a precondition of the invocation of the individual communication procedure. This provision mirrors the equivalent accommodation in Article 5(2)(a) of the OP to ICCPR, but adds some further detail. Under the OP to the ICCPR, any matter which is not 'being examined' under another procedure of international investigation or settlement is capable of being adjudicated upon by the HRC. This means that the HRC can hear communications after the petitioner has exhausted other avenues of relief in other tribunals or treaty monitoring bodies such as the ECtHR, the Inter-American Court of Human Rights, CERD, CAT or CEDAW. Only simultaneous consideration is prevented. This caused Council of Europe countries substantial difficulties as it was thought to be tantamount to allowing appeals against the decision of the Strasbourg Court to the HRC in Geneva. The difficulty was exacerbated by the restrictive interpretation given to the words 'the same matter', allowing the HRC maximum penetration into the sphere of operation of regional courts by declaring that the issue before the HRC

[60] See also *NSF v UK* (CEDAW/C38/D/10/2005) and *Salgado v UK* (CEDAW/C/37/D/11/2006).

[61] CEDAW/C/32/D/2/2003.

was not indeed 'the same matter' as had been investigated before by other jurisdictions. Accordingly, the competence of the HRC to examine communications when 'the same matter' is not being examined under another procedure of international investigation was narrowed in many cases by reservations entered to Article 5(2)(a) by a number of Council of Europe countries which made reservations precluding any consideration of the matter by the HRC where 'the same matter' had already been examined in another procedure of international investigation. These reservations were prompted by a resolution of the Committee of Ministers of the Council of Europe.[62] The solution adopted by the drafters of the OP to the Women's Convention was to take the wider view and add the further requirement that CEDAW be debarred from hearing a communication if 'the same matter' has already been dealt with by another procedure of international investigation or settlement by adding the words 'has been' to 'is being examined'. The solution adopted is different to that adopted by the HRC in its jurisprudence, but no less valid. It is the one adopted in Article 22(5)(a) of the Torture Convention. Nevertheless, it is suggested that it would have been more appropriate to have followed the drafting pattern of the OP to the ICCPR in the case of discrimination against women, which could conceivably come before a variety of international human rights instances with different normative conclusions. Thus, CEDAW sitting in New York or now also in Geneva (the 40th session of CEDAW was the first to be held there) will not be able to entertain any communications that relate to 'the same matter' that have been litigated in any other international human rights forum. As a result of pre-existing provisions conflicting with each other (HRC and CAT), this is a situation in which there was bound to be fragmentation, whatever solution was adopted by the drafters of the OP to the Women's Convention. It is suggested that in this case the drafters adopted the wrong solution for the reasons given above.

CEDAW has only had one occasion to consider this provision. The issue which arose in *Kayhan v Turkey*[63] was dismissal of a school teacher for wearing a head scarf. A key admissibility issue to be considered by CEDAW was whether the communication was inadmissible under Article 4(2)(a) of the OP because the ECtHR had examined a case (*Sahin v Turkey*) that was very similar. The author pointed out that she had not submitted her complaint to any other international bodies and that her case was rather different to the one heard in Strasbourg. CEDAW cited the decision of the HRC in *Fanali v Italy* (communication no 075/1980) that the identity of the author was a critical feature in deciding whether the 'same

[62] (1970) Yearbook of the European Convention on Human Rights 74–76.
[63] CEDAW/C/34/D/8/2005.

matter' had been litigated elsewhere at another international instance.[64] Following the precedent set by the HRC, CEDAW held that this ground of admissibility was no bar as the author was an entirely different person to the applicant at the ECtHR.[65] Thus, it can be seen that complementary treaty body jurisprudence is being developed in this regard.

Article 5 of the OP to CEDAW represents a radical textual departure from the OP to the ICCPR, or indeed any other international human rights treaty; it could be described correctly as ground-breaking in character. It seeks to assert the responsibility of CEDAW to ensure that States parties are accountable for any unjustifiable interference with the individual once a communication has been lodged. It states that:

> 1. At any time after receipt of a communication and before a determination on the merits has been reached, the Committee may transmit to the State party concerned for its urgent consideration a request that the State party take such interim measures as may be necessary to avoid possible irreparable damage to the victim or victims of the alleged violation.
> 2. Where the Committee exercises its discretion under paragraph 1, this does not imply a determination on admissibility or on the merits of a communication.

Thus, CEDAW is explicitly given the power to request interim measures of relief in the OP treaty itself. This gives CEDAW an immensely valuable tool, which, in theory at least, could prove to be a formidable weapon in protecting the rights of petitioners in a vulnerable position at the time of submission of the communication or who become so subsequently as a result of the communication. Every human rights tribunal requires the ability to issue interim orders to protect the rights of applicants pending a final determination on the merits of the case; this is particularly important where the life of the author may be at stake. This is in sharp contradistinction to the OP to the ICCPR which makes no mention at all of interim measures. However, at its first session after some considerable discussion, the HRC adopted a Rule on interim measures (which some members of the HRC felt went beyond the power conferred on it by the OP). The HRC's current provision is contained in Rule 92 of its Rules of Procedure. It states:

> [t]he Committee may, prior to forwarding its Views on the communication to the State party concerned, inform that State of its Views as to whether interim measures may be desirable to avoid irreparable harm to the victim of an alleged violation. In doing so, the Committee shall inform the State party concerned

[64] The *Fanali* case is discussed fully in PR Ghandhi, above n 42 at 223–24.

[65] For a discussion of these issues, see JG Merrills, 'The Mosaic of International Dispute Settlement Procedures: Complementary or Contradictory' (2007) 54 *Netherlands International Law Review* 361, 387–88; C Phuong, 'The Relationship between the European Court of Human Rights and the Human Rights Committee: Has the "Same Matter" already been "Examined"'? (2007) 7 *Human Rights Law Review* 385.

> that such an expression of its Views on interim measures does not imply a determination on the merits of the communication.[66]

Originally, the Special Rapporteur on Death Penalty cases was authorised to take Rule 92 decisions on behalf of the Committee (at that point these cases raised the issue most starkly), but since 1992 this power has been vested in the Special Rapporteur on New Communications in view of the wide range of circumstances that may give rise to a request for interim measures. It should be observed also for the HRC that interim measures are excluded from the Rules concerning confidentiality stipulated in Rule 102, and 'shall be made public'.[67] The twin principles of preservation and protection pending the resolution of the communication are at the jurisprudential heart of the interim measures doctrine. It may be observed that the Rules of Procedure of CEDAW also authorise a Working Group or Rapporteur to issue requests in the same manner as the plenary Committee.[68] In addition, Rule 63(3) states that, where an interim measures request is made by a Working Group or Rapporteur, those bodies must inform immediately CEDAW members of the nature of the request and the communication to which it relates.

The formulation in the OP to the Women's Convention differs in one material respect to that contained in the HRC's Rule 92. In particular, the formulation adopted by the OP provision may at first glance be thought to be marginally stronger as it uses the word 'request' rather than the terminology used by Rule 92, which uses the word 'Views'; however, given the HRC's difficulties with ensuring compliance with its interim measures requests, as they are to all intents and purposes termed, this benefit may be illusory. Other differences include the request on States parties to the Women's Convention to give 'urgent consideration' to a request from CEDAW for interim measures. Also, it may be noticed that the OP to the Women's Convention provision makes it clear that a request for interim measures does not imply any determination on admissibility either. However, strangely Rule 63(4) of CEDAW's Rules of Procedure only mentions that a request for interim measures does not imply a determination of the merits.

There are six broad categories in which interim measures requests have been granted by the HRC:

(1) where the health and well-being of an individual is concerned;
(2) where the life or lives of individuals (or groups of individuals) may be in jeopardy;

[66] Rules of Procedure of the HRC, CCPR/C/3/Rev 8, 22 September 2005.
[67] R 102(5).
[68] R 63(2) of the Rules of Procedure of CEDAW, UN GAOR, 56th Session, Supp No 38 (A/56/38) annex 1.

(3) deportation and extradition cases;
(4) threats to the way of life of a community;
(5) preservation of evidence pendente lite; and
(6) death penalty cases.

Several of these instances could arise in the context of discrimination against Women. The record of the HRC in obtaining compliance with its requests has been chequered. Since the mid-1990s, there has been a worrying increase in the number of stays of execution in death penalty cases which have been ignored deliberately by the States parties. The list of States ignoring Rule 92 requests for stays includes: the Philippines, Trinidad and Tobago, Guyana, Sierra Leone, Tajikistan and Uzbekistan; Austria and Canada have ignored such requests in other cases, such as those involving extradition or deportation. This has raised serious issues regarding the authority of the HRC.[69]

Naturally, the question arises therefore as to how the HRC can implement effectively compliance with its interim measures requests. The HRC has made it clear through a series of decisions originating with the *Piandiong v The Philippines* case that requests for interim measures are binding. It has done this through the medium of the provisions of the OP to the ICCPR, incorporating the right of individual communication. The HRC's constant jurisprudence since has been that unfettered access to it and cooperation with it in good faith is essential and implicit under the terms of the OP. Accordingly, it is axiomatic that if a State party acts in such a way that prevents or frustrates the consideration of the communication by the HRC or renders the expression of its Views nugatory or futile, then a State commits a grave breach of the OP.[70]

Nevertheless, the HRC has still faced a considerable degree of non-compliance with its interim measures requests. Examples include cases such as: *Ashby v Trindad and Tobago*,[71] *Weiss v Austria*,[72] *Ahani v Canada*,[73]

[69] See particularly: *Ashby v Trinidad and Tobago*, UN GAOR, 49th Session, Supp No 40 (A/49/40), Report of the Human Rights Committee, vol 1, 70–71; *Bullock v Trinidad and Tobago*, UN GAOR, 50th Session, Supp No 40 (A/50/40), Report of the Human Rights Committee, vol 2, 168; and *Ross v Guyana*, UN GAOR, 53rd Session, Supp No 40 (A/53/40), Report of the Human Rights Committee, vol 1, 71.

[70] UN GAOR, 56th Session, Supp No 40 (A/56/40), Report of the Human Rights Committee, vol 1, 181, 185–86.

[71] UN GAOR, 57th Session, Supp No 40 (A/57/40), Report of the Human Rights Committee, vol 2, 22.

[72] UN GAOR, 58th Session, Supp No 40 (A/58/40), Report of the Human Rights Committee, vol 2, 384.

[73] UN GAOR, 59th Session, Supp No 40 (A/59/40), Report of the Human Rights Committee, vol 2, 273; see generally on the *Ahani* case: J Harrington, 'Punting Terrorists, Assassins and Other Undesirables: Canada, The Human Rights Committee and Requests for Interim Measures of Protection' (2003) 48 *McGill Law Journal* 55.

and *Ruzmetov v Uzbekistan* and *Shukurova v Tajikistan*.[74] Thus, the HRC has been forced to endorse the proclaimed binding nature of its requests for interim measures with elaboration in a General Comment. In General Comment No 31 [80] on the Nature of the General Legal Obligation Imposed on States Parties to the Covenant, the Committee addressed the issue of non-compliance with requests for interim measures. It stated in paragraph 19 that:

> [t]he Committee further takes the view that the right to an effective remedy may in certain circumstances require States parties to provide for and implement provisional or interim measures to avoid continuing violations and to endeavour to repair at the earliest possible opportunity any harm that may have been caused by such violations.[75]

Thus, it can be envisaged easily that CEDAW will face similar problems to the HRC in the future in obtaining compliance with its interim measures requests. It is true that the wording of the provision in the OP to the Women's Convention is marginally stronger and it has the benefit of being in the text of the OP itself rather than inserted by appropriately adopted Rules of Procedure. Nevertheless, it is predicted that some States may decline similarly to give effect to CEDAW's requests for interim measures.[76] Unsurprisingly, CEDAW has experienced already some difficulties in the application of interim measures. In *AT v Hungary*[77] (discussed above), on 10 October 2003, with her initial submission, the author requested effective interim measures under Article 5(1) urgently in order to avoid irreparable harm to her person; she feared for her life, which she felt was threatened by her former partner. On 20 October 2003 (with a *corrigendum* dated 17 November 2003), a note verbale was sent to the State party for its urgent consideration, requesting the State party to provide immediate, appropriate and concrete preventive interim measures of protection to the author as may be necessary in order to avoid irreparable damage to her. The State party was given until 20 December 2003 to provide details of the measures it had initiated to protect the author. On 20 April 2004, the State party responded by detailing that the Governmental Office for Equal Opportunities had retained a lawyer with experience

[74] UN GAOR, 61st Session, Supp No 40 (A/61/40), Report of the Human Rights Committee, vol 1, 86.

[75] UN GAOR, 59th Session, Supp No 40 (A/59/40), Report of the Human Rights Committee, vol 1, 175–79, 179. On General Comments generally, see: T Opsahl, 'The General Comments of the Human Rights Committee' in J Jekewitz et al. (eds), *Des Menschen Recht zwischen Freiheit und Verantwortung, Festchrift für Karl Josef Partsch zum 75. Geburtstag* (Berlin, Duncker & Humblot, 1989).

[76] See generally S Ghandhi, 'The Human Rights Committee and Interim Measures of Relief' (2007) 13 *Canterbury Law Review* 203.

[77] CEDAW/C/32/D/2/2003.

of domestic violence cases to assist the author, which had set up contact with the local government in order to stop the domestic violence against the author; the State party also indicated that a request for a case conference had been issued to the local authority (which had not met with any response). Clearly these steps were inadequate to assure the author of her safe being. Thus, on 13 July 2004 the Working Group on Communications sent another *note verbale* as a follow-up to the previous requests, conveying the Working Party's regret that the State party had furnished very little information on the interim measures taken. The Working Group requested that the author be given immediately a safe place of refuge for her and her children and appropriate financial assistance. The State party was invited to inform the Working Group as soon as possible of any concrete action taken in compliance with the request for interim measures. On 27 August 2004, the State party simply repeated information that it had given before. In its consideration of the merits, CEDAW deplored the lack of effective legal and other measures that prevented the State party from dealing with CEDAW's interim measures request in a satisfactory manner. Thus, it can be seen that CEDAW will be faced with problems of implementation, just like the HRC before it, in spite of having the interim measures provision inserted in the text of the treaty, rather than simply as a rule of procedure.[78] Nevertheless, the inclusion of this power to request interim measures in the text of the treaty itself is a significant development, particularly in the case of CEDAW, which meets less frequently than the HRC.[79]

Article 7(1) of the OP to the Women's Convention states that: '[t]he Committee shall consider communications received under this Protocol in the light of *all information* made available to it'.[80] The significance of this innovation is that it deletes the word 'written' from the equivalent provision of Article 5(1) of the OP to the ICCPR. Thus, under the express terms of the OP to the ICCPR the HRC is confined to an evaluation in the light of all written information only. The question arises how significant this omission is for the HRC. In 1979, shortly after the HRC began its functions as a monitoring body, it held a private discussion on whether it

[78] Interim measures of relief were requested also by CEDAW in *NSF v UK* CEDAW/C/38/D/10/2005.

[79] In Resolution 62/218, the General Assembly has granted an extension of its meeting time to three annual sessions of three weeks, each preceded by a one-week working group from 2010 onwards; the Assembly approved also with some modification, the Committee's request for extended meeting time and chambers for 2008/09; in particular, it authorised the Committee to hold a total of five sessions, on an exceptional and temporary basis, three of these in parallel chambers; see statement of chairperson of CEDAW (Ms Dubravka Šimonović) to 52nd Session of Commission on the Status of Women, 25 February–7 March 2008.

[80] Emphasis added.

would be possible to hear witnesses or to inspect any relevant object with the consent of the State party concerned.[81] There may well be considerable advantages in some cases in introducing oral evidence: for example, in some very complex cases (and many cases are becoming increasingly so), it could be that oral proceedings might be able to shed more light and clarify some of the factual issues that are in dispute between the parties; the resolution of any dispute between the parties is more likely to become crystallised. On the other hand, the practicalities of such an arrangement, given the part-time nature of human rights treaty monitoring bodies, their restricted budget and given that the work load of members of such bodies is now at saturation point, would only get worse with the introduction of oral evidence. Legal representation would have to be permitted and this would escalate the costs of the action. And what would be the position where applicants could not afford to travel to New York or Geneva to present their case or employ counsel to represent them? Presumably, some sort of legal aid fund would need to be established. Indeed, the issue of resources is fundamental to the question of allowing oral hearings and, given the current financial climate both globally and at the UN, it is not likely that the situation will permit an experiment such as this. Thus, although this innovation in the text of the OP to the Women's Convention opens up the possibility of oral testimony thus enhancing the evidentiary evaluation capacity of CEDAW, many difficulties will have to be addressed before such a procedure can function efficiently and fairly.[82] In the meantime, the systems will remain unified with no admission of oral evidence permitted.

It should also be noted that, under Article 7(3) of the OP to the Women's Convention, CEDAW can make 'recommendations' together with its 'views'. The case of *AT v Hungary*[83] (discussed above) is significant for showing that CEDAW can make both specific and general recommendations under Article 7(3) of the OP (as indeed are subsequent cases). In this case, the specific recommendation made by CEDAW was that the author be given a safe home in which to live with her children, appropriate child support and legal assistance in addition to reparation proportionate to the physical and mental harm suffered and to the gravity of the violations of her rights. CEDAW also made a wide-ranging number of general recommendations, (as in other cases also), including the key one that a specific law be introduced prohibiting domestic violence against women, which should provide for a panoply of protection and exclusion orders, in addition to support services, including shelters. Accordingly, it can be

[81] UN doc CCPR/C/S.R. 138, paras 105–21.
[82] See PR Ghandhi, above n 42 at 309–11.
[83] CEDAW/C/32/D/2/2003.

seen readily that the scope of pronouncements of CEDAW is much wider than that of the HRC, and amply justifies the insertion of the provision for making recommendations in the OP. These recommendations lay down explicitly what the State party must do to be in compliance with its international obligations; they will enhance the authority of CEDAW in its function of assisting in the eradication of all forms of discrimination against women at the international level.

Articles 8 and 9 of the OP to Women's Convention represent considerable other radical departures from the precedent set of the OP to the ICCPR. It institutes a system of inquiries to include a visit to the State party concerned. The provisions are modelled closely on Article 20 of the Torture Convention, but introduce some improvements in procedures.[84] The precedent set under the Torture Convention was an important one. Under these Articles, if CEDAW receives reliable information indicating grave and systematic violations by a State party of the rights contained in the Convention, then CEDAW must invite that State party to cooperate in the examination of that information and to submit observations with regard to the information concerned. There is no doubt that reliable information can emanate from individuals, groups of individuals, the NGO community or UN sources. Taking account of any observations submitted to it by the State party concerned, plus any reliable information made available to it (for example, by the Specialised Agencies, Special Rapporteurs of the Human Rights Council and relevant NGOs or indeed by another State party), CEDAW may designate one or more of its members to conduct an inquiry and to report back urgently to it; where warranted and only if the State party consents, may the inquiry include an on site visit to the territory of the State party concerned; after CEDAW has examined the findings of the inquiry, it must transmit these findings to the State party concerned together with any comments and recommendations; within six months (180 days) of receiving these findings, comments and recommendations the State party must submit its observations to CEDAW. Any inquiry must be conducted confidentially and the cooperation of the State party concerned must be sought at all stages of the proceedings. In respect of follow-up procedure, after expiry of the six-month time period for the submission by the State party of its observations, CEDAW may invite the State party concerned to inform it of measures taken in response to such an inquiry. In addition, CEDAW can invite the State party to include in its report under Article 18 of the Convention details of any measures taken in response to any such inquiry. The greatest fault in these procedures is its optional nature: under Article 10(1) of the OP to CEDAW, a State party may at the time of signature, ratification or accession to the OP declare

[84] 1465 UNTS 85.

that it does not recognise the competence of CEDAW in regard to the provisions provided for in Articles 8 and 9.[85] Of course, any State party that has made such a declaration may withdraw it any time by notice to the Secretary-General of the UN. On the other hand, the ability to opt out of this procedure may make States parties more willing to accept the right of individual communication in the OP to CEDAW.

In practice, this tool has proved immensely valuable. Commensurate with these provisions CEDAW completed its first inquiry under Article 8 in July 2004 in relation to Mexico, as a result of a letter received dated 2 October 2002 from Equality Now and *Casa Amiga*, a rape crisis centre in Cuidad Juárez, Mexico.[86] This case illustrates vividly the important contribution and engagement of the NGO community to the inquiry procedure, in contradistinction to their involvement in individual cases. The full cooperation of the Mexican Government was received for the visit of the two Committee members under this procedure. Aside from the negative feature of the optional applicability of this procedure, on the positive side, it does allow a detailed investigation of serious abuses of women's rights by CEDAW, a body of independent experts. Often individual communications fail to reflect any systematic and widespread abuse of human rights and this procedure may be important in that regard. In addition, there may be cases where individuals or groups of individuals are unable to submit communications, such as for fear of reprisals. In sum, it allows CEDAW to address a wide range of issues stemming from deep structural violations and to make recommendations thereon.[87] Rules 76–90 provide the detail of the inquiry and visit procedure.[88] The procedure permits reasonably rapid investigation of egregious or gross violations to be uncovered and dealt with. Of course, it goes without saying that if CEDAW were to make regular use of the power to instigate inquiries, there would be significant resource implications that would have to be resolved. This fairly novel provision certainly assists CEDAW in the fulfilment of its function as protector of the group rights of women in holding States parties accountable for grave collective breaches of women's rights.

Finally, mention must be made of Article 11 of the OP to the Women's Convention which states that: '[a] state party shall take all appropriate steps to ensure that individuals under its jurisdiction are not subjected

[85] So far, Bangladesh, Belize, Colombia and Cuba have made declarations opting out of the inquiry procedure.

[86] CEDAW/C/2005/OP.8/MEXICO, Report on Mexico produced by CEDAW under Art 8 of the OP to the Convention, and reply from the Government of Mexico.

[87] www.un.org/womenwatch/daw/cedaw/protocol/whatis.htm.

[88] Rules of Procedure of CEDAW, UN GAOR, 56th Session, Supp No 38 (A/56/38), annex 1.

to ill-treatment or intimidation as a result of communicating with the Committee pursuant to this Protocol'. This formalises into the text of the treaty itself the practice of the HRC in upholding vigorously the rights of victims to unfettered access to the international instance specified as the monitoring body, otherwise the right of communication could be rendered illusory by retaliatory action by the State party.[89] Thus, the OP to the Women's Convention imposes effectively an undertaking by the State party not to hinder in any way the effective exercise of the right of individual communication. Under Rule 91 of the Rules of Procedure, CEDAW must bring to the attention of States parties their obligation under Article 11 to take appropriate steps to ensure that petitioners are not subjected to 'ill-treatment' or 'intimidation'. Furthermore, if CEDAW receives reliable information that a State party has breached its Article 11 obligations, it can invite the State party concerned to submit written explanations or statements clarifying the matter and describing any action it is taking to ensure that its obligations under Article 11 are fulfilled.[90] Clearly, such a provision is an essential part of CEDAW's armoury in upholding its responsibility to protect the rights of women.[91]

V. CONCLUSIONS

John Merrills has stated aptly that '[t]he peaceful settlement of disputes is the most critical issue of our time'.[92] To what extent, if at all, do the provisions of the OP to the Women's Convention meet this challenge? The purpose of the OP was to reach deep into the heart of a State's domestic legal order to uncover individual cases where the State party had failed to observe the standards of the Women's Convention. This penetration was designed to operate at a much deeper level than that provided for by the usual reporting procedure adopted also by the Convention under Article 18, as a method of implementation of the State party's obligations. The OP was designed also to heighten awareness of women's rights generally, and violence against women in particular. The absence of an individual petition procedure in contrast with the other UN Treaty Body

[89] *Sendic Antonaccio v Uruguay*, UN GAOR, 37th Session, Supplement No 40 (A/37/40), Report of the Human Rights Committee, 114 and *Hammel v Madagascar*, UN GAOR, 42nd Session, Supplement No 40 (A/42/40), Report of the Human Rights Committee, 130.

[90] Rules of Procedure of CEDAW, UN GAOR, 56th Session, Supplement No 38 (A/56/38), annex 1.

[91] For a comparison with the jurisprudence on maintaining the effectiveness of the right of individual petition of the ECtHR at Strasbourg, see J G Merrills, *The Development of International Law by the European Court of Human Rights* (Manchester, Manchester University Press, 1993) 51–54.

[92] *International Dispute Settlement* (Cambridge, Cambridge University Press, 2005) 334.

Systems (with the exception of the International Covenant on Economic, Social and Cultural Rights for which one was adopted on 10 December 2008 but is not yet in force) was seen to be a mark of the lower importance of Women's Rights generally in the UN scheme of things. This had to be put right. Of course, once CEDAW had begun to develop a systematic and coherent jurisprudence over a period of time, it was considered that its authority and prestige would be cemented. Indeed, the status of the Women's Convention is still not on an equivalent footing with other UN Treaty Body Systems as there is no provision for an inter-State disputes procedure.[93] On the other hand, the inter-State procedure in the other UN Treaty Body Systems has never been used. It is obvious that the procedures are unsatisfactory and that the inter-State procedure is rather an ineffective technique for enforcing human rights law for political reasons. In this connection John Merrills has remarked in relation to the ICCPR that:

> indeed, it is hard to believe that many governments, other than those of democracies with genuine guarantees of freedom of expression and association, free elections, protection against arbitrary arrest and due process of law, will ever expose themselves to the possibility of complaints by other States that they are violating civil and political rights.[94]

Accordingly, the omission of this procedure from the Women's Convention is more symbolic than substantive. On the other hand, it should be observed that Article 29 allows the submission of a dispute between States parties to arbitration, and thereafter to the ICJ. However, this complete lack of use of the inter-State procedure has prompted the HRC to remind States parties of the desirability of making declarations accepting the HRC's jurisdiction in such cases and further reminding States which have already made the declaration (under Article 41(1) of the ICCPR) of availing themselves of this procedure.[95] Despite these exhortations, it is not considered that this is likely to arouse much interest from States parties in the immediate future.

It is obvious from the above analysis of cases decided by CEDAW that the main admissibility issues to date have concerned inadmissibility *ratione temporis* and exhaustion of domestic remedies. This should not come as a great surprise. In the early days of CEDAW's individual communication jurisprudence, it is hardly exceptionable that the Committee has had to grapple with facts that occurred before the OP entered into force for the State party concerned. This is likely to continue for a while with new

[93] See generally S Leckie, 'The Inter-State Complaint Procedure in International Human Rights Law: Hopeful Prospects or Wishful Thinking?' (1988) 10 *Human Rights Quarterly* 249.

[94] See JG Merrills above n 65 at 55–56.

[95] General Comment 31 [80], Nature of the General Legal Obligation Imposed on States Parties to the Covenant, CCPR/C/21/Rev.1/Add.13, 26 May 2004.

States parties to the OP against which individual cases are filed. CEDAW has been zealous in following the precedent set by the HRC, which is in perfect harmony with the principles of general international law in this respect, that it cannot examine alleged breaches of the Convention occurring prior to entry into force of the OP for the State party concerned, unless the facts continued thereafter. Similarly, CEDAW has followed the jurisprudence of the HRC in its resolution of issues relating to exhaustion, such as the proposition that only those remedies that are both available and in principle effective need be exhausted. Again, this is in line with general principles of international law. The HRC's jurisprudence is replete with examples of inadmissibility for failure to exhaust local remedies and it is interesting that every case that CEDAW has had to examine to date has also involved such issues. One case (*Kayhan*) has concerned issues involving multiple jurisdictions (under Article 4(2)(a) OP), where again CEDAW has followed the jurisprudence of the HRC in its resolution of what amounts to 'the same matter'. It seems that CEDAW will be faced with similar problems to the HRC regarding States parties' compliance with its interim measures requests, as illustrated by *AT v Hungary* above, despite the interim measures provision being inserted in the Women's Convention itself, unlike under the ICCPR where it is only to be found in the HRC's Rules of Procedure.

On 4 December 2008, The Minister of State, Ministry of Justice (Michael Wills MP) announced the publication of a report on the UK's experience under the OP to the Women's Convention to Parliament. The Report is entitled: 'The Optional Protocol to the United Nations Convention for the Elimination of All Forms of Discrimination Against Women (CEDAW): The Experience of the UK'.[96] The Report was prepared by Professor Jim Murdoch of The School of Law, University of Glasgow. Part of the justification for the review was 'to gain greater empirical evidence on the value of individual petition to the UN generally'.[97] It is arguable that, if the Government wanted empirical evidence of the operation of individual communication procedures in the UN, it should have chosen other more established treaty bodies such as CERD, HRC and CAT as the yardstick on which to base its judgment, rather than the relatively new and inexperienced CEDAW system. Professor Murdoch is particularly critical of CEDAW's admissibility jurisprudence. Overall, Professor Murdoch can discern no 'attempt on the part of the Committee to develop settled case-law in this area' which may cause 'some frustration to State parties'.[98]

[96] www.justice.gov.uk/whatwedo/humanrights.htm.

[97] Statement of Michael Wills MP, Minister of State, Minister of Justice; Hc Deb, 4 December 2008, c12Ws.

[98] Report, 13.

In particular, Professor Murdoch criticises that: (1) CEDAW is reluctant to canvass all the grounds of admissibility advanced by the State parties, preferring to base its decision on one or two grounds only, failure to exhaust domestic remedies and inadmissibility *ratione temporis* (this is certainly factually correct); he suggests that this weakens the normative value of the views of CEDAW and that CEDAW 'appears unwilling to build up a coherent jurisprudence'; and, (2) the reasoning of CEDAW on admissibility issues is particularly thin.[99] However, Professor Murdoch does concede that if his criticisms are valid, 'it may nevertheless be readily addressed by the Committee, if and when the Committee has the opportunity to develop a settled body of case-law. This will, of course, be dependent upon greater use being made of the right of complaint'.[100] It is true that that CEDAW routinely uses expressions such as: 'the Committee sees no reason to find the communication inadmissible on any other grounds'. However, any detailed examination of the early admissibility jurisprudence of the HRC, CERD or CAT would have encountered the same problem; indeed the same criticism could be made of the early admissibility jurisprudence of the now abolished European Commission on Human Rights under the Strasbourg machinery. In their formative period, all international human rights tribunals have proceeded cautiously and incrementally until self-confidence and weight of cases makes it possible to develop coherent principles. As Professor Murdoch acknowledges, these are very early days in the development of CEDAW's admissibility jurisprudence—the 10 cases submitted to CEDAW to date are hardly sufficient to form a considered evaluation. The HRC has carved out a prestigious niche for itself since it began hearing individual cases in 1977. Today, its authority in the UN Treaty Body System is unrivalled. Any judgment reached a couple of years after it had started its implementation function under the ICCPR's OP would have come to a very different conclusion. In sum, it is submitted that it is premature to be overly critical of CEDAW's jurisprudence. Time is needed for the case law to formulate and to mature.

On the contrary, it is suggested that this study shows that CEDAW is intent on developing a jurisprudence that is both congruent and consistent with that of the other UN treaty-monitoring bodies, especially the HRC. This is only to be expected, as the drafters clearly had in mind the experience and case law of these bodies as a whole as a model from which to develop the text of the OP to the Women's Convention. Time will tell whether CEDAW can vindicate the rights of women in the individual communication procedure as successfully as the HRC. What can be seen

[99] Ibid.
[100] Ibid 18.

emerging is an attempt by CEDAW to create a harmonious and unified jurisprudence with other UN Treaty Body Systems, especially the HRC, in order to discharge its mandate to make States parties accountable for violations of the Women's Convention. Of course, there will be a number of challenges ahead, notably the whole issue of reform of the form and working methods of the various treaty bodies that implement the current eight main UN human rights treaties in force. Although this issue has been highlighted recently by 'Concept Paper on the High Commissioner's Proposal for a Unified Standing Treaty Body',[101] the issue has been exercising the UN for several decades.[102] In contrast to the procedures under the reporting mechanisms of the various UN human rights treaties, which are fragmentary and disjointed, the attempt being made by CEDAW to develop, albeit incrementally, a congruent and unified jurisprudence with the HRC, CERD and CAT is to be welcomed.

[101] HRI/MC/2006/CRP.1, 14 March 2006.

[102] HB Shöpp-Schilling, 'Treaty Body Reform: the Case of the Committee on the Elimination of Discrimination Against Women' (2007) 7 *Human Rights Law Review* 201.

6

Trends in Dispute Settlement in the Law of the Sea: Towards the Increasing Availability of Compulsory Means

ROBIN CHURCHILL

I. INTRODUCTION

ANYONE WANTING AN introduction to the ambitious and complex system of dispute settlement contained in the 1982 UN Convention on the Law of the Sea can do no better than read the excellent chapter on this subject in John Merrills' book, *International Dispute Settlement*. It is thus appropriate that in this *festschrift* there should be a chapter on dispute settlement in the law of the sea. I am delighted to have been asked to write this chapter as I have long admired and profited from John Merrills' extensive writings, especially those on dispute settlement.

The aim of this chapter, in keeping with the theme of this book, is to explore developments and trends in dispute settlement in the law of the sea. The focus will be on judicial and quasi-judicial means, in other words settlement by international courts, arbitral tribunals and bodies that exercise a quasi-judicial function but do not necessarily make legally binding decisions. Although the law of the sea is a discrete and fairly self-contained branch of international law, it is still, of course, part of international law, and indeed is almost as old as international law itself. It is therefore not surprising that the mechanisms that are used for dispute settlement in the law of the sea are largely those that have traditionally been used in general international law. Nevertheless, there have been a number of innovations in recent years that in part reflect the rather specialised nature of some of the matters with which the international law of the sea deals.

Although the 1982 UN Convention on the Law of the Sea (UNCLOS)[1] represents a major codification and is regarded as having a kind of 'constitutional' status in the law of the sea,[2] it is by no means the only treaty, or the only treaty containing judicial dispute settlement mechanisms, in the law of the sea. There are, in fact, many other treaties, a number of which are indeed called for, or whose existence is assumed, by UNCLOS. Many of those treaties have dispute settlement machinery containing judicial or quasi-judicial means.

This chapter begins with a discussion of the dispute settlement mechanisms of UNCLOS, focusing on their innovative aspects, the reasons for such innovation, and their practical application. Using the same focus, the following sections of the chapter look at dispute settlement in relation to two areas of the law of the sea that are regulated not only by UNCLOS but also by a considerable number of other multilateral treaties containing dispute settlement mechanisms—fisheries and the prevention of marine pollution. After that, there will be some consideration of how far traditional judicial means of settlement—the International Court of Justice, arbitration and regional courts of general competence—are still available for settling law of the sea disputes. The chapter ends with some conclusions about trends in dispute settlement in the law of the sea.

II. DISPUTE SETTLEMENT UNDER UNCLOS

Part XV of UNCLOS is dedicated to dispute settlement. It contains provisions both on what may be labelled for convenience as the general scheme of dispute settlement, as well as provisions dealing with a number of specialised dispute settlement mechanisms.

A. The General Scheme of Dispute Settlement

Shorn of its complex detail, the general UNCLOS scheme of dispute settlement essentially amounts to a compromissory clause of a fairly traditional kind. It provides that disputes concerning the interpretation or application of UNCLOS that cannot be settled by the parties to the dispute by diplomatic or judicial means of their own choice may, with some exceptions, be unilaterally referred by any party to the dispute to one of

[1] United Nations Convention on the Law of the Sea (adopted 10 December 1982, entered into force 16 November 1994) 1833 UNTS 396.

[2] See further S Scott, 'The LOS Convention as a Constitutional Regime for the Oceans' in AG Oude Elferink (ed), *Stability and Change in the Law of the Sea: The Role of the LOS Convention* (Leiden, Martinus Nijhoff, 2005).

four possible fora for binding settlement. Those fora are: the International Tribunal for the Law of the Sea (ITLOS), the International Court of Justice (ICJ), an arbitral tribunal constituted in accordance with Annex VII of UNCLOS, and a special arbitral tribunal constituted in accordance with Annex VIII. At any time following its signature of UNCLOS, a State may make a written declaration specifying one or more of those four fora as its preferred means for settling disputes. If the parties to a dispute have made declarations expressing a preference for the same forum, that will be the forum for hearing the dispute. Where the parties' choice of forum does not coincide, or where one or more of the parties to the dispute has not made a declaration, the dispute will be dealt with by an Annex VII arbitral tribunal.[3] Currently only around a quarter of the 157 States parties to UNCLOS have made declarations.[4] Statistically, therefore, the likelihood is that most disputes will be referred to Annex VII arbitration. Giving parties to UNCLOS a choice of forum was apparently considered essential in order to obtain agreement on the settlement of dispute provisions during the negotiation of UNCLOS.[5] It is therefore surprising that there have not been more declarations. This may be due as much to bureaucratic inertia in national governments as anything else.

Of the four possible fora for settling UNCLOS disputes, the ICJ requires little comment. Its role under Part XV of UNCLOS is essentially no different to its role under any other compomissory clause in a treaty giving it jurisdiction in accordance with Article 36(1) of its Statute. Consequently it cannot hear disputes involving parties to UNCLOS that are not States, of which there are currently three: the European Community (EC), the Cook Islands and Niue. Likewise little need be said about Annex VII arbitration, which functions very much like a typical inter-State arbitration.

The ITLOS and Annex VIII arbitration require more comment. The ITLOS is a new international court, established by Annex VI of UNCLOS. It is largely modelled on the ICJ, but there are some significant differences. It has 21, rather than 15, judges, presumably in order to allow for somewhat greater geographical representation. The judges are elected, and the ITLOS as a whole is financed, by the States parties to UNCLOS rather than the UN. Judges are required to be persons 'enjoying the highest reputation for fairness and integrity and of recognised competence in the field of the law of the sea,'[6] rather than simply international law, as is the case with the ICJ. The main reason for establishing a new international

[3] UNCLOS Art 287(1), (3), (4) and (5).

[4] Details of such declarations can be found on the website of the UN's Division for Oceans and Law of the Sea (DOALOS), www.un.org/Depts/los.

[5] AO Adede, *The System for Settlement of Disputes under the UN Convention on the Law of the Sea* (Dordrecht, Martinus Nijhoff, 1987), 49–54, 243–44 and 283.

[6] UNCLOS Annex VI, Art 2(1).

court as an alternative to the ICJ was because at the time that UNCLOS was being negotiated, there was considerable distrust of the ICJ by both developing States (the UNCLOS negotiations began only a few years after the *South-West Africa* case) and Communist States.[7] That situation has, of course, since changed, and if UNCLOS were being negotiated today, the ITLOS might not be thought necessary.

Annex VIII arbitration has several noteworthy features. It is limited to four kinds of dispute: those concerning fisheries, protection and preservation of the marine environment, marine scientific research and navigation. Each Annex VIII tribunal normally consists of five members, with each party to the dispute appointing two members and the remaining member, who acts as President of the tribunal, being appointed by agreement between the parties or, failing agreement, by the UN Secretary-General. Arbitrators are preferably to be chosen from a list of experts in each of the four fields referred to above, drawn up and maintained by the FAO, UNEP, the Inter-Governmental Oceanographic Commission and the International Maritime Organisation (IMO), respectively. Each State party may nominate to each of the four lists two experts in each field 'whose competence in the legal, scientific or technical aspects of such field is established and generally recognised and who enjoy the highest reputation for fairness and integrity.'[8] Thus, arbitrators need not be, and in most cases probably will not be, legally qualified. In addition to their normal arbitration function, Annex VIII tribunals may also be used at any time, if the parties to a dispute so agree, to 'carry out an inquiry and establish the facts giving rise to the dispute,' and, if the parties so request, 'formulate recommendations'.[9] Thus, rather unusually, an Annex VIII tribunal may engage in both diplomatic and judicial methods of dispute settlement. However, the chances of such a tribunal being used in any capacity are at present rather remote, as only nine parties to UNCLOS (three of which are land-locked) have chosen Annex VIII arbitration as a preferred means of settlement.

As already mentioned, the possibility for a party to a dispute to refer it unilaterally for binding settlement is subject to a number of exceptions. First, Article 297 provides that disputes concerning the exercise by a coastal State of its rights within its EEZ are exempt from compulsory dispute settlement unless the dispute concerns the exercise of other States' rights under the Convention of navigation, overflight and the laying of cables and pipelines or the dispute concerns allegations that a

[7] N Klein, *Dispute Settlement in the UN Convention on the Law of the Sea* (Cambridge, Cambridge University Press, 2005) 54–55.

[8] UNCLOS Annex VIII, Art 2(3).

[9] Ibid Art 5.

coastal State has acted in contravention of specified international rules for the protection of the marine environment. The reason for this exception is because of political sensitivity concerning the EEZ provisions of UNCLOS, which represent a careful and delicate balance between the interests of coastal States and the interests of other States.[10] Secondly, Article 298 provides that a State may at any time after signing the Convention make a declaration stating that it does not accept compulsory dispute settlement in relation to disputes relating to maritime boundaries with neighbouring States or those involving historic bays or titles, disputes concerning military activities and certain kinds of law enforcement activities in the EEZ, and/or disputes in respect of which the Security Council is exercising the functions assigned to it by the UN Charter. Only 27 parties to UNCLOS have so far made declarations under Article 298,[11] of which only 10 have excluded all the matters listed in that Article completely. The low number of declarations is rather surprising, as Article 298 is said to have been necessary in order to secure agreement on a system of compulsory dispute settlement being included in UNCLOS.[12] More specifically, the reason why maritime boundaries may be excepted from compulsory settlement is because of fundamental disagreement during the negotiation of UNCLOS over the rules that should govern delimitation of boundaries, a disagreement that is reflected in the vagueness of the substantive provisions of UNCLOS on this question. The exceptions relating to military activities, law enforcement and the Security Council reflect the political and security sensibilities of many States. The low number of declarations under Article 298 suggests that the assumptions on which those exceptions are based may be questionable. Some of the matters excepted from compulsory judicial settlement under Articles 297 and 298, namely certain kinds of disputes relating to fisheries and marine scientific research in the EEZ and maritime boundary delimitation, are subject to compulsory conciliation.[13] The latter functions in much the same way as compulsory conciliation under the Vienna Convention on the Law of Treaties and some other multilateral treaties,[14] including the fact that the report of the conciliation commission setting out its recommendations for settlement is not binding. There have been no instances of compulsory conciliation under UNCLOS to date.

[10] Klein, above n 7 at 125–26 and 225–26.

[11] See n 4 above.

[12] See S Rosenne and LB Sohn (eds), *United Nations Convention on the Law of the Sea 1982: A Commentary*, vol V (Dordrecht, Martinus Nijhoff, 1989) 109–10.

[13] Arts 297(2), 297(3), 298(1)(a) and Annex V, UNCLOS.

[14] See JG Merrills, *International Dispute Settlement*, 4th edn (Cambridge, Cambridge University Press, 2005) 77–82, 190–92.

Seven disputes have so far been referred to binding legal settlement under UNCLOS. Of these, three have been decided on the merits (two maritime boundary delimitation cases, between Barbados and Trinidad and Tobago, and between Guyana and Suriname, respectively,[15] and the *Saiga* case[16]). One case, the *Land Reclamation* case, in which Malaysia claimed that certain of Singapore's land reclamation activities breached its rights under UNCLOS, was settled out of court.[17] In the *Southern Bluefin Tuna* case, in which Australia and New Zealand claimed that an experimental fishing programme for southern bluefin tuna by Japan breached UNCLOS obligations relating to the conservation of fishery resources on the high seas, the arbitral tribunal concerned found that it lacked jurisdiction.[18] In the *MOX Plant* case Ireland withdrew its complaint that the United Kingdom had breached UNCLOS by the construction and operation of a plant to make mixed oxide fuel (MOX) at Sellafield[19] following a ruling from the European Court of Justice that in instituting proceedings Ireland had breached EC law.[20] Finally, in the *Swordfish* case, in which Chile alleged that the EC had breached UNCLOS through the activities of its vessels fishing for swordfish in the south-east Pacific, proceedings have been suspended almost since the day it was brought because the parties came to a provisional arrangement.[21] All the cases were originally referred to arbitration under Annex VII arbitration as one or more of the parties had not selected a preferred means of settlement under Article 287, but two of the cases (the *Saiga* and *Swordfish* cases) were subsequently transferred by agreement to the ITLOS for settlement.

The seven cases that have so far been referred to compulsory judicial settlement were brought during a period of just over six years, ending

[15] *Barbados/Trinidad and Tobago Maritime Boundary Case*, Award of 11 April 2006, available on the website of the Permanent Court of Arbitration, www.pca-cpa.org and (2006) 45 ILM 798; and the *Guyana/Suriname* case, Award of 17 September 2007, www.pca-cpa.org/upload/files/Guyana-Suriname%20Award.pdf.

[16] *The M/V Saiga No 2 Case (St Vincent and the Grenadines v Guinea)*, Judgment of 1 July 1999. Like all the orders and judgments of the ITLOS, the text of the judgment may be found on its website: www.itlos.org. It is also reproduced in (1999) 38 ILM 1323. The ITLOS found that the arrest by Guinea of the *Saiga*, an oil tanker that was supplying fuel oil to vessels fishing off the West African coast, was unlawful and ordered Guinea to pay compensation to St Vincent.

[17] *Case concerning Land Reclamation by Singapore in and around the Straits of Johor (Malaysia v Singapore)*, Award on Agreed Terms of 1 September 2005, www.pca-cpa.org/upload/files/MASI%20Award.pdf.

[18] *Southern Bluefin Tuna Case (Australia and New Zealand v Japan)*, Award on Jurisdiction and Admissibility, 4 August 2000, (2000) 39 ILM 1359.

[19] *The MOX Plant Case (Ireland v UK)* Order No 6 of 6 June 2008. Termination of Proceedings, www.pca-cpa.org/upload/files/MOX%20Plant%20Order%20No.%206.pdf.

[20] Case C-459/03 *Commission v Ireland* [2006] ECR I-4635.

[21] *Case concerning the Conservation and Sustainable Utilisation of Swordfish Stocks in the South-Eastern Pacific Ocean (Chile/European Community)*, Orders of 15 March 2001, 16 December 2003, 29 December 2005 and 30 November 2007, all www.itlos.org.

in February 2004. In the four and a half years since then (to the time of writing) no further cases have been brought. Should we be surprised or concerned at this lack of cases? Inter-State litigation is still generally occasional and sporadic, the large number of cases brought under the WTO's Dispute Settlement Understanding being very much the exception. It is true that there are a large number of disputes (at least in the sense of a difference of views) in the law of the sea, in particular some 200 unresolved maritime boundaries and a considerable amount of national legislation that is (arguably) inconsistent with UNCLOS and that has been protested by one or more other States.[22] Some such disputes may involve non-parties to UNCLOS, others may fall within the exceptions to compulsory judicial settlement. In many other instances States will lack sufficient interest to consider litigation, or will be dissuaded by its costs and bother,[23] or will wish to retain the flexibility and control offered by diplomatic means of settlement and avoid the risk of a judicial body coming to a conclusion on an unclear or ambiguous provision of UNCLOS that goes against their interests. Some disputes concern widespread, systemic matters, such as illegal, unreported and unregulated fishing, sub-standard ships and threats to the marine biodiversity of the deep seabed, that are not easily susceptible to compulsory judicial settlement under UNCLOS because would-be applicant States may lack a sufficient legal interest or feel that a judicial decision in a single case will not solve what is a widespread and deep-rooted problem and consider that such matters are better addressed through the development of treaties or soft law instruments. The most important point is that disputes should ultimately be settled (and often the time factor is not important), and that they should be settled peacefully. The means by which they are settled is not significant. If all future law of the sea disputes were to be settled by diplomatic means, that would not necessarily mean that the availability of judicial settlement under UNCLOS was pointless or its non-use a failure. It might well mean that that availability had induced the diplomatic settlement of some disputes that otherwise might not have been settled at all.

[22] For surveys of such legislation, see RR Churchill, 'The Impact of State Practice on the Jurisdictional Framework contained in the LOS Convention' in Oude Elferink (ed), above n 2; JA Roach and RW Smith, *United States Responses to Excessive Maritime Claims*, 2nd edn (The Hague, Nijhoff, 1996); and T Scovazzi, 'The Evolution of International Law of the Sea: New Issues, New Challenges' (2000) 286 *Recueil des Cours* 39.

[23] As to the costs of litigation, it should be noted that in 2000 the UN General Assembly established a voluntary Trust Fund to assist States in cases before the ITLOS: see UN General Assembly Resolution 55/7 of 30 October 2000, para 9 and Annex I. No money has yet been paid out from this Fund, which at the end of 2007 totalled a rather modest $104,412: see Annual Report of the International Tribunal for the Law of the Sea for 2007, SPLOS/174, para 95.

B. Disputes Relating to Mining in the International Seabed Area

There are separate procedures for the settlement of disputes relating to mining for minerals in the International Sea-Bed Area (the Area). These procedures are set out, not in Part XV of UNCLOS, but in section 5 of Part XI of UNCLOS, which must be read together with the 1994 Agreement relating to the Implementation of Part XI of UNCLOS.[24] The primary forum for dealing with mining disputes in the Area is the Sea-Bed Disputes Chamber of the ITLOS, an 11-member body, selected by and from the judges of the ITLOS, who must ensure that there is representation of the principal legal systems and equitable geographical distribution.[25] The Chamber may also establish an *ad hoc* three-member chamber for dealing with certain kinds of dispute.[26] The Sea-Bed Disputes Chamber has jurisdiction to hear disputes between States parties relating to the provisions of UNCLOS concerning the Area; disputes between States parties and the International Sea-Bed Authority; disputes between the parties to a contract (which may be States, the Authority, the Enterprise (the mining arm of the Authority), State enterprises or natural or legal persons); and disputes between the Authority and prospective contractors.[27] Thus, most unusually, the Chamber, as an international court, may hear disputes involving not only States and international organisations but also State enterprises and natural and legal persons; and may apply legal instruments which include not only a treaty (UNCLOS) but also regulations made by an international organisation (the Authority)[28] and contracts. As an alternative to the Chamber, certain kinds of contractual dispute may be referred by any of the parties to binding commercial arbitration, although any arbitral tribunal has no competence to interpret UNCLOS and must refer questions of interpretation of UNCLOS to the Chamber for a ruling.[29] Furthermore, disputes concerning the application of GATT rules to the Authority's production policy are to be settled in accordance with the WTO's Dispute Settlement Understanding (DSU) where the States parties concerned are members of the WTO:[30] the purpose of this provision is to ensure that the GATT is interpreted by the DSU, not the Chamber. Finally, it should be noted that the Chamber may also give advisory opinions at the request of the Assembly or the Council of the

[24] (1994) 33 ILM 1309.
[25] Annex VI, Art 35.
[26] Annex VI, Art 36.
[27] UNCLOS Art 187.
[28] It should be noted that the Chamber may not question the way that the Authority has exercised its discretion nor declare its regulations invalid: see Art 189.
[29] Art 188(2).
[30] 1994 Implementation Agreement, Annex, s 6, para 1(f).

Authority on legal questions arising within the scope of their activities.[31] The Chamber's power here is similar to that of the ICJ under Article 65 of its Statute and Article 96 of the UN Charter.

Given that the first contracts for exploration of the Area were not signed until 2001,[32] that commercial mining in the Area is unlikely to begin for some time, and the fact that decision-making in the Authority is largely by consensus, it is not surprising that none of the above provisions has yet been invoked.

C. Provisional Measures

Article 290 of UNCLOS gives the court or tribunal hearing the case, or the ITLOS if an arbitral tribunal is still to be constituted, the power to prescribe provisional measures. Most of this provision is similar to the competence that the ICJ has to indicate provisional measures under Article 41 of its Statute. Thus, the forum hearing the case must *prima facie* have jurisdiction and may prescribe measures where this is necessary to preserve the respective rights of the parties to the dispute pending the final decision. One novel aspect of Article 290 is that measures may be prescribed in order to 'prevent serious harm to the marine environment,' a phrase that the ITLOS has interpreted as also including the conservation of fishery resources.[33] This ground was the basis of the order for the provisional measures prescribed not only in the *Southern Bluefin Tuna* case but also in the *MOX Plant*[34] and *Land Reclamation* cases.[35] Other points of interest are that the body prescribing provisional measures may substitute its own measures, in whole or in part, for those requested by the parties;[36] provisional measures are binding on the parties to the case;[37] and the ITLOS may (and in practice invariably does) require the

[31] UNCLOS Art 191.

[32] Report of the twelfth Meeting of States Parties [to UNCLOS] SPLOS/91, 10.

[33] *Southern Bluefin Tuna Cases (New Zealand v Japan); (Australia v Japan),* Order for Provisional Measures of 27 August 1999, para 70, (1999) 38 ILM 1624.

[34] *The MOX Plant Case (Ireland v UK),* Request for Provisional Measures, Order of 3 December 2001, paras 82–84, (2002) 41 ILM 405.

[35] *Case concerning Land Reclamation by Singapore in and around the Straits of Johor (Malaysia v Singapore),* Request for Provisional Measures, Order of 8 October 2003, para 99.

[36] In the case of the ITLOS, see Art 89(5) of its Rules. The Annex VII Tribunal in *The MOX Plant Case* considered that it had a similar power: see *The MOX Plant Case (Ireland v UK),* Order No 3 of 24 June 2003. Suspension of Proceedings on Jurisdiction and Merits and Request for Further Provisional Measures, para 43, www.pca-cpa.org/upload/files/MOX%20Order%20no3.pdf.

[37] UNCLOS Art 290(6).

parties to report to it on the steps that they have taken to give effect to the provisional measures prescribed.[38]

The most interesting aspect of the UNCLOS provisional measures procedures is the way that they have been used in practice. The ITLOS, which has heard all but one of the five applications for provisional measures that have so far been made, has used its competence to prescribe provisional measures to play a conflict-management role and to engender better relations between the parties to the dispute, albeit that at times its actions seem difficult to reconcile with a strict reading of Article 290. Thus, in the *Southern Bluefin Tuna* case, the provisional measures prescribed by the ITLOS, which required the parties to avoid action that would aggravate the dispute, limit their catches and resume negotiations on conservation and management measures without delay, prompted the parties towards renewing such negotiations in a more cooperative spirit and are credited by several commentators with playing a significant role in the eventual resolution of the dispute.[39] In the *MOX Plant* case the ITLOS found the parties (Ireland and the United Kingdom) under a legal obligation to cooperate[40] and ordered them to exchange information as to the possible consequences for the Irish Sea from the operation of the MOX plant, to monitor its effects, and to devise measures to prevent pollution from the plant. Those measures have led to increased exchanges of information and cooperation between Ireland and the United Kingdom. This has undoubtedly taken a good deal of the heat out of the dispute, which still persists (albeit in a fairly subdued manner because the MOX plant has not yet become operational) since (as seen earlier) Ireland withdrew the matter from arbitration. Finally, in the *Land Reclamation* case the ITLOS, having also found the parties (Malaysia and Singapore) under an obligation to cooperate and having noted various undertakings unilaterally given by Singapore during the proceedings (which the ITLOS held were legally binding), ordered the parties to enter into consultations to establish a group of independent experts to conduct a study to determine the effects of Singapore's land reclamation activities on the marine environment of the Straits of Johor and to propose, as appropriate, measures to deal with

[38] ITLOS Rules Art 95(1).

[39] See, eg B Mansfield, 'Compulsory Dispute Settlement after the Southern Bluefin Tuna Award' in AG Oude Elferink and DR Rothwell (eds), *Oceans Management in the 21st Century: Institutional Frameworks and Responses* (Leiden, Martinus Nijhoff, 2004) 259–61, 263–69; and T Stephens, 'The Limits of International Adjudication in International Law: Another Perspective on the Southern Bluefin Tuna Case' (2004) 19 *International Journal of Marine and Coastal Law* 177, especially at 183–87.

[40] The basis of this obligation appears to be that it is a 'fundamental principle in the prevention of pollution of the marine environment under Part XII of the [Law of the Sea] Convention and general international law', and also that it is dictated by 'prudence and caution': see the *MOX Plant* Order, above n 34, paras 82 and 84.

any adverse effects of such reclamation.[41] Proceedings before the Annex VII Tribunal that was due to deal with the merits phase of the case were effectively suspended while the group of independent experts established pursuant to the ITLOS Order carried out its work. On the basis of a report from the group, the parties were able to conclude an agreement, signed in 2005,[42] that constituted a full and final settlement of the dispute.[43]

D. Prompt Release of Vessels

Article 292 of UNCLOS provides that where a State party has detained a vessel flying the flag of another State party and it is alleged that the detaining State has not complied with the provisions of UNCLOS requiring the prompt release of the vessel and its crew upon the posting of a reasonable bond or other financial security, the flag State of the detained vessel may seek the release of the vessel by applying to an international court or tribunal, including the ITLOS. That court or tribunal is to determine the bond or other financial security, and once the latter has been posted, the detaining State must promptly release the vessel. There are two provisions of UNCLOS on prompt release of the kind referred to in Article 292. The first is Article 73, which provides for the prompt release of foreign vessels arrested for alleged illegal fishing in the EEZ of a coastal State. The second is Article 226, which deals with the release of vessels detained in connection with alleged pollution of the marine environment.

The provisions of Article 292 are quite novel: nothing like them exists in any other treaty. Their purpose is to prevent foreign vessels and their crews from being detained for a possibly prolonged period of time while the alleged fisheries or pollution offence is being dealt with by the domestic courts of the detaining State, while at the same time providing surety (in the form of the bond or other security) to cover any penalties that may be imposed by domestic courts.[44] In essence prompt release proceedings are a form of diplomatic protection, where a State acts on behalf of a ship having its nationality. However, prompt release differs from traditional diplomatic protection in one significant respect. There is no obligation to exhaust domestic remedies before its case is taken up by the flag State,[45]

[41] Order, above n 35, para 106.

[42] The text of the Settlement Agreement is annexed to the Award on Agreed terms, above n 17.

[43] See Award on Agreed terms, above n 17.

[44] See *Monte Confurco Case (Seychelles v France) Prompt Release*, Judgment of the ITLOS of 18 December 2000, para 71. The texts of the judgments in this and other prompt release of vessel cases are available on the website of the ITLOS, www.itlos.org/start2_en.html.

[45] *Camouco Case (Panama v France) Prompt Release*, Judgment of the ITLOS of 7 February 2000, paras 57–58.

unlike the general position in international law.[46] Indeed, if all domestic remedies have been exhausted, it will probably be too late for the flag State to make an application under Article 292.[47]

There has been a fair amount of use of Article 292 by flag States. Nine applications for prompt release had been made up to September 2008 (one of which was withdrawn before it could be heard), all to the ITLOS, and all concerning fisheries. The ITLOS has held that it has a twofold function in prompt release proceedings: either to set a bond where none has been set by the detaining State or, more usually, to determine whether the amount, form and nature of the bond or other financial security that has been set is reasonable; and, if not, to substitute that bond with a different (and usually lower) bond of its own. The practical application of prompt release proceedings has not been free of difficulties. One of the central problems is that there is something of an inherent tension in UNCLOS between its provisions on prompt release and its provisions designed to protect the exercise of the coastal State's fisheries rights in the EEZ from international judicial scrutiny. The latter provisions include Article 297(3), which (as seen earlier) stipulates that a coastal State is not obliged to accept the submission of a dispute concerning the exercise of its sovereign rights relating to fisheries in its EEZ to compulsory judicial settlement; and Article 292(3), which provides that a court or tribunal hearing a prompt release application 'shall deal only with the question of release, without prejudice to the merits of any case before the appropriate domestic forum against the vessel.' Those provisions make it difficult for a court or tribunal to look at the circumstances of the arrest (in particular whether the arrest was actually for an alleged fisheries offence in the EEZ) or to review the reasonableness of a bond set by the detaining State without straying into territory over which Articles 297(3) and 292(3) have erected a 'keep out' notice. There have been times when the ITLOS has strayed into that territory.[48] Another problematic issue concerning the practical application of Article 292 relates to the way in which the size of the bond or other financial security is to be calculated. While the ITLOS has helpfully

[46] See International Law Commission Draft Articles on Diplomatic Protection Art 14 [2006] *Yearbook of the International Law Commission* 16.

[47] This is the implication of the judgment of the ITLOS in the *Tomimaru case (Japan v Russian Federation) Prompt Release*, Judgment of the ITLOS of 6 August 2007, (2007) 46 ILM 1185.

[48] For fuller consideration of this point, see R Churchill, 'The Jurisprudence of the International Tribunal for the Law of the Sea relating to Fisheries: Is there much in the Net?' (2007) 22 *International Journal of Marine and Coastal Law* 383, 402–04 and S Oda, 'Dispute Settlement Prospects in the Law of the Sea' (1995) 44 ICLQ 863, 865–67. See also T Mensah, 'The Tribunal and the Prompt Release of Vessels' (2007) 22 *International Journal of Marine and Coastal Law* 425, 444–47; and the declaration of Judge Mensah and the dissenting opinions of Judges Anderson and Jesus in the *Monte Confurco* case, above n 44, and the dissenting opinion of Judge Wolfrum in the *Camouco Case*, above n 45, paras 13–15.

set out the criteria that it believes should govern this question,[49] it would have been even more useful guidance for detaining and flag States if the ITLOS had shown in the cases in which it has set a bond how the size of that bond was derived from its criteria, rather than seemingly appearing to pluck a figure from thin air. The prompt release procedures have also thrown up a number of other problems, but for reasons of space they cannot be dealt with here.[50]

E. Evaluation of the UNCLOS Dispute Settlement Machinery

At the time of its adoption in 1982, UNCLOS contained arguably the most far-reaching, detailed and ambitious system of dispute settlement found in any multilateral treaty. Since then it has perhaps been rivalled by the WTO's Dispute Settlement Understanding, adopted in 1994. Some features of the UNCLOS dispute settlement system are, as pointed out earlier, fairly traditional; others are quite innovative. The UNCLOS system presents a marked contrast to the dispute settlement system adopted at the previous codification of the law of the sea at the First UN Conference on the Law of the Sea in 1958. In line with other codifying conventions adopted at around that time that were based on draft articles prepared by the International Law Commission, such as the 1961 Vienna Convention on Diplomatic Relations and the 1963 Vienna Convention on Consular Relations, dispute settlement was made optional (albeit providing for the possibility of unilateral reference of disputes to the ICJ for States that accepted it). Those arrangements were contained in a protocol attached to the four Geneva Conventions of 1958.[51] That protocol was never accepted by more than a small minority of parties to the Conventions,[52] and was never invoked by any of them.

There are various reasons why UNCLOS, unlike the 1958 Conventions, provides for compulsory dispute settlement. First, a number of developed

[49] See, in particular, the *Camouco* case, above n 45, para 67 and the *Hoshinmaru case (Japan v Russian Federation) Prompt Release*, Judgment of the ITLOS of 6 August 2007, para 82.

[50] For consideration of these matters, see E Franckx, '"Reasonable Bond" in the Practice of the International Tribunal for the Law of the Sea' (2002) 32 *California West International Law Journal* 303; Klein, above n 7 at 85–119; Mensah, above n 48; A Serdy and M Bliss, 'Prompt Release of Fishing Vessels: State Practice in the Light of the Cases before the International Tribunal for the Law of the Sea' in Oude Elferink and Rothwell, above n 39; and Y Tanaka, 'Prompt Release in the United Nations Convention on the Law of the Sea: Some Reflections on the ITLOS Jurisprudence' (2004) 51 *Netherlands International Law Review* 237.

[51] Optional Protocol of Signature concerning the Compulsory Settlement of Disputes arising from the Law of the Sea Conventions (adopted 29 April 1958, entered into force 30 September 1962) 450 UNTS 169.

[52] Of the 70 or so states that were parties to one or more of the Geneva Conventions, only 28 accepted the Protocol.

States, including the United Kingdom and the USA, made it clear that they could not accept some of the proposed substantive innovations of UNCLOS, which they thought would produce disputes, without compulsory dispute settlement.[53] Secondly, it was thought that the possibility of compulsory settlement would protect the integrity of the UNCLOS text, particularly the many delicate compromises with which it abounds, from unravelling in the face of unilateral State action and would ensure its uniform interpretation.[54] Thirdly, compulsory dispute settlement was also seen by developing and weaker States as a means of countering the political, economic and military pressures of more powerful, developed States.[55] Interestingly, the UNCLOS system has not so far in practice greatly functioned in line with those expectations. Few of the cases brought have involved disputes over the application of the innovative and compromise provisions of UNCLOS or over the meaning of its provisions that are unclear or ambiguous: most differences of view on those matters have simply not been litigated at all. Nor, with the possible exception of the *Swordfish* case, have any cases involved parties that were markedly unequal.

III. DISPUTE SETTLEMENT UNDER FISHERIES TREATIES

As far as the legal regulation of fisheries is concerned, UNCLOS makes a sharp distinction between the legal regime applying within the 200-mile exclusive economic zone (EEZ), where the coastal State has the exclusive right to manage the fisheries and to decide which other States (if any) should be permitted to fish there, and the high seas beyond, where all States in principle have the freedom to fish. As far as the EEZ is concerned, we have already seen that Article 297(3) of UNCLOS provides that disputes concerning EEZ fisheries may not be submitted to judicial settlement without the consent of the coastal State, a consent that is unlikely to be forthcoming in most cases.[56] Since the general establishment of EEZs by coastal States from the late 1970s onwards, there have been scores of bilateral agreements providing for the access (usually on a

[53] C Chinkin, 'Dispute Resolution and the Law of the Sea: Regional Problems and Prospects' in J Crawford and DR Rothwell (eds), *The Law of the Sea in the Asian-Pacific Region* (Dordrecht, Nijhoff, 1995) 245; AE Boyle, 'Dispute Settlement and the Law of the Sea Convention: Problems of Fragmentation and Jurisdiction' (1997) 46 ICLQ 37, 38–39.

[54] Adede, above n 5 at 241.

[55] Klein, above n 7 at 52–53. See also TA Mensah, 'The Role of Peaceful Dispute Settlement in Contemporary Ocean Policy and Law' in D Vidas and W Østreng (eds), *Order for the Oceans at the Turn of the Century* (The Hague, Kluwer, 1999) 82.

[56] For a discussion of the situations in which a coastal State might be prepared to agree to an UNCLOS judicial body hearing a dispute, see Churchill, above n 48 at 420–22.

fairly temporary basis) of foreign vessels to the EEZs of coastal States. In the light of Article 297(3), it is not surprising that such agreements do not as a rule provide for compulsory dispute settlement.[57]

On the high seas, matters are very different. There, fisheries are usually regulated at the regional level by what were originally called international fisheries commissions but are now known as regional fisheries management organisations (RFMOs). The treaties establishing the early international fisheries commissions (concluded from the 1930s onwards), reflecting prevalent attitudes to dispute settlement at the times that those treaties were negotiated, generally contained no provisions on dispute settlement. As they were gradually replaced (from the late 1970s onwards) by RFMOs, more far-reaching dispute settlement procedures were introduced. The most significant development was the adoption in 1995 of the Agreement for the Implementation of the Provisions of the United Nations Convention on the Law of the Sea relating to the Conservation and Management of Straddling Fish Stocks and Highly Migratory Fish Stocks, generally known as the UN Fish Stocks Agreement.[58] Article 30(1) of the Agreement stipulates that the provisions of Part XV of the Law of the Sea Convention apply, *mutatis mutandis*, to any dispute relating to the interpretation and application of the Agreement. Given that the Agreement implements UNCLOS, it is not surprising that it also incorporates the dispute settlement procedures of UNCLOS. It is possible for a State to be a party to the Agreement without being a party to UNCLOS[59] (and in practice one State, the USA, is at present in this position). Article 30(1) states explicitly that such a State may utilise the dispute settlement machinery of UNCLOS. It is highly unusual in international law for a State that is party to one treaty being able to use the dispute settlement procedures of another treaty to which it is not a party.

The dispute settlement provisions of the Fish Stocks Agreement contain several other interesting and novel features. First, Article 30(2) of the Agreement stipulates that

> the provisions relating to the settlement of disputes set out in Part XV of [UNCLOS] apply, *mutatis mutandis*, to any dispute between States Parties to this Agreement relating to the interpretation or application of a subregional,

[57] For a rare example, see Treaty on Fisheries between Certain Pacific Island States and the USA (adopted 2 April 1987, entered into force 15 June 1988) (1987) 26 ILM 1048, Art 6 of which provides for compulsory arbitration. See also text at n 68 below.

[58] Agreement for the Implementation of the Provisions of the United Nations Convention on the Law of the Sea relating to the Conservation and Management of Straddling Fish Stocks and Highly Migratory Fish Stocks (adopted 4 August 1995, entered into force 11 December 2001) (1995) 34 ILM 1542.

[59] Agreement Art 1(2)(e).

regional or global fisheries agreement relating to straddling fish stocks or highly migratory fish stocks to which they are parties.

This remarkable provision at one stroke makes the dispute settlement machinery of UNCLOS applicable to some 20 fisheries treaties.[60] Secondly, Article 29 of the Agreement provides that States parties may refer disputes of a 'technical nature' to an 'ad hoc expert panel' which is to 'resolve the dispute expeditiously without recourse to binding procedures for the settlement of disputes.' This is a useful provision that should facilitate the speedy and informal resolution of disputes that do not turn on points of law. Thirdly, Article 28 of the Agreement requires States to cooperate to prevent disputes, in particular by adopting 'efficient and expeditious decision-making procedures' within RFMOs. Furthermore, where coastal States and high seas fishing States cannot reach agreement on compatible conservation and management measures, Article 7(5) of the Agreement provides that the States concerned must make every effort to enter into provisional arrangements of a practical nature. Both Article 28 and Article 7(5) seek to prevent, or at least delay, disputes being referred to binding third party settlement. Where, nevertheless, a dispute under the Fish Stocks Agreement is ultimately referred to a judicial body for settlement, it may be possible for such a body to depart from a strictly legal approach in settling the dispute as Article 30(5) of the Agreement (on applicable law) allows a court or tribunal to apply, in addition to relevant legal rules, 'generally accepted standards for the conservation of living marine resources … with a view to ensuring the conservation of' the stock concerned.

A number of treaties establishing RFMOS have provisions that are similar to Article 30(1) of the Fish Stocks Agreement and therefore apply the UNCLOS dispute settlement machinery to disputes relating to those treaties. Such treaties include the Convention on the Conservation and Management of Highly Migratory Fish Stocks in the Western and Central Pacific Ocean,[61] the Convention on the Conservation and Management of Fishery Resources in the South-East Atlantic Ocean,[62] the Convention on Future Multilateral Cooperation in the North-East Atlantic Fisheries,[63]

[60] For a list of the main such treaties, see nn 61–65 and 67–82 below.

[61] Convention on the Conservation and Management of Highly Migratory Fish Stocks in the Western and Central Pacific Ocean (adopted 5 September 2000, entered into force 19 June 2004), Art 31 (2001) 40 ILM 278.

[62] Convention on the Conservation and Management of Fishery Resources in the South-East Atlantic Ocean (adopted 20 April 2001, entered into force 13 April 2003), Art 24 (2002) 41 ILM 40.

[63] Convention on Future Multilateral Co-Operation in the North-East Atlantic Fisheries (adopted 18 November 1980, entered into force 17 March 1982) 1285 UNTS 129. The Convention originally had no machinery on dispute settlement, but in 2004 the Commission established by the Convention adopted a recommendation (which is legally binding)

the Southern Indian Ocean Fisheries Agreement,[64] and the Convention on Future Multilateral Cooperation in the Northwest Atlantic Fisheries.[65] Those treaties have either been adopted or amended since the Fish Stocks Agreement. It is clear from the relevant drafting history that the dispute settlement provisions of those treaties have been inspired by the Agreement. Given that all the treaties in question are concerned with straddling or highly migratory fish stocks and that Article 30(2) of the Agreement extends the UNCLOS dispute settlement machinery to such treaties, it might be thought that the dispute settlement provisions of those treaties were redundant. However, for Article 30(2) to operate, it is necessary that both/all the parties to a dispute relating to a treaty concerned with straddling or highly migratory stocks are parties to the Agreement as well as to the treaty to which the dispute relates. With the exception of the North-East Atlantic Convention, each of the treaties mentioned has several parties that are not parties to the Agreement. As long as that remains the case, it is useful for those treaties to have their own compulsory dispute settlement procedures. Some of them also have informal dispute resolution procedures for technical disputes or for reviewing decisions of the RFMO, along the lines of Article 29 of the Fish Stocks Agreement.[66]

There are quite a number of other treaties falling within the scope of Article 30(2) of the Fish Stocks Agreement that have their own dispute settlement machinery, but machinery that is less far-reaching than that of UNCLOS. As with the first group of treaties mentioned above, the dispute settlement machinery of this second group of treaties will continue to apply where one or more of the parties to the dispute are not parties to the Agreement. This second group of treaties includes the Agreement establishing the General Fisheries Commission for the Mediterranean, which provides that any dispute not settled by a specially appointed committee shall be referred to the ICJ or, if one of the parties to the dispute is a regional economic integration organisation, to arbitration unless the parties to the dispute otherwise agree;[67] the Treaty on Fisheries between

providing for the settlement of disputes in accordance with the UNCLOS machinery: see North-East Atlantic Fisheries Commission, *Report of the 23rd Annual Meeting*, vol II, 28–29.

[64] Southern Indian Ocean Fisheries Agreement (adopted 7 July 2006, not yet in force), Art 20 [2006] OJ L196/15.

[65] Convention on Future Multilateral Co-Operation in the Northwest Atlantic Fisheries (adopted 24 October 1978, entered into force 1 January 1979) 1135 UNTS 369. The Convention originally had no machinery on dispute settlement, but in 2007 it was amended to provide for the settlement of disputes in accordance with the UNCLOS machinery: see Art XV(8) of the amended Convention, www.nafo.int/publications/frames/general-a17.html.

[66] South-East Atlantic Convention Art 24(3); North-East Atlantic Convention Recommendation, para 3; and Revised NAFO Convention Art XV(3).

[67] Agreement establishing the General Fisheries Commission for the Mediterranean (adopted 24 September 1949, entered into force 20 February 1952, amended October 1997), Art XVII [1998] OJ L190/36. Originally the Agreement had no provisions on dispute settlement.

Certain Pacific Island States and the USA, which provides that any dispute that cannot be settled through consultations may be referred by any party to the dispute to arbitration;[68] the Western Indian Ocean Tuna Organization Convention, which has similar provisions;[69] the Agreement for the Establishment of the Indian Ocean Tuna Commission, which provides that any dispute that cannot be settled through compulsory conciliation may be referred to the ICJ unless the parties to the dispute otherwise agree;[70] and the Galapagos Agreement, which provides that any dispute not settled by a conciliation commission or a technical arbitration body, and not referred by agreement to the ICJ or the ITLOS, may be submitted by either party to the dispute to arbitration.[71] All those treaties, as can be seen, provide for some form of compulsory judicial settlement. All have been concluded after the adoption of UNCLOS and before the entry into force (and, in most cases, adoption) of the Fish Stocks Agreement, and were presumably influenced by the emphasis put on dispute settlement by UNCLOS. In addition, there are some other treaties concerned with straddling or highly migratory fish stocks, which provide only for consensual means of dispute settlement, often for no more than diplomatic means. Treaties in this category include the Convention for the Conservation of Southern Bluefin Tuna,[72] the Convention on the Conservation of Antarctic Marine Living Resources,[73] the Niue Treaty on Cooperation in Fisheries Surveillance and Law Enforcement in the South Pacific Region,[74] the Convention on Fisheries Cooperation among African States Bordering the Atlantic Ocean,[75] the Arrangement for the Conservation and Management of the Western Pacific Purse Seine

[68] Treaty on Fisheries between Certain Pacific Island States and the USA (adopted 2 April 1987, entered into force 15 June 1988) Art 6 (1987) 26 ILM 1048.

[69] Western Indian Ocean Tuna Organization Convention (adopted 19 June 1991, entered into force 15 December 1992) Art 18, text available on the website of Ocean Law, www.oceanlaw.net

[70] Agreement for the Establishment of the Indian Ocean Tuna Commission (adopted 25 November 1993, entered into force 27 March 1996) Art XXIII 1927 UNTS 329.

[71] Framework Agreement for the Conservation of Living Marine Resources on the High Seas of the South Pacific (adopted 14 August 2000, not yet in force) Art 14 (2001) 45 *Law of the Sea Bulletin* 70.

[72] Convention for the Conservation of Southern Bluefin Tuna (adopted 10 May 1993, entered into force 1994) Art 16 1819 UNTS 360.

[73] Convention on the Conservation of Antarctic Marine Living Resources (adopted 20 May 1980, entered into force 7 April 1982) Art XXV 1329 UNTS 47.

[74] Niue Treaty on Co-Operation in Fisheries Surveillance and Law Enforcement in the South Pacific Region (adopted 9 July 1992, entered into force 20 May 1993) Art IX (1993) 32 ILM 136.

[75] Convention on Fisheries Co-Operation among African States Bordering the Atlantic Ocean (adopted 5 July 1991, entered into force 11 August 1995) Art 21 (1991) 19 *Law of the Sea Bulletin* 33.

Fishery,[76] the Convention on the Conservation and Management of Pollock Resources in the Central Bering Sea,[77] the Federated States of Micronesia Arrangement for Regional Fisheries Access,[78] the 'Loophole Agreement',[79] and the Convention for the Strengthening of the Inter-American Tropical Tuna Commission.[80] The reasons for less far-reaching dispute settlement provisions in those treaties may be because some of their parties include States traditionally opposed to compulsory dispute settlement and because of the rather limited institutional arrangements of some of those treaties. For them Article 30(2) of the Agreement is especially significant since it offers the possibility of compulsory judicial dispute resolution, at least where the parties to the dispute are parties to the Agreement. The same is true for those few treaties concerned with straddling or highly migratory species that have no provisions at all on dispute settlement. Such treaties include the International Convention for the Conservation of Atlantic Tunas[81] and the Nauru Agreement concerning Cooperation in the Management of Fisheries of Common Interest.[82]

There are a number of treaties concerned with types of high seas fisheries other than those for straddling or highly migratory species. The majority of those treaties contain no provisions on dispute settlement; a few provide for dispute settlement by consensual means. For reasons of space only one of those treaties is mentioned here,[83] and that is because it utilises the UNCLOS machinery to a degree. Article IX of the FAO Agreement to

[76] Arrangement for the Conservation and Management of the Western Pacific Purse Seine Fishery (adopted 28 October 1992, entered into force 8 December 1995) Art 10, text available on the website of Ocean Law, www.oceanlaw.net.

[77] Convention on the Conservation and Management of Pollock Resources in the Central Bering Sea (adopted 16 June 1994, entered into force 8 December 1995) Art XII (1995) 34 ILM 67.

[78] Federated States of Micronesia Arrangement for Regional Fisheries Access (adopted 30 November 1994, entered into force 23 September 1995) Art 19, text available on the website of Ocean Law, www.oceanlaw.net.

[79] Agreement between Iceland, Norway and Russia concerning Certain Aspects of Co-Operation in the Area of Fisheries (signed 15 May 1999, entered into force 15 June 1999) Art 10 (1999) 14 IJMCL 484.

[80] Convention for the Strengthening of the Inter-American Tropical Tuna Commission (adopted 14 November 2003, not yet in force) Art XV [2006] OJ L224/22. The original Convention establishing the Commission had no provisions on dispute settlement. Art XV(3) provides for the settlement of technical dispute along the same lines as Art 29 of the Fish Stocks Agreement.

[81] International Convention for the Conservation of Atlantic Tunas (adopted 14 May 1966, entered into force 21 March 1969), 673 UNTS 63.

[82] Nauru Agreement concerning Co-Operation in the Management of Fisheries of Common Interest (adopted 11 February 1982, entered into force 4 December 1982), text available on the website of Ocean Law, www.oceanlaw.net.

[83] For a slightly out of date list of such treaties, see J Peel, 'A Paper Umbrella which dissolves in the Rain? The Future for resolving Fisheries Disputes under UNCLOS in the Aftermath of the Southern Bluefin Tuna Arbitration' (2002) 3 *Melbourne Journal of International Law* 53, 76–78.

Promote Compliance with International Conservation and Management Measures by Fishing Vessels on the High Seas[84] provides that any dispute relating to the interpretation or application of the Agreement that cannot be settled by other means agreed by the parties to the dispute may be referred, with the consent of both/all the parties to the dispute, to the ICJ, the ITLOS or arbitration.

Although there are now a considerable number of high seas fisheries treaties providing for compulsory judicial settlement of disputes, either directly or through the Fish Stocks Agreement, no use has yet been made of those provisions. Possible explanations include the relatively recent conclusion or entry into force of most of the treaties concerned; the relatively limited number of parties to the Fish Stocks Agreement;[85] a reluctance to use judicial means to settle disputes that have a strong policy (rather than legal) content; problems of *locus standi*, especially in relation to disputes between members of RFMOs and non-members; the loss of control and inability to reach a compromise solution where a dispute is referred to a third party; and a desire to avoid the costs and bother of litigation. It is also possible that the threat (or even possibility) of unilateral referral of a fisheries dispute to a judicial body has induced parties to a dispute to settle it by diplomatic means.[86] What is not a factor in the non-use of judicial dispute settlement machinery is a lack of fisheries disputes. Increasing competition between fishermen (exacerbated by over-capacity in many of the world's fishing fleets) for fish stocks that are mostly fully or over-exploited has already led to, and will inevitably continue for some time to produce, a number of serious disputes. An interesting suggestion has been made recently that the decisions of RFMOs should be capable of being subjected to judicial review. This would avoid having to frame differences as contentious disputes and could also allow NGOs to intervene.[87]

A final point that may be made about the settlement of fisheries disputes is that some trade disputes that have been litigated have their origins in fisheries disputes, where one State has imposed trade sanctions against other States engaging in fishing practices that are considered undesirable

[84] Agreement to Promote Compliance with International Conservation and Management Measures by Fishing Vessels on the High Seas (adopted 24 November 1993, entered into force 24 April 2003) (1994) 33 ILM 968.

[85] The Agreement had 71 parties as of September 2008.

[86] These factors are explored further in Churchill, n 48 above at 417–23. See also TL McDorman, 'The Dispute Settlement Regime of the Straddling and Highly Migratory Fish Stocks Convention' (1997) 35 *Canadian Yearbook of International Law* 57, 59–62; TL McDorman, 'Global Ocean Governance and International Adjudicative Dispute Resolution' (2000) 43 *Ocean and Coastal Management* 255, 269–71, 273; and A Serdy, 'The Paradoxical Success of UNCLOS Part XV: A Half-Hearted Reply to Rosemary Rayfuse' (2005) 36 *Victoria University of Wellington Law Review* 713, 715, 717.

[87] MW Lodge et al, *Recommended Best Practices for Regional Fisheries Management Organisations* (London, Chatham House, 2007) 82–83.

or illegal. Examples include the two tuna/dolphin cases litigated under the pre-WTO GATT, which concerned a US ban on imports of tuna caught in ways that harmed dolphin populations;[88] the shrimp/turtle case heard under the WTO Dispute Settlement Understanding (DSU), which concerned a US ban on imports of shrimp from a number of States because the shrimp had been caught in a way that harmed turtles;[89] and a case brought under the DSU by the EC against Chile, where the EC challenged Chile's ban on EC vessels landing catches in Chile, imposed because of alleged violation of UNCLOS by EC vessels fishing for swordfish on the high seas.[90]

IV. DISPUTE SETTLEMENT UNDER MARINE POLLUTION TREATIES

UNCLOS identifies six sources of marine pollution (shipping, dumping of waste, seabed mining within the limits of national jurisdiction, seabed mining in the International Seabed Area, land-based sources and the atmosphere),[91] but leaves their detailed regulation to other instruments. Pollution from shipping is regulated by three global treaties; dumping of waste by both a global treaty and regional treaties; and pollution from seabed mining within the limits of national jurisdiction, land-based pollution and atmospheric pollution by a mixture of regional treaty and global soft law instruments (the latter, by their nature, are of no interest as far as dispute settlement is concerned). Pollution from mining in the International Seabed Area is and will be controlled through regulations already adopted and to be adopted by the International Seabed Authority. Most of the treaties referred to have provisions on dispute settlement. Disputes relating to the Authority's regulations will be settled according to the procedures governing seabed mining, outlined in section II B above.

The main treaty regulating pollution from shipping is the International Convention for the Prevention of Pollution from Ships (known as the MARPOL Convention).[92] It provides that disputes relating to its

88 GATT, *United States: Restrictions on Imports of Tuna—Report of GATT Panel* (16 August 1991) (1991) 30 ILM 1594; and GATT, *United States: Restrictions on Imports of Tuna—Report of the Panel* (20 May 1994), (1994) 33 ILM 839.

89 WTO, *United States: Import Prohibition on Certain Shrimp and Shrimp Products—Report of the Appellate Body* (12 October 1998), WT/DS58/AB/R.

90 WTO, *Chile—Measures affecting the Transit and Importing of Swordfish*, WT/DS193/3 (6 April 2001). Proceedings in the case are currently suspended. Following the EC's initiation of proceedings under the DSU, Chile referred its allegations of breaches of UNCLOS by the EC for compulsory settlement under UNCLOS—the *Swordfish* case, discussed at n 21 above.

91 See Arts 207–12.

92 International Convention for the Prevention of Pollution from Ships (adopted 2 November 1973, entered into force 2 October 1983), 1340 UNTS 61.

interpretation or application that cannot be settled by consensual means may be referred by either party to the dispute to arbitration.[93] The other two global treaties dealing with pollution from shipping, the International Convention on the Control of Harmful Anti-Fouling Systems on Ships[94] and the International Convention for the Control and Management of Ships' Ballast Water and Sediments,[95] although concluded much more recently than the MARPOL Convention, do not, unlike the latter, provide for compulsory judicial settlement but only for settlement by any peaceful means of the parties' choice.[96] The explanation why the dispute settlement machinery of those two treaties is more modest than that of the MARPOL Convention may be because treaties negotiated under the auspices of the IMO, as those two treaties were, have in the past usually contained no or very limited dispute settlement machinery (the MARPOL Convention being a notable exception). The reason for that may be because the IMO sees itself as primarily a technical organisation seeking to avoid all political controversy and dispute, and thus would not wish to encourage the publicising of disputes through the provision of compulsory dispute settlement procedures in its treaties. Marine pollution caused by the dumping of waste is regulated at the global level by the London Convention.[97] This provides that disputes relating to the Convention that cannot be settled by diplomatic means may be referred, by agreement, to arbitration or the ICJ.[98] In 1996 a protocol to the Convention was adopted which, for parties to it, supersedes the original convention. Reflecting developments in dispute settlement since the original convention was adopted, it provides that disputes that cannot be settled by diplomatic means may be referred by either party to the dispute to arbitration unless the parties agree to use one of the UNCLOS dispute settlement fora.[99]

Most of the regional treaties regulating various sources of marine pollution (including dumping) are the product of UNEP's Regional Seas Programme. They have a common format, comprising a framework convention for a particular region together with a number of protocols

[93] Art 10 and Protocol II.

[94] International Convention on the Control of Harmful Anti-Fouling Systems on Ships (adopted 5 October 2001, entered into force 17 September 2008), text available on the website of Ocean Law, www.oceanlaw.net.

[95] International Convention for the Control and Management of Ships' Ballast Water and Sediments (adopted 13 February 2004, not yet in force), (2004) 19 *International Journal of Marine and Coastal Law* 446.

[96] Arts 14 and 15, respectively.

[97] Convention on the Prevention of Marine Pollution by Dumping of Wastes and Other Matter (adopted 29 December 1972, entered into force 30 August 1975) 1046 UNTS 120.

[98] Art 11, as amended in 1978.

[99] Protocol to the Convention on the Prevention of Marine Pollution by Dumping of Wastes and Other Matter (adopted 8 November 1996, entered into force 24 March 2006) Art 16 (1997) 36 ILM 1.

addressing different sources of marine pollution and broader aspects of the protection of the marine environment. Dispute settlement provisions are generally found in the framework conventions (of which there are currently 10) rather than the protocols, although such provisions apply both to the protocols as well as the conventions. They invariably provide for consensual dispute resolution, some by diplomatic means only, others also by arbitration. The reason for a consensual approach is probably due to the fact that many of the States participating in those conventions have traditionally not been keen on compulsory judicial means and to the fact that marine pollution is seen as a problem that needs to be addressed through the greatest degree of cooperation and thus it is desirable to avoid the kind of bad feeling that might be engendered by unilaterally initiated litigation. The regional marine pollution treaties for the Baltic Sea and North-East Atlantic (including the North Sea) have been negotiated outside the framework of UNEP's Regional Seas Programme. The 1992 Baltic Convention, like the 1974 Convention which it replaced, provides that disputes that cannot be settled by diplomatic means may be referred with the agreement of both/all the parties to the dispute to arbitration or the ICJ.[100] The reason for consensual settlement is no doubt explained by the fact that the parties to the 1974 Convention included three Communist States (Russia, Poland and East Germany), which traditionally emphasised the consensual nature of international law and were opposed to compulsory dispute settlement. That appears still largely to be the position of Russia, even after the collapse of Communism, and this explains why the dispute settlement provisions of the 1974 Convention were reproduced unchanged in the 1992 Convention. In the case of the North-East Atlantic, under both the current regional convention and the convention of 1974 which it replaced, disputes that cannot be settled by diplomatic means may be referred by either party to the dispute to arbitration.[101] This is the only regional pollution treaty that provides for compulsory dispute settlement. The explanation for this is probably that the parties to the Convention are all from Western Europe, a region that has traditionally been sympathetic to compulsory dispute settlement.

In spite of the fact that quite a number of treaties concerned with marine pollution provide for the judicial settlement of disputes, albeit in most cases only if both/all the parties to the dispute agree, this dispute settlement machinery has so far been invoked only once. That was by Ireland, which unilaterally referred its dispute with the United Kingdom

[100] Convention on the Protection of the Marine Environment of the Baltic Sea Area (adopted 9 April 1992, entered into force 17 January 2000) Art 26 2009 UNTS 195.

[101] Convention for the Protection of the Marine Environment of the North-East Atlantic (usually known as the Ospar Convention) (adopted 22 September 1992, entered into force 25 March 1998) Art 32 (1993) 32 ILM 1072.

over the latter's refusal to provide it with certain information relating to the construction and operation of the MOX plant to an arbitral tribunal set up under the Ospar Convention. Ireland was unsuccessful in its action.[102] There are a number of possible reasons why there has been so little use so far of the judicial settlement machinery of marine pollution treaties. States may consider that disputes over the interpretation of a marine pollution treaty or measure adopted thereunder are better dealt with by the institutional machinery that those treaties establish or utilise (commission, meeting of the parties, or the Marine Environment Protection Committee of the IMO) than by a court or tribunal. Disputes over application of a treaty are likely usually to involve issues of non-compliance. In this situation States may refrain from invoking dispute settlement procedures because they are not directly affected by another State's non-compliance or because they are not complying themselves, which is frequently the position:[103] in any case, most dispute settlement procedures cannot be utilised without the consent of the other party/parties to the dispute.

V. JUDICIAL SETTLEMENT OF LAW OF THE SEA DISPUTES BY THE MEANS OF GENERAL INTERNATIONAL LAW

Where a law of the sea dispute cannot be settled by the judicial means provided by the treaties considered above, either because one or more of the parties to the dispute is not a party to the treaty in question or because the dispute does not relate to the interpretation and application of such a treaty, the general judicial mechanisms of international law—the ICJ, arbitration and regional courts with broad competence—may be available for settling the dispute. Even if a dispute concerns UNCLOS and both/all the parties to the dispute are parties to UNCLOS, it is possible, nevertheless, to refer the dispute for settlement to one of the general international law judicial means because UNCLOS does not claim a monopoly for its specialist dispute settlement procedures. Indeed, the position is rather the reverse. Article 280 provides that nothing impairs the right of any States parties to UNCLOS to agree at any time to settle a dispute by any peaceful means of their own choice. Article 281 goes on to provide that if the parties to a dispute concerning UNCLOS have agreed to settle that dispute by peaceful means of their own choice, the dispute settlement procedures

[102] Dispute concerning Access to Information under Article 9 of the Ospar Convention (2003) 42 ILM 1118.

[103] See further E Hey, T Ijlstra and A Nollkaemper, 'The 1992 Paris Convention for the Protection of the Marine Environment of the North-East Atlantic: A Critical Analysis' (1993) 8 *International Journal of Marine and Coastal Law* 1, 43; and EA Kirk, 'Noncompliance and the Development of Regimes addressing Marine Pollution from Land-Based Activities' (2008) 39 *Ocean Development and International Law* 235.

of UNCLOS apply only where no settlement has been reached by utilising those means and the agreement does not exclude recourse to any further procedure. Article 282 provides that if the parties to a dispute concerning UNCLOS have agreed, through a general, regional or bilateral agreement 'or otherwise',[104] that such a dispute shall, at the request of any party to the dispute, be submitted to a procedure that entails a binding decision, that procedure shall apply instead of the procedures of UNCLOS, unless the parties to the dispute agree otherwise. In practice, general international law judicial means have been used to settle a number of law of the sea disputes since UNCLOS entered into force in 1994: a brief survey of such settlement will now be made.

A. The ICJ

Since the entry into force of UNCLOS in 1994, five disputes concerning the law of the sea have been referred to the ICJ. They have all concerned matters dealt with by UNCLOS, but in all but one case one or more of the parties to the dispute was not a party to UNCLOS at the time that the dispute was referred to the ICJ. The exception is the *Romania/Ukraine* case,[105] where the parties had concluded an agreement in 1997 whereby if they could not settle their maritime boundary by agreement, either of them could refer the matter unilaterally to the ICJ. This is a classic application of Article 282 of UNCLOS. It is noteworthy that none of the five cases was referred to the ICJ by special agreement. The basis of the ICJ's jurisdiction was either the optional clause (the *Spain/Canada* case[106]), a compromissory clause in an existing treaty (the *Peru/Chile*[107] and *Romania/Ukraine* cases) or both (the *Nicaragua/Honduras* and *Nicaragua/Colombia* cases[108]). All but one of the five cases concern maritime boundary delimitation (the fifth

[104] The phrase 'or otherwise' is generally taken to refer to the optional clause of Art 36(2) of the ICJ's Statute. See Rosenne and Sohn (eds), above n 12 at 26–27.

[105] *Maritime Delimitation in the Black Sea Case (Romania v Ukraine)*, www.icj-cij.org/docket/index.php?p1=3&p2=3&code=ru&case=132&k=95.

[106] *Fisheries Jurisdiction Case (Spain v Canada)* [1998] ICJ Rep 463. The Court found that it lacked jurisdiction due to a reservation made by Canada to its optional clause declaration.

[107] *Maritime Dispute Case (Peru v Chile)*, referred to the ICJ in January 2008. See ICJ Press Release 2008/1, 16 January 2008. Peru has invoked the Pact of Bogotà as the basis of the ICJ's jurisdiction.

[108] *Case concerning Territorial and Maritime Dispute between Nicaragua and Honduras in the Caribbean Sea (Nicaragua v Honduras)* Judgment of 8 October 2007, www.icj-cij.org/docket/files/120/14075.pdf and (2007) 46 ILM 1053. *Territorial and Maritime Dispute (Nicaragua v Colombia)*, Preliminary Objections, Judgment of 13 December 2007 www.icj-cij.org/docket/files/124/14305.pdf. In each case the compromissory clause relied on by Nicaragua was the Pact of Bogotà. In the *Nicaragua/Colombia* case the ICJ decided that it did not need to consider the ICJ's optional clause as a basis of jurisdiction: see paras 132–40 of the Judgment.

concerned the arrest by Canada of a Spanish fishing vessel on the high seas). Together with the two arbitrations under Annex VII of UNCLOS (referred to above) and the arbitration referred to below, as well as a dozen or so maritime boundary cases referred to the ICJ or arbitration before 1994, these four cases show the continuing popularity among States for the resolution of maritime boundaries by judicial means (although it must also be remembered that the overwhelming majority of maritime boundaries are determined by agreement between the parties following negotiations). Indeed, apart from international trade disputes, maritime boundaries are the most litigated matter between States.

B. Arbitration

Some treaties provide for the possibility for one party to a dispute unilaterally to refer the dispute to arbitration. Those relevant to the law of the sea have already been referred to above. But arbitration by agreement remains an option, especially where one or both of the parties to a dispute are not parties to UNCLOS. So far one law of the sea dispute has been settled through consensual arbitration since the entry into force of UNCLOS in 1994. That was the maritime boundary dispute between Eritrea and Yemen, where Eritrea was not a party to UNCLOS at the time that the parties agreed to arbitration. Interestingly, in spite of this, the tribunal was directed to take UNCLOS into account in determining the boundary.[109]

C. Regional Courts With Broad Subject Matter Jurisdiction

Arguably the leading court of this type is the European Court of Justice (ECJ). It has held that treaties to which the EC is a party, whether together with its Member States (such as UNCLOS, the Fish Stocks Agreement and some regional pollution treaties) or to the exclusion of its Member States (most fisheries treaties), are part of Community law.[110] Thus, a dispute between two EC Member States relating to a treaty to which both they and the EC are parties will be a dispute relating to Community law, at least if the dispute concerns a matter that falls within the competence of the EC. Such disputes not only may be heard before the ECJ but must be heard there if the parties to the dispute refer it to judicial settlement, since

[109] Arbitration Agreement (adopted 3 October 1996, entered into force 2 November) Art 2(3), annexed to the Award of the Arbitral Tribunal in the Second Stage (Maritime Delimitation), *Eritrea/Yemen Arbitration* (2001) 40 ILM 983.

[110] Case 13/00 *Commission v Ireland* [2002] ECR I-2943, para 14; and Case 239/03 *Commission v France* [2004] ECR I-9325, para 25.

under Article 292 of the EC Treaty Member States are obligated not to refer disputes concerning Community law to any other court or tribunal. Accordingly, the ECJ held that Ireland violated Article 292 by referring its dispute with the United Kingdom over the MOX plant to arbitration under UNCLOS Annex VII.[111]

The ECJ may deal not only with inter-State disputes concerning treaties to which the EC is a party (although no such cases have yet been referred to it) but also disputes concerning such treaties that involve other actors. First, it is possible for the Commission to bring a case against a Member State before the ECJ under Article 226 of the EC Treaty if it considers that the Member State is not complying with a treaty to which both that State and the EC are parties: that is because such non-compliance will be a breach of Community law if it concerns a provision of a treaty that falls within the EC's competence. There is at least one such case involving a law of the sea treaty. In *Commission v France* the Commission alleged that France had failed to comply with the protocol on land-based sources of marine pollution to the Mediterranean Convention by permitting a State-owned energy concern to pollute a salt marsh: the allegation was upheld by the ECJ.[112] It would also be possible for a Member State, or conceivably an EC institution (the Commission or the European Parliament would seem the most likely), to argue that the EC had violated a treaty to which it was a party and bring an action before the ECJ under Article 230 (breach of EC law) or Article 232 (failure to act where required to do so). The same possibility is unlikely to be open to individuals (ie, natural and legal persons) because they have restricted *locus standi* under Article 230 and 232. It is possible for individuals to challenge the legality of EC acts incidentally in proceedings before national courts. However, in its recent judgment in the *Intertanko* case, in which a group of tanker owners sought to argue that an EC directive dealing with criminal liability for causing marine pollution breached UNCLOS, the ECJ held that individuals could not invoke a treaty before national courts to challenge the validity of EC legislation unless the treaty in question established 'rules intended to apply directly and immediately to individuals and to confer upon them rights or freedoms capable of being relied upon against States'.[113] The ECJ found that UNCLOS was not a treaty of that type. It seems likely that the ECJ would reach the same conclusion in respect of all the other law of the sea treaties referred to above. On the other hand, the ECJ has held that individuals may rely on treaties, at least if their provisions are sufficiently clear and precise, to challenge before national courts acts of Member States that

[111] Case C-459/03 *Commission v Ireland* [2006] ECR I-4635.
[112] Case C-239/03 *Commission v France*, above n 110.
[113] Case C-308/06 *Intertanko*, Judgment of 3 June 2008 (not yet reported), para 64.

are alleged to contravene treaties to which the EC is a party. This was the situation, for example, in a case where individual fishermen were held by the ECJ to be competent to rely on the protocol to the Mediterranean Convention to challenge the same pollution of a salt marsh that was in issue in *Commission v France*.[114] However, it is difficult to see that the protocol, any more than UNCLOS, conferred rights directly on individuals. It would therefore seem, assuming that this case is still good law following *Intertanko*, that individuals wishing to challenge the non-compliance by the EC with a treaty are in a markedly inferior position to individuals who wish to challenge the non-compliance by a Member State with a treaty to which both it and the EC are parties. There seems no obvious reason for such differentiation.

Another regional court with broad subject matter jurisdiction is the Central American Court of Justice. The Court has heard at least one law of the sea case. In 1999 Nicaragua asked the Court to rule that the planned ratification by Honduras of a bilateral maritime boundary agreement with Colombia would breach the Tegucigalpa Protocol to the Charter of the Organisation of Central American States. After making an order of provisional measures in 1999, the Court gave a judgment finding in favour of Nicaragua in 2001.[115]

VI. CONCLUSIONS

Provision for the compulsory settlement of disputes in treaties relating to the law of the sea was not unknown before the adoption of UNCLOS in 1982, but UNCLOS marked a major advance with the comprehensiveness of its dispute settlement machinery and the wide range of potential disputes subject to it. Since then compulsory dispute settlement has become a feature of many other law of the sea treaties, While much of the dispute settlement machinery of UNCLOS and those other treaties is fairly traditional, there are, nevertheless, some significant innovations. The latter include: the establishment by UNCLOS of a new international court, the ITLOS, which is the only international court of global application with the jurisdiction to hear inter-State disputes apart from the ICJ, although the scope of its jurisdiction is obviously more restricted *ratione materiae* (though somewhat broader *ratione personae*); the wide choice of forum given to States parties to UNCLOS; the combination of diplomatic and judicial means of settlement, and the use of specialist arbitrators, in

[114] Case 213/03 *Syndicat professionnel coordination des pêcheurs de l'étang de Berre et de la région v Électricité de France* [2004] ECR I-7357, paras 39–47.

[115] Text of the judgment available on the website of the Central American Court of Justice, www.ccj.org.ni.

tribunals established under Annex VIII of UNCLOS; the access of natural and legal persons to the Sea-bed Disputes Chamber of the ITLOS; aspects of the system of provisional measures under UNCLOS (including the prescription of such measures in order to protect the marine environment; the obligation on parties to the dispute to report on their implementation of provisional measures; and the practice of the ITLOS in prescribing measures to promote confidence building between the parties and to manage the dispute); the jurisdiction of the ITLOS to order the release of vessels detained for alleged fisheries and pollution offences upon the posting of a bond or other security; the extension of the UNCLOS dispute settlement machinery to a number of other law of the sea treaties and, through Article 30(2) of the Fish Stocks Agreement, to some 20 treaties concerned with straddling and highly migratory fish stocks; and provision for the use of less formal procedures to resolve technical disputes under the Fish Stocks Agreement and some other fisheries treaties. So far much of this diverse dispute settlement machinery is unused. Part of the explanation is because a good deal of it is of very recent origin. It may well come to be used in the future. All those with an interest in dispute settlement in international law would therefore do well to keep developments in dispute settlement in the law of the sea under fairly close observation.

7

The WTO Dispute Settlement Mechanism as a New Technique for Settling Disputes in International Law

SURYA P SUBEDI*

I. INTRODUCTION

THE WTO DISPUTE settlement mechanism (DSM) is a novelty in international law in so many respects.[1] Although it is an improvement on the old GATT dispute settlement mechanism, it is quite different in nature from other international mechanisms available for resolving international disputes between States. Unlike other mechanisms, the rules and procedures of this mechanism, especially the provisions relating to the appellate body, follow the principles of common law rather than civil law. This mechanism is a blend of diplomacy, negotiation, mediation, arbitration and adjudication. It is neither fully judicial nor completely a non-judicial mechanism.

Although the mechanism as a whole could best be described as quasi-judicial, this term too would not be wholly accurate description of this

* Email: s.p.subedi@leeds.ac.uk.

[1] See generally, S Lester, B Mercurio, A Davies and K Leitner, *World Trade Law: Text, Materials and Commentary*, pt III, Dispute Settlement in the WTO (Oxford, Hart Publishing, 2008); K Bagwell, PC Mavroidis, and RW Staiger, 'The case for tradable remedies in WTO dispute settlement' in SJ Evenett and BM Hoekman (eds), *Economic Development and Multilateral Trade Cooperation* (Washington DC, World Bank, 2006) 395–413; WJ Davey, 'The WTO Looking Forwards' (2006) *Journal of International Economic Law* 9–23; E Petersmann 'Strategic Use of WTO Dispute Settle Proceeding for Advancing WTO Negotiations on Agriculture' in *Reforming the World Trading System: Legitimacy, Efficiency, and Democratic Governance* (Oxford, Oxford University Press, 2005) 127–44; WJ Davey 'Dispute Settlement in the WTO and Regional Trade Agreements: A comment' in Lorand, Bartels and Federico (eds), *Regional Trade Agreements and the WTO Legal System* (Oxford, Oxford University Press, 2006); AF Lowenfeld, *International Economic Law Part III, Dispute Solution*, 2nd edn (Oxford, Oxford University Press, 2008) 143–211.

mechanism. This is because, while the first stage of the proceedings—ie up to the panel stage, which is modelled largely on arbitration—could be regarded as quasi-judicial, the second stage of the dispute—ie the work of the appellate body—is very much like a judicial mechanism with some exceptions. For instance, unlike in a court of law, the proceedings of the appellate body are confidential.

The decision of the Appellate Body of the WTO is not a judgment either; it issues reports in the form of recommendations to both the Dispute Settlement Body (DSB), a committee comprised of all WTO Members, and the WTO members concerned. Thus this mechanism is quite a complex one in many respects, but has been regarded as quite an efficient one in resolving international trade disputes. Furthermore, it was perhaps the first international dispute settlement mechanism which embraced the idea of an appeal against the decisions of dispute settlement panels.

The claim often made by both scholars in their writings and WTO officials is that the WTO, which came into existence on 1 January 1995, has passed its infancy successfully[2] and its dispute settlement body (DSB) has been a success.[3] Indeed, within a relatively short period of time the WTO has become one of the most important international organisations with nearly 153 States, developed and developing, small and big, powerful and weak, as its members. Since its inception nearly 400 cases have been referred to the DSM, which is a great deal more than have been referred to the International Court of Justice (ICJ) established nearly 60 years ago. Some of the cases decided by the DSB have had far-reaching implications, involving billions of dollars, and received prominent treatment in the media.

However, this is not a perfect mechanism by any means. It is not free of constraints, deficiencies and some inherent weaknesses. Critics argue that the DSB is not as effective as it appears to be on the surface, especially when it comes to enforcing the rulings of the DSB against major powers.[4]

[2] The Uruguay Round of Multilateral Negotiations launched under the auspices of GATT in 1986 concluded in December 2003. Among the agreements concluded by the Uruguay Round was the one establishing a Multilateral Trade Organization which was later named as WTO and the agreement to establish this organisation was formally signed in Marrakesh, Morocco, on 15th April 1994. In accordance with the provisions of the Final Act embodying the results of the Uruguay, the WTO came into existence on 1 January 1995.

[3] See, eg D McRae, 'What is the Future of WTO Dispute Settlement?' (2004) 7 *Journal of International Economic Law* 3 ff; WJ Davey, 'The WTO Dispute Settlement System: The First Ten Years', (2005) 8 *Journal of International Economic Law* 17 ff.

[4] M Bronckers and M Djordjevic, 'Financial Compensation in the WTO: Improving the Remedies of WTO Dispute Settlement' (2005) 8 *Journal of International Economic Law* 101 ff; Y Fukunaga, 'Securing Compliance through the WTO Dispute Settlement System: Implementation of DSB Recommendations' (2006) 9 *Journal of International Economic Law* 383 ff.

They also argue that it does not provide effective remedies for those non-State business actors which suffer from injustices and distortions in international trade.

Although the passage of a mere 15 years is not a long period of time to assess the performance of the WTO dispute settlement mechanism, it should be noted that this mechanism was not created as an entirely new one in 1995 but as an improvement on the previous dispute settlement mechanism under the GATT. In other words, the new mechanism was reborn in its present form in January 1995. It is in this context that this chapter aims to examine the framework of the DSB, highlight its salient features and provide an overall assessment of this special dispute settlement mechanism.

II. AN OVERVIEW OF THE MECHANISM

A. The objective of the DSB

The main aim of the dispute settlement mechanism of the WTO is to secure a positive solution to a dispute.[5] Through this mechanism the WTO seeks to provide legal certainty to producers and exporters around the globe that foreign markets remain open to them. This certainty has been provided by creating a rule-based, fully-fledged international organisation and an effective dispute settlement mechanism. Indeed, a mechanism for resolving trade disputes under the DSU is vital for enforcing the rules and therefore for ensuring that trade flows smoothly.

B. Powers and Functions of the DSB

The Dispute Settlement Body was established to settle trade related disputes between WTO members arising under several WTO agreements such as the Marrakesh agreement establishing the WTO, multilateral agreements on trade in goods, the general agreement on trade in services and the agreement on trade-related aspects of intellectual property rights

[5] See generally on the WTO law and policy, B Hoekman and M Kostecki, *The Political Economy of the World Trading System: From GATT to WTO* (Oxford, Oxford University Press, 1995); MJ Trebilock and R Howse, *The Regulation of International Trade*, 2nd edn (London, Routledge, 1999); JH Jackson et al, *Legal Problems of International Economic Relations: Cases, Material and Text* (Minnesota, West Publishing, 2002); A Lowenfeld, *International Economic Law* (Oxford, Oxford University Press, 2002); DLM Kennedy and JD Southwick (eds), *The Political Economy of International Trade Law: Essays in Honour of Robert E Hudec* (Cambridge, Cambridge University Press, 2002).

and the plurilateral trade agreements listed in the appendices of the DSU.[6] The establishment of the DSB and its powers and functions are outlined in Article 2 of the DSU in the following terms:

> The Dispute Settlement Body is hereby established to administer these rules and procedures and, except as otherwise provided in a covered agreement, the consultation and dispute settlement provisions of the covered agreements. Accordingly, the DSB shall have the authority to establish panels, adopt panel and Appellate Body reports, maintain surveillance of implementation of rulings and recommendations, and authorize suspension of concessions and other obligations under the covered agreements.[7]

The importance of the dispute settlement mechanism and the nature of obligations of the member of the WTO in this regard are outlined in Article 3(2) of the DSU:

> The dispute settlement system of the WTO is a central element in providing security and predictability to the multilateral trading system. The Members recognize that it serves to preserve the rights and obligations of Members under the covered agreements, and to clarify the existing provisions of those agreements in accordance with customary rules of interpretation of public international law. Recommendations and rulings of the DSB cannot add to or diminish the rights and obligations provided in the covered agreements.[8]

Article 3(7) goes on to outline the purposes and scope of the dispute settlement mechanism in the following words:

> The aim of the dispute settlement mechanism of the WTO is to secure a positive solution to a dispute. A solution mutually acceptable to the parties to a dispute and consistent with the covered agreements is clearly to be preferred. In the absence of a mutually agreed solution, the first objective of the dispute settlement mechanism is usually to secure the withdrawal of the measures concerned if these are found to be inconsistent with the provisions of any of the covered agreements. The provision of compensation should be resorted to only if the immediate withdrawal of the measure is impracticable and as a temporary measure pending the withdrawal of the measure which is inconsistent with a covered agreement. The last resort which this Understanding provides to the Member invoking the dispute settlement procedures is the possibility of suspending the application of concessions or other obligations under the covered

[6] The Plurilateral Agreements are the Agreement on Trade in Civil Aircraft, Agreement on Government Procurement, International Dairy Agreement and the International Bovine Meat Agreement. The applicability of the DSU to the Plurilateral Trade Agreements would be subject to the adoption of a decision by the parties to each agreement setting out the terms for the application of the DSU to the individual agreement.

[7] GATT Secretariat (it now would be WTO), The Results of the Uruguay Round of Multilateral Trade Negotiations (Geneva, 1994), 405.

[8] Ibid.

agreements on a discriminatory basis vis-à-vis the other Member, subject to authorization by the DSB of such measures.[9]

Thus, the message in the DSU is that the main object and purpose of the dispute settlement mechanism is to persuade the WTO members to be compliant with the law rather than punish the guilty. What is aimed at here is the resolution of a dispute in an amicable manner rather than adjudication of it by the DSB.

C. Establishment of Panels

Panels function like tribunals and usually consist of three members. Panellists are usually chosen in consultation with the countries in dispute. If the two sides cannot agree on the appointment of panellists then the Director-General of the WTO will appoint them. They are chosen either from a permanent list of well-qualified candidates, or from elsewhere. They serve in their individual expert capacities.[10] Standard terms of reference as specified in the DSU would apply to panel proceedings unless the parties agree to special terms within 20 days of the panel's establishment. Rulings in a trade dispute are made by a panel and endorsed (or rejected) by the entire membership of the WTO since their report is passed to the DSB for final approval. If the panel decides that the disputed trade measure does break a WTO agreement or an obligation, it recommends to the State concerned that the measure be brought in compliance with WTO rules.[11] The report of the panel becomes the ruling or recommendation of the DSB within 60 days unless a consensus rejects it. This notion of 'negative consensus' is considered further later. Either side can appeal the findings in the report.

D. Appeal Mechanism

The Appellate Body of the WTO was established in 1995 under Article 17 of the DSU. It is a standing body of seven persons created to hear appeals from reports issued by panels. The seven members are elected by the DSB for a term of four years. The concept of appellate review of the report of a panel is an important new feature of the DSB which did not exist under the old GATT system. Any of the parties to the dispute can appeal a panel's ruling. Appeals have to be based on points of law such as legal

[9] Ibid 406.
[10] DSU Art 8.
[11] DSU Art 12 and App 3.

interpretation. The Appellate Body cannot re-examine existing evidence or examine new issues. Each appeal is heard by three members of a permanent seven-member Appellate Body, and it can uphold, modify or reverse the panel's legal findings and conclusions. Neither the panels nor the Appellate Body pass judgment.

The Appellate Body is also required to work within a tight time-frame when considering appeals. Once the Appellate Body has concluded its report it is circulated to all WTO members within 90 days of the date when the notice of appeal was filed, and it becomes public immediately upon circulation to members. Within 30 days of the circulation of an Appellate Body report, the DSB has to meet to adopt it, unless the DSB decides by consensus not to adopt that Report. In practice almost all reports of the appellate body are automatically and unconditionally adopted by the DSB.[12]

E. Implementation of the Rulings

The aim of the dispute settlement mechanism of the WTO is persuasive rather than punitive. The losing State party is required to bring its policy, a trade measure, a legal provision or an administrative decision into line with the ruling or recommendations so that the State concerned becomes compliant with WTO rules. The losing State party must follow the recommendations of the panel report or the appeals report. It must state its intention to do so at a DSB meeting held within 30 days of the adoption of the report of this body.

If compliance with the recommendation immediately proves impractical, the losing party will be given a 'reasonable period of time' to do so. The length of a reasonable period of time should be decided either by agreement of the parties and approval by the DSB within 45 days of adoption of the report or through arbitration within 90 days of adoption. If the State concerned fails to act within the reasonable period of time so specified it has to enter into negotiations with the other disputing parties in order to determine mutually-acceptable compensation which may include measures such as tariff reductions in areas of particular interest to the winning party. If no satisfactory compensation is agreed within 20 days, the winning party may ask the DSB for permission to impose limited trade sanctions against the other party and the DSB is under an obligation to grant this authorisation within 30 days of the expiry of the 'reasonable period of time' unless there is a consensus against the request.[13]

[12] DSU Arts 17, 18 and 19.
[13] DSU Arts 20 and 21.

III. SOME SALIENT FEATURES OF THE DSB

A. Compulsory Jurisdiction

The DSB of the WTO is the first major international dispute settlement mechanism with compulsory jurisdiction. States which are members of the WTO have no choice but to submit their trade disputes to the DSB. This is not the case with many other mechanisms for the settlement of international disputes. For instance, the ICJ itself has no compulsory jurisdiction. It can entertain cases only when States issue a declaration accepting its compulsory jurisdiction or agree through a special agreement to refer the matter to the Court.

The system of dispute settlement under the 1982 UN Convention on the Law of the Sea (UNCLOS)[14] comes close to the DSB of the WTO in the sense that it too has a compulsory jurisdiction on many aspects of the law of the sea. However, both in terms of the number of cases referred to the International Tribunal for the Law of the Sea (ITLOS) and other arbitral tribunals and the significant exceptions to compulsory jurisdiction means the WTO-DSM remains the only truly compulsory system currently extant in the international field.

B. The Mechanism for Appeal

Another major improvement on the GATT dispute settlement under the WTO DSB is the provision for appeal on questions of law. No judgment of the ICJ can be appealed nor can the awards of international investment tribunals. But within the WTO, the reports of a panel, that is, the findings of a Panel, can be appealed to the Appellate Body which functions like an appeal court.

Most significantly, there is now a much more effective system for implementation of the rulings of the DSB. When the Panel or the Appellate Body report is adopted, the party concerned will have to notify its intentions with respect to implementation of adopted recommendations. In cases where it is impracticable to comply immediately, as already noted, the party concerned is given a reasonable period of time—determined either by agreement of the parties concerned and approval by the DSB within 45 days of adoption of the report, or through arbitration within 90 days of adoption.

If the Panel or the Appellate Body report recommends payment of compensation, parties can enter into negotiations to agree on mutually acceptable compensation. If no agreement could be reached, a party to

[14] See Churchill, ch 6 of this book.

the dispute may request authorisation of the DSB to suspend concessions or other obligations to the other party concerned under the WTO agreements.

Any disagreements over the proposed level of suspension can be referred to arbitration. Normally, concessions should be suspended in the same sector as that in the issue in the case concerned and if this is not practicable or effective, the suspension can be made in other sectors of the same agreement. If this too is not effective or practicable and if the circumstances are serious enough, the suspension of concessions under another agreement is also possible.

C. Strict Timetable for Settling Disputes

The DSB of the WTO is also credited for providing a strict time-frame for the settlement of trade disputes. Unlike the ICJ or the ITLOS, where it can take a long time before a final judgment is delivered, the cases referred to the DSB have to follow a rigid time-frame designed for a swift conclusion of the case. Within nine months of the establishment of a panel, the DSB has to deliver its report and if the report is appealed, the consideration of appeal should be completed within 12 months in total. Apart from arbitration, no national or international dispute settlement mechanism can rival this timing.

The timetable of the DSB to settle a trade dispute runs as follows: The first stage is for consultation for up to 60 days. The DSU requires that before taking any other actions the countries in dispute have to talk to each other to see if they can settle their differences by themselves. If they fail to resolve the dispute in an amicable manner they can also ask the Director-General of the WTO to mediate or try to help in any other way, including offering his good offices. If this all fails, then the second—more legalistic—stage of the dispute will commence, under which the complaining State party to the dispute can ask for a panel to be appointed, following which the panel has to be appointed within 45 days. Once a panel has been constituted it can take up to six months to conclude its examination of the dispute concerned and produce its report. When the ruling of a panel has been appealed the appeal process must not last more than 60 days, with an absolute maximum of 90 days. The DSB on its part has to accept or reject the appeals report within 30 days.

D. Flexibility in Settling Disputes

The WTO system is designed to settle disputes as amicably as possible through consultations whenever possible. Consequently, many of the disputes referred to the DSB have been notified as settled 'out of court' or have remained in consultation phase. The whole approach in the DSB mechanism is a persuasive one: to persuade the disputing parties to discuss their problems and settle the dispute by themselves. It is not surprising therefore that the first stage of the disputes is consultations between the governments concerned. Furthermore, even when the case has progressed to other stages, consultation and mediation are still always possible, thereby allowing the disputing parties to come to an amicable resolution of the dispute. Article 5(3) reads as follows:

> Good offices, conciliation or mediation may be requested at any time by any party to a dispute. They may begin at any time and be terminated at any time. Once procedures for good offices, conciliation or mediation are terminated, a complaining party may then proceed with a request for the establishment of a panel.[15]

This high degree of flexibility provided by the DSU to the parties has enabled member States of the WTO to settle their differences prior to proceeding to the more formal stage of composition of panels. The informality of the process is also conducive to arriving at a mutually acceptable solution. This is one reason why many disputes between WTO members have not resulted in formal rulings by the DSB.

E. Transparency for WTO Members

Unlike other international dispute settlement mechanisms, the procedure of the DSB is actually quite transparent—not to the outside world, but to the disputing parties themselves and the general membership of the WTO. Although the panel is required to meet in closed session, the parties to the dispute and interested parties can attend the meetings when invited by the panel to appear before it. The deliberations of the panel and the documents submitted to it are also to be kept confidential. However, the disputing parties are allowed to comment on the work of the panel. This is not the case with other international dispute settlement mechanisms.

The panel will submit the descriptive (factual and argument) sections of its report to the two sides, giving them two weeks to comment. Secondly, the panel submits an interim report including its findings and conclusions to the two sides, giving them one week to ask for a review. Thirdly, a final report is submitted to the two sides before circulating it to the general membership of the WTO. The presentations, rebuttals and statements made by a party to the dispute before the panel have to be made in the

[15] GATT Secretariat (it now would be WTO), *The Results of the Uruguay Round of Multilateral Trade Negotiations* (Geneva, 1994) 409–10.

presence of the other parties. Each party's written submissions, including any comments on the descriptive part of the report and responses to questions put by the panel, are also made available to the other party or parties.

However, the practice of the Appellate Body in recent years has been to open its hearing to the public at the request of the parties in the dispute concerned. For instance, in March 2009 in the case entitled '*United States—Laws, Regulations and Methodology for Calculating Dumping Margins (Zeroing)—Recourse to Article 21.5 of the DSU by the European Communities*',[16] the Appellate Body decided to open its hearing to public viewing at the WTO Headquarters in Geneva at the request of the participants (the European Communities and the United States).

F. The Requirement of Consensus

Unlike the GATT system which required a positive consensus to establish a panel, under the new DSU a panel has to be established unless the DSB decides by consensus against establishment. One of the major improvements on the old GATT dispute settlement system was to make it impossible for the country losing a case to block the adoption of the ruling. Under the old GATT system—also known as the 'positive consensus' procedure—rulings could only be adopted by consensus. This meant that a single objection could block the ruling. However, under the new WTO system also known as 'negative consensus' procedure, rulings are automatically adopted by the DSB unless there is a consensus to reject a ruling.[17] This means that any country wanting to block a ruling by the DSB (it is the General Council, consisting of representatives of all WTO members, that serves as DSB when considering reports of panels or the Appellate Body) has to persuade all other WTO members (including its adversary in the case) to share its view on the matters raised in the dispute concerned.

G. Sequencing

The word 'sequencing' in WTO parlance signifies the procedural steps and time-periods needed to deal with a situation where the complaining country claims that the defending country has not implemented the rulings. Articles 21(5), 22(2) and 22(6) of the DSU deal with the basic elements

[16] WT/DS294/RW.

[17] GATT Secretariat (it now would be WTO), 'The WTO Dispute Settlement Mechanism', *GATT Focus* (Special Issue, May 1994) 12–14.

of sequencing. According to Article 21(5), where the two parties disagree whether the rulings have been implemented or not, a panel examines the dispute and reports within 90 days. This article reads as follows:

> Where there is disagreement as to the existence or consistency with a covered agreement of measures taken to comply with the recommendations and rulings such dispute shall be decided through recourse to these dispute settlement procedures, including wherever possible resort to the original panel. The panel shall circulate its report within 90 days after the date of referral of the matter to it. When the panel considers that it cannot provide its report within this time frame, it shall inform the DSB in writing of the reasons for the delay together with an estimate of the period within which it will submit its report.

Under Article 22(2) if the defending country fails to implement, the complaining country can ask the DSB to authorise it to retaliate. Consequently, according to Article 22(6), within 30 days from the end of the reasonable period of time for implementation, the DSB authorises the complaining country to retaliate. Thus, there are two key steps with their own time-periods: 90 days for a panel to examine whether a ruling has been implemented; and 30 days for DSB to authorise retaliation. However, there is some uncertainty raised by the wording of the DSU as it does not specify whether these steps have to come one after the other. Therefore, the issue is part of the main agenda for negotiations with the DSB as part of the Doha mandate to improve the DSU of the WTO.

H. *Amicus Curiae* Submissions

One of the controversial issues in the operation of the rules of the DSU of the WTO has been whether panels and the Appellate Body may accept and consider unsolicited submissions—commonly referred to as *amicus curiae* briefs—which they receive from entities not a party or third party to the dispute, including NGOs, INGOs, academics and other individuals. Known in common parlance as 'friend of the court', the notion of '*amicus curiae*' is not new to the world of law or jurisprudence. However, the problem is that neither the DSU nor the Working Procedures for Appellate Review specifically addresses this issue and different States and scholars have different views in this regard. The admittance of such briefs in the US-Shrimp/Turtle dispute[18] in 1998 stirred a debate among WTO Member States as to whether this should be permissible under the DSU. The view advanced by the Appellate Body seems to be that the panel's comprehensive authority to seek information from any relevant source

[18] *United States—Import prohibition of certain shrimp and shrimp products* WT/DS58/AB/R, 12 October 1998.

under Article 13 of the DSU and to add to or depart from the Working Procedures in Appendix 3 to the DSU (Article 12.1, DSU) permits panels to accept and consider or to reject information and advice, even if submitted in an unsolicited fashion. However many Members of the WTO, especially the developing ones, are of the view that the DSU does not allow panels to accept and consider non-requested *amicus curiae* briefs. In their view the DSM of the WTO is a mechanism available purely to members of the organisation and there is no role whatsoever for non-parties, particularly NGOs.

Although only a few panels have in fact made use of their discretionary right to accept and consider *amicus curiae* briefs, such briefs have frequently been filed in Appellate Body proceedings and the Appellate Body maintains that it has the authority to accept and consider any information it considers pertinent and useful in deciding an appeal, including *amicus curiae* submissions. The Appellate Body has taken the view that it has such a right flowing from its broad authority to adopt procedural rules, provided they do not conflict with the DSU or the covered agreements. Nevertheless, the Appellate Body has stated that it does not need to take into account the views in *amicus curiae* briefs filed by non-parties to the dispute. In clarifying its position on this matter, the Appellate Body held in the *US–CVDs on Steel* that:

> Individuals and organizations, which are not Members of the WTO, have no legal *right* to make submissions to or be heard by the Appellate Body. The Appellate Body has no legal *duty* to accept or consider unsolicited *amicus curiae* briefs submitted by individuals or ogranizations, not Members of the WTO. The Appellate Body has a legal *duty* to accept and consider *only* submissions from WTO Members which are parties or third parties in a particular dispute.[19]

The Appellate Body went on to assert that '[we] are of the opinion that we have the legal authority under the DSU to accept and consider *amicus curiae* briefs in an appeal in which we find it pertinent and useful to do so.'[20] The Appellate Body had the opportunity to further clarify its position in the *Asbestos* case[21] in which it decided to invite briefs from all interested sources relying on Article 16(1) of the Working Procedures for Appellate Review. Article 16(1) reads as follows:

> In the interest of fairness and orderly procedure in the conduct of an appeal, where a procedural question arises that is not covered by these Rules, a Division

[19] Para 41, of the Appellate Body report on United States - Imposition Of Countervailing Duties On Certain Hot-Rolled Steel Products Originating In The United Kingdom, WTO Doc WT/DS138/AB/R of 10 May 2000.

[20] Para 42, Report of the Appellate Body.

[21] *European Communities—Measures affecting asbestos and products containing asbestos* (DS135/R) and (DS135/R/Add 1). Document inviting briefs: DS135/9.

> may adopt an appropriate procedure for the purpose of that appeal only provided that it is not inconsistent with the DSU, the other covered agreements and these Rules.

Thus, the legal position on this matter seems to be that individuals and organisations have no legal right to make submissions to or to be heard by the Appellate Body. Accordingly, it has no legal duty to accept or consider *amicus curiae* briefs submitted by individuals or organizations. It should be noted here that the issue relating to what kind of access the public might have to panel proceedings or their input into the procedure by means of *amicus curiae* briefs is one of the subjects being discussed within the DSB under the Doha mandate to improve the DSU.

I. Role of Public International Law in WTO Treaty Interpretation

Whether the WTO legal regime is a fully self-contained body of trade rules or a part of public international law, and to what extent rules and principles of public international law could be taken into account in interpreting the rules of WTO law, have been issues which have been debated both within and outside the WTO. While many scholars such as Pauwelyn[22] argue that WTO rules are part of the wider corpus of public international law, others, such as Trachtman,[23] take a more cautious approach. For instance, Trachtman argues that 'WTO negotiators in 1994 did not intend other international law to be used as potential defences to WTO obligations.' Citing the decisions of the WTO Appellate Body in the *Hormones and Poultry*[24] cases, he asserts that

> [t]he clear and general practice of international tribunals is to limit the scope of applicable law to that specified in their particular mandates. In the case of the DSU, its affirmative mandate is clearly and repeatedly limited to WTO law: the 'covered agreements'. Therefore, the only law that WTO panels and the Appellate Body are authorised to apply (directly) is WTO law.[25]

Although it can be submitted that nothing in the DSU precludes WTO panels from applying certain principles of public international law in deciding cases before them, the WTO agreements, resulting from substantial political negotiation focussing on the creation of a separate and specific legal regime, do not contain any explicit provisions concerning

[22] J Pauwelyn, 'The Role of Public International Law in the WTO: How Far Can We Go?' (2001) 95 AJIL, 535–52.

[23] J Trachtman, 'Conflict of Norms in Public International Law: How WTO Law Relates to Other Rules of International Law' (2004) 98 AJIL, 855–61.

[24] WT/DS48/AB/R.

[25] See above n 24.

the relationship between WTO rules and the rules of public international law. Nevertheless, it also is clear that WTO agreements were not designed and do not cover all aspects of the process involved in settling a trade dispute between States. Therefore, it can be submitted that international law, especially that concerning the interpretation of treaties contained in the 1969 Vienna Convention on the Law of Treaties, would apply to the interpretation of WTO treaties by WTO panels and the Appellate Body.

Whether or not the WTO regime can be regarded as a fully self-contained body of rules, it is plausible to conclude that international law can and will play a role in settling trade disputes by the DSM of the WTO. For instance, WTO panels or the Appellate Body would not be able to interpret any WTO rules in contravention of the principles of *jus cogens* or the principles enunciated in the UN Charter. Moreover, the mention of the principle of sustainable development, a principle of international environmental law, in the preamble to the Agreement Establishing the WTO—and the rulings of the WTO Appellate Body in cases such as *Shrimp-Turtle*[26] demonstrate that public international law principles will have a measure of influence in the interpretation of the WTO agreements by WTO panels and the Appellate Body.

IV. OVERALL ASSESSMENT OF THE MECHANISM

It has been submitted generally that the DSB has worked well and contributed to strengthening the rules-based system of the WTO. While around 300 cases in total were referred to the old GATT dispute settlement mechanism during the entire 47 years of its existence, more than 400 cases had already been referred to the DSB of the WTO in the first 15 years of its existence. This demonstrates a growth in confidence in the dispute settlement mechanism of the WTO. Because of the flexibility offered by the DSU, well over 100 cases have been settled or defused as a result of bilateral consultations. This quasi-judicial characteristic of the DSB, combining political flexibility and legal integrity, makes this a unique process for settling international disputes peacefully. Some of the cases decided by the DSB have had far-reaching implications, involved billions of dollars and received prominent treatment in the media.[27]

However, critics have pointed out a trade-liberalisation bias of the DSB in its consideration of the cases referred to it. Of course, since the DSB

[26] *United States—Import Prohibition of certain Shrimp and Shrimp Products*, Appellate Body Report, WTO/DS58/AB/R, circulated on 12 October 1998.

[27] See for an overview of the operation of the WTO since its inception, SP Subedi, 'The Notion of Free Trade and the First Ten Years of the World Trade Organization: How Level is the "Level Playing Field"?' (2006) 53(2) *The Netherlands International Law Review* 273–96.

is part of the WTO structure designed to promote trade liberalisation it seems natural for the DSB to have this bias. After all, it is supposed to apply and interpret WTO law—which is pro-trade liberalisation. This inherent limitation of the DSB is not conducive to making it a body capable of balancing trade concerns with other legitimate concerns, required to promote international justice. The *Tuna-Dolphin I* and *II*[28] and *Shrimp-Turtle*[29] cases could be cited as examples of such trade bias.[30] Various proposals have been made to reform the DSB in line with the statements made in the Doha Declaration of 2001, to correct this bias.[31]

The effectiveness of the DSB depends on the remedy actually received by the aggrieved party at the end of the day. There are doubts as to the effectiveness of the WTO rulings because some of the more powerful States have not internalised the WTO framework. There have been difficulties in implementing certain panel and Appellate Body rulings and in bringing the laws of such powerful States into conformity with WTO rules, especially if it involves enacting new legislation in order to comply with the WTO ruling. The risk here is that some of the more powerful States would use the WTO when it suits them and disregard it when their own vital interests are at stake.

The DSB adopts the international law approach of persuasion, designed to encourage States to participate in the regime created rather than award huge amounts of compensation to the States which are victims of violation of international trade law.[32] In other words, in most of the WTO cases the losing State is required to comply with the WTO rulings by making its laws consistent with its WTO obligations. This works if the impact of the dispute is limited to the State as a collective entity.

However, when individual interests are involved, the mere promise by a losing party of compliance with WTO obligations in the future may not be satisfactory for the individual business parties—whether natural or juridical—who may have suffered huge financial losses as a result of the breach of WTO law in the first place. Only when non-performance continues can a losing party demand 'compensatory measures'. As highlighted in a report prepared by the Consultative Board to the Director-General of

[28] GATT Panel Report on *United States—Restrictions on Imports of Tuna*, 18 February 1992, GATT BISD (39th Supp) at 205 (1993) and (1994) 33 ILM 839.

[29] *United States—Import Prohibition of certain Shrimp and Shrimp Products*, Appellate Body Report, WTO/DS58/AB/R, circulated on 12 October 1998.

[30] There are of course some commentators who have suggested that *Shrimp-Turtle II* has gone too far against trade liberalisation.

[31] See generally, W Weiss, 'Reforming the Dispute Settlement Understanding' in H Hohmann (ed), *Agreeing and Implementing the Doha Round of the WTO* (Cambridge, Cambridge University Press, 2008) 269–93.

[32] It has generally been regarded that it is a *lex specialis* exception to the usual rules of State responsibility.

the WTO and entitled *The Future of the WTO*, the stick applied in the WTO system is curbing future market access rather than the 'cheque in the mail' approach.[33] Even when compliance is not forthcoming, and compensatory measures are not agreed, the fallback is 'suspension of obligations' or the so-called 'retaliation' by the aggrieved party with the authorisation of the DSB.

V. CURRENT NEGOTIATIONS TO IMPROVE THE DSM

Soon after the conclusion of the Uruguay Round of multilateral trade negotiations, it was agreed in a Ministerial Decision of 1994 that dispute settlement rules should be reviewed by 1 January 1999. The review started within the DSB in 1997 and the deadline was extended to 31 July 1999. However, there was no agreement on the subject matter.

When the trade ministers of the WTO Member countries met in Doha, Qatar, in November 2001 for the Doha Ministerial Conference, they agreed to negotiate to improve and clarify the DSU, stating that:

> We agree to negotiations on improvements and clarifications of the Dispute Settlement Understanding. The negotiations should be based on the work done thus far as well as any additional proposals by Members, and aim to agree on improvements and clarifications not later than May 2003, at which time we will take steps to ensure that the results enter into force as soon as possible thereafter.[34]

It should be noted that the Doha Declaration (in paragraph 47) also states that the negotiations on the DSU will not be part of the single undertaking—that is, that they will not be tied to the success or failure of the other negotiations mandated by the declaration.

Since then negotiations have taken place within the DSB and member governments have participated actively in these talks, resulting in well over 80 WTO members having subscribed to more than 40 proposals, each of which containing several suggested changes, covering virtually all stages of the dispute settlement system.

While some of the proposals are related to housekeeping issues such as how to deal with inactive cases which remain dormant for several years without any indication that the complaining countries want to pursue these any further, many others are focussed on certain fundamental issues such as sequencing, external transparency, enhancing third-party rights,

[33] P Sutherland et al, *The Future of the WTO: Addressing Institutional Challenges in the New Millennium* (Report by the Consultative Board to the Director-General Supachai Panitchpakdi) (Geneva, WTO, 2004).

[34] Doha Declaration WT/MIN(01)/DEC/W/1 of 14 November 2001, para 30.

enhancing compensation, strengthening notification requirements for mutually agreed solutions, strengthening special and differential treatment for developing countries at various stages of the proceedings and composition of panels.

With regard to the composition of panels, negotiators are discussing the possibility of a permanent roster of individuals, retained on a full-time basis, from which panelists would be drawn for each case to speed up the process and to reinforce the independence of panels and quality of their reports. However, although all proposals are still on the table, no major breakthrough was achieved in this regard within the Doha Round of multilateral trade negotiations which itself is suspended at the moment. The Hong Kong Declaration of the WTO issued by the Sixth Ministerial Conference of December 2005 simply noted the progress made in the DSU negotiations as reflected in the report by the Chairman of the Special Session of the DSB to the Trade Negotiations Committee (TNC) and directed the Special Session to continue to work towards a rapid conclusion of the negotiations.

VI. CONCLUSIONS

The new dispute settlement mechanism of the WTO was a new experiment in international law and is a new technique for settling international trade disputes. Purely as a trade body, the WTO has done well and simply as a quasi-judicial mechanism for settling technical trade disputes, the DSB too has done reasonably well. But the DSB has no powers to go beyond the WTO law that already exists and many developing countries believe that this law is not as fair as it should be.[35] It is therefore debatable whether the DSB is capable of ensuring a level playing field and thereby delivering justice in the broader sense of the term, or ensuring fairness and justice in the narrow sense of applying and interpreting the existing body of law as objectively, independently and impartially as possible.

In order to enable the DSB to play the role of a real international trade court capable of promoting and ensuring fairness and justice for all in the broader sense of the terms, certain changes will have to be made to WTO law, in line with the aims and objectives of the Doha Declaration of the WTO of 2001.[36] For this, the Doha Trade Round initiated by the Declaration would have to be revived and compromises found among the

[35] See for a detailed analysis of the difficulties within the WTO system, Oxfam, *Rigged Rules and Double Standards: Trade, Globalisation, and the Fight Against Poverty* (Oxford, Oxfam, 2002).

[36] WT/MIN(01)/DEC/1 of 20 November 2001.

major trading nations of the world, to make the WTO legal regime itself fair for all.

Whether the WTO is able eventually to revive the Doha Round and move forward the multilateral trade negotiations on wider, complex and more fundamental issues such as the liberalisation of trade agriculture and acceleration in the liberalisation of the services sector, the WTO could make various changes to the DSU to in order to make the workings of the DSB more transparent to the public in general interested in its work rather than keeping much of its proceedings confidential. At present, only the final outcome of a dispute is made available to the public.[37] The enforcement mechanism of the decisions of the DSB could be improved and more certainty achieved. Rather than focusing largely on the objective of compliance by WTO members with international trade rules, the DSU could include some more robust punitive mechanisms such as compensation to those directly affected by a deliberate trade-distorting measure adopted by a WTO member.

Although the dispute settlement mechanism of the WTO is an intergovernmental mechanism available only to WTO member States, the time has perhaps come to look at the possibility of allowing non-State actors an opportunity, under certain narrowly defined conditions, to bring a claim to the WTO against a State. The actual victims of a distorting measure adopted by a WTO member are often non-State actors—companies and other business organisations—but the WTO dispute settlement mechanism does not allow them any access to it. This state of affairs somehow does not look satisfactory in a world where the stated aim has been to achieve greater legitimacy, transparency and democracy in the conduct of international relations.

[37] As stated earlier, this issue is one of the main items on the agenda of the Doha Round of negotiations to improve the DSU of the WTO. Therefore, the future of the negations on these issues seems to depend on the success or failure of the Doha Round as a whole. It remains to be seen whether and if so when the stalled negotiations would be revived.

8

Legal Means of Dispute Settlement in the Field of Collective Security: The Quasi-Judicial Powers of the Security Council

NIGEL D WHITE AND MATTHEW SAUL

I. INTRODUCTION

THE INTERNATIONAL COURT of Justice (ICJ), not the Security Council (SC) is the 'principal judicial organ' of the UN.[1] Rather, the SC is a political organ with 'primary responsibility for the maintenance of international peace and security',[2] mandated under Chapter VII to take decisions relating to threats to the peace, breaches of the peace, and acts of aggression.[3] However, the SC's express and implied powers show that its role in collective security is not purely an executive one. In relation to the settlement of international disputes the UN Charter Chapter VI allocates to the SC non-binding powers of recommendation. In the light of its practice of determining what recommendations and measures should be taken in the interests of international peace, it is reasonable to identify a quasi-judicial role for the SC, in terms of judgment and capacity for implementation (enforcement) of that judgment.[4] In effect this amounts to a utilisation of powers drawn from Chapters VI and VII, both express and implied to fulfil one of the purposes of the UN set out in

[1] UN Charter Art 92. On the ICJ's contribution to international peace and security see D Akande, 'The Role of the International Court of Justice in the Maintenance of International Peace' (1996) *African Journal of International and Comparative Law* 592.

[2] UN Charter Art 24(1).

[3] Ibid Arts 39–42.

[4] See R Higgins, 'The Place of International Law in the Settlement of Disputes by the Security Council' (1970) 64 *American Journal of International Law* (*AJIL*) 1–18; E Lauterpacht, *Aspects of the Administration of International Justice* (Cambridge, Cambridge University Press, 1991) 37–48; V Gowlland-Debbas, *Collective Responses to Illegal Acts in International Law* (Dordrecht, Martinus Nijhoff, 1990) 265–69.

Article 1(1) of the Charter, namely to 'bring about by peaceful means, and in conformity with the principles of justice and international law, adjustment or settlement of international disputes or situations which might lead to a breach of the peace'.

Of course, with regards dispute settlement in collective security it does not follow from this recognition of quasi-judicial competence that the SC is effective, but, amidst the present range of threats and challenges for international peace, it is clearly important that the SC strives to be as effective as possible, but that effectiveness must be balanced against its obligations under international law. In trying to achieve order in international relations, the Security Council must also strive to achieve justice, and it is this constant balancing which permeates all decisions on matters of collective security—where the security imperative meets the rights of States or individuals.[5] Thus, in the course of examining the role of and problems faced by the SC in relation to collective security and dispute settlement, this chapter is particularly interested in its effectiveness and how this could be improved, but a central argument is that effectiveness is dependent upon legitimacy, which in large part includes respect for the canons of international law. Analysis is centred on the key dispute-settlement functions undertaken by the SC: investigation, judgment, and implementation (enforcement). The focus is on the SC because it alone has the power to bind Member States, a power which is not shared by the General Assembly (GA), except in budgetary matters. This is not to suggest, of course, that the GA has no role in international dispute settlement, nor that it does not act in a quasi-judicial manner,[6] but the absence of binding powers limits its impact. Similarly, mention of the SC as a legislature is only to the extent that a particular action is relevant for the analysis of its dispute settlement function.[7]

Before examining in more detail the Security Council's quasi-judicial role, it is necessary to outline its functions more broadly and the legal order within which it operates. The aim is not to reprise the question whether the Security Council is bound by international law, but to identify those laws that it should respect if its decisions and judgments are to gain maximum support amongst Member States and the wider international community. Some of these laws are binding per se, others may be more arguable, but all should form part of the Security Council's 'jurisprudence' when attempting to settle disputes.

[5] See generally R Foot, JL Gaddis and A Hurrell (eds), *Order and Justice in International Relations* (Oxford, Oxford University Press, 2003).

[6] See Legal Consequences for States of the Continued Presence of South Africa in Namibia (South West Africa) notwithstanding Security Council Resolution 276, 1971 ICJ Rep 16, 49, paras 102–03.

[7] See S Talmon, 'The Security Council as World Legislature' (2005) 99 *AJIL* 175–93.

II. THE MANY ROLES OF THE SECURITY COUNCIL

Paul Kennedy in his recent work on the UN concludes that 'even if the world body is constitutionally one organism, there are in practice many UNs',[8] referring to the different elements of the UN system. Indeed, this point can be taken further when considering the most influential and powerful organ in the UN system—the SC. There are many SCs: the public one where Resolutions are adopted and the private one where deals are made; the executive one where action is taken against recalcitrant States who are in breach of UN law, and the legislative one that adopts broad-ranging Resolutions that address world problems such as terrorism and the proliferation of weapons of mass destruction; the quasi-judicial one where judgments are made on the behaviour of States and individuals, and the political one which ignores egregious acts such as genocide and aggression when it either suits the interests of the permanent members or they cannot agree on action; the corporate one when the Council agrees on a course of action and adopts a decision binding on the membership, and the concert one when it simply facilitates discussions between States; the organ where the veto is abused to prevent action to deal with serious breaches of international law, and the one where it is used to prevent authorisation of illegitimate actions; the interventionist Council addressing what have traditionally been seen as domestic matters, and the non-interventionist one when one or more permanent members (currently China and Russia) decide that the proposal is going too far; the traditional body basing its Resolutions upon Chapter VI and thereby respecting the principles of consent and sovereignty and the modern centralised authority adopting coercive measures under Chapter VII to deal with the constantly changing security landscape; the organ that is concerned about preventing the use of force between States, and the organ that has the power to authorise military action; the body that is subject to international law, and the one that can by dint of Articles 25 and 103 of the Charter override treaty obligations that are inconsistent with its decisions.

There are so many facets to the Security Council, some of them hugely controversial, arguably in their development unconstitutional, that it proves very difficult, almost impossible, to pin down its true nature and character. Arguably because of this it has proven impossible to reform. Arguments about size, effectiveness, legitimacy and democracy tend to stand or fall on which particular vision of the SC the proponent has—ranging from its being solely an executive organ to it being a nascent form of world government. In these circumstances with no consensus, States fall back on self-interest and argue for instance that they should be

[8] P Kennedy, The Parliament of Man: The Past, Present and Future of the United Nations (New York, Random House, 2006) xvi.

permanent members even though they may contribute little to international peace and security; and despite their claims will not represent the States in their region.

What is clear though is that the SC has exceptional powers in that the Charter expressly recognises that it is an exception to both the norm of non-intervention in Article 2(7) and that prohibiting the use of force in Article 2(4). The latter has two express exceptions in Chapter VII, the right of self-defence belonging to States in Article 51 and the power to authorise military action in Article 42. The former states that:

> Nothing contained in the present Charter shall authorize the United Nations to intervene in matters which are essentially within the domestic jurisdiction of any State ... but this principle shall not prejudice the application of enforcement measures under Chapter VII.

In granting these exceptional powers States recognise that the SC can by-pass the traditional limbs of international law—consent and sovereignty—but only when acting under Chapter VII. Furthermore, the SC is empowered to make binding decisions mainly under Chapter VII, which can create obligations that override conflicting obligations—not simply in response to acts of aggression that breach Article 2(4), but in response to 'threats to the peace' as determined by the Council itself not necessarily by international law. The real problem is not so much the SC's alleged abuse of power—it is the amount of power it has got, especially under Chapter VII.

III. THE SECURITY COUNCIL WITHIN THE INTERNATIONAL LEGAL ORDER

Can such an organ fit into the wider international legal order or is it so unbound as to be a like Frankenstein's monster, an analogy currently favoured by institutional lawyers sceptical of the growing power of international institutions. In the most crucial scene of Mary Shelley's nineteenth century gothic novel the monster declares to its maker Dr Frankenstein—'you are my creator, but I am your master: obey!'[9] When considering the federal competence of the EC and the spreading supranationality of the SC it is tempting to see such bodies in this light—with States as the creators but organisations as the masters. In reality though it is unnecessary to engage in such scare-mongering for the simple fact is that it is not international organisations that commit genocides, or widespread human

[9] J Klabbers, *An Introduction to International Institutional Law* (Cambridge, Cambridge University Press, 2002) v; J Alvarez, *International Organizations as Lawmakers* (Oxford, Oxford University Press, 2005) 585.

rights abuses, or invade States. At worst the UN may ignore genocides, or its peacekeepers may be unable to prevent human rights violations and a minority might themselves be in violation, though this is as much the fault of the Member States. On the other hand, it might be persuaded to authorise the use of force by willing States to combat genocide if the cause convinces the members of the UN Security Council.

Organisations are not (yet) the monsters of Mary Shelley's nightmare, but governments can be. If organisations can regulate, can govern States, then the benefits of having relatively powerful organisations may well outweigh the preservation of full State sovereignty in the traditional anarchic State-dominated system of international relations. With this in mind we can make some remarks about the role of the SC in the international legal order. Some are relatively uncontroversial, but a number are arguable. All, though, contribute to the legitimacy of Council decisions and actions.

The first point to note is that the SC is an integral part of the post-1945 international legal order; it is not somehow outside that order. It does possess exceptional powers that enable it to disregard the norms of non-intervention and that prohibit the use of force that bind other international legal actors, but even when using these exceptional powers it is required to act within the purposes and principles of the UN Charter. In the case of the Security Council its function is to maintain or restore international peace and security—one of the purposes of the UN—but it must, according to Article 24(2), act in accordance with the whole range of purposes and principles of the UN, which includes respect for human rights.

The SC is also bound by *jus cogens* so that it should not commit acts in violation of these norms,[10] but there is also an expectation that it should take action to combat serious violations of peremptory norms such as genocide and crimes against humanity, or where there are systematic war crimes being committed. The 'responsibility to protect' debate is where this argument currently lies;[11] and the inadequacies of the SC's response to the situations in Darfur and the Democratic Republic of the Congo reflect the reality of the progress that has been made. The SC is also bound by customary international law by dint of the overall international legal

[10] *Application of the Convention on the Prevention and Punishment of the Crime of Genocide (Bosnia and Herzegovina v Serbia and Montenegro)* 1993 ICJ Rep 325, 440–41 (separate opinion of Judge *ad hoc* Lauterpacht).

[11] E McLean, 'The Responsibility to Protect: The Role of International Human Rights Law' (2008) 13 *Journal of Conflict and Security Law* 123; C Focarelli, 'The Responsibility to Protect Doctrine and Humanitarian Intervention: Too Many Ambiguities for a Working Doctrine' (2008) 13 *Journal of Conflict and Security Law* 191.

personality of the UN.[12] This means that it should respect basic human rights found in customary law when making judgments about States and individuals, an obligation reinforced by the need for its decisions to respect the purposes and principles of the UN which include the promotion of human rights. Furthermore, the legitimacy of its decisions would be enhanced if when acting in a quasi-judicial way—in deciding that a State is guilty of supporting terrorism for instance or in listing individuals suspected of terrorism—it recognised basic principles of due process and natural justice by giving those targeted a chance to challenge the decisions taken against them. It must recognise that while it has binding powers and powers of enforcement, it still relies on the legitimacy of its decisions to ensure compliance by the wider membership.

By the terms of Article 103 only inconsistent treaty law can be overridden by a Charter obligation. To argue that Article 103 should be interpreted to override customary duties as well, on the basis that the Charter is a global constitution and Article 103 is evidence of this,[13] fails to recognise that the Charter is an imperfect constitution that creates a powerful organ with weak constitutional constraints. To argue the supremacy of SC imposed obligations over any inconsistent duty under such a constitution will further the dominance of politics over law and thus in reality weaken the claim made that the Charter is a world constitution. Care should be taken in interpreting Article 103 too widely.[14] Further, when deciding which treaty obligations can be overridden by SC-imposed duties, the resolution should not be interpreted with too broad a footprint. In acting within the purposes and principles it must allow States to uphold their human rights obligations, for instance, as far as is possible.[15]

Article 103 was intended to allow UN obligations to displace those treaty obligations directly in their path, so that an arms embargo would require a State to suspend any agreement it has to supply arms to the target government.[16] It should not be used as an excuse to override any treaty obligation that might prevent the efficient application of the

[12] Interpretation of the Agreement of 25 March 1951 between the WHO and Egypt, 1980 ICJ Rep 73, 89–90.

[13] R Bernhardt, 'Article 103' in B Simma (ed), *The Charter of the United Nations: A Commentary* (Oxford, Oxford University Press, 2002) 1299.

[14] R Liivoja, 'The Scope of the Supremacy Clause of the United Nations Charter' (2008) 57 ICLQ 586.

[15] Joined Cases C-402/05 P and C-415/05 P *Yassin Abdullah Kadi, Al Barakaat International Foundation v Council of the European Union and Commission of the European Communities*, Judgment of the Court (Grand Chamber) of 3 September 2008, para 375; *R (Al-Jedda) v Secretary of State for Defence* [2007] UKHL 58, [30] (Lord Bingham), [126] (Baroness Hale), [130] (Lord Carswell).

[16] N Bentwich and A Martin, *A Commentary on the Charter of the United Nations* (New York, Macmillan, 1950) 179–80.

sanctions. States should freeze the assets of individuals as required by the SC, but should still as far as possible protect the human rights of those individuals in accordance with their international treaty obligations. Though some governments (and domestic courts) have interpreted Articles 25 and 103 quite broadly, it is not clear that this is the intention of the SC as a whole. In its declaration on combating terrorism (Resolution 1456, 2003) the SC, meeting at the level of foreign ministers, declared that States 'must ensure that any measure taken to combat terrorism comply with all their obligations under international law, and should adopt measures in accordance with international law, in particular international human rights, refugee, and humanitarian law'. This is hardly institutional *opinio juris* to the effect that its Resolutions enable States to by-pass their human rights obligations.

It may be argued that some of these limitations are *de lege ferenda* or are more broadly about the legitimacy of the Council, anyway unenforceable, but the point is that the Security Council's legitimacy, and therefore its effectiveness as an organ whose purpose is to maintain or restore peace and security, will only be secured if we recognise that it has got exceptional powers, but these are not exceptional to the international legal order (somehow existing outside of it with no reference to it), but exceptional within the international legal order (operating with regard to the existing laws).

This outline of applicable law will inform our analysis of the development of the SC's quasi-judicial role. The analysis considers the various aspects of the quasi-judicial process that has been imperfectly developed in SC practice, from the initial seizure of the dispute, through investigation, adjudication (including the use of other courts) and enforcement.

IV. SEIZURE OF THE DISPUTE

In domestic legal systems, gaining the consent of parties to any dispute is not generally a prerequisite for a criminal or civil court to have jurisdiction over the case, though broader dispute Resolution mechanisms may be more dependent upon consent. As Professor Merrills has illustrated in his examination of the different forms of dispute settlement within the international legal order,[17] consent has traditionally been the foundation

[17] JG Merrills, *International Dispute Settlement* (Cambridge, Cambridge University Press, 2005); JG Merrills, 'The Means of Dispute Settlement' in MD Evans (ed), *International Law* (Oxford, Oxford University Press, 2006). See also JG Merrills, *Anatomy of International Law* (London, Sweet & Maxwell, 1981) 87: 'International law has not been imposed on states, but springs from their collective decision that it should exist'.

of any judicial, quasi-judicial or indeed any peaceful method of settlement a dispute. The ICJ is founded on both parties consenting to the jurisdiction of the court before it can hear the case.[18]

This book shows that the exceptions to the consensual approach have grown in recent years, but the SC was a much earlier exception. There are various avenues into the SC which are not dependent upon the consent of the disputing parties: by a Member State bringing the Council's attention to any dispute or situation endangering the peace;[19] by the Secretary-General bringing to the attention of the SC 'any matter which in his opinion may threaten the maintenance of international peace and security';[20] or by the SC itself determining the 'existence of any threat to the peace, breach of the peace, or act of aggression'.[21] The first of these is the gateway to Chapter VI and the pacific settlement powers of the SC; while the latter is the gateway to Chapter VII and the coercive powers of that body. In addition the General Assembly has a 'right to submit disputes to the Council, under Articles 11 and 12 of the Charter.[22] Once a dispute is submitted to the Council it must decide whether to include it on its agenda by means of a procedural decision under Article 27(2). Once seized of a dispute the Council should invite States who are parties to the dispute to participate in discussions without a vote according to Article 32. Furthermore, any Member State may be invited (without any voting rights) to any SC discussion under Article 31.[23]

V. INVESTIGATION

The Security Council requires knowledge of the facts of a particular situation so that it can act in the manner best suited for international peace and security. As John Merrills makes clear, investigation is of importance in dispute settlement.[24] If there is no sound grasp of the facts from which the dispute has arisen, the rest of the settlement process will be flawed. Hence, the importance that the action of the SC has a sound factual basis is amplified when it is engaged in matters of dispute settlement. This section considers the techniques by which the SC gains its factual

[18] Statute of the ICJ Art 36(1).
[19] UN Charter Art 35(1).
[20] UN Charter Art 99.
[21] UN Charter Art 39.
[22] P Sands and P Klein, *Bowett's Law of International Institutions* (London, Sweet & Maxwell, 2001) 44.
[23] See B Conforti, *The Law and Practice of the United Nations*, 2nd edn (Leiden, Martinus Nijhoff, 2000) 83; SD Bailey and S Daws, *The Procedure of the UN Security Council*, 3rd edn (Oxford, Clarendon Press, 1998) 22.
[24] Merrills, *International Dispute Settlement*, above n 17 at 63.

information and the issues this raises in terms of the legitimacy and effectiveness of dispute settlement, particularly with regard to its quasi-judicial role.[25]

Investigatory bodies established by the Security Council to ascertain the facts of a dispute are relatively rare. The Charter basis for such bodies is to be located in a combination of Articles 34 and 29, although they are rarely cited in the enabling Resolutions. Article 34 provides that 'the Security Council may investigate any dispute or situation in order to determine whether' its continuance 'is likely to endanger the maintenance of international peace and security', while Article 29 permits the SC to 'establish such subsidiary organs as it deems necessary for the performance of its functions'. Often the body's function will go beyond mere fact-finding and enter the realm of good offices and peacekeeping.

During the early years of SC practice, some confusion arose from the fact that this provision did not confer a general power of investigation on the SC. The power appears to be confined to ascertaining whether the dispute or situation comes within the parameters of Chapter VI. Indeed, the sub-committee on the Spanish question established in 1946 was directed to ascertain whether the activities of the Franco regime constituted a situation within the meaning of Article 34 or Article 39.[26]

However, shortly afterwards, the SC showed its willingness to go beyond a strict interpretation of Article 34 when, in 1946, it established a commission of investigation to examine certain frontier incidents on the Greek borders. The Commission not only ascertained the facts but made several wide ranging recommendations, which were not adopted by the Council because of Soviet opposition.[27]

The agreement at Yalta in 1945—that established to all intents and purposes that the veto could be applied to virtually any Resolution so long as it was not clearly procedural—severely hampered the development of a regular process of fact-finding by the SC.[28] There was an isolated instance of the majority in the SC adopting a Resolution by a procedural vote in 1959 to establish a sub-committee to investigate a complaint by Laos despite the negative Soviet vote.[29] The legality of this method is doubtful

[25] Drawing attention to the importance of fact-finding missions, see DW Bowett, 'The United Nations and Peaceful Settlement' in Report of a Study Group of the David Davies Memorial Institute of International Studies, *International Disputes: The Legal Aspects* (London, Europa Publications, 1972) 179, 186–87; for a substantial critique of the present approach to fact-finding, see MC Bassiouni, 'Appraising UN Justice-Related Fact-Finding Missions' (2001) 4 *Journal of Law and Policy* 35–49.

[26] UNSC Res 4 (29 April 1946).

[27] UNSC Res 15 (19 December 1946) UN Doc S/360/Rev 1 (1946).

[28] ND White, Keeping the Peace: The United Nations and the Maintenance of International Peace and Security (Manchester, Manchester University Press, 1997) 9.

[29] UNSC Res 132 (7 September 1959).

and it did not become an established feature in the practice of the Security Council.

Another problem as regards fact-finding during the Cold War was that even in the areas beyond the superpowers' interests where Council investigation was possible, the body established to undertake the task was often faced with a *fait accompli*. After alleged attacks by Portuguese forces on the independent African States of Guinea in 1970 and Senegal in 1971, the Council established special missions to ascertain whether such attacks had occurred. The mission's report on Guinea led to the Council determining that the attack constituted a threat to the peace. However, since the attacks were over, the Council could only condemn them, warn Portugal against further attacks, and demand that Portugal pay compensation to Guinea.[30]

Often in these cases where the aggression was short-lived and the *status quo* had been re-established, the investigation's only purpose was to find the guilty party—which proved to be virtually impossible in the case of mercenary aggression and difficult in the case of guerrilla activities. After a mercenary attack in 1977 aimed at overthrowing the government of Benin, a special mission could only report that the attackers worked for pecuniary motives and that the financiers could not be found.[31] This resulted in a general Council condemnation of mercenary aggression.[32]

Although there were other examples of fact-finding during the Cold War, they can be characterised generally as being selective and often ineffectual, although on some occasions they did form the basis of a later peaceful settlement or at least a stabilisation of the conflict with the assistance of a UN peacekeeping force.[33] As early as 1988, with superpower relations beginning to thaw, there was an indication of greater fact-finding by the SC, when a mission was sent to Nicaragua, and was a foretaste of the regional settlement process started by the Guatemala Accords of 1987, and culminating in the UN supervision of peaceful elections in Nicaragua in 1990.

Nevertheless, fact-finding by the SC is not undertaken as a matter of course; it often relies on a patchwork of sources, including established peacekeeping or observation teams, the Secretary-General and his staff, and the occasional formal fact-finding body mandated by a SC Resolution. For instance in April 1996, while calling for a cease-fire in Lebanon between Israel and Hezbollah, the SC deplored the shelling of a UNIFIL base at Qana in Lebanon which resulted in over 100 deaths

[30] UNSC Res 289 (23 November 1970); UNSC Res 290 (8 December 1970).
[31] SCOR Special Supp No 3 (1977).
[32] UNSC Res 419 (24 November 1977).
[33] See, eg UNSC Res 377 (22 October 1975) re Western Sahara.

(mainly civilians sheltering from the hostilities).[34] No determination was made as to the extent of Israel's guilt in committing this atrocity, nor did the Council formally dispatch a commission of inquiry to undertake such a task. Instead the Secretary-General sent his military adviser to investigate. Despite the military adviser's report stating that 'it is unlikely that gross technical and/or procedural errors led to the shelling of the United Nations compound',[35] no action was taken against Israel.

The situation in the Middle East shows that in the post-Cold War era fact-finding is still selective and largely dependent upon the will (or whim) of the permanent members. The major influence of the US on the extent of fact-finding in relation to Israel's actions is shown by the apparent willingness of Israel to allow a fact-finding mission to investigate events in the Palestinian refugee camp in Jenin during a Israeli military action there in 2002, which led to the deaths of as many as 500, according to Palestinian sources, or 50, from Israeli sources.[36] After considerable direct US engagement with Israel by US Secretary of State, Colin Powell,[37] Israeli consent to fact-finding was confirmed in a series of telephone conversations between the UN Secretary-General and Israeli Defence and Foreign Ministers. These calls preceded the vote on Resolution 1405 for the establishment of a UN fact-finding mission, which was tabled by the US and adopted unanimously.[38] However, with the mission waiting to deploy, Israel raised concerns about the mission's personnel and investigation priorities.[39] A telephone call from the US to Israel revealed that the US could not influence the Secretary-General in his selection or supervision of the mission.[40] The apparent decrease in the level of US pressure and the failure of the UN Secretary-General to resolve Israeli concerns led to the withdrawal of Israeli consent and the disbanding of the mission. Accordingly, the Secretary-General's report was prepared without the full cooperation of both parties to the dispute or a visit to the area.[41]

34 UNSC Res 1052 (18 April 1996).

35 UN Doc S/1996/337 (1996).

36 Death toll as reported by CNN: 'Security Council calls for "fact-finding" mission in Jenin' (CNN 20 April 2002) http://archives.cnn.com/2002/WORLD/meast/04/19/mideast/index.html.

37 See US comments from SC4515th mtg 19 April 2002, 17–19.

38 UNSC Res 1405 (19 April 2002) para 2; see Report of the Secretary-General prepared pursuant to General Assembly Resolution ES-10/10, attached to UNGA Res A/ES-10/186, 30 July 2002, 3–4.

39 Embassy of Israel Briefing, 1 May 2002, 'The Israeli Cabinet Decision regarding the UN Fact-finding Team', www.israelemb.org/articles/embassy-briefing/2002050100.html.

40 R Trounson and W Orme, 'U.N. Delays Fact-Finding Mission to West Bank Camp' *LA Times* (Los Angeles 27 April 2002) http://articles.latimes.com/2002/apr/27/news/mn-40329.

41 See Report of the Secretary-General above n 38.

Despite occasions of overtly power influenced decision-making, the Council does recognise the importance of impartial fact-finding. A good example of this is the Council's response to the report of the fact-finding mission sent to Lebanon to inquire into the terrorist bombing that killed the former Prime Minister Rafiq Hariri in Beirut on 14 February 2005. This mission identified acute difficulties with the impartiality of the Lebanese investigation, which threatened to impede the realisation of the truth and aggravate the fragile political situation surrounding the withdrawal of the 29-year Syrian military presence from Lebanon.[42] This prompted the Security Council to establish an International Independent Investigation Commission to assist Lebanese authorities in their investigation of all aspects the terrorist bombing.[43] The Commission conducted an extensive criminal and judicial investigation and found 'converging evidence pointing at both Lebanese and Syrian involvement in this terrorist act'.[44] This underlined:

> [a] shared assumption [on behalf of the Lebanese government and the SC] that a purely national tribunal would not be able to effectively fulfil the task of trying those accused of the crime[45]

and led to the Council completing a sensible approach to the incident by setting up a special tribunal, composed of Lebanese and international judges, to try the accused under Lebanese criminal law (the rules of procedure draw on Lebanese and international criminal law), rather than passing judgment itself.[46] This is a more specific example of the SC establishing judicial bodies to deal with aspects of dispute, as in the former Yugoslavia and Rwanda, where in 1992 and 1994 respectively commissions of experts were dispatched to investigate violations of international humanitarian law in those countries as a prelude to the establishment of international criminal tribunals (discussed further below).

Whatever the source, fact-finding can only normally be undertaken with the consent of the State or States involved in the dispute. The SC

[42] Report of the Fact-finding Mission to Lebanon inquiring into the causes, circumstances and consequences of the assassination of former Prime Minister Rafik Hariri, UN Doc S/2005/203, para 62.

[43] UNSC Res 1595 (7 April, 2005) para 1.

[44] Report of the United Nations International Independent Investigation Commission Prepared Pursuant to Resolution 1595 (2005), 19 October 2005, UN Doc S/2005/622, 5.

[45] Report of the Secretary-General pursuant to para 6 of Res 1644 (2005), 21 March 2006, UN Doc S/2006/176, 2, para 5.

[46] UNSC Res 1757 (30 May 2007) para 1; initially, it was intended that the Court would find its authority through an agreement between the UN Secretary-General and Lebanon, but Lebanese political disagreements meant the speaker of the Lebanese Parliament would not convene a parliamentary session to ratify the agreement that the government had signed as required by the constitution; see further F Megret, 'A Special Tribunal for Lebanon: The UN Security Council and the Emancipation of International Criminal Justice' (2008) *Leiden Journal of International Law* 485.

has not attempted to invoke a mandatory power to send a fact-finding mission into a State, although after the conflict between Iraq and coalition forces ended in March 1991, Iraq was subjected to very intrusive disarmament missions. Although Iraq consented to them when it agreed to the permanent cease-fire in SC Resolution 687 on 3 April 1991, it really had little choice, given the threat of further military actions against it. Without a mandatory power to order a State to accept a fact-finding mission, and in view of the fact that the Gulf crisis was exceptional in the sense that military action preceded the missions when normally they should be one of the first steps taken by the Council, fact-finding is not going to be properly institutionalised. If all members of the SC accepted that it did have the power to oblige States to accept a fact-finding mission by making it clear in the enabling Resolution that it was a binding Resolution under Articles 34 and 25, there does not appear to be any legal limitation on this power.[47] Article 34 is not restricted to recommendations, although if one accepts the predominant (western) view that it is only under Chapter VII that binding decisions can be made, then such a power is not contained in the Charter.[48] Recent SC practice shows the weakness of requiring consent in all cases. When tension arose on the Djibouti–Eritrea border in June 2008 the SC called on the Secretary-General to send a fact-finding mission to the area, but the mission was not granted permission to enter Eritrean territory, thus the report transmitted to the Security Council on 11 September 2008 was based only on Dijbouti's version of events.[49] This highlights the difficulties encountered without consent. When one side will not cooperate this frustrates the system as the initial report is the starting point for subsequent action, but its lack of impartiality impacts on the legitimacy of the whole settlement process.

As has been seen from the introduction to this chapter, the SC has an inherent quasi-judicial power, one that it has used sparingly for most of its life as the political pressures of the Cold War led to Resolutions based on compromise rather than on judicial-type rulings. However, with the end of the Cold War the Council has increasingly used this power to condemn States for breaches of international law, rather akin to the GA. Any basic judicial process would commence with a determination of the facts before moving on to the judicial decision,[50] yet in the SC the facts are often not clarified—or if they are, the Council has already condemned.

As well as inconsistently investigating the facts of disputes brought before it, the presentation of fact to the Council falls far beneath the

[47] T Schweisfurth, 'Article 34' in Simma, above n 13 at 605.

[48] White, above n 28 at 59–63.

[49] SC 5924th mtg, 24 June 2008; UN Doc S/2008/602.

[50] E Lauterpacht, *Aspects of the Administration of International Justice* (Cambridge, Cambridge University Press, 1991) 42.

minimum standards of natural justice. For example, following disturbances in Jerusalem on 8 October 1990 when Palestinians were killed apparently by Israeli security forces, following Israel's refusal to agree to a fact-finding mission, the Council watched amateur video footage suggesting that the shootings were unprovoked.[51] Another instance of failure to observe basic due process in gathering facts was shown by the actions taken by the SC against Libya in 1992 as a result of its alleged support for terrorism (including the Lockerbie bombing of 1988), when:

> without undertaking its own investigation, the Council imposed sanctions on Libya on the strength of information supplied by the United States and Britain.[52]

In addition to lack of fact-finding when action is taken against States, there is a similar problem when targeted sanctions are taken against individuals.

The targeted sanctions regime against the Taliban/Al-Qaeda established by Resolution 1267 of 1999 (as developed in subsequent Resolutions),[53] in view of its subject matter and scope, is the most well-known of a considerable number of such regimes set up by the Council under Chapter VII.[54] Targeted or smart sanctions single out particular individuals to be the target of restrictions on personal and financial freedoms, and consequently do not impact on innocent civilian populations in the same way as comprehensive sanctions. Still, leaving aside debate about the legal status of targeted sanctions,[55] mistaken targeting has a hugely negative impact on an innocent person's life, and is one reason why attention should be paid to the investigation that precedes a decision to target a particular individual. The vast majority of targeted sanctions regimes include a listing committee.[56] These committees rely

[51] UNSC Res 672 (12 October 1990); UNSC Res 673 (24 October 1990); SC 2953rd mtg, 1990.

[52] J Quigley, 'Security Council Fact-finding: A Prerequisite to the Effective Prevention of War' (1992) 7 *Florida Journal of International Law* 192.

[53] See UNSC Res 1333 (19 December 2000), UNSC Res 1390 (28 January 2002), UNSC Res 1526 (30 January 2004), UNSC Res 1617 29 July (2005), UNSC Res 1735 22 December (2006) and UNSC Res 1822 (30 June 2008).

[54] See, eg UNSC Res 1132 (8 October 1997)—Sierra Leone; UNSC Res 1518 (24 November 2003)—Iraq; UNSC Res 1521 (22 December 2003)—Liberia; UNSC Res 1533 (12 March 2004)—Democratic Republic of the Congo; UNSC Res 1572 (15 November 2004)—Côte d'Ivoire; UNSC Res 1591 (29 March 2005)—Sudan; UNSC Res 1636 (31 October 2005)—Lebanon/Syria; UNSC Res 1718 (14 October 2006)—North Korea; and UNSC Res 1737 (23 December 2006)—Iran.

[55] TJ Biersteker and SE Eckert, *Strengthening Targeted Sanctions Through Fair and Clear Procedures*, White Paper prepared by the Watson Institute Targeted Sanctions Project, Brown University, 30 March 2006, at 13.

[56] All the regimes listed in n 54 above include listing committees; examples of target sanctions regimes without a listing committee include UNSC Res 917 (6 May 1994)—against the military junta in Haiti. UNSC Res 1127 (28 August 1997)—against senior officials of the National Union for Total Independence of Angola (UNITA) and their family members there.

in terms of investigation on the statement of the case from the Member State(s) that submitted the individual's name in light of a belief that the relevant criteria, such as 'associated with Al-Qaida and the Taliban',[57] have been satisfied. This dependency on information from individual Member States raises doubts about impartiality, which, along with the consequences of a general lack of guidance on the quality and amount of information required from a Member State,[58] undermines the legitimacy of a decision to list a particular individual.[59]

Putting to one side for a moment the potential abuse of human rights law caused by targeted sanctions,[60] this summary approach to justice found in the SC is inconsistent with the standards set by the UN itself. In 1992 the GA, by consensus, adopted the Declaration on Fact Finding by the United Nations in the Field of the Maintenance of Peace and Security. The Resolution recognised:

> that the ability of the United Nations to maintain international peace and security depends to a large extent on its acquiring detailed knowledge about the factual circumstances of any dispute or situation,[61]

so that the competent organs of the UN should endeavour to undertake fact-finding activities that should be 'comprehensive, objective, impartial and timely'.[62] It reiterated that 'the sending of a United Nations fact-finding mission to the territory of any State requires the prior consent of that State', although it encouraged States to adopt 'a policy of admitting … fact-finding missions to their territory'.[63]

The key point from the above discussion is that there are clearly occasions when the Security Council may struggle for comprehensive knowledge of a particular situation. If the required action is of an immediate and responsive type without a major dispute settlement element, then in some instances it might be necessary for the SC to act without comprehensive knowledge. But when the anticipated action is more squarely directed at dispute settlement, the legitimacy and consequently effectiveness of the action taken can be more seriously undermined by the approach taken to gathering the facts. This is amplified with regard to action of a judicial nature directed at individuals. Hence, when dispute settlement

[57] UNSC Res 1617 (29 July 2005) para 2 provided a much needed elaboration on what it means to be 'associated with'.

[58] See Biersteker and Eckert above n 55 at 26–28.

[59] See further E Rosand, 'The Security Council's Efforts to Monitor the Implementation of Al Qaeda/Taliban Sanctions' (2004) *AJIL* 745–63, 750.

[60] See European Court of Justice's judgment in the *Kadi* case, 2008, above n 15 at paras 283–85.

[61] UNGA Res 46/59, 9 December 1991.

[62] Ibid.

[63] Ibid.

is involved, greater efforts should be made to acquire comprehensive knowledge.

VI. ADJUDICATION

According to Article 1(1) of the Charter, one of the main purposes of the UN is to 'maintain international peace and security', and to that end 'to take effective collective measures' to tackle threats to or breaches of the peace; and

> to bring about by peaceful means, and in conformity with the principles of justice and international law, adjustment or settlement of situations which might lead to a breach of the peace.[64]

The SC's competence under Chapter VII is shaped to allow it to take collective measures, but this tends to eclipse its competence under Chapter VI to settle disputes, which according to Article 1 must be undertaken in accordance with the principles of justice and international law. Although it shares its pacific settlement role with the GA and ICJ, the SC still has 'primary responsibility' for peace and security under Article 24, which in paragraph 2 points to the SC's powers under both Chapters VI and VII, a provision which also reminds the Council that it must act 'in accordance with the Purposes and Principles' of the UN.

However, although Article 1 and Chapter VI arguably point to a SC with a quasi-judicial function where it applies principles of justice and international law, a function distinct from its executive one under Chapter VII, an examination of most SC debates leading to the adoption of a recommendation towards the pacific settlement of a dispute illustrates that it is often arrived at by political consensus, and that law is often merely a 'tactical device' and a 'weapon in the armoury of rhetoric'.[65] The law of nations could be said to play a residual role in the work of a political body such as the SC, although the ending of the Cold War witnessed an increase in judicial-type determinations by the SC. These judgments though are not often arrived at after proper fact-finding or by the applications of any basic principles of natural justice.

The contention that, although the Council does not decide cases in accordance with international law as does the ICJ, it is still constrained by a 'broad framework of legally acceptable solutions',[66] did appear to be

[64] UN Charter Art 1.

[65] R Higgins, 'The Place of International Law in the Settlement of Disputes by the UN Security Council' (1970) 63 *AJIL* 1, 4.

[66] Ibid. See also O Schachter, 'The Quasi-Judicial Role of the Security Council and the General Assembly' (1964) 58 *AJIL* 960.

somewhat flawed during the Cold War, in that some SC-inspired pacification attempts sought solutions which appeared to contradict the tenets of international law. For example, the Council-supervised negotiations on the Gulf War between Iran and Iraq in the 1980s were premised on the non-identification of the aggressor, namely Iraq. Indeed, this neutral approach persisted with SC inaction despite the fact that the Secretary-General apportioned responsibility to Iraq for its attack on Iran in 1980 in a report to the Security Council 11 years later.[67]

Alternatively, it may be argued that the SC often fails to identify breaches of international law but it does not adopt Resolutions which are in breach of international law. However, this is a long way from the position that law plays an important role in the Council's pacification function. The SC's failure to establish a solution is mainly due to it often being faced with the situation of an aggressor country gaining, with little possibility of it handing back its gains when faced with a Council recommendation. This is an inevitable flaw in any system based on recommendation and voluntary acceptance. Nevertheless, in order to ensure that the recommendation has a chance of success, it should be clear and unambiguous. Unfortunately, the necessities of consensus dictate that clarity is often unattainable. Resolution 242, adopted on 6 November 1967 five months after the Israeli victory in the Six Day War, is an example of an ambiguous recommendation. The Resolution stated, inter alia, that the Council,

> Affirms that the fulfilment of Charter principles requires the establishment of a just and lasting peace in the Middle East which should include the application of both the following principles:
>
> (i) Withdrawal of Israeli armed forces from territories occupied in the recent conflict;
> (ii) Termination of all claims or states of belligerency and respect for and acknowledgement of the sovereignty, territorial integrity and political independence of every State in the area and their right to live in peace within secure and recognised boundaries free from threats or acts of force.

This appears to be a clear legal framework for the settlement of the Middle East problem, although the two principles outlined in the Resolution miss the root cause, namely the homeless Palestinians and their right to self-determination. Nevertheless, the Resolution is based on legal principles, namely, that Israel has the right to exist, the non-use of force, and the return of territories occupied by Israel in the Six-Day War. However, the fact that the Resolution does not state whether this means 'all' or 'some' of the territories detracts from its value. Law and justice point to the former interpretation, otherwise Israel would be gaining by the use of force,

[67] UN Doc S/232743 (1991).

although it could be argued that the occupied territories, or at least some of them, are essential for the security and defence of Israel. Although Perry argues that if an advisory opinion of the ICJ were sought, there would be no doubt that Resolution 242 would be interpreted to mean 'all' the territories,[68] the doubt and confusion created by the British-proposed text has not helped to end the conflict. Besides although the ICJ may opt for this solution, it is not unforeseeable that the Council may promote peace on the basis of Israel handing back some of its territories but not all. It must not be forgotten that international law is greatly tempered by political considerations in the Council forum.

Generally, when attempting to settle a dispute, the Security Council tends to adopt recommendations which are aimed at not causing offence to either party in order to induce them to come to an agreement. Determinations of legal guilt may come later if the parties remain recalcitrant. The initial recommendations are usually based on broad principles of international law and justice centred on the fundamental principles of international law contained in Article 2 of the UN Charter and the principle that a State should not gain from its breach. It may be argued that more concrete legal determinations should be made even under purely recommendatory Chapter VI Resolutions. There are both pitfalls and advantages in this approach. A 'once and for all' legal determination may make a State more intransigent and so work against the settlement process, and at the same time it may mobilise international opinion which will work in its favour. Witness the determination by the ICJ in 2004 that the construction of a security wall by Israel in occupied Palestinian territory constituted a violation of international law,[69] a judgment which proved a focus for world opinion but did not lead to Israel removing the wall or even stopping its construction. Nor did the judgment receive any backing from the Security Council.

With the end of the Cold War, the Council has been more willing to make legal determinations even if they might inhibit the settlement process by branding one of the disputants as the guilty party. Part of the reason for this is that the Council is more willing to enter into the enforcement provisions of Chapter VII if the parties do not comply with the determination (see enforcement section below). Although this approach is somewhat selective and is mainly directed at the so-called 'pariah' States, it must be remembered that these States have often breached international law.

[68] G Perry, 'Security Council Resolution 242: The Withdrawal Clause' (1977) 31 *Middle East Journal* 413 and 432.

[69] Legal Consequences of the Construction of a Wall in the Palestinian Occupied Territory, Advisory Opinion, 2004 ICJ Rep 136.

The post-Cold War practice of the Council has not only taken on greater judicial overtones, but has increasingly extended to enforcement of its determinations utilising the powers of Chapter VII of the UN Charter. This was the case in the early 1990s, for example, as regards Iraq, following its aggression against Kuwait in August 1990, which was followed by a determination that Iraq's annexation of Kuwait was null and void,[70] building upon its determinations of illegality made during the Cold War against Rhodesia for its unilateral declaration of independence, against Northern Cyprus for a similar act, and against South Africa for its continued occupation of Namibia.[71] In this period a similar approach was taken against Libya for its support for terrorism, and the remnants of the Yugoslavian State (Serbia and Montenegro) for its intervention in the emerging State of Bosnia in May 1992. In these instances, the SC condemned the State in question and then went on to enforce that decision using its non-forcible powers, and in the case of Iraq, its power to authorise military action under Chapter VII of the Charter.

The rush to Chapter VII in recent disputes and conflicts is contrary to the structure of the SC's powers, where Chapter VII, as has been argued, is exceptional to the normal approach of international law. Ratner also makes the point that

> [h]eightened respect for Chapter VII turns upon an understanding that it represents a *last* resort, and one that the key Member States will back up with their political weight and levers. Chapter VI provides a mechanism to keep Chapter VII the exception. It also offers the link with consent and 'sovereignty' that most States find necessary to accept expanding the UN's authority in new directions.[72]

This might be the ideal scenario, but the SC has increasingly taken it upon itself to act under Chapter VII in relation to disputes, and this cannot be ignored. Other organs have not proven robust enough to take a centre stage in performing a judicial function or indeed a policy-making role, where the GA has lost its voice in the post-Cold War era.[73]

Although we can decry the absence of a proper separation of power within the UN, the fact is that the Council has developed competence in all three areas, making it both dangerous and potentially key to solving world problems. Nevertheless, in accepting that it may have these powers, we should also recognise that these powers are limited by principles of international law and the requirement of legitimacy, so that

[70] UNSC Res 662 (9 August 1990).

[71] UNSC Res 217 (20 November 1965); UNSC Res 276 (30 January 1970).

[72] SR Ratner, 'Image and Reality in the UN's Peaceful Settlement of Disputes' (1995) 6 *European Journal of International Law* 426–444, 444.

[73] See M Koskenniemi, 'The Police in the Temple, Order Justice and the UN: A Dialectical View' (1995) *European Journal of International Law* 325, 338–39.

when acting in a judicial manner the SC should include basic respect for natural justice such as the *audi alteram partem* principle (referring to the importance of the accused being given an opportunity to be heard).[74] The Council should also avoid using a combination of powers in the same Resolution; the move from judgment to enforcement, for instance, should be taken in separate steps after a fair appraisal of the evidence. In addition, the Council should show a greater willingness to utilise the whole range of its powers before it enforces its judgment by using non-forcible or forcible measures under Articles 41 and 42. This would include making greater use of its powers to order provisional measures under Article 40 of the Charter, especially when it is not fully apprised of the facts.[75]

The importance of the legitimacy of the procedure in making judgments and thereby encouraging States towards compliance is difficult to prove empirically, but possible examples can be given. SC Resolution 1718 of 2006,[76] reacting to the announcement on 9 October 2006 by North Korea (DPRK) that it had conducted an underground nuclear weapon test, is a useful example. The Resolution made a number of legal determinations. In operative paragraph 3, the SC demanded that the DPRK 'immediately retract its announcement of withdrawal from the Treaty on the Non-Proliferation of Nuclear Weapons'. In paragraph 4, the SC demanded 'further that the DPRK return to the Treaty on the Non-Proliferation of Nuclear Weapons and International Atomic Energy Agency (IAEA) safeguards'. In paragraph 6, it decided:

> that the DPRK shall abandon all nuclear weapons and existing nuclear programmes in a complete, verifiable and irreversible manner, shall act strictly in accordance with the obligations applicable to parties under the Treaty on the Non-Proliferation of Nuclear Weapons and the terms and conditions of its International Atomic Energy Agency (IAEA) Safeguards Agreement (IAEA INFCIRC/403) and shall provide the IAEA transparency measures extending beyond these requirements, including such access to individuals, documentation, equipments and facilities as may be required and deemed necessary by the IAEA.[77]

Given the rogue nature of the North Korean regime it is difficult to correlate its (non-)compliance with the legitimacy of these determinations. Had it been another State, one can start to see how compliance could correlate

[74] M Stephen, 'Natural Justice at the United Nations: The Rhodesia Case' (1973) 67 *AJIL* 479. See further Lauterpacht n 4 above, 42.

[75] DW Bowett, 'The Impact of Security Council Decisions on Dispute Settlement Procedures' (1994) 5 *European Journal of International Law* 97. See further P Kooijmans, 'Provisional Measures of the UN Security Council' in E Denters and N Schrijver (eds), *Reflections on International Law from the Low Countries: in Honour of Paul de Waart* (The Hague, Martinus Nijhoff, 1998) 289–300.

[76] UNSC Res 1718 (14 October 2006).

[77] Ibid para 6.

with the legitimacy of the legal determination and the fact that the SC did not give North Korea any opportunity to argue its case or to dispute the facts (returned to below); but even in such circumstances thoroughness in procedure is vital if the Council is to avoid giving the targeted State an excuse for non-compliance. If, for example, North Korea had been invited to present its case to the Council before the drafting of Resolution 1718, this would have demonstrated a much keener interest to hear evidence from both sides, rather than reliance on a short (apparently unsolicited) letter from North Korea.[78] Consequently it would have helped to dampen the strength of North Korea's challenges to the impartiality of the SC, which were made at the Council meeting where the Resolution was adopted (which North Korea requested to attend).[79] Similarly, some effort to make public the prior consultations between members of the Council which led to the formulation of Resolution 1718 would have been useful.[80]

VII. ENFORCEMENT

With the Council moving towards enforcement of its judgments and thereby increasingly using its binding powers under Chapter VII, there is little need to decipher whether the SC has or could develop a power of binding settlement. Articles 36 and 37 are firmly premised on the Security Council simply having the ability to recommend terms of settlement. There has been little suggestion that the SC has the power to impose a mandatory settlement by a combination of Article 25 and Chapter VI. Nevertheless, on occasions, the Council's recommendations for settlement based on a combination of Article 24 and Chapter VI, are more comprehensive and detailed so that they suggest a more intense and concerted effort by the Council to achieve a settlement than on other occasions.[81]

Although the provisions of Chapter VI do not expressly allow for the Council to impose a mandatory settlement, it is able to use a combination of powers under Chapters VI and VII to the same effect if it determines that the situation or conflict is a threat to or breach of the peace. Indeed, the gateway to Chapter VII, Article 39, provides that the SC can 'make recommendations' for settlement 'or decide what measures shall be taken in accordance' with Articles 41 and 42. This allows the SC to propose pacific settlement, and if it is not accepted, to take economic or military action.

[78] Letter dated 11 October 2006 from the Permanent Representative of the Democratic People's Republic of Korea to the United Nations addressed to the President of the Security Council, UN Doc S/2006/801.
[79] UNSC 5551st mtg, 14 October 2006, 7–8.
[80] See comments of the President, ibid 2.
[81] See discussion of the situation in Namibia in White, above n 28 at 94.

Such a combination of powers allowing enforcement of a settlement is arguably tantamount to a binding (or at least coerced) settlement. The SC acted in this manner in relation to the Yugoslav crisis of the mid-1990s when it imposed sanctions against the Serbian-led remnants of that State for interfering in the emerging State of Bosnia, imposing quite restrictive sanctions in May 1992, and authorising military action by NATO against Bosnian Serb forces.[82] Following a settlement on Bosnia agreed to by the parties at Dayton Ohio in November 1995, sanctions were formally terminated in October 1996 following elections in Bosnia, and the peace was policed by a SC-authorised stabilisation force (IFOR/SFOR/EUFOR).[83] Although the Dayton Accords were formally a product of the consent of the parties, they were in reality arrived at as a result of coercion authorised by the Security Council, and are being complied with because of the threat of further Council sanctioned coercion by NATO/EU.

The SC also effectively imposed terms of settlement on Iraq in 1991 following the successful prosecution of a UN-authorised war against it to counter the Iraqi invasion of Kuwait in August 1990. This is a reversal of the normal process whereby the Council proceeds in an incremental fashion from settlement proposals to enforcement action. The Iraqi aggression was met with economic and military enforcement action authorised by the SC. With the Iraqis in Kuwait defeated in March 1991, the Council imposed the most draconian measures seen in the organ's lifetime. Resolution 687 was adopted on 3 April 1991 by 12 votes to one (Cuba) with Yemen and Ecuador abstaining. Its preamble contained, inter alia, an affirmation of the 'sovereignty, territorial integrity and political independence of Kuwait and Iraq' and called on States taking military action under UN authority to 'bring their military presence in Iraq to an end as soon as possible'.

Although this statement satisfied sufficient members that the Council's intention was not to overthrow the Iraqi regime, the thrust of the Resolution was to oblige Iraq to compensate for its aggression, to severely curtail that regime's ability to wage further aggressive wars by intrusive disarmament provisions, and also, by maintaining the sanctions regime, to gradually undermine its grip on the country. It also demanded that Iraq and Kuwait respect the 'inviolability of the international boundary and the allocation of islands' as agreed by them in 1963. It authorised the Secretary-General to make arrangements to demarcate the boundary between Iraq and Kuwait, and finally decided to guarantee the inviolability of the demarcated international boundary. This, as with the rest of the

[82] UNSC Res 757 (30 May 1992); UNSC Res 942 (23 September 1994). Also UNSC Res 816 (31 March 1993); UNSC Res 998 (16 June 1995).

[83] UNSC Res 1031 (15 December 1995).

Resolution, was a measure taken under Chapter VII and therefore binding on Iraq. The disputed boundary had been used as an excuse by Iraq for its invasion and so the Council was coercing the Iraqis into settling their dispute with Kuwait to prevent it being used in a similar fashion in the future. The Iraqi government had no choice but to accept this and all the other aspects of the Resolution. A boundary commission was established in May 1991 with three independent experts and a representative each from Iraq and Kuwait. Despite Iraq's complaints about the legality of imposing a boundary, the commission completed its task and its demarcation was endorsed by the SC.[84]

On the issue of responsibility, Resolution 687 reaffirmed that Iraq 'is liable under international law for any direct loss, damage ... or injury to foreign Governments, nationals and corporations, as a result of Iraq's unlawful invasion and occupation of Kuwait', reaffirming its Resolution 674 of 29 October 1990. This clearly shows the Council acting in a judicial capacity. It also decided to establish a fund to pay compensation and a commission to administer it. The Secretary-General was requested to report with a recommendation for:

> mechanisms for determining the appropriate level of Iraq's contribution to the fund based on a percentage of the value of the exports of petroleum and petroleum products ... taking into account the needs of the people of Iraq.[85]

In SC Resolution 705 adopted on 15 August 1991, the SC decided that the figure should be that suggested by the Secretary-General of 30 per cent.[86]

The remainder of Resolution 687 of 1991 also contained a mixture of judicial determinations and executive action to enforce those judgments. In addition to a continuing arms embargo against Iraq, Resolution 687 included a decision that 'Iraq shall unconditionally accept the destruction, removal or rendering harmless, under international supervision' of its chemical and biological weapons, development and support systems, as well as 'all ballistic missiles with a range greater that 150 kilometres'. Iraq was put under an obligation to fully report, within 15 days, on its weapons systems and to undertake not to develop ones in the future. A special mission was created to inspect and verify the destruction of these weapons as well as to develop a plan for the ongoing monitoring of the state of Iraqi armament. Furthermore, Resolution 687 decided that 'Iraq shall unconditionally agree not to acquire and develop nuclear weapons' and to report to the IAEA within 15 days on its nuclear weapons facilities. Iraq was also obliged to allow the IAEA to remove, render harmless

[84] UNSC Res 833 (27 May 1993).
[85] UNSC Res 687 (8 April 1991).
[86] UN Doc S/22661 (1991).

or destroy such facilities and weapons, and to develop a plan for the on-going monitoring of Iraq's nuclear programme.

The difficult task of disarming Iraq eventually led to the ill-conceived and unauthorised US and UK invasion of March 2003. Both invaders were disenchanted with the lack of progress on disarmament, but also claimed that their actions were justified under the terms of Resolutions 678, 687 and 1441 of 2002, allowing them to enforce 'material breaches' of Resolution 687. Although the argument was admittedly weak,[87] it shows the danger in the SC passing judgments on States and then failing to take effective executive action against States in breach. In these circumstances, powerful States will point to non-compliance as a justification for taking action. Arguably if the Council is going to use its quasi-judicial powers to condemn a State for aggression, and decide that it must give up its weapons, then it has to deal with the consequences if that State fails to comply.

Once a judgment has been made by the SC, what follows by way of implementation of the judgment is dependent on the context in which the judgment was made. In relation to judgments of the SC, a number of different scenarios have occurred.

The judgment might come with specific orders for implementation; this can be with judgments directed at States as well as at individuals; for example, sanctions against North Korea in Resolution 1718 (which included prohibitions on transfer of arms and related material, materials related to nuclear capacity, and luxury goods),[88] and sanctions imposed on individuals listed by the 1267 Committee. In relation to such listed individuals, all States are required to freeze assets, prevent travel through their territory, and support an arms embargo. While the extent to which a particular State will comply with such obligations is dependent on a number of factors, an important issue in terms of effectiveness of implementation is whether the envisaged process of implementation actually complies with international law. The legitimacy of a judgment is undermined if the action required for its implementation is contrary to international law. Some leeway might be given in the interests of international peace and security, but some fundamental principles of international law should not be expendable. With regard to States, from an international order perspective, it would be counter-productive if measures required for a judgment's implementation operated with a disregard for the essential core of sovereignty by, for example, imposing a particular form of government or extinguishing statehood. In terms of individuals, to safeguard human welfare, at least those human rights that the ICCPR

[87] ND White, 'The Will and Authority of the Security Council after Iraq' (2004) 17 *Leiden Journal of International Law* 645 at 654–63.

[88] UNSC Res 1718 (14 October 2006), para 8.

does not permit derogation from in any circumstances—Articles 6, 7, 8 (paragraphs 1 and 2), 11, 15, 16 and 18—should be upheld, and derogation from any other human rights reasoned on the basis of a direct and compelling link to international peace and international security.

This point is well illustrated by the measures that follow a listing (a judgment) that an individual should be on the 1267 Committee's list. The travel ban clearly interferes with the right to freedom of movement,[89] and the freezing of assets, specifically 'freeze without delay the funds and other financial assets or economic resources of designated individuals and entities',[90] brings into question the right to property.[91] It might be accepted that the threat to international peace and security, which legitimate targets represent, justifies interference with these human rights.[92] However, such interference is more problematic when seen in the context of a regime which struggles for consistency with the international human rights to a fair trial and an effective remedy,[93] particularly because of the 1267 Committee's failure to grant individuals proposed for listing a hearing, and the delisting procedure being dependent on diplomatic protection.[94] This is because these process rights operate as a safeguard against wrongful interference with any substantive rights at stake. Hence disregard of process rights is more difficult to justify and increases the significance of interference with the substantive rights. Moreover, if the Council does not incorporate adequate provision for a fair trial and effective remedy into a targeted sanctions regime, this leaves it more open to challenge in domestic and regional courts. A judgment that Council implementation measures are not compliant with fundamental rights clearly undermines the legitimacy and therefore effectiveness of those measures and the judgment that underlies them.

In this respect, the recent September 2008 *Kadi & Al Barakaat* decision from the ECJ on the Regulation of the Council of the EU implementing the decision of the 1267 Committee to list the appellants, has come the closest. The ECJ found that the relevant Regulation infringed the appellants'

[89] ICCPR Art 12.

[90] UNSC Res 1822 (30 June 2008), para 1(a).

[91] Protocol 1 to the ECHR Art 1.

[92] See, eg Judgment of the ECJ in Joined Cases C-402/05 P and C-415/05 P *Yassin Abdullah Kadi and Al Barakaat International Foundation v Council of the EU and Commission of the EC* (ECJ Judgment), 3 September 2008, http://curia.europa.eu/jurisp/cgi-bin/form.pl?lang=EN&Submit=rechercher&numaff=C-402/05.

[93] See, eg Art 8 UDHR 'Everyone has the right to an effective remedy by the competent national tribunals for acts violating the fundamental rights granted him by the constitution or by law'; Art 10 UDHR 'Everyone is entitled in full equality to a fair and public hearing by an independent and impartial tribunal, in the determination of his rights and obligations and of any criminal charge against him'; see further B Fassbender, *Targeted Sanctions and Due Process* (2006) (study commissioned by the UN Office of Legal Affairs) 15–16.

[94] See Biersteker and Eckert, above n 55 at 49.

fundamental individual rights, including the right to be heard before a court of law,[95] the right to an effective legal remedy,[96] and the right to property,[97] and so overruled the Court of First Instance and annulled the Regulation. By treating the Regulation like any other, the ECJ did not consider it necessary to address the validity of the relevant SC Resolutions. Nonetheless, the obvious causal link between the 1267 regime and the failings of the annulled regulation must be seen as a major a blow to the legitimacy of the 1267 regime.

It is important to keep action taken under review, particularly where sanctions have been introduced, or else the incentive for compliance is reduced. This generally depends on the SC and/or the wider membership continuing to show concern about a situation. In terms of monitoring the compliance of States with a particular sanctions regime, this task is delegated to a sanctions committee which always consists of representatives of all 15 members of the Council, and tends also to have an administrative function, such as deciding on exemptions to travel bans for humanitarian needs.[98] In terms of legitimacy and effectiveness, these bodies have been criticised for being overly secretive and suffering from lack of overall coherence in their activities.[99] Moreover, they rely heavily on information supplied in individual Member State reports on implementation, which links effectiveness of the committees to the willingness of Member States to actually submit the reports,[100] and then the amount of information provided can vary in length and detail. This concern about the quality of the information is addressed to some extent when the Council instructs the Secretary-General to appoint groups or panels of experts to visit and investigate targeted and neighbouring States and report to the relevant committee on matters related to the implementation of the sanctions.[101] The effectiveness of implementation and review is also complicated if the Council does not set out the sanctions in sufficiently precise terms. For example, Resolution 1718 specified that Member States 'shall prevent the direct or indirect supply, sale or transfer to the DPRK of … luxury goods'. Despite a number of

[95] *Kadi* case, above n 92 at para 334.

[96] Ibid para 349.

[97] Ibid paras 368–70: the lack of guarantee that he could put his case to the relevant authorities was fundamental to the finding that the interference was unjustified.

[98] See, eg Security Council Committee established pursuant to Res 1718 (2006), 20 June 2007, guidelines of the committee for the conduct of its work, para 11, www.un.org/sc/committees/1718/index.shtml.

[99] See Koskenniemi, above n 73 at 345.

[100] As of 31st December 2007, 71 countries and one organisation (EU) had provided reports to the 1718 Committee, by 31 December 2008, two additional countries had provided reports (Luxembourg and Brunei Darussalam), www.un.org/sc/committees/1718/mstatesreports.shtml.

[101] See, eg Report of the Panel of Experts submitted pursuant to para 1 of SCouncil Res 1819 (2008) concerning Liberia UN Doc S/2008/785.

Member States raising concerns about what is covered by the term 'luxury goods' in their reports,[102] with at least India indicating that it was waiting for the Committee to draw up a list before it would take action,[103] the Committee only went so far as to stress that definition was a matter for Member States to determine in line with the objective that it was

> not intended to restrict the supply of ordinary goods to the wider population of the country or to have a negative humanitarian impact on the Democratic People's Republic of Korea.[104]

These points about the review process relate back to fact-finding and the difficulties therein. It is also worth noting that as a sanctions regime lengthens in time the political significance of the initial judgment diminishes, with fewer and fewer States supporting their continuation, shown by the sanctions regime and military action against Iraq over its failure to fully cooperate on disarmament. Support for military action to enforce 'material breaches' of Resolution 687 diminished from an initial high between 1991–93, to a handful of States by the invasion in 2003.

It is important to have the ability to respond when there is a lack of compliance.[105] In this respect, the SC struggles because of its nature as a political body and the different views amongst its membership, particularly in terms of the deference that is given to sovereignty. One sees this later point in the language in Resolution 687 requiring Iraq to 'undertake' and 'agree' to take steps, but also acting in a binding fashion under Chapter VII, reflecting the political and diplomatic turmoil in the Council when it came to deciding what to do at the end of Operation Desert Storm. Additionally, members of the Council might be split in their understanding as to what represents an adequate level of compliance from a targeted State. As regards Resolution 1718, North Korea has not complied with all its obligations, so the sanctions regime continues. But North Korea has resumed participation in the six-party talks—with China, Japan, the Republic of Korea, the Russian Federation and the United States—aiming to achieve the verifiable denuclearisation of the Korean Peninsula as required by paragraph 14 of Resolution 1718. In such a context, greater efforts to coerce fuller compliance with the requirements of Resolution 1718, or indeed to implement the sanctions

[102] See, eg Letter dated 30 November 2006 from the Permanent Representative of Germany to the United Nations addressed to the Chairman of the Committee S/AC 49/2006/33 at 2.

[103] Letter dated 20 February 2007 from the Permanent Representative of India to the United Nations addressed to the Chairman of the Committee S/AC 49/2007/23, para 6.

[104] Annual report of the Security Council Committee established pursuant to Res 1718 (2006) 31 December 2007, UN Doc S/2007/778 at 3, para 5.

[105] See Koskenniemi, above n 73 at 346.

more effectively,[106] could risk the progress that North Korean engagement in dialogue represents in terms of addressing a threat to international peace and security. However, a relaxation of the sanctions before all the requirements of 1718 have been complied with would risk undermining the future deterrent effect of sanctions. It is therefore easy to see how members of the Council might come to opposite views as to when the 1718 sanctions regime should end, potentially resulting in deadlock.

Failures in relation to implementation stem ultimately from the political nature of the SC. There needs to be political will for implementation to be seen through to a successful conclusion but also in a proper manner: in relation to individuals, some of the impetus for this is likely to come from the challenges that are being made in domestic and regional settings which will hopefully help force the SC to rethink how it approaches these matters. Indeed, this is seen in the improvements that have been made in the procedures associated with the 1267 Committee over the period of its operation. These include a requirement of greater detail in the statement of case from a Member State which proposes a listing, the submission of additional information on an individual as and when it becomes available, and an undertaking from the Committee to notify the country of residence or nationality of the listed individual within two weeks.[107]

But when it comes to direct actions against States that do not comply, the responses of the SC are likely to remain fickle given the reluctance and restrictions on the ICJ becoming an organ of judicial review. Accordingly, there is a need for self-improvement as regards the procedure that is gone through at the fact-finding and judgment stages to improve the legitimacy of the judgment and thereby increase the likelihood of compliance, as well as to incline Member States to view the decision as one worth pursuing over time.

VIII. USE OF OTHER COURTS

Article 36(3) of the Charter states that the 'Security Council should also take into consideration that legal disputes should as a general rule be referred by the parties to the International Court'. A number of factors act against increased reference to the ICJ. Many countries are not willing to gamble losing a dispute in an all or nothing legal ruling; they prefer, if anything, political compromises. In addition, a strict delineation between

[106] See, querying the rigour with which the economic sanctions against North Korea have been implemented, M Noland, 'The (non) Impact of UN Sanctions on North Korea' December 2008, Peterson Institute Working Paper, www.petersoninstitute.org.

[107] UNSC Res 1735 (22 December 2006); see further the chapter on Recommendations and Options to Enhance Fair and Clear Procedures in Biersteker and Eckert, above n 55.

the Council and the ICJ on the basis of whether the dispute is political or legal fails to take account of the fine and often blurred distinction between law and politics and the fact that the Council has a quasi-judicial role anyway.

In fact the Council has made little use of Article 36(3).[108] In the dispute between Albania and the United Kingdom over aspects of passage through the Corfu Channel in 1947, the Security Council recommended that the parties 'immediately refer the dispute' to the ICJ.[109] The case was argued before the Court and the judgment found both parties had breached international law,[110] but it found Albania responsible for the damages and losses caused to British warships as a result of mines in the Corfu Channel and ordered Albania to pay compensation. Albania did not pay, and the SC did not attempt to enforce the Court's judgment. That the Council, under Article 36(3), can do no more than make a recommendation which the parties are free to accept or reject was made clear by the Court. The United Kingdom argued that the SC's Resolution had established the Court's jurisdiction. Although the Court found it unnecessary to rule on this point, a majority pointed out that Article 36(3) did not introduce a new case of compulsory jurisdiction.[111]

The division of competence between the SC and the ICJ has not been changed significantly by the advent of SC-created criminal tribunals since these have jurisdiction over individuals whereas the Court exercises jurisdiction over States. Nevertheless, as the *Bosnia v Serbia* case of 2007 shows, the jurisprudence of the International Criminal Tribunal for the former Yugoslavia (ICTY) on individual criminal responsibility was taken into account in the judgment of the ICJ on the issue whether Serbia had breached the convention prohibiting genocide.[112] The Court stated that it

> attaches utmost importance to the factual and legal findings made by the ICTY on ruling on the criminal liability of the accused before it and, in the present case, the Court takes the fullest account of the ICTY's trial and appellate judgments dealing with the events underlying the dispute[113]

before the Court. Thus, while there is a clear demarcation between the criminal tribunals and the ICJ, the ICJ at least is keen to take on board the ICTY's jurisprudence when relevant. The Court though did make it clear

[108] T Stein, 'Article 36', in Simma above n 13 at 627.

[109] UNSC Res 22 (9 April 1947).

[110] *Corfu Channel Case (Merits)* 1949 ICJ Rep 4, 22, 35.

[111] *Corfu Channel Case (Preliminary Objections)* 1947–48 ICJ Rep 15, 31–32 (joint separate opinion).

[112] 1948 Convention on the Prevention and Punishment of the Crime of Genocide, Adopted by UNGA Res 260 (III) A, 9 December 1948.

[113] *Case Concerning the Application of the Convention on the Prevention and Punishment of the Crime of Genocide (Bosnia and Herzegovina v Serbia and Montenegro)* [2007] ICJ Rep, para 403.

that it did not have to follow the ICTY's judgments on 'issues of general international law which do not lie within the specific purview of its jurisdiction and, moreover, the Resolution of which is not always necessary for deciding the criminal cases before it', in refusing to adopt the ICTY's 'overall control' test for attributability over the ICJ's settled 'effective control' test.[114] Thus while the UN Courts (the ICJ as the principal judicial organ of the UN, and the criminal tribunals as creations of the SC) do try to be complementary, there will be issues on which they clash.

The end of the Cold War not only saw the expansion of the use of established powers by the SC, but also the development of new powers. There is no express mention in the Charter of a power to create international criminal tribunals to try individuals charged with breaches of international humanitarian law, and yet in February 1993 the Security Council decided 'that an international tribunal shall be established for the prosecution of persons responsible for serious violations of international humanitarian law committed in the territory of the former Yugoslavia since 1991', after concluding that 'widespread violations of international humanitarian law' constituted a threat to international peace and security,[115] and after having established in October 1992 a Commission of Experts to collect evidence.[116] After requesting and receiving a report from the Secretary-General on the structure and functions of the tribunal, the Security Council, 'acting under Chapter VII of the Charter', established the ICTY.[117]

The Security Council took similar steps of 'condemnation; publication; investigation; and by establishing the tribunal, punishment',[118] as regards the genocide occurring in Rwanda in 1994. A Commission of Experts was established in July 1994, and the International Tribunal for Rwanda (ICTR) was established under Chapter VII of the Charter in November 1994

> for the sole purpose of prosecuting persons responsible for genocide and other serious violations of international humanitarian law committed in the territory of Rwanda and Rwandan citizens responsible for genocide and other such violations committed in the territory of neighbouring States, between 1 January 1994 and 31 December 1994

after determining that 'genocide and other systematic, widespread and flagrant violations of international humanitarian law' committed in Rwanda constituted a threat to international peace and security'.[119] Although the

[114] Ibid.

[115] UNSC Res 808 (22 February 1993).

[116] UNSC Res 780 (6 October 1992).

[117] UNSC Res 827 (25 May 1993).

[118] JC O'Brien, 'The International Tribunal for Violations of International Humanitarian Law in the Former Yugoslavia' (1993) 87 *AJIL* 639, 640.

[119] UNSC Res 955 (8 November 1994).

tribunals are separate with the ICTY having its seat at the Hague and the ICTR at Arusha, a single Appeals Chamber was established 'to ensure that the international norms of international humanitarian law, crimes against humanity and genocide will be interpreted and applied consistently by both new international tribunals, whose case law will have considerable impact on the development of these norms'.[120]

The competence of the Council to establish tribunals has been challenged before both the ICTY and ICTR and questioned in the literature,[121] on the basis that there is no express power in the Charter to create such courts, and that they do not contribute to international peace and security. While we can debate such issues, the point of relevance here is whether the Council has judicial competence which it can delegate to a subsidiary organ to exercise.[122] The above analysis shows the SC acting in a quasi-judicial manner increasingly against individuals, and identifies provisions in the Charter that can be construed to give the SC this power. Indeed, it seems preferable for the SC to create a proper judicial body that will give individuals a fair trial rather than delivering a form of rudimentary justice itself. The real problem for the SC when it creates such tribunals to address particular threats to the peace is the charge of inconsistency: why Yugoslavia and Rwanda and not Chechnya, the Democratic Republic of the Congo or Darfur?

This problem has been answered to some extent by the creation of the International Criminal Court (ICC) in 2002 to which the SC can refer cases.[123] Still, the jurisdictional limitations on the ICC help to explain why the SC continues to be involved in the creation of internationalised criminal tribunals. Specifically, the Special Tribunal for Lebanon (STL), and the Special Court for Sierra Leone, which mix national judges with international judges, and domestic law with international law in situations where a purely domestic approach to criminal justice has been deemed inadequate.[124]

[120] J Karhilo, 'The Establishment of the International Tribunal for Rwanda' (1995) 64 *Nordic Journal of International Law* 683, 697.

[121] *Tadic* case before the ICTY IT-94-1-AR72 (2 October 1995); *Kanyabashi* case before the ICTR ICTR-96-15-I (18 June 1997); TD Mak, 'The Case Against an International War Crimes Tribunal for the Former Yugoslavia' (1997) 4 *International Peacekeeping* 536.

[122] D Sarooshi, *The United Nations and the Development of Collective Security* (Oxford, Oxford University Press,1999) at 20: 'An organ cannot delegate powers which it does not itself possess'.

[123] Rome Statute Establishing an International Criminal Court 1998 Art 13; UNSC Res 1593 (31 March 2005) re referral of the situation in Darfur to the ICC.

[124] Other internationalised criminal tribunals include the Special Panels for Kosovo, and East Timor, created by the respective UN administrations; the Extraordinary Chambers in the Courts of Cambodia, created by agreement between the UN Secretary-General and the Government of Cambodia on the initiative of the General Assembly; and the international judges that serve on the Special Chambers of the Bosnian State Court.

This proliferation of Council-initiated tribunals introduces further consistency issues. In particular, the ICTY and ICTR, when created, were granted Chapter VII powers, which enable these courts to compel third-party States to comply with their orders with respect to surrender of suspects or removal of immunities, for example.[125] While the difficulties in capturing leading war criminals in Bosnia and Serbia shows that in reality it is not possible to completely eradicate the link between dependency on the cooperation of third States and a court's effectiveness, the point remains that the ICTR and ICTY have been bestowed with extensive compliance powers that even the STL, the only other tribunal expressly created by a Chapter VII Resolution, does not appear to possess.[126] Indeed, had the Special Court for Sierra Leone, created by an agreement at the direction of the SC between the UN Secretary-General and Government of Sierra Leone, been granted Chapter VII powers,[127] it is reasonable to believe that Nigeria would have handed over Charles Taylor to the Court with greater haste; a matter which affected the perceived utility of the Court in relation to the post-conflict context in which it was situated for a considerable period of time. To avoid further undermining its own legitimacy, when the SC does deem a situation worthy of an internationalised criminal tribunal, it should strive to be consistent or offer a reasoned basis for differences in the powers it bestows.

IX. CONCLUSION

Concrete suggestions for reform of the SC made by Bowett would mean that the SC should make clear the legal basis for its actions and should seek legal advice whenever there is a prospect that legal rights might be affected; as well as giving affected States the right to speak and undertake proper fact-finding.[128] These have not been adopted by the SC though certain areas have seen improvement, for instance in the procedures of the 1267 Committee and the practice of the Council to consult the membership more widely when adopting legislative measures of general

[125] See, eg UNSC Res 827 (25 May 1993) para 4.

[126] Earlier Council Resolutions on the situation in Lebanon under Chapter VII had called on States to comply with the international investigation which preceded the tribunal, see UNSC Resolutions 1595 (7 April 2005), 1636 (31 October 2005), and 1644 (15 December 2005); Resolution 1757 (30 May 2007) which created the STL, however, made no mention of whether third States were obliged to comply with the Court.

[127] Agreement between the United Nations and the Government of Sierra Leone on the Establishment of a Special Court for Sierra Leone (16 January 2002).

[128] D Bowett, 'The Impact of Security Council Decisions on Dispute Settlement Procedures' 5 *European Journal of International Law* (1994) 93–99, 100.

effect.[129] Sanctions regimes do not fare well when judged against basic rule of law requirements. Farrall identifies five rule of law principles which he suggests should influence the decision making-procedure of the SC. These principles are: 'transparency, consistency, equality, due process, and proportionality'.[130] For Farrall, the principles are related but distinct, they feature in most politico-legal systems which promote the rule of law; and reflect recurring themes from the SC's own deliberation and practice concerning both the rule of law and UN sanctions regimes. They also reflect principles contained in the UN Millennium Declaration, as well as the approach employed with regard to the rule of law by the UN Secretary-General.[131]

Farrall identifies that there are failings across the board in relation to the principles, and, focusing on the sanctions regime, suggests how things could be improved. One point that comes across from Farrall's set of proposals is how failings in relation to transparency and due process could be improved with relative ease, by, for example, holding discussions about a potential new sanctions regime in public,[132] and offering potential targets of sanctions the opportunity to present their case.[133] Indeed, as Johnstone has argued, the legitimacy of Council decisions in general could readily be improved through an increase in reasoned deliberation at the Council.[134]

An important point to add to the debate is that there is a need for the Council to be more aware when it is acting judicially, this is not just in relation to sanctions or individuals, but generally so that it will become more accustomed to a using a more judicial approach in its procedure. When making determinations of rights and duties, or of rights and wrongs under international law, it should act in a judicial manner to the greatest extent possible; and as Bowett suggests it should take independent legal advice on how to achieve this.

The key point of this chapter is that when the SC acts in a judicial manner in relation to either States or individuals, how it acts has long-term consequences for implementation and enforcement of its decisions. This chapter has suggested how the legitimacy of the action taken is affected by whether or not the SC has due regard to the judicial process when making judgments of a legal nature, especially when enforcement action follows

[129] See I Johnstone, 'Legislation and Adjudication in the UN Security Council: Bringing Down the Deliberative Deficit' (2008) 102 *AJIL* 275, 290–294, discussing the more inclusive and process surrounding the adoption of UNSC Res 1540 (28 April 2004) in contrast with UNSC Res 1373 (28 Sept 2001).

[130] J M Farrall, *United Nations Sanctions and the Rule of Law*, (Cambridge, Cambridge University Press, 2007) 40.

[131] Ibid.

[132] Ibid 230.

[133] Ibid 237.

[134] Johnstone, above n 129 at 276.

upon those judgements. When judicial determinations were less frequent it may have been acceptable not to make a distinction, but as they have increased in frequency, and individuals have increasingly become the targets, there is a need for greater consideration of the failings of the SC as a venue for judicial activity. A flawed process of judgment is likely to undermine adherence to that judgment and lead to a need for greater recourse to enforcement measures if implementation is to be realised.

The SC is not a judicial body, but it has an important role in dispute settlement in matters of collective security. It should make more use of its Chapter VI powers, especially where it has not managed to gain a comprehensive impartial knowledge of the factual situation. Still, an active SC, whose reach in terms of subject matter is ever-growing, will encounter situations where determinations of law and the extent of legal obligations are required as matter of practical necessity. When this is the case the SC should not hide behind its executive function and processes, rather, the SC should be open about its quasi-judicial function and strive to the greatest extent possible to reach standards that would be expected in relation to such a function (standards of proper fact-finding, key aspects of natural justice and due process, the right to a remedy etc.). This will help to improve the legitimacy of the decision and the likelihood of compliance, which in turn would help both to encourage those targeted to comply and—should there be a lack of adherence—encourage political will for subsequent activity in relation to implementation which can be sustained over time. A final point in relation to the importance of the SC taking its quasi-judicial role seriously: if the SC gets its legal determinations wrong there are significant implications for the international order, so striving for the standards expected of a judicial body could help guard against such an occurrence and perhaps provide some mitigation should it occur.

9

Non-compliance Procedures and Dispute Resolution Mechanisms under International Environmental Agreements

KAREN N SCOTT

I. INTRODUCTION TO NON-COMPLIANCE PROCEDURES IN INTERNATIONAL ENVIRONMENTAL AGREEMENTS

THE DEVELOPMENT OF so-called non-compliance procedures (NCPs) in international environmental law is a relatively recent phenomenon. It is notable, for example, that in their seminal and influential text on strategies for managing compliance with international environmental agreements published in 1995,[1] Abram and Antonia Chayes do not discuss NCPs at any length despite their evident centrality to the authors' theme. More recently, Markus Ehrmann writing in 2002 commented that the number of compliance control procedures associated with international environmental agreements is low.[2] Today, there are over 20 non-compliance procedures that actively seek to support and facilitate compliance with international obligations in areas such as air pollution, climate change, marine environmental protection, biodiversity conservation, environmental impact assessment, fisheries management, freshwater resources and transboundary movement of chemicals, pesticides and waste. Many of these procedures have been adopted in the last five years.[3] One of the earliest NCPs (although not officially so-called) was developed under the auspices of the 1979 Bern Convention on the

[1] A Chayes and A Chayes, *The New Sovereignty: Compliance with International Regulatory Agreements* (Cambridge, MA, Harvard University Press, 1995).

[2] M Ehrmann, 'Procedures of Compliance Control in International Environmental Treaties' (2002) 13 *Colorado Journal of International Environmental Law and Policy* 377, 388.

[3] A further four such procedures are currently in advanced stages of development. See App I at the end of this chapter.

Conservation of European Wildlife and Habitats.[4] Notwithstanding its age, the case-file procedure created by the parties to the Bern Convention remains innovative almost 30 years on owing to its status as one of the few NCPs to permit non-governmental organisations (NGOs) and individuals to indirectly initiate action against a party in alleged non-compliance with their obligations under the Convention. This facility is not provided for in connection with the non-compliance procedure developed under the auspices of the 1987 Montreal Protocol on Substances that Deplete the Ozone Layer,[5] which is generally considered to be among the first global NCPs to be adopted. Nevertheless the Montreal Protocol's non-compliance procedure remains one of the most complex and sophisticated NCPs, and has provided a model for numerous subsequent NCPs adopted in other areas, most notably climate change.

Although non-compliance procedures vary in their complexity, scope and effectiveness, a number of typical features common to most if not all NCPs can be identified. First, and most notably, these procedures emphasise the importance of providing assistance and facilitating cooperation in order to enable States to comply with their international obligations.[6] This approach is sometimes described as 'soft enforcement' of treaty norms.[7] Many compliance institutions work closely with funding bodies established under the treaty or external bodies associated with treaty activities (such as the Global Environmental Facility (GEF)) in order to provide resources to assist State compliance with their treaty obligations. Nevertheless, it should be noted that increasingly, non-compliance procedures also provide for the adoption of coercive measures where facilitative measures fail or are otherwise deemed inappropriate. This good-cop-bad-cop approach to compliance underpins the NCPs operating in areas such as climate change and fisheries management in particular. The second feature common to most (although not all) non-compliance procedures is the creation of designated institutions such as a compliance committee, commission or group to oversee and implement the procedure. These institutions are generally provided with a mandate to consider not only individual cases of non-compliance, but also issues relating to compliance

[4] 1979 Convention on the Conservation of European Wildlife and Natural Habitats (Bern Convention) (in force 1982) 19 ILM 15 (1980).

[5] 1987 Protocol on Substances that Deplete the Ozone Layer (Montreal) (in force 1989) 26 ILM 1550 (1987).

[6] M Fitzmaurice and C Redgwell, 'Environmental Non-compliance Procedures and International Law' (2000) XXXI *Netherlands Yearbook of International Law* 35, 40; G Handl, 'Compliance Control Mechanisms and International Environmental Obligations' (1997) 29 *Tulane Journal of International and Comparative Law* 29, 34.

[7] O Yoshida, 'Soft Enforcement of Treaties: The Montreal Protocol's Non-compliance Procedure and the Functions of Internal International Institutions' (1999) 10 *Colorado Journal of International Environmental Law and Policy* 95, 95.

with, and implementation of, treaty obligations more generally. Third, the majority of NCPs permit complaints against a State alleged to be in non-compliance with its treaty obligations to be initiated by that State itself, a treaty institution (such as the secretariat) and other State parties. This clearly emphasises the NCPs' multilateral as opposed to bilateral approach to compliance and the resolution of disputes under the treaty. In the overwhelming majority of cases in all areas of international environmental law, non-compliance proceedings are initiated by either the State itself alleged to be or about to be in non-compliance or by a treaty institution rather than by other State parties. Fourth, many (but by no means all) non-compliance procedures permit some form of public participation within the procedure. Whilst the majority of such NCPs permit the public to observe proceedings and require the compliance institution to make its decisions publicly available, a growing number of procedures allow individuals or appropriately qualified NGOs to initiate non-compliance proceedings, to provide technical or expert information in connection with proceedings and/or (in exceptional cases) to participate in decision-making on compliance matters. Finally, a small number of recently adopted non-compliance procedures have recognised the importance of institutional cooperation and coordination with other NCPs that are operating within the same area or which otherwise impact upon the obligations or activities of State parties alleged to be in non-compliance with their treaty obligations.

Non-compliance procedures have been developed in order to respond to the very specific challenges faced by traditional dispute resolution mechanisms within environmental regimes, which generally create *erga omnes*—as opposed to strictly reciprocal—obligations. For example, where the consequences of non-compliance impact on a commons resource such as the oceans or the atmosphere, other States may lack the standing to bring an action under the traditional head of State responsibility.[8] Even where an individual State or group of States can point to environmental damage specific to them, as is arguably the case with respect to a number of small island developing States already experiencing negative impacts of climate change, such States may find it challenging to establish the 'wrongfulness' of the conduct in question and causality between the conduct and the resulting damage.[9] The latter challenge may be compounded where the impacts on the environment are subtle and cumulative.[10] Moreover, the traditional remedies under international law

[8] M Ehrmann, above n 2 at 380.

[9] M Koskenniemi, 'Breach of Treaty or Non-compliance? Reflections on the Enforcement of the Montreal Protocol' (1992) 3 *Yearbook of International Environmental Law* 123, 125–127.

[10] M Fitzmaurice and C Redgwell, above n 6 at 41.

associated with State responsibility are often inappropriate in the context of environmental damage where prevention is generally prized above cure and the failure to comply is more often the result of incapacity or lack of priority rather than a deliberate decision to abandon or renege upon previously agreed treaty commitments.[11] Furthermore, whilst alternative courses of action can be found under treaty law, the *erga omnes* as opposed to reciprocal nature of environmental obligations again renders traditional remedies inappropriate. Suspending or even excluding a State party from a treaty in order to punish that State's failure to comply with its obligations to protect a natural resource, ecosystem or species is, in practice, only likely to compound the damage or risk of damage to that same natural resource, ecosystem or species. Finally, reliance on external bodies such as the International Court of Justice (ICJ), the International Tribunal for the Law of the Sea (ITLOS), *ad hoc* arbitral tribunals and mediators to resolve individual disputes relating to compliance under a treaty may risk disturbing the normative expectations of all parties under that treaty.[12] As Thomas Gehring has perceptively noted, disputes within an environmental context will often involve both an individual and a group aspect.[13] In contrast to the individual, the group's interest is in protecting the stability of the regime and guarding against 'incidental or unintended modification' of treaty obligations resulting from the external resolution of individual disputes.[14] As Gehring concludes: '[t]his "group aspect" calls for a different procedure for dispute settlement.'[15]

In an attempt to respond to these challenges, non-compliance procedures have been described variously as 'occupying a function between conciliation and traditional dispute settlement'[16] or a form of 'alternative dispute resolution'.[17] However, most NCPs are considerably more complex than implied by either description. The typical non-compliance committee constitutes a political as opposed to an arbitral or judicial body. Nevertheless, a trend towards the 'legalisation' of NCPs can undoubtedly be detected. The NCP developed under the auspices of the 1997 Kyoto Protocol[18] for example, provides for complex rules of procedure,

[11] M Koskenniemi, above n 9 at 127.

[12] T Gehring, 'International Environmental Regimes: Dynamic Sectoral Legal Systems' (1990) 1 *Yearbook of International Environmental Law* 35, 50.

[13] Ibid.

[14] Ibid 51.

[15] Ibid.

[16] P Sands, *International Environmental Law* (Cambridge, Cambridge University Press, 2003) at 205.

[17] P Birnie and A Boyle, *International Environmental Law* (Oxford, Oxford University Press, 2002) at 206.

[18] 1997 Protocol to the UN Framework Convention on Climate Change (Kyoto Protocol) (in force 2005) (1998) 37 ILM 22.

permits the presentation of expert testimony at hearings, requires that the Compliance Committee delivers a reasoned decision in each case and provides for a limited right of appeal against that decision to the Meeting of the Parties. This procedure is undeniably 'quasi-judicial' in nature despite the political constitution of the Compliance Committee. Most compliance institutions, in addition to their being political and/or quasi-judicial in nature, are also technical bodies in terms of many of their functions. For example, most compliance-related institutions are mandated to monitor and report to the conference of the parties on compliance issues generally. The Implementation Committee established under the 1979 Convention on Long-range Transboundary Air Pollution (LRTAP)[19] is required to ensure that data submitted by parties has been evaluated by the appropriate technical body or expert. The Compliance Committee established by the parties to the 1997 Kyoto Protocol has been given a number of technical tasks connected to the collation and interpretation of data, which clearly extends its mandate beyond compliance per se. Moreover, in resolving individual or general compliance issues, compliance bodies may be required to interpret the scope and meaning of complex norms to the extent that their functions may be described as effectively law-making as well as law-enforcing.[20] A recently published guide to the case law of the 1998 Aarhus Convention[21] Compliance Committee[22] demonstrates not only the judicial nature of this body, but the inevitable consequences of this for law-creation in practice. Arguably the term which best combines these various functions is 'administrative'. Non-compliance procedures (along with many other aspects of international environmental law) operate within the so-called 'global administrative space', which is defined by international administrative lawyers as

> a space in which the strict dichotomy between domestic and international has largely broken down, in which administrative functions are performed in often complex interplays between officials and institutions on different levels, and in which regulation may be highly effective despite its predominately non-binding norms.[23]

[19] 1979 Convention on Long-Range Transboundary Air Pollution (LRTAP) (in force 1982) (1979) 18 ILM 1442.

[20] G Handl, above n 6, 32, 37.

[21] 1998 Convention on Access to Information, Public Participation in Decision-making and Access to Justice in Environmental Matters (Aarhus Convention) (in force 2001) (1999) 38 ILM 519.

[22] A Andrusevych, T Alge and C Clemens (eds), *Case Law of the Aarhus Convention Compliance Committee (2004–2008)* (Lviv, RACSE, 2008), http://doku.cac.at/case_law_accc.pdf.

[23] N Krish and B Kingsbury, 'Introduction: Global Governance and Global Administrative Law in the International Legal Order' (2006) 17 *European Journal of International Law* 1, 1.

Despite the fact that this description of international administrative law was not written with NCPs in mind, and, that surprisingly, leading international administrative lawyers have paid little attention to the institutions established by international environmental agreements in their development of this sub-discipline to date,[24] the aptness of this description to NCPs is undeniable.

Nevertheless, non-compliance procedures do not replace the traditional rules of international law which are potentially applicable in cases of non-compliance and dispute as between treaty parties. Non-compliance procedures operate in addition to, and alongside, dispute-resolution mechanisms and rules relating to State responsibility, countermeasures and the implementation, interpretation and termination of treaties. The relationship between non-compliance procedures and these areas of law and, the impact of NCPs on these areas, is unclear and, to an extent, disputed. Some of these themes will be returned to at the end of this chapter.

II. THE NATURE OF COMPLIANCE AND NON-COMPLIANCE MECHANISMS

The term 'compliance'[25] is generally defined as referring to behaviour which conforms to a specific or explicit treaty or customary norm.[26] It should be distinguished from the related but conceptually distinct notions of implementation—the rendering of an obligation into national law[27]—and effectiveness, which focuses on changes in State behaviour[28] or the success that an individual treaty has in addressing the problem it was intended to solve.[29]

The perplexing question as to why nations comply with their international environmental commitments has received considerable attention in

[24] See especially C Harlow, 'Global Administrative Law: The Quest for Principles and Values' (2006) 17 *European Journal of International Law* 187; N Krisch, 'The Pluralism of Global Administrative Law' (2006) 17 *European Journal of International Law* 247; B Kingsbury, N Krisch and R Stewart, 'The Emergence of Global Administrative Law' (2004–05) 15 *Law and Contemporary Problems* 15.

[25] See generally B Kingsbury, 'The Concept of Compliance as a Function of Competing Conceptions of International Law' (1997–1998) 19 *Michigan Journal of International Law* 345.

[26] See especially: R Mitchell, *International Oil Pollution at Sea: Environmental Policy and Treaty Compliance* (Cambridge, MA, MIT Press, 1994) at 30; K Raustiala, 'Compliance and Effectiveness in International Regulatory Cooperation' (2000) 32 *Case Western Reserve Journal of International Law* 387, 391; E Weiss and H Jacobson, *Engaging Compliance with International Environmental Accords* (Cambridge, MA, MIT Press, 1998) at 40. But see B Kingsbury, ibid 346.

[27] G Handl, above n 6 at 30, fn 4.

[28] K Raustiala, above n 26 at 394.

[29] M Ehrmann, above n 2 at 378.

legal, political and international relations literature.[30] Realist or rationalist scholars argue that nations only comply when it is in their interests to do so.[31] Thus in situations where it is easy or cost-effective to comply with international norms (such as the moratorium on commercial whaling agreed under the auspices of the 1946 International Convention on the Regulation of Whaling[32]), compliance is high. Where, on the other hand, it is more difficult from a political, technical or economic perspective to comply with obligations (as in the case of greenhouse gas emissions reductions agreed to under the 1997 Kyoto Protocol), compliance is (relatively) low.[33] A related theory of compliance focuses on self-interest in terms of international reputation. States value their reputation on the international stage as good global citizens and, consequently, comply with their environmental commitments in order to maintain and enhance that reputation.[34] By contrast, liberal theorists emphasise the importance of strong democratic traditions and respect for the rule of law as an important factor as to why nations comply with their international commitments. In a study carried out in 2002, Eric Neumayer concluded that there is evidence to support the contention that democracies are more strongly committed to international environmental norms than non-democracies.[35] Supporters of the transnational legal process theory of compliance also emphasise the importance of the relationship between international commitments and the domestic implementation of those commitments as key to supporting compliance at the

[30] See especially: J Cameron, J Werksman and P Roderick, *Improving Compliance with International Environmental Law* (London, Earthscan Publications, 1996) ch 1; T Crossen, 'Multilateral Environmental Agreements and the Compliance Continuum' (2004) 16 *Georgetown International Environmental Law Review* 473; H Koh, 'Why do Nations Obey International Law?' (1996–97) 106 *Yale Law Journal* 2599; R Mitchell, 'Compliance Theory: Compliance Effectiveness, and Behaviour Change in International Environmental Law' in D Bodansky et al (eds), *The Oxford Handbook of International Environmental Law* (Oxford, Oxford University Press 2007) 893.

[31] K Raustiala, above n 26 at 400; G Vigneron, 'Compliance and International Environmental Agreements: A Case Study of the 1995 United Nations Straddling Fish Stocks Agreement' (1998) 10 *Georgetown International Environmental Law Review* 581.

[32] In force 1948, 161 UNTS 72.

[33] See especially S Barrett, *Environment and Statecraft: The Strategy of Environmental Treaty Making* (Oxford, Oxford University Press, 2003) ch 7.

[34] See especially A Guzman, 'A Compliance-Based Theory of International Law' (2002) 90 *California Law Review* 1823.

[35] E Neumayer, 'Do Democracies Exhibit Stronger International Environmental Commitment? A Cross-Country Analysis' (2002) 39 *Journal of Peace Research* 139. Edith Brown Weiss has notably challenged liberal theory supporters, perspicuously noting that whilst democracies may be more responsive to public opinion, it cannot be assumed that public opinion is always sympathetic to environmental commitments. The ambivalent attitude of (arguably) a large proportion of the general public in the West towards making personal changes in their lives with the aim of minimising greenhouse gas emissions would appear to support Weiss' conclusion. See E Weiss, 'Understanding Compliance with International Environmental Agreements: The Baker's Dozen Myths' (1999) 32 *University of Richmond Law Review* 1555, 1579.

international level.[36] Other scholars focus on the nature of the international norms themselves and on the power of shared ideas[37] or the perception that those norms are fair or legitimate[38] as influencing the extent to which nations are prepared to comply with those norms. Whilst coercion and sanctions in connection with non-compliance with international norms undoubtedly have a role to play in some areas of international law[39] many scholars argue that its relevance is limited within the area of international environmental law.[40] Abram and Antonia Chayes have explored at length the notion that in respect of international environmental commitments, non-compliance does not generally result from wilful disobedience but is due to a lack of capacity, priority or information. In this situation they conclude that 'coercive enforcement is as misguided as it is costly'.[41] The Chaysian (or managerial) approach as to why nations comply with their international environmental commitments emphasises the dynamic role played by treaties and treaty institutions in actively managing compliance. They and other scholars have identified certain factors in treaty and institutional design, which are key to promoting and facilitating compliance: the creation of clear, precise and legitimate legal norms; transparent procedures and access to information (including the facilitation of NGO participation); reporting, verification and monitoring obligations; capacity building and technical assistance; dispute resolution mechanisms; and procedures for the review and assessment of treaty performance with a view to facilitating its adaptation and amendment.[42] Scholars belonging to the managerial theory of compliance conclude that the extent to which States will comply with their international environmental obligations is largely dependent upon effective, responsive and ultimately dynamic treaty design.

[36] See especially: C Kelly, 'Enmeshment as a Theory of Compliance' (2005) 37 *New York University Journal of International Law and Politics* 303; H Koh, 'Transnational Legal Process' (1996) 75 *Nebraska Law Review* 181.

[37] K Raustilia, above n 26 at 405.

[38] See especially: T Franck, *The Power of Legitimacy Among Nations* (Oxford, Oxford University Press, 1990); T Franck, *Fairness in International Law and Institutions* (Oxford, Clarendon Press, 1995).

[39] See especially: G Downs, D Rocke and P Barsoom, 'Is the Good News about Compliance Good News about Cooperation?' (1996) 50 *International Organisation* 379; T Yang, 'International Treaty Enforcement as a Public Good: Institutional Deterrent Sanctions in International Environmental Agreements' (2006) 27 *Michigan Journal of International Law* 1131.

[40] See especially A Chayes and A Chayes, above n 1 at 29–108. However, as will be discussed below, a number of NCPs, notably that developed by the 1997 Kyoto Protocol combine a facilitative/soft approach to compliance with sanctions. On sanctions and the climate change regime, see C Hagem and H Westskog, 'Effective Enforcement and Double-edged Deterrents: How the Impacts of Sanctions also Affect Complying Parties' in O Schram Stokke, J Hovi and G Ulfstein (eds), *Implementing the Climate Regime: International Compliance* (London, Earthscan, 2005) 107.

[41] A Chayes and A Chayes, above n 1 at 22.

[42] A Chayes and A Chayes, ibid.

Non-compliance procedures undoubtedly constitute a significant mechanism for managing and facilitating compliance with international environmental commitments.[43] Non-compliance bodies are themselves an important and integral component of the institutional infrastructure[44] of an increasing number of international environmental agreements. As such, they clearly support the managerial theory of compliance. However, a number of such procedures (such as the mechanism devised by the parties to the 1997 Kyoto Protocol) can also be described as coercive in nature. To this extent, they can also be used to support an enforcement or coercive theory of compliance. Many NCPs are open to the public or at least to NGO presence, and the initiation of non-compliance proceedings against a treaty party may impact upon the reputation of that party as a good international citizen at the international and/or domestic level. Non-compliance procedures thus have the potential to support a reputational theory of compliance. The facilitation of public participation within non-compliance proceedings as observers, experts or even complainants provides further practical support for compliance theories based on democracy, legitimacy or transnational process. Moreover, the extent to which these procedures seek to facilitate compliance through assistance and capacity building with the involvement of all treaty parties arguably contributes to the general perception that the treaty norms are both legitimate and fair, which in and of itself also promotes compliance with treaty obligations. Finally, the fact that most if not all non-compliance procedures emphasise the role of financial, technical and information-based assistance in facilitating a State to comply with its obligations, means compliance is likely to be justified on the grounds of self-interest supporting a rational theory of compliance.

[43] Other mechanisms which support compliance with international environmental commitments (beyond the scope of this chapter) include reporting requirements, monitoring, fact-finding, inspection/observation schemes, verification processes, funding mechanisms and action supporting compliance taken outside of the treaty regime. See especially: D Bodansky et al (eds), *The Oxford Handbook of International Environmental Law* (Oxford, Oxford University Press 2007) chs 41, 42 and 43; J Cameron, J Werksman and P Roderick, above n 31; D Victor, K Raustiala and E Skolnikoff (eds), *The Implementation and Effectiveness of International Environmental Commitments: Theory and Practice* (Cambridge, Massachusetts, MIT Press, 1998); E Weiss and H Jacobson, above n 27; R Wolfrum, 'Means of Ensuring Compliance with and Enforcement of International Environmental Law' (1998) 272 *Recueil des Cours* 9. See also the *Guidelines for Strengthening Compliance with and Implementation of Multilateral Environmental Agreements (MEAs) in the ECE Region* (2003) ECE/CEP/107 (20 March 2003); Decision SS VII/4 of the UNEP Governing Council (Special Session) (2002), *Guidelines on Compliance with and Enforcement of Multilateral Environmental Agreements.*

[44] The institutional infrastructure of international environmental agreements comprises what has been aptly described by Robin Churchill and Geir Ulfstein as an 'autonomous institutional arrangement'. See R Church and G Ulfstein, 'Autonomous Institutional Arrangements in Multilateral Environmental Agreements: A Little-Noticed Phenomenon in International Law' (2000) 94 *American Journal of International Law* (*AJIL*) 623.

III. COMMON FEATURES OF NON-COMPLIANCE PROCEDURES

For the purposes of this section of the Chapter, 20 active non-compliance procedures and four procedures in advanced stages of development have been assessed. Although this does not represent an exhaustive list of non-compliance mechanisms, the procedures surveyed are drawn from a wide range of international environmental treaties of application to pollution prevention and control, biodiversity conservation, transboundary movements of waste and dangerous substances, as well as fisheries management. Owing to space constraints the references in this section of the chapter will be kept to a minimum. The relevant articles of each instrument plus associated decisions and resolutions related to compliance are listed in Appendix I at the end of this chapter. In Appendix II detailed (although inevitably incomplete) information relating to the non-compliance procedure established by each instrument is displayed in tabular form.

Although the non-compliance procedures surveyed in this Chapter vary to a greater or lesser extent from one another, certain common features can be identified, and these are used as a basis for the discussion in this section. Many of these NCPs are complex and took many years negotiate and develop. For example, although the 1987 Montreal Protocol itself took only 10 months to negotiate, the non-compliance procedure took a further five years to develop.[45] Whilst the Montreal Protocol's NCP was the subject of specific negotiations by State parties, other non-compliance procedures such as those which operate under the 1973 Convention on International Trade in Endangered Species (CITES)[46] and the 1979 Bern Convention[47] evolved on a more organic or *ad hoc* basis through State practice. At least two of the treaties included (the 1971 Ramsar Convention[48] and the 1972 World Heritage Convention[49]) have developed procedures for considering a party's compliance with a small number of its obligations under the treaty analogously to, but distinct from, non-compliance procedures considered under other treaties. In both cases the relevant treaty body is limited to an examination of the status of sites listed as deserving special protection and the host State's

[45] M Ehrmann, above n 2 at 394.

[46] 1973 Convention on International Trade in Endangered Species of Fauna and Flora (CITES) (in force 1975) (1973) 21 ILM 1085. See especially: R Reeve, *Policing International Trade in Endangered Species: The CITES Treaty and Compliance* (London, Earthscan, 2002).

[47] See especially S Jen, 'The Convention on the Conservation of European Wildlife and Natural Habitats (Bern 1979): Procedures of Application in Practice' (1999) 2 *Journal of International Wildlife Law and Policy* 224.

[48] 1971 Convention on Wetlands of International Importance (Ramsar Convention) (in force 1975), (1972) 11 ILM 963.

[49] 1972 UNESCO Convention Concerning the Protection of the World Cultural and Natural Heritage (World Heritage Convention) (in force 1975) (1972) 11 ILM 1358.

action (or inaction) in connection with those sites. Nevertheless, the Bureau (in respect of the 1971 Ramsar Convention) and World Heritage Committee (in respect of the 1972 World Heritage Convention) conduct a relatively formal examination of the status of sites at risk, and attempt to persuade States to comply with their international obligations by means of assistance (financial and technical) and sanction (ultimate removal from the list). As such, their inclusion within this survey is appropriate. Finally, it is worth noting that some non-compliance procedures are much more active than others. Compliance bodies established by the 1987 Montreal Protocol, 1979 Bern Convention, 1998 Aarhus Convention and the 1991 Espoo Convention,[50] for example, are all extremely active. By contrast, minimal use has been made of the equivalent procedures under the 1992 OSPAR Convention[51] and 1989 Basel Convention.[52] In respect of the latter instrument, the Conference of the Parties to the Basel Convention has formally called upon State parties to make use of the non-compliance procedure.[53] More recently, the Compliance Committee has recommended that the Basel Secretariat make use of its mandate to make submissions to the Committee, particularly in cases where national reports have not been submitted or which are incomplete.[54] This advice has yet to be heeded by the Parties to, and institutions established under, the Basel Convention.

A. Institutional Infrastructure

i. Institutions and Composition Thereof

Most (although not all) instruments surveyed establish a specific institutional mechanism central to the implementation of the non-compliance procedure.[55] Variously described as a Compliance, Implementation or Standing Committee, Commission or Bureau, these bodies normally comprise representatives drawn from a small number of State parties. The

[50] 1991 Convention on Environmental Impact Assessment in a Transboundary Context (Espoo Convention) (in force 1997) (1991) 30 ILM 802.

[51] 1992 Convention for the Protection of the Marine Environment of the North East Atlantic (OSPAR) (in force 1998) (1993) 32 ILM 1072.

[52] 1989 Convention on the Control of Transboundary Movements of Hazardous Wastes and Their Disposal (Basel Convention) (in force 1992) (1989) 28 ILM 657.

[53] Decision VII/30 Mechanism for Promoting the Implementation and Compliance: Work Programme 2005–2006 (2004).

[54] Report of the sixth session of the Basel Convention Implementation Committee (Geneva, 28–29 February 2008), UNEP/CHW/CC/6/7 (18 March 2008) para 17.

[55] The 1992 OSPAR Convention unusually has not established a separate body to address compliance issues, which are considered by the OSPAR Commission established under Art 10 of the Convention.

number of representatives varies from five[56] to 21[57] and are commonly selected on the basis of geography (eg, the 1987 Montreal Protocol Implementation Committee) and/or individual expertise (eg, 1991 Aarhus Convention Compliance Committee) or a combination of both (eg, the 1997 Kyoto Protocol Compliance Committee). Where geography is not the primary criterion for selection it is often a factor which must be considered along with other criteria[58] such as cultural representation,[59] equity between developed and developing States, gender,[60] representation from regional organisations,[61] and representation of States responsible for hosting the conference or meeting of the parties.[62] Where compliance matters are dealt with by a pre-existing treaty body (as is the case of the 1992 OSPAR Convention and 1979 Bern Convention) it is common that all States parties are involved in decisions relating to compliance issues.[63] It would also appear to be standard practice that all States parties are represented on compliance institutions established by treaties focusing on fisheries management. Exceptionally, expert NGOs or industry representatives may be appointed to the compliance body. For example, three expert NGOs and three industry representatives are entitled to be appointed as members of the International Review Panel established to assess compliance with the 1999 Agreement on the International Dolphin Conservation Programme.[64] Also unusually, the selection of Compliance Committee members may be required to take into account proposals made by qualified NGOs in connection with Committee membership.[65]

[56] The normal composition of the Implementation Committee under the 1991 Espoo Convention is eight. However, it may function where membership falls to five. Should membership fall below five the matter must be referred to the Meeting of the Parties.

[57] 21 members make up the World Heritage Committee established under Arts 8–10 of the 1972 World Heritage Convention.

[58] Consideration of geographical representation must be given when selecting members of the Aarhus Compliance Committee and the Compliance Committee established under the 1999 Protocol on Water and Health to the 1992 Convention on the Protection and Use of Transboundary Water Courses and International Lakes (Protocol on Water and Health) (in force 2005), (1999) 29 EPL 200.

[59] 1972 World Heritage Convention.

[60] These factors are currently being considered by the parties to the 2001 Stockholm Convention on Persistent Organic Pollutants (in force 2004) (2001) 40 ILM 532, in their ongoing negotiations for the development of a non-compliance procedure under Art 17 of the POPs Convention. See the Annex to Decision SC-3/20 (2005) *[Non-compliance] [Compliance] Procedures under Article 17 of the Stockholm Convention* at para 6.

[61] 1995 Barcelona Convention (in respect of the European Community).

[62] 1973 CITES.

[63] It should be noted that the executive arm of the non-compliance procedure under the 1979 Bern Convention is the Bureau, which consists of the chairman, vice-chairman and previous chairman.

[64] 1999 Agreement on the International Dolphin Conservation Programme (Dolphin Conservation Agreement) (in force 1999), www.iattc.org/PDFFiles2/AIDCP-(amended-Oct-2007).pdf.

[65] 1999 Protocol on Water and Health.

A number of compliance institutions also include within their members representatives from other treaty bodies or closely associated financial mechanisms. For example, the ozone secretariat, Ozone Multilateral Fund secretariat and representatives from the international and bilateral implementing agencies of the GEF are included in the membership of the 1987 Montreal Protocol Implementation Committee. Finally, it should be noted that in all cases the State under investigation is entitled to be represented in the compliance institution and to participate in the consideration of the complaint or allegation against it. Unsurprisingly in no case is the State under investigation able to participate in the elaboration and adoption of recommendations relating to its situation, although a number of procedures permit that State to comment in writing on the recommendations prior to, or immediately after, their formal adoption.[66]

Of all the non-compliance institutions established to date, the most complex body has been created by the parties to the 1997 Kyoto Protocol.[67] The Kyoto Compliance Committee comprises a plenary, a bureau and two branches: the Facilitative Branch and the Enforcement Branch. The 20 State representatives (divided equally between both branches) serve in their individual capacity and have been selected on the basis of their scientific, legal and/or socio-economic expertise. Nevertheless, the chair and vice-chair of each branch must comprise an Annex I and non-Annex I representative, and each branch must include one member from each of the five UN geographical groupings, one member from the small island developing States, two members from Annex 1 parties and two members from non-Annex 1 parties. The result has been described as 'an elaborate, complex structure, which gives the impression of a judicial organ dressed up in political (or bureaucratic) garb'.[68]

ii. Functions

The majority of compliance institutions have very similar mandates setting out their functions. Typical functions include: receiving (regular and *ad hoc*) reports; information-gathering within the territory of the State

[66] Eg 1995 Barcelona Convention; 2000 Protocol on Biosafety to the 1992 Convention on Biological Diversity (Biosafety Protocol) (in force 2003) (2000) 39 ILM 1027; 1999 Protocol on Water and Health.

[67] On the Kyoto non-compliance procedure more generally, see: R Lefeber, 'From the Hague to Bonn to Marrakesh and Beyond: A Negotiating History of the Compliance Regime under the Kyoto Protocol' (2001) 14 *Hague Yearbook of International Law* 25; O Schram Stokke, J Hovi and G Ulfstein (eds), *Implementing the Climate Regime: International Compliance* (London, Earthscan, 2005); J Werksman, 'Compliance and the Kyoto Protocol: Building a Backbone into a "Flexible" Regime' (1998) 9 *Yearbook of International Environmental Law* 48.

[68] J Klabbers, 'Compliance Procedures' in D Bodansky et al (eds), *The Oxford Handbook of International Environmental Law* (Oxford, Oxford University Press, 2007) 995, 999.

party under investigation; providing advice and recommendations on individual and general cases of compliance to the conference/meeting of the parties or directly to individual parties; monitoring compliance with NCP measures; and exchanging information with other bodies such as the secretariat, financial mechanisms or, to a more limited extent, with external institutions connected to financial assistance or non-compliance. Some compliance bodies such as 1979 LRTAP Implementation Committee and the 1997 Kyoto Compliance Committee have additional technical functions connected to the collation, evaluation and interpretation of data. Finally, it should be noted that a minority of institutions have a more limited mandate in connection with compliance. For example, the 1992 OSPAR Commission is apparently able only to call upon parties to take steps to bring about compliance and to adopt measures to assist compliance.

iii. Decision-making

All compliance institutions require their members to reach decisions on compliance-related issues by means of consensus in the first instance. However, it should be noted that in some cases 'consensus' is given a very particular meaning. For example, 'consensus' for the purposes of the 1987 Montreal Protocol Implementation Committee includes the situation where one State objects to the measure adopted provided that the position of the objecting State is made clear in the report of the Implementation Committee.[69] Where consensus is not achievable decisions may be taken in the majority of non-compliance institutions on the basis of a three-quarters or two-thirds majority. In two cases—the 1973 CITES and the 1991 Espoo Convention—a simple majority will suffice.[70] A minority of instruments require a majority vote in favour of a measure by a particular category of parties. For example, measures may only be adopted by the Enforcement Branch of the Kyoto Compliance Committee where three-quarters of the parties vote in favour of the measure including a majority of Annex 1 parties and a majority of non-Annex 1 parties. In the event that a compliance measure is adopted by a majority vote rather than consensus, a number of compliance institutions require that the views of all parties be reflected in the report dealing with that measure.[71]

[69] M Ehrmann, above n 2 at 408.

[70] In the case a tie within the Standing Committee established under the 1973 CITES the depository government has the casting vote.

[71] 2000 Biosafety Protocol; 1991 Espoo Convention; 1996 Protocol to the London Dumping Convention (London (Dumping) Protocol) (in force 2006) (1997) 36 ILM 7.

B. Treaty Provisions Subject to Review

The issue of which of the treaty provisions should be subject to review under the non-compliance procedure is regularly the most controversial and difficult part of the compliance negotiations as a whole. In particular, the issue of whether obligations connected to the provision of financial and technical assistance should be subject to the non-compliance process has proven particularly challenging to resolve. In light of this it is perhaps understandable that a number of non-compliance procedures provide no guidance as to which treaty obligations are subject to review.[72] In this situation it is presumably the role of the compliance body to decide the extent of its review mandate on an evolving or *ad hoc* basis. It is notable that with respect to three of these instruments for which no formal review mandate is articulated (1973 CITES, 1979 LRTAP and the 1999 Water and Health Protocol) the practice of the relevant compliance body has been to interpret its mandate broadly and to consider compliance issues connected to both substantive and reporting obligations under the treaty.

Other instruments omit a formal mandate but provide guidance as to the treaty provisions which may be considered by the compliance body in connection with compliance-related matters. Guidance issued under the auspices of the 1998 Aarhus Convention for example, permits the Compliance Committee to consider complaints connected to access to information, public participation in environmental decision-making, access to justice as well as general failures to implement correctly certain provisions of the Aarhus Convention within national law. This is clearly an expansive and comprehensive mandate and, as noted above, the 1998 Aarhus Convention Compliance Committee is one of the most active compliance bodies within the field of international environmental law.

The majority of non-compliance procedures specify (in varying degrees of detail) the precise treaty provisions which may be considered by the compliance body in connection with compliance-related complaints. For example, the 2000 Biosafety Protocol expansively permits the Compliance Committee to consider compliance with 'the provisions of this Protocol'.[73] The Implementation Committee established under the 1991 Espoo Convention is provided with a similarly broad mandate to consider all matters related to compliance except those submitted to the enquiry procedure under Article 3(7) of the Convention. This generous mandate was

[72] Treaties included in this category include: 1973 CITES; 1979 LRTAP; 1992 OSPAR; and the 1999 Water and Health Protocol.

[73] 2000 Biosafety Protocol Art 34. It should be noted that this provision does not refer to *all* provisions, and thus the option to exclude review of selected provisions has arguably been preserved.

arguably expanded further in 2007 when the members of the Compliance Committee agreed that:

> If a contradiction were to be identified between provisions in the [Espoo] Convention and provisions in other agreements to which a Party to the Convention is also a Party, then it might consider it as a compliance matter provided that such a contradiction can be construed as a compliance issue under the Convention.[74]

By contrast, the 1987 Montreal Protocol Implementation Committee is provided with the mandate to examine compliance with the reporting obligations under the Protocol as well as obligations connected to the phasing out of production and consumption of designated substances, trade with non-parties and the issue of licences connected to substances covered by the Protocol. Similarly, both the Facilitative and Enforcement Branches of the 1997 Kyoto Protocol Compliance Committee are permitted to examine State compliance with only nine separate provisions of the Kyoto Protocol.[75] In providing a detailed and precise mandate specifying treaty provisions subject to review, the thorny issue of whether obligations relating to financial and technical assistance may be subject to the compliance procedure is neatly avoided.[76]

Finally, it should be noted that the review mandate of a small number of non-compliance procedures varies according to who initiates proceedings. For example, the Compliance Committee established under the 1989 Basel Convention may examine compliance-related issues connected to any treaty provision where the State in non-compliance or about to be in non-compliance itself refers the issue of non-compliance to the Committee. Where proceedings are initiated by another State however, the Committee may only examine treaty provisions of direct relevance to the actual dispute between the party initiating proceedings and the party alleged to be in non-compliance. The Committee's mandate is most restricted in cases where the secretariat initiates non-compliance proceedings. In this situation the Committee may only examine non-compliance in connection with the reporting obligations under the treaty. Finally,

[74] Report of the Eleventh Meeting of the Implementation Committee (2007) ECE/MP.EIA/WG.1/2007/4, para 26.

[75] Arts 3(1), 3(14), 6, 12, 17, 5(1), 5(2), 7(1) and 7(4) of the 1997 Kyoto Protocol are subject to consideration by the Facilitative Branch of the Compliance Committee. The Enforcement Branch has a similar mandate but is not able to examine compliance with Art 3(14). In contrast to the Facilitative Branch it is able to consider compliance with Art 8 in addition to the other provisions listed.

[76] It should nevertheless be noted that Art 4(7) of the 1992 UN Framework Convention on Climate Change (in force 1994) (1992) 31 ILM 851, stipulates that the extent to which developing countries will effectively implement their commitments under the Convention will depend on the effective implementation by developed country parties of their commitments under the Convention related to financial resources and transfer of technology.

when reviewing compliance issues generally with a view to reporting to the Conference of the Parties, the Committee may look at a wide range of issues including waste management, training, access to assistance and enforcement. As noted above, despite or perhaps because of this complex mandate, the Basel Compliance Committee has yet to be referred a substantive non-compliance issue to decide.

C. Initiation of Non-compliance Proceedings

The majority of non-compliance procedures provide for three broad mechanisms in connection with the initiation of compliance proceedings. The first mechanism is self-referral whereby a State party which has failed to comply with treaty obligations or fears that it will not be able to comply with its obligations in the near future initiates proceedings preemptively. The emphasis on self-referral is an important component of most non-compliance proceedings and reflects the precautionary approach endorsed by these mechanisms and the importance of addressing issues of non-compliance in their early stages.[77] It also reflects the emphasis of most of these procedures on facilitating compliance through the provision of assistance as opposed to coercive measures such as sanctions. Often initiating non-compliance proceedings provides a means to obtain technical or financial assistance under the treaty which will enable the struggling State to comply with its international obligations. It is notable that NCPs which do not appear to permit self-referral (such as the 1992 OSPAR Convention, the 1979 Bern Convention, the 1999 Dolphin Conservation Agreement and the 1966 International Commission for the Conservation of Atlantic Tunas (ICCAT)[78]) all provide for minimal measures connected to the provision of financial and technical assistance to States in non-compliance with their treaty obligations. The first non-compliance procedure to permit self-referral was the 1987 Montreal Protocol, and this mode of initiating proceedings was used relatively extensively in the 1990s, where a number of States with economies in transition declared themselves or were deemed to have declared themselves in non-compliance with their ozone commitments.[79] Since then self-referral has been used regularly to initiate proceedings before the Montreal Implementation Committee as

[77] O Yoshida, above n 7 at 121.

[78] 1966 International Commission for the Conservation of Atlantic Tunas (ICCAT) (in force 1969), 37 UNTS 63.

[79] Belarus, Bulgaria, Poland, Russia and the Ukraine attempted to request a five-year grace period from the Conference of the Parties with respect to various commitments connected to the phase out of ozone-depleting substances in 1995. However, the request was treated as a self-referral in connection with anticipated non-compliance and directed to the Implementation Committee. See D Victor, 'The Operation and Effectiveness of the Montreal

well as on a less regular basis to initiate proceedings before compliance bodies established by other treaties.

The second mechanism by virtue of which non-compliance proceedings may be initiated relies on the submission of a compliant by a State party in connection with another party's failure to comply with its treaty obligations. Whilst the majority of non-compliance procedures permit States to initiate proceedings against other parties,[80] a small number of NCPs (such as the procedure established by the parties to the 1996 London Protocol) require that the complainant State must be especially affected by the alleged non-compliance.[81] Although this requirement is consistent with the traditional rules of State responsibility and treaty suspension and termination, it introduces an arguably undesirable element of bilateral reciprocity into what is otherwise a multilateral process. Nevertheless, despite the absence of this restriction in the vast majority of non-compliance procedures, very few States initiate non-compliance proceedings against other States. For example, out of 29 submissions to date to the 1998 Aarhus Convention Compliance Committee in connection with allegations of non-compliance only one complaint was made by a State party with respect to the conduct of another party under the Convention.[82]

It is highly likely that the absence of examples of States initiating proceedings against other States alleged to be in non-compliance with their treaty commitments is due to the fact that most NCPs permit action to be initiated by treaty bodies. This third initiating mechanism is extremely significant and, in practice, is used to initiate the vast majority of non-compliance proceedings under most treaties. In most cases the treaty secretariat is provided with the mandate to initiate non-compliance proceedings against a State believed to be in or about to be in non-compliance with its treaty obligations. Some treaties—such as the 1973 CITES—provide the secretariat with a substantial investigative

Protocol's Non-Compliance Procedure' in D Victor, K Raustiala and E Skolnkioff (eds), above n 43, 137, 155–156.

[80] Notable exceptions include the 1992 OSPAR, the 1999 Dolphin Conservation Agreement and the 1966 ICCAT. These three treaties permit proceedings to be initiated by treaty institutions only (on which see below).

[81] This requirement is also contained in a two draft non-compliance procedures in the process of being developed under the 2001 Stockholm Convention on Persistent Organic Pollutants (see the Annex to Decision SC-3/20 (2005) *[Non-compliance] [Compliance] Procedures under Article 17 of the Stockholm Convention* at para 17(b)) and the 1998 Rotterdam Convention on the Prior Informed Consent Procedure for Certain Hazardous Chemicals and Pesticides in International Trade (in force 2004) (1999) 38 ILM 1 (see Decision RC-3/4 (2008) *Draft text of the procedures and mechanism on compliance with the Rotterdam Convention,* Annex, para 12(b)).

[82] See submission ACCC/S/2004/01 by Romania with respect to the alleged non-compliance of the Ukraine with Art 6(2)(e) of the Convention in connection with the provision of information to the public affected by the construction of the Bystroe Canal in the Danube Delta.

role before passing the matter on to the compliance body—in the case of CITES—the Standing Committee. Others require the secretariat to work closely with the party alleged to be in non-compliance in order to try to resolve the issue before passing the matter to the compliance body if resolution proves unattainable.[83] A number of treaties permit the compliance body itself[84] or the meeting of the parties[85] to initiate proceedings rather than the secretariat. Many non-compliance procedures specify the information which can be used by treaty institutions as a basis for initiating non-compliance proceedings against a State party. The NCP established by the parties to the 1991 Espoo Convention takes a notably expansive approach towards the information which may be deemed relevant in considering a party's alleged non-compliance with its obligations. Such information includes: questionnaire responses; party reports; information provided by the secretariat; bilateral and multi-lateral agreements; national legislation; information resulting from the Implementation Committee's work-plan; information from NGOs and any public sources of information including the media.[86] A small number of NCPs (such as the procedure established by the parties to the 1989 Basel Convention) provide only a limited mandate for the initiation of non-compliance proceedings by treaty institutions,[87] or no mandate at all. Non-compliance proceedings under the 1997 Kyoto Protocol may only be formally initiated by means of self-referral or by a State party in connection with the alleged non-compliance by another State party. Given the sophisticated and complex nature of the Kyoto non-compliance procedure this is a surprising and regrettable omission, which is only partially addressed by the fact that the Compliance Committee receives the final reports on State parties compiled by the expert review teams. Although receipt of these reports provides the Committee with a basis for initiating action where a party appears to be in non-compliance with its obligations (action was recently taken against Greece on this basis[88]) this is arguably not a

[83] Eg the 1995 Barcelona Convention and the 1999 Protocol on Water and Health.

[84] Eg the 1991 Espoo Convention.

[85] Eg the 1996 London Protocol.

[86] See the *Report of the Ninth Meeting of the Implementation Committee*, ECE/MP.EIA/WG.1/2006/4 (28 April 2006) para 6.

[87] The secretariat to the Basel Convention is permitted to initiate proceedings in respect of alleged non-compliance with reporting obligations only although the Conference of the Parties may initiate a general review of compliance issues.

[88] Reports submitted by both Greece and Canada at the December 2008 meeting of the Compliance Committee raised questions related to implementation. The question of Greece's compliance with Decision 19/CMP.1 and Decision 15/CMP.1 was referred to the Enforcement Branch of the Compliance Committee. The Enforcement Branch determined that Greece was temporarily unable to participate in the flexible mechanisms under the 1997 Kyoto Protocol but revised this decision on receipt of a revised plan of implementation from Greece with respect to these decisions. (See FCCC/KP/CMP/2008/5 at paras 23–25 and 30).

complete substitute for permitting the secretariat or other treaty body to initiate non-compliance procedures. For example, reports are only submitted periodically and, depending on the nature of the report, will not necessarily provide information on all obligations subject to review under the Kyoto Protocol.

Finally, a small number of non-compliance procedures permit the initiation of proceeding directly or indirectly by individuals or appropriately qualified NGOs. Procedures established under both the 1998 Aarhus Convention and 1999 Protocol on Water and Health permit individuals and NGOs to initiate proceedings against States alleged to be in non-compliance with their treaty obligations.[89] In respect of the Aarhus Convention the overwhelming majority of non-compliance proceedings to date have been initiated by members of the public.[90] Case-file investigations under the 1979 Bern Convention may be initiated by the Convention secretariat or Bureau on receipt of a communication from an individual or an NGO, and in practice, a large number of case-files have been opened on the basis of information provided by the public. Similarly, under the 1971 Ramsar Convention NGOs or other interested bodies can draw the attention of the Bureau to examples of, or issues relating to, non-compliance under the Convention. On a rather more limited basis the Compliance Committee established by the parties to the 2000 Biosafety Protocol may consider information it receives from a State not party to the Protocol and invite the party referred to in the communication to indicate whether it would like the Committee to consider the issue with a view to providing assistance. It would appear that in such situations the matter is considered under the heading of something other than non-compliance.

D. Non-compliance Measures

i. Typical Non-compliance Measures

Typical non-compliance measures are facilitative or supportive and tend to focus on assistance and cooperation rather than coercion or sanctions. It

Canada was assessed to be in compliance with Decision 15.CMP.1, Decision 13, CMP.1 and the Annex to Decision 5/CMP.1 and no further action was taken against it (see FCCC/KP/CMP/2008/5 at paras 27–30).

[89] The procedures under both instruments permit state parties to exclude the option of public initiation of non-compliance proceedings for an initial period of four years following the entry into force of the procedure. The Compliance Committee under the Protocol on Water and Health must consider the availability of domestic remedies when reviewing submissions from individuals or NGOs.

[90] The NCP operating under the 1999 Protocol on Water and Health was adopted in 2007 and thus has been active for a very short period of time.

is this feature which sets non-compliance procedures apart from the more traditional areas of dispute resolution, State responsibility and treaty law. In fact the very term 'non-compliance' rather than 'breach' represents a clear intention to avoid pejorative language which is regarded as inappropriate in the context of *erga omnes* obligations and environmental protection.[91] This trend is developed further by the use of the term 'compliance committee' (rather than 'non-compliance committee') or the even more innocuous appellation: 'implementation committee'. The majority of non-compliance procedures permit the issue of measures calling for, or even providing, financial, technical or knowledge-based assistance. Some treaty regimes such as the 1987 Montreal Protocol, 1997 Kyoto Protocol, 1989 Basel Convention and 1971 Ramsar Convention provide for a fund or financial mechanism to assist States in complying with their obligations. In the case of the 1987 Montreal Protocol, the provision of additional funding may be made formally conditional on compliance, and it has been suggested that this feature has made a significant contribution to the success of the Protocol.[92] The 1991 Espoo Convention Implementation Committee may issue recommendations to potential donors on the assistance likely to be needed by States struggling to meet their obligations under the Convention. Both the Standing Committee established under the 1973 CITES and Bureau established under the 1971 Ramsar Convention can issue recommendations for the provision of training and in-country assistance to support a State in the implementation of its international commitments.

Nevertheless, it is misleading to categorise non-compliance procedures as being solely concerned with supportive and assistance-focused measures. Increasingly, these procedures are prioritising measures which are undoubtedly coercive or sanction-focused in nature. The NCP established by the parties to the 1997 Kyoto Protocol is at the forefront of such developments and, as noted above, establishes a specific 'Enforcement Branch' which focuses on the 'coercive' enforcement of Kyoto commitments, working alongside the Facilitative Branch. Although no other non-compliance procedure has to date embraced an equivalent formal institutional divide between facilitative and coercive measures, most procedures provide for some form of sanction in connection with non-compliance. For example, the majority of non-compliance procedures permit their compliance bodies to issue declarations of non compliance, cautions, formal statements of concern and to condemn States failing to comply with their treaty obligations. Most procedures also permit the appropriate body to request/require

[91] M Koskenniemi, above n 9 at 128.
[92] D Victor, above n 78 at 138.

that the State party in non-compliance develop a compliance plan, and to provide regular progress reports. As a last resort sites listed under the 1971 Ramsar Convention and the 1972 Heritage Convention can be removed from those lists where they have deteriorated to such an extent that inclusion is no longer appropriate.[93] Under fishery management conventions compliance bodies are increasingly able to publish lists of vessels engaged in illegal, unreported and unregulated (IUU) fishing and lists of parties engaged in or facilitating such damaging fishing practices. All of these measures, provided that they are given appropriate publicity, may damage a State's international reputation and can serve to shame a State into compliance. A smaller number of NCPs permit the suspension of a party's rights and privileges under the treaty for sustained or serious cases of non-compliance. Such action is permitted under instruments such as the 1998 Aarhus Convention, the 1991 Espoo Convention, the 1999 Protocol on Water and Health, the 1987 Montreal Protocol and the 1997 Kyoto Protocol. Such action may result in the suspension of voting rights previously enjoyed by the State in non-compliance and may significantly hinder the access of that party to financial and other technical assistance under those instruments. Furthermore, the suspension of treaty privileges under the Montreal and Kyoto Protocols may indirectly impose trade restrictions on the non-complying State. Parties under the 1987 Montreal Protocol may be prohibited from trading in substances covered by the Protocol, for example, and parties failing to comply with their obligations under the 1997 Kyoto Protocol may be forbidden to participate in any international emissions trading scheme. Trade-related measures are also permitted under the 1973 CITES in circumstances where the Standing Committee recommends the suspension of commercial trade in one or more CITES species with parties in non-compliance with their obligations under the Treaty.[94] In a related development an increasing number of non-compliance procedures developed under the auspices of fishery management conventions permit the issue of recommendations calling upon State parties to deny fishing vessels suspected of IUU fishing access to their ports or transhipment facilities.[95] Finally, at least two instruments

[93] It should be noted that sites may only be removed from the Ramsar list with permission from the host state. The removal of sites from both the Ramsar and the Heritage lists may have negative financial implications for the host state if they are no longer able to access funds available under both Conventions or as a result of lost tourist revenue resulting from negative publicity.

[94] Currently only Nigeria is subject to wildlife-related trade sanctions authorised by the 1973 CITES. Non-discriminatory trade measures are also permitted under the 2000 Convention on the Conservation and Management of Highly Migratory Fish Stocks in the Western and Central Pacific Ocean (WCPFC) (in force 2004) www.wcpfc.int/.

[95] See Conservation Measure 10-06 (2008).

provide for the imposition of specific penalties on States failing to comply with certain treaty obligations. For example, where the Enforcement Branch of the 1997 Kyoto Protocol Compliance Committee determines that a Party has exceeded its emissions allowance assigned under the Protocol for the first commitment period, it shall (amongst other measures) deduct from that Party's assigned allowance for the second commitment period, a number of tonnes equal to 1.3 times the amount in tonnes of excess emissions. Similarly, parties exceeding their annual catch limit for tuna under the 1966 ICCAT may be liable to have their catch limit reduced in the subsequent year.

ii. Binding and Final Measures

The majority of non-compliance procedures do not permit the designated compliance body to issue binding recommendations. In the majority of cases measures recommended by the compliance body must be ratified by the meeting or conference of the parties.[96] Notable exceptions to this trend include the 1992 OSPAR Convention, 1979 Bern Convention and the 1973 CITES. However, in the case of both the OSPAR and Bern Conventions the compliance body relies on a pre-existing institution and is comprised of all State representatives. Moreover, decisions made by the 1973 CITES Standing Committee related to compliance are deemed to have been made under the delegated authority of the conference of the Parties. The 1998 Aarhus Convention Compliance Committee may issue final measures pending consideration of the non-compliance issue by the conference of the parties, and the compliance bodies established by the 2000 Biosafety Protocol, 1995 Barcelona Convention and 1999 Protocol on Water and Health may issue final recommendations in respect of selected measures only.[97] The most complete jurisdiction to issue final measures has been granted to the Compliance Committee established by the parties to the 1997 Kyoto Protocol. However, parties benefit from a limited right of appeal—on the basis that due process has been denied—to the Meeting of the Parties in connection with compliance decisions issued by the Enforcement Branch.

The more fundamental question relates to the issue as to whether final compliance measures, (irrespective of whether they are issued by the compliance body or by the conference of the parties), are binding, either as a matter of treaty law or as a matter of law relating to the international

[96] Measures issued by the executive treaty body (such as the COP or MOP) are not necessarily binding. See the text accompanying nn 97–112 below.

[97] These measures are generally limited to the provision of advice and assistance as well as requests for further information and the development of action plans.

organisation itself.[98] A very small number of non-compliance procedures (but forming a majority within the fisheries management sector) explicitly indicate that compliance measures are binding upon State parties.

A greater number of instruments indicate clearly that measures are not formally binding and constitute recommendations only. The 1989 Basel Convention, 1973 CITES, the 1971 Ramsar Convention and the 1979 Bern Convention are included within this category. The non-binding status of measures risks, in situations where they are not implemented, ultimately undermining the non-compliance procedure as a whole. For example, a case-file opened under the Bern Convention concerning the protection of turtles in Greece was eventually closed in 1999 after 14 years without resolution.[99] This precedent might suggest that if States refusing to comply with their treaty obligations resist compliance recommendations for long enough, the Standing Committee (in the case of the Bern Convention) will ultimately admit defeat and cease issuing measures or recommendations with respect to that State.

Most instruments do not explicitly designate non-compliance measures as binding or non-binding and thus their status is uncertain. For example, the non-compliance procedure adopted by the Parties to the 1987 Montreal Protocol is based on Article 8 of the Protocol. Whilst Article 8 of the Protocol is obviously binding, decisions of the Meeting of the Parties (such as those which established the procedure and determine the compliance or otherwise of States parties) are not normally legally binding.[100] Nevertheless, the Montreal Protocol NCP is generally regarded as one of the most successful non-compliance procedures of any international environmental agreement. In practice, the extent of engagement between the parties to the Protocol and the Implementation Committee means that the issue as to whether Committee recommendations are formally binding is largely irrelevant.[101] This pragmatic conclusion is also likely to apply to the 1997 Kyoto Protocol. Although the Kyoto NCP itself appears to indicate that decisions of the Compliance Committee are binding (subject to a limited right of appeal to the Conference of the Parties) Article 18 of the Protocol stipulates that '[a]ny procedures and mechanisms under this Article entailing binding consequences shall be adopted by means of an amendment to this Protocol.' The Protocol has yet to be amended to formally include the non-compliance procedure, despite

[98] M Fitzmaurice and C Redgwell, above n 6 at 48–49.
[99] Description of the 'Specific Sites' Case-File System under the Bern Convention, T-PVS (2000) 35 at page 7.
[100] M Ehrmann, above n 2 at 393.
[101] Ibid 394.

the fact that the procedure is now operational.[102] Provided that States continue to engage with the non-compliance procedure this is not likely to be an issue. However, as noted above the ability of the Kyoto Compliance Committee to sanction States in non-compliance extends substantially beyond the mandate granted to the Montreal Implementation Committee. Moreover, it appears inevitable that a large number of States will be in non-compliance with their emissions commitments by the end of the first commitment period (2012).[103] It is thus possible that States failing to meet their emission reductions commitments may be more inclined to argue that Compliance Committee measures are not formally binding in the absence of an appropriate amendment to the Kyoto Protocol.[104]

E. Public Participation in Non-compliance Proceedings

Public participation in the form of permitting individuals or NGOs to attend compliance related-meetings as observers or even to initiate non-compliance proceedings is a growing feature of many NCPs. Opening up non-compliance proceedings to the public partially responds to the criticism that too many of the current NCPs rely upon States to take action against one another or to provide information to the compliance body with regard to non-compliance.[105] More generally, improving the transparency of non-compliance proceedings also has the potential to indirectly improve compliance with treaty obligations, as States seek to protect their reputation as good international citizens and avoid being publicly sanctioned for non-compliance. Examples of prominent (and effective) NGO participation within international regimes include Greenpeace and the 1972 London (Dumping) Convention,[106] TRAFFIC and the WWF and the 1973 CITES and the IUCN and the 1972 World Heritage

[102] Saudi Arabia presented a proposal for amendment in 2005 but this was not adopted. See doc UNFCCC/KP/CMP/2005/2 (26 May 2005).

[103] See the *National Greenhouse Gas Inventory Data for the Period 1990–2006* FCCC/SBI/2008/12, http://unfccc.int/resource/docs/2008/sbi/eng/12.pdf.

[104] Nevertheless, F Yamin and J Depledge have pertinently observed in connection with the political as opposed to legal character of COP/MOP decisions that 'the extent to which something is considered "legally binding" in international law is ultimately an expression of political will. Thus it will be up to Parties whether or not they choose to regard a COP/MOP decision as having only political consequences or legally binding consequences.' See F Yamin and J Depledge, *The International Climate Change Regime: A Guide to Rules, Institutions and Procedures* (Cambridge, Cambridge University Press, 2004) 397.

[105] J Varuhas, 'One Person Can Make a Difference: An Individual Petition System for International Environmental Law' (2005) 3 *New Zealand Journal of Public and International Law* 329, 333.

[106] 1972 Convention on the Prevention of marine Pollution by Dumping of Wastes and other matter (in force 1975) (1972) 11 ILM 1294.

Convention.[107] In many situations NGOs are better informed and more appropriately placed to respond to non-compliance than affected States. For example, immediately after the Ukraine announced a proposal to construct the Danube–Black Sea Shipping Canal in the vulnerable Bystroe estuary of the Danube Delta in 2004, a concerned NGO (Ecopravo-Lviv or EPL) submitted communications to the 1998 Aarhus Convention Compliance Committee and the 1991 Espoo Convention Implementation Committee alleging that the Ukraine was in non-compliance with a number of its international obligations under those treaties. The Espoo Implementation Committee concluded that it did not have the mandate to consider communications received from NGOs, (it has since amended its rules of procedures to permit the receipt of communications from organisations such as the EPL), and had to wait a further year before it was able to consider the Bystroe estuary development following a compliant made by Romania. By this time the shipping canal was already under construction.[108]

Most (if not all) non-compliance procedures require the publication of reports and measures related to non-compliance proceedings, except where they contain information relating to matters deemed confidential. The majority of NCPs now also permit suitably qualified NGOs to attend non-compliance meetings as observers[109] although a number of procedures allow meetings to be closed at the request of the compliance body or the State party under investigation. NGOs are not generally given voting rights but a small number of non-compliance procedures permit NGOs to speak at meetings.[110] For example, individuals or NGOs initiating non-compliance proceedings under the auspices of the 1999 Protocol on Water and Health are permitted to participate in discussions relating to that non-compliance issue and to comment on draft recommendations. Proposals put forward by observers in the Standing Committee established under the auspices of the 1979 Bern Convention can be put

[107] E Brown Weiss, above n 35 at 1579–80. See also A Chayes and A Chayes, above n 1, ch 6; O Schram Stokke, J Hovi and G Ulfstein, above n 40, ch 8.

[108] See especially T Sobol, 'An NGO's Fight to Save Ukraine's Danube Delta: The Case for Granting Non-governmental Organisations Formal Powers of Enforcement' (2006) 17 *Colorado Journal of International Environmental Law and Policy* 123.

[109] Notable exceptions include the 1987 Montreal Protocol, the 1979 LRTAP and the 1992 OSPAR Convention. Although NGOs have requested observer status in the past with respect to the 1987 Montreal Protocol this has been denied on the basis that sensitive and confidential information was due to be discussed (D Victor, above n 78 at 142. Victor notes that although in principle NGO issues can be raised via a sympathetic party or the secretariat, this has yet to happen in practice.)

[110] Eg the 2003 Convention for the Strengthening of the Inter-American Tropical Tuna Commission Established by the 1949 Convention between the United States of America and the Republic of Costa Rica (IATTC) (in force 2008), www.iattc.org/PDFFiles2/Antigua_Convention_Jun_2003.pdf.

to a vote if they are sponsored by a State delegation.[111] A small number of non-compliance procedures permit NGOs and individuals to submit information or briefs to the compliance body. For example, competent NGOs may submit relevant factual information to either branch of the Compliance Committee established by the parties to the 1997 Kyoto Protocol. The World Heritage Committee may engage in consultation with the public over the status of individual World Heritage sites and is entitled to receive information about those sites from sources other than the host State. The Compliance Group recently established by the parties to the 1996 London Protocol may receive information submitted by interested NGOs about allegations of non-compliance, but is under no obligation to consider that information. As discussed above[112] very few NCPs permit NGOs and individuals to actually initiate proceedings against States alleged to be in non-compliance and/or to allow NGOs to nominate members for election to the compliance body itself.[113] Only the 1999 Dolphin Conservation Agreement includes NGO and industry representation actually on the International Review Panel, although the International Whaling Commission is considering permitting similar representation on the proposed Compliance Review Committee currently under development.[114] The 1998 Aarhus Convention appears to permit the greatest level of public participation in non-compliance proceedings overall, and this is unsurprising given the focus of the Convention on public participation in environmental decision-making and access to environmental justice. NGOs and members of the public are able to observe meetings, initiate proceedings against States alleged to be in non-compliance and to nominate persons for election to the Compliance Committee.[115] Nevertheless, the Aarhus Convention is not the only instrument to facilitate extensive public participation in its non-compliance procedures[116] and this is undoubtedly a growing and important trend.

[111] Three NGOs (the RSPB, SEH and WWF) were heavily involved in drafting the current procedures (dating from 1993) relating to non-compliance under the 1979 Bern Convention. The original proposal submitted by these three NGOs is reproduced in the Annex to document T-PVS(93) 22 *Implementation of the Bern Convention—Opening and Closing of Files and Follow Up Recommendations* (1993).

[112] See text accompanying n 88 above.

[113] See text accompanying nn 64 and 65 above.

[114] See the 2006 Annual Report of the International Whaling Commission, Annex F, App 5, 12.

[115] See especially S Kravchenko, 'The Aarhus Convention and Innovations in Compliance with Multilateral Environmental Agreements' (2007) 18 *Colorado Journal of International Environmental Law and Policy* 1.

[116] It should be noted that the 1999 Protocol on Water and Health permits the same level of public participation within its non-compliance procedure.

F. Relationship Between Non-compliance Proceedings and Dispute Resolution and Other Non-compliance Processes

i. Non-compliance Procedures and Dispute Resolution Processes

A significant number of non-compliance procedures established under international environmental agreements specify that their operation is without prejudice to the dispute resolution provisions under that agreement or under international law more generally. This preserves the formal primacy of the dispute resolution procedure but does not provide guidance on how the procedures interact in specific cases. Most treaties which provide for additional or alternative means for assessing compliance with, or implementation of, treaty commitments also specify the relationship between those mechanisms and the non-compliance procedure. For example, the Kyoto NCP operates without prejudice to the multilateral review process,[117] and the Implementation Committee established under the 1991 Espoo Convention is unable to consider matters already the subject of an enquiry procedure under Article 3(7) of the Convention. Otherwise, treaties provide no guidance as to how non-compliance procedures interact with dispute resolution provisions or indeed other areas of international law. The relationship between non-compliance procedures and dispute resolution will be discussed in the final section of this chapter.

ii. Non-compliance Procedures as Between Treaties

As non-compliance procedures proliferate within the field of international environmental law it is inevitable that major developments or activities are likely to raise questions of non-compliance with respect to any number of treaties. Consequently, the relationship between, and interaction among, compliance bodies is becoming an increasingly important issue. The complexities arising from the multiple application of non-compliance proceedings has recently been illustrated by the Ukraine's controversial decision to construct the Danube–Black Sea Shipping Canal in the Bystroe estuary of the Danube Delta as previously referred to. Neighbouring States (in particular, Romania) and an interested NGO (Ecopravo-Lviv (EPL)) alleged that the Ukraine was in breach of a number of its obligations under several treaties: the 1998 Aarhus Convention; 1979 Bern Convention; 1979 Bonn Convention on the Conservation of Migratory

[117] Arts 13 and 16 of the 1997 Kyoto Protocol. Under Art 13 of the Protocol the MOP is provided with the mandate to assess the overall implementation of the Protocol by the Parties and to periodically examine the obligations of the Parties in light of the object of the UNFCCC, experience related to implementation and developments in scientific and technological knowledge. See further, F Yamin and J Depledge above n 104, ch 11.

Species of Wild Animals;[118] 1991 Espoo Convention; and the 1971 Ramsar Convention. Whilst the obligations alleged to have been breached under these various conventions are not identical,[119] they are undoubtedly closely related and mutually reinforcing.

Relatively few non-compliance procedures have included explicit provisions dealing with their relationship and interaction with external non-compliance procedures. The four NCPs which currently address this issue (the 1998 Aarhus Convention, 1995 Barcelona Convention, the 1999 Protocol on Water and Health and 2000 WCPFC)[120] permit their associated compliance bodies to solicit and provide information as appropriate from and to other non-compliance bodies. No non-compliance procedure has as yet developed formal procedures for coordinating on-the-ground information gathering missions and facilitating the issue of coherent and complementary non-compliance measures. Despite the absence of such guidelines, in the case of the Danube–Black Sea Canal development, representatives from the institutions noted above plus the European Commission and the International Commission for the Protection of the Danube River (ICPDR) conducted a joint fact-finding mission to the Ukraine in 2004.[121] Moreover, in 2008 the Secretariat of the 1991 Espoo Convention organised an informal consultation among interested treaty bodies dealing with the Danube–Black Sea Shipping Canal issue with a view to considering possible measures that might be taken to support the Ukraine with its international obligations.[122] The Ukraine has consented to both

[118] In force 1983 (1980) 19 ILM 15.

[119] Alleged breaches variously referred to issues connected to an apparent failure to provide for appropriate public participation in the decision to build the canal, a lack of consultation with neighbouring states and the impact of the scheme on a vulnerable ecosystem and associated migratory and wetland species.

[120] Two non-compliance procedures in the process of being developed would appear to favour including provisions permitting their compliance body to solicit information from other NCPs operating in the same area. See: Annex to Decision SC-3/20 (2005) *[Non-compliance] [Compliance] Procedures under Article 17 of the Stockholm Convention* at para 35, which outlines the proposed non-compliance procedure in connection with the 2001 Stockholm Convention on Persistent Organic Pollutants. See also Decision RC-3/4 (2008) *Draft text of the procedures and mechanism on compliance with the Rotterdam Convention*, Annex, para 28, which outlines the proposed non-compliance procedure with respect to the 1998 Rotterdam Convention on PIC. Rather surprisingly, the final terms of reference of the Compliance Group established by the Parties to the 1996 London Protocol does not permit the Group to solicit information from or provide information to other relevant compliance bodies with overlapping or closely related mandates (such as the 1992 OSPAR Commission, the 1989 Basel Convention Compliance Committee and institutions established under other regional seas conventions).

[121] Joint Mission of the Expert Team of the European Commission and International Conventions to the 'Bystroe project' in the Ukrainian part of the Danube Delta (6–8 October 2004) Report, http://ec.europa.eu/environment/enlarg/bystroe_docs/bystroe_joint_mission_report.pdf.

[122] Letter from the Executive Secretary of the UNECE to the Ministry of Environmental Protection of Ukraine (Ref ECE/EHLM/105/2008/1) and Background Note dated 8 May 2008 on file with the author.

missions and is actively engaged with these various treaty organisations in connection with the Bystroe Canal development. This *ad hoc* informal arrangement between the institutions of up to seven different treaties, which focuses on not only information sharing but also the development of mutually reinforcing non-compliance measures, demonstrates the possible extent and depth of potential cooperation between non-compliance institutions. Nevertheless, without the ultimate development of procedures designed to govern cooperation and interaction, the extent to which these bodies can coordinate their activities will remain uncertain.

IV. IMPLICATIONS OF NON-COMPLIANCE PROCEDURES FOR DISPUTE RESOLUTION MECHANISMS

Whilst the creation of non-compliance procedures within international environmental agreements can generally be considered a positive development from the perspective of environmental protection, there remain a number of challenging unanswered questions as to how these procedures interact with general principles of international law relating to dispute resolution, countermeasures and termination of treaty relations.[123] As discussed above, non-compliance procedures function alongside rather than replace traditional dispute resolution mechanisms. This raises the immediate question as to whether a natural hierarchy exists between the two parallel systems or whether they are mutually exclusive.[124] To the extent that non-compliance procedures apply only to selected obligations under the treaty, a natural demarcation between the jurisdictional extent of these procedures is clearly visible. In practice however, this may be a difficult distinction to draw, particularly where the NCP does not specify in clear terms its scope of application.

A significant proportion of treaties are silent as to the relationship (or hierarchy) between their NCPs and other dispute resolution mechanisms where both processes are of potential application to the treaty provisions in dispute. In this situation it might be argued that the very existence of the NCP automatically excludes the invocation of external dispute resolution mechanisms or even unilateral action against a State alleged to be in non-compliance with its treaty obligations. Some support for this proposition might be found in Article 60(4) of the 1969 Vienna Convention on the Law of Treaties,[125] which stipulates that the provisions permitting action in response to a material breach of the

[123] See especially M Fitzmaurice and C Redgwell, above n 6; G Handl, above n 6; M Koskenniemi above n 9.

[124] M Fitzmaurice and C Redgwell, above n 6 at 44.

[125] In force 1980 (1969) 8 ILM 689.

treaty 'are without prejudice to any provision in the treaty applicable in the event of breach.' A similar (although not identical) provision can be found in Article 55 of the 2001 Draft Articles on State Responsibility and is of application to the adoption of countermeasures. However, it is more likely that where the treaty is silent as to the relationship between the NCP and dispute resolution a State can choose to initiate either non-compliance proceedings or dispute resolution proceedings or (potentially) both. As noted above, States seeking to invoke international rules operating externally to the NCP established under the treaty would normally have to prove that they have been, or are, especially affected by the consequences of non-compliance. The dispute between Ireland and the UK over the opening of the MOX nuclear reprocessing plant at Sellafield and access to information under Article 9 of the 1992 OSPAR Convention provides a rare example of an environmental non-compliance issue being subjected to arbitration.[126] Although OSPAR provides for a basic NCP (under Article 23 of the Convention), proceedings were not initiated against the UK and no State suggested that the matter should have been considered by the Commission before going to arbitration.[127]

The majority of non-compliance procedures indicate that their operation is without prejudice to the formal dispute resolution provisions of the treaty. This would appear to establish a hierarchy between the parallel processes with formal dispute resolution at its apex. Nevertheless, a basic clause confirming the non-prejudicial impact of NCPs on dispute resolution does little to clarify the relationship between these two processes at an operational level. For example, a without prejudice clause provides no indication as to whether it is permissible to subject a State in non-compliance with its treaty obligations to multiple proceedings. Martti Koskenniemi suggests that (in the case of the 1987 Montreal Protocol) a party initiating formal dispute resolution proceedings before the ICJ under Article 11(3) of the Protocol is estopped (on at least a temporary basis) from simultaneously initiating non-compliance proceedings within the Implementation Committee.[128] But would this principle apply where the issue of non-compliance is submitted to a non-binding dispute resolution process such as mediation? Moreover, the multilateral focus of non-compliance procedures means that normally *any* State can initiate proceedings and, in most cases, proceedings may be also begun

[126] Dispute Concerning Access to Information under Article 9 of the OSPAR Convention, *Ireland v UK*, Final Award (2 July 2003) (2003) 42 ILM 1118.

[127] It should be noted that it would appear that proceedings can only be initiated by the OSPAR Commission although reports relating to compliance issues can be submitted by the Parties to the Commission (see Art 23).

[128] M Koskenniemi, above n 9 at 159.

by a treaty institution or even an NGO. It is thus quite foreseeable that a State especially affected by non-compliance under a treaty may decide to respond by initiating dispute resolution proceedings against the State alleged to be in non-compliance, whilst, simultaneously, the NCP under that treaty may be initiated by another State or a treaty institution. In principle (and indeed in practice) the issue of multiple proceedings is not inevitably problematic. Although remedies under both processes may differ,[129] they should normally be mutually reinforcing. However, it is not inconceivable that the non-compliance body and the dispute resolution mechanism may reach quite different conclusions as to whether a State is in compliance (or not) with its treaty obligations. This raises the issue as to whether each body should take account of the proceedings taking place within the other body. In other words, if the Compliance Committee established under a treaty determines that a State is in non-compliance with its treaty obligations, should the International Court of Justice or arbitral tribunal be required to accept those findings, and proceed from that basis when determining issues connected to State responsibility or treaty law, or, is it permitted to determine the issue of non-compliance itself without reference to the conclusions reached by the Compliance Committee? As noted above, a finding of non-compliance will not inevitably lead to the imposition of State responsibility as separate questions relating to damage, causation and even special defences will have to be addressed.

A related issue focuses on whether dispute resolution mechanisms can be invoked, or unilateral counter measures adopted, after non-compliance proceedings have been completed. For instance, if a State found to be in non-compliance with its treaty obligations refuses to comply with NCP measures adopted by the appropriate compliance body, can especially affected States take unilateral action external to the treaty against that State or, do they have to continue to work through the non-compliance procedure? An example of such a situation occurred in 1995 when Russia declared that it would be in non-compliance with its obligations to phase out ozone-depleting substances under the 1987 Montreal Protocol from the 1 January 1996 and requested a five-year grace period within which to comply. This request was refused and numerous measures were adopted designed to persuade Russia to comply with its obligations, which it eventually did, after five years! Although the Implementation Committee regularly threatened tougher sanctions against Russia it never actually imposed them.[130] In this situation there would appear to be no practical

[129] The focus on reparation and compensation under dispute resolution mechanisms is normally entirely absent from non-compliance procedures, which prioritise measures designed to promote future compliance.

[130] T Yang, above n 39 at 1144–45.

nor principled difficulty with resorting to alternative measures, especially where the non-compliance procedure has arguably been unsuccessful. But what about a situation where a party or small number of parties do not agree with the conclusion of the Compliance Committee or conference of the parties? The vast majority of NCPs do not require consensus for decision-making so such disagreement is not an unrealistic possibility. For example, in 2008 Bangladesh informed the 1987 Montreal Protocol Implementation Committee that it is likely to be in non-compliance with its obligation to phase out metered-dose inhalers by 2010. Recognising the difficulty that some States would experience in meeting this deadline the Meeting of the Parties had previously adopted Decision XVIII/16, which requested the Implementation Committee 'to give special consideration to such Parties'. The Committee interpreted this Decision as providing it with a mandate to recommend that the non-compliance procedure should not be applied to Bangladesh and that its consideration of this issue should be deferred. A number of States including New Zealand and the Netherlands objected strongly to this conclusion and expressed concern that the decision to defer would imply that the Implementation Committee had simply given up on Bangladesh and, moreover, that the decision would simply encourage other States to refuse to comply with their obligations when facing technological or economic difficulties.[131] In this particular situation the options of both New Zealand and the Netherlands would appear to be limited, given that neither State is apparently especially affected by Bangladesh's non-compliance with its treaty obligations. Nevertheless, it is not inconceivable that a State party may be especially affected by the issue of non-compliance and wish to take additional external action where it is dissatisfied with the (final) decision of the compliance body established by that treaty. The inherent risk in permitting such action is that it is likely to undermine confidence in, and operation of, the non-compliance procedure as a whole.

The potential problems associated with the interaction between non-compliance procedures and other areas of international law highlighted in this section do not represent an exhaustive list of such problems, but do indicate the potential depth and complexity of the challenges generated by NCPs. Pragmatically, the most significant impact that non-compliance procedures are likely to have on dispute resolution mechanisms is a reduction in the (already low) use of those mechanisms to resolve environmental disputes between States. It is highly likely that States in dispute over an environmental matter will choose to address

[131] See the Report of the Implementation Committee under the Non-compliance Procedure for the Montreal Protocol on he work of its forty-first meeting (UNEP/OzL.Pro/ImpCom/41/8, 24) at paras 54, 57, 65, 67, 71 and 72.

that matter through the multilateral non-compliance process established under a treaty rather than directly, on a bilateral basis, with its inevitable attendant political and diplomatic consequences. This trend has significant implications for the international legal system more generally. The multilateral non-compliance process increasingly involves at high levels of engagement entities other than States. International institutions, NGOs and even individuals are now intimately involved in processes which impact upon issues of State responsibility and treaty relations, previously belonging to the exclusive preserve of States. Moreover, to the extent that compliance bodies become involved in interpreting treaty obligations, they are also effectively contributing to the law-creation process, which similarly is traditionally regarded as exclusive to States.[132] Thus, to a greater or lesser extent, non-compliance procedures as developed under international environmental agreements are challenging not only our traditional views on international dispute resolution but also on how international law is made and who (or what) is regarded as a legitimate participant within the international legal system.

[132] Although some NCPs have formally confirmed that compliance institutions do not interpret treaty obligations and have no role in law-creation (a position which was confirmed by the fourth meeting of the parties to the 1987 Montreal Protocol in 1992 (see David Victor, above n 78 at 164)), others have clearly permitted their institutions to become involved in such tasks. For example, the Compliance Committee established by the parties to the 1998 Aarhus Convention has thus far engaged in extensive interpretation of treaty obligations, taking into account general rules of international law and is developing a sophisticated body of case law in a manner analogous to domestic judicial or administrative institutions. This is a particularly significant development in light of the composition of the Aarhus Convention Compliance Committee and the ability of NGOs to nominate its members.

Appendix I to Chapter 9

INTERNATIONAL ENVIRONMENTAL INSTRUMENTS AND DECISIONS/RESOLUTIONS RELATED TO NON-COMPLIANCE PROCEDURES

1966 International Commission for the Conservation of Atlantic Tunas (ICCAT) (in force 1969) Article IX; Recommendation 95-15 Mandate and Terms of Reference Adopted by the Commission for the ICCAT Conservation and Management Measures Compliance Committee;

1971 Convention on Wetlands of International Importance (Ramsar Convention) (in force 1975) Article 6; Recommendation 4.7: Mechanisms for improved application of the Ramsar Convention; Resolution VI.1: Working definitions of ecological character, guidelines for describing and maintaining the ecological character of listed sites, and guidelines for operation of the Montreux Record;

1972 UNESCO Convention Concerning the Protection of the World Cultural and Natural Heritage (World Heritage Convention) (in force 1975) Article 11(4);

1973 Convention on International Trade in Endangered Species of Fauna and Flora (CITES) (in force 1975), Articles XII, XIII; Conf 11.3 (Rev CoP14) Compliance and Enforcement; Conf 14.3 CITES Compliance Procedures; Conf 11.1 (Rev CoP14) Establishment of Committees; Rules of Procedure of the Standing Committee (as amended at the 53rd meeting, Geneva, June–July 2005);

1979 Convention on the Conservation of European Wildlife and Natural Habitats (Bern Convention) (in force 1982), Articles 13, 14; Decision T-PVS (93) 22 (1993) Implementation of the Bern Convention; Opening and Closing of Files and Follow-up Recommendations;

1979 Convention on Long-Range Transboundary Air Pollution (LRTAP) (in force 1982) Article 10(2); Decision 1997/2 (ECE/EB.AIR, annex V)•;

1980 Convention on the Conservation of Antarctic Marine Living Resources (CCAMLR) (in force 1982), Article XI; Standing Committee on Implementation and Compliance (SCIC) Terms of Reference and Organisation of Work agreed at the XXI Meeting of the CCAMLR Commission (2002), XXI (2002) CCAMLR Commission Report, Annex 5, Appendix VII;

1987 Protocol on Substances that Deplete the Ozone Layer (Montreal) (in force 1989) Article 8; Decision IV/5 Non-compliance procedure; Decision X/10 Review of the non-compliance procedure; Decision III/20 Composition of the Implementation Committee; Decision XIV/37 Interaction between the Executive Committee and the Implementation Committee;

1989 Convention on the Control of Transboundary Movements of Hazardous Wastes and Their Disposal (Basel Convention) (in force 1992), Article 15(5)(e); Decision VI/12 (2002) Establishment of a Mechanism for Promoting

• Articles and decisions related to the various protocols under LRTAP omitted.

Implementation and Compliance; Decision IX/2 Work Programme for the Committee for Administering the Mechanism for Promoting Implementation and Compliance of the Basel Convention for the period 2009–2011;

1991 Convention on Environmental Impact Assessment in a Transboundary Context (Espoo Convention) (in force 1997), Article 11(2); Decision III/2 Review of Compliance (and appendix); Decision IV/2 Operating Rules of the Implementation Committee;

1992 Convention for the Protection of the Marine Environment of the North East Atlantic (OSPAR) (in force 1998) Article 23; Rules of Procedure of the OSPAR Commission (Reference Number 2005–17);

1995 Convention for the Protection of the Marine Environment and the Coastal Region of the Mediterranean (Barcelona Convention) (in force 2004), Articles 18, 27; Decision IG 17/2 (2008) Procedures and Mechanisms on Compliance under the Barcelona Convention and its Protocol;

1996 Protocol to the London Dumping Convention (London (Dumping) Protocol) (in force 2006) Article 11; Compliance Group established in 2003 (Report of the 25th Meeting of the London Convention LC/25/16, Annex 2); Compliance Procedures and Mechanisms agreed in 2007 (Report of the 29th Meeting to the London Convention LC 29/17, Annex 7);

1997 Protocol to the UN Framework Convention on Climate Change (Kyoto Protocol) (in force 2005) Article 18; Decision 27/CMP.1 Procedures and mechanisms relating to compliance under the Kyoto Protocol; Decision 4/CMP.2 Rules of procedure of the Compliance Committee of the Kyoto Protocol; Decision 4/CMP.4 Amendments to the rules of procedure of the Compliance Committee of the Kyoto Protocol;

1998 Convention on Access to Information, Public Participation in Decision-making and Access to Justice in Environmental Matters (Aarhus Convention) (in force 2001), Article 15; Decision I/7 (2004) Review of Compliance;

1999 Agreement on the International Dolphin Conservation Programme (Dolphin Conservation Agreement) (in force 1999), Articles XII, XVI, Annex VII; 2002 Resolution on the Definition of a Pattern of Infractions;

1999 Protocol on Water and Health to the 1992 Convention on the Protection and Use of Transboundary Watercourses and International Lakes (Protocol on Water and Health) (in force 2005), Article 15, Decision I/2 (2007) Review of Compliance;

2000 Protocol on Biosafety to the 1992 Convention on Biological Diversity (Biosafety Protocol) (in force 2003), Article 34; Decision BS I/7 (2005) Establishment of Procedures and Mechanisms on Compliance under the Cartagena Protocol on Biosafety; Decision BS II/1 (2006) Rules of Procedure for Meetings of the Compliance Committee; Decision BS III/1 (2007) Compliance; Decision IV/1 (2007) Compliance;

2000 Convention on the Conservation and Management of Highly Migratory Fish Stocks in the Western and Central Pacific Ocean (WCPFC) (in force 2004), Articles 11, 14, 25; Western and Central Pacific Fisheries Commission Rules of Procedure (2004);

2003 Convention for the Strengthening of the Inter-American Tropical Tuna Commission Established by the 1949 Convention between the United States of America and the Republic of Costa Rica (IATTC) (in force 2008)

Articles VII(5), XVIII(6) and (10), Annex 3; 1999 Resolution on the Establishment of a Permanent Working Group on Compliance; 2000 Permanent Working Group on Compliance—Rules of Procedure;

INSTRUMENTS WITH NON-COMPLIANCE PROCEDURES IN ADVANCED STAGES OF DEVELOPMENT

1946 International Convention on the Regulation of Whaling (ICRW) (in force 1948) Article IX, 2006 Report of the International Whaling Commission, Annex F, Appendix 5;

1998 Rotterdam Convention on the Prior Informed Consent Procedure for Certain Hazardous Chemicals and Pesticides in International Trade (Rotterdam PIC) (in force 2004), Article 17; Decision RC-4/7 (and Annex) Procedures and Mechanisms on Compliance with the Rotterdam Convention;

2001 International Treaty on Plant Genetic Resources for Food and Agriculture (Plant Genetic Resources Treaty) (in force 2004) Articles 19(3)(e), 21; Resolution 3/2006 Draft Procedures and Operational Mechanisms to Promote Compliance and to Address Issues of Non-compliance; Resolution 1/2007 Compliance;

2001 Stockholm Convention on Persistent Organic Pollutants (POPs Convention) (in force 2004) Article 17; Decision SC-3/20 (and Annex) [Non-compliance] [Compliance] Procedures under Article 17 of the Stockholm Convention;

Appendix II to Chapter 9

FEATURES OF NON-COMPLIANCE PROCEEDINGS (NCPS)

Instrument	Institutional Infrastructure	Functions	Provisions Subject to Review	Initiation of NCPs	NCP Measures	Public Participation	Relationship between NCP and Dispute Resolution; NCPs between Treaties
1966 ICCAT							
Conservation and Management Measures Compliance Committee	H; N	2; 5; 67; 8; 11	c	IV	kk; mm; qq; rr	iii	22
1971 Ramsar Convention		3; 4; 7	c	I; IV; VII	bb; ll1; nn; ss	ii; v	22
Bureau	H						
1972 WHC	21 members.						
Committee	A; C; I; M	2; 3; 4	c	I; IV	bb; ll; mm; nn; rr	v; vi	22
1973 CITES	18 members.						
Standing Committee	A; G; J; N	2; 3; 4; 6; 7; 8	a	I; II; IV; VII	bb; cc; dd; ee; gg; jj; nn; ss	ii; iii; v	22

Instrument	Institutional Infrastructure	Functions	Provisions Subject to Review	Initiation of NCPs	NCP Measures	Public Participation	Relationship between NCP and Dispute Resolution; NCPs between Treaties
1979 Bern Convention Standing Committee	H; M	3; 4; 7; 8	a	IV; VII	aa; ss	ii; iii; v	22
1979 LRTAP Implementation Committee	9 members. J	1; 2; 3; 4; 6; 7; 12	a	I; II; IV	aa; qq; tt		11
1980 CCAMLR Standing Committee on Implementation and Compliance	H; P	2; 5; 6; 7; 11	a	II; IV	gg; mm; qq; rr	iii	22
1987 Montreal Protocol Implementation Committee	10 members. A; D; J; P (including 1 dissent)	1; 2; 4; 5; 7; 8	c	I; II; IV	bb; dd; ee; hh; qq; tt		11

1989 Basel Convention Compliance Committee	15 members. A; J; K; M	1; 2; 3; 4; 6; 8	c; e; g	I; III; IV	bb; dd; ee; ff; qq; ss	iv	11
1991 Espoo Convention Implementation Committee	8 members. J; N; O	1; 2; 3; 4; 6; 7; 8	c; j	I; II; IV; VII	bb; cc; dd; ff; hh; qq; tt	ii; iii	11
1992 OSPAR Commission	H; L	1; 3; 7	a	IV	aa		22
1995 Barcelona Convention (Compliance Committee)	7 members. A; E; F; J; K; L	2; 3; 4; 6; 8	c; e; g	I; II; IV	bb; dd; ee; ff; oo; rr	iii	11; 33
1996 London Protocol (Dumping) Compliance Group	15 members. A; E; J; K; L; O	1; 2; 3; 5; 6; 7; 8; 9; 10	a	I; III; IV	bb; dd; ee; qq; tt	v	11
1997 Kyoto Protocol Compliance Committee	20 members. A; E; F; J; L	1; 2; 3; 6; 7; 8; 12	c	I; II; IV (limited)	bb; cc; dd; ee; ff; hh; kk; nn; pp; rr (?)	v	11

(continued)

Instrument	Institutional Infrastructure	Functions	Provisions Subject to Review	Initiation of NCPs	NCP Measures	Public Participation	Relationship between NCP and Dispute Resolution; NCPs between Treaties
1998 Aarhus Convention (Compliance Committee)	9 members. B; E; J; K; O	1; 2; 3; 4; 5; 6; 7; 8; 9; 11	b	I; II; IV; VI	bb; dd; ee; ff; hh; mm; oo; tt	i; iii; vii	11; 33
1999 Dolphin Conservation Agreement International Review Panel	H; I	2, 8	c	IV	aa	iv; vi	22
1999 Protocol on Water and Health Compliance Committee	9 members. B; E; J; K; M	1; 2; 3; 4; 6; 7; 8; 9	a	I; II; IV; VI	bb; cc; dd; ee; ff; gg; hh; mm; nn; rr	i; ii; vii; viii	11; 33
2000 Biosafety Protocol Compliance Committee	15 members. A; E; J; K; M; O	1; 2; 3; 6; 7; 8; 9	d	I; II; V	bb; dd; ee; ff; oo; tt	iii	11

2000 WCPFC Commission	H; L; O	1; 2; 5; 6; 7; 8	a	IV	ff; gg; kk; qq; tt	iii	33
2003 IATTC Permanent WG on Compliance	H	2, 6, 7, 8	c	II	aa	iii	22
1946 ICRW *(in negotiation)* (as of April 2009)	*H; I?*	*1; 2; 6; 7; 8; 12*	*a*	*IV*	*? ee; gg; hh; jj; kk*	*? iii*	
1998 Rotterdam PIC (in negotiation) (as of April 2009)	*15 members.* A; E	*2; 3; 6; 7; 9*		*I; III; IV*	*bb; cc; ee; gg; qq; rr*	*iii (general meetings);* iv (individual cases)	*11; 33*
2001 Plant Genetic Resources Treaty	*14/10/7? members.* A; E?	*1; 2; 3; 6; 7; 8; 9; 12*		I; II?; IV?	*bb; dd; ee; gg*	*v*	*11*
2001 POPs Convention (in negotiation) (as of April 2009)	*10–20 members* E; B; F; J; K; O; (L or M)	*2; 4; 5; 6; 7; 8; 9*	*b*	*I; III; IV*	*bb; dd; ee; gg; hh; qq; ss*	*iii*	*11; 33*

Key to the Table

Instruments in *italics* are in the process of developing NCPs, which are currently under negotiation.

Institutional Infrastructure

A = required geographical representation;
B = geographical representation to be considered when electing/selecting members;
C = cultural representation to be considered when electing/selecting members;
D = members include other treaty institutions such as representative from the financial mechanism;
E = members must be independent experts in relevant fields such as law, science and economics;
F = members must represent developed/developing States/must be drawn from other groups such as small island States;
G = members include depository government/previous and next host governments.
H = institution is comprised of all contracting parties;
I = institution includes NGO/industry members;
J = State under investigation may be represented at meetings but may not participate in determination of findings or adoption of recommendations;
K = State under investigation may comment in writing on recommendations;
L = decision-making by consensus or 3/4 majority;
M = decision-making by consensus or 2/3 majority;
N = decision-making by consensus or bare majority;
O = where institution is divided all views must be reflected in final report;
P = consensus only.

Functions

1 = receive/consider regular/special reports from parties;
2 = make recommendations to the COP/MOP/treaty bodies;
3 = make recommendations/provide advice to parties;
4 = information gathering within the territory of the State under investigation with the permission of that State;
5 = exchanging information with other treaty bodies;
6 = prepare general reports on compliance issues;
7 = monitoring implementation of compliance measures;
8 = make a formal determination of non-compliance in connection with specified treaty provisions;
9 = seek expert information;
10 = provide advice to non-parties considering membership;
11 = communicate with appropriate bodies established under other treaties;
12 = other technical functions;

Provisions Subject to Review

a = not specified;
b = not specified but guidance provides assistance;
c = specified in detail;

d = specified in outline;
e = primary obligations such as emission reductions or the protection of species/areas;
f = limited mandate (such as reviewing inclusion of a site on the Heritage/Ramsar list);
g = reporting obligations;
h = compliance decisions;
j = situations involving contradictory treaty obligations.

Initiation of NCPs
I = self (State in/potentially in non-compliance)
II = other treaty party (no restriction)
III = other treaty party (non-compliance must specifically affect complaining State);
IV = treaty institution such as secretariat/MOP/COP/compliance body itself;
V = non-party States;
VI = public (direct) (individuals/NGOs etc.)
VII = public (indirect through submission of information to secretariat/compliance body) (individuals/NGOs etc);

NCP Measures
aa = not specified;
bb = recommendations re: assistance/advice (finance/technical/training);
cc = recommendations to other parties to provide assistance (finance/technical/training);
dd = request party in non-compliance submit a report and timetable on measures taken/to be taken;
ee = formal cautions;
ff = declarations of non-compliance;
gg = formal public notification (including lists of States/vessels in non-compliance);
hh = suspension of treaty privileges;
jj = trade measures;
kk = reductions in emissions/fishing quotas for next year/commitment period;
ll = remove sites from treaty based lists (ll1 with permission of the party in non-compliance only);
mm = other measures;
nn = compliance body can issue final recommendations;
oo = compliance body can issue final recommendations in limited circumstances (such as pending a COP/MOP or in relation to selected matters);
pp = there is a right of appeal from the decision of the compliance body;
qq = compliance body cannot issue final recommendations
rr = final recommendations from the COP/MOP are binding;
ss = final recommendations from the COP/MOP are not binding;
tt = it is not stipulated whether final recommendations from the COP/MOP are binding.

Public Participation
i = direct initiation of proceedings (see above);
ii = indirect initiation of proceedings (see above);
iii = observers (generally permitted as of right);
iv = observers (may be permitted by special decision);
v = submission of expert evidence/reports/information;
vi = NGO/industry representation on compliance body;
vii = NGO may make proposals in connection with membership of compliance body;
viii = NGO/individual may comment on draft recommendations where NGO/individual initiated proceeding.

Relationship between NCPs and Dispute Resolution; NCPs between Treaties
11 = NCP is expressly without prejudice to the treaty's dispute resolution proceedings;
22 = treaty is silent on relationship between NCP and dispute resolution proceedings;
33 = compliance body may seek information from/provide information to compliance bodies under other treaties relating to specified subject matter.
? = unclear as to whether the feature identified is provided for in the instrument or in the case of instruments under negotiation (in italics) whether this feature will ultimately be included in the compliance mechanism.

10

The Antarctic Treaty after 50 Years

JAMES CRAWFORD*

I. INTRODUCTION

EVERYONE HAS THEIR favourite cynical saying about treaties. 'A treaty is a disagreement reduced to writing'.[1] 'It's called a treaty but it's only a truce'.[2] 'Treaties, you see, are like girls and roses: they last while they last'.[3] These (and no doubt all other witty remarks about treaties) could be applied to the Antarctic Treaty, concluded 50 years ago, on 1 December 1959.[4] The Antarctic Treaty is the reduction to writing of a disagreement about status; a truce called on claims. But it has lasted and produced a family of treaties, the Antarctic Treaty System (ATS), the world's only continental system of government not based on sovereignty but on the non-recognition of sovereignty. Moreover, what this chapter will also reveal is that despite the absence of 'formal' dispute settlement procedures within the Treaty regime, it is the Treaty regime itself that provides the principal device for the resolution of disputes.

The Treaty was signed and eventually ratified by the 12 States which participated in the Washington Conference: Argentina, Australia, Belgium, Chile, France, Japan, New Zealand, Norway, South Africa, the Soviet Union, the United Kingdom and the United States. Poland became the first State to accede to the Treaty, so that on its entry into force on 23 June 1961 there were 13 parties. The Treaty is a rather simple document: its

* This chapter is based on a conference paper given at Cumberland Lodge, UK, on 10–12 June 2009 commemorating the 50th anniversary of the Antarctic Treaty. Opinions expressed are those of the author alone. Thanks to Federica Paddeu, Research Associate, Lauterpacht Centre for International Law, for help in preparation.

[1] P Allott, 'The Concept of International Law' in M Byers (ed), *The Role of Law in International Politics* (Oxford, Oxford University Press, 2000) 81.

[2] My own periphrasis of Marshal Foch's statement at the conclusion of the Treaty of Versailles: 'This is not a peace treaty, it is an armistice for twenty years', as quoted by P Reynaud, *Mémoires—Envers et contre Tous* (Paris, Flammarion, 1963) vol II.

[3] Charles de Gaulle, Speech at the Elysée Palace, 2 July 1963, quoted in A Passeron, *De Gaulle Parle 1962-6* (Paris, Fayard, 1966).

[4] 402 UNTS 71.

flexibility has allowed for additional measures to be implemented, leading to the growth of a Treaty System much more extensive than the 14 Articles of the Treaty itself. But it remains useful to review those Articles.[5]

The Preamble asserts that Antarctica is to 'continue forever to be used for peaceful purposes and not become the scene or object of international discord', and this is reinforced in the main body of the Treaty. Article I provides that Antarctica is to be used for peaceful purposes only. No military bases are to be established or military manoeuvres conducted. Article V furthers the effort to demilitarise the continent by prohibiting nuclear explosions and the disposal of nuclear waste. These two provisions have been effective: not even the 1982 Falklands War between Argentina and the United Kingdom resulted in any breach.

Science was the other key factor behind the Treaty. Article II aims to promote the continuation of the 'freedom of scientific investigation' which occurred during the International Geophysical Year (IGY). Article III provides for the exchange of information about scientific programs and personnel and for the results of scientific research to be made freely available. By and large these provisions have also been effective, with scientific research continuing in Antarctica unhindered by excessive Treaty restrictions or by the assertion of jurisdiction by claimant States.[6]

Article IV is the key to the Treaty, without which it could not have been concluded.[7] It seeks to take into account the positions of each of the parties which had an interest in Antarctica at the time of the Treaty's negotiation. It provides that:

1. Nothing contained in the present Treaty shall be interpreted as:
   (a) a renunciation by any Contracting Party of previously asserted rights of or claims to territorial sovereignty in Antarctica;
   (b) a renunciation or diminution by any Contracting Party of any basis of claim to territorial sovereignty in Antarctica which it may have whether as a result of its activities or those of its nationals in Antarctica, or otherwise;
   (c) prejudicing the position of any Contracting Party as regards its recognition or non-recognition of any other State's rights of or claim or basis of claim to territorial sovereignty in Antarctica.
2. No acts or activities taking place while the present Treaty is in force shall constitute a basis for asserting, supporting or denying a claim to

[5] This section draws on J Crawford and DR Rothwell, 'Legal Issues Confronting Australia's Antarctica' (1992) 13 *Australian Yearbook of International Law* 53, 81.

[6] See EF Roots, 'The Role of Science in the Antarctic Treaty' in *Antarctic Treaty System: An Assessment* (Washington DC, National Academy Press, 1986).

[7] R Trolle-Anderson, 'The Antarctic Scene: Legal and Political Facts' in GD Triggs (ed), *The Antarctic Treaty Regime: Law, Environment and Resources* (Cambridge, Cambridge University Press, 1987) 59.

> territorial sovereignty in Antarctica or create any rights of sovereignty in Antarctica. No new claim, or enlargement of an existing claim, to territorial sovereignty in Antarctica shall be asserted while the present Treaty is in force.

Article IV has three basic provisions. By entering into the Treaty no claimant State can be considered to have prejudiced its position, while other potential claimant States, such as the United States and Russia, also do not prejudice their position. No activities which take place while the Treaty is in force are to constitute a basis for 'asserting, supporting, or denying' a claim to territorial sovereignty. And no new claim and no enlargement of an existing claim is to be asserted while the Treaty is in force.

The area of application of the Treaty is defined in Article VI, which provides that the Treaty extends south from 60°S latitude to the South Pole. It specifically includes ice shelves. But Article VI states that

> nothing in the present Treaty shall prejudice or in any way affect the rights, or the exercise of the rights, of any State under international law with regard to the high seas within that area.

There has been some debate as to the effect of this exclusion. Initially it was thought that the Treaty did not apply to the high seas within the zone of application, but subsequent practice within the Antarctic Treaty system has demonstrated that this is not so. The better view is that the Treaty does not affect existing rights of high seas navigation in the Southern Ocean but that subject to this proviso, it does apply there.

As with other international legal regimes, implementation of the Antarctic Treaty represented a problem, especially as there was initially no attempt to establish a Secretariat.[8] The approach adopted was a system of self-policing in which under Article VII the parties could designate observers to carry out inspections. Initially, the purpose of the inspections was to ensure that the provisions of the Treaty were being adhered to, but as the Antarctic Treaty System developed it grew to encompass the various recommendations agreed to at Antarctic Treaty Consultative Meetings (ATCM). All areas of Antarctica are open to inspection, with the consequence that all scientific research, especially that conducted at scientific stations, is subject to periodic scrutiny by designated observers. In order to resolve any potential jurisdictional problem regarding observers, Article VIII makes provision for exclusive jurisdiction by the party of which they are nationals.

[8] An Antarctic Treaty Secretariat was eventually created in 2004, pursuant to a decision taken in ATCM 2003: it is based in Buenos Aires. See: www.ats.aq/index_e.htm.

If the core of the Antarctic Treaty is Article IV, it is Article IX which has provided the foundation for the development of the Antarctic Treaty System. Article IX establishes the mechanism under which meetings are held on a regular basis and recommendations made by the participants to their governments on measures including, under Article IX(1):

a. [the] use of Antarctica for peaceful purposes only;
b. facilitation of scientific research in Antarctica;
c. facilitation of international scientific cooperation in Antarctica;
d. facilitation of the exercise of the rights of inspection provided for in Article VII of the Treaty;
e. questions relating to the exercise of jurisdiction in Antarctica;
f. preservation and conservation of living resources in Antarctica.

None of the numerous recommendations adopted has covered the subject of Article IX(1)(e), 'questions relating to the exercise of jurisdiction in Antarctica'.

The important provisions dealing with amendment of the Treaty are found in Article XII. This creates two procedures. One applies if there is to be an amendment during the course of the Treaty's operation; the other provides for a Review Conference. Both provisions reinforce the important position of the Consultative Parties within the Treaty, and the need for consensus on any amendment or modification to the Treaty. A regular modification or amendment of the Treaty only enters into force after it has been ratified by all Consultative Parties. This was the procedure adopted with respect to the 1991 Madrid Protocol.[9]

Article XII(2)(a) provides that after 30 years a conference may be called to review the operation of the Treaty. It does not provide for the expiry, as distinct from review, of the Treaty at the end of the 30 year period. If amendments agreed to at a Review Conference do not subsequently enter into force, then a procedure exists allowing any party to the Treaty to withdraw.[10] But a Review Conference is not automatic and in fact has never been convened.

The position of the Claimant States has considerably changed: from an initial numerical dominance within the Antarctic Treaty, they now constitute seven out of 28 Antarctic Treaty Consultative Parties, and seven out of 47 Antarctic Treaty Parties. According to some authors, these changes disturb the Claimant States' negotiating position in discussions

[9] Protocol on Environmental Protection to the Antarctic Treaty, Madrid, 4 October 1991, in force 15 January 1998, (1991) 30 ILM 1455.

[10] For a discussion of these provisions see SKN Blay, BM Pietrowicz and RW Tsamenyi, 'Antarctica after 1991: The Legal and Policy Options' (1989) *Antarctic and Southern Oceans Law and Policy Occasional Paper* 2, 1–5.

'affecting regime development and resource management'.[11] Nonetheless it remains the case that Claimants States have retained a special status in the Antarctic Treaty system.

Evidently the Antarctic Treaty System faces a variety of threats: climate change and its consequences, the increased environmental and safety burden of tourism, uncertainties about sustainability of stocks from the very large—whales—to the very small—krill. As to the 'health' of the Treaty this seems more a function of the still limited value of actual and potential resources compared with the costs of winning them, and of the much greater significance, still, of the scientific effort as compared with alternative uses. If the Treaty remains a success after 50 years, one major reason for its stability is the continued relative isolation of Antarctica and the relative absence of economically exploitable resources.

II. SOVEREIGNTY CLAIMS AND ARTICLE IV OF THE TREATY

From a legal point of view, the most important provision of the Treaty is Article IV(2), which applies against the background of a denial that the Treaty involves 'a renunciation by any Contracting Party of previously asserted rights of or claims to territorial sovereignty in Antarctica' (Article IV(1)(a)). There are two quite different aspects to Article IV(2). The first sentence is concerned with the legal effects, on the international plane, of 'acts or activities taking place while the present Treaty is in force'. It should be stressed that this sentence does not prohibit any particular conduct, including the making and enforcement of laws. It simply qualifies or removes the international legal consequences of such conduct, to the extent that it would otherwise reinforce, consolidate or extend a claimant's sovereignty. By contrast the second sentence does require abstention, the abstention from making a 'new claim', or from 'enlarging' an existing claim. What are the implications of this?

So far as the ordinary exercise of legislative powers goes, they are not extensive. When a State legislates for territory over which it asserts sovereignty, it does not make a 'new claim' to that sovereignty: it just exercises it. No doubt such legislation, if it is enforced, may further consolidate that sovereignty, if it is in dispute. But issues of consolidation are dealt with in the first sentence of Article IV(2), not the second. The enactment of laws by Claimant States is not prohibited by the Treaty.

Is the position any different when it comes to their enforcement? It is difficult to see why it should be. The enforcement of an existing law is no

[11] PJ Beck and CH Schofield, *Who Owns Antarctica? Governing and Managing the Last Continent* (Durham, International Boundaries and Research Unit, 1994) 13.

more a new claim to sovereignty than its enactment. The only hypothesis on which the exercise of a jurisdiction under a law would involve a 'new claim' would be that the original right was a mere right to make laws which were not to be enforced. That would not be a claim to territorial sovereignty.

But legislation can also be the vehicle for the extension of a sovereignty claim, for example in the context of off-shore resources. Would legislation defining and regulating the continental shelf off the Antarctica or enacting a fisheries zone or an exclusive economic zone, involve an 'enlargement of an existing claim' contrary to Article IV(2)? One possibility is that Article IV is addressing only territorial claims to the Antarctic continent itself, and not maritime claims at all. But in other contexts a reference to the territory of a State includes reference to at least some of its off-shore zones, especially where what is in dispute is the extent of jurisdiction.

In analysing the sovereignty claims, a distinction must be made between claims relating to maritime areas off the Antarctic continent, where the question of sovereignty has not been agreed and therefore the existence of coastal States not determined, and maritime areas appurtenant to the sub-Antarctic islands, over which sovereignty is recognised under international law, even if in certain cases these islands are the subject of a sovereignty dispute. It may also be necessary to distinguish between the maritime areas that inhere in the coastal State (eg, the continental shelf) and those that need to be expressly proclaimed (eg, the Exclusive Economic Zone (EEZ)).

A. The Continental Shelf

With the continental shelf, the position is complicated by two factors. First, the continental shelf doctrine was well established before the Antarctic Treaty came into force, and although there have been significant changes in that doctrine as a result of the negotiation of the 1982 UN Convention on the Law of the Sea,[12] the underlying concept of the continental shelf has not changed.[13] If the continental shelf doctrine antedated the Antarctic Treaty, claimant States would not be making a new claim, or enlarging an existing claim, in asserting rights to a continental shelf off their Antarctic claimed sectors. On that basis Article IV(2) would simply not apply.

[12] 1833 UNTS 396.

[13] See the Geneva Convention on the Continental Shelf, 29 April 1958: 499 UNTS 311 (entry into force, 10 June 1964, after the Antarctic Treaty).

Secondly, it is established that the continental shelf inheres in a coastal State by virtue of its sovereignty over the land territory. It does not need to be claimed, or proclaimed. Thus Article 2(3) of the 1958 Geneva Convention on the Continental Shelf provides that:

> The rights of the coastal State over the continental shelf do not depend on occupation, effective or notional, or on any express proclamation.[14]

To take one example, Australia proclaimed a continental self around its coastline, including that of the Australian Antarctic Territory (AAT), in 1953.[15] But having regard to the terms of Article 2(3), it could be argued that even if the continental shelf doctrine was a post-Antarctic Treaty innovation, Australia had not made a new claim or enlarged an existing one. Even so, if Australia then legislated to give effect to its 'sovereign rights' over the continental shelf of the AAT, the issue would be whether it had 'asserted' such a claim. If so, it might be the case that under Article IV Australia would have the rights, but could not exercise them.

B. The Outer Continental Shelf

This issue has arisen most particularly in relation to the outer continental shelf of Antarctica. According to Article 76 of UNCLOS, coastal States are entitled to the continuation of their continental margin, that is, the prolongation of their land mass, whenever this margin extends beyond 200 nautical miles from the baselines from which the breadth of the territorial sea is measured. The limit of the outer continental shelf of the coastal State is defined in complex terms in Article 76 of UNCLOS, which also requires States to provide the Commission on the Limits of the Continental Shelf, a body created under Annex II to the Convention, with information on the limits of their outer continental shelf. The Commission is to make recommendations to coastal States in relation to the limits of their continental

[14] In the *North Sea Continental Shelf* cases, ICJ Rep 1969, 6, 31, the ICJ expressed the view that certain articles of the Convention (including Art 2) were declaratory of general international law. As to the automatic attribution of a continental shelf, see now Art 77(3) of the 1982 Convention.

[15] See WM Bush, *Antarctica and International Law* (New York, Oceana, 1988) vol 2, 172. The Proclamation did not expressly refer to the AAT, but it did so by clear implication ('any part of the coasts and territories under its authority other than territories administered under the trusteeship system of the United Nations'). The Continental Shelf (Living Natural Resources) Act 1968 (Cth) formally applies to the AAT (see ss 5(1), 9), but has not been applied in practice. The Petroleum (Submerged Lands) Act 1967 (Cth) does not apply: ss 5(1), 5A, 7. On the other hand the Seas and Submerged Lands Act 1973 (Cth), which is in declaratory form and provides a legal basis for delimiting the Australian territorial sea and continental shelf, applies to all Australian territories (see s 4). See also Bush, n 15 above, 173, 174.

shelf, and 'the limits of the shelf established by a coastal State on the basis of these recommendations shall be final and binding.'

It appears that, pursuant to the definition contained in Article 76, most of the continental shelf of Antarctica might extend beyond 200 nautical miles from the baseline, wherever that may be.[16] Moreover, some of the sub-Antarctic Islands have continental shelves that extend south of 60°S, into the Antarctic Treaty Area (ATA).

To date, of the seven States that claim territory in Antarctica, five (Australia, Argentina, New Zealand, Norway and the UK) have presented submissions to the Commission on the Limits of the Continental Shelf which include data on the outer continental shelf of their Antarctic sectors or on the outer continental shelf of their sub-Antarctic Islands. Australia's submission, presented on 15 November 2004,[17] was the first to be reviewed by the Commission, which issued recommendations on 9 April 2008.[18] Australia's submission included the outer continental shelf of sub-Antarctic islands which extended into the Antarctic Treaty Area. It also included data on the extended continental shelf of its claimed Antarctic Sector. The submission, however, was accompanied by a note requesting the Commission not to deal with the Antarctic outer continental shelf claim for the time being.[19] This position eventually became known as the 'Australian method'.

New Zealand submitted the information on its outer continental shelf on 19 April 2006. In a separate communication accompanying the submission, it reserved the right to submit information on the outer continental shelf of its Antarctic claimed sector at a later moment, notwithstanding the provision in Article 4 of Annex II, establishing a 10-year time-limit for

[16] AG Oude Elferink, 'The Continental Shelf of Antarctica: Implications of the Requirement to Make a Submission to the CLCS under Article 76 of the LOS Convention' (2002) 17 *International Journal of Marine and Coastal Law* 485, 503. Problems regarding the determination of baselines in Antarctica are discussed below.

[17] Continental Shelf Submission of Australia, www.un.org/Depts/los/clcs_new/submissions_files/aus04/Documents/aus_doc_es_web_delivery.pdf.

[18] Summary of the Recommendations of the Commission on the Limits of the Continental Shelf (CLCS) in Regard to the Submission made by Australia on 15 November 2004, recommendations adopted by CLCS, 9 April 2008, www.un.org/Depts/los/clcs_new/submissions_files/aus04/aus_summary_of_recommendations.pdf.

[19] Many States presented submissions in reaction to Australia's outer-continental shelf submission. In them, recalling Art IV of the Antarctic Treaty, these States re-formulated their non-recognition of claims to Antarctic territory and consequent non-recognition of claims over the seabed and subsoil of the submarine areas beyond and adjacent to Antarctic. See statements by: USA, Russia, Japan, Netherlands, Germany and India. Other States that presented submissions are East Timor and France. East Timor's submission dealt with the question of the delimitation of maritime boundaries between Timor-Leste and Australia; and France's submission was a confirmation of Australia's assertion that the delimitation of the outer continental shelf in areas bordering with France would be without prejudice to any delimitation subsequently concluded between the two countries. See www.un.org/Depts/los/clcs_new/submissions_files/submission_aus.htm.

the submission of information on the limits of the extended continental shelf.[20] This way of doing things has become known as the 'New Zealand method'.

Norway's submission relates both to the island of Bouvetøya in the South Atlantic Ocean (a part of whose outer continental shelf continues into the Antarctic Treaty Area) and its Antarctic claimed sector. However, the Norwegian submission expressly requested the Commission not to take any action in relation to this part of the continental shelf 'for the time being'. Norway recalled 'the unique and comprehensive Antarctic cooperation and the need to ensure the continuing peaceful cooperation and harmony in the Antarctic Area. Norway remains fully committed to its obligations and the cooperation under the Antarctic Treaty System.'[21]

Argentina's submission includes data for its Antarctic outer continental shelf and the continental shelves of the Malvinas (Falklands) and South Georgia and South Sandwich islands, sovereignty over which is disputed with the UK. Part of the outer continental shelf of these islands extends into the Antarctic Treaty Area.[22] But whereas Australia and Norway have expressly requested the Commission not to take any action in respect of the information submitted relating to the outer continental shelf of their sectors, Argentina has made no such request.

The UK's submission does not include data on the outer continental shelf of the claimed sector of Antarctica.[23] It relates solely to the Falkland, South Georgia and South Sandwich Islands, a part of whose outer continental shelf extends south of 60°S latitude into the Antarctic Treaty Area.

[20] Note from the Permanent Mission of New Zealand to the Secretary-General of the UN accompanying the lodgement of New Zealand's submission, Note No NZ-CLCS-TPN-02, www.un.org/Depts/los/clcs_new/submissions_files/nzl06/nzl_doc_es_attachment.pdf. Japan and the Netherlands submitted notes in reaction to New Zealand's submission, reaffirming that they did not recognise any claims to territorial sovereignty in Antarctica. See www.un.org/Depts/los/clcs_new/submissions_files/submission_nzl.htm.

[21] Continental Shelf Submission of Norway in respect of Bouvetøya and Dronning Maud Land, Executive Summary, 6, submitted on 4 May 2009, www.un.org/Depts/los/clcs_new/submissions_files/nor30_09/nor2009_executivesummary.pdf. In June 2009, the US and Russia filed their reactions to the Commission in relation to Norway's submission to the CLCS, they both stated that they do not recognise any State's claim to Antarctica, and consequently, they do not recognise any maritime rights in the coasts adjacent to Antarctica. See www.un.org/Depts/los/clcs_new/submissions_files/submission_nor_30_2009.htm.

[22] Outer Limit of the Continental Shelf Argentine Submission, 21 April 2009, www.un.org/Depts/los/clcs_new/submissions_files/arg25_09/arg2009e_summary_esp.pdf.

[23] Submission to the Commission on the Limits of the Continental Shelf pursuant to Article 76, para 8 of the United Nations Convention on the Law of the Sea 1982 in respect of the Falkland Islands, and of South Georgia and the South Sandwich Islands, UK, 11 May 2009, www.un.org/Depts/los/clcs_new/submissions_files/gbr45_09/gbr2009fgs_executive%20summary.pdf.

Several difficulties arise in relation with claims over the Antarctic continental and outer continental shelf. The first, fundamental and much debated, problem relates to the status of Antarctica and, consequently, the status of the territories claimed. Do the claims over Antarctic territory grant the respective claimant States the character of 'coastal States'? Not surprisingly, claimant States have answered this question affirmatively, whereas non-claimant States have rejected the existence of coastal States and coastal State jurisdiction for territories in the ATA. This question has been considered as a 'dispute touching upon the fundamental underpinnings of the ATS and the status of Antarctica under general international law'.[24]

Similarly, scholars have differed in their conclusions as to the status of the Antarctic continent. For Kohen, Antarctica as a '*territoire terrestre*' has the same characteristics as other terrestrial territories, including the character as a space capable of being subject to sovereignty.[25] In the opposite sense Joyner expresses 'serious' doubts in relation to this possibility.[26]

The existence of coastal States in Antarctica was at the heart of the arguments presented to the Commission on the Limits of the Continental Shelf in reaction to Australia's inclusion of data on its Antarctic outer continental shelf in its submission. The reacting States did not protest the submission on the basis of it constituting a 'new claim' contrary to Article IV of the Antarctic Treaty. They rather protested the existence of *any* territorial sovereignty over Antarctica, which in consequence meant that they would not recognise any maritime claims appurtenant to the area: the land dominates the sea, as the International Court of Justice has held on numerous occasions.[27]

Thus Germany maintained that it does not

> recognize any State's claim to territory in Antarctica and does not recognize that a State's claim to territorial sovereignty in Antarctica is capable of creating any rights over the seabed and subsoil of the submarine areas beyond and adjacent to the Continent of Antarctica.[28]

[24] Oude Elferink, above n 16 at 505.

[25] MG Kohen, *Possession Contestée et Souveraineté Territoriale* (Geneva, Presses Universitaires de France, 1997) 106.

[26] CC Joyner, 'The Antarctic Treaty System and the Law of the Sea—Competing Regimes in the Southern Ocean?' (1995) 10 *International Journal of Marine and Coastal Law* 301, 309–11. Rothwell and Joyner affirm that no coastal states exist in Antarctica: DR Rothwell and CC Joyner, 'The Polar Oceans and the Law of the Sea' in AG Oude Elferink and DR Rothwell (eds), *The Law of the Sea and Polar Maritime Delimitation and Jurisdiction* (The Hague, Martinus Nijhoff, 2001) 2.

[27] See, eg *Case Concerning Maritime Delimitation in the Black Sea (Romania v Ukraine)*, judgment of 3 February 2009, para 77.

[28] Communication by Germany, Note No 88/2005, at 1, www.un.org/Depts/los/clcs_new/submissions_files/aus04/clcs_03_2004_los_deu.pdf.

Any action by the Commission in this respect would negatively affect the 'balance of rights and obligations in the Antarctic Treaty'.[29]

India noted that it did not recognise

> any state's rights or claims to territorial sovereignty in the Antarctic Treaty area, and consequently does not recognize any state's right over or claims to the water, seabed and subsoil of the submarine areas adjacent to the continent of Antarctica.[30]

Japan stressed the importance of maintaining the balance of rights and obligations in the Antarctic Treaty, and called upon the Commission not to alter that balance by taking action with respect to Australia's submission on the Antarctic. It then recalled Article IV of the Treaty and indicated that it does not

> recognise any State's right of or claims to territorial sovereignty in the Antarctic, and consequently does not recognize any State's rights over or claims to the water, seabed and subsoil of the submarine areas adjacent to the continent of Antarctica.[31]

Russia said that it did not recognise

> any claims in relation to territories located in the area covered by the Treaty, nor does it regard the assertion of such claims by any State as establishing rights with respect to the seabed (continental shelf) and its mineral resources in areas appurtenant to Antarctica.[32]

The Netherlands reiterated its 'longstanding' position that it

> does not recognize any claim to territories in Antarctica and does not recognize that a claim to territorial sovereignty in Antarctica is capable of creating any sort of rights over continental shelf adjacent to Antarctica.

It added that:

> It is well-established that the principle of sovereign rights over continental shelf adjacent to the coast, for the purposes of exploring and exploiting the natural resources of the shelf, derives from sovereignty of the coastal State over adjacent land territory. Accordingly, the Netherlands does not consider that the continental shelf adjacent to Antarctica is subject to the sovereign rights of any State.[33]

[29] Ibid 2.

[30] Communication by India, Note No NY/PM/443/1/98, at 2, www.un.org/Depts/los/clcs_new/submissions_files/aus04/clcs_03_2004_los_ind.pdf.

[31] Communication by Japan, Note No SC/05/ 039, at 2, www.un.org/Depts/los/clcs_new/submissions_files/aus04/clcs_03_2004_los_jap.pdf.

[32] Communication by Russia, Note No 739/n, at 1, www.un.org/Depts/los/clcs_new/submissions_files/aus04/clcs_03_2004_los_russiantext.pdf.

[33] Communication by the Netherlands, Note No NYV/2005/690, at 1, www.un.org/Depts/los/clcs_new/submissions_files/aus04/clcs_03_2004_los_nl.pdf.

The US submission maintained that:

> The US does not recognize any State's claim to territory in Antarctica and consequently does not recognize any State's rights over the seabed and subsoil of the submarine areas beyond and adjacent to the continent of Antarctica.[34]

By contrast, none of the States which claim sovereignty over the Antarctic reacted to the Australian inclusion of its Antarctic outer continental shelf in the submission. France, the only other claimant State to react to Australia's submission, did not touch upon this matter, simply consenting to the establishment of limits on the outer continental shelf in areas where French and Australian claims may overlap, as required by the Rules of Procedure of the Commission.

Assuming, however, that Antarctic claimant States can in principle claim maritime areas adjacent to their respective Antarctic sectors, another question arises from Article IV of the Antarctic Treaty: is the claim to the outer continental shelf of Antarctica an 'enlargement of an existing claim'?[35] Similar issues arise from the establishment of baselines as for claims to the outer continental shelf. This can be seen from two perspectives: some argue that drawing of a straight baseline, enclosing internal waters, is the assertion of a sovereign claim which extends to the water and the superjacent seabed, subsoil, and airspace.[36] Others, emphasising the fact that Article IV of the Antarctic Treaty refers to 'territorial sovereignty', maintain that since the assertion of baselines is properly an exercise of 'maritime sovereignty', for it is regulated by the law of the sea and does not relate the acquisition of title to territory, it falls outside the scope of Article IV.[37] I will return to this issue shortly.

C. Sub-Antarctic Continental Shelf Extending into the Treaty Area

Many of the islands north of the 60°S parallel have continental shelves which extend into the Antarctic Treaty Area. Sovereignty over these islands may give rise to maritime rights to the States exercising sovereignty over them, including rights to the continental shelf and extended continental shelf, and over the territorial sea and exclusive economic

[34] Communication by the United States of America, www.un.org/Depts/los/clcs_new/submissions_files/aus04/clcs_03_2004_los_usatext.pdf.

[35] See SB Kaye, 'The Outer Continental Shelf in the Antarctic' in Oude Elferink and Rothwell, above n 26 at 133–37.

[36] R Churchill and V Lowe, *The Law of the Sea* (Manchester, Manchester University Press, 1999) 60–61.

[37] SB Kaye and DR Rothwell, 'Southern Ocean Boundaries and Maritime Claims: Another Antarctic Challenge for the Law of the Sea?' (2002) 33 *Ocean Development & International Law* 359, 379.

zone, pursuant to UNCLOS. In consequence, these claims have encountered little opposition.

True, some have argued that these islands must be qualified as 'rocks which cannot sustain human habitation or economic life of their own', pursuant to Article 121(3) of UNCLOS, and that in consequence, they should not give rise to maritime rights to the States which exercise sovereignty over them. For instance, Judge Vukas, speaking of the Kerguelen Islands, considered it highly questionable that the proclamation of an EEZ off 'uninhabitable and uninhabited' islands was in accordance with the spirit of UNCLOS.[38]

Nevertheless, State practice does not accept this view: maritime zones off the sub-Antarctic Islands have been proclaimed by a number of States and other States have accepted these claims. No State contested Australia's right to the extended continental shelf off Heard Island and the McDonald Islands or Macquarie Island, and similarly no protests were made when the limits of these outer continental shelves were recommended by the Commission early in 2008.

The extension of the continental shelf into the Antarctic Treaty area may cause regulatory problems in two areas: (i) problems of delimitation between the continental shelf of the Antarctic Territory and that of islands north of the 60°S parallel but continuing into the Antarctic Treaty Area; and, (ii) the regime applicable to the continental shelf south of 60°S latitude.

So far, only Australia has received the recommendation by the Commission on the Limits of the Continental Shelf on the limits of its outer continental shelf extending into the Antarctic Treaty Area. These areas include the outer continental shelves of the Heard and MacDonald Islands (the Kerguelen Plateau) and that of Macquarie Island, which together make up around half of the extension of the outer continental shelf confirmed by the Commission. The problem of continental shelf delimitation would seem not to arise: only the Kerguelen Plateau extends into the outer continental shelf of Antarctica, and it does so in the shelf of the Australian Antarctic Territory.[39]

The regulation of these areas is more complex. It raises, in general, similar normative problems that the regulation of the outer continental shelf of Antarctica may raise, but there is a fundamental difference between the two: the rights of coastal States over these islands are not contested.

[38] *Monte Confurco (Seychelles v France)*, ITLOS, Prompt Release, Case No 6, 2000, 125 ILR 220, 254. Judge Vukas repeated his position in a Declaration appended to the *Volga Case (Russia v Australia)*, ITLOS, Prompt Release, Case No 11, 2002, 126 ILR 433, 460–65, but in relation to the Heard Island and the McDonald Islands.

[39] SB Kaye, 'Antarctic Maritime Delimitation' in Oude Elferink and Rothwell, above n 26 at 173.

This would entail greater clarity and, probably, less controversy in the determination of the regime applicable. Clearly, though, different considerations will be relevant, and the sovereign rights of coastal States may have greater influence, as evidenced by the application of the Convention on the Conservation of Antarctic Marine Living Resources (CCAMLR)[40] in areas outside the Antarctic Treaty Area which include sub-Antarctic Islands over which sovereignty is not contested.

D. The Exclusive Economic Zone

As noted, the position with the 200 mile EEZ may be different. The EEZ has developed since the Antarctic Treaty, and may well entail a 'new claim' in a way that the continental shelf may not. Moreover, unlike the continental shelf, the practice is for these zones to be expressly claimed by proclamation pursuant to legislation passed for that purpose.

In fact most States which have claims over the Antarctic or that have sovereignty over sub-Antarctic islands have recently sought to expand their maritime areas, and have therefore expressly claimed an EEZ. Chile has gone so far as to create a new maritime area: the 'presential sea', although it does not involve any claim to exclusive rights.[41]

The practice of claimant States in making maritime claims has not disclosed a pattern. Of the five claimants that recognise each other's claim to Antarctica (Australia, France, New Zealand, Norway, and the United Kingdom), only Australia has formally proclaimed an EEZ around its Antarctic territory, on the basis that the EEZ is an attribute of sovereignty, and consequently, not a 'new claim'. Both Argentina and Chile have also claimed all of their maritime zones around their Antarctic sectors.[42] The remaining claimants have not taken steps to regularise their maritime arrangements off their Antarctic territories.[43]

[40] 1329 UNTS 47.

[41] The 'presential sea' is the maritime area which departs from the outer limit of the Chilean EEZ and extends to the South Pole, therefore including Antarctic sea. The basis of the claim, however, is not Chile's claim over the Antarctic territories: P Vigni, 'Antarctic Maritime Claims: "Frozen Sovereignty" and the Law of the Sea', in AG Oude Elferink and DR Rothwell (eds), *The Law of the Sea and Polar Maritime Delimitation and Jurisdiction* (The Hague, Martinus Nijhoff, 2001) 88–89. Orrego-Vicuña clarified that the Chilean action was not designed to signal a new maritime zone, but was intended simply to identify an area of the high seas where Chilean interests were directly involved. The status of the area as high seas has never been contested: F Orrego-Vicuña, *The Changing International Law of High Seas Fisheries* (Cambridge, Cambridge University Press, 1999) 107–08.

[42] Argentina has claimed the EEZ off all of its territory, which includes the claimed sector of Antarctica, www.dna.gov.ar/DIVULGAC/ARGANT.HTM. However, through Law No 23968 (1991), Argentina established the baselines for all of its territory, expressly excluding its Antarctic claimed sector: see art 1.

[43] Kaye and Rothwell, above n 37 at 372–73.

So far as the responses by non-claimant States are concerned, of course they are no more disposed to recognise EEZ claims than claims to land territory in Antarctica. But it may be relevant that—neither in respect of outer continental shelf nor EEZ—has any State taken the point that these claims are independently prohibited by Article IV of the Treaty. That is at least modest support for the proposition that Article IV is not concerned with maritime claims *as such*.

III. EXERCISE OF JURISDICTION IN THE ANTARCTIC TREATY AREA

According to one view:

> The agreement to disagree on the question of sovereignty as laid down in Article IV of the Antarctic Treaty precludes the exercise of unilateral jurisdiction over the continent and adjacent maritime areas. The regulation of human activities on the Antarctic continent and in its adjacent maritime areas therefore has many similarities with that of the high seas, whose regime relies on the freedom of the high seas and the primacy of flag state jurisdiction.[44]

Whether or not this is right (and I have suggested it may not be), it is a fact that the claimant States have shown considerable restraint in exercising jurisdiction over the various zones.

A. The Antarctic Treaty

The Antarctic Treaty says little about jurisdiction. This is a consequence of the division of opinion on sovereignty claims, and the division between States advocating a nationality based jurisdictional approach and a territoriality based one (not reflecting the claimant/non-claimant State divide).[45] Article VIII contains the only definitive rule related to jurisdiction, according to which:

> 1. In order to facilitate the exercise of their functions under the present Treaty, and without prejudice to the respective positions of the Contracting Parties relating to jurisdiction over all other persons in Antarctica, observers designated under paragraph 1 of Article VII and scientific personnel exchanged under sub-paragraph 1(b) of Article III of the Treaty, and members of the staffs accompanying any such persons, shall be subject only to the jurisdiction of the Contracting Party of which they are nationals in respect of all acts or

[44] EJ Molenaar, 'Sea-Borne Tourism in Antarctica: and Further Governmental Regulation' (2005) 20 *International Journal of Marine and Coastal Law* 247, 249.

[45] R Davis and E Lee, 'Marine Environmental Protection and the Southern Ocean: The Maritime Jurisdictional Dimension of the Antarctic Treaty System' in Oude Elferink and Rothwell, above n 26 at 206.

omissions occurring while they are in Antarctica for the purpose of exercising their functions.

2. Without prejudice to the provisions of paragraph 1 of this Article, and pending the adoption of measures in pursuance of subparagraph 1(e) of Article IX, the Contracting Parties concerned in any case of dispute with regard to the exercise of jurisdiction in Antarctica shall immediately consult together with a view to reaching a mutually acceptable solution.

This rule has been described as 'basically a transactional formula which is not intended to prejudge the substantive problem'.[46] Attempts to achieve a general solution to the substantive jurisdictional question under Article IX(1)(e), which allows parties to agree on measures relating to the exercise of jurisdiction, have failed. In practice, controversies have been avoided by the cautiousness with which the Antarctic Claimant States have asserted their jurisdiction, especially over marine areas. In fact, the practice has been not to apply their laws to foreigners, even when they are expressed to apply broadly to both nationals and aliens.[47]

A further question is that of jurisdiction over the high seas within the Antarctic Treaty Area, for Article VI of the Treaty expressly indicated that:

> Nothing in the present Treaty shall prejudice or in any way affect the rights, or the exercise of the rights, of any State under international law with regard to the high seas within that area.

This provision, the result of compromise during the drafting of the Convention between opposite positions, has been the subject of ample debate. Article VI does not deny the Treaty application over the high seas south of the 60th parallel: the Treaty does not say that it does not apply to the high seas, but merely that it is not applicable insofar as it conflicts with the rights relating to the high seas, as they exist at any given time.[48]

B. The Convention on the Conservation of Antarctic Marine Living Resources

CAMLR raises particular issues of jurisdiction in respect of the maritime areas adjacent to sub-Antarctic islands. First, according to Article I(1), the Convention's scope of application extends beyond 60°S and includes the

[46] F Orrego-Vicuña, *Antarctic Mineral Exploitation—The Emerging Legal Framework* (Cambridge, Cambridge University Press, 1988) 2.

[47] Davis and Lee, above n 45 at 201–02, 207.

[48] T Scovazzi, 'The Application of the Antarctic Treaty System to the Protection of the Antarctic marine Environment' in F Francioni (ed), *International Environmental Law for Antarctica* (Milano, Giuffré Editore, 1992) 115, quoted by KR Wood, 'The Uncertain Fate of the Madrid Protocol to the Antarctic Treaty in the Maritime Area' (2003) 34 *Ocean Development & International Law* 139, 158.

area within the Antarctic Convergence. This is an ecological boundary that divides the ecosystems of the Antarctic from those situated to the north.[49] The Convention centralises the conservation of marine living resources on the Commission created by that instrument. States parties are requested to notify to the Commission activities, both by contracting and non-contracting parties, which may affect the implementation of the objective of the Convention. All of the Antarctic claimant States are parties to the CCAMLR and are members of the CCAMLR Commission.[50]

In fact claimant States have mostly not controlled marine living resources off the coasts of their claimed sector as coastal States would do elsewhere. Australia has excluded the EEZ of its Antarctic Territory from the Fisheries Management Act (1991). Argentina and Chile have taken a more assertive attitude by prescribing activities within their claimed maritime zones adjacent to Antarctica. But, they have never pursued a rigorous policy of enforcement vis-à-vis foreign vessels and nationals.[51]

These problems have also arisen in relation to sub-Antarctic Islands. Under the law of the sea, the regulation of marine resources in these areas is within the coastal State's jurisdiction, under the CCAMLR the regulation of these resources is allocated to the Commission on the Conservation of Antarctic Marine Living Resources.

This conflict has been seemingly resolved by the statement of the Chairman of the Conference on Antarctic Marine Living Resources, from which the Convention originated.[52] According to this statement, there are three main exceptions to the Convention, in favour of coastal State jurisdiction:

- — National measures aimed at conserving marine living resources that were adopted before the entry into force of the convention, remain valid.
- — No specific conservation measure within the CCAMLR zone, which is also within the maritime zone of a coastal State, may be adopted without the consent of said State.
- — Scientific observation and inspection cannot be carried out within areas over which a State has sovereign rights without its consent.

[49] The Convergence is the boundary between the cold Antarctic surface water and the warmer sub-Antarctic water: see Rothwell and Joyner, above n 26 at 3.

[50] See the Commission's website: www.ccamlr.org/pu/E/ms/contacts.htm.

[51] EJ Molenaar, 'CCAMLR and Southern Ocean Fisheries' (2001) 16 *International Journal of Marine and Coastal Law* 465, 478.

[52] The statement refers mainly to the French islands of Kerguelen and Crozet; however, the text extends to 'waters adjacent to the islands within the area to which this convention applies over which the existence of State sovereignty is recognized by all the Contracting Parties'. See the Statement of the Chairman of the Conference on the Conservation of Antarctic Marine Living Resources, attached to the CCAMLR, para 5.

There exist serious controversies as to the legal value of this statement.[53] But it has also been noted that, at least with respect to the French islands, this position has generally been respected.[54]

This statement is said to reconcile the regimes under CCAMLR and the law of the sea, by providing for the priority of coastal State rights under the law of the sea. In practice, on the basis of this statement, States have been allowed to exercise jurisdiction over their maritime areas, and they have done so, for instance, in relation to the regulation of fishing of the Patagonian toothfish (*Dissostichus eleginoides*) in the South Georgia, Price Edward, Crozet, Kerguelen and Heard Island and the McDonald Islands.[55]

This solution has, nevertheless, been the subject of mixed reviews. It has been supported on the argument that the conservation of resources in these areas may be easier to achieve by coastal States in the exercise of their sovereign rights, rather than to count on flag State enforcement. The reason for this is that coastal States could enforce the provisions of the CCAMLR which have been incorporated into their domestic laws even as against States not parties to the Convention.[56]

The enforcement of conservation measures for the protection of the Patagonian toothfish may be quoted as an example of the more efficient enforcement of conservation and protection measures by coastal States,[57] which was the subject of various prompt release disputes before ITLOS.[58] The dispute between Australia and Russia in the *Volga case* concerned Australia's prosecution of the *Volga* and its crew, a Russian-flagged vessel, engaged in illegal fishing of Patagonian toothfish, in the fishing zone off Heard Island and the McDonald Islands. Australia partly justified

[53] DR Rothwell, *The Polar Regions and the Development of International Law* (Cambridge, Cambridge University Press, 1996) 127; Vigni above n 41 at 100.

[54] Molenaar, above n 51 at 480. In any event, it must be noted that, under CCAMLR, substantive issues must be decided by consensus, including the consent of those States with sovereignty over sub-Antarctic islands which are members of the Commission. Similarly, Australia applies its laws on its sub-Antarctic islands, the contents of which are consistent, but not identical, with CCAMLR conservation measures.

[55] D Miller, EN Sabourenkov and DC Ramm, 'Managing the Antarctic Marine Living Resources: The CCAMLR Approach' (2004) 19 *International Journal of Marine and Coastal Law* 317, 350.

[56] See DR Rothwell and SB Kaye, 'Law of the Sea and the Polar Regions' (1998) 18 *Marine Policy* 41; Vigni, above n 53 at 100. Miller, Sabourenkov and Ramm, above n 55 at 353, who recognise the inherent difficulty of the Commission's enforcement of conservation measures in the Convention Area.

[57] Ibid 350, 356.

[58] *The 'Camouco' Case (Panama v France)*, ITLOS, Prompt Release, Case No 5, 2000, 125 ILR 164; *The 'Monte Confurco' Case (Seychelles v France)*, ITLOS, Prompt Release, Case No 6, 2000, 125 ILR 220; *The 'Grand Prince' Case (Belize v France)*, ITLOS, Prompt Release, Case No 8, 2001; 125 ILR 272; *The 'Volga' Case (Russian Federation v Australia)*, ITLOS, Prompt Release, Case No 11, 2002, 126 ILR 433.

its actions on the basis of the CCAMLR and the seriousness of illegal harvesting of Patagonian toothfish in the area covered by the treaty. The Tribunal limited itself to noting the submissions made by Australia in relation to the international concern raised by illegal, unregulated and unreported fishing in the Southern Ocean. Some judges were, however, more explicit. Judge Cot expressly endorsed Australia's exercise of jurisdiction off Heard and McDonald Islands, and held this action to be not only compatible with UNCLOS rights, but also to uphold an international system for the protection of a 'common heritage'.[59] By contrast Judge Vukas maintained that, in view of the Commission inspection procedures established in the CCAMLR itself:

> It is ... unnecessary and confusing if individual States adopt and apply their own measures in the exclusive economic zone they have proclaimed inside the area of application of the CCAMLR.[60]

C. The Madrid Protocol on Environmental Protection to the Antarctic Treaty

The Madrid Protocol on Environmental Protection to the Antarctic Treaty, adopted in 1991, is intended for the 'planning and conduct of all activities in the Antarctic Treaty Area' and has as its goal 'the comprehensive protection of the Antarctic environment and dependent associated ecosystems'. This wording may imply that the Madrid Protocol's scope of application is not limited to the Antarctic Treaty Area, but may instead extend beyond that boundary. The Madrid Protocol, read together with its annexes, relies implicitly on nationality jurisdiction, but also on 'extended notions of control, through a system of inspection by observers arranged by the [Antarctic Treaty Consultative Parties]'.[61]

Annex IV of the Madrid Protocol establishes a comprehensive regime for the prevention of marine pollution in Antarctica: it is essentially precautionary in nature.[62] On the other hand, under Article 234 of UNCLOS, States enjoy jurisdiction to prescribe and enforce laws in relation to the prevention, reduction and control of marine pollution from vessels in ice-covered areas within the limits of the EEZ.

It has been argued that Article 234 of UNCLOS is not applicable to Antarctica since the Third UN Conference on the Law of the Sea expressly excluded Antarctica from its area of application. But even if this was the position adopted or assumed by some delegations at the

[59] Ibid 468–69 (separate opinion of Judge Cot).
[60] Ibid 464 (declaration of Judge Vukas).
[61] Davis and Lee, above n 45 at 213.
[62] Wood, above n 48 at 141.

Conference, nothing in the Convention suggests that it has a limited area of application.[63]

Davis and Lee argue that the development in the ATS has led to the creation of a 'special competence and joint jurisdiction'. In their view, the growing concern for environmental protection, the development of an ecosystem focus and the perception of the parties to the Antarctic Treaty that they have special rights and obligations to protect the Antarctic environment, all have 'encouraged the ATP to cooperate in the implementation of environmental measures, rather than to seek precise delineation of each party's jurisdictional reach'.[64]

Likewise Orrego-Vicuña considers that traditional international law rules are difficult to apply in Antarctica and that their application must take special account of the unique context of Antarctica.[65] In his view 'jurisdiction over Antarctic maritime areas has developed in a collective manner whereby it tends to be exercised jointly by the consultative parties, or by other countries participating in the … specific resource regimes'.[66]

It may be that joint jurisdiction could resolve the problem of allocation of responsibilities within the ATS. But there are many problems with the idea, including the uniform application of standards by all treaty parties and the enforcement of the rules against third States. As to uniform application of standards, there is no agreement between the parties as to the basic definitions of environmental protection. For instance, the classification of the environmental impact assessment into 'less than minor or transitory', 'minor or transitory' and 'more than minor or transitory' has proved to be unhelpful in the absence of guidance in the interpretation of these terms.[67] As concerns third parties, the polar opposite—so to speak—of the enforcement of standards by the claimant State is not joint jurisdiction: it is no effective jurisdiction at all.

IV. REGULATION OF DEVELOPING USES

Further problems arise in relation to the regulation of developing uses of Antarctica. Prominent among which are the issues of Antarctic tourism,

[63] See Rothwell and Kaye, above n 56 at 41.

[64] Davis and Lee, above n 45 at 216–17.

[65] This position is also held by Rothwell and Kaye, above n 56 at 41.

[66] F Orrego-Vicuña, 'The Law of the Sea and the Antarctic Treaty System: New Approaches to Offshore Jurisdiction' in CC Joyner and SK Chopra (eds), *The Antarctic Legal Regime* (The Hague, Martinus Nijhoff, 1988) 121.

[67] Davis and Lee, above n 45 at 219–20; DR Rothwell, 'Polar Environmental Protection and International Law: The 1991 Antarctic Protocol' (2000) 11 *European Journal of International Law* 591, 600.

conservation of marine living resources and the harvesting of whales. I will deal with these in turn.

A. Antarctic Tourism

After fishing, tourism is the second main commercial activity in the Area. It has grown considerably in the past years. The number of participants in Antarctic tourism in the 1992–93 season was about 6,500 passengers. In the 2007–08 season the number was 46,069 passengers, of which 13,015 were air-overflight and cruise-only tourists and 33,054 were sea-borne and air-borne landed tourists.[68]

Regulation is not absent. Several Antarctic Treaty Parties have implemented domestic legislation, and industry regulation occurs through the International Association of Antarctic Tour Operators (IAATO), which has taken an active role in ensuring member compliance with the Protocol and the ATS, in general. IAATO also engages in the collection and dissemination of information regarding the scale and scope of tourist activities in Antarctica.

One of the main problems of tourism in Antarctica is related to ship operations and the risk of pollution.[69] Once more, normative problems arise, for both the Madrid Protocol and MARPOL[70] could be applicable to vessel related pollution. The solutions adopted in the framework of the Antarctic Treaty are essentially two: either MARPOL should have priority because it is seen as the most appropriate international convention, or both conventions are to be applied concurrently.

The United States, Japan, Norway and New Zealand, among others, follow the first approach. In their view land-based stations should follow Madrid Annex III on Waste Disposal and Waste Management, and ships should follow MARPOL and only Madrid Annex IV on Prevention of Marine Pollution. The reason is that MARPOL is seen as the most appropriate instrument to regulate ship operations in the maritime area of Antarctica.

Under the second approach, MARPOL provides the general basis for the regulation of ships in the maritime areas of Antarctica, but when a certain subject is not addressed, is beyond the scope of MARPOL or is specifically regulated by the Madrid Protocol, the latter should apply.[71] This approach is followed by States like Australia and the UK. It can also be

[68] See IAATO Tourism Statistics, www.iaato.org/tourism_stats.html.

[69] Molenaar, above n 44 at 249.

[70] International Convention for the Prevention of Pollution from Ships, 1973, as modified by the Protocol of 1978 relating thereto (MARPOL), 1340 UNTS 61.

[71] Wood, above n 62 at 142–43.

evidenced in the practice of the Antarctic Treaty Consultative Meetings, such as Recommendation XVIII-1, on 'Guidance for those conducting tourism and non-governmental activities in Antarctic', which states:

> Dispose of waste materials in accordance with Annexes III and IV of the Protocol. These annexes prohibit, among other things, the discharge of plastics, oil and noxious substances into the Antarctic Treaty Area; regulate the discharge of sewage and food waste; and require the removal of most waste from the area.'[72]

According to Molenaar, the current situation is that no State can unilaterally regulate or prohibit activities by foreign vessels or foreign nationals: rather, regulation of tourist activities in Antarctica is governed by a 'complex web of concurrent (overlapping) international regimes', relying predominantly on the freedom of the high seas, flag State jurisdiction and the core elements and objectives of the Antarctic Treaty.[73]

B. Marine Living Resources

Despite the growth in tourism, marine living resources are the principal Antarctic resources subject to exploitation.[74] Their conservation is carried out under the Convention on the Conservation of Antarctic Marine Living Resources, concluded in 1980. The Convention's objective is the conservation (including rational use) of Antarctic marine living resources on the basis of a precautionary, multi-species management and ecosystem approach. But as we will see, this approach has its limits when it comes to whales.

The Convention's main regulatory body is a Commission of 25 members. Pursuant to Article IX, the Commission operates by facilitating research, compiling data, adopting and reviewing Conservation Measures and implementing the system of observation and inspection established in Article XXV of the Convention. The Commission is assisted by the Scientific Committee, whose recommendations and advice must be fully taken into account by the Commission, pursuant to Article IX(4).

The main target species are the Patagonian- and the Antarctic toothfish and krill. Toothfish is especially vulnerable due to its slow growth and low productivity, and in recent years the stock has come under a lot of pressure, especially through illegal, unreported and unregulated (IUU) fishing.[75] At present, it seems that krill is not overexploited, but information in relation to the impact of krill fishing upon the abundance

72 See www.ats.aq/documents/recatt%5Catt245_e.pdf.
73 Molenaar, above n 44 at 255.
74 Rothwell and Joyner, above n 26 at 8.
75 Molenaar, above n 51 at 465.

of its major predators is lacking, and a highly precautionary approach is called for.[76]

The area of application of the CCAMLR overlaps with the coverage of the Convention on the Conservation of Southern Bluefin Tuna (CCSBT) and,[77] potentially, with the International Convention for the Conservation of Atlantic Tuna (ICCAT).[78] Similarly, the southern boundaries of other Regional Fisheries Management Organizations (RFMO) coincide with the northern boundary of the CCAMLR area. These Agreements are the Indian Ocean Tuna Commission (IOTC) agreement,[79] the Honolulu Convention on the Conservation and Management of Highly Migratory Fish Stocks in the Western and Central Pacific Ocean,[80] the Convention on the Conservation and Management of the Fishery Resources in the South East Atlantic Ocean (SEAFO),[81] and the Galapagos Agreement for the Conservation of the Living Marine Resources on the High Seas of the Southeast Pacific.[82]

Cooperation is required to harmonise the conservation measures of these areas and those of the CCAMLR in zones of convergence. For this purpose, the CCAMLR established in Article IX(5) that the Commission shall take account of regulatory efforts established or recommended

> by existing fisheries commissions responsible for species which may enter the area to which this Convention applies, in order that there shall be no inconsistency between the rights and obligations of a contracting party under such regulations or measures and conservation measures which may be adopted by the Commission.

Clearly, the same is required by the other commissions in respect of CCAMLR protected species: for instance, the Patagonian toothfish is caught not only in the CCAMLR area but also in adjacent areas in the Atlantic, Indian and Pacific Ocean.

The travails of toothfish in the ATA are paralleled by the slaughter of southern blue-fin tuna. An unhappy jurisdictional decision of 2000 held in effect that the compulsory jurisdiction provisions of the 1982 Convention are not applicable in the case of any treaty containing a version of the ATS jurisdictional clause.[83] The SBT Convention coexists with the conservation

[76] OS Stokke, 'The Effectiveness of CCAMLR' in OS Stokke and D Vidas, *Governing the Antarctic* (Cambridge, Cambridge University Press, 1996) 144.

[77] 1819 UNTS 360.

[78] 637 UNTS 63.

[79] 1927 UNTS 330.

[80] (2001) 40 ILM 277.

[81] (2001) 41 ILM 257.

[82] See www.cpps-int.org/spanish/tratadosyconvenios/tratadosregionales/acuerdodegalapagos.htm (14 August 2000).

[83] *cf Southern Bluefin Tuna (Australia and New Zealand v Japan)* ITLOS Order of 27 August 1999, 117 ILR 148, with the Tribunal's Award of 4 August 2000 denying jurisdiction, 119 ILR 508.

obligations under UNCLOS. But jurisdictionally there seems to be nothing the parties to the SBT Convention can do about it.

C. Whaling

Finally, I should say a word on the contentious subject of whaling. The primary regime for regulating whaling is the International Convention for the Regulating of Whaling (ICRW) of 1946.[84] Commercial whaling was put under a moratorium in 1986 by the International Whaling Commission (IWC), which in 1994 also established a Southern Ocean Sanctuary.[85] But under a long-running program of special permit whaling (JARPA I and JARPA II) Japan continues to catch especially minke whales in the Southern Ocean.[86]

Regulation of whaling under CCAMLR is not necessarily excluded from a legal point of view. Under Article I(2) of CCAMLR, "Antarctic marine living resources" is defined to mean the populations of 'fin fish, mollusks, crustaceans and all other species of living organisms, including birds, found south of the Antarctic Convergence'. This evidently includes Antarctic marine mammals as well.[87]

But there are both legal and political problems. The legal problem is embodied in CCAMLR Article VI, which provides that

> [n]othing in this Convention shall derogate from the rights and obligations of contracting parties under the International Convention for the Regulation of Whaling and the Convention for the Conservation of Antarctic Seals.

The political problem is that the main antagonist States to IWC are also parties to the CCAMLR Commission and there is pronounced aversion to importing the highly-charged problems of the IWC into the ATS. The result for the time being is an impasse.

Into that impasse national regulations may intrude. An exception from a general practice of non-enforcement of EEZ jurisdiction against non-nationals is the injunction against whaling issued by the Federal Court of Australia in *Humane Society International Inc v Kyodo Senpaku Kaisha Ltd*.[88] The injunction was issued under the Environment Protection and Biodiversity Conservation Act 1999 (Cth), which applies to the Australian EEZ including off the AAT. In issuing the injunction despite

[84] 161 UNTS 74.

[85] See A Gillespie, 'The Southern Ocean Sanctuary and the Development of International Environmental Law' (2005) 15 *International Journal of Marine and Coastal Law* 293.

[86] See generally A Gillespie, *Whaling Diplomacy* (Cheltenham, Edward Elgar, 2005), esp ch 5.

[87] Molenaar, above n 51 at 474.

[88] [2008] FCA 3.

the defendant's refusal to accept service and its practical unenforceability, Alsop J said:

> The question of futility can, however, also be seen from a perspective of disobedience. To do so requires the setting to one side of the refusal by Japan to recognise Australia's claim to Antarctica. It is not for this Court to question Australia's claim or Parliament's mandate in the EPBC Act, which is based on Australia's claim. Thus, this perspective can be seen to be relevant for this Court to take into account (even if from another perspective, for instance that of Japan, the perspective is flawed) …
>
> Further, one cannot ignore the public interest nature of the claim and the complete recognition by the Parliament of that type of claim and of the lack of wide international recognition of Australia's claim to the relevant part of Antarctica …
>
> In the light of the reasons of the majority of the Full Court, I cannot conclude that the practical difficulty (if not impossibility) of enforcement is a reason to withhold relief.[89]

Of course Japan does not recognise Australian EEZ jurisdiction off Antarctica and it has protested the injunction.

V. CONCLUSION

The legal difficulties outlined here are intriguing, especially for the light they shed on the relations between legal regimes: UNCLOS and the ATS, CCAMLR and the ICRW, etc. They indicate some of the weaknesses of a treaty system based on non-recognition. For example, one reason why the Madrid Protocol of 1991 triumphed over the Wellington Convention of 1988 (CRAMRA)[90]—apart from the merits of the anti-mining case—was that it was easier to get agreement on an outright prohibition than a system of permissions and controls.[91]

But the legal difficulties have not stood in the way of the continuing political success of the Antarctic Treaty and its system. For example the earlier assault on the exclusivity of the ATS, mounted through the United Nations, is now a thing of the past.[92] The ATS parties have managed to incorporate aspirants and even opponents into the system without—apparently—diluting it too much. If one may suspect that the absence of a compelling case for resource exploitation (certain fish stocks apart) has

[89] Ibid paras 51–53.
[90] (1988) 27 ILM 868.
[91] See Crawford and Rothwell, above n 5 at 71 and 86–87.
[92] See UNGA 60/47, 8 December 2005; PJ Beck, 'The United Nations and Antarctica, 2005: the end of the "Question of Antarctica"?' (2006) 42 *Polar Record* 217.

been a significant factor, so too has been the willingness of the Consultative Parties not to press their claims at the expense of the system as a whole: to rely, paradoxically, on the sovereign act of non-enforcement.

In the end one should be careful about the search for definitive solutions if these are not in truth available. International lawyers are used to the stability which is based on a definitive resolution of claims to sovereignty; they are fond of invoking it as a problem-solving device.[93] But it is a stability not available in Antarctica and one which the Treaty deliberately eschews.[94]

[93] See, eg *Territorial Dispute (Libya v Chad)* [1994] ICJ Rep 6, 37, paras 72–73.
[94] *cf* Crawford and Rothwell, above n 5 at 88.

11

Cross-border Family Mediation

KISCH BEEVERS

I. INTRODUCTION

> Mediation is essentially an adjunct of negotiation, but with the mediator as an active participant, authorised, and indeed expected, to advance fresh proposals and to interpret, as well as to transmit, each party's proposals to the other.[1]

I CAN STILL visualise Professor John Merrills standing at the front of the lecture theatre, hearing his carefully measured words as he lectured to our cohort of students on a variety of aspects of public international law and international dispute settlement. Although my own research took me into the world of private international law, in particular international family law and now into the world of cross-border family mediation, much of the wisdom contained in his book, *International Dispute Settlement*, is equally relevant to the solving of disputes in the private world. John Merrills writes that 'mediation can only be as effective as the parties wish it to be', but that:

> It would be quite wrong to think that a mediator is merely someone who lends authority to an agreement that is already virtually made. On the contrary, by facilitating the parties' dialogue, providing them with information and suggestions, identifying and exploring their aims and canvassing a range of possible solutions, mediation can play a vital role in moving them towards agreement.[2]

These are sentiments that are equally pertinent to mediation in family disputes, as we will see.

Family mediation has long been established in many countries as an alternative, or as complementary, to litigation,[3] the use of which has

[1] JG Merrills, *International Dispute Settlement*, 4th edn (Cambridge, Cambridge University Press, 2005) 28.
[2] Ibid 44.
[3] L Webley, A Review of the Literature on Family Mediation For England and Wales, Scotland, the Republic of Ireland, France and the United States, prepared for the Lord Chancellors's Advisory Committee on Legal Education and Conduct (London, Institute of

been developing in the UK since the 1970s,[4] and has attracted a wealth of literature from academics and practitioners alike.[5] Cross-border family mediation, in contrast, has only just caught the imagination of international players and has been very slow to develop. The main reason for this is the increased complexity of dealing with family law cases in an international setting. Mediators must deal with the problems associated with at least two languages, two cultures, and the geographical distance between the parties requiring at least one party to travel, thus incurring extra cost and causing delay. Coupled with this, any mediated settlement must bear in mind two different legal systems and be capable of enforcement in at least two States. The European Union and the Hague Conference on Private International Law have both recently turned their attention to cross-border mediation, and various national and international initiatives have begun to take shape dealing with situations where cross-border family mediation can make a difference. These initiatives have had to develop specific models of mediation in order to deal with the complexity of the barriers presented by its international context. However, before considering the specific issues relating to cross-border family mediation, the contribution of the EU and the Hague Conference to its regulation, and exploring two areas in which it is being used, it is worth briefly highlighting the fundamentals of family mediation theory and practice.

II. MEDIATION IN FAMILY DISPUTES

Family law mediation is both widespread and various in its models. Some of the earliest forms of family dispute resolution can be found in tribal custom,[6] while in the modern world family law mediation has become compulsory in some jurisdictions (either by law or court order),[7]

Advanced Legal Studies, 1998); R Pawlowski, 'Alternative Dispute Resolution for Hague Convention Child Custody Disputes' (2007) 45(2) *Family Court Review* 302.

4 For discussions of the history of family mediation see, eg: A Diduck and F Kaganas, *Family Law, Gender and the State*, 2nd edn (Portland, Hart Publishing, 2006) ch 11; S Roberts, 'Family Mediation in the New Millenium' in S Cretney (ed), *Family Law: Essays for the New Millennium* (Bristol, Jordan Publishing Ltd, 2000) 33–42; M Roberts, *Mediation in Family Disputes: principles of practice*, 2nd edn (Aldershot, Ashgate Publishing, 1997) ch 2; H Irving and M Benjamin, *Family Mediation: Contemporary Issues* (California, Sage Publications, 1995).

5 See, eg the very comprehensive bibliography contained in the Civil Mediation Council's website, www.civilmediation.org.

6 Still sometimes arranged by a specific community; see *P v P* [2006] EWHC 2410 (Fam), [2007] 2 FLR 439, where mediation was undertaken by three members of the Nepalese community in the UK.

7 Mandatory family mediation can be found in certain US and Australian jurisdictions as well as New Zealand; and court-ordered mediation in South Africa.

but purely voluntary in others.[8] The need to find the best solution for a particular family to take it from crisis to a workable future arrangement that can be accepted by both parties, while at the same time bearing in mind the need to reduce court costs and workload, has fuelled the development of family mediation in our modern societies. In the UK, family law mediation is thriving despite the failure of the Family Law Act 1996, which contained a range of mediation incentives.[9]

The vast majority of the published literature supports the premise that family mediation should be undertaken on a purely voluntary basis. A variety of reasons are put forward to support this approach, ranging from a theoretical stance that mediation is a consensual process, through to more practical arguments that, although our laws and courts could require the parties to mediate, they cannot force that mediation to succeed nor force the parties to sign an agreement, and that voluntary mediation is more likely to produce an agreed settlement.[10] As Dyson LJ has stated:

> If the court were to compel parties to enter into a mediation to which they objected, that would achieve nothing except to add to the cost to be borne by the parties, possibly postpone the time when the court determines the dispute and damage the perceived effectiveness of the ADR process.[11]

However, not every family dispute is suitable for mediation. If the dispute is one where there is a fundamental disagreement on the facts or the legal norms to be applied, then litigation will probably be more suitable.[12] Moreover, there is much literature on the question of whether mediation is suitable where there has been a history of domestic violence. There is always the risk of an imbalance of bargaining power and a continuance of the coercion by one party based on the fear of the other.[13] The Draft Code of Practice for Family Mediators issued by the Legal Aid Board in 1997 contains the instruction that family mediators must ensure that 'clients participate in mediation only if willing and not influenced by fear or violence or other harm to themselves or any child of the family …'.[14]

[8] The UK Government has declared that it does not intend 'to make mediation compulsory but will strongly promote its use', White Paper, *Parental Separation: Children's Needs and Parents' Responsibilities: Next Steps* (CM 6452, 2005).

[9] For a discussion of the failure of the Family Law Act 1996 including the mediation incentives see, eg: S Roberts, above n 4 at 38–40; A Diduck and F Kaganas, above n 4 at 420.

[10] For a range of responses on this issue, see the *Next Steps* White Paper, n 8 above.

[11] *Halsey v Milton Keynes General NHS Trust* [2004] EWCA Civ 576, [2004] 1 WLR 3002, at para 10.

[12] M Roberts, n 4 above, 129.

[13] See L Webley, n 2 above, para 5.4.

[14] Franchising Family Mediation Services: The Legal Aid Board's Approach to the Piloting of Franchise Contracts for the Provision of Family Mediation Services, (Legal Aid Board, February 1997).

It is argued that the 'welfare of the child' principle[15] is not paramount in family mediation itself; rather it serves to inform the framework in which mediation takes place.[16] However, it could also be argued that since one of the aims of mediation is to encourage parents to resolve their disputes by putting the needs of the children first, that the mediation process is consistent with the welfare principle. Research shows that as it is the prevalence of conflict between parents that most affects children,[17] and since mediation is designed to reduce such conflict, this must be in the best interests of the children. Certainly there is no absolute requirement to place the welfare of the child as paramount within the mediation sessions as there is in court litigated disputes. There is a general assumption that it is best for parents to make their own decisions in the best interests of the child, and for this reason the Children Act 1989 contains the 'no order principle',[18] whereby the courts can refuse to make an order if it considers that the parents are making suitable arrangements based on the welfare of the child.

However, in the family mediation process, there is no control other than the guidance of the mediator. Therefore, it is argued, it must always be possible for a mediated settlement to be in the best interests of the parents rather than the best interests of the children.[19] This potential problem is exacerbated by the fact that the child's views are very rarely canvassed during a mediated settlement,[20] although the UK Government is examining ways of developing more child-centred mediation practices.[21] Article 12 of the UN Convention on the Rights of Child 1989 requires States to ensure that a child who is capable of forming their own views is given the right to express those views freely, either directly or indirectly in a manner consistent with the procedure of national law. To this end, s 1(3)(a) of the Children Act 1989 states that courts must have regard to the ascertainable wishes and feelings of the child concerned, as do various international

[15] Children Act 1989 s 1(1).

[16] M Roberts, above n 4 at 29.

[17] See G Harrold and M Murch, 'Inter-parental conflict and children's adaptation to separation and divorce: theory, research and implications for family law, practice and policy' [2005] *Child and Family Law Quarterly* 185.

[18] Children Act 1989 s 1(5).

[19] A Diduck and F Kaganas, above n 4 at 439.

[20] Ibid; G Douglas M Murch L Scanlan and A Perry, 'Safeguarding Children's Welfare in Non-Contentious Divorce: Towards a New Conception of the Legal Process' [2000] *Modern Law Review* 177, 191; House of Commons Public Accounts Committee, Fifty-first Report, Conclusions and Recommendations No 7, www.publications.parliament.uk/pa/cm200607/cmselect/cmpubacc/396/39602.htm.

[21] 'HM Government, 'Parental Separation: Children's Needs and Parents' Responsibilities: Next Steps. Report of the Responses to Consultation and Agenda for Action' (Cm 6452, 2005) para 52.

instruments focussing on family law disputes.[22] Additionally, the UK College of Family Mediators encourages mediators to consider ways in which a child may be involved or consulted during the decision-making process.[23] However, to date, one of the main problems appears to be that mediators are not trained to deal with children directly and prefer to work purely with the parents.[24] This does not necessarily mean that the mediation is not child-centred—indeed the UK College also requires mediators to encourage parents to talk with and listen to their children—but where mediators do not directly consider the wishes of the child, there may be certain cases in which the parents' expression of the child's wishes do not conform with reality.[25]

So what qualities do mediators need to work in this delicate area of family law? According to Piper, the most important quality of a mediator is 'an eclectic and pragmatic frame of mind,'[26] and that '[u]nderstanding what is taking place during the course of mediation is … the mediators' main tool of their trade.'[27] Indeed, the mediator is seen as the manager of the parties' negotiations, steering them through the mediation process in such a way to facilitate discussion and ultimately resolve the dispute with an agreed settlement,[28] and it almost goes without saying that a mediator must be completely neutral, impartial and independent.[29] Family mediation in the UK is carried out by trained family mediators offered by a variety of court schemes and outside organisations, who may also be family lawyers, although this is not a necessary prerequisite. All providers of family mediators must be approved by the Family Mediation Council,[30] and those assisting in publicly funded mediation must be from a provider that has a contract with the Legal Services

[22] Hague Convention on the Civil Aspects of International Child Abduction Art 13 contains a possible defence to the return of the child if the child objects and is of an age and maturity to have the objections taken into account; Regulation 2201/2003 Art 11(2), going further, states that a child must be given the opportunity to be heard in child abduction proceedings but contains no similar provision for non-abduction family law disputes.

[23] UK College of Family Mediators, 'Children, Young People and Family Mediation: Policy and Practice Guidelines' (2002), www.ukcfm.co.uk.

[24] Ibid; Douglas et al, above n 20.

[25] G Harrold and M Murch, above n 17 at 199. See also M Roberts, 'Children and the Mediation Process' in UK College of Family Mediators, *Directory and Handbook 1998/9* (London, Sweet & Maxwell, 1988).

[26] C Piper, 'Norms and Negotiation in Mediation and Divorce' in M Freeman (ed), *Divorce: Where Next?* (Aldershot, Dartmouth Publishing, 1996) 195.

[27] Ibid 184.

[28] J Haynes, *The Fundamental of Family Mediation* (Horsmonden, Old Bailey Press, 1993) 28.

[29] UK College of Family Mediators, *Code of Practice for Family Mediators*, www.collegeofmediators.co.uk/Downloads/PoliciesStandards/tabid/365/Default.aspx.

[30] www.familymediationcouncil.org.uk.

Commission.[31] Trained mediators will be skilled in conflict management strategies and in the arts of communication, listening and evaluation, as well as possessing the ability to guide the mediation appropriately taking into account the wider issues, influences and legal backdrop. Whether or not the mediator needs to be legally trained will depend on the individual case. Many parents will have consulted solicitors previously and may be referred to mediation during the litigation process; in these cases they will already have been informed of the legal procedures and their legal rights. However, where a couple comes to mediation first to try to sort out their differences without going to court, a legally trained mediator would be preferable to ensure that the parties' rights are protected and that they are aware of the family law constraints within which a negotiated settlement should take place.

The National Audit Office found that between October 2004 and March 2006 only 20 per cent of legally aided family disputes had attempted mediation[32]; and based on their studies, the House of Commons Public Accounts Committee reported in 2007 that an estimated £10 million per year could be saved from the legal aid budget if only 14 per cent more cases went to mediation.[33] Not only is mediation cheaper, many judges advocate the use of family mediation to reduce court time,[34] court costs and the overall time taken to arrive at the dispute resolution.[35] Although these practical benefits are extremely important, the merit of family mediation must also been seen through the huge intangible benefits it brings to the parties, their children and various third parties. Mediation is a flexible, client-centred process using a 'holistic approach in an air of complete neutrality'.[36] Its intangible benefits are widely reported in the family mediation literature referenced in this chapter, and include the facilitation of better communication and understanding between the parties in a safe environment and improvement in their ongoing relationship through the development of constructive workable solutions to their dispute. The avoidance of litigation brings more than its practical benefits, for it reduces the conflict often attached to the adversarial process, and it

[31] The Legal Services Commission 2008, Strategy Document, www.legalservices.gov.uk/docs/cls_main/FamilyMediationStrategy_140808.pdf.pdf.

[32] National Audit Office, *Legal aid and mediation for people involved in family breakdown* 10, www.nao.org.uk/publications/nao_reports/06-07/0607256.pdf.

[33] Above n 20, para 3.

[34] Eg *S-M (Children)* [2004] EWCA Civ 1238, [9].

[35] See, eg: *Re H (A Child)* [2002] EWCA Civ 2005, [58] (Ward LJ); *Headicar v Headicar* [2004] EWCA Civ 1867, [2005] 2 FCR 1, [22] (Dame Butler-Sloss); *Moore v Moore* [2004] EWCA Civ 1243, [2005] 1 FLR 666, [22] (Thorpe LJ); *W v H* [2004] EWHC 526, [2006] 2 FLR 258, [18] (Munby J). See also the House of Commons Public Accounts Committee report, above n 20 at para 4.

[36] K Clarke, 'Lawyer Mediators: The Unsung Heroes of Family Dispute Resolution' [2008] *Family Law* 76.

is the level of exposure to conflict that causes greater or lesser harm to the children both in the short and long term.[37] The flexibility of the process also allows the needs and desires of third parties (such as grandparents) to be taken into account, so that an ongoing relationship can be maintained between the child and the extended family. Moreover, if mediation achieves an agreed settlement, then this settlement is perceived to have been achieved through a self-determinative process: a process that the parties entered into voluntarily, participated in and ultimately resolved without that resolution being imposed by the courts.

III. CROSS-BORDER FAMILY DISPUTES

There are now a number of cross-border family mediation initiatives that are taking shape around the world and, in particular, in Europe. This chapter considers the initiatives that affect the United Kingdom directly, with references where appropriate to further reading on initiatives being developed in other countries.

A. European Initiatives

The revised Brussels II Regulation[38] governs the private international law issues concerned with parental responsibility as between its Member States. Building on the success of the Hague Conference's development and use of a network of Central Authorities that work closely together behind the legal scenes, this Regulation includes the requirement that Central Authorities cooperate with each other, providing information and assistance, and 'facilitate agreement between holders of parental responsibility through mediation or other means'.[39] The Practice Guide[40] to the Regulation makes it clear that although Central Authorities may use other agencies to carry out such mediation, it is important that mediation is not used as a way to unduly delay any proceedings.[41] In this regard,

[37] PR Amato and JM Sobolewski, 'The effects of divorce and marital discord on adult children's psychological well-being' (2001) 66 *American Sociological Review* 900; EM Hetherington and J Kelly, *For better or for worse: divorce reconsidered* (New York, Norton, 2002); V King and JM Sobolewski, 'Nonresident fathers' contributions to adolescent well-being' (2006) 68 *Journal of Marriage and Family* 537.

[38] Council Regulation (EC) 2201/2003 of 27 November 2003 concerning jurisdiction and the recognition and enforcement of judgments in matrimonial matters and the matters of parental responsibility, repealing Regulation No 1347/2000; [2003] OJ L338/1.

[39] Ibid Art 55.

[40] For the 2005 updated version of the Practice Guide to the revised Brussels II Regulation, see http://ec.europa.eu/justice_home/doc_centre/civil/doc/parental_resp_ec_vdm_en.pdf.

[41] Ibid 44.

the Practice Guide is referring in particular to incidents of international parental child abduction where speed is of the essence and where the Regulation itself imposes a maximum six-week time limit for the determination of such applications.[42] However, the revised Brussels II Regulation does little in general to promote mediation since the combination of multiple grounds of jurisdiction and a *lis pendens* 'first past the post' rule means that each party may rush to litigate in the court of their choice rather than wait for the outcome of mediation.[43]

On 11 June 2008 the European Directive on certain aspects of mediation in civil and commercial matters came into force,[44] and Member States have three years in which to implement its provisions. The Directive applies to cross-border mediation only, although it does state that there is nothing to prevent its provisions being applied to domestic mediation as well.[45] The Directive applies to all Member States of the European Union with the exception of Denmark[46] and, in line with the European Council's[47] desire to encourage better access to justice within Europe, is designed to promote amicable settlement of disputes through mediation.[48]

For the purposes of the Directive, cross-border disputes are defined as being where one party is domiciled or habitually resident in a Member State other than that of any other party to the dispute.[49] However, the definition of domicile is the civil and commercial definition under Regulation 44/2001[50] rather than the family law definition of each country.[51] Mediation is defined as a process for reaching agreement, which is voluntary[52]; although the Directive also covers cross-border mediation that is compulsory under the national system as long as it does not preclude the parties having recourse to the judicial system.[53] The crux of the Directive is to promote mediation in the first place[54]; to provide the right for any court to direct the parties to a dispute to mediation; to promote

[42] Regulation 2201/2003, Art 11(3).

[43] *cf* Commission Staff Working Document, Annex to the proposal for a Council Regulation amending Regulation (EC) No 2201/2003 as regards jurisdiction and introducing rules concerning applicable law in matrimonial matters—Impact Assessment COM (06) 399 final, (Sec(2006) 950).

[44] Directive 2008/52/EC [2008] OJ L136/3.

[45] Ibid recital para 8.

[46] Ibid Art 1(3).

[47] Determined at the European Council meeting at Tampere in October 1999.

[48] Directive 2008/52/EC [2008] OJ L136/3, Art 1(1).

[49] Ibid art 2(1).

[50] Council Regulation (EC) 44/2001 of 22 December 2000 on jurisdiction and the recognition and enforcement of judgments in civil and commercial matters [2001] OJ L12/1.

[51] The English law on both types of domicile can be found in L Collins (ed), *Dicey, Morris and Collins on The Conflict of Laws*, 14th edn (London, Sweet & Maxwell, 2006).

[52] Directive 2008/52/EC [2008] OJ L136/3, Art 3(a).

[53] Ibid Art 5(2).

[54] Ibid Art 1(1).

the development of and adherence to codes of conduct for mediators ensuring that they are adequately trained and impartial[55]; to ensure confidentiality[56]; and to ensure that mediated settlements can become enforceable, and that enforceable settlements are recognised and enforced in other Member States.[57] There are, however, no provisions concerning the mediation process itself.

The provisions of the Directive are very general and do not provide any specific safeguard for cross-border family mediation as opposed to other civil and commercial mediation. However, one key provision for attempting to ensure the continued adherence to the mediated settlement is the requirement under Article 6 that agreements can be converted into enforceable instruments, and that these shall be recognised and declared enforceable in all other Member States (except Denmark) by virtue of Regulation 2201/2003, the revised Brussels II Regulation.[58] This means that, for the purposes of ensuring the agreement is enforced in another European jurisdiction, any mediated settlement, agreement or memorandum of understanding must be converted into an enforceable Consent Order that can be ratified by the courts. As we will see, this is an extremely important provision for cross-border mediation in the case of international parental abduction since it is crucial that the agreement be registered and enforced in the country of the child's habitual residence at the time of the Hague Convention application.[59]

The 2008 European Directive is the second of two specific European initiatives designed to promote and enhance alternative dispute resolution by way of mediation. The European Code of Conduct for Mediators,[60] drawn up by the Commission in conjunction with a group of stakeholders was launched at a European Commission Justice Directorate conference in July 2004. It contains a number of principles to which it is hoped mediators will voluntarily adhere to ensure competent and impartial mediated settlements. The Code is intended to apply to all types of mediation in civil and commercial matters and addresses issues of competence, impartiality, fairness of procedures, fees and confidentiality. The principles contained in the Code are in no way controversial, but provide a baseline of good practice to which mediators across Europe should adhere.

55 Ibid Art 4.
56 Ibid Art 7.
57 Ibid Art 6.
58 Enforcement by way of the Regulation is not spelt out in the articles of the Directive itself but mentioned specifically in paras 20 and 21 of the Recital.
59 See below n 61.
60 See http://ec.europa.eu/civiljustice/adr/adr_ec_code_conduct_en.pdf.

B. International Child Abduction: the Hague Convention

The Hague Convention on Child Abduction[61] provides for the semi-automatic return of children abducted from the country of their habitual residence by one parent in breach of rights of custody pertaining to either the other parent or an institution.[62] This highly successful Convention has been ratified by 80 States around the world,[63] and its provisions have been adopted and fortified by the EC revised Brussels II Regulation. In a nutshell, courts or administrative bodies of a receiving State must order the return of the child[64] unless one of the very limited grounds of defence have been made out: that the rights of custody were not being exercised at the time of the abduction[65]; that the child has been resident and settled in the receiving State for at least 12 months[66]; that the left-behind parent has consented or acquiesced to the removal or retention of the child in the new State[67]; that the return of the child would expose the child to a grave risk of physical or psychological harm or place the child in an intolerable situation[68]; or that the child is of an age and mature enough to express their wish not to return.[69] These defences to the return of the child provide the receiving court with the discretion only not to return the child[70]; the ultimate decision is made by balancing the defence, once it has successfully been made out, against the underlying principles of the Convention, being that it is generally contrary to the welfare of children to be abducted, and that the courts of the child's habitual residence are generally best placed to decide on the future upbringing of the child.[71]

The success of the Convention relies heavily on the operation of the Central Authorities appointed by each State to secure the return of wrongfully abducted children.[72] According to the Convention, one of the key duties of the Central Authorities is 'to secure the voluntary return

[61] Hague Convention of 25 October 1980 on the Civil Aspects of International Child Abduction.

[62] Ibid Art 3(a).

[63] See www.hcch.net/index_en.php?act=conventions.status&cid=24.

[64] Art 12.

[65] Art 3(b).

[66] Art 12.

[67] Art 13(a).

[68] Art 13(b).

[69] Art 13.

[70] *P v P (Minors) (Child Abduction)* [1992] 1 FLR 155; *N v N (Abduction: Art 13 Defence)* [1995] 1 FLR 107; *TB v JB (Abduction: Grave Risk of Harm)* [2001] 2 FLR 515.

[71] See generally: E Pérez-Vera, Explanatory Report of the Hague Convention on the Civil Aspects of International Child Abduction, *Actes et Documents* of the XIVth Session, Vol III, 1982, 426, paras 19–26; PR Beaumont and PE McEleavy, The Hague Convention on International Child Abduction (Oxford, Oxford University Press, 1999) 28–35.

[72] See Art 7, Hague Convention, for details of the responsibilities of Central Authorities.

of the child or to bring about an amicable resolution of the issues'[73]; and the explanatory report makes it clear[74] that some cases may be resolved without recourse to the courts, it being up the to Central Authorities to determine when such measures have failed. The Fifth Meeting of the Special Commission of 2006 to review the operation of the Hague Child Abduction Convention reiterated, within its conclusions and recommendations,[75] that Central Authorities should seek the voluntary return of the child wherever possible but this should not result in any undue delay in the return proceedings.[76] Having considered a report on the development of mediation and the extent to which it is being undertaken,[77] the Special Commission welcomed the mediation initiatives taking place in various Contracting States[78] and noted that the Permanent Bureau was looking at the possible inclusion of an instrument on cross-border family mediation in the future.[79]

Indeed in 2007, the Permanent Bureau of the Hague Conference published a Feasibility Study on Cross-Border Mediation in Family Matters[80] noting that

> [t]he divergent development of domestic mediation in family matters poses challenges for the development of international mediation, both in terms of legal issues such as confidentiality and enforceability and practical issues such as costs and accommodating different styles and structures of mediation.[81]

Pursuant to this, the Council on General Affairs and Policy of the Conference met in April 2008 and invited the Permanent Bureau to develop a Good Practice Guide for consideration at the Special Commission, likely to meet in 2011.

C. International Child Abduction: The Reunite Pilot Project

One of the initiatives considered by the Special Commission was a pilot scheme in the United Kingdom on mediation in child abduction

[73] Ibid Art 7(c).
[74] Para 92.
[75] www.hcch.net/upload/concl28sc5_e.pdf.
[76] Ibid para 1.3.1.
[77] S Vigers, Preliminary Document No 5 of October 2006 for the attention of the Fifth meeting of the Special Commission to review the operation of the Hague Convention of 25 October 1980 on the Civil Aspects of International Child Abduction (a copy of the report can be requested from secretariat@hcch.net).
[78] Para 1.3.2. *cf* Vigers, n 77 above; Pawlowski, 'Alternative Dispute Resolution for Hague Convention Child Custody Disputes' (2007) 45 *Family Court Review* 302.
[79] Para 1.3.3.
[80] See www.hcch.net/upload/wop/genaff_pd20e2007.pdf.
[81] Ibid 3.

cases, funded by The Nuffield Foundation and carried out by Reunite International Child Abduction Centre.[82] Reunite recognised that, in contrast to the norm when the Convention was first drawn up, the majority of abduction cases today feature the custodial parent as the abductor[83] and the left-behind parent seeking the return of the child not necessarily to take over the custodial role but to retain and possibly improve regular contact with the child. Therefore, it was perceived that mediation may be able to provide a way for the parties to settle their differences and make proper arrangements for the children acceptable to both, rather than fighting for their 'rights' in court. It was hoped that this in turn would not only reduce the cost of such cases, but also limit the potential damage to the child of continued conflict between the parents as they face further court battles upon the merits of the case once the return order has been implemented.

The objectives of the pilot scheme were threefold:

1. to establish how mediation could work in legal conformity with the principles of the Hague Convention;
2. to develop a mediation structure that would fit in practically with the procedural structure of an English Hague Convention case;
3. to test whether such a model would be effective in practice.[84]

The methodology employed by the study included safeguards to ensure that mediation only happened after a Hague Convention application had been made and that it did not prejudice the rights of the parties or the outcome of case should the mediation not be successful. Moreover, since the Hague Convention and the revised Brussels II Regulation call for abduction cases to be dealt with within a six-week period, the mediation was designed to run in parallel to the court proceedings and be completed within that time frame. Owing to the complexity of the issues and the very limited time frame in which the mediation was to take place, the mediation model used was one of co-mediation with two independent mediators who were able to undertake interchangeably the various roles that mediators adopt during the sessions. Indeed, one of the conclusions of the research states that it is 'essential that these high conflict cases should only be mediated in a co-mediation setting'.[85]

The aim of each mediation was to achieve a Memorandum of Understanding that could be converted into a 'Consent Order' to be

[82] See www.reunite.org/pages/mediation.asp. See: *Recent Developments at the Hague Conference on Private International Law* [2007] IFLJ 101 for a list of a number of other cross-border initiatives.

[83] It is estimated that these cases account for 60–70% of applications; see report above n 82 at 4.

[84] The Reunite Report, above n 82 at 6.

[85] Ibid 54.

approved by the court to which the Convention application had been made and also hopefully registered in the overseas jurisdiction, the country of habitual residence to which return of the child was initially sought. Until the Consent Order had been made, the Memorandum of Understanding would be simply as its words denote: a non-binding record of the parties' agreement at that time.

The target number of cases for this project was set at 20, and Reunite screened 80 referrals from solicitors and judges for their suitability to undertake mediation, finally taking on 28 of those cases, of which 75 per cent achieved a Memorandum of Understanding. The screening process ensured that both parties to each mediation were willing to mediate and were prepared to be in the same room as each other, and that the case would otherwise have been determined under the Hague Convention. Cases were also rejected where the level of violence was of concern and where the views of the parties were so polarised that there were no grounds upon which the mediation could hinge.

The mediation model devised needed to reflect the tight time-scale in which Hague Convention cases must be finalised, coupled with the additional costs of travel and hotel expenses for one of the parties. A maximum of three 3-hour sessions over two days were provided with the two co-mediators and an interpreter if required, the intensity of these sessions leading to one of the conclusions by all concerned that child abduction cases should always be co-mediated. Where the child involved was of an age that its views should be heard, a Children and Family Court Advisory Support Service (CAFCASS) report was ordered at screening stage. The parties were also able to refer to their lawyers for advice at any stage during the mediation.

The experience of all concerned in these mediations—the parties, solicitors and mediators—was that the scheme was a resounding success. The parties in the main reported that the mediation had the effect of reducing conflict and improving communication, thus helping towards the resolution of the dispute. The vast majority would consider using mediation again and would recommend it to others. Where dissatisfaction was expressed, the criticism was not of the mediation or of the mediators but of the attitude or conduct of the other party.[86] Every one of the solicitors who responded to Reunite's questionnaire commented that they would like to see mediation offered as good practice in cases of international parental child abduction.[87]

Cross-border family mediation confronts many additional challenges to the process of mediation due to the complexity and number of barriers to

[86] Ibid 22–28.
[87] Ibid 34, 38.

its success. This pilot study identifies many of these issues and thus is of great value to those promoting not only mediation in international parental child abduction cases, but in the broader cross-border family dispute.

i. Jurisdiction

The Reunite study identifies that the tangible outcome of mediation, in this case the Memorandum of Understanding, must bear in mind the legal norms and procedures of at least two legal systems. The difficulties involved in expecting an Order from one jurisdiction concerning the upbringing of a child to be respected and upheld in another have been discussed elsewhere,[88] but suffice to say that there is very little preventing a parent from attempting to vary the terms of custody or contact when the child is present in the other jurisdiction. For this reason, not only should the mediated settlement be the product of voluntary consensus, rather than be enforced by reason of the prevailing situation, but the result of that settlement, the ensuing Consent Order, should be capable of registration or ratification in the foreign jurisdiction. The Reunite scheme was careful to ensure that the Memorandum of Understanding was capable of being converted into a Consent Order by being 'sufficiently formed and sufficiently specific to avoid unnecessary future litigation'[89] and by requesting the party's overseas lawyer to arrange for the order to be registered or mirrored in the overseas jurisdiction.[90] However, it was identified that at least one of the Memoranda of Understanding had to be modified to ensure that the provisions were acceptable or enforceable in the other jurisdiction.[91] Unfortunately, there is no information in the Reunite report informing us of the outcome of such requests.

The new recognition and enforcement provisions of the 2008 European Directive on cross-border mediation will no doubt form an important part of the mediation process in ongoing international parental child abduction mediations. As explained above, the Directive provides that enforceable orders in one Member State shall be recognised and declared enforceable in all other Member States (with the exception of Denmark) by virtue of the revised Brussels II Regulation.

Once the Memorandum of Understanding has been translated into a Consent Order and ratified by the courts, the hope is that the child's

[88] McClean, 'International Child Abduction—some recent trends' [1997] *Child and Family Law Quarterly* 387; Reunite, 'The outcomes for children returned following an abduction' September 2003, www.reunite.org/pages/outcomes_research.asp; Beevers, 'Non-Convention Child Abduction—Consideration of Welfare and Undertakings' [2003/4] *Contemporary Issues in Law* 302.

[89] The Reunite Report, above n 81, 9.

[90] Ibid 11.

[91] Ibid 32.

relationship with the parties will stabilise and flourish. However, the nature of family life is such that the Consent Order can always be the subject of variation by the courts. Moreover, it is always a possibility that although agreement is reached during mediation, one of the parties decides not to abide by that agreement. The question then becomes to what extent does the mediated Consent Order bind the courts. The answer is that it does not. The English courts have held that the withdrawal of the Hague Convention proceedings does not amount to an adjudication, thereby allowing a further return application to be made should the Consent Order not be adhered to; and that the Consent Order itself does not amount to acquiescence to the original abduction, which would otherwise amount to a defence to the wrongful abduction.[92] This then allows the parties to argue their positions under the Hague Convention application without one party being able to depend on the broken mediated settlement to support their cause.

ii. Mediation issues

Although one of the strengths of the Hague Child Abduction Convention is that, except in certain situations, the abducted child is quickly returned to the country of habitual residence in order for the court there to decide on the future of the child in the light of all the evidence available to it, this does little to assist the family in terms of reducing conflict, cost and litigation. The availability of mediation once a Hague Convention application has been made means that the parties can address all the issues leading up to, as well as further to, the abduction. Rather than reaching an agreement as to whether the child should be returned or not, the Memoranda of Understanding are able to cover the whole panorama of the family's life, thus enabling the child to enjoy a positive relationship not only with the parents but also with the extended family. The settlements achieved by the Reunite mediators contained provisions not only for custody and access, but also included agreements over education, health and financial matters. Thus, a dispute that began with an abduction and an application for return can lead to a holistic agreed plan for the future of the divided family. This reduction in conflict and continued trauma to the child can seldom be achieved by the adversarial court system even outside the confines of the Hague Convention, no doubt one reason why Thorpe LJ has constantly been at pains to extol the virtues of a mediated settlement in such disputes.[93]

[92] *Re G (Abduction: Withdrawal of Proceedings, Acquiescence and Habitual Residence)* [2007] EWHC 2807 (Fam), [2008] 2 FLR 351.

[93] See, eg: *Re S (a child)* [2002] EWCA Civ 1941, [43]; *Re G (children) (foreign contact order: enforcement)* [2003] EWCA Civ 1607, [2004] WLR 521, [49]; *Re M (children)* [2004] EWCA Civ

An important issue to be considered when deciding whether or not to mediate is that of the existence of domestic violence, since the experience of most family law mediators and the opinion of most writers researching and publishing in the area of family law mediation appears to be that the existence of domestic violence in the parties' pre-mediation relationship is normally a counter-indicator to the wisdom of attempting mediation.[94] This position is not reflected to the same extent in the Reunite pilot scheme, although great care was taken to screen out cases where the degree of violence would make the case unsuitable for mediation. Where allegations of domestic violence were part of the background to the case, but the case was accepted for mediation, mediators reported initial nervousness, but that once the mediation commenced the victim parent felt safe.[95] However, in one case the feedback from a defence lawyer demonstrated fear that the other parent might have wielded excessive influence.[96]

In screening out cases where there is an allegation of domestic violence, it must always be remembered that one of the defences that an abducting parent can attempt to make out under the Hague Convention is that the return will place the child in a grave risk of physical or psychological harm.[97] Many of the cases where this defence is argued revolve around allegations of domestic violence towards the abducting parent, which, it is argued, puts the child in a grave risk of harm. The English courts have insisted on a very restrictive approach to this defence and repeatedly held that the grave risk of harm must be to the child and not just to the parent and that, even if the parent is a victim of domestic violence, that parent should resolve the issues in the country of habitual residence and not abduct the child to another country.[98] Therefore, realistically, it could be argued that the victim parent has nothing to lose but everything to gain by being subject to a safe environment where the best interests of the child can be discussed and a mediated settlement agreed, rather than being sent back to the country of the child's habitual residence to litigate

1574, [2004] 1 FLR 656; Thorpe LJ, 'The role of the judge in international mediation', www.era.int/web/en/resources/5_2341_5009_file_en.7092.pdf; Thorpe LJ, 'The case for judicial activism' (2007) 9 EUJLR 1.

[94] See above nn 13 and 14.

[95] The Reunite report, above n 82 at 48.

[96] Ibid 39.

[97] Hague Convention on international child abduction Art 13(b).

[98] *K v K (child abduction)* [1998] 3 FCR 207; *H (Children) (Child Abduction: Grave Risk)* [2003] EWCA Civ 355, [2003] 2 FLR 141; *Re W (Abduction: Domestic Violence)* [2004] EWHC 1247, [2004] 2 FLR 499; *Re HE (a child); Re W (A Child) (Conditions for Return)* [2004] EWCA Civ 1366, [2005] 1 FLR 727. See N Lowe and A Perry, 'International Child Abduction—the English Experience' (1999) 48 ICLQ 127.

in the hope that the undertakings[99] submitted to court by the other party will be respected.

iii. Mediators

The chosen model for the child abduction mediation was that of co-mediators because of the complexity of the issues and also the required speed of the mediation process. On reflection, all of the mediators involved in the scheme strongly advocated this model because of the complex, intense, urgent, volatile and emotional nature of this type of mediation. Moreover, every mediator involved in this pilot scheme reported that it was essential that they had specialist knowledge of international parental child abduction and the Hague Convention, although only 50 per cent thought that a specialist family law background was necessary, and only 50 per cent thought that legal expertise was necessary.

With regard to the gender of the mediators, although 50 per cent of the mediators advocated mixed gender mediation,[100] only a very small number of the parties thought that the sex of the mediator was of relevance.[101] However, it must be noted that very few of the participants represented cultures that are particularly distinct from our own; so that while gender did not figure importantly in this study, any cross-border family mediation should continue to identify its relevance prior to the mediation commencement.

Where requested by one of the parties, an interpreter was provided for the mediation proceedings. The mediators reported that the use of interpreters did extend the mediation time, but that in one case the interpreter was particularly helpful, 'almost becoming a third mediator'.[102] Although this comment appears on face value to be positive, it must be of concern that an interpreter becomes so involved in the mediation in view of the fact that all the mediators were of the opinion that at least specialist knowledge of child abduction and the Hague Convention is vital.

A number of the cases studied were found to be the cause of a delay of three or four weeks in the Hague Convention proceedings, these being due to a late decision to mediate or due to travel difficulties.[103] Although the time frame for determination of Hague Convention applications is six

[99] Eg, that the child will remain with the mother in residence provided for by the father, that the father will not remove the child, and that the father will withdraw criminal proceedings, etc. See above n 26.

[100] The Reunite Report, above n 82 at 43.

[101] Ibid 19–20.

[102] Ibid 49.

[103] Ibid 34. Delay is also reflected in the case law where mediation has proved unsuccessful and the court continues to hear the application for return; see, eg: *C v W* [2007] EWHC 1349 (Fam), [2007] 2 FLR 900.

weeks, and the additional mediation process can prejudice adherence to this requirement, it must be highlighted that a successfully mediated agreement avoids the delay in arriving at the ultimate decision on the upbringing of the child when the child has to be returned to the country of habitual residence for litigation to take place there.

Overall, the Reunite mediation pilot scheme has been held to be a resounding success.[104] Although more than 25 per cent of the mediated cases did not result in a Memorandum of Understanding, all parties to the mediation and their lawyers reported that this was not because of the mediation process nor because of the mediators, but simply because the parties were not open to mediation or believed in its benefits, or that the parties did not stick to the agreement reached. Reunite now continues to offer mediation in cases of international parental child abduction, focussing on the best interests of the child.

D. Mediated Contact in the Cross-Border, Cross-Cultural Setting

Outside the confines of legislation and international agreements, cross-border mediation can provide a successful avenue through which to explore dispute resolution between parents of different nationalities and cultures. The International Social Service (ISS) is an international non-governmental organisation dedicated to helping individuals and families with personal or social problems resulting from migration and international movement.[105] Within this international network, ISS UK provides a range of different social services to protect children who are subject to cross-border family difficulties and is involved in various family dispute resolution initiatives.

Although much of its work is within the public law arena, ISS UK does take on private law cases and is currently involved in mediating between parents of children who have been abducted to certain non Hague Convention countries. During the last 10 years ISS UK have been engaged in a specific project with Libya, mediating between mothers whose children have been abducted to Libya, and the fathers and other family members in Libya who have the effective care of the children. This type of mediation is very different from the classic style of mediation discussed above: the distance and expense involved, the risk of criminal charges, the reluctance or refusal of the fathers to travel to the UK, and the extreme differences in cultural expectation make the Reunite-style

[104] Preface to the Reunite Report, above n 82 at 3, per W Duncan, Deputy Secretary General of the Hague Conference on Private International Law.
[105] www.iss-ssi.org/.

mediation service an impossibility. However, mediation does take place and achieves results, even though such mediation is protracted and not as effective as the more classic format of mediation. Through taking a group of mothers on successive trips to Libya, ISS UK has managed to open and maintain lines of communication between the parties and to mediate contact between the mothers and their children. With the United Nations Convention on the Rights of the Child as the only legal basis for their intervention, ISS UK endeavours to seek and respect the views of the children where appropriate, some of those children now being in their 20s. To facilitate this mediated contact between mothers and their children, ISS UK now works in partnership with a leading Libyan charity. This charity also covers most, if not all, of the costs involved in this group of mothers visiting Libya, which means that many women with very limited means have the opportunity of seeing their children, something that, without the aid of this particular charity, they would not be able to do. The semi-official nature of these group visits creates a more positive environment in which the mediated contact can take place: the mothers feel relatively safe and the fathers feel that there is less likelihood of the children being removed from Libya.

Apart from the cultural barriers that need to be respected and overcome, and the problems with distance and cost, there is the issue of the language barrier. In effect, the success of these trips depends on the ability of at least one of the mediators to speak, to a high standard, the language of the other. As with the more classic form of mediation, there must always be doubt as to how accurate the views of each party is translated bearing in mind the nuances involved in the discussion of emotional issues.

However, the ISS UK Libyan project experience has been extremely good, with not one single case where contact did not take place. Indeed, one of the cases recently resulted in an award of custody to the mother, albeit through the litigation process rather than a mediated settlement. In the words of the ISS Senior Project Manager, the mediation process is all about 'building bridges and keeping them open'.[106]

IV. CONCLUSION

Throughout the world, domestic family law mediation has been judged to be widely successful, bringing benefits to not only the family members but also to the public purse. The limited amount of cross-border family mediation now taking place—although not without its problems—not

[106] The author would like to thank Marek Ganther of ISS UK for his comments and provision of an unpublished report on the Libyan project.

only replicates these benefits, but can be seen as providing a solution for family disputes where litigation simply does not work. Cross-border mediation will often mean cross-cultural mediation where differing underlying traditions, presumptions, beliefs and expectations need to be dealt with sympathetically.[107] The adversarial nature of the litigation process does not allow for these elements to be dealt with satisfactorily, leading to the perception of one winner and one loser. Even if a satisfactory solution can be found by the court, at least one party is bound to feel that they have 'lost', and there is no guarantee than any ensuing order will be recognised and enforced in the other country or countries represented by this international family.

One of the advantages of cross-border family mediation is that such alternative dispute resolution methods can be found in the problem-solving traditions of many ancient cultures. Indeed, it is central to the Koranic tradition and as such provides the crucial link between western and Islamic cultures that, to date, international legal conventions have failed to do. However, these benefits should not be overstated: the ISS experience shows us that although cross-border mediation can achieve incredible results in a particularly difficult international environment, these results are precarious in nature, depending on voluntary or persuaded compliance for continuing affect.

The Reunite pilot scheme tells us much about the wider issues of cross-border family mediation and demonstrates the additional complexities brought by the international backdrop to the dispute. Domestic family law mediation is set against the principles of domestic family law, whereas cross-border family mediation is set against the constraints of differing laws from at least two legal systems where laws regarding the custody of and contact with the children of the family can simply be incompatible.

On top of this, cross-border family mediation must deal with the problem of at least one of the parties not being a native speaker of the language of the mediation. Although an interpreter can assist, problems were perceived during the Reunite study: one of the parties can end up feeling marginalised from the process and doubting that their views are properly represented. The problem of language is also exacerbated by the differences in cultural expectations; for example, expectations based on gender. The way forward from both the experience of Reunite and ISS seems to be that of the co-mediation model, the mediators themselves reflecting linguistic and cultural backgrounds of the parties. Each party can then feel their views are being adequately represented, with each also being treated equally as an integral part of the process.

[107] *cf* SN Shah-Kazemi, 'Cross-Cultural Mediation: a critical view of the dynamics of culture in family disputes' (2000) 14 *International Journal of Law, Policy and the Family* 302.

Future cross-border family mediation initiatives must also take account of the additional cost and time involved as opposed to domestic family law mediation. At least one of the parties may have to travel, incurring considerable expense. Litigation may have to be adjourned for the mediation to be set up and the parties assembled, affecting, in particular, the time constraints imposed on child abduction disputes.[108] Moreover, such initiatives will also need to provide for the wishes of the child to be represented in accordance with the United Nations Convention on the Rights of the Child, a requirement that does not appear to have received the same priority in cross-border mediation as it has in many domestic family law mediation models. It has already been noted that the lack of proper consideration of the views of the children involved can result in a mediated settlement that represents the best interests of the parents rather than the best interests of the child.

One crucial difference between domestic and cross-border family mediation is the need for any settlement to be recognised and enforced in at least one other country. Whereas domestic family mediation is capable of standing on its own and respecting the 'no order' principle of the Children Act 1989, the settlement achieved through cross-border mediation will need to be converted into a legal instrument for subsequent recognition and enforcement to take place. This has been recognised in Article 6 of the European Directive on certain aspects of mediation in civil and commercial matters. The need to convert the voluntary mediated agreement into a binding legal order to secure its recognition can be seen to indirectly militate against the attractiveness of mediation as opposed to litigation, at least in Europe. This is because the basis of jurisdiction and, therefore, recognition and enforcement is the *lis pendens* first–past-the-post rule. Therefore, any future initiatives to be considered by the EU in particular will need to build in safeguards to ensure that a party who looks to mediation to resolve a dispute is not prejudiced by the other party who dashes to the court to apply for a court-imposed order.

Notwithstanding all of these difficult issues, cross-border family mediation has the important effect of reducing conflict in these complex and highly charged international family disputes, which not only enables the parties to move forward in their relationship with each other, but also provides a far better psychological environment in which their children can grow and thrive.[109]

[108] Both Art 11, Hague Convention on Child Abduction and Art 11(3), revised Brussels II Regulation require a decision within six weeks of the application for return being lodged.

[109] PR Amato and JM Sobolewski, above n 27; for an excellent review of the literature and research concerning potential psychological harm to children of divorce, albeit concentrating on the effects of residential mobility, see WG Austin, 'Relocation, Research and Forensic Evaluation' (2008) 46 Family Court Review 137 and 347.

Family law mediation is not always successful,[110] nor is its agreed settlement always upheld in its entirety by the courts.[111] In fact, it has been reported that it attracts less than a 50 per cent success rate overall,[112] and we have seen that the National Audit Office reported that only 20 per cent of legally aided family law clients attempt mediation. More positively, although based on only a small sample, the Reunite pilot study reported a 75 per cent success rate in terms of reaching a mediated settlement. So, cross-border family mediation is not the ultimate answer, or the only answer; but its results reported to date show that further initiatives are very worthwhile pursuing.

110 See, eg *Re J (children) (abduction: child's objections to return)* [2004] EWCA Civ 428, [2004] 2 FLR 64.

111 *Morgan v Hill* [2006] EWCA Civ 1602, [2007] 1 FLR 1480.

112 A Diduck and F Kaganas, above n 4 at 445.

Part 3

The Regional Dimension

12

Aspects of the African Court of Justice and Human Rights

GINO J NALDI*

I. INTRODUCTION

AFRICAN LEADERS MEETING in Libya in 1999 resolved to establish a new pan-African organisation to replace the wearied Organization of African Unity (OAU), the African Union (AU).[1] The AU was founded in the belief that current and future social, political and economic realities, both in Africa and globally, could only be effectively addressed by a dynamic and empowered body.[2] The Constitutive Act of the AU was adopted in July 2000, entering into force on 26 May 2001.[3] The official launch of the AU was effected in July 2002 in Durban, South Africa.[4]

An important innovation that signaled a welcome departure from the OAU's hesitation to put in place a judicial body is the fact that the Constitutive Act makes provision for a Court of Justice for the resolution

* I am indebted to Professor Konstantinos Magliveras, University of the Aegean. Any errors remain my own.

[1] Sirte Declaration of 9 September 1999, OAU Doc EAHG/Decl (IV) Rev 1, reproduced in (1999) 11 *African Journal of International and Comparative Law* 803.

[2] According to the OAU Secretary-General, '[The African leaders] certainly had in mind an organization that would provide a framework for enhanced cohesion, co-operation, integration and strengthened capacity to deal with the crises that face the African continent today', *Report of the Secretary General on the Implementation of the Sirte Decision on the African Union*, OAU Doc CM/2210 (LXXIV), para 26.

[3] The Constitutive Act is available at the AU's website, www.africa-union.org. Also reproduced in (2000) 12 *African Journal of International and Comparative Law* 629. See C Heyns, E Baimu and M Killander, 'The African Union' (2003) 46 *German Yearbook of International Law* 252; K Magliveras and G Naldi, 'The African Union—A New Dawn for Africa?' (2002) 51 ICLQ 415; C Packer and D Rukare, 'The New African Union and its Constitutive Act' (2002) 96 *American Journal of International Law* 365.

[4] *Durban Declaration in Tribute to the Organization of African Unity and on the Occasion of the Launching of the African Union*, AU Doc ASS/AU/Decl 2 (I), reproduced in (2002) 41 ILM 1029.

of inter-African disputes. Accordingly the Court of Justice is established as the principal judicial organ of the AU.[5] Beyond this the Constitutive Act itself is largely silent, referring crucial questions relating to the composition and functions of the Court of Justice to a future Protocol. The only indication given as to the competences of the Court of Justice is Article 26 of the Constitutive Act, indicating that it shall be seized of matters of interpretation arising from the Constitutive Act's application or implementation. The Protocol of the Court of Justice of the African Union was duly adopted on 11 July 2003.[6] The adjudicatory jurisdiction of the Court of Justice was to cover all disputes and applications envisaged in the Constitutive Act and in the Protocol of the Court of Justice relating to various categories of cases,[7] including the interpretation and application of the Constitutive Act, the interpretation, application or validity of AU treaties and all subsidiary legal instruments adopted within the framework of the AU, any question of international law, all acts, decisions, regulations and directives of the AU organs, all matters specifically provided for in other agreement/s that State parties may conclude among themselves or with the AU conferring jurisdiction on the Court of Justice, the existence of any fact, which, if established, would constitute a breach of an obligation owed to a State party or to the AU, and the nature or extent of the reparation to be made for the breach of an obligation. However, the Protocol of the Court of Justice was stillborn, as the AU decided that the Court of Justice should be merged with the African Court on Human and Peoples' Rights into one single judicial body.[8]

II. THE MERGER OF THE COURT OF JUSTICE AND THE AFRICAN COURT ON HUMAN AND PEOPLES' RIGHTS

The creation of an African Court on Human and Peoples' Rights was a development that appeared to signal that the OAU was serious about

[5] Constitutive Act Art 18. The Court of Justice is additionally listed as one of the principal organs of the AU, see Constitutive Act Art 5(1). See also Protocol of the Court of Justice of the African Union 2003 Art 2(2), www.africa-union.org. See K Magliveras and G Naldi, 'The African Court of Justice' (2006) 66 *Zeitschrift für ausländisches öffentliches Recht und Völkerrecht* 187.

[6] *Decision on the Protocol of the Court of Justice of the African Union*, AU Doc Assembly/AU/Dec.25 (II), based on the recommendations made by the Executive Council, *Decision on the Draft Protocol of the Court of Justice*, AU Doc Dec EX/CL/58 (III). It does not seem unkind to observe that the Protocol's substantive clauses have been heavily influenced by the Statute of the International Court of Justice (ICJ).

[7] Protocol Art 19.

[8] The Protocol on the Court of Justice never entered into force notwithstanding the fact that in 2007 the 15th instrument of ratification necessary for it to do so under Art 60 thereof was deposited.

solving an apparently intractable problem that embarrassed the whole continent. The Protocol on the Establishment of an African Court on Human and Peoples' Rights, adopted in 1998, came into force on 25 January 2004.[9] The African Court on Human and Peoples' Rights was to be the ultimate guarantor of human rights and peoples' rights in Africa as set out in the African Charter on Human and Peoples' Rights (African Charter), adopted by the OAU in 1981.[10] The task of promoting and protecting the rights enshrined in the African Charter was originally entrusted to the African Commission on Human and Peoples' Rights (African Commission),[11] a quasi-judicial organ with powers akin to those of the UN Human Rights Committee or the now defunct European Commission on Human Rights.[12] The failure to establish a human rights court was criticised on the basis that without such an organ human rights

[9] Upon ratification by 15 States, see Art 34(3), African Charter. At the time of writing it has been ratified by 25 States: Algeria, Burkina Faso, Burundi, Côte d'Ivoire, Comoros, Gabon, Gambia, Ghana, Kenya, Libya, Lesotho, Malawi, Mali, Mauritania, Mauritius, Mozambique, Niger, Nigeria, Rwanda, Senegal, South Africa, Tanzania, Togo, Tunisia and Uganda. For analysis, see F Viljoen, *International Human Rights Law in Africa* (Oxford, Oxford University Press, 2007) 418–75; J Harrington, 'The African Court on Human and Peoples' Rights', in MD Evans and R Murray (eds), *The African Charter on Human and Peoples' Rights: The System in Practice, 1986–2000* (Cambridge, Cambridge University Press, 2002) 305–34; N Krisch, 'The Establishment of an African Court on Human and Peoples' Rights' (1998) 58 *Zeitschrift fur auslandisches offentliches Recht und Volkerrecht* 713; G Naldi and K Magliveras, 'Reinforcing the African System of Human Rights: The Protocol on the Establishment of a Regional Court on Human and Peoples' Rights' (1998) 16 *Netherlands Quarterly on Human Rights* 431; NJ Udombana, 'Toward the African Court on Human and Peoples' Rights: Better Late than Never' (2000) 3 *Yale Human Rights and Development Law Journal* 45. For basic facts on the African Court on Human and Peoples' Rights, see www.aict-ctia.org/courts_conti/achpr/achpr_home.hmtl.

[10] See www.africa-union.org; (1982) 21 ILM 58. Entered into force on 21 October 1986. All the Member States of the AU have ratified the African Charter. See K Magliveras and G Naldi , *The African Union* (The Hague, Kluwer Law International, 2009) 155–99; F Viljoen, n 9 above, 235–53; UO Umozurike, *The African Charter on Human and Peoples' Rights* (The Hague, Martinus Nijhoff, 1997) 29–61. The African Charter has been described as 'modest in its objectives and flexible in its means': B Obinna Okere, 'The Protection of Human Rights in Africa and the African Charter on Human and Peoples' Rights: A Comparative Analysis with the European and American Systems' (1984) 6 *Human Rights Quarterly* 141 at 158. Other important human rights treaties are the African Charter on the Rights and Welfare of the Child 1990, and the Protocol to the African Charter on Human and Peoples' Rights on the Rights of Women in Africa 2003, www.africa-union.org. See K Magliveras and G Naldi, above n 10, 226–34; F Viljoen, *International Human Rights Law in Africa* 260–75; F Banda, 'Blazing a Trail: The African Protocol on Women's Rights Comes into Force' (2006) 50 *Journal of African Law* 72.

[11] African Charter Arts 30 and 45.

[12] On the African Commission's mandate, see K Magliveras and G Naldi, *The African Union* above n 19, 199–217; F Viljoen, *International Human Rights Law in Africa,* 216–19, 310–417; A Ankumah, *The African Commission on Human and Peoples' Rights: Practice and Procedure* (The Hague, Martinus Nijhoff, 1996) 20–110. On the European Commission on Human Rights see, JG Merrills and AH Robertson, *Human Rights in Europe,* 4th edn (Manchester, Manchester University Press, 2001) 271–87.

in Africa could never be adequately protected.[13] The African Commission was, for various reasons, perceived as too weak to undertake this role effectively.[14] The parlous state of human rights in much of Africa, often on a large scale, rendered opposition to a court untenable. The Protocol on the Establishment of an African Court on Human and Peoples' Rights was finally adopted by the OAU in 1998.[15]

However, in a decision that was initially greeted with dismay,[16] in July 2004 the AU resolved that the African Court on Human and Peoples' Rights and the Court of Justice should be merged.[17] This development may have been prompted on practical grounds,[18] including a desire for

[13] RM D'Sa, 'The African Charter on Human and Peoples' Rights: Problems and Prospects for Regional Action' (1981–83) 10 *Australian Yearbook of International* Law 101; R Gittleman, 'The African Charter on Human and Peoples' Rights: A Legal Analysis' (1982) 22 *Virginia Journal of International Law* 667.

[14] G Robertson, *Crimes Against Humanity: The Struggle for Global Justice* (London, Penguin, 1999) 58–59; KO Kufuor, 'Safeguarding Human Rights: A Critique of the African Commission on Human and Peoples' Rights' (1993) 18 *Africa Development* 65, 74; Z Motala, 'Human Rights in Africa: A Cultural, Ideological, and Legal Examination' (1989) 12 *Hastings International and Comparative Law Review* 373, 405; M wa Mutua, 'The African Human Rights System in Comparative Perspective' (1993) 3 *Review of the African Commission on Human and Peoples' Rights* 5, 11. However, it must be acknowledged that the African Commission has grown into its protective roles in recent years and has become a much more forceful defender of human and peoples' rights, see K Magliveras and G Naldi, above n 10, 199–217.

[15] Protocol to the African Charter on Human and Peoples' Rights on the Establishment of an African Court on Human and Peoples' Rights, adopted by the Assembly of Heads of State and Government, 34th Ordinary Session, Ouagadougou, Burkina Faso, 8–10 June 1998, www.africa-union.org. Note that mention in the Protocol to the OAU should now be taken to refer to the African Union.

[16] Thus Amnesty International criticised the decision on the ground that it undermined the effective functioning of the African Court on Human and Peoples' Rights (African Union: Assembly's decision should not undermine the African Court, http://web.amnesty.org/library/print/ENGIOR300202004). The African Commission itself expressed concern at the 'negative impact' that the decision could have on the establishment of an effective African Court on Human and Peoples' Rights, drawing attention to the different mandates and litigants of the two courts (Resolution on the Establishment of an Effective African Court on Human and Peoples' Rights, ACHPR/Res 76 (XXXVII) 05 (2005), www1.umn.edu/humanrts/africa/resolutions/rec81.html). See also F Viljoen and E Baimu, 'Courts for Africa: Considering the Co-Existence of the African Court on Human and Peoples' Rights and the African Court of Justice' (2004) 22 *Netherlands Quarterly on Human Rights* 241.

[17] Decision on the Seats of the African Union, Assembly/AU/Dec.45 (III), para 4 (2004); Decision on the Merger of the African Court on Human and Peoples' Rights and the Court of Justice of the African Union, Assembly/AU/Dec.83 (V). See F Viljoen, above n 9, 457–58; I Kane and AC Motala, 'The Creation of a New African Court of Justice and Human Rights' in MD Evans and R Murray (eds), *The African Charter on Human and Peoples' Rights: The System in Practice, 1986–2006*, 2nd edn (Cambridge, Cambridge University Press, 2008) 406, 409–13.

[18] According to the AU, the 'institutional merging of the two courts is aimed at integrating justice more concretely into the institutional mechanism of the African Union. It will also make it possible to bring together the competences of these two statutory organs of the AU': Press Release No 66/2008.

rationalisation,[19] and the potential problem of overlapping jurisdiction between the two courts.[20] A draft protocol on the merger of the two courts was submitted for consideration in 2006,[21] proposing the creation of a single Court composed of two sections,[22] a General Affairs Section and a Human Rights Section with jurisdiction over alleged violations of human rights.[23] Pending further development on the draft statute the AU nevertheless decided to allow the African Court on Human and Peoples' Rights to become operational.[24] Steps were therefore taken to make the African Court on Human and Peoples' Rights functional, and judges have been elected.[25] However, progress towards the merger was by now gaining impetus and at its summit in Sharm El-Sheikh, Egypt, in 2008 the AU Assembly took the momentous decision to adopt the Protocol on the Statute of the African Court of Justice and Human Rights (hereafter Protocol).[26] The Protocol replaces the Protocol on the African Court on Human and Peoples' Rights and the Protocol on the Court of Justice,[27] and merges the African Court on Human and Peoples' Rights and the Court of Justice into a single Court, the African Court of Justice and Human Rights.[28] A number of transitional arrangements regarding the African Court on Human and Peoples' Rights are made.[29]

[19] I Kane and AC Motala, above n 18, 416; NJ Udombana, 'An African Human Rights Court and an African Union Court: A Needful Duality or a Needless Duplication?' (2003) 28 *Brooklyn Journal of International Law* 811. According to Interights, the merger was motivated by the desire to ensure adequate funding for an effective court: see www.interights.org/AfricanSingleProtocolAdopted/index.htm.

[20] The African Court on Human and Peoples' Rights appears to have the capacity to pronounce on the Constitutive Act, given that the promotion and protection of human rights are stated as core principles and objectives, under Protocol on an African Court on Human and Peoples' Rights Art 3(1), whereas the African Court of Justice seemed to have jurisdiction over the African Charter on Human and Peoples' Rights under Protocol of the Court of Justice Art 18(1)(b).

[21] Draft Protocol on the Statute of the African Court of Justice and Human Rights, EX.CL/211 (VIII) Rev. 1. See F Viljoen, above n 9, 458; I Kane and AC Motala, above n 19, 406–40.

[22] Draft Statute of the African Court of Justice and Human Rights Art 16.

[23] Draft Statute of the African Court of Justice and Human Rights Arts 17(2) and 35.

[24] Assembly/AU/Dec 83 (V), para 3.

[25] See www.aict-ctia.org/courts_conti/achpr/achpr_bios.hmtl. See also Assembly/AU/Dec 202 (XI).

[26] Decision on the Single Legal Instrument on the Merger of the African Court on Human and Peoples' Rights and the African Court of Justice, Assembly/AU/Dec 196 (XI). The text of the Protocol is available at the AU's website, www.africa-union.org. 15 ratifications are required for it to enter into force: Protocol Art 9(1). There are none at the time of writing.

[27] Protocol Art 1.

[28] Protocol Art 2.

[29] Protocol Arts 4 and 5. Following the Protocol's entry into force, the Protocol on the African Court on Human and Peoples' Rights is to remain in force for a transitional period no longer than one year or any other period as determined by the Assembly: Protocol Art 7.

III. THE ESTABLISHMENT OF THE AFRICAN COURT OF JUSTICE AND HUMAN RIGHTS

It need hardly be articulated that the African Court of Justice and Human Rights is allocated a fundamental role in helping the AU achieve its objectives. It is now stated to be 'the main judicial organ of the African Union.'[30] The Statute of the African Court of Justice and Human Rights (the Statute) is annexed to the Protocol and constitutes an integral part thereof.[31] The Protocol effectively amends the Constitutive Act in that references to the Court of Justice in the Constitutive Act must henceforth be read as references to the African Court of Justice and Human Rights (the Court).[32] The roles of the African Court on Human and Peoples' Rights and the Court of Justice are essentially retained in that the former is replaced by a Human Rights Section and the latter by a General Affairs Section.[33] Yet one of the effects of the single instrument is that the distinctive identities of the two separate African Courts is diminished because both sections share features in common. Considered overall, it will become apparent that the Statute appears to have drawn inspiration from the Statute of the International Court of Justice. This chapter will focus particularly on the General Affairs Section of the Court.

The Statute proclaims that the seat of the Court is the same as that of the African Court on Human and Peoples' Rights but it may sit in another Member State if necessary with its consent.[34] The official and working languages of the Court are those of the AU.[35]

IV. THE COMPOSITION OF THE COURT

The Court of Justice consists of 16 judges,[36] who must be impartial and independent.[37] The Human Rights and General Affairs Sections are each composed of eight judges.[38] To be quorate the General Affairs Section must consist of six judges.[39] In the normal course of events cases will be

[30] Statute Art 2(1). See further n 5 above.

[31] Protocol Art 1.

[32] Protocol Art 3.

[33] Statute Art 16.

[34] Statute Art 25(1). The Court will therefore be based in Arusha, Tanzania, AU Press Release No 66/2008.

[35] Statute Art 32. See further, Constitutive Act Art 25.

[36] Statute Art 3(1). The Assembly may review the number of judges at the request of the Court, ibid.

[37] Ibid Art 4. See also Art 11(1) on the oath of office and ibid Arts 12 and 13.

[38] Ibid Art 16.

[39] Ibid Art 21(2). A quorum of nine judges is specified for the Full Court, Art 21(1), Statute.

heard by one of the Sections as appropriate but cases may be referred to the full Court if circumstances dictate.[40] Provision is made for the constitution of one or several chambers by the Sections.[41] The judges must be nationals of State parties, that is, nationals of a State that has ratified the Protocol,[42] but no two judges may be nationals of the same State.[43] Each State party may nominate up to two candidates, and in a progressive move, consideration must be given to adequate gender representation.[44] Article 4 of the Statute, which is virtually identical to Article 2 of the Statute of the ICJ, requires the judges to possess the appropriate qualifications required for appointment to the highest judicial offices or be jurists of recognised competence in international law.[45]

The procedure for the election of judges is set out in Article 7 of the Statute. The judges are elected by the Executive Council in a secret ballot, and appointed by the Assembly.[46] A two-thirds majority of the AU Member States is required, which is a significant hurdle.[47] This fact will give rise to non-State Parties being able to exercise a vote, an undesirable circumstance, and it is submitted that voting rights should have been restricted to State parties. The same procedure applies where vacancies result from death, resignation or removal from office.[48] Equitable gender representation in the election of the judges must be secured,[49] which demands that the candidatures of a certain number of women must survive the nomination process.[50] Africa's regions and its principal legal traditions, which must be interpreted to include the civil, Roman–Dutch, common, and Islamic legal systems, must also be represented on the Court.[51]

[40] Ibid Art 18.

[41] Ibid Art 19(1). *cf* Statute of the ICJ Art 26.

[42] Statute Art 3(1). *cf* Statute of the ICJ Art 2, where the nationality of the judges is not a consideration.

[43] Statute Art 3(2). *cf* Statute of the ICJ Art 3(1).

[44] Statute Art 5(2). See also Protocol on the African Court of Human and Peoples' Rights Art 14(3). The AU is committed to the promotion of gender equality, see Constitutive Act Art 4(l) and Protocol on Amendments to the Constitutive Act Art 3(i). There are two lists of candidates, one for each of the Sections, and States can choose the list on which their candidates are placed: Statute Art 6.

[45] But with the added proviso, in an implied reference to the Human Rights Section, that expertise in human rights law may also be required.

[46] Statute Art 7(1)–(2).

[47] Statute Art 7(2). See also para 3 thereof. See further Constitutive Act Art 9(h).

[48] Statute Art 10(3).

[49] Statute Art 7(5).

[50] Provided the policy is proportionate and based on objective and reasonable criteria and is neutral and specific to individual candidates. See Case No 943/2000 *Guido Jacobs v Belgium*, UN GAOR A/59/40, vol II, annex IX, s S (Human Rights Committee, 7 July 2004).

[51] Statute Art 7(4). Art 3(3) of the Statute states that where possible each geographical region of Africa is to represented by three judges except for the Western Region which will have four judges. *cf* Statute of the ICJ Art 9.

The judges are elected in an individual capacity, that is, they do not represent States or other agencies nor must they be under their control or direction.[52] They must therefore abstain from any pursuit that is incompatible with their independence or impartiality or the demands of their office.[53] This obligation accompanies the commitment to the independence of the bench which seeks to ensure that the judges are not subjected to inducements, pressure, influence, threats or other interference.[54] Judges are, of course, under a general duty to consider all cases impartially.[55] The corresponding obligation on the Court to act impartially, fairly and justly is expressly spelt out in Article 12(2) of the Statute. The Statute seeks to avoid conflicts of interest by requiring the recusal of a judge who has had previous involvement with a case.[56] In fact, in order to avoid any semblance of partiality, a judge who is a national of a State that is a party to a case is not permitted to hear the case.[57] Not only is this a departure from accepted international practice but it does not appear to be reconcilable with the assertion of the judges' independence.[58] No provision is made for replacing a judge in such circumstances with an interim or substitute judge.

In fact, in a departure from usual practice, the Protocol makes no provision for the appointment of judges *ad hoc*. This is an obvious difference from the ICJ.[59] However, the fact that a judge who is a national of a State party to a case cannot hear that case would appear to obviate the need for *ad hoc* judges, and consequently the omission may be justified on this ground.

The judges serve for six years and may be re-elected for one further period.[60] The President and Vice-President are elected by the Court for a period of three years and are eligible for re-election for one further period.[61] Vacancies may arise from death, resignation or removal from office.[62] In such circumstances, another judge is elected to complete the

52 Statute Art 12(3).

53 Ibid Art 13. *cf* Statute of the ICJ Art 16(1).

54 Statute Art 12(1). See also ibid Art 4.

55 See Statute on the oath of office Art 11(1).

56 Statute Art 14(1). Additionally, if the President is of the view that a judge should not participate in a case that judge, with the agreement of the Court, will be excluded from the case: Statute Art 14(2). *cf* Statute of the ICJ Art 17(2).

57 Statute art 14(3).

58 *cf* Statute of the ICJ Art 31(1), which provides that in such circumstances the judge retains the right to in the case. However, see further Rules of the ICJ Art 32(1), www.icj-cij.org.

59 *cf* Statute of the ICJ Art 31(2)–(3).

60 Statute Art 8(1). The elections are held on a staggered basis: Statute Art 8(1). The judges of the ICJ are elected for a period of nine years and may be re-elected and there are no limits on their re-election: Statute of the ICJ Art 13(1).

61 Protocol Art 22(1).

62 Statute Arts 9 and 10(1).

predecessor's term of office.[63] A judge may be suspended or removed from office when two-thirds of the other members of the Court are of the view that s/he no longer fulfils the requirements of office.[64] However, the Court's recommendation must then be accepted by the Assembly, which has the final say.[65] The Protocol does not expressly address the question of a judge whose term of office expires while hearing a case.[66]

V. THE COMPETENCE OF THE COURT

It has been noted that the Court is composed of two Sections; a General Affairs Section and a Human Rights Section.[67] The General Affairs Section is competent to hear all cases except for those involving human and peoples' rights,[68] which is expressly reserved for the Human Rights Section.[69] However, any case may be referred to the Full Court.[70] Although no guidance is provided as to when a referral from the General Affairs Section may be considered appropriate this could happen where a particularly complex point of law is at issue or where sensitive matters of high politics and diplomacy are at stake.

The central question of who has standing to submit cases to the Court, although in the guise of the General Affairs Section, is determined by Article 29 of the Statute.[71] Three groups are listed: all State parties to the Protocol; the Assembly, the Parliament[72] and any other AU organ authorised by the Assembly; and staff cases on appeal. The reference to 'other organs of the Union' in the second indent of the provision may include

[63] Statute Art 8(3).

[64] Statute Art 9(2). *cf* Statute of the ICJ Art 18(1), which requires the unanimous opinion of the other judges.

[65] Statute Art 9(4).

[66] *cf* Statute of the ICJ Art 13(3).

[67] Statute Art 16, .

[68] Ibid Art 17(1).

[69] Ibid Art 17(2).

[70] Ibid Art 18.

[71] Entities'eligibility to submit cases to the Human Rights Section alleging violations of human rights is governed by Art 30 of the Statute. According to Art 33(1) of the Statute, disputes are submitted to the General Affairs Section by means of a written application to the Registrar, indicating the subject of the dispute, the applicable law and the basis of jurisdiction.

[72] According to Protocol to the Treaty Establishing the African Economic Community Relating to the Pan-African Parliament 2001 Art 2(2), www.africa-union.org, which entered into force on 27 November 2003, the role of the Pan-African Parliament is to represent the peoples of Africa, and in accordance with Constitutive Act Art 17(1), to ensure the full participation of African peoples in the development and economic integration of the Continent. The Pan-African Parliament's powers are for now consultative and advisory rather than legislative although in time it is expected to evolve full legislative powers, Protocol Relating to the Pan-African Parliament Arts 2(3) and 11. See K Magliveras and G Naldi, above n 10, 110–16.

the Executive Council, the Commission, and Peace and Security Council. The African Commission and the African Committee on the Rights and Welfare of the Child are specifically excluded since they have standing under Article 30 of the Statute.[73]

Article 29(2) of the Statute makes it plain that non-AU Member States are not allowed to submit cases to the Court. Neither does the Court have jurisdiction over disputes involving AU Member States that have not ratified the Protocol. It is therefore evident that the Court only has jurisdiction over those States that have expressly accepted its jurisdiction. Moreover, its jurisdiction is not compulsory over AU Member States by mere virtue of membership of the organisation but States must take the deliberate step of signing up to the Protocol.[74] But what should be noted is that once the Protocol has been ratified, State parties are immediately subject to the jurisdiction of the court and do not need to provide express consent for each and every dispute arising: in other words, jurisdiction is compulsory for State parties.[75] There is one important exception, however. The standing of individuals and NGOs before the Human Rights Section is subject to the condition set out in Article 8(3) of the Protocol, the substantive section of which states that, 'Any Member State may … make a declaration accepting the competence of the Court to receive cases under Article 30(f) [of the Statute] involving a State which has not made such a declaration'. The Section's jurisdiction to receive petitions from these complainants is thus made contingent upon States making a separate declaration recognising its competence in this particular area. It is likely that in time the Court will become operational but with jurisdiction over a limited number of States. This situation may be considered unsuitable for an organisation such as the AU which has embarked on a journey towards economic and political union since such a goal cannot be reasonably realised without a large degree of harmonisation and common purpose, and it might have been preferable for the Court to have been conferred automatic jurisdiction over AU Member States. However, the possible undesirable consequences of such a scenario are partially mitigated by the fact that the decisions of the Court on the interpretation and application of the Constitutive Act are binding on all the Member States of the AU even if they have not accepted the Protocol.[76]

[73] Neither are they AU organs.

[74] While all UN Member States are *ipso facto* parties to the Statute of the ICJ under UN Charter Art 93(1), acceptance of the ICJ's compulsory jurisdiction is dependent on a declaration to that effect pursuant to Statute of the ICJ Art 36(2). The AU departs significantly from the European Community in this respect since the jurisdiction of the European Court of Justice is an integral aspect of membership of the EC.

[75] This conclusion is based on the combined effect of Protocol Art 8(1) and Statute Arts 28 and 29.

[76] Statute Art 50(3).

Although Article 29(2) of the Statute is clear, the possibility of a challenge to the Court's jurisdiction cannot be ruled out. The ICJ makes provision for preliminary objections in its Rules.[77] It is therefore curious that the crucial question as to the competence of the Court to determine its jurisdiction should it be disputed is not explicitly addressed. Such a power is exercised by other comparable tribunals[78] but a provision to this effect was dropped from the final version of the Protocol.[79] Since this authority corresponds to a fundamental principle of international law, namely, 'the inherent power of a tribunal to interpret the text establishing its jurisdiction',[80] it seems likely that the Court will assert this capacity.

Article 28 of the Statute stipulates that the jurisdiction of the Court covers all cases and legal disputes relating to eight categories of cases. While this provision is similar to Article 36(2) of the Statute of the ICJ, the former is broader in scope than the latter and reflects an African perspective. First, the jurisdiction of the Court covers the interpretation and application of the Constitutive Act.[81] Secondly, the interpretation, application or validity of AU treaties and all subsidiary legal instruments adopted within the framework of the AU/OAU.[82] This competence is rational given that the Constitutive Act is the 'constitution' of the AU while the other provision confers upon the Court the power of judicial review over AU/OAU documents. The term 'Union treaties' encompasses a wide range of treaties including, inter alia, the Convention on Refugee Problems in Africa 1969, the Convention on the Elimination of Mercenarism in Africa 1977, the Treaty Establishing the African Economic Community 1991, the Convention on the Prevention and Combating of Terrorism 1999, the Convention on Preventing and Combating Corruption 2003,[83] and the Protocols to the Constitutive Act relating to the function and competencies of the AU organs.[84] The meaning of the term 'subsidiary legal instruments' is unclear. It does not appear to be intended to refer to the Protocols since these form an integral part of the Constitutive Act, but it certainly cannot mean the decisions taken by AU organs as these are the express subject of the fifth category.

[77] Rule 79, ICJ, and Rule 36, Inter-American Court of Human Rights.

[78] See Statute of the ICJ Art 36(6) and Protocol on the African Court of Human and Peoples' Rights Art 3(2).

[79] I Kane and AC Motala, 'The Creation of a New African Court of Justice and Human Rights' in MD Evans and R Murray (eds), *The African Charter on Human and Peoples' Rights: The System in Practice, 1986–2006*, 2nd edn (Cambridge, Cambridge University Press, 2008) 406, 428.

[80] See Judge Lauterpacht's Separate Opinion in the *Norwegian Loans Case (France v Norway) (Judgment)* [1957] ICJ Rep 9, 34.

[81] Statute Art 28(a).

[82] Ibid Art 28(b).

[83] The texts of all these treaties are available at www.africa-union.org.

[84] For example, the Protocol relating to the Pan-African Parliament 2001, and the Protocol establishing the Peace and Security Council 2002, www.africa-union.org.

The third category is especially relevant to the Human Rights Section, the interpretation and application of the African Charter, the African Charter on the Rights and Welfare of the Child 1990, the Protocol on the Rights of Women 2003 or any legal instrument relating to human rights ratified by the States Parties concerned.[85] The inclusion of 'any other legal instrument relating to human rights' is noteworthy because the Court has potentially been granted jurisdiction to pronounce on UN treaties such as the International Covenants on Human Rights, the Convention on the Elimination of Discrimination Against Women, but also the treaties of African sub-regional organisations such as the Economic Community of West African States (ECOWAS), and the Southern African Development Community (SADC), which contain commitments to human rights.[86]

The fourth category covers any question of international law.[87] The inclusion of this category in the Statute may perhaps be questioned in view of the ICJ's role as the principal judicial organ of the United Nations. The primary responsibility for determining questions of international law should lie with the ICJ, which is uniquely placed to examine such issues. In recent years, fears have been expressed that the proliferation of international judicial bodies could lead to the fragmentation of international law.[88] It is possible to speculate whether the drafters of the Statute intended to establish an alternative forum to the ICJ for African States or whether they merely intended to ensure that the Court of Justice would have the specialised jurisdiction to consider questions of international law. Of course, the Court, as any other institutionalised judicial body, should have the right to determine international law issues on a case-by-case basis.[89] It would be undesirable for the Court to have to decline

[85] Statute Art 28(c).

[86] See Revised Treaty on the Economic Community for West African States 1993 Art 4(g), www.ecowas.int, reprinted in (1996) 35 ILM 660, and *Hadijatou Mani Koraou v Republic of Niger*, Judgment No ECW/CCJ/JUD/06/08 (27 October 2008), paras 41–42; Treaty on the Southern African Development Community 1992 Art 4(c), as amended 2001, www.sadc.int, reprinted in (1993) 32 ILM 116, and Case No 2/2007 *Mike Campbell (Pvt) Ltd et al v The Republic of Zimbabwe*, SADC (T) (November 2008), www.saflii.org/sa/cases/SADCT/2008/2.pdf. This had been the experience of the American human rights system, see *'Other Treaties' Subject to the Consultative Jurisdiction of the Court (Art. 64 of the American Convention on Human Rights)* (Advisory Opinion) [1982] (Ser A), No 1; *Right to Information on Consular Assistance Within the Framework of the Guarantees of Legal Due Process* (Advisory Opinion) [1999] (Ser A), No 16. See further, Pasqualucci, *The Practice and Procedure of the Inter-American Court of Human Rights* 56–57.

[87] Statute Art 28(d).

[88] See, eg G Guillaume, 'The Future of International Judicial Institutions' (1995) 44 ICLQ 848; CPR Romano, 'The Proliferation of International Judicial Bodies: The Pieces of the Puzzle' (1999) 31 *New York Journal of International Law and Policy* 709.

[89] For example, the ECJ does not have a specific mandate to deal with matters of international law but may do so if they derive from an infringement of the EC Treaty; see L Neville Brown and T Kennedy, *The Court of Justice of the European Communities*, 5th edn (London, Sweet & Maxwell, 2000) 112–13.

jurisdiction because it had not been given the explicit mandate to rule on matters of international law. The fifth category specifies all acts, decisions, regulations and directives of the AU organs.[90] It would seem that the Court has been given the authority to entertain requests for judicial review[91] questioning the validity, interpretation and the effects of application of such measures. There is no suggestion that the jurisdiction of the Court is limited to reviewing legally binding measures only.[92] However, it is not clear whether the Court's decisions in such cases are purely of a declaratory nature or whether it can actually annul a measure.[93]

The sixth condition refers to compromissory clauses,[94] stipulating all matters specifically provided for in other agreement/s that State parties may conclude among themselves or with the AU and which confer jurisdiction on the Court.[95] An example of such a treaty is the Non-Aggression and Common Defence Pact of the African Union 2005, Article 16 thereof stating that contracting parties are under the obligation to refer all disputes over its interpretation, implementation and validity to the Court.[96]

The seventh category refers to the existence of any fact, which, if established, would constitute a breach of an obligation owed to a State party or to the AU.[97] This provision is capable of bestowing upon the Court a wide jurisdiction. The difficulty that may arise in this context is the fact that the Court will share this competence with other AU organs. Both the Assembly and the Peace and Security Council have the authority to impose sanctions on Member States for breaches of certain fundamental obligations of AU law.[98] However, unlike the UN context, it will be recalled that Article 28(e) of the Protocol confers upon the Court powers of judicial review.[99] Furthermore, if we choose to be guided by the ICJ's

[90] Statute Art 28(e).

[91] *cf* EC Treaty Art 230.

[92] The ECJ has decided that it possesses the capacity to review non-binding measures, Case C-322/88 *Grimaldi v Fonds des Maladies Professionelles* [1989] ECR 4407.

[93] *cf* EC Treaty Art 231.

[94] *cf* Statute of the ICJ Art 37.

[95] Statute Art 28(f).

[96] Available at www.africa-union.org.

[97] Statute Art 28(g). *cf* Statute of the ICJ Art 36(2)(c), referring to 'a breach of an international obligation'.

[98] See: Constitutive Act Art 23(1), authorising the Assembly to impose sanctions on a Member State for defaulting in its contributions; Constitutive Act Art 23(2), for failure to comply with AU decisions and policies; and Constitutive Act Art 30, which prevents governments coming to power through unconstitutional means to participate in AU activities. In relation to the latter scenario, Protocol of the Peace and Security Council Art 7(1)(g) authorises the Peace and Security Council, in conjunction with the Comission's Chairperson, to institute sanctions. See also African Charter on Democracy, Elections and Governance 2007 Art 25, unratified.

[99] Compare *Legal Consequences for States of the Continued Presence of South Africa in Namibia (South West Africa) notwithstanding Security Council Resolution 276* [1971] ICJ Rep 16 and *Questions of Interpretation and Application of the 1971 Montreal Convention arising from the Aerial Incident at Lockerbie (Provisional Measures)* [1992] ICJ Rep 3.

practice, it is evident that the ICJ does not decline jurisdiction simply because other UN organs are considering other aspects of a case.[100]

The final category bestows upon the Court competence to determine the nature or extent of the reparation to be made for the breach of an obligation.[101] This provision enables the Court to grant remedies which should extend to damages or other forms of compensation.

It is unfortunate that the Statute fails to specify in explicit terms whether inter-State cases are permissible, whether AU organs can institute proceedings against States and vice versa, or whether one AU organ can bring an action against another AU organ. It is likely that the Court will find that the Statute does indeed provide for these different bases of jurisdiction but it would have been better to have had them enumerated for the removal of doubt.

It should be observed that, while Article 28 of the Statute states that, 'The Court shall have jurisdiction over … all legal disputes submitted to it', Article 29(1) of the Statute says that entities can submit cases to the Court 'on any *issue or* dispute provided for in Article 28' (emphasis added). While the word 'dispute' has a technical meaning in international law[102] it is not clear whether the different form of words used in Article 29(1) of the Statute is intended to make a substantive difference by allowing the petitioners the capacity to submit to the Court questions of law other than disputes and without invoking the Court's Advisory Jurisdiction, or whether this is an infelicitous use of language. The ICJ has definitely expressed the view that a dispute is a prerequisite for exercising its judicial function[103] and it will not entertain cases where a dispute no longer exists.[104]

An important matter that is omitted from the Protocol and Statute is the question of reservations. It appears that agreement on this issue could not be reached at the drafting stage.[105] By way of contrast, acceptance of the ICJ's jurisdiction under Article 36(2) of its Statute, the optional clause, is very often subject to conditions.[106] In accordance with the rules of general international law silence on this issue allows States to enter reservations

[100] See, eg *Legal Consequences of the Construction of a Wall in Occupied Palestinian Territory Case* [2004] ICJ Rep 134.

[101] Statute Art 28(h). *cf* Statute of the ICJ Art 36(2)(d). The ICJ has awarded damages in a number of cases: see MN Shaw, *International Law*, 6th edn (Cambridge, Cambridge University Press, 2008) 1101–04.

[102] An international dispute has been defined as 'a disagreement on a point of law or fact, a conflict of legal views or of interests', *Mavrommatis Palestine Concessions Case* (1924) 2 AD 27.

[103] *Nuclear Tests Cases* [1974] ICJ Rep 253, 270–71.

[104] Ibid 271.

[105] I Kane and AC Motala, above n 17, 423–24.

[106] See generally, JG Merrills, 'The Optional Clause Today' (1979) 50 BYIL 87; JG Merrills, 'The Optional Clause Revisited' (1993) 64 *British Yearbook of International Law* 197.

on condition that the reservations are not incompatible with the object and purpose of the treaty in conformity with Article 19(c) of the Vienna Convention on the Law of Treaties 1969. Answers will be forthcoming only if States enter reservations when ratifying the Protocol, and only if the Court is called upon to address this question.

VI. SOURCES OF LAW

Article 31(1) of the Statute sets out in descending order the applicable law which the Court must have regard to in determining the cases before it:

(a) The Constitutive Act;
(b) International treaties, general or particular, ratified by the contesting States;
(c) International custom, as evidence of a general practice accepted as law;
(d) General principles of law recognised either universally or by African States;
(e) As subsidiary means for the determination of the rules of law, judicial decisions[107] and the writings of the most highly qualified publicists of various nations as well as the regulations, directives and decisions of the AU; and
(f) Any other law relevant to the case.

The Court has additionally the power to decide a case *ex aequo et bono* if the parties agree.[108]

It will also be observed that this clause is very similar to Article 38(1)–(2) of the Statute of the ICJ. In keeping with the generally accepted view that Article 38(1) of the Statute of the ICJ does not enumerate a formal hierarchy of sources, although in practice they may be applied sequentially,[109] the same may be said of Article 31(1) of the Statute, save for the obvious 'subsidiary means' listed in sub-paragraph (e). Some differences may be observed, however, reflecting the Statute's regional setting in light of Article 28 of the Statute. Thus, as has been previously stated, the Court must have regard to the Constitutive Act. This is hardly surprising in view of the fact that the Constitutive Act is the constitutional document of the AU. Again, the reference to international treaties in sub-paragraph (b) must necessarily encompass all OAU/AU treaties, for example, the

[107] It is clearly stated that that judicial decisions have no binding force except as between the parties to a particular case in accordance with Statute Art 46(1).

[108] Statute Art 31(2).

[109] I Brownlie, *Principles of Public International Law*, 6th edn (Oxford, Oxford University Press, 2003) 5.

Convention on Refugees, the African Charter, and the Protocol on the Rights of Women.[110] The language of this provision differs from its analogous provision in the Statute of the ICJ by referring to 'treaties ... ratified by the contesting States.' However, the linguistic difference is probably of little consequence as it is a basic rule of international law that a State is not bound by a treaty it has not ratified.[111] Significantly, given the context, account should also be taken of regional customary law. In light of the reference to general principles of law, the development of such principles by the Court must be contemplated.[112] Consequently, whether or not the reference is to general principles of international law or of municipal law accepted in different parts of Africa, included in such principles could be a right to development[113] and second and third generation human rights.[114] That the decisions of the AU may also be taken into account if appropriate appears to be an eminently sensible step in this context as they could assist the Court in the clarification of any dispute but it could also be interpreted as an acknowledgement of the norm generating possibilities of soft law.[115] Finally, the reference in sub-paragraph (f) to any other relevant law should avoid any possibility of *non-liquet*. In light of the evolution of international law since the Statute of the ICJ was adopted in 1945 it may seem curious that the AU omitted any express reference to the concept of *jus cogens*.

VII. PROVISIONAL MEASURES

Article 35(1) of the Statute empowers the Court to indicate provisional, or interim, measures of protection 'on its own motion or on application by the parties ... if it considers that circumstances so require ... which

[110] The texts of these treaties are available at www.africa-union.org.

[111] Vienna Convention on the Law of Treaties 1969 Art 34.

[112] On the use of general principles by the World Court see Shaw, *International Law*, 98–109; Sir Hersch Lauterpacht, *The Development of International Law by the International Court of Justice* (Cambridge, Cambridge University Press, reprint, 1996) 158–72.

[113] Such a right has been asserted by the African Commission, see, eg *The Social and Economic Rights Action Center and the Center for Economic and Social Rights v Nigeria*, Communication No 155/96, Fifteenth Annual Activity Report 2001–2002; *Bissangou v Republic of Congo*, Communication No 253/2002, Twenty-first Annual Activity Report 2005–2006. See further, K Magliveras and G Naldi, above n 9, 196–97; R Murray, *Human Rights in Africa: From the OAU to the African Union* (Cambridge, Cambridge University Press, 2004) 240–41.

[114] *The Social and Economic Rights Action Center and the Center for Economic and Social Rights v Nigeria*, Communication No 155/96, Fifteenth Annual Activity Report 2001–2002; K Magliveras and G Naldi, *The African Union*, 191–99; Murray, *Human Rights in Africa*, 245–59.

[115] *Military and Paramilitary Activities In and Against Nicaragua* (*Nicaragua v USA*) [1986] ICJ Rep 14, 99–100; *Legality of the Threat or Use of Nuclear Weapons Case* [1996] ICJ Rep 226, para 70.

ought to be taken to preserve the respective rights of the parties'.[116] This provision leaves a number of issues unaddressed but the experience of the ICJ should provide guidance. Therefore, the first point to be made is that a request for provisional measures, or the authority of the Court to do so *propio motu*, may be entertained only once a case has been filed. While the Statute does not specify at which stage of the proceedings the Court may indicate provisional measures, the language used in paragraph 2 stipulating that pending the final decision notice of the measures shall immediately be given, inter alia, to the parties, strongly suggests that they could be indicated at any stage of the proceedings before the final judgment has been delivered. The ICJ's practice accepts that a request for provisional measures may be filed by a party at any time during the case, including with the initial application instituting proceedings, pending the final judgment.[117] Neither does the Statute address the question of whether the Court must first ascertain whether it has jurisdiction on the merits before ordering the provisional measures. The long established principle applied by the ICJ is that as long as prima facie jurisdiction is manifest it will entertain the request for interim measures, even if it later turns out that it lacks jurisdiction.[118] A somewhat recent example is the *Case Concerning Application of the International Convention on the Elimination of All Forms of Racial Discrimination (Georgia v Russian Federation)*.[119]

The Statute is silent on another crucial matter, namely whether or not provisional measures are of a legally binding nature.[120] The recent practice of the ICJ[121] and other international bodies[122] establishes a compelling trend towards considering them binding.

[116] This provision reflects the combined effect of Statute of the ICJ Art 41(1) and ICJ's Rules of Procedure Arts 73–78.

[117] ICJ's Rules of Procedure Art 73(1).

[118] H Lauterpacht, above n 112, 110–12. See also *Military and Paramilitary Activities in and against Nicaragua, Provisional Measures*, [1984] ICJ Rep 169; *Application of the Convention on the Prevention and Punishment of the Crime of Genocide (Bosnia and Herzegovina v Yugoslavia (Serbia and Montenegro)), Provisional Measures* [1993] ICJ Rep 3.

[119] *Provisional Measures* [2008] ICJ Rep www.icj-cij.org, at paras 113, 117. See also *Case Concerning the Arrest Warrant of 11 April 2000 (Democratic Republic of Congo v Belgium), Provisional Measures* [2000] ICJ Rep 182, para 67.

[120] The Protocol refers to 'judgments' only having a legally binding effect, see arts 37 and 51 thereof.

[121] *LaGrand Case (Germany v USA)* [2001] ICJ Rep 466, paras 99–103; *Application of the Convention on the Prevention and Punishment of the Crime of Genocide (Bosnia and Herzegovina v Serbia and Montenegro)* [2007] ICJ Rep, paras 452, 468.

[122] For the European Court of Human Rights, see *Momatkulov and Abdurasuloviv v Turkey*, Judgment of 6 February 2003, www.echr.coe.int/ENG/Judgments.htm. For the UN Human Rights Committee, see Communication No 869/1999, *Piandiong, Morallos and Bulan v The Philippines*, UN Doc CCPR/C/70/D/869/1999 (19 October 2000). See also G Naldi, 'Interim Measures in the UN Human Rights Committee' (2004) 53 ICLQ 445.

VIII. INTERVENTION

Article 49(1) of the Statute permits any Member State or AU organ that has a legal interest in a case before the Court which could be affected by a decision to request the Court to intervene in the case. The decision on the request rests with the Court so that the views of the parties to the case cannot bind the Court.[123] The practice of the ICJ under Article 62 of its Statute demonstrates that the ICJ has applied a very strict test in this area.[124] The use of the phrase 'Any Member State' suggests that the permission to intervene extends to AU Member States which are not contracting parties to the Protocol. This follows from the definition of the term 'Member State' provided in Article 1 of the Statute. It also corresponds with the practice of the ICJ which has established that a 'jurisdiction link' by the intervening party is not required.[125] Extending this right to AU organs is also understandable given the nature and purposes of the organisation.

Article 50 of the Statute allows for intervention in a case where the interpretation of the Constitutive Act arises. The wording of Article 50 gives rise to some confusion. Paragraph 1 thereof says that interested 'Member States' will receive notification, the definition of which, as has been established above, refers to non-contracting parties. However, paragraph 2 declares that, 'Every State Party and organ of the Union' has the right to intervene. Based on the definition of the term 'State Parties' provided in Article 1 of the Statute the right to intervene appears to be limited to only those States that are parties to the Protocol. It is not apparent why a distinction appears to have been drawn in this instance with Article 49(1) discussed above, particularly in view of the fact that all AU Member States potentially have an interest in the interpretation of the Constitutive Act. It may be a 'slip of the pen'.

Article 51(1) of the Statute makes provision for Member States and AU organs to be notified where the interpretation of a treaty which the former

[123] *Continental Shelf* (*Tunisia v Libya*) (*Malta Intervening*) [1981] ICJ Rep 3. The State seeking to intervene has the burden of proof: *Land, Island and Maritime Frontier Dispute (El Salvador v Honduras) (Nicaragua Intervening)* [1990] ICJ Rep 92, 117.

[124] See C Chinkin, 'Third party Intervention Before the International Court of Justice' (1986) 80 AJIL 495. ICJ's Rules of Procedure Art 81(2)(a) requires the intervening State to set out the interest of a legal nature that will be affected; and see *Indonesia/Malaysia (Philippines Intervening)* [2001] ICJ Rep 575, where the ICJ explained the meaning of an 'interest of a legal nature'. For the factors that will persuade the ICJ to accept a request for intervention, see *Land, Island and Maritime Frontier Dispute (El Salvador v Honduras) (Nicaragua Intervening)* [1990] ICJ Rep 92. Furthermore, in *Request for Interpretation of the Judgment of 31 March 2004 in the Case concerning Avena and Other Mexican Nationals (Mexico v United States of America)* [2009] ICJ Rep, para 44 (www.icj-cij.org), the ICJ observed that a question that was not decided in the initial case cannot be submitted for interpretation.

[125] *Land and Maritime Boundary (Cameroon v Nigeria) (Equatorial Guinea Intervening)* [1999] ICJ Rep 1029.

have ratified is at issue. This provision potentially confers upon the Court an extremely wide competence, which again raises concerns about possible divergent interpretations of international law. Under paragraph (2) thereof every State and AU organ taking advantage of this right is bound by the interpretation given by the Court. However, Article 51 of the Statute differs from the corresponding provision in the Statute of the ICJ, Article 63, in one important respect: Article 51(3) of the Statute excludes cases of alleged violations of human and peoples' rights. It should be observed that Article 51(1)–(2) of the Statute repeats the 'Member States'/'State Party' issue discussed above in relation to Article 50.

IX. NON-APPEARANCE

Pursuant to Article 41(1) of the Statute, should one of the parties not appear before the Court, or fails to defend the case against it, the Court is authorised to consider the case and give its judgment.[126] However, the Court must satisfy itself that it has jurisdiction, that the claim is well founded in fact and in law, and that the defaulting party had due notice.[127] The practice of the ICJ in relation to Article 53 of its Statute reveals that the ICJ acts on behalf of the absent party by submitting legal argument in support of its case.[128] This fact notwithstanding, the party that chooses not to appear is likely to prejudice its case.[129] Perhaps with a view to this prospect, Article 41(3) of the Statute allows the non-appearing party 90 days from the date of notification to lodge an objection to the judgment which, however, shall not stay its enforcement unless the Court decides to the contrary.

X. JUDGMENTS

According to Article 42(1)–(2) of the Statute the general rule is that decisions of the Court are decided by a majority of the judges present and, in case of a tie, the presiding judge has the casting vote.[130] The exception relates to intervention in a case concerning the Constitutive Act where it is specified that decisions shall be made by a qualified majority of at least

[126] Non-appearance does not seem to amount to a violation of international law but certainly goes against the spirit of the obligations assumed under the Statute of the ICJ: A Verdross and B Simma, *Universelles Voelkerrecht*, 3rd edn (Berlin, Duncker & Humblot, 1984) 124–25.

[127] Statute Art 41(2).

[128] See, eg *US Diplomatic and Consular Staff in Tehran Case* (*United States of America v Iran*) [1980] ICJ Rep 3; *Fisheries Jurisdiction Cases* [1974] ICJ Rep 3.

[129] *Military and Paramilitary Activities In and Against Nicaragua (Nicaragua v United States of America)* [1984] ICJ Rep 14, 544, (Judge Jennings, dissenting).

[130] *cf* Statute of the ICJ Art 55. According to Protocol Art 57, a judgment given by a chamber is considered as rendered by the Court.

two votes in the presence of at least two thirds of the judges.[131] The use of the word 'decisions' in this context appears to signify the various rulings made by an international court, for example, on the granting of interim measures, or on the taking of evidence.

The Court is required to render its judgment within 90 days of having completed its deliberations.[132] Judgments must state the reasons on which they are based and must state the names of the Judges who have taken part in the decision.[133] They are read in open court.[134] Separate or dissenting opinions are expressly allowed under Article 44 of the Statute. There are similarities to Articles 56 and 57 of the Statute of the ICJ.

Article 46(1) of the Statute specifies that judgments are binding on the parties.[135] It is important to note that a judgment of a Chamber or a Section is considered as rendered by the Court.[136] The binding nature of the judgments is to be given effect through paragraph 3 thereof which lays down that the parties to the dispute must not only comply with the judgment within the time stipulated by the Court but also guarantee its execution.[137] The latter requirement is commendable because it expressly sets down what is expected of States parties and places upon them the onus of compliance.[138] This commitment is reinforced by paragraph 4 which requires the Court to refer the matter to the Assembly if a party fails to comply with a judgment.[139] It follows that the Court must examine the validity of a claim of non-compliance before referring it to the Assembly.[140] The Assembly may impose sanctions pursuant to Article 23(2) of the Constitutive Act.[141] The Assembly has an element of discretion

[131] Statute Art 50(4).

[132] Ibid Art 43(2)–(3).

[133] Ibid Art 43(1).

[134] Ibid Art 43(4).

[135] *cf* Statute of the ICJ Art 59, which has been drafted in an *a contrario* fashion, ie, that judgments have no binding force except between the parties.

[136] Statute Art 19(2).

[137] *cf* UN Charter Art 94(1), which, however, is silent on the issue of the execution of the judgment.

[138] According to Shaw, the record of compliance with judgments of the ICJ has improved in recent years: Shaw, *International Law* 1104.

[139] This contrasts with the position of the ICJ, which does not concern itself with the question of compliance: *Nuclear Tests Cases* [1974] ICJ Rep 253, 477. However, UN Charter Art 94(2) allows the other party to the case to appeal directly to the Security Council. On art 94(2), see G Guillaume, 'De l'exécution des décisions de la Cour International de Justice' (1997) 4 *Revue Suisse de droit international and de droit européen* 431; C Schulte (ed), *Compliance with Decisions of the International Court of Justice* (Oxford, Oxford University Press, 2004).

[140] See also Statute Art 57, which requires the Court to submit an annual report to the Assembly, where it will, inter alia, specify those cases where parties have not complied with its judgments.

[141] Under UN Charter Art 94(2), the Security Council has a discretion as to what measures to take. Theoretically, these could include the adoption of sanctions. On the Assembly's power to impose sanctions, see K Magliveras and G Naldi, above n 10, 98–103.

and is not compelled to act even if it were found that a State had failed to comply. While it is unlikely that the Assembly will seek to exercise this power except in the most blatant cases, a pusillanimous attitude by the Assembly will probably replicate the 'do nothing' stance of the UN Security Council, thereby rendering Article 46 of the Statute ineffective.

According to Article 46(2) of the Statute, judgments, which includes those of the Chambers and Sections,[142] are final.[143] It might have been preferable to repeat verbatim the corresponding provision in Article 60 of the Statute of the ICJ, which benefits from legal clarity, stipulating that judgments are additionally 'without appeal'. It must simply be accepted as a fact of life that if, for the sake of argument, the Court were to issue a judgment that was perceived to be 'wrong', no possibility of lodging an appeal against that judgment would exist.[144] However, requests for the interpretation or revision of a judgment may be made. Article 48 of the Statute, an almost verbatim repetition of Article 61 of the Statute of the ICJ, permits the revision of judgments subject to a number of mandatory and discretionary conditions. First, that the application for revision is based on the discovery of a new fact which, if it had been known at the time to the Court and the party claiming revision, would have been a decisive factor, provided that such ignorance was not due to negligence, presumably on the part of the party. Secondly, that a double statute of limitations has been observed: the application was lodged no later than six months of the new fact's discovery and not later than ten years from the date of the judgment. Thirdly, that the Court first may require the party in question to comply with the judgment.

XI. ADVISORY JURISDICTION

In accordance with Article 53(1) of the Statute the Court has the competence to give advisory opinions on any legal question at the request of the Assembly, the Parliament, the Executive Council, the Peace and Security Council, the Economic, Social and Cultural Council, the Financial institutions or any AU organ authorised by the AU.[145] The authority of the Court to render advisory opinions is discretionary, as evidenced by the inclusion

[142] Statute Art 19(2).

[143] Subject to Statute Art 41(3) (default judgments).

[144] The international furore caused by the ICJ's decision in *South West Africa Cases (Second Phase)* [1966] ICJ Rep 6 comes to mind.

[145] It should be observed that the African Commission has the power to interpret the Banjul Charter under Art 45(3) thereof, described by an eminent author as amounting to authorisation 'to issue what are in effect advisory opinions': see AH Robertson and JG Merrills, *Human Rights in the World*, 3rd edn (Manchester, Manchester University Press, 1992) 221.

of the verb 'may' in the provision.[146] However, Article 53(3) of the Statute states an explicit exception in that a request must not relate to a pending application before the African Commission or the African Committee of Experts. This should ensure that the jurisdiction of these bodies is not undermined. It remains to be seen in what other circumstances the Court may choose to decline to exercise its advisory jurisdiction. The ICJ is of the view that it may do so for 'compelling reasons'.[147]

The range of applicants authorised to request an opinion is noteworthy and there is no explicit indication that the AU organs are restricted to their sphere of competence, although this may turn out to be the case.[148] A further point worth drawing attention to is the wide-ranging scope of the issues subject to the Court's advisory jurisdiction.[149]

The Court must give its opinions in open court.[150] With respect to other procedural aspects of the advisory jurisdiction Article 56 of the Statute states that the Court will be guided by the procedure applicable in contentious cases.[151] Amongst other things, judges should be allowed to deliver separate or dissenting opinions.

XII. CONCLUSION

It is not possible to predict with a given degree of certainty when the Statute of the Court will come into force. At the time of writing there have been no ratifications of the Protocol. The requisite fifteen ratifications seems few, as it corresponds to less than one-quarter of the AU membership. Thus, at the initial stages of its operations, the role played by the Court could be limited to only a fraction of the Member States. For this reason, it might have been more appropriate for the Protocol to require ratification by the whole membership, or certainly by a large enough number to be representative of Africa's principal legal traditions. Until such time as the Court becomes operational, the Assembly is the body authorised to interpret the Constitutive Act.[152]

The other challenge facing the Court is its relationship with the African Court on Human and Peoples' Rights. The Statute ingeniously preserves the autonomy of the human rights organ through the establishment of a clearly defined Human Rights Section and there does not seem to be

[146] *cf* Statute of the ICJ Art 65.
[147] *Legality of the Threat or Use of Nuclear Weapons Case* [1996] ICJ Rep 226, 235.
[148] *cf* UN Charter Art 96(2), and see *Legality of the Use by a State of Nuclear Weapons in Armed Conflict Case* [1996] ICJ Rep 66.
[149] On the ICJ, see Shaw, n 101 above, 1108–09.
[150] Statute Art 55.
[151] *cf* Statute of the ICJ Art 68.
[152] Constitutive Act Art 26.

in principle much reason to fear that human rights protection will be diminished in future. Of course, the Statute is not as detailed as the Protocol on the African Court on Human and Peoples' Rights but it may be that the Rules will address some of these gaps.

It will have been noted that the Statute is heavily influenced by the Statute of the ICJ, but notwithstanding that, a number of *lacunae* and badly drafted provisions have managed to slip through. Given that the Court will have a role in interpreting and implementing aspects of economic law it is regrettable that the experience of the ECJ appears to have been largely overlooked.[153] Perhaps in time, as Africa proceeds towards greater economic and political integration, it may be that the Court will be given competences similar to those of the ECJ.[154] Undoubtedly, the Court will be called upon to clarify the meaning of certain vague or badly drafted passages. Notwithstanding this criticism, the Statute, together with the Rules, should be adequate for the Court to fulfill its role as the 'principal judicial organ' of the AU. Indeed, if allowed to operate efficiently, and the Court must be adequately resourced to enable it to fulfil its mandate properly,[155] it should help bring about the much needed rule of law in the Continent. But to do so both the AU organs and the Member States need to be convinced of the advantages of judicial settlement in their dealings, otherwise the Court could end up as another false dawn for Africa.

[153] It has been argued that the Treaty Establishing the African Economic Community 1991 would likely lead the then envisaged Court to develop the law in line with that of EC Law: see G Naldi and K Magliveras, 'The African Economic Community: Emancipation for African States or Yet Another Glorious Failure? (1999) 24 *North Carolina Journal of International Law and Commercial Regulation* 601.

[154] Two separate procedures for amending the Statute are envisaged. Under Art 58(1) a State party may make a written request to the Chairperson of the Commission, who forwards it to the Member States. In accordance with para 2, the Assembly may adopt the proposed amendment by a simple majority and after the Court has given its opinion on it. Under Art 59 the Court may propose to the Assembly any amendments that it deems necessary through the Chairperson of the Commission. The procedure specified in Art 58(2) then applies.

[155] Attention has already been drawn to the fact that the decision to amalgamate the two courts, was partially motivated by a desire for economy, above n 19. Inadequate funding has been a perennial problem for the OAU/AU, hampering the work of its institutions and its programmes. To take one example, the Office of the UN High Commissioner for Human Rights identified the limited resources allocated by the OAU to the African Commission as one of the major obstacles to its effective functioning: see UN Doc E/CN.4/1999/93, para 6.

13

The EU, the ECHR and the Effective Protection of Human Rights for Individuals

TAWHIDA AHMED

I. INTRODUCTION

THE DIRECTION AND development of international dispute settlement is certainly being challenged, as well as enhanced, by the multiplicity of international courts and tribunals.[1] In the sphere of human rights protection in Europe, the most salient concerns relate to relationship between the European Court of Human Rights (ECtHR) of the Council of Europe (CoE) and the European Court of Justice (ECJ) of the European Union (EU). Several recent works have highlighted proposals from the ECJ and the ECtHR for responding to actual and potential overlaps.[2] The ruling of the ECtHR in *Bosphorus Hava Yollari Turizm v Ticaret Anonim Sirket v Ireland*[3] (*Bosphorus*) is the latest in a line of cases attempting a solution to a specific part of the wider debate on human rights dispute settlements: the judgment by one international system

[1] Generally on dispute settlement, see JG Merrills, *International Dispute Settlement*, 4th edn (Cambridge, Cambridge University Press, 2005); specifically on the multiplicity of international courts and tribunals, see JG Merrills, 'The Mosaic of International Dispute Settlement Procedures: Complementary or Contradictory?' (2007) *Netherlands International Law Review* 361–93 and R Higgins, 'A Babel of Judicial Voices? Ruminations from the Bench' (2006) 55(4) ICLQ 791–804.

[2] See, eg S Peers, 'Bosphorus, European Court of Human Rights, case note' (2006) *European Constitutional Law Review* 443–55; B Davies, '*Segi* and the Future of Judicial Rights Protection in the Third Pillar of the EU' (2008) 14(3) *European Public Law* 309–19; P Manzini, 'The Priority of Pre-Existing Treaties of EC Member States within the Framework of International Law' (2001) 12 *European Journal of International Law* 781–92; H Schermers, '*Matthews v United Kingdom*' (1993) 36 CMLRev 673–81; T King, 'Ensuring Human Rights Review of Intergovernmental Acts in Europe' (2000) 25 ELR 79–88; I Canor, 'Who is the Ultimate Guardian of Fundamental Rights in Europe' (2000) 25 ELR 3–21; K Lenaerts, 'Fundamental Rights in the European Union' (2000) 25 ELR 575–600.

[3] (2006) 42 EHRR 1.

(under the European Convention on Human Rights (ECHR; Convention)) on the protection of human rights by another (the EU), where the application of legal rules arising from the latter cause a (potential) breach to the human rights of natural or legal persons within the jurisdiction of the former. The ruling has, however, been severely criticised. The objective of this chapter is not to add generally to the existing studies, but rather to focus on the specific implications raised by that case for the attainment of a 'practical and effective' international human rights dispute settlement system: an objective often keenly declared by the ECtHR in its case law. The issues concerning 'practical and effective' protection of human rights for individuals raised by the case include the following: (a) contribution to the rhetoric of universality of human rights; (b) participation by individuals in challenging potential breaches; (c) judicial declarations as a means of deterring human rights breaches; and (d) judicial monitoring which is independent from the potential human rights violator. The chapter thus identifies and elaborates upon the ideals which underlie the contention that the ECtHR should undertake a stricter review of the EU's commitment to Convention rights and the ECJ's monitoring of the same. As a result of this approach, the specific problems associated with the current test presented by the ECtHR in *Bosphorus* are highlighted and a revised test suggesting a more tailored response is put forward.

It will be argued that the ECtHR's response, in *Bosphorus*, to the challenges of international cooperation with the EU impacts on the guarantee of individuals' rights before the ECtHR, by failing to give sufficient significance to certain principles and values necessarily attached to that protection, such as those embodied within the four factors above. It is suggested that the ECtHR has thereby neglected the opportunity to strengthen human rights protection under the ECHR and, moreover, it has affected the *status quo* beyond what was necessary in accommodating the autonomy of the EU and the ECJ. In other words, the ECtHR has not simply missed an opportunity to do more, but has positively *taken away from the procedural and substantive rights individuals already had* (or should have been entitled to) under the ECHR and that this is not proportionately justified by the aim of achieving international cooperation with the EU and ECJ.

In examining these claims, Part II of this chapter introduces *Bosphorus* and the unique EU–ECHR relationship and examines the concerns arising from the *Bosphorus* principles with respect to the four elements of effective protection for individuals outlined above. Although the challenges of the EU–ECHR relationship cannot be wholly reconciled with the provision of optimal rights protection for individuals, Part III suggests ways in which any disproportionately detrimental effects of the judgment could be limited, before the chapter concludes in Part IV. In addition to the specificities of the chapter, it is hoped that the examination serves as a general account of the current stage of the law in relation to the interactions (conflicting or otherwise) in human rights dispute settlement between the two European courts in focus.

II. THE FAILURE OF THE ECTHR TO UPHOLD EFFECTIVE RIGHTS PROTECTION

It is uncontroversial to argue that the development of human rights in international dispute settlement systems aims to provide in depth monitoring of the effective protection of human rights *for individuals* as against the State. By operating on a system of obligations owed directly to individuals and not only as between States, human rights law differs remarkably from the rest of international law.[4] In addition, not only States, but individuals themselves are to be given the capacity to raise a matter of breach of human rights before international tribunals. The ECHR was one of the first international mechanisms to give effect to this through an individual petition system which provides the individual with direct access to the ECtHR.[5] The ECtHR has the role of securing the human rights of individuals who seek its protection. If these principles exist based on the rationale that States are capable of adopting laws and policies which can conflict with human rights (here Convention rights), then it makes sense for that rationale to also extend to the rules adopted by other bodies—in this case international organisations like the EU—which also affect States' abilities to meet their human rights obligations to individuals.[6] Hence, from the viewpoint of effective individual protection, the duty (on the participating States) not to violate human rights ought to remain unaltered and the task of human rights courts, such as the ECtHR, should remain intact: to ensure the effective protection of individual human rights by State parties (even in the cases of rules originating from non-State bodies, like the EU). Legislation originating from the EU and applied by the ECHR States parties should therefore respect the Convention rights of those within the jurisdiction of the States parties in accordance with Article 1 ECHR, and it should be possible to have those rules scrutinised by the ECtHR for their compatibility with ECHR norms.

[4] Rosalyn Higgins, *Problems and Process, International Law and How We use it* (Oxford, Oxford University Press, 1994), 95–96.

[5] The League of Nations (the predecessor to the UN) had a system to take matters before the Permanent Court of International Justice, but individuals were required to petition the Council, which could act on their behalf.

[6] Whether bodies such as the EU are directly bound by rules of other international organisations, like the Council of Europe, is not the focus of this chapter, but has been dealt with elsewhere. See T Ahmed and I Butler, 'The European Union and Human Rights: An International Law Perspective' (2006) 17(4) *European Journal of International Law*, 771–801 and the references therein.

In reality, complications in applying the above rationale have arisen for two main reasons. First, the Council of Europe and the EU are separate international entities. The EU has not acceded to the ECHR and is not legally bound to comply with its standards of protection and the ECtHR consequently has no authority to review challenges against the EU per se. Since the review of Member States' EU-related actions may place Member States in the difficult position of either applying EU law or continuing to breach ECHR rules, the ECtHR has been in a political dilemma as to how to implement ECHR standards in the cases of such review. Secondly, the EU has developed an internal framework for safeguarding human rights within the EU. Within that framework, the EU declares itself to strive for compatibility with ECHR standards of protection, though it is under no legal obligation to faithfully apply those standards. The existence of this parallel commitment to Convention rights, whilst an active demonstration of the value attached to the human rights of individuals in Europe, again presents political complications which can result in reducing the effectiveness of the ECHR protection available to individuals. This is a combined consequence of: a) the actual or potential conflicts which arise from overlaps and particularly the danger that the EU provides a lower level of human rights protection; and b) the absence of a presupposed hierarchical relationship between the two organisations. These complications have direct implications for the quality of the rights granted to individuals and ultimately therefore for the upholding of the values of the international human rights system. A brief analysis of the ECtHR's *Bosphorus* case provides a current example of how a dispute might arise. It further provides the fruit to demonstrate how the ECtHR's proposed solution might fail to give sufficient weight to the role played by individuals in the aims and enforcement of ECHR rights.

The relevant facts of *Bosphorus* can be presented reasonably briefly. Based on a UN Security Council Resolution,[7] the EU adopted a Regulation[8] requiring that the property of companies thought to violate the Resolution be impounded by Member States. Ireland, as a Member State of the EU applied the EU legislation in its domestic law. Bosphorus' property rights were affected after its aircraft was impounded by Ireland and compensation denied by Ireland and confirmed later by an ECJ ruling.[9] Under ECHR rules, Bosphorus, as a legal entity, has the right to petition the ECtHR in respect of that breach. Again, however, the ECtHR held that the legal rights of Bosphorus had not been breached. How did the Court

[7] UBSC Res 820 (17 April 1993), UN Doc S/RES/820.

[8] Council Regulation (EEC) 990/93 of 26 April 1993, Concerning Trade between the European Economic Community and the Federal Republic of Yugoslavia (Serbia and Montenegro) [1993] OJ L102/14.

[9] Case C-84/95 *Bosphorus Airways* [1996] ECR I-3953.

reach this conclusion? Previously in *Matthews*, the ECtHR held that for breaches arising from EU primary Treaty law, the participating States of the ECHR are obliged to 'secure' convention rights.[10] In *Bosphorus*, for breaches arising from secondary EU law or from the application of EU judicial decisions, the ECtHR devised a different route. According to *Bosphorus*, the ECtHR will automatically regard the case as a direct claim by the applicant against the Member States: thus far it is in line with *Matthews*. However, in deciding whether to scrutinise the claim in depth and also as justification for any breaches of human rights found thereafter, the court will take account of the fact that the domestic law was applied pursuant to EU law obligations (ie, that Ireland's actions were dictated by strict 'international legal obligations' under the EU Regulation). To 'take account of' in this context means that the Court will presume that the EU provides a level of protection 'equivalent' ('comparable', not identical) to those found in the ECHR system in both substance and procedure and therefore closer scrutiny of whether the EU law in question specifically guarantees the right in the case before it is unnecessary. This presumption of comparable protection will apply unless it can be shown that the EU presents a manifest deficiency in the protection of Convention rights, in which case 'the interest of international cooperation would be outweighed by the Convention's role as a "constitutional instrument of European public order" in the field of human rights.'[11] Alternatively, if the presumption is deemed applicable, then the State in question is regarded as fulfilling ECHR obligations. In *Bosphorus*, the ECtHR held that the current level of the EU's commitments to the protection of fundamental rights and the mechanisms available for individuals, Member States or EU institutions to challenge EU law were sufficient to engage the presumption of equivalence. That presumption was not rebutted in the instant case by the applicant company, as there was no dysfunction in the EU's mechanisms of control for the observance of Convention rights.[12] The presumption could, however, be rebutted in the future. The ECtHR thus retains the right to re-visit the existence of equivalence from time to time. The equivalence doctrine (and therefore the weaker level of scrutiny by the ECtHR) only applies where actions of the Member States are challenged and the Member State does no more than implement EU obligations, that is, where 'the Member State has no discretion whatsoever in applying the international law, such that its actions are effectively subsumed as those

[10] *Matthews v UK* [1999] 28 EHRR 361.

[11] *Bosphorus*, above n 9, para 156, citing *Loizidou v Turkey* (preliminary objections) judgment of 23 March 1995, (1995) 20 EHRR 99, Series A no 310, 7–8, para 75.

[12] *Bosphorus*, above n 9, para 166.

of the international entity'.[13] In *Bosphorus*, the court accepted that the EU Regulation in question and ECJ preliminary ruling decision left no discretion for their implementation in Ireland. For EU actions which leave discretion in the manner of implementation, the Member States' actions will be fully scrutinised for their compatibility with the ECHR.

What can we make of this ruling? A general positive observation is that, short of the EU's accession to the ECHR, the case makes progress in the process of the ECtHR dealing with States' transfers of powers to international organisations and their implications on Convention rights. The ECtHR's declaration of its authority to review EU secondary legislation was not previously so clearly declared and 'viewed as part of a process ... is a step towards greater control over the EU.'[14] It furthers the workings of public international law and the mutual existence or operations of international courts whose legal jurisdictions either directly or indirectly overlap. It maintains EU supremacy and autonomy (both internally (vis-à-vis its own States) and externally (vis-à-vis the ECHR), but significantly, it does not exempt all EU-related situations from ECtHR scrutiny. These situations are aptly analysed by Costello,[15] some of which are integrated into the discussions to follow in this chapter. It can further be argued that the ECHR took a sensible step to remain passive on the ruling of EU-related issues in which it is, between the two European courts, the lesser expert.

However, as an answer to the dilemma of the EU's relationship with the ECHR, where the goal of effective individual rights protection is concerned, it arguably falls short of promoting the importance attached by the international human rights regime, and especially the ECHR, to that goal. The ruling causes one to be uncomfortable on several fronts relating to individual protection: a) it discredits the rhetoric of universality of human rights; b) it limits the participation rights of individuals in ECHR litigation; in particular it limits access to the full scrutiny available under the ECHR mechanism; c) it may not deter future ECHR breaches; and d) it does not provide robust independent judicial monitoring of Member States' ECHR commitments in the context of EU regulation. A closer look at these four points will demonstrate how these issues pose threats to the effectiveness of individual human rights protection under the ECHR. These threats are all the more significant because they not only represent an abstinence from further enhancing or progressing protection, but more importantly they undermine the *status quo*.

[13] C Costello, 'The *Bosphorus* Ruling of the European Court of Human Rights: Fundamental Rights and Blurred Boundaries in Europe', (2006) 6(1) HRLR 87–103, 107.
[14] Ibid 90.
[15] Ibid 107 ff.

A. The Universality Of Human Rights—Uniformity

Human rights are universal in that all human beings possess them and they hold as against all other institutions and individuals.[16] This principle underlies, shapes, and is an inspiration for, other important indicators of effective rights protection for individuals. In the specific case study of the ECHR at hand, that indicator refers to the full and invariable application of the Convention's protection, as existed prior to the ruling in *Bosphorus*. It entails, broadly speaking, an emphasis on the uniform and equal treatment of like cases which come before the ECtHR.

To begin with, one can agree with the judges providing the concurring judgment in *Bosphorus* that:

> It has now been accepted and confirmed that the principle that Article 1 of the Convention makes 'no distinction as to the type of rule or measure concerned' and does 'not exclude any part of the member States' 'jurisdiction' from scrutiny under the Convention' (see *United Communist Party of Turkey and Others v. Turkey*, judgment of 30 January 1998, *Reports of Judgments and Decisions* 1998-I, pp. 17–18, § 29) also applies to Community law. It follows that the member States are responsible, under Article 1 of the Convention, for all acts and omissions of their organs, whether these arise from domestic law or from the need to fulfil international legal obligations.[17]

Hence, the exemption of some EU-related areas from the full application of the ECHR creates the risk of the double standard application of the ECtHR's jurisdiction and undermines the uniform application of the Convention rights. The double standards claim arises in two ways. It is applicable to the fact that State actions involving EU-related scenarios are dealt with in a different way to those involving non-EU-related scenarios or States which are not members of the EU. The claim of double standards may also be invoked in respect of the risk that the assumption of equivalence and hence the lack of ECtHR supervision may lead to the ECJ not fully applying Convention standards within the EU. Clearly, the application of *Bosphorus* in this manner creates arbitrary hierarchies between the cases which will and will not be subject to ECtHR scrutiny. This decision is taken not according to internal Convention rules and values, but because of the presence of an external (political) factor: the ECHR's relationship with the EU and the respective jurisdictions of the two courts. This in itself is not regarded as a problem if an appropriate balance is struck in the application of these external forces.

[16] J Donnelly, *Universal Human Rights in Their and Practice*, 2nd edn (Ithaca, Cornell University Press, 2003) 1.

[17] *Bosphorus*, above n 9, Joint concurring opinion of Judges Rozakis, Tulkens, Traja, Botoucharova, Zagrebelsky and Garlicki, 50.

A relevant factor negating that appropriateness is that the ECtHR has outlined that for those individuals falling within the EU's (as opposed to the ECtHR's) bracket of protection, the presumption that the EU (and therefore also the State) has not breached human rights is only rebuttable in the event of finding a 'manifest deficiency' with the EU's mechanisms for human rights protection. Arguably, this sets a high threshold before the ECtHR's closer monitoring role is applied, and therefore a low threshold of human rights protection for the EU to actually meet in order to secure its independence. The equivalence doctrine also affects the national level application of the ECHR: national courts have two (possibly contradictory) sources of interpretative guidance on human rights guarantees.[18] Delegation to the ECJ of the application of the ECHR creates unpredictability of results for victims[19] and presents a higher risk of legal uncertainty than in the situation where all cases were dealt with by the ECtHR.

The ECtHR, through its ruling in *Bosphorus*, has created divisions in the application of the ECHR. Such divisions have the potential to undermine the integrity of the ECHR's system of judicial protection of individuals. Whilst the aim of maintaining respect for EU law and the ECJ is a legitimate reason for limiting the ECHR's 'universal' applicability and is in line with the ECtHR's emerging approach to accommodating other elements of 'international' law[20] in cases that come before it, the solution adopted was perhaps too lenient on the EU and disproportionately detrimental for individual rights. The threshold of manifest deficiency is arguably inappropriate for a system devoted to individual rights protection which is enforceable by those individuals and the lack of a case by case review permits an unacceptable number of loopholes and legal uncertainty in respect of cases involving EU law. Accordingly, the nature of the framework through which this is carried out in relation to the EU could be adjusted, as discussed in part III below.

B. Access to Justice—'Full' ECHR Participation Rights

The correlation between the existence, or holding, of rights and their enforceability is long standing. Participation in the enforcement of one's rights through judicial means is an important element of that.[21] It is part of the wider right to a remedy, which 'would include both the "procedural right of effective access" and "the substantive right to a

[18] Costello, above n 12 at 119.

[19] D Shelton, *Remedies in International Human Rights Law* (Oxford, Oxford University Press, 1999) 55.

[20] *Behrami and Behrami v France* (2007) 45 EHRR10, 4, para 122.

[21] Higgins, above n 3, ch 6; Shelton, above n 18, 183–89.

remedy"'.[22] The terms of this chapter concern the implications of *Bosphorus* on the former[23]—effective access to the ECtHR. Indeed in the ECHR, access to justice refers largely to the right of individuals to apply for and receive the full judicial procedure before the ECtHR. The rationale of the equivalence doctrine requires comments to be made regarding participation in both the ECHR system and the EU system.

In terms of participation at the ECtHR, it can be argued that refusal by the ECtHR to adjudicate on the specific facts of the case before it denies individual applicants the right to a full litigious process before the ECtHR itself. Although access to the ECtHR is technically granted to the individual in that the case reaches the court, the court in the first place undertakes only a general review of the EU's ability to protect human rights.[24] This general review cannot adequately identify the deficiencies that a specific case by case review could. It therefore does not induce 'practical and effective' protection of Convention rights which the ECtHR has time and again asserted[25] and will likely deny the full jurisdiction of the ECtHR in cases which require urgent attention. Dembour notes that:

> The effectiveness principle has been established on the ground that the Convention is intended to guarantee rights that are 'practical and effective' rather than 'theoretical and illusory'. It looks beyond the letter of the law to assess concretely the position of the individual. For example, the right to a fair trial amounts to nothing if access to a tribunal is denied in the first place.[26]

Though the ECtHR's development of this principle of practical and effective protection relates to evaluation of domestic tribunals, there is no reason why these principles do not equally apply to the ECtHR. Specifically in relation to access to tribunals, Article 13 ECHR coupled with Article 6(1) ECHR has been invoked by the ECtHR to provide a strong level of access to justice before national law.[27] In *Leander v Sweden*, the ECtHR held that an individual applicant 'must have a *bona fide* opportunity to have his case tested on its merits and, if appropriate, to obtain redress.'[28] And in

[22] K Wellens, *Remedies against International Organizations* (Cambridge, Cambridge University Press, 2002), 17, citing Shelton, above n 18 at 14–15.

[23] Because the ECtHR did not find a procedural deficiency in the EU mechanisms, it did not move on to consider the subjective right to property in the case.

[24] Unless there can be shown a manifest deficiency in the EU's level of protection under the terms of *Bosphorus*.

[25] *Airey v Ireland* (1979–80) 2 EHRR 305; *Vilvarajah v UK* (1991) 215 ECtHR Ser A, para 125.

[26] M Dembour, *Who Believes in Human Rights? Reflection on the European Convention* (Cambridge, Cambridge University Press, 2006) 21. See also Shelton, above n 18 at 22–23.

[27] As confirmed in *Golder v UK* (1975) 18 ECtHR Ser A, (1975) 1 EHRR 524; Shelton, above n 18, 22–32; A Mowbray, *Cases and Materials on the European Convention on Human Rights* (Oxford, Oxford University Press, 2007), chs 8 and 15.

[28] *Leander v Sweden* (1987) ECtHR Ser A, (1987) 9 EHRR 453 at para 77 cited in Shelton, above n 18 at 26.

Silver v UK, the Court said that this is to be available to everyone who claims to be a victim.[29] And while the ECtHR allows national law to impose restrictions, there are rules to follow:

> Limitations must not restrict exercise of the right in such a way or to such an extent that the very essence of the right is impaired. They must pursue a legitimate aim and there must be reasonable proportionality between the means employed and the aim sought to be achieved.[30]

However, *Bosphorus* applies a different set of standards to the Convention mechanism. Understandably, the ECtHR had ambitions to strike a balance which dealt with the EU–ECHR and ECJ–ECtHR relations in a fashion politically appealing to both systems. The procedure established in *Bosphorus* enables the EU to maintain its independence of and autonomy from the ECHR system, whilst nevertheless leaving ultimate authority with the ECtHR to oversee that the EU's system does not use its independence to violate human rights in a manner manifestly deficient of ECHR standards. This *Bosphorus* solution is 'a' means of achieving the legitimate political aim the court set out to achieve. However, whether it is a proportionate means is another question. Different views have been expressed in scholarship.[31] While a thorough examination of this balance is outside the scope of this chapter, one or two points on individuals' access to the full jurisdiction of the ECtHR can be brought forward. Denying a specific judgment on the merits of an alleged convention violation carries the risk of neglecting potential breaches of rights and therefore of impairing the essence of any right which comes within the realm of *Bosphorus*, since a detailed examination of that right will not take place. In addition, it attaches less value to the rights of the EU-related claimant to full ECHR judicial scrutiny on the merits than it attaches to the non-EU-related individual. Overall, as Eckes notes, the ECtHR abstains from adjudicating in instances where it is needed the most:

> The function of the ECtHR is to assure justice in cases where usually well-functioning judicial systems exceptionally fail to comply with the Convention. Its role is not to review cases coming from jurisdictions which as a rule do not respect the ECHR. Therefore, the fact that the European legal system principally

[29] Shelton, above n 18 at 24, citing *Silver v UK* (1983) 61 ECtHR Ser A, (1983) 5 EHRR 347 at para 113.

[30] Shelton, above n 18 at 26, citing *Ashingdale v UK* (1985) 93 ECtHR Ser A, (1985) 7 EHRR 528 24–25, para 57 and *FE v France* judgment of 30 October 1998, (1998) 29 EHRR 435; *Fayed v UK* (1994) 294-B ECtHR Ser A, 49–50, (1994) 18 EHRR 393, para 65.

[31] On the one hand, see Costello, above n 12; and on the other hand, see Peers, above n 1 and C Eckes, 'Does the European Court of Human Rights Provide Protection from the European Community? The Case of *Bosphorus Airways*' (2007) 13(1) *European Public Law* 47–67.

provides for an 'equivalent' protection cannot justify the Court's decision not to apply fully the ECHR.[32]

In relation to the EU forum, several comments in respect of access to the court can be made. There are numerous deficiencies in the participation rights of individuals in the EU's judicial mechanisms, where the potential application of the *Bosphorus* principles by the ECtHR would lead to either no participation of affected individuals in the judicial process or a limited level of participation. As noted on many occasions, the possibility for individuals to challenge community measures before the ECJ is weak on a general level[33] but is weaker still in respect of certain subject-areas. Thus, on the general level, the ECtHR in *Bosphorus* itself notes that individuals have no *locus standi* under the EC Treaty (ECT),[34] they have restricted rights to initiate judicial review proceedings in Article 230(4) EC Treaty and have no right to take an action against another individual.[35] This falls short of specific requirements under Article 6(1) ECHR. Further, there is no mechanism in the EU to challenge the validity of primary law (there is only the possibility to interpret primary law).[36] In addition, specific subject areas provide further restrictions on participation rights before the EU judicial bodies. These are in the fields of common foreign and security policy (CFSP) in Treaty on European Union (TEU) Title V, police and judicial cooperation in criminal matters (PJCC) in TEU Title VI and visas, asylum and immigration in ECT Title IV.[37] For instance, in relation to the third pillar, natural and legal persons have no right to bring a case before the ECJ and indirect access to the Court through the preliminary ruling process is optional for the Member States.[38] Only national courts of final instances may make preliminary references to the ECJ under Title IV ECT on visas, immigration and asylum[39] and finally based on Article 6 TEU, the ECJ cannot review acts adopted under CFSP, such as Joint Actions and Common Positions.[40]

32 Eckes, above n 30 at 64.

33 See A Arnull, *The European Union and its Court of Justice* (Oxford, Oxford University Press, 2006), chs 3 and 4; Eckes, above n 30 at 56–60 and see refs therein at fn 52.

34 EC Treaty Arts 226–28.

35 *Bosphorus*, above n 9 at paras 162–63.

36 Costello, above n 12 at 115.

37 See further Costello, above n 12, Peers, above n 1 and Eckes, above n 30. Though NB the progress made in Case C-355/04 P *Segi et al v Council of the European Union*, judgment of 27 February 2007 and Case C105/03 *Pupino* [2005] ECR I5285: Davies, above n 1 and M Fletcher, 'Extending "indirect effect" to the third pillar: the significance of Pupino' (2005) 30(6) ELR, 862–77. These pieces also highlight the remaining obstacles to protection in these areas.

38 TEU Art 35; Davies, above n 1 at 311. In relation to Title VI EU acts, see Fletcher, above n 36.

39 EC Treaty Art 68.

40 As listed in Costello, above n 12 at 116–18.

Costello argues that in relation to these areas of EU law, protection by the EU equivalent to that of the ECHR is lacking and the ECtHR *should*, in future cases, scrutinise the EU measures which concern these areas. In respect of the right to property in *Bosphorus*, the ECtHR felt that the EU's general mechanisms for challenging EU measures which restricted that right were sufficient to meet Article 6(1) ECHR requirements, even though, as outlined above, the EU mechanisms encompassed a number of shortcomings. The ECtHR made reference to those shortfalls in the judgment of *Bosphorus*,[41] yet it was satisfied that the EU provides a comparable level of access to court as required by the Convention. This view of access to the ECJ is rather generous and unsupportive of the principle of effective individual participation in relation to the enforcement of Convention rights.

It may be asked whether our assessment of the ECHR is harsh here, especially since the ECtHR must accommodate the competing interests of the EU and because effective participation by those who have suffered rights breaches is not guaranteed so satisfactorily in other human rights systems at the international level, even today.[42] Is the ECHR system being unfairly singled out here? Such a case could be put forward, but the Convention system is different to other international human rights dispute settlement mechanisms: it has sought, from its inception, to provide a higher degree of individual participation in its judicial enforcement mechanism. This is noted by the ECtHR, which comments that individual participation 'is one of the keystones in the machinery for the enforcement of the rights and freedoms set forth in the Convention'.[43] This point was emphasised by the judges providing a concurring opinion in *Bosphorus*.[44] The participative apparatus of the ECHR was developed explicitly and purposefully to counteract the failings of States and international institutions to protect individuals. In this respect, the ECHR aims to provide protection on a *direct* case-by-case basis. Thus, as measured against its own standards, failure by the ECtHR to guarantee this destabilises the *status quo*. As opined by the judges delivering the concurring opinion in *Bosphorus*,

> the right of individual application is one of the basic obligations assumed by the States on ratifying the Convention. It is therefore difficult to accept that they should have been able to reduce the effectiveness of this right for persons within their jurisdiction on the ground that they have transferred certain

[41] *Bosphorus*, above n 9 at paras 162–63.

[42] See discussion in Higgins, above n 3 at 48–55.

[43] *Mamatkulov and Askarov v Turkey* ([GC], nos 46827/99 and 46951/99, ECHR 2005-I), (2005) 41 EHRR 494, para 122.

[44] *Bosphorus*, above n 9, Joint Concurring Opinion of Judges Rozakis, Tulkens, Traja, Botoucharova, Zagrebelsky and Garlicki, at 52.

> powers to the European Communities. For the Court to leave to the Community's judicial system the task of ensuring 'equivalent protection', without retaining a means of verifying on a case-by-case basis that that protection is indeed 'equivalent', would be tantamount to consenting tacitly to substitution, in the field of Community law, of Convention standards by a Community standard which might be inspired by Convention standards but whose equivalence with the latter would no longer be subject to authorised scrutiny.[45]

The court did, in the main judgment, after noting the lack of direct individual participation in EU mechanisms, suggest that alternative avenues for the protection of human rights within the EU, such as actions instituted by Member States and EU institutions, provide ample scope for *indirect* benefits to the applicant. It is questionable, however, whether these adequately compensate for the lack of direct access to the ECtHR. Equally, the use of the preliminary reference procedure for individuals, who, through national courts, can direct questions to the ECJ,[46] does not provide an adequate substitute. In particular, the lower courts at national level have discretion as to whether they submit a question to the ECJ and subsequently on how they apply the ECJ's ruling to the case before them. ECJ scrutiny is thus not always available or strictly final, yet this is not, as outlined by the concurring judgment in *Bosphorus*, accounted for by the equivalent protection doctrine.[47] Rather, it may simply constitute an additional burden in that individuals would be required to take action before two international tribunals,[48] further curtailing access to the ECtHR.

Human rights protection is best achieved where breaches can be challenged by those individuals who are the victims of human rights violations.[49] Neither the general review of the ECJ nor the indirect State- or institutional means could guarantee this in the quest to maintain full ECHR standards. *Bosphorus* instead leaves clear gaps in the participation rights of individuals in both its own system and that of the EU. The promotion of international relations can justify some limits on participation rights of individuals, but not to this extent.

[45] Ibid.

[46] On the interpretation of primary and secondary law and the validity of secondary law.

[47] *Bosphorus*, n 9 above, Joint Concurring Opinion of Judges Rozakis, Tulkens, Traja, Botoucharova, Zagrebelsky and Garlicki, at 52: 'However, it is clear from paragraph 157 of the [Bosphorus] judgment and the reference to *Cantoni v France* (judgment of 15 November 1996, *Reports* 1996-V) that the use of discretion in implementing a preliminary ruling by the European Court of Justice is not covered by the presumption of "equivalent protection".'

[48] K Kuhnert 'Bosphorus: Double Standards in European Human Rights Protection' (2006) 2(2) *Utrecht Law Review* 177–89 and Costello, n 12 above at 119.

[49] U Baxi, 'Too Many of Too Few' (2001) *HRLR* 1(1) 1–9; see also E Shmidt-Assmann and L Harrings, 'Access to Justice and Fundamental Rights', *European Review of Public Law* (1997) 9, 529–49.

C. Deterrence Effect: Declaratory Judgments

Effective protection of human rights also requires an element of enforcement,[50] or broadly speaking the provision of a form of remedy. In the global context, Theo van Boven's study on remedies revealed two goals:

> First to provide individual remedies for the victim; secondly, to uphold the public interest by deterring future violations. In this way the principles take into account the object and purpose of human rights treaties and the concept of obligations *erga omnes*.[51]

Judicial enforcement is thus associated with the principle of deterrence[52] where the judicial pronouncement of a breach and perhaps also any subsequent remedy acts as a deterrent to prevent governing authorities committing the same or similar breaches. A concern of the *Bosphorus* test is that its application to the EU is unlikely to contribute to the creation of an ECHR system robust enough to deter EU institutions and Member States in EU-related contexts from breaching human rights in the establishment and implementation of EU law. Rather, instead of settling the dispute before it, the ECtHR hands general authority back to the domain wherein the conflict arose, with a strong mark of approval that that domain 'presumably' complies with Convention rights.

This decreases the number of opportunities in which the ECtHR acts as the remedy provider and its judgments act as a deterrent to human rights breaches. This is not to judge the ECHR's current provision of remedies to be an optimal form of deterrence: there is a widely held belief that the consequences of Convention breaches may not exceed the social value of continuing to breach.[53] However, remedies are wide-ranging and begin first of all with declaratory judgments. Though declarations do not automatically entail additional penalties, for example of the financial type, on the State and 'merely pronounce a particular practice or condition to be illegal, leaving officials free to choose if and how to remedy the situation',[54] in terms of political pressures in a system of international adjudication, the declaratory judgments of the ECtHR hold enormous symbolic value.

[50] Shelton, above n 18 at 56.

[51] Shelton, above n 18 at 22, referring to Revised Set of Basic Principles and Guidelines on the Right to reparation for victims of [Gross] Violations of Human Rights and International Humanitarian Law, Prepared by Mr Theo van Boven E/CN.4/1997/104, App and Shelton, above n 18 at 49–51.

[52] O De Schutter and P Alston, 'Introduction, Addressing the Challenges Confronting the EU Fundamental Rights Agency' in P Alston, and O De Schutter (eds), *Monitoring Fundamental Rights in the EU* (Oxford, Hart Publishing, 2005), 1–21, 1.

[53] Shelton, above n 18 at 51; A Mowbray, *Cases and Materials on the European Convention on Human Rights* (Oxford, Oxford University Press, 2007) ch 19; A Mowbray, 'The European Court of Human Right's Approach to Just Satisfaction' (1997) PL 647, 658–59.

[54] Shelton, above n 18 at 55.

It was noted above that the ECtHR favoured a political balance to the EU–ECHR situation. However, Shelton has argued in another context that balancing in human rights cases 'may lead to undervaluing individual rights if the 'costs' being evaluated include the risk of non-compliance.'[55] The balance must therefore be carefully constructed to ensure against the ECtHR tolerating an environment of non-compliance. By not making declarations on Convention breaches, the ECtHR leaves scope to the ECJ to decide on the EU's level of compliance with Convention standards, especially as there are no additional safeguards before that compliance becomes 'manifestly deficient'. By delegating a monitoring role to the ECJ on matters of human rights falling under the convention, the ECtHR leaves unmonitored the risk of the ECJ adopting standards of protection far lower than that available under the ECHR, thus negatively affecting the *status quo* for individuals and creating circumstances to continue violations. It may in fact encourage the ECJ to take a lax approach to human rights protection. This is difficult to reconcile with the principle of deterrence of human rights breaches. The procedures adopted in *Bosphorus* do not even permit the ECtHR to provide guidance on the means of protection at EU level, general reviews being insufficient to fulfil this. Thus, the EU is not deterred from violating Convention rights unless it will be manifestly deficient of ECHR standards. One issue of course is that the existence of a manifest deficiency is not always clear *ex ante* and thus the lack of guidance from the ECtHR is of further concern.

The ambiguities and disappointment of *Bosphorus* also leave one unclear as to how the ECtHR might approach cases where it ought to review Member States' EU-related actions. For instance, under a strict reading of *Bosphorus*, the ECtHR should scrutinise Member States' actions where they have had discretion in the implementation of secondary legislation. However, it is unclear whether the ECtHR will take a firm approach to the existence of discretion and thus tighten the State's margin of appreciation in order to provide a heightened level of individual protection. Failure to do so would result in a wider range of EU-related actions being brought within the immunity of *Bosphorus*. As a final point, the granting of authority to the ECJ in ECHR-related matters has further implications for the principle of deterrence. It gives power to the EU to rule on the standards of the ECHR. Apart from the ECJ not being in a position to give authoritative rulings of the ECHR,[56] such a situation also takes opportunities away from the ECtHR to develop positive obligations

[55] Ibid 54.

[56] R Lawson, 'The Contribution of the Agency to the Implementation in the EU of International and European Human Rights Instruments' in P Alston and O De Schutter above n 51, 229–52 at 250.

under the Convention: the ECJ certainly has no authority to rule on such obligations for the Convention regime as a whole.

Overall, delegation of ECtHR authority to the ECJ decreases respect for the ECtHR.[57] Shelton warns of the dangers of having rights without remedies by saying that such circumstances

> call[s] into serious question the integrity of human rights norms and the rule of law. If the primary purpose of rights is to affect the distribution of power between individual and state—specifically, to protect individuals from the abuse of state power—then rights without remedies are ineffectual for this purpose. The government's duty to respect such rights then would be illusory. Even the symbolic value of rights could disappear once it becomes obvious that rights could be violated with impunity. The structural limits on the powers of government would exist only in the unlikely event that those with government power did not seek to aggrandize it.[58]

This last point is engaged in the next section concerning conflict of interests and independent monitoring. In relation to the first point, the ECtHR's solution to the EU–ECHR conundrum does little to protect the individual from the powers of governing authorities. Although, as noted earlier, *Bosphorus* applies in a discrete situation, for a political purpose, and seeks to provide a compromise within the wider European institutional setting, it does not provide the individual in the specific cases with a solution which guarantees their faith in the ECHR system and as such does not deter specific breaches of human rights by the EU at least until it reaches the stage of manifest deficiency. The importance of human rights protection should be visible not only when viewed as part of the broader political context, but also in each and every specific case.

D. Conflict of Interests—External Supervision of Human Rights Protection

Linked to the idea of deterrence is that of the provision of independent monitoring to ensure the guarantee of Convention standards. The ECHR applies this in respect of all its States parties. To a large extent, where state action is intertwined with those of the EU, *Bosphorus* transfers that monitoring role to the EU: it endorses internal EU supervision of EU activities. The general argument is that the optimal level of human rights protection (in the current analysis, the optimal level is that of the ECHR) cannot be achieved when the potential offender (here the EU) is also the guarantor of those rights[59] and the final arbiter on the matter to the exclusion of

[57] Shelton, above n 18 at 50.
[58] Ibid 52.
[59] U Baxi, 'Too Many of Too Few' (2001) HRLR 1(1) 1–9, 6.

further monitoring of its actions (ie through the ECJ). Seen in this light, the EU therefore cannot be a strong guarantor of individual human rights, against violations of human rights arising from its own activities, neither in respect of its internal human rights standards and especially not those of the ECHR.

O'Connell, more specifically, raises questions about the nature of organisations purporting to protect human rights. He takes issue with the proposition that neo-liberal organisations (like the World Bank or the International Monetary Fund, to use his examples) which aim to pursue free market based, privatisation agendas can ensure human rights protection.[60] Along the lines of this argument, the EU, whilst displaying such features,[61] cannot thus provide the same level of human rights protection that independent monitors could provide.[62] The economic aims and objectives of the EU have been clear from its very beginnings, and although there is a greater integration of the human rights language within its activities and case law, the basic foundations of the EU remain the same. O'Connell argues that neo-liberal strategies always undermine and conflict with the protection of human rights, because the former flourishes on inherent features which violate the latter. The two principles cannot be simultaneously preserved: whilst O'Connell backs up this point with talks of the characteristics of neo-liberal models (such as the decreasing role of the State and the reduction of positive regulation in favour of de-regulation) which are the opposite to the needs of the human rights model,[63] Williams raises the concern of EU decision-making being influenced by actors with primarily economic aims.[64] These factors fail to provide a foundation for the flourishing of human rights protection.

Baxi raises another point in relation to global corporations which, for example, seek to fund human rights initiatives. He argues that such acts 'carr[y] the potential symbolic costs for legitimation of human rights cultures'.[65] There is a conflict of interest within the organisation: the same organisation which is driven by its own goals of economic success is the same one charged with promotion of rights which may obstruct that success. Whilst the EU has progressed in attempts to establish a human rights

[60] P O'Connell, 'On Reconciling Irreconcilables: Neo-Liberal Globalisation and Human Rights' (2007) 7(3) *Human Rights Law Review* 483–509.

[61] Despite its attempts at regulating social rights and human rights.

[62] P O'Connell, above n 59 at 483–509; for similar arguments, see J Donnelly, 'The Social Construction of International Human Rights', in T Dunne and N Wheeler, *Human Rights in Global Politics* (Cambridge, Cambridge University Press, 1999), 71–102 at 94–95.

[63] O'Connell, above n 59 at 495–501.

[64] A Williams, 'The (Im)possibility of the European Union as a Global Human Rights Regime' in R Brownsword (ed), *Global Governance and the Quest for Justice, Volume IV: Human Rights* (Oxford, Hart Publishing, 2004) 69–87, 79.

[65] Baxi, above n 48 at 6.

dimension within its system of operations, this is not always comparable to ECHR standards. Because a conflict of interests exists in the manner argued by Baxi and O'Connell, the CoE ought not to entrust the EU with guaranteeing ECHR standards of human rights protection, at least not without closer parallel supervision by the ECtHR itself—a body external to the EU. The case would be different if the EU was providing external monitoring of Member States' measures affecting human rights protection, rather than internal monitoring of its own measures.

The preliminary ruling procedure of the EU again may be invoked as a forum for bringing forth human rights concerns, but it could not constitute an adequate remedy because, although it provides individuals with access to the ECJ, it still does not provide external supervision of EU compliance with the Convention.[66] Shelton's study on remedies confirms that human rights treaties need supervisory bodies[67] and these must be external bodies, because

> [i]t is to his own government that the individual will look for his most basic needs. At the same time, it is from his own government that an individual often most needs protection.[68]

This is because it is the State which has the power to impact on the lives of individuals and thus affect their rights. It was argued earlier that where international organisations, like the EU, hold similar governing powers which can affect individual human rights, then they should similarly be held accountable for affecting individual's human rights, or at least affecting the States' capabilities of fulfilling those rights. Otherwise, the individual is left without redress against the governing body[69] and the State is free to breach international human rights standards through the use of international organisations. The weakness in external ECHR supervision of the EU denoted by *Bosphorus* is all the more problematic because civil society is not adequately represented within the EU and arguably therefore people's interests are not well served.[70] The weak form of individual participation in EU mechanisms, as set out earlier, is an example of this.

III. A REVISED TEST

As alluded to throughout part II, the critique embodied in this analysis is not intended to dispute the necessity of devising a compromise in the

[66] *Bosphorus*, above n 9, Joint Concurring Opinion of Judges Rozakis, Tulkens, Traja, Botoucharova, Zagrebelsky and Garlicki, 52.
[67] Shelton, above n 18 at 52.
[68] Higgins, above n 3 at 95.
[69] Ibid.
[70] O'Connell, above n 59 at 494.

context of European human rights challenges. It rather aimed to explore in more detail the roots of the contention that the compromise adopted in *Bosphorus* is likely to impact negatively on human rights protection, particularly on what is seen as the very essence of the protection promised by the ECHR: the guarantee of Convention rights *to individuals*, which are *enforceable by those individuals*. More specifically, it has indicated that some of those negative impacts may be excessive and disproportionate to the legitimate aim of international cooperation on which the ruling is based. To follow on from that, this section pulls together these different threads and arguments and presents a modified *Bosphorus* test which could avoid these excessive impacts. Since the chapter has not examined the entirety of the EU–ECHR debate, the revisions do not claim to offer a full package solution. The preceding sections did, however, indicate the centrality of individuals in the identity of the ECHR system of human rights protection as primarily developed by its court and the revisions outlined below are proposals for a way forward in the future application of the *Bosphorus* rules to preserve that identity more effectively. The key elements consist of the following.

In the first place, the threshold of 'manifest deficiency' ought to be changed to 'deficiency' only. Though there is insufficient explanation of this concept in the *Bosphorus* judgment to decipher its meaning, the term 'manifest' does suggest that the ECHR will only review EU law in cases of extremely serious violations, leaving the EU to account internally for all other violations, *albeit* that these may also be of a serious nature. If the essence of the ECHR as developed by its court is to protect individuals, then the application of such a high threshold in the quest to secure a harmonious EU–ECHR relationship is excessive. Surely, where 'equivalent' has been indicated to mean 'comparable' by the ECtHR, then 'equivalent' cannot also mean 'everything that is not manifestly deficient'. Although the ECtHR need not demand identical protection from EU measures, a more suitable balance between the aims of international cooperation and those of individual protection would be to require the EU to provide protection that is not 'deficient' so that the EU is forced to tighten the attention it pays to human rights in its internal legal order. Conversely then, it is not essential that the EU provide protection identical to the ECHR level in order to fulfil ECHR standards. It can fulfil those standards by ensuring that its economic aims do not 'seriously' impair the essence of the right in question. In this sense, for example, the lack of capacity for individuals under EU mechanisms to challenge third pillar measures which directly impact on their human rights 'ought' to be considered a deficiency in the EU's human rights protection system, until such a time as the EU broadens the scope of application of the ECJ's jurisdiction to cover all third pillar measures which *affect individual rights*. This type of refinement of *Bosphorus* will affect several of the factors of human rights protection explored in part II above. For instance, although it will not eliminate the two principal charges of double standards (vis-à-vis non-EU related scenarios and vis-à-vis the possible divergent applications of the Convention standards by the ECJ), it will limit the extent of the potential inconsistencies in those two situations and the scope for legal uncertainty. Additionally, it would demand a greater degree of participation in European measures by individuals than would be required by the 'manifest deficiency' standard. Moreover, it would increase the instances in which the ECtHR continues to play an external supervisory role in relation to the application of Convention rights in the jurisdiction of its States parties.

A second suggestion is that in future cases, the ECtHR should fully apply the *Bosphorus* test by undertaking assessments of both the EU's *procedural* and *substantive* protection of human rights.[71] This is not, therefore, a suggestion for change in the *Bosphorus* test, but an appeal for its proper application. In *Bosphorus*, the judges conducted a review of the EU's general mechanisms for human rights protection with no specific regard to the right to property. The ECtHR should ensure that its review of the EU's comparability of human rights protection is conducted on a case by case basis, in relation to the specific mechanism for protection of the human right in question and in relation to the substantive protection of that right (even if it is only scrutinised for evidence of 'deficient' protection). This would ensure a greater level of uniformity in the application of Convention rights; it demands a greater level of individual participation in the enforcement of Convention rights; it increases the possibilities for the ECtHR to declare on potential breaches, which in turn enhances its deterrent effect and provides an improved level of independent monitoring of EU rules which may affect a State's ability to secure Convention rights. Finally, that external review by the ECtHR could be stricter where the EU's interests continue to raise a question of conflict of interests with human rights protection, and especially in cases where the participation of individuals in the making and enforcement of EU law is weak. This should result in the EU adopting a higher standard of internal human rights supervision.

In sum, *Bosphorus* ought to be read as or interpreted in future cases in the following way: EU Member States remain responsible for the application of EU law over which they have discretion in implementation. Member States will be presumed to have complied with the Convention rights of individual applicants, where the EU provides human rights protection of equivalent (comparable) standard to the ECHR. The ECtHR will undertake subject-specific substantive and procedural reviews of the EU

[71] *Bosphorus*, above n 9 at para 155.

in relation to all the cases before it. Where the EU's protection is considered deficient of ECHR standards, then the presumption of equivalence is rebutted.

IV. CONCLUSION

Today's human rights dispute settlement mechanisms face an ongoing range of complexities. This chapter has sought to assess the success of the ECtHR in upholding its self-declared ideals of 'practical and effective' enforcement of individual human rights in the face of such complexities. *Bosphorus* presented a typical case for the dispute, involving Member States' obligations to apply Convention rights versus contradictory EU legislation. The difficulties arise from the fact that the membership of the two organisations overlap; the EU is not bound by the ECHR; and that there is no hierarchy between the ECJ and ECtHR. The solution outlined by the ECtHR in *Bosphorus* aptly preserves harmonious relations both between the EU and ECHR and between the ECJ and the ECtHR. Whilst this is a legitimate goal, it leaves much to be desired when the measure of effectiveness concerns the preservation of individual human rights.

Moreover, the ruling by the ECtHR in *Bosphorus* can be criticised for creating both procedural and substantive gaps in the ECHR's protection of human rights. When dealing with measures arising from other international organisations, the ECtHR is no doubt in a difficult position of devising ways to ensure effective rights protection whilst reconciling the autonomy and authority of two separate legal orders. The EU has developed a highly sophisticated framework of European integration and the ECHR has developed the reputation of being the guardian of human rights protection within Europe and in particular all EU Member States have signed up to its commitments. The *Bosphorus* scenario is not the first time that the ECtHR has been faced with a case of potential violation of human rights arising from EU law. To date, it has avoided passing judgment on rules adopted by the EU institutions. In *Bosphorus*, the Court finally faced the issue head-on. However, in the solution suggested, the ECtHR arguably lost sight of the aim of individual human rights protection, a goal which is not only a foundation of regional human rights law, but also a central goal of the development of the Convention system. The chapter presented the view that the decision in *Bosphorus* weighed too greatly in favour of international cooperation, to the detriment of individuals. This was explained through the examination of four criteria: the universal application of ECHR rights; access to justice before the ECtHR; the effect of deterring EU violations of the ECHR; and the need for external monitoring by the ECtHR of Convention rights. This chapter has argued that a stricter level of scrutiny of EU measures would provide a better balance in achieving both aims than is currently formulated in *Bosphorus*. To this end, whilst the proposed revised test would still pose threats to the goal of individual human rights protection, it provides the ECtHR with greater scope for monitoring the 'comparable' protection of Convention rights in the EU.

In addition to the specific issues arising from *Bosphorus*, the case also exemplifies some general developments in international dispute settlement mechanisms. In the first place, it highlights the multiple existence of international mechanisms in similar fields and particularly their overlap in terms of geography, membership and/or substance. This is testament to the claim that States see an increasing value in conducting international relations and addressing challenges through international organisations and their courts and tribunals. Nevertheless, in the second place, the case also demonstrates these organisations give rise to new and ongoing problems. Thus, whilst a commitment to human rights by both the CoE and the EU is of enormous positive significance to the human rights cause, it also presents complications which may negatively affect those rights and in particular halt the speed of progress an organisation wishes to make in that field. Finally, the *Bosphorus* case is an example of the power and relevance of courts in providing solutions to these new problems in relation to which the legislative and political bodies have yet to provide decisive direction.

14

The European Court of Justice as a Constitutional Court: Implications for the EU and International Legal Orders

PAUL JAMES CARDWELL

I. INTRODUCTION

THE EUROPEAN COURT of Justice (ECJ) is a constituent part of the most developed example of a system of regional governance currently in existence.[1] The extensive contribution of the ECJ in shaping the legal framework of the European Community (EC)/European Union (EU) and furthering the process of European integration is well-known and well-documented.[2] From early seminal decisions recognising the 'new legal order' created by the EC Treaty[3] and the supremacy of EC law over the national law of the Member States,[4] through decisions which drove the legal orders of the Member States towards harmonisation in the absence of sustained EC legislative activity in the 1970s and early 1980s,[5] the ECJ's role cannot be understated. Innovations by the ECJ have also filled gaps in the Treaty-based constitutionalism of the EC/EU; for example, the principle and conditions of State liability for harm caused to individuals through breaches of EC law.[6] Read alongside

[1] See further: R Kirkham and PJ Cardwell, 'The European Union: A Role Model for Regional Governance?' (2006) 12 *European Public Law* 403.

[2] See generally: JHH Weiler, 'A Quiet Revolution: The European Court of Justice and its Interlocutors' (1994) 24 *Comparative Political Studies* 510; A Arnull, *The European Union and its Court of Justice* (Oxford, Oxford University Press, 1999); A Stone Sweet, *The Judicial Construction of Europe* (Oxford, Oxford University Press, 2004).

[3] Case 26/62 *Van Gend en Loos* [1963] ECR 13.

[4] Case 6/64 *Costa v ENEL* [1964] ECR 585.

[5] See, esp Case 120/78 *Rewe-Zentral AG v Bundesmonopolverwaltung für Branntwein* ('Cassis de Dijon') [1979] ECR 649.

[6] Case C-6/90 and C-9/90 *Francovich and Bonifaci v Italy* [1991] ECR I-5357.

the Union's Treaty arrangements, the ECJ's jurisprudence has provided a more holistic template for the founding charters/treaties of more recent regional entities.[7] Despite this influence, however, some of the distinctive hallmarks of EC/EU law (especially the principle of supremacy of EC/EU law over national law) remain absent from the text of the Treaty arrangements of the EU.[8] As such, any understanding of the nature of EC/EU law must pay strong heed to the case law of the Court in addition to the Treaty texts.

The implications of the 'new legal order' for the now-27 legal systems of the Member States and the relationships between the Member States, EC/EU law and international law has not, however, been without controversy. By using the language of the Treaty as an inspiration for laying down some of the principles commonly associated with the nature of European law, the ECJ has often been accused of exceeding the role accorded to it in the Treaties and creating a legal order which bears only partial resemblance to the words found in the Treaty.[9] Certainly, the work and methodology of the ECJ in establishing general *principles* of law distinguishes it as a court from other international courts, in particular the International Court of Justice.[10] Evaluating whether the early innovations by the ECJ and the techniques it has employed are justifiable or not is beyond the scope of this chapter. What is important to note however is that the success of the ECJ as a court in a regional system of governance, and the growth in competence and powers of the EU and its institutions, has resulted in the raising of pertinent questions of jurisdiction and competence between the various institutions and the Member States. Such issues have arisen in a variety of situations, often in relation to the external sphere. Within the wider context of a growth in the creation of tribunals/arbitration mechanisms at the global level, the potential for overlapping or contradictory dispute resolution mechanisms is clear. As

[7] See esp the Treaty Creating the Court of Justice of the Cartagena Agreement (the Andean Community) Art 30, which covers a *Francovich* situation by stating that 'A verdict of non-compliance issued by the Court … shall constitute legal and sufficient grounds for the party to ask the national judge for compensation for any damages or loss that may be due'.

[8] This would not have been the case if the Treaty Establishing a Constitution for Europe had come into force, as it contained the following Art I-6: 'The Constitution and law adopted by the institutions of the Union in exercising competences conferred on it shall have primacy over the law of the Member States'. The Treaty of Lisbon does not contain any reference to primacy or supremacy over national law, although Declaration no 17 attached to the Treaty recognises the principle 'in accordance with well settled case law of the Court of Justice'.

[9] See, especially, H Rasmussen, *On Law and Policy in the European Court of Justice* (Dordrecht, Martinus Nijhoff, 1986).

[10] T Tridimas, *The General Principles of EU Law*, 2nd edn (Oxford, Oxford University Press, 2006) 57.

John Merrills himself notes, this phenomenon is 'something all courts and tribunals must work with as the legal world becomes more complex'.[11]

Since the Treaty on European Union (TEU) 1992, the activities of the EU have diversified into more widespread areas which move it away from being characterised as a merely economic entity, if indeed such a characterisation was ever wholly accurate. These areas cover foreign and security policy, and freedom, security and justice, including cooperation in criminal law and military issues. Although aspects of these areas have arguably been long present (often indirectly) within the European integration process, it is only recently that they have come to the fore to the extent that they are now commonly cited as key priorities for the Union by the institutions.[12] The legal framework at the institutional level is made more complex by the 'pillar' structure of the EU, where the jurisdiction of the ECJ is limited in the second and third pillars. Given this complexity, the ECJ has hence been faced with a number of difficult issues, not only in terms of its own competence, but also in the relationship between the Community/Union legal order and public international law and human rights. Recent cases before the ECJ have shown that settling disputes between the Member States, even on issues which do not directly concern the implementation of EC/EU law, and issues which involve the impact of international law in domestic legal systems, is becoming increasingly important in testing the boundaries between the EC/EU legal order and international law. The stated values of the Union, including its commitment to human rights, are also being tested within the search for a greater global role for the Union. As the most prominent example of the development of a regional system of law (and one which has supranationalism at the heart of most of its policy-making areas) the EU is a major contributor to the increasingly blurred nature of the boundaries of international law.

Taking the need for dispute resolution in the international legal order in the twenty-first century as a starting point, the purpose of this chapter is to explore some of the case law of the ECJ since 2005 in order to consider the dynamism of the relationship between EC/EU law and international law. The argument is made that the ECJ continues to resemble a 'constitutional court' for the EU and its emphasis on the requirement of Member States to uphold the treaty in all ways has significant implications for the application and effectiveness of international law in Europe. The chapter draws out two related points: the increasingly blurred nature

[11] JG Merrills, *International Dispute Settlement*, 4th edn (Cambridge, Cambridge University Press, 2005) 124.

[12] See, eg the Conclusions of the European Council, 19–20 June 2008 (European Council, 11018/08).

of international dispute resolution between States who are also members of the European Union, and the complexity of recognising how the EU's distinct legal order fits in the international legal system, within the context of the growth of new dimensions in the European integration process.[13] The chapter proceeds by setting the context of these recent developments, before focussing discussion on three major judgments of the ECJ since 2005 and drawing out what they tell us about the present state of the constitutional order of the EU and dispute resolution.

II. THE NATURE OF THE 'NEW LEGAL ORDER'

The European Union is founded upon treaties concluded by sovereign States and it can thus be correctly described as a 'creature of international law'.[14] The ECJ's role was defined in the original EC Treaty in terms which remain relatively unchanged today, with the exception of the re-defining of its role in relation to more recent policy areas, particularly those in the second and third pillars of the EU's constitutional structure as created by the TEU and amended by the subsequent Treaties of Amsterdam and Nice. In essence, the Court must ensure that 'in the interpretation and application of this Treaty the law is observed'.[15] A cursory reading of the Treaty provisions on the powers and competence of the ECJ,[16] along with the conferred powers principle of Article 5 EC ('The Community shall act within the limits of the powers conferred upon it by this Treaty and of the objectives assigned to it therein') gives little indication of the extent to which the ECJ has developed the nature of the Treaty in the ways that it has over the past fifty years by pushing the boundaries and depth of the legal provisions.[17] Its own role in consolidating its place at the heart of the constitutional structure of the EU cannot be ignored.

From the *van Gend en Loos* case, delivered only five years after the Treaty of Rome came into effect, the nature of EC law as a 'new legal order of international law for the benefit of which the states have limited their sovereign rights, albeit within limited fields, and the subjects of which comprise not only Member States but also their nationals'[18] has guided the ECJ in its subsequent jurisprudence. The ECJ was clearly minded to extend the traditional notion of international law (as represented by the

[13] The relationship between the EU, its Member States and the European Convention of Human Rights and European Court of Human Rights, is the subject of the chapter in this collection by Tawhida Ahmed and as such will not be covered here.

[14] J Shaw, *Law of the European Union*, 3rd edn, (Basingstoke, Palgrave Macmillan, 2000) 10.

[15] Art 220 EC.

[16] Arts 220–45 EC.

[17] J Shaw, 'Europe's Constitutional Future' (2005) PL 132–33.

[18] *Van Gend en Loos*, above n 3 at 10.

submissions of several Member States to the Court) as binding individuals as well as States.[19] Through the combination of the doctrines of direct effect of provisions of EC law in national courts (*Van Gend en Loos*) and supremacy of EC law over national law (*Costa v ENEL*) the Court found ways to ensure that the nature of EC law reached beyond the governmental-level into the national legal orders of the Member States. These two cases represented novel approaches of the ECJ using methods which had not previously been explicitly recognised in international law. Bruno de Witte has written that:

> the principle [of primacy] applies to 'relations between powers', that is, it merely implies that Community law prevails over national law on the international plane; and the procedure of Article 169 EEC Treaty[20] is meant to give effect to that principle. The *Costa* controversy, however, was about the *internal primacy* of EC law, that is, the duty of *national* courts to enforce EC rules even when they conflict with national legislation. Such a duty had never been considered to be part of international law, although the failure of courts to enforce international treaty rules could, of course, be a contributory factor in the establishment of State responsibility under international law. The preliminary reference mechanism allowed the Court, in *Costa*, to 'stop the clock'.[21]

The work of the Court in early cases has prompted prolonged academic debate, and it is not the purpose here to revisit the different arguments in depth. What is significant to note here, however, is that over the following decades, the ECJ consolidated its place as a key institution in the Community legal order in ensuring that, on one level, the Treaty Articles relating to such core issues as the 'four freedoms' ensured the moves towards a single market in the absence of (until the mid-1980s) strong legislative action and, on another level, ensuring that it remained the only body capable of authoritative guidance on the terms of the Treaty. In addition, as noted above, the creation of general principles of law which went beyond the positive law in force in all of the Member States set the workings of the Court apart from those of the International Court of Justice. The ECJ was not constrained by the lack of municipal authority for its decisions in the Member States.[22] Thus, it has gone beyond mere 'gap filling' in the Treaty arrangements towards expressing constitutional

19 See generally: P Pescatore, The Doctrine of 'Direct Effect': An Infant Disease of Community Law' (1983) 8 *European Law Review* (*EL Rev*)155; F Mancini, 'The Making of a Constitution for Europe' (1989) 26 *Common Market Law Review* (CML Rev) 595; A Arnull, 'Does the Court of Justice have Inherent Jurisdiction? (1990) 27 CML Rev 683; K Lenaerts and P van Nuffel, *Constitutional Law of the European Union*, 2nd edn (London, Sweet & Maxwell, 2005) 14–17.

20 Now Art 226 EC.

21 B de Witte, 'Direct Effect, Supremacy, and the Nature of the Legal Order' in P Craig and G de Búrca (eds), *The Evolution of EU Law* (Oxford, Oxford University Press, 1999) 182–83.

22 Tridimas, above n 10 at 57.

standards, giving 'complexity and coherence to the community legal system which goes beyond the skeletal legal system of the Community treaties'.[23] The effect of the ECJ distinguishing its work from that of existing international courts led Eric Stein to comment in 1981 that:

> Tucked away in the fairyland Duchy of Luxembourg and blessed, until recently, with benign neglect by the powers that be and the mass media, the Court of Justice of the European Communities has fashioned a constitutional framework for a federal-type structure in Europe. From its inception a mere quarter of a century ago, the Court has construed the European Community Treaties in a constitutional mode rather than employing the traditional international law methodology.[24]

Some years later, Martin Shapiro posited the view that the nature of the ECJ as 'a court clothed in constitutional law that it continues to stitch as it moves along' is indicative of a court which can be regarded not only as successful, but as a successful *constitutional* court.[25]

The questions of direct effect and supremacy are generally seen as settled within most areas of the EU legal order, although national constitutional courts in Member States both new and old continue to be faced with problematic issues in relation to their acceptance within national legal systems and their own constitutional law.[26] Such questions are likely to continue to arise in the context of the complexity of the EU's growing competence in areas which are inherently 'sensitive' in terms of the sovereignty of the Member States. Questions are particularly pertinent with regard to the second and third pillars of the EU's constitutional structure: Common Foreign and Security Policy (CFSP, second pillar) and Police and Judicial Cooperation (PJC, third pillar). These pillars are often characterised as 'intergovernmental' rather than 'supranational' within the Treaty provisions since their creation in the Treaty on European Union 1992. They constitute two dimensions of European integration which Member States have been more reticent to allow the same level of competence to the EU institutions than in the Community (first) pillar. This includes the lack of a general right of initiative on the part of the Commission, and also more limited jurisdiction of the ECJ. It is no accident that the focus of two of the three major cases fall within these areas which consider various important lessons about the role of the ECJ in the 21st century EU.

[23] P Allott, 'Preliminary Rulings—Another Infant Disease' (2000) *EL Rev* 538, 540–41.

[24] E Stein, 'Lawyers, Judges and the Making of a Transnational Constitution' (1981) 75 *AJIL* 1.

[25] M Shapiro, 'The European Court of Justice' in Craig and de Búrca, above n 21 at 326.

[26] See esp the cases of the Constitutional/Supreme Courts of Germany (*Brunner v The European Union* (Cases 2 BvR 2134/92 and 2159/92) [1994] CMLRev 57), Denmark (*Carlsen v Prime Minister* [1999] 3 CMLRev 854) and Poland (*European Arrest Warrant case*, decision of the Polish Constitutional Tribunal of 27 April 2005 [2005] no P 1/05).

III. *PUPINO*: EXPANDING THE CONSTITUTIONAL PRINCIPLES OF THE EU?

The case of *Pupino* brings into focus the role of the ECJ in the evolving domain of Police and Judicial Cooperation in Criminal Matters in the EU.[27] Here, the ECJ was asked to consider the effect of a Framework Decision concluded under Article 34 TEU, part of the 'third' pillar of Police and Judicial Cooperation. The subject matter of the Framework Decision was the standing and protection of victims in criminal proceedings and contained specific provisions on 'victims who are particularly vulnerable'. Maria Pupino, a nursery school teacher, had been accused of misusing disciplinary measures and injuring children in her care. The Italian law of criminal procedure consisted of two stages, and evidence was only heard at the second stage, unless limited exceptions provided for in the legislation applied. The exceptions did not apply in Pupino's case, but the Prosecutor nevertheless attempted to take evidence during the first stage. The Italian court did not accept the Prosecutor's arguments that taking evidence at the first stage was necessary. The Court was minded, however, to refer to the ECJ by means of the preliminary reference procedure (Article 234 EC) the question of whether it was obliged to interpret Italian law in the light of the provisions of the directive, which obliges Member States to pursue special arrangements for vulnerable victims (which includes minors according to the definition in the Framework Decision Article 2(2)).

The terms of Article 34 TEU exclude the possibility of direct effect of Framework Decisions.[28] However, the ECJ stated that as the binding character of Framework Decisions (in Article 34(2)(b)) is formulated in identical terms to Article 249 EC paragraph 3,[29] there is an obligation on national courts 'to interpret national law in conformity'.[30] This is substantially the same requirement as the Court has developed for Community law (the so-named 'indirect effect' of directives).[31] The Italian court was therefore bound to allow for special arrangements to be made for the childrens' evidence.

The Italian and UK governments submitted to the Court in *Pupino* that the third pillar does *not* have an equivalent of Article 10 EC,[32] the principle

[27] Case C-105/03 *Criminal Proceedings against Maria Pupino* [2005] ECR I-5285.

[28] Art 34(2)(c).

[29] 'A directive shall be binding, as to the result to be achieved, upon each Member State to which it is addressed, but shall leave to the national authorities the choice of form and methods'.

[30] *Pupino*, above n 27 at 34.

[31] Case 14/83 *Von Colson and Kamann v Land Nordrhein-Westfalen* [1984] ECR 1891.

[32] 'Member States shall take all appropriate measures, whether general or particular, to ensure fulfilment of the obligations arising out of this Treaty or resulting from action

of loyal cooperation, and therefore Member States cannot be bound in the same way. Nevertheless, AG Kokott was of the opinion that even in the absence of express words, the sense and spirit of Article 10 EC can be felt in the third pillar, considering the aim of the EU as articulated in Article 1 TEU: an 'ever closer Union among the peoples of Europe'. This aim cannot, in the view of the Advocate General, be achieved 'unless the Member States and institutions of the Union cooperate sincerely and in compliance with the law'.[33] AG Kokott went on to say that against this background:

> Article 10 EC lays down some axiomatic principles, namely, that obligations must be fulfilled and damaging measures refrained from. The same applies in Union law without needing to be expressly mentioned.[34]

The ECJ found that non-application of a 'general or particular' principle of cooperation would render the Union's tasks difficult to carry out effectively, and therefore national courts must interpret national law 'as far as possible in the light of the wording and purpose of the Framework Decision'.[35]

In coming to this reasoning, AG Kokott referred to the origins in international law of the EC Treaty and Treaty on European Union. As an international treaty it should be interpreted 'not only on the basis of its wording, but also in the light of its objectives', as according to the Vienna Convention on the Law of Treaties of 23 May 1969. The ECJ, in its judgment, did not refer to international law generally or the Vienna Convention, though it did agree with the Advocate General that Framework Decisions have a binding character and, coupled with the existence of an (implied) principle of loyal cooperation in the third pillar, Member States are obliged to interpret national law in accordance with the Framework Decision.[36] To do otherwise would deprive the Treaty provisions of their 'useful effect' vis-à-vis individuals who would not be able to rely on the Framework Decision.[37]

As previously mentioned, various Member States made submissions to the Court, several pointing to the lack of an explicitly worded Article 10 EC-style obligation of loyal cooperation within the TEU and arguing that since the third pillar was distinct from the Community pillar, there was no obligation to interpret national law in conformity with a

taken by the institutions of the Community. They shall facilitate the achievement of the Community's tasks. They shall abstain from any measure which could jeopardise the attainment of the objectives of this Treaty'.

33 *Pupino*, n 27 above, opinion of Kokott AG of 11 November 2004, para 26.
34 Ibid para 27.
35 Ibid para 43.
36 Ibid para 34.
37 Ibid para 38.

Framework Decision. Sweden's submission to the ECJ in *Pupino* was that the Framework Decision was an instrument of international law, suggesting that the ECJ would not be capable of construing the same legal effect as if it was a Community instrument. The argument behind this view was that the third pillar is more readily visible as an intergovernmental forum for cooperation; Member States may opt in or out of the preliminary reference procedure, in contrast to the mandatory provision in the Community pillar. Further, the institutional competences differ and are weighted more heavily towards the Council, with a more limited role for the Commission than in the first pillar.[38]

For the Advocate General, however, even if this was the case then the Courts of the Member States would be obliged to 'bring their conduct into compliance, as far as possible, with that obligation'.[39] This reasoning would seem to rely on an implied duty on national Courts to respect obligations derived from international law,[40] even though the unique nature of the EC/EU as an integration process and legal order is also stressed throughout. In this sense, it appears that international law is useful in the reasoning of the Advocate General, but only insofar as it serves as a reference point which *reinforces* the nature of the EC/EU as a separate legal order. As far as State sovereignty is concerned, however, international law references give way to references to the development of the new legal order and principles of supremacy as built up in the first pillar. This is not necessarily a negative development, since both the AG's opinion and the judgment of the ECJ are logical in the sense of consistent interpretation of the Treaty Articles. Had the ECJ not already laid down the obligation of indirect effect in *Von Colson*, then this decision would have been surprising and also had the effect of taking the EU legal order into new territory.[41] As it stands, the Court's reasoning relies more on the import of principles from the first pillar of the EU than insights from international law. It would seem strange to make a strong distinction between the first pillar of the EU as a substantial departure from 'traditional' international

[38] *cf* TEU Art 35(2): 'By a declaration … any Member State shall be able to accept the jurisdiction of the Court of Justice to give preliminary rulings'; and Art 234 EC: 'Where any such question is raised in a case pending before a court or tribunal of a Member State against whose decisions there is no judicial remedy under national law, that court or tribunal shall bring the matter before the Court of Justice'.

[39] *Pupino*, n 27 above, opinion of Kokott AG of 11 November 2004, para 37.

[40] In the case of the UK, for example, Lord Bingham of Cornhill noted in *A (FC) and Others (FC) v Home Secretary* [2004] UKHL 71, [27]: 'the well established principle that the words of a United Kingdom statute, passed after the date of a treaty and dealing with the same subject matter, are to be construed, if they are reasonably capable of bearing such a meaning, as intended to carry out the treaty obligation and not to be inconsistent with it: *Garland v British Rail Engineering Ltd* [1983] 2 AC 751, 771'.

[41] M Fletcher, 'Extending "Indirect Effect" to the Third Pillar: the Significance of *Pupino*?' (2005) 30 *EL Rev* 862, 866.

law and the second and third pillars. Nevertheless, as Spaventa has noted, *Pupino* may have a 'Pandora's box' quality in relation to other constitutional principles which may find their way into the third pillar too.[42]

Pupino could potentially have strong implications for the legal order in the second pillar (the CFSP), since the ECJ may try to read the obligation on Member States to support the CFSP 'actively and unreservedly in a spirit of loyalty and mutual solidarity'[43] in a similar way. There seems to be little room for doubt, therefore, that if the ECJ is prepared to extend the effect of Article 10 EC to the third pillar, the CFSP will not be immune from a reinforcement of the obligation of cooperation. This has been raised as a possibility by several commentators,[44] and whilst it may be welcome from the perspective of ensuring that the second and third pillars oblige Member States to respect their obligations, it is not difficult to imagine a certain nervousness in the capitals of some Member States, where governments may be worrying about the interpretation of the Treaty they have signed up to in 'sensitive' areas.

The point to make at this juncture is that measures which are taken within 'intergovernmental' frames should not be seen as immune from the legal techniques developed by the Court, such as indirect effect, which apply in the first pillar. Taken together, the pillar structure does not separate the EU's legal order into hermetically sealed parts and despite the 'intergovernmental' characteristics of the CFSP, important consequences on the legal order of the Member States may arise, and have effects on individual EU and non-EU citizens and their rights.[45] The ECJ can therefore be seen as responding to the new challenges posed within expanding areas of EU activity. Separating the pillars and labelling them as being based on 'Community' or 'international' law thus appears problematic, either for those Member States attempting to prevent the ECJ's application of first pillar principles or for the Court itself when justifying its decision by referring to international law obligations as the reason why compliance is required. Constraints, derived from Article 10 EC, do

[42] E Spaventa, 'Opening Pandora's Box: Some Reflections on the Constitutional Effects of the Ruling in Pupino' (2007) *European Constitutional Law Review* 5, 24.

[43] TEU Art 11(2).

[44] See especially: P Craig and G de Búrca, *EU Law Text, Cases and Materials*, 4th edn (Oxford, Oxford University Press, 2008) 191–92: 'a clear separation of the Union legal system from the Community legal system is impossible. Cross-fertilization between the two systems has taken place and is well exemplified in the Pupino ruling'. Gosalbo Bono concludes from this that, 'even the sacrosanct Community principles of direct effect and primacy over the law of the Member States cannot be said to be completely alien to the CFSP legal order' R Gosalbo Bono, 'Some Reflections on the CFSP Legal Order' (2006) 43 *CML Rev* 337, 378.

[45] K Lenaerts and T Courthaut, 'Of Birds and Hedges: the Role of Primacy in Invoking Norms of EU Law' (2006) 31 ELRev 287, 288.

exist on the Member States in the exercise of their foreign policies[46] and it would seem inadequate, in the light of the potential effects of *Pupino*, to understand CFSP instruments as 'international law decisions'.[47] The relationship between rights, foreign policy instruments and EU/international law was at the heart of the *Kadi* judgment, to which discussion now turns.[48]

IV. *KADI*: FUNDAMENTAL RIGHTS IN EU LAW, INTERNATIONAL LAW AND FOREIGN POLICY

In *Kadi*[49] the applicant challenged two Regulations made in furtherance of the CFSP Common Positions which had been created in order to implement a UN Security Council (UNSC) Resolution.[50] The measures aimed to freeze the assets of individuals suspected of supporting Osama Bin Laden, the Taliban and Al-Qaeda. Yassin Abdullah Kadi was named as a supporter by the UN Sanction Committee in 2001 and subsequently added to the Regulation annex.[51]

Kadi unsuccessfully challenged the freezing of his assets in Member States of the EU before the Court of First Instance (CFI) by way of the judicial review procedure set out in Article 230 EC. The basis of his challenge centred on a lack of competence on the part of the EU institutions to freeze his assets, and the infringement of his fundamental rights as a consequence of doing so. The CFI rejected all of the arguments. On the competence issue, the CFI found that although Articles 60 and 301 EC

[46] M Cremona, 'Defending the Community Interest: the Duties of Cooperation and Compliance' in M Cremona and B De Witte (eds), *EU Foreign Relations Law: Constitutional Fundamentals* (Oxford, Hart Publishing, 2008) 167.

[47] Craig and De Búrca, above n 44 at 192.

[48] The following section draws on PJ Cardwell, D French and ND White, 'Kadi: the Interplay between EU and International Law' (2009) 58(1) *International and Comparative Law Quarterly* (*ICLQ*) 229–40.

[49] Case T-315/01 *Yassin Abdullah Kadi v Council and Commission* [2005] ECR II-3649. Another individual, Ahmed Ali Yusuf, and the Al Barakaat International Foundation also challenged the Regulations on similar grounds and the CFI's judgment was given on the same day (Case T-306/01 *Ahmed Ali Yusuf and Al Barakaat International Foundation v Council and Commission* [2005] ECR II-3533). The Al Barakaat Foundation's appeal to the ECJ was joined with the *Kadi* appeal. Owing to the similar legal issues raised, only *Kadi* will be referred to in this section.

[50] Council Regulation (EC) 2062/2001 of 19 October 2001 amending, for the third time, Council Regulation (EC) No 467/2001 prohibiting the export of certain goods and services to Afghanistan, strengthening the flight ban and extending the freeze of funds and other financial resources in respect of the Taliban of Afghanistan and repealing Regulation (EC) No 337/2000 [2001] OJ L277/25 and Council Regulation (EC) 467/2001 of 6 March 2001 [2001] OJ L67/1 following Council Common Position 1999/727/CFSP [1999] OJ L294/1 and 2001/154/CFSP [2001] OJ L57/1 and United Nations Security Council Resolution 1267 (15 October 1999) UN Doc S/RES/1267.

[51] Regulation 467/2001, annex 1, as amended by Regulation 2026/2001.

only expressly mention sanctions which can be imposed on third countries (and not, therefore, individuals), recourse to the 'residual powers' of Article 308 EC[52] was justified.[53]

As regards the second issue, the CFI was unwilling to find that it had the power to review UNSC resolutions to assess their conformity with fundamental rights. The CFI concluded that since UNSC resolutions are binding on Member States and, as a matter of customary international law, a State 'may not invoke the provisions of its internal law as justification for its failure to perform a treaty',[54] such resolutions fall outside the ambit of the Court's judicial review. The Court felt it was not able to 'call in question, even indirectly, their lawfulness in the light of Community law'.[55] The CFI noted, however, one limit on the binding nature of UNSC resolutions, namely that they must observe peremptory norms of general international law, or *jus cogens*. If the resolution did not do so, then the Court would be empowered to carry out indirect judicial review; as the CFI noted:

> In connection with an action for annulment of a Community act adopted, where no discretion whatsoever may be exercised, with a view to putting into effect a resolution of the Security Council may therefore, highly exceptionally, extend to determining whether the superior rules of international law falling within the ambit of *jus cogens* have been observed, in particular, the mandatory provisions concerning the universal protection of human rights.[56]

On this basis, the CFI considered the claims founded on fundamental human rights and found that none could succeed.

Kadi appealed to the ECJ.[57] Advocate General Maduro's opinion, delivered in January 2008, proposed that the Court should set aside the CFI's decision and annul the Regulations insofar as they concern the applicant. The opinion places great emphasis on the right of the Community courts

[52] 'If action by the Community should prove necessary to attain, in the course of the operation of the common market, one of the objectives of the Community, and this Treaty has not provided the necessary powers, the Council shall, acting unanimously on a proposal from the Commission and after consulting the European Parliament, take the appropriate measures'.

[53] However, the Court refused to endorse the Commission's argument that the fight against international terrorism fell within its residual competence of Art 308 in order to achieve a Community objective. This, in the view of the CFI, would 'deprive many provisions of the Treaty on European Union of their ambit and would be inconsistent with the introduction of instruments specific to the CFSP' (para 156). Nevertheless, when the effects of Arts 60, 301 and 308 were combined, this justified their use in the present case and did not constitute a widening of 'the scope of Community powers beyond the general framework created by the provisions of the Treaty' (paras 132–33).

[54] Ibid para 182.

[55] Ibid para 225.

[56] Ibid para 231.

[57] Case C-402/05 *Yassin Abdullah Kadi and Al Barakaat International Foundation v Council and Commission* [2008].

to review whether the Regulation complies with the respect for the individual's fundamental rights within the legal order of the EU. In a strongly worded assertion, the Advocate General found that 'it would be wrong to conclude that, once the Community is bound by a rule of international law, the Community Courts must bow to that rule with complete acquiescence and apply it unconditionally in the Community legal order'.[58] As such, the institutions 'cannot dispense with proper judicial review proceedings when implementing the Security Council resolutions in question within the Community legal order'.[59] Given the proposed availability of review of these measures by the ECJ, the Advocate General found that the closely-connected rights invoked form part of the general principles of Community law as laid down by the ECJ in a series of cases.[60] The Court cannot necessarily know whether the sanctions are disproportionate or misdirected, but since there is no 'genuine and effective mechanism'[61] for allowing a right to be heard at the UN level, but merely an intergovernmental process to petition the Sanctions Committee, it must fall to the powers for judicial review within the Community legal order to ensure that a right to be heard is allowed.[62]

In September 2008, the ECJ set aside the ruling of the CFI and the Regulations freezing Kadi's funds on the basis that they constituted unjustified restrictions and unacceptable limits on the right to be heard and effective judicial review of those rights. The decision found that the Council was competent to adopt the Regulation on the legal basis it did, but that the CFI erred in holding that the Community courts had no jurisdiction to review the measure in light of the fundamental rights of the applicant. It accepted that Article 308 could be used jointly with Articles 60 and 301 'if such powers appear none the less to be necessary to enable the Community to carry out its functions with a view to attaining one of the objectives laid down by the Treaty'.[63] Such an objective in the present case was met, and the ECJ dismissed the appeal on this point.

[58] Ibid, opinion of Poiares Maduro AG of 16 January 2008, para 54.

[59] Ibid para 24.

[60] See esp Case C-32/95 P *Lisresal and others* [1996] ECR I-5373 and Case C-50/00 P *Unión de Pequeños Agricultores v Council* [2002] ECR I-6677.

[61] *Yassin Abdullah Kadi* above n 57 para 54.

[62] On the issue of competence, the Advocate General found that the CFI's interpretation of Arts 60 and 301 was too narrow in restricting the imposition of sanctions on the governing regimes of third countries only. The mentioning of 'third countries' in these Articles includes, according to the Advocate General, the economic relations with individuals and entities *within* third countries, since 'the sanctions necessarily affect the overall state of economic relations between the Community and that country' (paras 12–13). There was no need, in his view, to bring in Art 308 and to do otherwise would be to deprive Art 301 of much of its use.

[63] Ibid para 211.

As regards the substantive issues on the fundamental rights claims, the ECJ's approach is wholly different from that of the CFI. In his appeal, Kadi claimed that the CFI erred in law in accepting the nature of UNSC resolutions as automatically part of European law and stating that the Community Courts have no power to review the lawfulness of UNSC resolutions except in relation to *jus cogens*. The appellant referred to the judgment of the European Court of Human Rights in *Bosphorus*[64] as evidence of the requirement of judicial review to be available at Community level when rights are at stake, even if the measure is ultimately derived from international law.[65]

The ECJ confirmed that fundamental rights, in particular those found in the European Convention on Human Rights (ECHR), are an integral part of the general principles of law[66] and that the lawfulness of Community acts depends on their respect for human rights,[67] despite the general obligation on the Community to respect international law.[68] A review, such as the one in the present case, is of the *Community* act, and not the international agreement.[69] The ECJ utilised various EC Treaty provisions in support of its view that derogations from the principles of human rights are not possible and that these constitute a 'constitutional guarantee stemming from the EC Treaty as an autonomous legal system which is not to be prejudiced by an international agreement'.[70] The existence of the procedure whereby States may petition the Sanctions Committee on behalf of an individual did not constitute a generalised immunity from jurisdiction within the EC legal order.[71] The ECJ was therefore unimpressed with arguments that it should show full deference to the UN's legal order since the guarantees for judicial protection were not in place at the UN level. Since the ECJ found that the CFI was wrong to find that it had no jurisdiction to consider the claims based on fundamental rights, the ECJ felt no need to consider the aspects of the appeal dealing with *jus cogens*.

The ECJ did however consider the nature of the fundamental rights at stake. The Court felt that neither the Regulation nor the CFSP Common Position afforded Kadi the right to be heard and there was no means by which he could make his point of view known or exercise rights of

[64] *Bosphorus Hava Yollari Turizm ve Ticaret Anonim Sirketi v Ireland* (2006) 42 EHRR 1.
[65] This point is explored in more detail in the chapter by Tawhida Ahmed.
[66] *Yassin Abdullah Kadi* above n 57 at para 283.
[67] Ibid para 284. See also: *Opinion 2/94* [1996] ECR I-1759, para 34, and Case C-112/00 *Schmidberger* [2003] ECR I-5659, para 73.
[68] *Yassin Abdullah Kadi* above n 57 at para 291.
[69] Ibid para 286.
[70] Ibid para 316.
[71] Ibid paras 318–21.

defence.[72] The CFI had itself previously recognised a right to a fair hearing and the right to reasons, in *Organisation des Modjahedines du peuple d'Iran*.[73] This judgment, however, differed from the *Kadi* decision in that the CFSP measures challenged by the applicants were 'autonomous' and not the product of UNSC Resolutions. The CFI therefore held that the right to a fair hearing and the right to reasons should apply.[74] The ECJ has also ruled on challenges to the CFSP Common Positions using the power granted to it under Article 35(6) TEU.[75] In *Segi*[76] and *Gestoras Pro Amnistia*[77] the ECJ dismissed appeals from the CFI relating to claims for damages for inclusion on a list of suspected terrorist groups. The ECJ did not find any jurisdiction to award damages under Title VI of the TEU nor the right to directly or indirectly challenge a Common Position. Yet, given the potential effects on third party individuals of a CFSP measure, the Court found in *Gestoras Pro Amnistia* that

> it has to be possible to make subject to review by the Court a Common Position which, because of its content, has a scope going beyond that assigned by the EU Treaty ... Therefore, a national court hearing a dispute which indirectly raises the issue of the validity or interpretation of a Common Position adopted on the basis of Article 34 EU, as is the case in this instance for part of Common Position 2001/931 ... and which has serious doubts whether that Common Position is really intended to produce legal effects in relation to third parties, would be able, subject to the conditions fixed by Article 35 EU, to ask the Court to give a preliminary ruling. It would then fall to the Court to find, where appropriate, that the Common Position is intended to produce legal effects in relation to third parties, to accord it its true classification and to give a preliminary ruling.[78]

On the right to property, whilst a relationship of proportionality between the aim and means of the restrictive measure 'might, in principle, be justified',[79] the current application of the Regulation to Kadi infringed his fundamental right to respect for property. The ECJ's reasoning on this point was closely linked to the lack of opportunity for him to put his case

[72] Ibid para 348.

[73] Case T-228/02 *Organisation des Modjahedines du peuple d'Iran v Council* [2006] ECR II-4665.

[74] Ibid para 91.

[75] 'The Court of Justice shall have jurisdiction to review the legality of Framework Decisions and decisions in actions brought by a Member State or the Commission on grounds of lack of competence, infringement of an essential procedural requirement, infringement of this Treaty or of any rule of law relating to its application, or misuse of powers. The proceedings provided for in this paragraph shall be instituted within two months of the publication of the measure'.

[76] Case C-355/04 *Segi, Izaga and Galarraga v Council* [2007] ECR I-1657.

[77] Case C-354/04 *Gestoras Pro Amnistia, Olano and Errasti v Council* [2007] ECR I-1579.

[78] Ibid para 54.

[79] *Yassin Abdullah Kadi* above n 57 at para 366.

to the authorities.[80] However, since the ECJ was unaware of the evidence which had led to Kadi being placed on the Sanctions Committee list in 2001, it also stated that 'on the merits of the case, the imposition of those measures on the appellants may for all that prove to be justified'.[81] The result was that notwithstanding the upholding of the appeals, the effects of the regulation would be maintained (pursuant to Article 231 EC) for a period of three months until the Council could remedy the infringements, which it has now done.[82]

The *Kadi* decision is therefore instructive on several points, all of which contribute to the view of the ECJ consolidating its role as a constitutional court. The first is that an explicit link is created between foreign policy and fundamental rights. Even in domestic legal systems, foreign policy is often understood as an area removed from strong judicial oversight. In the EU sense, measures taken under the CFSP, the second pillar, are also beyond the general jurisdiction of the ECJ. Yet, as the *Kadi* decision shows, legal instruments taken under CFSP may have important effects on individuals as well as States, and as such the involvement of the ECJ is justified in upholding those rights.

Second, *Kadi* reflects the long-standing view of the Court that the EU legal system is an autonomous legal framework independent of, and not reliant upon, public international law. Although the CFI's step in acknowledging the primacy of the UN legal system over the Community legal order,[83] the argument that the EU was denied the right to judicially review one of its own measures simply because it was adopted to implement a UN resolution, particularly one that potentially infringed the fundamental rights inherent within the Union's legal framework seemed incompatible with the past emphasis within the ECJ's jurisprudence on fundamental rights. It is not sufficient for court-based fundamental rights protection to be left to the European Court of Human Rights and it is clear from this judgment that the ECJ is acting in a way which would be expected of a constitutional court, charged with a mission of ensuring that rights, either general or specific, are respected. The protection of constitutional guarantees, drawn from the principles common to the Member States, is again not new.[84]

[80] Ibid paras 372–73.

[81] Ibid para 374.

[82] Commission Regulation (EC) No 1190/2008 of 28 November 2008 amending for the 101st time Council Regulation (EC) No 881/2002 imposing certain specific restrictive measures directed against certain persons and entities associated with Usama bin Laden, the Al-Qaida network and the Taliban [2008] OJ L322/1.

[83] See, eg C Tomuschat, 'Note on Kadi v Council and Commission (CFI)' (2006) 43 CML Rev 537.

[84] See, eg Case 11/70 *Internationale Handelsgesellschaft* [1970] ECR 1125.

Third, the place of the ECJ in protecting fundamental rights places it in a unique position between the international legal order (in which the EU's official role in ambiguous) and the national legal orders of the Member States. The EU institutions are not members of the UN, but since measures pursued in furtherance of a UN Security Council Resolution are (as in the case here) put in place at the level of the EU, it has fallen to the ECJ to ensure the protection of fundamental rights. This has had the effect of elevating the constitutionally-grounded language of the ECJ in upholding 'the guarantee of judicial protection'[85] in the absence of a judicial mechanism at the international level, since the only way to be removed from the list was via the (politically-based) sanctions committee. The ECJ was extremely critical of this 'diplomatic and intergovernmental' procedure, which it states 'cannot give rise to generalised immunity from jurisdiction within the internal legal order of the Community'.[86] In developing this line of argument, the Court adopts the general view that 'the Community judicature must … ensure the review, in principle the full review, of the lawfulness of all Community acts in the light of the fundamental rights forming an integral part of the general principles of Community law'.[87] This places the measures which froze Kadi asset's clearly within the ambit of Community law, yet the Court also points to the requirement of EC law to 'respect international law in the exercise of its powers' and that 'a measure adopted by virtue of those powers must be interpreted, and its scope limited, in the light of the relevant rules of international law'.[88] Therefore, whilst the place of Community law within the broader scope of international law is affirmed, this is not where the emphasis of the decision lies. Rather, it is the autonomy of the EU's legal order which the ECJ sought to reaffirm through its constitutional guarantee 'stemming from the EC Treaty as an autonomous legal system which is not to be prejudiced by an international agreement'.[89]

As such, *Kadi* raises interesting questions about how the constitutional order of the EU relates to the international legal order from which it was essentially created. Notwithstanding the commitments to upholding the UN Charter in the preamble of the EU Treaty which suggests a level of deference within—and by—the EU as an international organisation, it appears that *Kadi* marks a significant, though not surprising, step towards the ECJ becoming a more generalised constitutional court for the EU.

[85] *Yassin Abdullah Kadi* above n 57 at para 322.
[86] Ibid para 321.
[87] Ibid para 326.
[88] Ibid para 291.
[89] Ibid para 316.

V. MOX PLANT: JURISDICTION AND COMPETENCE AS CONSTITUTIONAL QUESTIONS FOR THE ECJ

The MOX Plant dispute was a rare occurrence: a commencement of formal, legal proceedings by one Member State of the EU against another in an international tribunal. By and large, disputes between Member States of the EU have only rarely resulted in formal proceedings being brought before the ECJ or other dispute resolution mechanisms. In particular, the procedure laid down by Article 227 EC ('A Member State which considers that another Member State has failed to fulfil an obligation under this Treat may bring the matter before the Court of Justice') has been only used scarcely when compared with the similar provision in Article 226 EC, which grants the Commission the competence to deliver a reasoned opinion on the infringement, followed by recourse to the ECJ, in its role as guardian of the Treaties.[90] Recourse to judicial bodies other than the ECJ is even rarer.

The dispute between Ireland and the UK over the construction of the Sellafield Mixed Oxide (MOX) Plant on the UK's Irish Sea coast resulted in the start of two legal avenues by Ireland for redress.[91] The one of concern here was that of the 1982 United Nations Convention on the Law of the Sea (UNCLOS) of which Ireland, the UK and the EC are parties.[92] Ireland's claims were grounded on alleged failures of the UK to respect its environmental obligations. Ireland's arguments centred on alleged failures by the UK to assess potential damage to the Irish Sea and its marine environment and take steps to prevent it, and a failure to cooperate fully with Ireland as a neighbouring State.

Ireland's application to the UNCLOS tribunal prompted the Commission to start Article 226 EC proceedings, which eventually led to the instant case, *Commission v Ireland*.[93] In making its application to the UNCLOS tribunal, the Commission claimed, Ireland had breached its obligations under Articles 10 EC and 292 EC. Article 292 EC reads: 'Member States undertake not to submit a dispute concerning the interpretation or application of this treaty to any method of settlement other

[90] 'If the Commission considers that a Member State has failed to fulfil an obligation under this Treaty, it shall deliver a reasoned opinion on the matter after giving the State concerned the opportunity to submit its observations. If the State concerned does not comply with the opinion within the period laid down by the Commission, the latter may bring the matter before the Court of Justice'.

[91] This section draws on arguments developed in PJ Cardwell and D French, 'Who Decides? The European Court of Justice's Judgment on Jurisdiction in the MOX Plant Dispute' (2007) 19 *Journal of Environmental Law* 121.

[92] The other was the 1992 Convention for the Protection of the Marine Environment of the North East Atlantic (OSPAR). The OSPAR arbitral tribunal rejected Ireland's claims on 2 July 2003.

[93] Case C-459/03 [2006] ECR I-4635.

than those provided for therein'. Article 10 EC, the loyal cooperation Article, has already been discussed above in relation to *Pupino*, but the interpretation of its content is also notable here.

Advocate General Maduro pointed to the diametrically opposed arguments put forward by the Commission and Ireland over the jurisdiction of the ECJ to deal with the *MOX Plant* dispute. Though there is no doubt from the Treaties that the ECJ has exclusive jurisdiction to interpret the Treaty and EC law, the obligations invoked by Ireland against the UK were those arising under UNCLOS, not the EC Treaty. The argument put forward by Ireland was that the Articles invoked were not matters of EC law over which the ECJ enjoys jurisdiction. For the Commission, *all* the issues in question fell within the jurisdiction of the ECJ by virtue of the fact that even if only part of the dispute falls within EC law, the ECJ is thus competent. Whether that competence is exclusive was a further question for the ECJ to address.

The ECJ has been reluctant to set out strict demarcation lines between the respective competences of the EC and the Member States when concluding a Mixed Agreement, that is, an 'external' agreement within which the competence between the Community and the Member States is shared.[94] The EC enjoys competence in the external environmental field by means of Article 175 EC, under which the EC became party to UNCLOS alongside the Member States.

The question of delimiting the respective competences of the EC and the Member States in Mixed Agreements, a common feature of the EU's externally-focussed policies, has been confronted by the ECJ since as far back as the early 1970s. In the European Road Transport Agreement (*AETR*) judgment,[95] the ECJ recognised the implied competence of the EC in the external field arising from the conferment of internal competence in a specific field.[96] Here, the Community has fixed only minimum rules (as set out in the Declaration of Community competence attached to the EC's acceptance of UNCLOS) and therefore, according to Ireland, the nature of the dispute with the UK did not cover areas in which competence has been transferred to the Community.

The ECJ held, relying on *AETR*, that its jurisdiction extends to *all* mixed agreements. A detailed examination of the extent of Community

[94] See generally: P Eeckhout, *External Relations of the European Union* (Oxford, Oxford University Press, 2004) 190–223; P Koutrakos, *EU International Relations Law* (Oxford, Hart Publishing, 2006) 137–80; G De Baere, *Constitutional Principles of EU External Relations* (Oxford, Oxford University Press, 2008) 231–64.

[95] Case 22/70 *Commission v Council* [1971] ECR 263.

[96] Ibid para 17: 'each time the Community, with a view to implementing a common policy envisaged by the Treaty, adopts provisions laying down common rules, whatever form these may take, the Member States no longer have the right, acting individually or even collectively, to undertake obligations with third countries which affect those rules'.

competence within each provision is not required before recognising its jurisdiction. It thus followed that the ECJ viewed itself at the arbiter of questions where jurisdiction lay (thus upholding the *competenz-competenz* principle). Since the issues raised by Ireland in its complaints come (partially) within EC regulatory competence, they form part of the EC legal order and Article 292 EC is therefore applicable.[97]

The analysis of Article 10 by the ECJ is also interesting. The Court followed Advocate General Maduro's analysis of the Article as a general duty of cooperation, from which Article 292 is a more specific expression.[98] As the ECJ found that Ireland was in breach of Article 292, it was not therefore necessary to address whether engaging proceedings before the arbitral tribunal also resulted in a breach of Article 10 as a separate argument. It would, however, have been interesting to see how the ECJ would have approached Article 10 if the more precise obligation in Article 292 had been absent. *Pupino* suggests that the ECJ is willing to take a broad view of the implications of Article 10.

Ireland was found to have breached its Treaty obligations by not consulting the Commission before following this course of action. This is especially interesting because it suggests that even in an area over which the ECJ does not have competence (a particularly apt question in relation to mixed agreements), a Member State may breach Article 10 by not consulting with the Commission first. Article 10 is thus to be seen as an obligation on the Member States to consult with the Community institutions, even when they believe it is on a matter outside of the EC's competence, in case there is a risk of impinging on the Community's competence. Delimiting over what jurisdiction the ECJ has is not a straightforward question. For the ECJ, though Article 282 UNCLOS[99] was relevant in part, the principal issues were very much internal questions of competence rather than questions of international law.

The *MOX Plant* decision is, in effect, a continuation of the case law on international agreements before the ECJ since the 1970s. In the absence of comprehensive competence on the part of the EC institutions to sign international agreements, finding the middle-way between the respective competences of the EU institutions and the Member States is likely to be a continuing theme, in light of the increasingly complex and numerous instances of international legal agreements. Whilst the European

[97] *Commission v Ireland* above n 93 at paras 110, 127–28.

[98] Ibid, opinion of Poiares Maduro AG of 18 January 2006, para 55.

[99] 'If the States Parties which are parties to a dispute concerning the interpretation or application of this Convention have agreed, through a general, regional or bilateral agreement or otherwise, that such dispute shall, at the request of any party to the dispute, be submitted to a procedure that entails a binding decision, that procedure shall apply in lieu of the procedures provided for in this Part, unless the parties to the dispute otherwise agree'.

integration process has made disputes between the Member States much more likely to be solved at the political level, and recourse to dispute resolution mechanisms much less likely, in a continuously enlarging EU, the ECJ may be called on again to consider the extent of the loyal cooperation articles. From an EU point of view, the *MOX Plant* case is a welcome development in terms of ensuring that Member States use all the mechanisms available with the scope of the EC/EU Treaty arrangements, no matter how questionable the actual respective competences are. In terms of international law, however, the utility of specialist tribunals set up to deal with important areas, such as the law of the sea, could be diminished if regional governance becomes the norm. It is unlikely that this will be the case for some time, given the fragile nature of many other regional entities which have taken inspiration from the EU but have failed to make sufficient progress in integration.

VI. CONCLUSION

This chapter aimed to set out how the ECJ's recent case law seems, certainly to anyone unfamiliar with the past jurisprudence of the Court, to constrain or bind Member States with regard to both their domestic legal systems and their commitments under the international legal order. All three decisions covered here are significant in their different ways, and their importance for citizens (especially *Pupino* and *Kadi*) should not be understated.

It is possible to see that in the development of the general principles of EU law, Article 10 can be read as a particularly significant constitutional norm. In the absence of a 'written' constitution for the EU, the search for which in the form of the Constitutional Treaty and Treaty of Lisbon formed the backdrop to the cases explored here, the ECJ nevertheless continues to resemble a constitutional court. It continues to attach great importance to the commitment of the Member States in cooperating to meet the aims of the Treaties, first and foremost being an 'ever closer Union between the peoples of Europe'.

Professor (emeritus) JG Merrills List of Publications, May 2009

BOOKS

1. *A Current Bibliography of International Law* (London, Butterworths, 1978) 277 pp.
2. (a) *Anatomy of International Law*, 2nd edn (Andover, Sweet & Maxwell, 1981) 146 pp.
   (b) The first edition of this work (106 pp) was published by the same publisher in 1975.
3. (a) *The Development of International Law by the European Court of Human Rights*, 2nd edn (Manchester, Manchester University Press, 1993) 265 pp.
   (b) The first edition of this work (235 pp) was published by the same publisher in 1988.
4. (a) *Human Rights in the World*, 4th edn [with the late AH Robertson] (Manchester, Manchester University Press, 1996) 355 pp.
   (b) The third edition of this work (314 pp) was published by the same publisher in 1989.
5. *Judge Sir Gerald Fitzmaurice and the Discipline of International Law* (The Hague, Kluwer, 1998) 340 pp.
6. (a) *Human Rights in Europe*, 4th edn [with the late AH Robertson] (Manchester, Manchester University Press, 2001) 362 pp.
   (b) The third edition of the work (422 pp) was published by the same publisher in 1993.
7. (a) *International Dispute Settlement*, 4th edn (Cambridge, Cambridge University Press, 2005) 367 pp.
   (b) The third edition of this work (354 pp) was published by Cambridge University Press in 1998.
   (c) The second edition (288 pp) was published by Grotius Publications in 1991.
   (d) The first edition (211 pp) was published by Sweet & Maxwell in 1984.

Translations

Japanese translations of 2(a), 7(a), 7(c) and 7(d) by M Hasegawa were published in 1984, 2008, 1994 and 1987 respectively.

A Korean translation of 7(c) by Jae-Non Kim was published in 1998.

CHAPTERS IN BOOKS

1. 'The Role and Limits of International Adjudication' in Dhckaiia and Nirmal (eds), *International Court in Transition* (Allahabad, Chugh Publishers, 1994) 40–60.
   This is a revised version of Article No 30, below.
2. 'The Principle of Peaceful Settlement of Disputes' in Lowe and Warbrick (eds), *The United Nations and the Principles of international Law* (London, Routledge, 1994) 49–66.
3. 'Environmental Protection and Human Rights: Conceptual Aspects' in Boyle and Anderson (eds), *Human Rights Approaches to Environmental Protection* (Oxford, Oxford University Press, 1996) ch 2, 25–41.
4. 'The European Arrangements' and 'The European Convention on Human Rights' in Hanski and Suksi (eds), *An Introduction to the International Protection of Human Rights* (Turku, Abo Akademi University, 1997) chs 13 and 14, 209–43.
5. 'Aspects of the Incidental Jurisdiction of the International Court of Justice' in Evans and Konstadinidis (eds), *Remedies in International Law* (Oxford, Hart Publishing, 1998) 51–70.
6. 'Resolution of the Diaoyu (Senkaku) Islands Dispute by the International Court of Justice' in *International Law Conference on the Dispute over Diaoyu/Senkaku Islands*. (Taipei, Taiwan Law Society and Taiwan Institute of International Law, 1998) 89–101.
7. 'The Contribution of the Permanent Court of Arbitration to International Law and to the Settlement of Disputes by Peaceful Means' in Hamilton et al (eds) *The Permanent Court of Arbitration: International Arbitration and Dispute Resolution* (The Hague, Kluwer, 1999) 3–27.
8. *An Introduction to the International Protection of Human Rights*, 2nd edn [see 4 above] (Turku, Abo Akademi University, 1999) chs 16 and 17, 275–307.
9. 'International Boundary Disputes in Theory and in Practice' in Dahlitz (ed), *Peaceful Resolution of Major International Disputes* (New York, United Nations, 1999) 95–113.
10. 'The Optional Clause at Eighty' in Ando et al (eds), *Liber Amicorum Judge Shigeru Oda* (The Hague, Kluwer, 2002) 435–50.
11. 'The Means of Dispute Settlement' in Evans (ed), *International Law* (Oxford, Oxford University Press, 2003) ch 17, 528–59.
12. 'The Mutability of Treaty Obligations' in Craven and Fitzmaurice (eds), *Interrogating the Treaty. Essays in the Contemporary Law of Treaties* (Nijmegen, Wolf Publishers, 2005) ch 5, 89–103.
13. 'The Globalisation of International Justice' in Lewis (ed), *Global Governance and the Quest for Justice, Vol I International and Regional Organisations* (Oxford, Hart Publishing, 2006) 69–91.
14. 'The Means of Dispute Settlement' in Evans (ed), *International Law*, 2nd edn (Oxford, Oxford University Press, 2006) ch 18, 533–60. This is an updated version of 11 above.
15. 'Environmental Rights' in Bodansky, Brunnée and Hey (eds), *The Oxford Handbook of International Environmental Law* (Oxford, Oxford University Press, 2007) ch 29, 663–80.

In Press

16. 'Does the Optional Clause Matter?' in Bohlander and Kaikobad (eds), *Law, Order and Justice* (Nijhoff, forthcoming) (c 9,000 words).

ARTICLES

1. 'Morality and the International Legal Order' (1968) 31 MLR 520–35.
2. 'Francisco de Vitoria and the Spanish Conquest of the New World' (1968) 3 *Irish Jurist* (NS) 187–95.
3. 'Law, Politics and the Legislation of the Unrecognised Government' (1968) 3 *Ottawa Law Review* 1–25.
4. 'Two Approaches to Treaty Interpretation' (1968/69) 4 *Australian Yearbook of International Law* 55–83.
5. 'Law, Morals and the Psychological Nexus' (1969) 19 *University of Toronto Law Journal* 46–59.
6. 'The Justiciability of International Disputes' (1969) 47 *Canadian Bar Review* 241–70.
7. 'On Teaching International Law' (1969) 10 *SPTL Journal* 169–78.
8. 'Recognition and Construction' (1971) 20 ICLQ 476–500.
9. 'Fact and Fancy' (1971) 11 *SPTL Journal* 155–61.
10. 'Policy and Remoteness' (1973) 6 *Ottawa Law Review* 18–41.
11. 'One Nationality or Two?' (1974) 23 *International & Comparative Law Quarterly* 143–60.
12. 'Oppenheimer v Cattermole—The Curtain Falls' (1975) 24 *International & Comparative Law Quarterly* 617–35.
13. 'Sir Gerald Fitzmaurice's Contribution to the Jurisprudence of the International Court of Justice' (1976/77) 48 *British Year Book of International Law* 183–240.
14. 'Oil Exploration in the Aegean' (1977) 93 *Law Quarterly Review* 29–33.
15. 'Interim Measures of Protection and the Substantive Jurisdiction of the International Court' (1977) 36 *Cambridge Law Journal* 86–110.
16. 'Interpretation of the Bretton Woods Agreement' (1977) 26 *International & Comparative Law Quarterly* 218–24.
17. 'The Scope of Sovereign Immunity' (1977) 93 *Law Quarterly Review* 330–33.
18. 'Images and Models in the World Court: The Individual Opinions in the North Sea Continental Shelf Cases' (1978) 41 *Modem Law Review* 638–59.
19. 'Jurisdiction in the Aegean Sea Case' (1979) 95 *Law Quarterly Review* 340–46.
20. 'Trespass to Foreign Land' (1979) 28 *International & Comparative Law Quarterly* 523–25.
21. 'The Optional Clause Today' (1979) 50 *British Year Book of International Law* 87–117.
22. 'The United Kingdom—France Continental Shelf Arbitration' (1980) 10 *California Western International Law Journal* 314–64.
23. 'The International Court of Justice and the General Act of 1928' (1980) 39 *Cambridge Law Journal* 137–71.
24. 'Sir Gerald Fitzmaurice's Contribution to the Jurisprudence of the European Court of Human Rights' (1982) 53 *British Year Book of International Law* 115–62.

25. 'Decisions on the European Convention on Human Rights during 1983' (1983) 54 *British Year Book of International Law* 313–54.
26. 'Intervention in the International Court' (1985) 101 *Law Quarterly Review* 11–15.
27. 'Decisions on the European Convention on Human Rights during 1984' (1984) 55 *British Year Book of International Law* 363–99.
28. 'Decisions on the European Convention on Human Rights during 1985' (1985) 56 *British Year Book of International Law* 335–63.
29. 'Decisions on the European Convention on Human Rights during 1986' (1986) 57 *British Year Book of International Law* 449–75.
30. 'The Role and Limits of International Adjudication' (1987) 24 *Co-existence* 169–81, reprinted in WE Butler (ed) *International Law and the International System* (The Hague, Nijhoff, 1987) 169–81.
31. 'Decisions on the European Convention on Human Rights during 1987' (1987) 58 *British Year Book of International Law* 455–95.
32. 'Decisions on the European Convention on Human Rights during 1988' (1988) 59 *British Year Book of International Law* 365–408.
33. 'Decisions on the European Convention on Human Rights during 1989' (1989) 60 *British Year Book of International Law* 507–67.
34. 'Decisions on the European Convention on Human Rights during 1990' (1990) 61 *British Year Book of International Law* 409–49.
35. 'Decisions on the European Convention on Human Rights during 1991' (1991) 62 *British Year Book of International Law* 465–525.
36. 'Decisions on the European Convention on Human Rights during 1992' (1992) 63 *British Year Book of International Law* 533–98.
37. 'Emergency Measures and the European Convention' (1993) 7 *Interights Bulletin* 77.
38. 'Decisions on the European Convention on Human Rights during 1993' (1993) 64 *British Year Book of International Law* 481–541.
39. 'The Optional Clause Revisited' (1993) 64 *British Year Book of International Law* 197–244.
40. 'Decisions on the European Convention on Human Rights during 1994' (1994) 65 *British Year Book of International Law* 509–48.
41. 'Interim Measures of Protection in the Recent Jurisprudence of the International Court of Justice' (1995) 44 *International and Comparative Law Quarterly* 90–146.
42. 'Decisions on the European Convention on Human Rights during 1995' (1995) 66 *British Year Book of International Law* 513–59.
43. 'The Land and Maritime Boundary Case (Cameroon v Nigeria), Order of 15 March 1996' (1997) 46 *International and Comparative Law Quarterly* 676–81.
44. 'Decisions on the European Convention on Human Rights during 1996' (1996) 67 *British Year Book of International Law* 607–55.
45. 'The Land and Maritime Boundary Case, Preliminary Objections' (1999) 48 *International and Comparative Law Quarterly*, 651–58.
46. 'The International Court of Justice and the Adjudication of Territorial and Boundary Disputes' (2001) 13 *Leiden Journal of International Law* 873–901.
47. 'Human Rights and Democratic Values in the Strasbourg System' (2000) 29 *Thesaurus Acroasium* 41–106.

48. 'The Land and Maritime Boundary Case: The Intervention by Equatorial Guinea' (2000) 49 *International and Comparative Law Quarterly* 720–23.
49. 'The Management of International Disputes by Regional and Universal Organisations' (2001) 25 *Thesaurus Acroasium* 191–247.
50. 'The Aerial Incident of 10 August 1999 (Pakistan v India), Judgment on Jurisdiction' (2001) 50 *International and Comparative Law Quarterly* 657–62.
51. 'Sovereignty over Pulau Ligatan and Pulau Sipadan: The Phillipines' Intervention' (2002) 51 *International and Comparative Law Quarterly* 718–22.
52. 'The Belize-Guatemala Territorial Dispute and the Legal Opinion of January 2002' (2002) 2 *The Global Community Yearbook of International Law and Jurisprudence* 77–97.
53. 'The Land and Maritime boundary between Cameroon and Nigeria, Merits, Judgment of 10 October 2002' (2003) 52 *International and Comparative Law Quarterly* 787–97.
54. 'Sovereignty over Pulau Ligitan and Pulau Sipadan, Merits, Judgment of 17 December 2002' (2003) 52 *International and Comparative Law Quarterly*, 797–802.
55. 'The International Court of Justice in 2002' (2003) 3 *The Global Community Yearbook of International Law and Jurisprudence* 277–94.
56. 'The International Court of Justice in 2003' (2004) 4 *The Global Community Yearbook of International Law and Jurisprudence* 323–39.
57. 'The International Court of Justice in 2004' (2005) 5 *The Global Community Yearbook of International Law and Jurisprudence* 353–67.
58. 'New Horizons for International Adjudication' (2006) 6 *The Global Community Yearbook of International Law and Jurisprudence* 47–75.
59. 'The International Court of Justice in 2005' (2006) 6 *The Global Community Yearbook of International Law and Jurisprudence* 211–23.
60. 'The Mosaic of International Dispute Settlement Procedures: Complementary or Contradictory?' (2007) 54 *Netherlands International Law Review* 361–95.
61. 'The International Court of Justice in 2006' (2007) 7 *The Global Community Yearbook of International Law and Jurisprudence* 195–204.

In Press

62. 'The International Court of Justice in 2007' (2008, forthcoming) *The Global Community Yearbook of International Law and Jurisprudence* (c 6,000 words).

Index